Amsterdam

"All you've got to do is decide to go and the hardest part is over.

So go!"

TONY WHEELER, COFOUNDER – LONELY PLANET

THIS EDI

C

Karla Zimmerman

Contents

Plan Your Trip 4

Explore Amsterdam 62

Understand Amsterdam 237

Survival Guide 269

Amsterdam Maps 298

MARTIN CHILD / GETTY IMAGES ©

MERTEN SNIJDERS / GETTY IMAGES ©

JORG GREUEL / GETTY IMAGES ©

(left) **Bloemenmarkt p129** Wooden and fresh tulips are sold at this flower market.

(above) **Vondelpark p173** An urban escape.

(right) **Zuiderkerk p95** Get a great view from Groenburgwal canal.

Welcome to Amsterdam

Seventeenth-century buildings. Joint-smoking alien sculptures. Few cities meld history with modern urban flair like Amsterdam.

Admire Art

You can't walk a kilometre without bumping into a masterpiece in the city. The Van Gogh Museum hangs the world's largest collection by tortured native son Vincent. A few blocks away, Vermeers, Rembrandts and other Golden Age treasures fill the glorious Rijksmuseum. The Museum het Rembrandthuis offers more of Rembrandt via his etching-packed studio, while the Stedelijk Museum counts Matisses and Mondrians among its modern stock. And when the urge strikes for something blockbuster, the Hermitage Amsterdam delivers: the outpost of Russia's State Hermitage Museum picks from its three-million-piece home trove to mount mega exhibits.

Bike & Boat

Two-wheeling is a way of life here. It's how Amsterdammers commute to work, go to the shop and meet a date for dinner. With all the bike rental shops around, it's easy to gear up and take a spin. If locals aren't on a bike, they may well be in a boat. With its canals and massive harbour, this city reclaimed from the sea offers countless opportunities to drift. Hop in a canal boat (preferably an open-air one) or one of the free ferries behind Centraal Station for a wind-in-your-hair ride.

Feel Gezellig

Amsterdam is famously *gezellig*, a Dutch quality that translates roughly as convivial or cosy. It's more easily experienced than defined. There's a sense of time stopping, an intimacy of the here and now that leaves all your troubles behind, at least until tomorrow. You can get that warm, fuzzy feeling in many situations, but the easiest place is a traditional brown *café*. Named for their wood panelling and walls stained by smoke over the centuries, brown *cafés* practically have *gezelligheid* (cosiness) on tap, alongside good beer. You can also feel *gezellig* at any restaurant after dinner, when you're welcome to linger and chat after your meal while the candles burn low.

Wander into the Past

Amsterdam is ripe for rambling, its compact core laced by atmospheric lanes and quarters. You never know what you'll find: a hidden garden, a shop selling velvet ribbon, a *jenever* (Dutch gin) distillery, an old monastery-turned-classical-music-venue. Wherever you end up, it's probably by a canal. And a *café*. And a gabled building that looks like a Golden Age painting.

DENNIS VAN DE WATER / SHUTTERSTOCK ©

Why I Love Amsterdam

By Karla Zimmerman, Writer

I love walking around Prinsengracht in the morning. Houseboats bob, bike bells *cling cling,* flower sellers lay out their wares. The old merchants' houses tilt at impossible angles, and it's easy to imagine an era when boats unloaded spices out the front.

I love how cappuccinos appear and disappear in 350-year-old bars like Café Pieper, and how beers do the same in candlelit timewarps like Café de Dokter. It's all good fuel for ferrying across the IJ to see bands under twinkling lights at the Tolhuistuin come nightfall.

For more about our writers, see p328.

Top: Sunrise over an Amsterdam canal

Amsterdam's Top 10

1

Van Gogh Museum *(p170)*

1 Housing the world's largest collection by artist Vincent van Gogh, the museum is as much a tour through the driven painter's troubled mind as it is a tour through his body of work. More than 200 canvases are on display, from his dark, potato-filled early career in the Netherlands through to his later years in sunny France, where he produced his best-known work with its characteristic giddy colour. Paintings by contemporaries Gauguin, Toulouse-Lautrec, Monet and Bernard round out the retrospective.

Vondelpark & the Old South

Brown Cafés *(p49)*

2 For the quintessential bite of Amsterdam, pull up a stool in one of the city's famed brown *cafés* (traditional Dutch pubs). The true specimen has been in business a while and gets its name from centuries' worth of smoke stains on the walls. Brown *cafés* have candle-topped tables, sandy wooden floors and sometimes a house cat that sidles up for a scratch. Most importantly, brown *cafés* induce a cosy vibe that prompts friends to linger and chat for hours over drinks – the same enchantment the *cafés* have cast for 300 years. BELOW: HOPPE (P81)

Drinking & Nightlife

ATLANTIDE S.N.C./AGE / ROBERT HARDING ©

2

LONELY PLANET / GETTY IMAGES ©

3

JOE DANIEL PRICE / GETTY IMAGES ©

4

YADID LEVY / ROBERT HARDING ©

YADID LEVY / ALAMY STOCK PHOTO ©

Rijksmuseum *(p167)*

3 The Netherlands' top treasure house does not disappoint. The crowds huddle around Rembrandt's humongous *Night Watch* and Vermeer's *Kitchen Maid* in the Gallery of Honour, but that just means the remaining 1.5km of rooms are free for browsing antique ship models, savage-looking swords, crystal goblets and magic lanterns. You could spend days gaping at the beautiful and curious collections tucked into the nooks and crannies. What's more, free sculpture-studded gardens surround the monumental building.

Vondelpark & the Old South

Jordaan *(p147)*

4 If Amsterdam's neighbourhoods held a 'best personality' contest, the Jordaan (once the workers quarter) would win. Its intimacy is contagious, with modest old homes, offbeat galleries and vintage shops peppering a grid of tiny lanes. This is the place for jovial bar singalongs and beery brown *cafés*, the neighbourhood where you could spend a week wandering the narrow streets and still not discover all the hidden courtyards and tucked-away eateries. By now you know the Dutch propensity for *gezelligheid* (conviviality); the Jordaan is a font of it.

Jordaan & the West

Vondelpark *(p173)*

5 On a sunny day it seems the whole city converges on this sprawling equivalent of New York City's Central Park. Couples kiss on the grass, friends cradle beers at the outdoor cafes, while others trade songs on beat-up guitars. Street performers work the crowds and kids rush the playgrounds. It's all very democratic, and sublime for people watching. The English-style layout offers an abundance of ponds, lawns, thickets and winding footpaths that encourage visitors to get out and explore the free-wheeling scene.

Vondelpark & the Old South

Outdoor Markets *(p59)*

6 Amsterdam is market-mad, and its streets hold spreads from silks and coins to organic cheeses and bike locks. The Albert Cuypmarkt is king of the lot. Here Surinamese and Indonesian immigrants mix with locals at stalls hawking rice cookers, spices and Dutch snacks, such as sweet *stroopwafels* (syrup-filled waffles). Flowers fill the Bloemenmarkt, while porcelain teapots and other bric-a-brac tempt at Waterlooplein Flea Market. The Oudemanhuis Book Market has been selling tomes for a few centuries. Then there's the antiques market, farmers market, art market... BELOW: BLOEMENMARKT (P129)

Shopping

King's Day *(p23)*

7 For decades it was Queen's Day, but there's a new monarch in the house. So now it's King's Day (Koningsdag), celebrated on King Willem-Alexander's birthday of April 27 (unless it falls on a Sunday, in which case it's celebrated the day before). Whatever the name, whatever the date, it's really just an excuse for a gigantic drinking fest and for everyone to wear ridiculous orange outfits, the country's national colour. There's also a free market citywide (where anyone can sell anything) and rollicking free concerts.

Month by Month

MASSIMO BORCHI / CORBIS ©

7

COLLPICTO / ALAMY STOCK PHOTO ©

8

ALEKSANDAR VRZALSKI / GETTY IMAGES ©

Canal Trips *(p34)*

8 Amsterdam has more canals than Venice and getting on the water is one of the best ways to feel the pulse of the city. You could catch the vibe by sitting canal-side and watching boats glide by: myriad *cafés* seem purpose-built for this sport. Or you could stroll alongside the canals and check out some of the city's 2500 houseboats. Better yet, hop on a tour boat and cruise the curved passages. From this angle, you'll understand why Unesco named the city's waterways a World Heritage Site.

Canals

Anne Frank Huis *(p114)*

9 Seeing Anne Frank's melancholy bedroom and her actual diary, sitting alone in its glass case, is a powerful experience that draws a million visitors annually. Step behind the bookcase that swings open to reveal the 'Secret Annexe' and go up the steep stairs into the living quarters. It was in this dark and airless space that the Franks observed complete silence during the day, outgrew their clothes, pasted photos of Hollywood stars on the walls and read Dickens, before being mysteriously betrayed.

Western Canal Ring

DENNISVDW / GETTY IMAGES ©

PAULO AMORIM / GETTY IMAGES ©

Cycling *(p29)*

10 There are more bicycles in Amsterdam than cars. Everyone rides: young, old, club-goers in high heels, cops on duty, bankers in suits with ties flapping in the breeze. Pedal power is what moves the masses to work, to shop and to socialise at the *cafés*. Renting a bike not only puts you shoulder to shoulder with locals, it gives you easy access to the city's outer neighbourhoods and their cool architecture and museums, as well as the windmill-dotted countryside and its time-warped villages.

By Bike

What's New

De Hallen

Prepared food stalls, a cinema, hotel, bike recycling shop and fashion incubators now pack this century-old tram depot after its slick revamp. (p182)

A'DAM Tower

The abandoned Royal Dutch Shell offices have morphed into a hub for electronic dance music businesses. Meanwhile, cool spots continue to open in the surrounding district of Amsterdam-Noord. (p85)

Hoxton Amsterdam

The hotel sprawls through five canal houses and offers hip high style at affordable prices, plus gatherings on site with local artists and creative types. (p229)

Yellow Backie

The Yellow Backie program lets visitors catch a free ride on the back of a local's bike. It's basically bike hitchhiking, meant to foster good vibes between travellers and Amsterdammers. (p33)

CT Coffee & Coconuts

It's like a cathedral for divine brunch dishes: pancakes, French toast brioche, cheesy eggs. It's part of Amsterdam's larger brunch trend, with much of the deliciousness happening in De Pijp. (p193)

Brouwerij Troost

The craft brewery scene is booming in the city, and no one does it better than Troost. Mmm, saisons, blond ales and smoked porters. A second outpost opened in Westerpark. (p195)

Micropia

This museum about microbes sits on the Artis Zoo's premises and is way more entertaining than you think, with a wall of poop, kissing meter and other inventive exhibits. (p99)

Generator Amsterdam

Part of the burgeoning scene of poshtels (aka posh hostels) popping up around town, Generator brings its design-savvy twin and quad rooms to Oosterpark. (p230)

Jan Pieter Heijestraat

Stretching south from buzzing Kinkerstraat to busy Overtoom, backstreet Jan Pieter Heijestraat bursts with fresh boutiques, restaurants and bars. (p180)

Red Light Secrets Museum of Prostitution

Located in the thick of the Red Light District, the museum shows what is behind the crimson windows and answers basic questions about the industry. Also: dominatrix room. (p75)

Eurostar Direct Route

No more stopping to switch trains in Belgium. A direct London-to-Amsterdam route is slated to launch in late 2016 that will cut travel time to four hours. (p270)

For more recommendations and reviews, see **lonelyplanet.com/Amsterdam**

Need to Know

For more information, see Survival Guide (p269)

Currency
Euro (€)

Language
Dutch and English

Visas
Generally not required for stays up to three months. Some nationalities require a Schengen visa.

Money
ATMs widely available. Credit cards accepted in most hotels but not all restaurants. Non-European credit cards are sometimes rejected.

Mobile Phones
Local SIM cards can be used in European and Australian phones. Standard North American GSM 1900 phones will not work.

Time
Central European Time (GMT/UTC plus one hour)

Tourist Information
The VVV I Amsterdam Visitor Centre (Map p300; www.iamsterdam.com; Stationsplein 10; 9am-6pm; 4/9/16/24 Centraal Station), located outside Centraal Station, offers maps, guides, transit passes, accommodation booking services and ticket purchases for attractions.

Daily Costs

Budget: Less than €100
- Dorm bed €25–50
- Supermarkets and lunchtime specials for food €20
- Boom Chicago late-night show ticket €14
- GVB transit day pass €7.50

Midrange: €100–250
- Double room €150
- Three-course dinner in casual restaurant €35
- Concertgebouw ticket €40
- Canal Bus day pass €23

Top end: More than €250
- Four-star hotel double room €250
- Five-course dinner in top restaurant €60
- Private canal boat rental for two hours €90

Advance Planning

Six months before Book your hotel, especially if you'll be visiting in the summer or on a weekend.

Two months before Check calendars for the Concertgebouw (p185), Muziekgebouw aan 't IJ (p108), Melkweg (p143) and Paradiso (p143), and buy tickets for anything that looks appealing.

Two weeks before Make dinner reservations at your must-eat restaurants.

One week before Buy tickets online to the Van Gogh Museum (p170), Anne Frank Huis (p114) and Rijksmuseum (p167). Reserve walking or cycling tours.

Useful Websites

Lonely Planet (www.lonelyplanet.com/amsterdam) Destination information, hotel bookings, traveller forum and more.

I Amsterdam (www.iamsterdam.com) City-run portal packed with sightseeing, accommodation and event info.

Dutch News (www.dutchnews.nl) News tidbits and event listings.

Overdose.am (www.overdose.am) Art, music and fashion to-dos.

WHEN TO GO

Summer (June to August) is peak tourist season, with warm weather and lots of daylight for cycling. March to May is tulip time.

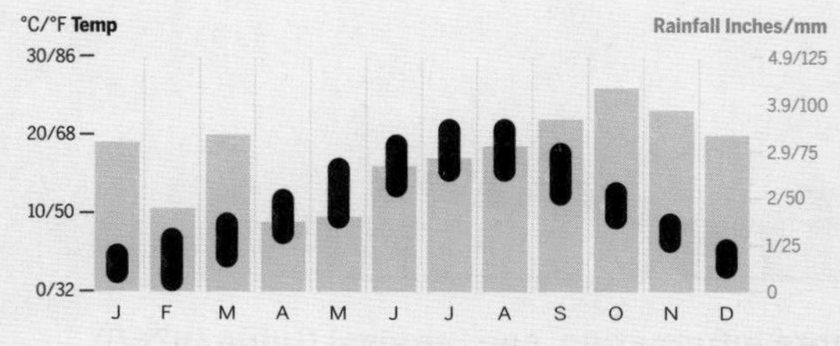

Arriving in Amsterdam

Schiphol Airport Trains to Centraal Station depart every 10 minutes or so from 6am to 12.30am; the trip takes 17 minutes and costs €5.10; taxis cost €47.

Centraal Station In central Amsterdam with most tram lines connecting it to the rest of the city; taxis queue near the front entrance (toward the west side).

Bus Station Eurolines buses arrive at Duivendrecht station, south of the centre, with an easy metro or train link to Centraal Station.

For much more on **arrival** see p270

Getting Around

GVB passes in chip-card form are the most convenient option for public transport. Buy them at visitor centres or from tram conductors. Always wave your card at the pink machine when entering and departing.

➡ **Walking** Central Amsterdam is compact and very easy to cover by foot.

➡ **Bicycle** This is the locals' main mode of getting around. Rental companies are all over town; bikes cost about €11 per day.

➡ **Tram** Fast, frequent and ubiquitous, operating between 6am and 12.30am.

➡ **Bus and Metro** Primarily serve the outer districts; not much use in the city centre.

➡ **Ferry** Free ferries depart for northern Amsterdam from docks behind Centraal Station.

➡ **Taxi** Expensive and not very speedy given Amsterdam's maze of streets.

For much more on **getting around** see p272

Sleeping

Resting your head in Amsterdam can be expensive. Book as far in advance as possible (especially for summer bookings, and for weekends anytime) to get the best deals and to secure the place you want. Hostels are plentiful, with most geared to youthful party animals. Hotels typically are small (less than 20 rooms) and ramble over several floors in charming old buildings. Canal-side addresses cost more, while places by the Red Light District or Damrak – though cheaper – tend towards the seedy side. In general, everything is pretty expensive.

Useful Websites

➡ **I Amsterdam** (www.iamsterdam.com) Wide range of options from the city's official website.

➡ **Hotels.nl** (www.hotels.nl) For deals on larger properties.

➡ **CityMundo** (www.citymundo.com) Reliable broker for apartment rentals; three-night minimum required for most.

For much more on **sleeping** see p224

First Time

For more information, see Survival Guide (p269)

Checklist

➡ Make sure your passport is valid for at least six months after your arrival date

➡ Inform your debit-/credit-card company of your travel plans

➡ Arrange appropriate travel insurance

➡ Call your mobile provider to enquire about roaming charges or getting an international plan

What to Pack

➡ Good comfortable shoes – Amsterdam is best appreciated on foot (or by bike)

➡ Umbrella or rain jacket, because it can be rainy

➡ Netherlands electrical adapter

➡ A small day pack (the smaller the better to avoid having to check it when visiting museums)

Top Tips for Your Trip

➡ Plan your time – lengthy queues can add an hour or so to each museum visit.

➡ Make reservations for dinner at midrange and top-end eateries. Many restaurants are small and customers like to linger. Without a reservation, you might well miss out on your favourite spot.

➡ Sightsee by foot. Walking is one of the best ways to get around the compact city – it's quick, free, and provides the opportunity to wander by hidden lanes and shops you might otherwise miss.

What to Wear

Locals dress stylishly, but practically. Most people wear jeans and hip boots for an evening out.

Pack layers of clothing, bearing in mind that Dutch weather is notoriously fickle and there can be chilly spells even in summer. In spring, summer and autumn, a light trench coat or jacket and a small travel umbrella will mean you're prepared for the weather, but will still blend in with the crowd. In winter, bring a proper heavy coat to ward off the near-freezing temperatures (and you'll still want that umbrella).

Be Forewarned

Amsterdam is a safe and manageable city, and if you use your common sense you should have no problems.

➡ Some restaurants and businesses close for two to six weeks in summer, usually in July or August, when owners go on holiday.

➡ Be careful around the canals. Almost none of them are fenced or otherwise blocked by barriers.

➡ Be alert for pickpockets in tourist-heavy zones such as the Bloemenmarkt and Red Light District; avoid deserted streets in the Red Light District at night.

➡ It is forbidden to take photos of women in the Red Light District windows, and this is strictly enforced.

➡ Trams stop running at 12.30am, after which you'll have to wait for less convenient and more expensive night buses.

Tours

The following tours provide a good introduction to Amsterdam, particularly if you're short on time:

➡ **Sandeman's New Amsterdam Tours** (p274) Pay-what-you-can walking tours that cover the Medieval Centre, Red Light District and the Jordaan.

➡ **Those Dam Boat Guys** (p37) Low-key canal tours on small, electric boats where you bring your own picnic.

➡ **Orangebike** (p29) Easy cycling jaunts that take in the city's sights, architecture and windmills.

Taxes & Refunds

Value-added tax (VAT, or 'BTW' in Dutch) is a sales tax levied on most goods and services. It's 6% for restaurants, hotels, books, transport and museum admissions, and 21% for most other items. The tax should already be included in stated prices.

It's sometimes possible for visitors to claim a VAT refund; see 59 for details.

Tipping

➡ **Bars** Not expected.

➡ **Hotels** €1 to €2 per bag for porters; not typical for cleaning staff.

➡ **Restaurants** Leave 5% to 10% for a cafe snack (if your bill comes to €9.50, you might round up to €10), 10% or so for a restaurant meal.

➡ **Taxis** Tip 5% to 10%, or round up to the nearest euro.

A canal tour at sunset

Etiquette

➡ **Greetings** Do give a firm handshake and a double or triple cheek kiss.

➡ **Marijuana & Alcohol** Don't smoke dope or drink beer on the streets.

➡ **Smoking** Don't smoke cigarettes in bars or restaurants.

➡ **Bluntness** Don't take offense if locals give you a frank, unvarnished opinion. It's not considered impolite, rather it comes from the desire to be direct and honest.

➡ **Cycling paths** Don't walk in bike lanes (which are marked by white lines and bicycle symbols), and do look both ways before crossing a bike lane.

Visitor Pass

The I Amsterdam Card (p273) is handy for quick visits to the city. It provides admission to more than 30 museums and includes a local transit pass, a canal cruise, and restaurant and shop discounts. If you visit three or more museums per day it'll pay for itself.

Language

English is widely spoken, especially by younger locals. Most restaurants and cafes have menus in Dutch and English; most museums have information posted in both languages.

Top Itineraries

Day One

Vondelpark & Old South (p165)

Begin with the biggies: tram to the Museum Quarter to ogle the masterpieces at the Van Gogh Museum (p170) and Rijksmuseum (p167). They'll be crowded, so make sure you've prebooked tickets. Modern-art buffs might want to swap the Stedelijk Museum (p172) for one of the others. They're all lined up in a walkable row.

Lunch Slow-food favourite Gartine (p76) grows ingredients in its garden.

Medieval Centre (p66)

Spend the afternoon in the Medieval Centre. Explore the secret courtyard and gardens at the Begijnhof (p69). Walk up the street to the Dam (p71), where the Royal Palace (p68), Nieuwe Kerk (p74) and Nationaal Monument (p71) huddle and provide a dose of Dutch history. Bend over and take your *jenever* (Dutch gin) like a local at Wynand Fockink (p84).

Dinner Do steak or fondue for dinner at Dwaze Zaken (p81).

Red Light District (p66)

Venture into the Red Light District. A walk down Warmoesstraat (p76) or Oudezijds Achterburgwal (p79) provides an eye-popping line-up of fetish-gear shops, live sex shows, smoky coffeeshops and, of course, women in day-glo lingerie beckoning from crimson windows. Then settle in to a brown *café* (pub), such as In 't Aepjen (p84), In de Olofspoort (p84) or 't Mandje (p84).

Day Two

De Pijp (p187)

Browse the Albert Cuypmarkt (p190), Amsterdam's largest street bazaar, an international free-for-all of cheeses, fish, *stroopwafels* (syrup-filled waffles) and bargain-priced clothing. Then submit to the Heineken Experience (p189) to get shaken up, heated up and 'bottled' like the beer you'll drink at the end of the brewery tour.

Lunch Bite into a burger at Butcher (p190) on Albert Cuypstraat.

Southern Canal Ring (p127)

Make your way over to the Southern Canal Ring and stroll along the grand Golden Bend. Visit Museum Van Loon (p130) for a peek into the opulent canalhouse lifestyle, or get a dose of kitty quirk at the Kattenkabinet (p130). Browse the Bloemenmarkt (p129) and behold the wild array of bulbs.

Dinner Fork into organic dishes canalside at Buffet van Odette (p135).

Southern Canal Ring (p127)

When the sun sets, it's time to partee at hyperactive, neon-lit Leidseplein (p129). If you get here before 7.30pm weekdays (6pm weekends), check at the Uitburo (p143) for concerts or show tickets. Paradiso (p143) and Melkweg (p143) host the coolest agendas. Otherwise the good-time clubs and *cafés* around the square beckon. Try beery Café de Spuyt (p140) or historic Eijlders (p138).

Day Three

Vondelpark & Old South (p165)

Take a spin around beloved Vondelpark (p173). Long and thin – about 1.5km long and 300m wide – it's easy to explore via a morning jaunt. All the better if you have a bicycle to zip by the ponds, gardens and sculptures.

Lunch Head to the Western Canals for Dutch classics at Bistro Bij Ons (p120).

Western Canal Ring (p112)

Immerse yourself in the Negen Straatjes (p125), or Nine Streets, a tic-tac-toe board of oddball speciality shops. The Anne Frank Huis (p114) is also in the neighbourhood, and it's a must. The claustrophobic rooms, their windows still covered with blackout screens, give an all-too-real feel for Anne's life in hiding. Seeing the diary itself – filled with her sunny writing tempered with quiet despair – is moving, plain and simple.

Dinner Balthazar's Keuken (p154) cooks whatever delights are on hand.

Jordaan (p147)

Spend the evening in the Jordaan, the chummy district touted as the Amsterdam of yore. Hoist a glass on a canalside terrace at 't Smalle (p157), join the houseboat party at Café P *96* (p159), or quaff beers at heaps of other *gezellig* (cosy) haunts.

Day Four

Nieuwmarkt, Plantage & Eastern Islands (p92)

Mosey through Waterlooplein Flea Market (p109) in Nieuwmarkt. Doc Martens? Buddha statues? Electric saw? These goods and more fill the stalls. Rembrandt sure loved markets, if his nearby studio is any indication. Museum het Rembrandthuis (p94) gives a peek at the master's inner sanctum, including his curio-packed cabinet and paint-spattered easel. Neighbouring Gassan Diamonds (p96) gives the bling lowdown via free tours.

Lunch Try a hot-spiced Surinamese sandwich at Tokoman (p101).

Nieuwmarkt, Plantage & Eastern Islands (p92)

Wander over to the Plantage to check out the intriguing Verzetsmuseum (p99), the Resistance Museum, or sea treasures at Het Scheepvaartmuseum (p98). Then it's time for an only-in-Amsterdam experience: drinking organic beer at the foot of an authentic windmill at Brouwerij 't IJ (p107). Snap your photos before knocking back too many glasses of the strong suds.

Dinner Dine in the glass greenhouse at De Kas (p204).

Oosterpark (p199)

You've been a sightseeing trooper, zipping through most of Amsterdam's neighbourhoods over the past four days. An evening spent plopped on the terrace at De Ysbreeker (p204), looking out over the bustling, houseboat-strewn Amstel river, is a well-deserved treat.

If You Like...

Art

Van Gogh Museum Has the world's largest collection of the tortured artist's paintings, from his early work to his final pieces. (p170)

Rijksmuseum The Netherlands' mightiest museum bursts with Rembrandts, Vermeers, delftware and more, all displayed in a dazzling neo-Gothic/Dutch Renaissance building. (p167)

Stedelijk Museum Bountiful modern trove including works by Picasso, Chagall, Mondrian, Warhol, Lichtenstein and the CoBrA school, much of it housed in the groovy 'Bathtub' wing. (p172)

Museum het Rembrandthuis You almost expect to find the master himself still nipping around his old paint-spattered studio and handsome home. (p94)

Hermitage Amsterdam This satellite of Russia's Hermitage Museum features one-off, blockbuster exhibits showing everything from Matisse cut-outs to Byzantine treasures. (p132)

FOAM (Fotografiemuseum Amsterdam) Changing exhibitions feature world-renowned photographers such as Sir Cecil Beaton, Annie Leibovitz and Henri Cartier-Bresson. (p130)

Markets

Albert Cuypmarkt Amsterdam's largest and busiest market has been selling flowers, clothing, food and household goods of every description for more than 100 years. (p190)

MASSIMO BORCHI / CORBIS ©

De Gooyer Windmill (p98)

Waterlooplein Flea Market The city's famous flea market piles up curios, used footwear, electronic gear, New Age gifts and cheap bicycle parts for bargain hunters. (p109)

Oudemanhuis Book Market Located in a moody, old, covered alleyway, this place is lined with secondhand booksellers and is a favourite with academics. (p89)

Noordermarkt The Noorderkerk's front plaza has been a market since the early 1600s; antiques and organic fare are the offerings these days. (p164)

Bloemenmarkt The 'floating' flower market (it actually sits on pilings) is the place to bag your beautiful bloomin' bulbs. (p129)

Romantic Spots

Sarphatipark Roam winding paths past idyllic ponds and fountains in the heart of village-like De Pijp. (p189)

Reguliersgracht The 'canal of seven bridges' enchants at night when its humpbacked arches glow with tiny gold lights. (p142)

Groenburgwal A drawbridge, church and canal so pretty even Claude Monet had to capture the image. (p108)

Vondelpark A hippie haven in the Flower Power era, this sprawling park still evokes the Summer of Love. (p173)

Schreierstoren The tower where women wept as their men set sail on Golden Age voyages is now a cosy cafe. (p72)

Canal Cruise Snuggle next to your sweetheart while gliding along the city's fairy-tale waterways. (p37)

Hedonistic Pursuits

Dampkring This coffeeshop stalwart has a comprehensive, well-explained menu, a Cannabis Cup–winning product and a Hollywood-backdrop pedigree. (p82)

Condomerie Het Gulden Vlies Puts the 'pro' back in prophylactic with its tasteful setting and huge array of condoms for sale. (p91)

Kokopelli Life gets a whole lot more colourful (literally) with a serving of magic truffles from this classy smart shop. (p91)

Prostitution Information Centre Get frank information about the women in the windows on the centre's walking tour. (p274)

Casa Rosso Jaw-dropping tricks with lit candles and more at the city's most popular sex show (a hen's-night favourite). (p88)

Webers When you need a PVC catsuit with whip holster, this little shop can do the fitting. (p110)

Windmills

De Gooyer It's hard to beat drinking freshly made organic beer at the foot of an 18th-century spinner. (p98)

Riekermolen Rembrandt used to sketch by this windmill, south of the city at Amstelpark's edge. (p203)

Zaanse Schans A whole village of blades turns in the North Sea breeze, a 20-minute train ride from the city. (p222)

National Mill Day Here's your chance to peek inside some of the country's 950 twirlers, including eight in Amsterdam. (p23)

For more top Amsterdam spots, see the following:

- Eating (p42)
- Drinking & Nightlife (p48)
- Entertainment (p56)
- Shopping (p58)

Parks & Gardens

Vondelpark A mash-up of ponds, lawns, thickets and winding footpaths beloved by picnickers, dope smokers, kissing couples and frolicking children. (p173)

Museumplein The festive green space between the Rijksmuseum, Van Gogh Museum and Stedelijk Museum packs a crowd for winter ice skating and summer lazing. (p174)

Oosterpark Political monuments and grey herons dot the sweeping expanse of this park, built for nouveau riche diamond traders a century ago. (p201)

Hortus Botanicus When Dutch ships sailed afar in the 1600s, the tropical seeds they brought back were grown in this wonderful garden. (p97)

Amsterdamse Bos The Amsterdam Forest sprawls with thick trees and open fields, criss-crossed with cycling and walking paths, and home to rowing ponds and a goat farm. (p202)

Westerpark Abutting a former-gasworks-building-turned-edgy-cultural-centre, the west side's rambling, reedy wilderness has become a hipster hang-out. (p151)

Park Frankendael Seek out the formal garden that sits behind the Louis XIV–style mansion. (p201)

Active Endeavours

Cycling in Amsterdam-Noord It's surprisingly easy to ride into the countryside and spin by time-warp villages and cow-dotted pastures. (p85)

Walking Tours The city has a slew of options for lacing up your shoes and seeing the sights. (p274)

Canal Bike Explore the city from a different perspective with a pedal around the canals. (p37)

Ice Skating Museumplein's pond turns into Amsterdam's favourite rink come winter, looking like the top of a wind-up jewellery box. (p174)

Friday Night Skate Strap on your skates and join the crowd for a 20km jaunt from Vondelpark through the city. (p186)

Sustainable Options

De Ridammerhoeve Feed the kids (both kinds) at the organic goat farm and cafe in Amsterdamse Bos. (p202)

De Kas Sit in a greenhouse and fork into meals, the components of which were grown just a few steps away. (p204)

Boerenmarkt This organic farmers market sets up on Saturdays at Noordermarkt and Nieuwmarkt at the Waag. (p110)

Instock This restaurant 'rescues' food that's about to reach its expiration date and be thrown out by shops, and transforms it into three-course meals. (p105)

Lot Sixty One Sniff out the roasting coffee beans from sustainable farms around the globe. (p181)

Architecture

Rijksmuseum Pierre Cuypers' magnificent, iconic design from 1875 harks back to earlier times, with Renaissance ornaments carved in stone around the facade. (p167)

ARCAM Amsterdam's Centre for Architecture is a one-stop shop for architectural exhibits, guidebooks and maps. (p100)

NEMO Renzo Piano's green-copper, ship-shaped science museum is a modern classic. (p100)

Scheepvaarthuis This grand 1916 building encrusted with nautical detailing and stained glass is the first true Amsterdam School construction. (p95)

Eastern Islands If you're looking for one place to see the cutting edge of Dutch architecture, the Eastern Islands is the place. (p98)

Beurs van Berlage The 1903 financial exchange building is a temple to capitalism, with tile murals and other decor that venerates labour. (p71)

Museum Het Schip A pilgrimage site for design buffs, this 1920s housing project is the pinnacle of Amsterdam School style. (p151)

Offbeat Museums

Kattenkabinet A creaky old canal house filled with kitty-cat art from the likes of Picasso, Steinlen and Rembrandt. (p130)

Houseboat Museum Get a feel for the compact, watery lifestyle aboard a 23m-long sailing barge. (p150)

Tassenmuseum Hendrikje This entire museum is devoted to handbags, from 16th-century pouches to Madonna's modern arm candy. (p131)

Amsterdam Pipe Museum Chinese opium pipes, Turkish water pipes, 1500-year-old Ecuadorian pipes and more cram the cabinets. (p129)

Pianola Museum Bursting with musical keys from the early 1900s, this little place is an extraordinary paean to the player piano. (p149)

Electric Ladyland Prepare for a trippy time at the world's first museum of fluorescent art, glowing with psychedelic rocks, rice and rabbits. (p149)

History Lessons

Anne Frank Huis The Secret Annexe, Anne's melancholy bedroom, and her actual diary are all here, serving as chilling reminders of WWII. (p114)

Oude Kerk The senior citizen of Amsterdam's structures, now more than 700 years old, with many famous Amsterdammers buried beneath the floor. (p70)

Amsterdam Museum Intriguing multimedia exhibits take you through the twists and turns of Amsterdam's convoluted history. (p73)

Verzetsmuseum Learn about WWII Dutch Resistance fighters during the German occupation. Learn, too, about the minority who went along with the Nazis. (p99)

Stadsarchief The city's rich archives offer remarkable displays, including Anne Frank's stolen-bike report from 1942. (p130)

Month by Month

TOP EVENTS

King's Day, April

Grachtenfestival, August

Amsterdam Gay Pride, August

Amsterdam Dance Event, October

Amsterdam Light Festival, early December to mid-January

January

Yes, it's cold. Yes, it's dark. But the museum queues are nonexistent and there is more time to relax in a cosy cafe in front of a crackling fireplace.

Amsterdam Fashion Week

Amsterdam's fashion scene takes flight during Fashion Week (www.fashionweek.nl), with catwalk shows, parties, lectures and concerts. Many events – both free and ticketed – are open to the public. They take place downtown and at the Westergasfabriek (p161). There's also a July fashion week.

March

Early spring weather can be fickle, but if it complies you can get a jump-start on tulip viewing (and the crowds) at Keukenhof.

5 Days Off

Electronic music festival 5 Days Off (www.5daysoff.nl) puts on dance parties at Melkweg (p143) and Paradiso (p143) toward the start of the month.

April

Days are getting longer, temperatures are rising and flowers are in full bloom in the lead-up to the show-stopping King's Day party, the highlight of Amsterdam's annual calendar.

King's Day

One of the biggest – and arguably best – street parties in Europe, King's Day (Koningsdag) celebrates the birthday of King Willem-Alexander on 27 April (26 April if the 27th is a Sunday). There's uproarious partying, music and *oranjekoorts* (orange fever), as well as a city-wide flea market.

World Press Photo

A gripping exhibition (www.worldpressphoto.org) of the year's best photojournalism debuts in the Nieuwe Kerk (p74) in late April, and stays on display until the end of June.

May

Amsterdam follows Remembrance Day (4 May) observances with Liberation Day (5 May) festivities, and flourishing cafe terraces make this mild month a perfect time to linger in the city.

National Mill Day

During the second weekend in May, some 950 windmills and watermills throughout the country welcome the public into their creaking innards (www.molens.nl). Look for mills flying a blue pennant.

Vondelpark Open-Air Theatre

A popular Amsterdam tradition, the Vondelpark Open-Air Theatre (p185) features world music, dance, theatre, cabaret and children's shows in a wonderful park setting from May to early September.

June

Visitors start flocking in for the summer peak season. It's typically sunny and warm, prime for bicycle rides and drinks on canal-side patios.

Holland Festival

Big-name theatre, dance and opera meet offbeat digital films and experimental music in the Netherlands' biggest performing-arts extravaganza (www.hollandfestival.nl). The month-long, highbrow-lowbrow mash-up happens at venues citywide.

Open Tuinen Dagen

Open Garden Days (www.opentuinendagen.nl), on the third weekend in June, brings a unique opportunity to view some 25 private gardens along the canals.

July

The days are long, the sun is shining, so who cares if the crowds are clogging Amsterdam's streets and canals? It only adds to the party atmosphere.

Amsterdam Roots Festival

Early July's four-day roots festival (www.amsterdamroots.nl) programs world music in key venues around town, culminating in the all-day Roots Open Air fest at Park Frankendael (p201).

Over het IJ Festival

Oddball venues at the NDSM-werf shipyards (p85) in Amsterdam-Noord host unconventional performing arts productions for 10 days in early July during the Festival across the IJ (www.overhetij.nl).

August

A welter of events take place during Amsterdam's high summer, yet the city has less sweltering temperatures than many other European cultural capitals and relatively few summer closures.

Amsterdam Gay Pride

The city flies the rainbow flag from late July to early August during Amsterdam Gay Pride (www.pride.amsterdam). Highlights of the week-long fest include the Drag Queen Olympics and the raucous, waterborne Pride Parade, on the Prinsengracht and Amstel.

Grachtenfestival

Classical musicians pop up in canal-side parks and gardens during mid-August's 10-day Canal Festival (www.grachtenfestival.nl). The highlight of the festival is the free concert on a floating stage in the Prinsengracht.

September

Summer may be technically over, but September is one of the best months to visit Amsterdam. There are some superb festivals along with fair weather and fewer crowds.

Amsterdam City Swim

More than 2500 people jump into the canals for the City Swim (www.amsterdamcityswim.nl) in early September to help raise money for charity. They splash through the waters of the IJ, Amstel and more on the lengthy course.

Jordaan Festival

Practitioners of the nostalgic, tears-in-your-beer folk music called *levenslied* – a speciality of the tight-knit Jordaan – take to the stage around mid-September for this weekend-long festival (www.jordaanfestival.nl).

October

A kaleidoscope of autumnal hues colour Amsterdam's parks and gardens, and while the weather may remain mild, low-season prices kick in and queues thin out.

Amsterdam Dance Event

An electronic music powwow on a massive scale, ADE (www.amsterdam-dance-event.nl) sees 2200 DJs and artists and more than 300,000 clubbers attending 450 events all over the city over five days and nights late in October.

November

Cultural events and reduced low-season rates make up for the shortening days and chilly nights, while the arrival of Sinterklaas heralds the start of the festive season.

Museumnacht

On the first Saturday in November around 50 museums throughout the city stay open until 2am for Museum Night, scheduling live music, DJs and art-fuelled parties. It's arranged by N8 (www.

(Top) Gay Pride Parade
(Bottom) Amsterdam Light Festival

ANJO KAN / SHUTTERSTOCK ©

ROB VAN ESCH / SHUTTERSTOCK ©

n8.nl), an organisation connecting under-35s with art.

Sinterklaas Intocht

St Nicholas arrives by boat from Spain for the Sinter klaas Intocht (www.sintinamsterdam.nl) in mid- to late November and parades on his white horse to the Dam and Leidseplein to the delight of the city's children.

International Documentary Film Festival

Ten days in late November are dedicated to screening fascinating true stories from all over the world (www.idfa.nl).

December

Winter magic blankets the city (as, some years, does snow), ice-skating rinks set up in open spaces, including the Museumplein, and the city is a vision of twinkling lights.

Amsterdam Light Festival

The twin highlights of this six-week-long festival (www.amsterdamlightfestival.com) include a Boulevard Walk of Light along the Amstel, passing magnificently lit monuments, and a magical, mid-December Christmas Canal Parade of illuminated boats along the canals.

New Year's Eve

Fireworks light up the skies in a sparkling spectacle and countless parties take place around the city. Locations vary; check with the I Amsterdam visitor centre to find out where to ring in the new year.

With Kids

Breathe easy: you've landed in one of Europe's most kid-friendly cities. The famous Dutch tolerance extends to children and Amsterdammers are cheerfully accommodating to them. You'll find that virtually all quarters of the city – except the Red Light District, of course – are fair game for the younger set.

FRANK WIJN / GETTY IMAGES ©

Ice skating at Museumplein (p174)

Outdoor Activities

Green spaces, parks and canals galore provide plenty of fresh-air fun for the little (and not so little) ones.

Parks & Playgrounds

A hot favourite with kids of all ages is the vast play space of the Vondelpark (p173), with leafy picnic spots and duck ponds, as well as cool space-age slides at its western end and a playground in the middle of the park. Westerpark (p151) also has a terrific playground, while Sarphatipark (p189) and Oosterpark (p201) shouldn't be overlooked as great open spaces to let the kids run free. Canoeing, a tree-climbing park, paddle boats and a goat farm are among the fun activities in the huge, forested Amsterdamse Bos (p202).

Winter Magic

Kids will love the skating rinks and outdoor merriment at the winter carnivals that spring up in public spaces such as the Museumplein (p174). Don't miss uniquely Dutch festive season treats such as *poffertjes* (small pancakes) and gingery-cinnamon *speculaas* (cookies), traditionally eaten around Sinterklaas (Saint Nicholas' Eve; 5 December), which are served up at rustic market stalls.

Canals

Take to the canals on a unique pedal-powered ride with Canal Bike (p37).

Artis Royal Zoo

The extrovert monkeys, big cats, shimmying fish and dazzling planetarium will keep young eyes shining for hours at Artis Royal Zoo (p99), while teenagers and adults will love the beautifully landscaped grounds. You can also peek inside Micropia, a building on the premises that is a 'zoo' for microbes. It's way more entertaining than you think, with exhibits that show how bacteria exchange when you kiss and what microbes live in the poop of anteaters, lions and other animals.

Museum Fun

Amsterdam has plenty of museums that are accessible, educational and above all, fun.

NEMO

A tailor-made, hands-on science museum, NEMO (p100) is useful for answering all those 'how' and 'why' questions.

Het Scheepvaartmuseum

The life-size ship moored beside the Martime Museum (p98) lets kids fire a (replica!) cannon, hoist cargo and skedaddle around a reproduced Dutch East India Company vessel from 1749.

Tropenmuseum

The children's section devoted to exotic locations at the Tropenmuseum (p201) is a winner in any language.

Joods Historisch Museum

There is a great kids' display on Jewish life in Amsterdam at the Joods Historisch Museum (p96).

Verzetsmuseum

A section at the Verzetsmuseum (p99) known as the Verzetsmuseum Junior puts the Dutch Resistance into context for kids through the experiences of four children: Eva, Jan, Nelly and Henk.

Van Gogh Museum

The Van Gogh Museum (p170) provides a free treasure hunt for kids to search for items in the paintings and displays. A small prize awaits those who complete the hunt.

Beaches & Castles

City Beaches

Around 10 'urban beaches' pop up on Amsterdam's outskirts each summer around the U. While most cater to adults (complete with cocktails and DJs), some are more family-friendly – check with the tourist office for locations. Enjoy the river views, but don't hope to swim.

Muiden Castle

It's a bit of a trek to get to, but the Muiderslot (p102) is a 700-year-old castle straight out of a fairy tale, with a drawbridge, moat, hulking towers and battlements. It offers special activities (like falconry) for kids on certain days. Combine it with a visit to the atmospheric fort on the nearby island of Pampus (p102).

Rainy-Day Ideas

It's prudent to have a rainy day plan in your back pocket. In fact, it might be so much fun that kids will hope the sun doesn't come back out all day.

TunFun

Set 'em loose for a romp in the underground, all-round pleasure centre TunFun (p111).

Cinema

Kids can eat popcorn and watch new releases at the art-deco Pathé Tuschinskitheater (p144) or the intimate, atmospheric Movies (p161) while adults revel in the historic environs.

Indoor Pools & Saunas

The recreational Zuiderbad (p186) is a good place to take the kids swimming on a rainy day. Adults will enjoy the palatial vintage interior.

Centrale Bibliotheek Amsterdam

The city's stunning, contemporary Centrale Bibliotheek Amsterdam (p100) has a whole floor dedicated to children's activities, including comfy reading lounges and plenty of books in English. Check out the weekly story times (some in English) for younger visitors. Teenagers can take advantage of the computer terminals and wi-fi.

Kid-Friendly Cuisine

While Amsterdam's foodie scene continues to explode with adventurous and sophisticated offerings, you can still find plenty of fare that junior diners will enjoy.

Sandwich Shops

A *broodje* (filled bread roll) or *tosti* (toasted sandwich) always hits the spot. Scores of shops throughout the city specialise in these staples; try Broodje Bert (p78).

KAVALENKAU / SHUTTERSTOCK ©

Kids outside the NEMO museum (p100)

Pancakes

The city is full of these kid-pleasing delights. Top choices include Pancakes! (p118) and Pancake Bakery (p120).

For true pancake aficionados, a trip aboard **De Pannenkoekenboot** (Pancake Boat; ☎626 88 17; www.pannenkoekenboot.nl; Ms Van Riemsdijkweg; adult/child from €18.50/12.50; ⏲by reservation), is definitely in order. Brunch and evening cruises depart from the NDSM-werf in Amsterdam-Noord, reached by a free ferry.

Burgers

Gourmet burgers made from organic ingredients are going gangbusters in Amsterdam. Best burger bets are Butcher (p190) and Geflipt (p191) in De Pijp, and Ellis Gourmet Burger (p152) in the Jordaan.

Fries

Fries slathered in mayonnaise or other sauces are favourites with all ages. Wil Graanstra Friteshuis (p121) is a local institution by the Anne Frank Huis. Frites uit Zuyd (p190) fires up crispy beauties in De Pijp.

Ice Cream

Many ice-cream shops are seasonal: come April or May, look out for them in most high foot-traffic areas. Year-round, try the chocolate-dipped waffle cones at Jordino (p154). IJsmolen (p104) has uniquely Dutch flavours such as *speculaas* (spicy Christmas biscuits) among its line-up. As a bonus, it's located by a windmill.

Cafes & Restaurants

Particularly kid-friendly cafes and restaurants include Moeders (p155), Het Groot Melkhuis (p184), Café Toussaint (p179) and NeL (p141).

Markets

Kids love browsing the markets for both familiar and exotic treats. Try the Albert Cuypmarkt (p190) for *stroopwafel* (syrup waffle), fruit smoothies, chocolates, sweets and fresh fruit. Or pick up ingredients here and take a picnic to the nearby Sarphatipark.

Kid-Friendly Shops

Dozens upon dozens of shops cater for children, who will adore deliberating over toys and sweet treats.

Check out Knuffels (p109) for stuffed-animal toys, Joe's Vliegerwinkel (p109) for kites, Mechanisch Speelgoed (p163) for nostalgic wind-up toys, De Winkel van Nijntje (p205) for merchandise related to Dutch illustrator Dick Bruna's most famous character – the cute rabbit Miffy (Nijntje in Dutch) – and Tinkerbell (p145), a toy-and-more store fronted by a mechanical bear blowing bubbles.

Het Oud-Hollandsch Snoepwinkeltje (p162) has jar after jar of Dutch penny sweets.

NEED TO KNOW

Admission prices 'Child' is defined as under 18 years. But at many tourist sites, the cut-off age for free or reduced rates is 12. Some sights may only provide free entry to children under six.

Bike seats Most bike rental shops rent bikes with baby or child seats.

Babysitting Many higher-end hotels provide babysitting services for a fee.

By Bike

Bicycles are more common than cars in Amsterdam, and to roll like a local you'll need a two-wheeler. Rent one from the myriad outlets around town or your accommodation, and the whole city becomes your playground. Cycling is the quintessential activity while visiting Amsterdam.

FUTURE LIGHT / GETTY IMAGES ©

Cyclists near canal houses

Hiring a Bike

Many visitors rent a bike late in their stay and wish they'd done so sooner. Rental shops are everywhere; you'll have to show a passport or European national ID card and leave a credit-card imprint or pay a deposit (usually €50). Prices for basic 'coaster-brake' bikes average €11 per 24-hour period. Bikes with gears and handbrakes cost more. Theft insurance costs around €3 extra per day.

Ajax Bike (p191) Off the beaten path in De Pijp, with bargain prices on city, kids', tandem and cargo bikes.

Bike City (p151) Jordaan shop; bikes carry no advertising, so you'll look like a local.

Black Bikes (Map p300, B6; ☎670 85 31; www.black-bikes.com; Nieuwezijds Voorburgwal 146; bike rental per 3/24hr from €6/8.50; ⏰8am-8pm Mon-Fri, 9am-7pm Sat & Sun; 🚋1/2/5/13/14/17 Dam/Raadhuisstraat) Signless company offering city, kids', tandem and cargo bikes at 10 shops, including this one in the centre.

Cycleswap (www.cycleswap.nl) Like Airbnb for bikes: rent a bike straight from an Amsterdammer. Prices vary.

Damstraat Rent-a-Bike (Map p304, E2; ☎625 50 29; www.rentabike.nl; Damstraat 20-22; bike rental per 3/24hr from €6.75/9.50; ⏰9am-6pm; 🚋4/9/16/24 Dam) Rents bikes of all types from its shop near the Dam.

MacBike (Map p300, G3; ☎620 09 85; www.macbike.nl; Stationsplein 5; bike rental per 3/24hr from €7.50/9.75; ⏰9am-5.45pm; 🚋4/9/16/24 Centraal Station) Among the most touristy of companies (bikes are bright red, with logos), but has a convenient location at Centraal Station, plus others at Waterlooplein (p100) and Leidseplein (p135). Big assortment of bikes available.

Bike Tours

A bike tour is an ideal way to get to know Amsterdam. Bike rental is included in prices (tour companies also rent bikes). Be sure to reserve in advance. Great options include the following:

Orangebike (www.orange-bike.nl; Buiksloterweg 5c; tours €22.50-32.50; ⏰office 9am-5.45pm Mon-Fri, 10am-5pm Sat & Sun; ⛴Buiksloterweg) Traditional city and countryside tours (including a beach tour), plus themed options like the Snack Tour, sampling *bitterballen* (croquettes) and *jenever* (Dutch gin), and architectural tours. The shop is in Amsterdam-Noord, a five-minute ferry ride from Centraal Station.

Mike's Bike Tours (p135) A range of fantastic, often youth-oriented tours around town, the harbour and further afield south along the Amstel river, past dairy farms and windmills.

Yellow Bike (Map p300, C5; ☎620 69 40; www.yellowbike.nl; Nieuwezijds Kolk 29; city/countryside tours €27.50/32.50; 🚋1/2/5/13/17 Nieuwezijds Kolk) The original. Choose from city tours or the longer countryside tour through the pretty Waterland district to the north.

Road Rules

➡ Helmets aren't compulsory. Most Dutch cyclists don't use them and they don't come standard with rental.

➡ Amsterdam has 500km of bike paths. Use the bicycle lane on the road's right-hand side, marked by white lines and bike symbols.

➡ Cycle in the same direction as traffic and adhere to all traffic lights and signs.

➡ Hand signal when turning.

➡ After dark, a white headlight and red tail light are required by law.

➡ Park only in bicycle racks near train and tram stations and in certain public squares (or risk the removal of your bike by the police).

Cycling Tips

➡ Most bikes come with two locks: one for the front wheel (attach it to the bike frame, too), the other for the back. One of these locks should also be attached to a fixed structure (preferably a bike rack).

➡ Cross tram rails at a sharp angle to avoid getting stuck.

➡ Watch out for vehicles, other bikes and oblivious pedestrians.

➡ Ring your bell as a warning as often as necessary.

Buying a Bike

Cheap, rebuilt bikes are available from ReCycle (p182). Or browse Waterlooplein Flea Market (p109) for used bikes.

NEED TO KNOW

Bike Paths Routecraft (www.routecraft.com) calculates the best bike routes in the city.

MacBike Maps Fun bike maps covering themes such as Jewish sites, canals, Amsterdam Noord's countryside and more. Maps cost a euro or two and are available at tourist offices, as well as MacBike shops.

Assistance If your bike goes missing, call the Fietsdepot (Bike Depository) at ☎334 45 22 to see if it was removed by the city (perhaps for being parked in an unsafe spot). If not, call the police on ☎0900 88 44 or visit the local station to report it as stolen.

Cycling Beyond the City

You don't have to pedal far from Amsterdam to reach idyllic, windmill-dotted landscapes. LF routes (*landelijke fietsroutes;* long-distance routes somewhat like bike highways) criss-cross the country. Look out for the widely available Falk/VVV *Fietskaart met Knooppuntennetwerk* (cycling network) map series, with keys in English.

By Numbers

➡ Total number of bikes in Amsterdam: 881,000

➡ Total number of cars: 263,000

➡ Total number of bike racks: 250,000

➡ Number of spaces at Centraal Station's bike-parking garage: 2500

➡ Number of bikes stolen in Amsterdam each year: 50,000 to 80,000

Top Cycling Spots

➡ Vondelpark (p173) Urban oasis.

➡ Eastern Islands (p98) Contemporary architecture.

➡ Amsterdamse Bos (p202) Enchanting woodlands.

➡ Amsterdam-Noord (p85) Windmills and bucolic farmland.

➡ Amstelsluizen (p132) Riverside riding by the locks.

Like a Local

Get on your bike, head to the nearest brown café *and take a free course in Dutch culture by simply observing what goes on around you. It's one thing to witness local life and another to actually immerse yourself in it.*

PETER PTSCHELINZEW / GETTY IMAGES ©

A canalside *café*

Embrace the Gezellig Culture

This particularly Dutch quality, which is most widely found in old brown *cafés* (traditional Dutch pubs), is one of the best reasons to visit Amsterdam. It's variously translated as snug, friendly, cosy, informal and convivial, but *gezelligheid* – the state of being *gezellig* – is something more easily experienced than defined. You can get this warm and fuzzy feeling in many places and situations, often while nursing a brew with friends during *borrel* – an informal gathering over drinks. And nearly any cosy establishment lit by candles probably qualifies.

Find Your Way Around

Navigate the Country

'Holland' is a popular synonym for the Netherlands, yet it only refers to the combined provinces of Noord (North) and Zuid (South) Holland. (Amsterdam is Noord-Holland's largest city; Haarlem is the provincial capital.) The rest of the country is not Holland, even if locals themselves often make the mistake.

Navigate the City

Amsterdam's concentric canals and similarly named streets make it all too easy to get lost. Some pointers: a *gracht* (canal), such as Egelantiersgracht, is distinct from a *straat* (street) such as Egelantiersstraat. A *dwarsstraat* (cross-street) that intersects a *straat* is often preceded by *eerste, tweede, derde* and *vierde* (first, second, third and fourth; marked 1e, 2e, 3e and 4e on maps). For example Eerste Egelantiersdwarsstraat is the first cross-street of Egelantiersstraat (ie the nearest cross-street to the city centre). Streets preceded by *lange* (long) and *korte* (short) simply mean the longer or shorter street. Be aware, too, that seemingly continuous streets regularly change name along their length.

Pedal Power

It takes spending all of five minutes in Amsterdam to realise that locals bike everywhere. Literally everywhere. They bike to the dentist, to work, to the opera and to brunch; they bike in snow, rain, sunshine and fog. So don't just rent a bike for a quick spin around the Vondelpark – get on the beaten path by biking everywhere, too. Dressing up to bike to dinner and a show, or to drinks and a club, is a typical Dutch pastime that locals shrug off but visitors marvel over. Put on a suit or a cocktail dress and pedal away. No matter what you wear or where you're going, you'll blend in (and have fun doing it).

Another great opportunity to join the locals is on National Cycling Day. It's held on the second Saturday in May, in conjunction with National Mill Day, and includes family cycling trips along special routes.

Soak Up Dutch History

One of the best ways to experience Amsterdam's unique history – from the highs of the Golden Age to the tragic years of German occupation – is to join the crowds at one of the city's many history-oriented celebrations. On Liberation Day (5 May) Amsterdammers join together to celebrate the end of German occupation in 1945; it's jubilantly commemorated with speeches, concerts and street parties. The Dam, Vondelpark and Museumplein are generally the focus of festivities.

Another interesting, if more sombre, local experience is to trek down to the Dam on Remembrance Day (4 May), when King Willem-Alexander lays a wreath for the victims of WWII at the Nationaal Monument on the Dam. At 8pm sharp, the city solemnly observes two minutes' silence.

Orange Fever

If you've ever attended a sporting event where the Dutch are playing, you'll already be familiar with *oranjegekte* (orange craze), also known as *oranjekoorts* (orange fever). The custom of wearing the traditional colour of the Dutch royal family, the House of Orange-Nassau, was originally limited to celebration days for the monarchy, such as Queen's Day (Koninginnedag), now King's Day (Koningsdag). But particularly since the 1974 FIFA World Cup, when tens of thousands of orange-clad football supporters cheered on every game, the ritual of wearing outlandish orange get-ups – clothes, scarves, wigs, fake-fur top hats, face paint, feather boas, you name it – has become a Dutch phenomenon. To really celebrate like a local, you know what colour to wear.

Burning of the Christmas Trees

It's a strange Dutch tradition that makes even normally jaded adults positively wide-eyed: the burning of the Christmas trees. Think of it as a pagan version of Sinterklaas – a time when people of all ages take to the streets to create massive bonfires of festive trees past their prime, to usher in the New Year without 'dead wood', so to speak. The event usually takes place about a week after New Year's. Museumplein is a good spot to check out the madness.

Join in the Festivities

Explore the unique character of Amsterdam's diverse neighbourhoods by partying with the locals at a neighbourhood festival.

Revel in the city's rich Surinamese and African heritage at the food-and-football **Kwaku** (www.kwakufestival.nl) festival, held in Nelson Mandelapark each weekend from mid-July to early August.

Listen to classic Jordaan ballads during the Jordaan Festival (p24).

Or grab your platinum-blonde wig and platform shoes for the hysterically fun Hartjesdagen Zeedijk (p276) festival, held on the third weekend of August. Dating back to medieval times, it features street theatre, a cross-dressing parade and all kinds of costumed extroverts on and around Zeedijk.

Locals party like it's King's Day during the **Uitmarkt** (www.uitmarkt.nl) festival, which kicks off the cultural season in late August.

For Free

Although the costs of Amsterdam's accommodation and dining can mount up, there is a bright side, too. Not only is the entire Canal Ring a Unesco World Heritage Site (read: free living museum), but virtually every day you'll find things to do and see that are free (or virtually free, at least).

Free Sights

The money-saving **I Amsterdam Card** (p273) offers discounts and freebies at shops, attractions and restaurants. Students and seniors should bring ID and flash it at every opportunity for reduced admission fees.

Civic Guard Gallery (p71) Stroll through the monumental collection of portraits, from Golden Age to modern.

Rijksmuseum Gardens (p167) Even many locals don't know that the Renaissance and baroque gardens are free and open to the public (including occasional sculpture exhibitions). Let your pre-Raphaelite spirit run free as you explore the rose bushes, hedges and statues.

Begijnhof (p69) Explore the 14th-century hidden courtyard and its clandestine churches.

Stadsarchief (p130) You never know what treasures you'll find in the vaults of the city's archives.

Gassan Diamonds (p96) Distinguish your princess from marquise, river from top cape.

Albert Cuypmarkt (p190) Amsterdam's biggest market, and the city's many other bazaars are all free to browse.

ARCAM (p100) A fascinating look at Amsterdam's architecture – past, present and future.

Stedelijk Museum Bureau Amsterdam (p150) This wee outpost of the city's modern-art museum shows cutting-edge works.

Free Entertainment

For discounted same-day tickets, visit the **Last Minute Ticket Shop** (www.lastminuteticketshop.nl).

Concertgebouw (p185) Sharpen your elbows to get in for Wednesday's lunchtime concert, often a public rehearsal for the performance later that evening.

Muziektheater (p108) Free classical concerts fill the air during lunch on Tuesdays.

Bimhuis (p108) Jazz sessions hot up the revered venue on Tuesday nights.

Openluchttheater (p185) Vondelpark's outdoor theatre puts on concerts and kids' shows throughout summer.

EYE Film Institute (p85) Has pods in the basement where you can watch free films.

North Sea Jazz Club (p161) Musicians on the come-up let loose in free 'Summer Sessions' during the week and late-night shows on Saturdays.

Mulligans (p140) Free music sessions and gigs at the city's best-known and -loved Irish pub.

Festivals Many festivals and events, including the ultimate party, King's Day (p23), are totally free. (Well, you might want to bring some euros for beer and a cheap orange wig.)

Free Transport

Yellow Backie (www.yellowbackie.org) A program that lets visitors catch a free ride on the back of a local's bike. When you see someone cycling by with a bright-yellow luggage rack on the rear, yell 'Backie!' The rider should stop, let you hop on, and pedal you onward.

Ferries Free ferries depart behind Centraal Station to NDSM-werf, northern Amsterdam's edgy art community 15 minutes up harbour, and to the EYE Film Institute, five minutes across the river.

Keizersgracht canal

Canals

Amsterdammers have always known their Canal Ring, built during the Golden Age, is extraordinary. Unesco made it official in 2010, when it listed the waterways as a World Heritage site. Today the city's canals outnumber those in Venice, and Amsterdam also has three times as many bridges – more than any other city worldwide.

History

Far from being simply decorative or picturesque, or even useful waterways for transport, the canals were crucial to drain and reclaim the waterlogged land. They solved Amsterdam's essential problem: keeping the land and sea separate.

Names & Layout

In Dutch a canal is a *gracht* (pronounced 'khrakht') and the main canals form the central *grachtengordel* (canal ring). These beauties came to life in the early 1600s, after Amsterdam's population grew beyond its medieval walls and city planners put together an ambitious design for expansion. The concentric waterways they built are the same ones you see today.

CORE CANALS

Starting from the core, the major semicircular canals are the Singel, Herengracht, Keizersgracht and Prinsengracht. An easy way to remember them is that, apart from the singular **Singel** (which originally was a moat that defended Amsterdam's outer limits), these canals are in alphabetical order.

The **Herengracht** is where Amsterdam's wealthiest residents moved once the canals were completed. They built their mansions alongside it (particularly around the Golden Bend), hence its name, which translates to Gentlemen's Canal.

Almost as swanky was the **Keizersgracht** (Emperor's Canal), a nod to Holy Roman Emperor Maximilian I.

The **Prinsengracht** – named after William the Silent, Prince of Orange and the first Dutch royal – was designed as a slightly cheaper canal with smaller residences and warehouses. It also acted as a barrier against the working-class Jordaan beyond.

RADIAL CANALS

The canals cutting across the core canals like spokes on a bicycle wheel are known as radial canals. From west to east the major radial canals are Brouwersgracht, Leidsegracht and Reguliersgracht, also in alphabetical order.

The **Brouwersgracht** (Brewers Canal) is one of Amsterdam's most beautiful waterways. It takes its name from the many breweries that lined the banks in the 16th and 17th centuries.

The **Leidsegracht** was named after the city of Leiden, to which it was the main water route.

Peaceful **Reguliersgracht** was named after an order of monks whose monastery was located nearby. Today it's often better known as the 'canal of seven bridges' and its iconic scenery isn't lost on canal-boat operators.

Bridges

Some truly striking bridges straddle the city's waterways.

Spanning the Singel, the **Torensluis** (Map p310; Singel 165a) was built in 1648, making it Amsterdam's oldest bridge (also, at 39m, its widest). The Blauwbrug (p132) crosses the Amstel river, with fish sculptures and imperial-crowned street lamps dotting the way. And you've probably seen the iconic Magere Brug (p132) in photos or appearing in films, stretching over the Amstel, glowing beneath the twinkle of 1200 tiny lights. In the Western Islands, look out for the narrow, charming Drieharingenbrug (p152).

NEED TO KNOW

Canal Safety

Virtually none of Amsterdam's canals are fenced or otherwise blocked off by barriers. If you're travelling with young children, keep a close eye out to ensure they don't take an unexpected plunge.

Ice skating was part of the Dutch psyche long before scarfed figures appeared in Golden Age winterscapes. The first skates were made from cow shanks and ribs, had hand-drilled holes and were tied to the feet. When canals and ponds freeze over, everyone takes to the ice. Beware, though: drownings occur each year. Stay away from the ice unless you see large groups of people and be very careful at the edges and under bridges – areas with weak ice.

Boating Rules & Advice

- Stay on the waterways' right (starboard) side.
- Commercial traffic (including tour boats) has right of way.
- The speed limit is 7.5km per hour (the top speed for many electric rental boats).
- Life jackets/vests aren't compulsory (but are strongly recommended).
- Drinking alcohol while in control of a boat is illegal.
- Shouting and amplified music is also illegal on board.
- Many bridges have low clearance (less than 2m).
- Docking is permitted anywhere in the city except beneath bridges, on narrow waterways, junctions or adjacent to rescue steps, or locations signposted as prohibited.
- Switch on your lights at dusk.

Houseboats

Some 2500 houseboats line Amsterdam's canals. Living on the water became popular after WWII, when a surplus of old cargo ships helped fill the gap of a housing shortage on land. The Prinsengracht displays

Canals by Neighbourhood

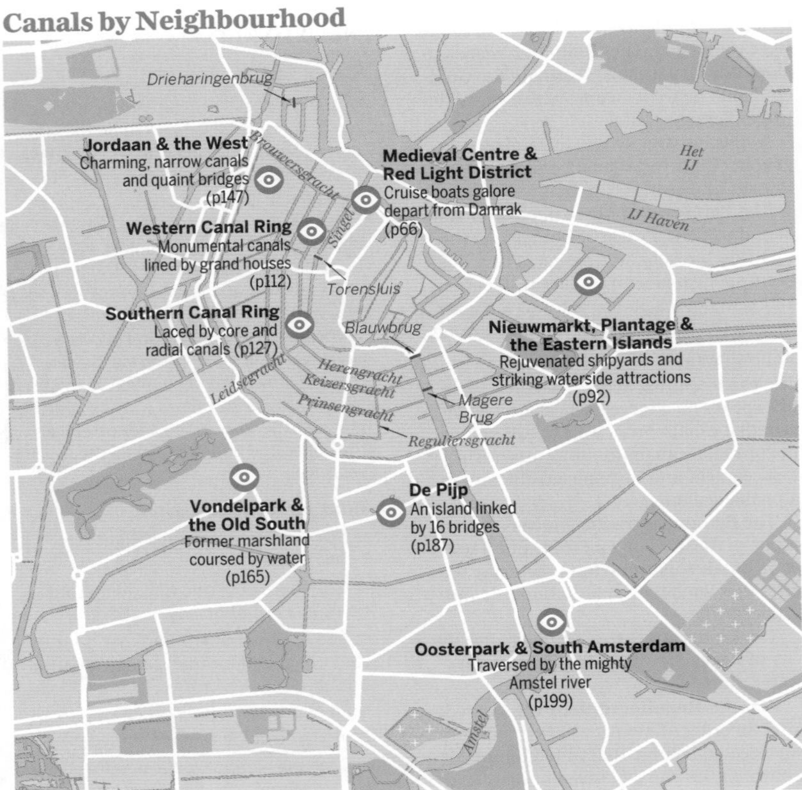

a particularly diverse mix of houseboats. You can climb aboard one and explore the cramped, er, cosy interior at the Houseboat Museum (p150), or book to stay overnight on the water yourself in true Amsterdam style.

Greener Canals

While Amsterdam's canals certainly aren't crystal clear (around 12,000 to 15,000 bicycles are pulled from the canals each year), they're cleaner today than ever before in the city's history.

In part this is due to the locks, most of which close three times per week to allow fresh water to be pumped from the IJsselmeer lake. This creates a current that flushes the stagnant canal water out through open locks on the other side of the city and out to sea – check out the mighty Amstelsluizen (p132) on the Amstel in the Southern Canal Ring. What's more, the canals are regularly patrolled by specialised cleaning boats. And since 2005, houseboats have been required to connect to the city's sewerage system. All should be connected by 2017.

These efforts have made a significant difference, as evidenced by the wildlife the canals now attract. Some 20 fish and crab species now live happily below the water's surface. They, in turn, attract a wide variety of water birds such as gulls, herons, ducks, coots and cormorants. You might even see – or more likely, hear – neon-green ring-necked parakeets circling above. These, of course, aren't native; their presence in the city dates from 1976, when a pet-shop owner, tormented by a pair of parakeets screeching in store, high-tailed them to the Vondelpark and let them loose. The birds soon bred, and now more than 3700 parakeets shriek around town.

As part of its comprehensive sustainability plan, Amsterdam is working toward a goal of allowing only electric tour boats on its central canals. It's also considering a one-way boat-traffic system to further reduce emissions and noise pollution, and to keep the waterways as pristine as possible.

Boat Tours

Sure they're touristy, but canal cruises are also a delightful way to see the city. Several operators depart from moorings at Centraal Station, Damrak, Rokin and opposite the Rijksmuseum. Costs are similar (around €16 per adult). To avoid the steamed-up-glass-window effect, look for a boat with an open seating area. On a night tour you'll see the bridges lit up (though these tours usually cost a bit more).

Those Dam Boat Guys Map p314 (☎06 1885 5219; www.thosedamboatguys.com; per person €20; ⌚1pm, 3pm & 5pm; 🚋13/14/17 Westermarkt) Here's your least-touristy canal-cruise option. The guys offer cheeky small tours (no more than 11 people) on electric boats. Feel free to bring food, beer, smoking material and whatever else you want for the 90-minute jaunt. Departure is from Cafe Wester (Nieuwe Leliestraat 2).

Canal Bus (☎217 05 00; www.canal.nl; day pass adult/child €23/11.50; ⌚10am-6pm; 📶; 🚋1/2/5 Leidseplein) Offers a handy hop-on, hop-off service. Its 16 docks around the city are located near the big museums and landmarks.

Blue Boat Company Map p322 (☎679 13 70; www.blueboat.nl; Stadhouderskade 30; 75-minute tour adult/child €16/8.50; ⌚half-hourly 10am-6pm Mar-Oct, hourly Nov-Feb; 🚋1/2/5/7/10 Leidseplein) Blue Boat's 75-minute main tour glides by the top sights. Ninety-minute evening cruises (adult/child €19.50/15.50) are offered at 8pm, 9pm and 10pm from March to October and at 8pm November to February. Other cruises include a children's pirate-themed tour, a dinner cruise and a tour in a smaller, open-top boat. The dock is near the Max Euweplein.

Wetlands Safari Map p300 (☎06 5355 2669; www.wetlandssafari.nl; incl transport & picnic adult/child €48/29; ⌚9.30am Mon-Fri, 10am Sat & Sun mid-Apr–Sep) OK, so it's not a canal tour, but it is an exceptional 5½-hour boat trip. Participants take a bus to just north of the centre, then canoe through boggy, froggy wetlands and on past windmills and 17th-century villages. Departure is from behind Centraal Station at the 'G' bus stop.

Boat Rentals

Canal Bike (www.canal.nl; per person per hr €8; ⌚10am-6pm Apr-Oct) These pedal boats allow you to splash around the canals at your own speed. Landing stages are by the Rijksmuseum, Leidseplein and Anne Frank Huis. Deposit of €20 required. Affiliated with Canal Bus.

Boaty (p191) Rents cool little electric boats near the Hotel Okura in De Pijp. It's a less-traffic-filled place to launch from, and lets you get your bearings before hitting the crowded city-centre waterways.

Kanoschool (www.kanoschool.nl; Admiralengracht 60; rental per hr €10; ⌚hours vary) Rents one- and two-person kayaks for paddling along the canals (waterway map and tips supplied; photo ID required as a deposit). Also has SUPs (stand up paddleboards). Located in the west, near Rembrandtpark.

Canal Motorboats Map p313 (☎422 70 07; www.canalmotorboats.com; Zandhoek 10a; rental 1st hour €50; ⌚10am-10pm; 🚌48 Barentszplein) Has small, electric aluminium boats (maximum seven passengers) that are easy to drive (no boat licence required). Staff give you a map and plenty of advice, and will come and rescue you if need be. Credit-card imprint or €150 cash deposit required. Reduced rates after the first hour.

Lonely Planet's Top Choices

Prinsengracht (p122) The liveliest of Amsterdam's inner canals, with cafes, shops and houseboats lining the quays.

Reguliersgracht (p131) From here you can peer through the arches of seven bridges.

Brouwersgracht (p149) Among some seriously tough competition, Amsterdammers swear this is the city's most beautiful canal.

Herengracht (p117) Amsterdam's stateliest canal takes in the city's most prestigious real estate along the Golden Bend.

Bloemgracht (p150) This gorgeous canal is home to a large number of fine, gabled houses.

Egelantiersgracht (p149) An elegant and serene canal that feels like you have it (practically) to yourself.

Best Canal-Related Museums

Houseboat Museum (p150) Discover how *gezellig* (convivial, cosy) houseboat living can be aboard this 1914 sailing-barge-turned-museum.

Het Grachtenhuis (p116) Inventive multimedia displays explain how the Canal Ring and its amazing houses were built.

Best Canal Festivals & Events

King's Day (p23) During one of Europe's biggest street parties, plenty of action takes place around the city's famous waterways.

Grachtenfestival (p24) The Canal Festival sees classical musicians play alongside and on the water aboard a barge.

Amsterdam Gay Pride (p24) Amsterdam proudly hosts the only waterborne gay pride festival in the world.

Open Tuinen Dagen (p24) Open Garden Days offer the opportunity to view dozens of private gardens along the canals.

Sinterklaas Intocht (p25) Even St Nicholas sails into town; his arrival by boat heralds the Christmas season.

Amsterdam Light Festival (p25) Highlights include a magical, mid-December Christmas Canal Parade of illuminated boats floating along the waterways.

Amsterdam City Swim (p24) Locals kick and splash through the canals to raise money for charity.

Best Houseboat Accommodation

Houseboat Ms Luctor (p228) A beautiful 1913-built self-contained boat with mahogany panelling, moored in a quiet location near Centraal Station.

B&B Le Maroxidien (p231) Dutch hospitality in a former freighter with three exotically themed cabins in its guest wing.

Frederic Rentabike (p229) Not only rents bikes, but a range of houseboats on the Prinsengracht, Brouwersgracht and Bloemgracht.

Best Canal-Side Dining

De Belhamel (p120) At the head of the Herengracht, this superb restaurant's canal-side tables are an aphrodisiac.

Buffet van Odette (p135) Simple, creative cooking overlooking the Prinsengracht's crooked canal houses.

Gebr Hartering (p104) Exquisitely presented modern Dutch dishes compete with an impossibly romantic canal-side location.

De Prins (p156) This brown *café* serves delicious fondue at tables sprinkled along the Prinsengracht.

Best Canal-Side Drinking

't Smalle (p157) Dock right by the stone terrace of the 18th-century former *jenever* (Dutch gin) distillery.

Café P 96 (p159) The summertime terrace of this late-night watering hole is aboard a houseboat.

Hannekes Boom (p107) Local favourite with a gorgeous leafy beer garden on the water.

Café Papeneiland (p159) A 1642 gem on the corner of the Prinsengracht and Brouwersgracht canals.

De Ysbreeker (p204) Hot spot overlooking the houseboat-dotted Amstel.

Café de Jaren (p82) Sit on the balcony, watch the Amstel flow by, and the afternoon vanishes.

Waterkant (p158) Big, buzzy patio on the Singelgracht prime for gin and tonics and Surinamese snacks.

Café Binnen Buiten (p196) The best canal-side terrace in Amsterdam's 'Latin Quarter', De Pijp.

Museums & Galleries

Amsterdam's world-class museums draw millions of visitors each year. The art collections take pride of place – you can't walk a kilometre here without bumping into a masterpiece. Canal-house museums are another local speciality. And, of course, the freewheeling city has a fine assortment of oddball museums dedicated to everything from hash to houseboats.

All the Art

The Dutch Masters helped spawn the prolific art collections around town. You've probably heard of a few of these guys: Johannes Vermeer, Frans Hals and Rembrandt van Rijn. They came along during the Golden Age when a new, bourgeois society of merchants and shopkeepers were spending money to brighten up their homes and workplaces with fresh paintings. The masters were there to meet the need, and their output from the era now fills the city's top museums.

Other Treasures

The Netherlands' maritime prowess during the Golden Age also filled the coffers of local institutions. Silver, porcelain and colonial knick-knacks picked up on distant voyages form the basis of collections in the Rijksmuseum (p167), Amsterdam Museum (p73), Het Scheepvaartmuseum (p98) and Tropenmuseum (p201).

Canal-House Museums

There are two kinds: the first preserves the house as a living space, with sumptuous interiors that show how the richest locals lived once upon a time, as at Museum van Loon (p130). The other type uses the elegant structure as a backdrop for unique collections, such as the Kattenkabinet (p130) for cat art.

Contemporary Galleries

Van Gogh and the Golden Age masters grab all the glory, but Amsterdam's art scene goes well beyond them. Several contemporary galleries dot the city, providing outlets for avant-garde and emerging artists. Many galleries, such as W139 in the Red Light District, began as squats and then moved into the mainstream over the years. Gallery-dense neighbourhoods include the Jordaan and the Southern Canal Ring.

How to Beat the Crowds

Queues at the Van Gogh Museum, Rijksmuseum, Anne Frank Huis and others can easily reach an hour, particularly in summer. Want to avoid the mobs? Here are some strategies:

Take advantage of e-tickets Most sights sell them and there's little to no surcharge. They typically allow you to enter via a separate, faster queue. Note that, in many cases, you need to be able to print the tickets (though mobile phone tickets are becoming increasingly common).

Go late Queues are shortest during late afternoon and evening. Visit after 3pm for the Rijksmuseum and Van Gogh Museum (also open Friday nights), and after 6pm for the Anne Frank Huis (open late nightly in summer).

Try tourist offices You can also buy advance tickets at visitor info centres, but often the queues there are as lengthy as the ones at the sights.

Buy a discount card In addition to saving on entrance fees, discount cards commonly provide fast-track entry.

NEED TO KNOW

Opening Hours

- Most museums open 10am to 5pm, some close on Monday.
- The Van Gogh Museum stays open to 10pm on Friday.
- The Anne Frank Huis stays open to 9pm or 10pm daily in summer and on Saturday year-round.

Costs

- Tickets are typically €8–18.
- Kids under 13 often get in for free or half-price.
- Audio guides are €2–5.

Top Tips

- Pre-book tickets for the big museums.
- Queues are shortest during late afternoon and evening.
- Friday, Saturday and Sunday are the busiest days.
- Many hotels sell surcharge-free tickets to the big museums as a service to guests; be sure to ask your front-desk staff.

Advance Purchase Recommendations

- **Van Gogh Museum & Rijksmuseum** No surcharge for e-tickets; puts you in a faster queue.
- **Anne Frank Huis** Small surcharge for e-tickets with set entry times; lets you bypass the queue.
- **Stedelijk Museum** No surcharge for e-tickets; lets you bypass the queue.
- **Heineken Experience & Madame Tussauds Amsterdam** E-tickets provide a small discount over regular admission; puts you in a faster queue.
- **Het Grachtenhuis** E-tickets provide a small discount over regular admission, but mostly they ensure access for the limited-space tours.

How to Save Money

Discount cards (p275) can save you lots of cash, as long as you choose wisely. There are three main options:

I Amsterdam Card Good for quick visits to the city. Provides admission to more than 30 museums (many of the same venues as the Museumkaart, though not the Rijksmuseum), plus a GVB transit pass (p273), a canal cruise, and restaurant and shop discounts. You'll need to visit three or so museums per day to make it pay for itself.

Museumkaart This card works well if you plan to be in the Netherlands a while. It provides free entry to some 400 museums nationwide for a year. Great for queue-jumping; no transit pass or other perks though.

Holland Pass It's similar to the I Amsterdam Card, but without the rush for usage; you can visit sights over a month. It gets a bit tricky to figure out how much money you're saving because you pick from tiers of attractions (the most popular/expensive sights are gold tier, others are silver tier). It also includes a train ticket from the airport.

Museums & Galleries by Neighbourhood

- **Medieval Centre & Red Light District** Spans the sacred (several church museums) to the profane (Sexmuseum; Hash, Marijuana & Hemp Museum).
- **Nieuwmarkt, Plantage & Eastern Islands** Museum het Rembrandthuis, NEMO, Het Scheepvaartmuseum and the Verzetsmuseum scatter around the neighbourhood.
- **Western Canal Ring** Anne Frank Huis draws the mega-crowds; smaller, canal-focused museums pop up, too.
- **Southern Canal Ring** Home to the Hermitage Amsterdam plus several quirky museums.
- **Jordaan & the West** Off-the-beaten path collections from tulips to houseboats to fluorescent art.
- **Vondelpark & the Old South** Holds the Museum Quarter and its big three: Van Gogh Museum, Rijksmuseum and Stedelijk Museum.
- **De Pijp** Crowds amass to learn about brewing at the Heineken Experience.
- **Oosterpark & South Amsterdam** Colonial trinkets at Tropenmuseum, avant-garde art at Cobra Museum.

Lonely Planet's Top Choices

Van Gogh Museum (p170) Hangs the world's largest collection of the tormented artist's vivid swirls.

Rijksmuseum (p167) Rembrandts, Vermeers, crystal goblets and magic lanterns pack the nation's sprawling treasure chest.

Anne Frank Huis (p114) The Secret Annexe and Anne's claustrophobic bedroom provide an unnerving insight into life during WWII.

Pianola Museum (p149) Listen to rare jazz and classical tunes unrolling on vintage player pianos.

Best Art Museums

Museum het Rembrandthuis (p94) Immerse yourself in the old master's paint-spattered studio and handsome home.

Stedelijk Museum (p172) Renowned modern art from Picasso to Mondrian to Warhol fills the newly revamped building.

Hermitage Amsterdam (p132) The outpost of Russia's Hermitage Museum picks from its rich home trove to mount mega exhibits.

FOAM (p130) Hip photography museum with changing exhibits by famous shutterbugs.

Best History Museums

Amsterdam Museum (p73) Whiz-bang exhibits take you through seven centuries of the city's intriguing history.

Verzetsmuseum (p99) Find out how the Dutch Resistance operated when the Germans occupied the country during WWII.

Best Unusual Museums

Kattenkabinet (p130) Art devoted to cats (including works by Picasso and Rembrandt) fills a rambling old canal house.

Tassenmuseum Hendrikje (p131) A museum of handbags and purses throughout history, with lots of sparkling celebrity clutches.

Sexmuseum Amsterdam (p71) The naughty art and artefacts make for a fun, silly browse.

Electric Ladyland (p149) The world's first museum of fluorescent art offers a trippy glow-in-the-dark experience.

Torture Museum (p73) Eerie galleries show branding tongs, skull crackers, a guillotine and the Iron Maiden of Nuremberg.

Best Canal-House Museums

Museum Van Loon (p130) This opulent old manor whispers family secrets in its shadowy rooms.

Museum Willet-Holthuysen (p131) Peruse sumptuous paintings, china and a French-style garden with sundial.

Best Underappreciated Museums

Tropenmuseum (p201) Contains a whopping collection of ritual masks, spiky spears and other colonial booty.

Het Scheepvaartmuseum (p98) The Maritime Museum features ancient globes, spooky ship figureheads and a replica schooner to climb.

Museum Ons' Lieve Heer op Solder (p76) Looks like an ordinary canal house, but hides a relic-rich 17th-century church inside.

Best Galleries & Arts Centres

Walls Gallery (p145) Edgy space in a former garage that shows up-and-coming artists.

W139 (p76) Ponder political, hot-button multimedia works in the thick of the Red Light District.

Civic Guard Gallery (p71) Check out the collection of enormous portraits, from Golden Age to modern day.

De Appel (p95) Count on having your mind expanded at this hip, contemporary-arts centre.

KochxBos (p149) Peculiar pop surrealism and underground art brighten a corner in the Jordaan.

Best for Kids

NEMO (p100) Kid-focused, hands-on science labs inside and a terrace with a splashy summer water feature on the roof.

Joods Historisch Museum (p96) The children's section replicates a Jewish home, with a hands-on music room and kitchen for baking.

Madame Tussauds Amsterdam (p71) Youth get excited to see their favourite celebrities and heroes up close (albeit in wax).

Micropia (p99) The world's first microbe museum has a wall of poop, kissing meter and other inventive exhibits.

Various cheeses for sale

Eating

Amsterdam's food scene is woefully underrated. Beyond pancakes and potatoes, Dutch chefs put their spin on all kinds of regional and global dishes using ingredients plucked from local seas and farms. Wherever you go, meals are something to linger over as the candles burn low on the tabletop.

FEBO (p45)

Specialities

TRADITIONAL DUTCH

Traditional Dutch cuisine revolves around meat, potatoes and vegetables. Typical dishes include *stamppot* (mashed pot) – potatoes mashed with another vegetable (usually kale or endive) and served with smoked sausage and strips of bacon. *Erwtensoep* is a thick pea soup with smoked sausage and bacon that's usually served in winter.

Pannenkoeken translates to pancakes – the Dutch variety is huge, served one to a plate and topped with sweet or savoury ingredients. The mini version, covered in sugar or syrup, is *poffertjes*. You can often find these fresh at markets.

Many snack bars and pubs serve *appeltaart* (apple pie). For breakfast it's common to eat *hagelslag* (chocolate sprinkles) on buttered bread.

CONTEMPORARY DUTCH

Fresh winds are blowing through the Dutch traditional kitchen, breathing new life into centuries-old recipes by giving them a contemporary twist. Creative Dutch chefs are taking concepts from the rest the world and melding them with locally sourced meats, seafood and vegetables. Amsterdam is ground zero for this type of 'contemporary Dutch' fare.

INDONESIAN & SURINAMESE

The most famous dish is rijsttafel (Indonesian banquet): a dozen or more tiny dishes such as braised beef, pork satay and ribs served with white rice. Other popular dishes are *nasi goreng* – fried rice with onion, pork, shrimp and spices, often topped with a fried egg or shredded omelette – and *bami goreng*, the same thing, but with noodles in place of rice. Indonesian food is

NEED TO KNOW

Price Ranges

Prices listed are for the cost of a main dish at dinner:

€ less than €12

€€ €12–25

€€€ more than €25

Opening Hours

Most restaurants open 11am to 2.30pm for lunch and 6pm to 10pm for dinner.

Reservations

Phone ahead to make a reservation for eateries in the middle and upper price brackets. Nearly everyone speaks English. Many places offer online booking options.

Service

Service in Amsterdam may be impersonal, off-putting and slow. Don't take it personally, it's not directed at you.

Tipping

Diners do tip, but modestly. Leave 5% to 10% for a cafe snack (if your bill comes to €9.50, you might round up to €10), leave 10% to 15% for a restaurant meal (the higher end for particularly good service).

Cash Rules

Many restaurants, even top-end, don't accept credit cards. Or if they do, there's often a 5% surcharge. Check first.

Saving Money

Dagschotel is dish of the day; heartier appetites might go for a *dagmenu* (a set menu of three or more courses).

Best Websites

- **Amsterdam Foodie** (www.amsterdamfoodie.nl) Restaurant reviews galore.
- **IENS** (www.iens.nl) Everyday eaters give their restaurant opinions; in Dutch.
- **Your Little Black Book** (www.yourlittleblackbook.me) What's new and hot in the city.

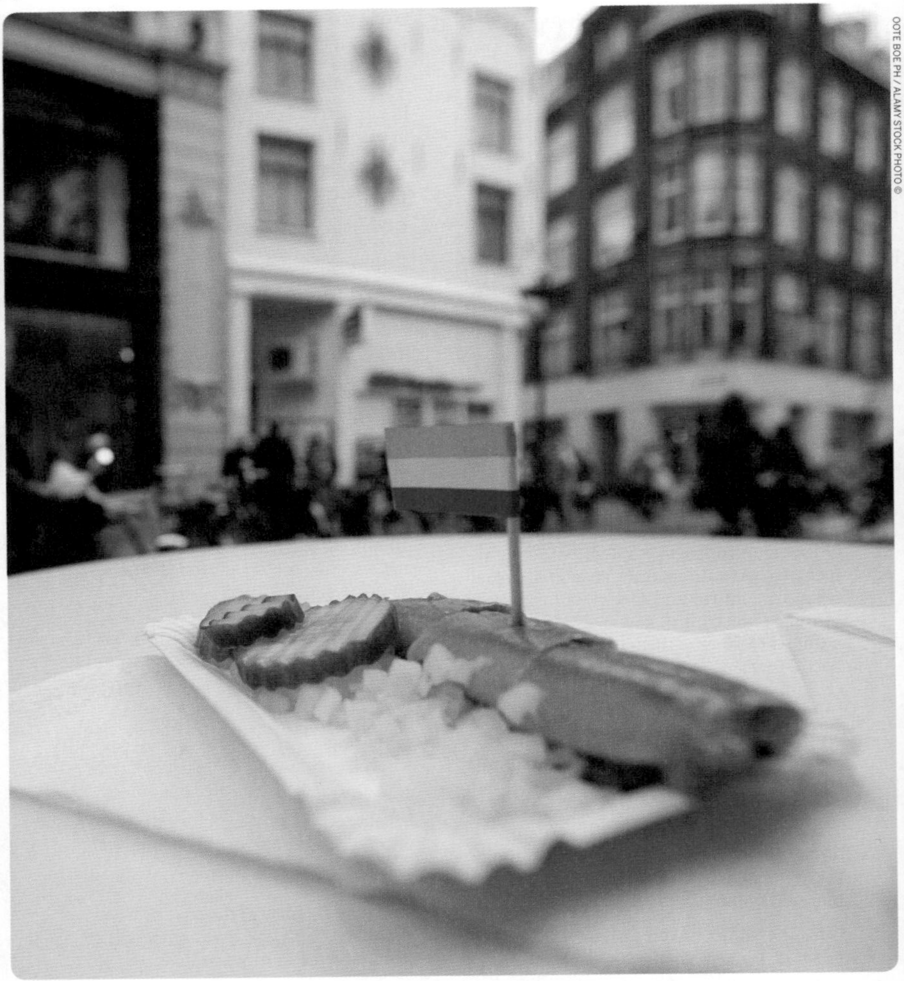

OOTE BOE PH / ALAMY STOCK PHOTO ©

LONELY PLANET / GETTY IMAGES ©

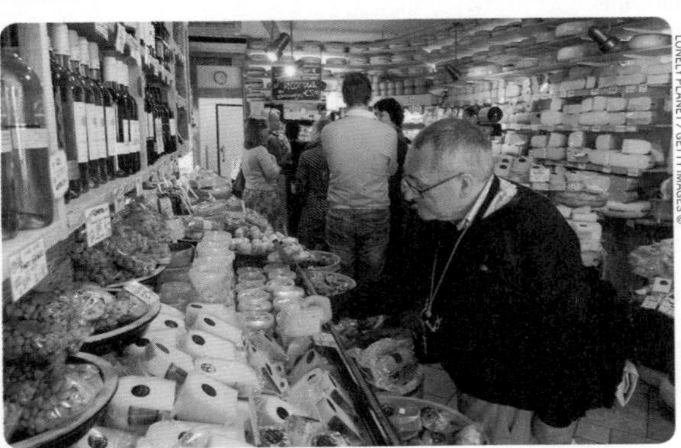

Above: *Haring* (herring)

Left: De Kaaskamer (p124), a cheese shop

usually served mild for Western palates. If you want it hot (*pedis,* pronounced 'p-*dis*'), say so, but be prepared for the ride of a lifetime.

Surinamese Caribbean-style cuisine prominently features curries (chicken, lamb or beef). Roti are burrito-like flatbread wraps stuffed with curried meat or veg; they're delicious, filling and cheap.

Snacks

Vlaamse *frites*/patat The iconic 'Flemish fries' are cut from whole potatoes and smothered in mayonnaise or myriad other gooey sauces.

Kroketten Croquettes are dough balls with various fillings that are crumbed and deep-fried; the variety called *bitterballen* are a popular brown-*café* snack served with mustard.

Haring Herring is a Dutch institution, sold at stalls around the city. It's prepared with salt or pickled, but never cooked, and served with diced onion and sometimes sweet-pickle chips.

Cheese

Locals love their *kaas* (cheese). Nearly two-thirds of all cheese sold is Gouda. The tastiest varieties have strong, complex flavours. Try some *oud* (old) Gouda, hard and rich in flavour and a popular bar snack with mustard. Edam is similar to Gouda, but slightly drier and less creamy. Leidse or Leiden cheese is another export hit, laced with cumin or caraway seed and light in flavour.

LOCAL EAT STREETS

These streets are stocked with popular local restaurants, where you can wander and choose whatever takes your fancy.

Jan Pieter Heijestraat Sociable spots keep popping up on this artery between Vondelpark and De Hallen cultural complex.

Amstelveenseweg Loads of international options along the western edge of Vondelpark.

Utrechtsestraat Chock-a-block with cafes where cool young Amsterdammers hang out; in the Southern Canal Ring.

Haarlemmerstraat & Haarlemmerdijk Adjoining streets north of the Jordaan that burst with trendy spots.

Sweets

The most famous candy is *drop,* sweet or salty liquorice sold in a bewildering variety of flavours. It's definitely an acquired taste. *Stroopwafels* hide their filling – usually thick caramel syrup – inside two cookie-esque waffles.

Quick Eats

Besides restaurants and *eetcafés* (pub-like eateries serving affordable meals), there are several quick options for feeding your face. *Broodjeszaken* (sandwich shops) are everywhere. Stroll up to the counter and pick the meat and/or cheese to go on a fluffy white or wheat roll for a few euros. Snack bars are also ubiquitous; FEBO is the most well-known, with its long rows of coin-operated yellow windows from which you pluck out a deep-fried treat. Branches are open into the wee hours, and stopping by for a greasy snack after a hard night of drinking is a Dutch tradition.

Eating by Neighbourhood

➡ **Medieval Centre & Red Light District** (p66) Name your price: from elegant Dutch to Zeedijk's Asian restaurants to alley-side sandwich shops.

➡ **Nieuwmarkt, Plantage & Eastern Islands** (p92) Nieuwmarkt's lively main square brims with locals digging in at outdoor terraces, while eateries beyond offer dramatic waterfront settings.

➡ **Western Canal Ring** (p112) Cute cafes and small restaurants surround the Negen Straatjes.

➡ **Southern Canal Ring** (p127) Cheap and cheerful around Leidseplein; diverse, quality options on Utrechtsestraat.

➡ **Jordaan & the West** (p147) Convivial little spots are the Jordaan's hallmark; scenester eats dot Westerpark.

➡ **Vondelpark & the Old South** (p165) Terrific area to dine with locals, from squats serving organic fare to cool-cat international restaurants to the big, airy Food Hall.

➡ **De Pijp** (p187) Grazing galore in the Albert Cuypmarkt; exotic ethnic places west on Albert Cuypstraat and Ferdinand Bolstraat; brunch spots everywhere.

➡ **Oosterpark & South Amsterdam** (p199) Indonesian, Moroccan, Turkish and Surinamese abounds.

Lonely Planet's Top Choices

Ron Gastrobar (p178) Ron Blaauw converted his swank, Michelin-starred eatery into this democratic spot serving Dutch-style tapas.

Greetje (p105) Resurrects and recreates Dutch classics, with mouthwatering results.

Gartine (p76) Slow-food sandwiches and a dazzling high tea hide in the Medieval Centre.

De Kas (p204) Dine in the greenhouse that grew your meal's ingredients.

Restaurant Fyra (p137) An elegant setting, and vegetables and herbs from the chef's own garden.

Best by Budget

€

Fat Dog (p190) Ultra-gourmet hot dogs by star chef Ron Blaauw.

Butcher (p190) Quite possibly the biggest, freshest burgers you'll ever taste, made right in front of you.

Braai BBQ Bar (p175) Street-food-style hot spot barbecuing tangy ribs.

Sterk Staaltje (p101) Greengrocer-like shop filled with ready-to-eat savoury treats.

De Laatste Kruimel (p77) Munch fab sandwiches and quiches amid repurposed-pallet decor.

€€

Dikke Graaf (p178) Cooking so delicious the aromas lure you in from the street.

La Cacerola (p135) Rustic, romantic gem featuring sublime Brazilian slow food.

Restaurant Bloem (p101) Exceptional meals prepared by passionate Italian chefs.

Balthazar's Keuken (p154) Ever-changing, Mediterranean-tinged dishes served in a revamped blacksmith's forge.

Buffet van Odette (p135) Airy, canal-side terrace for creative pastas and sandwiches.

€€€

Marius (p157) The chef whips up a four-course menu from his daily market finds.

Ciel Bleu (p195) Mind-blowing, two-Michelin-starred haute cuisine with 23rd-floor views over Amsterdam.

Blauw aan de Wal (p81) A 17th-century herb warehouse turned romantic restaurant in the Red Light District.

Best by Cuisine

Traditional Dutch

Bistro Bij Ons (p120) Honest-to-goodness classics include *stamppot*.

Letting (p118) Skip your hotel dining room and start the day with authentic Dutch breakfast dishes.

La Falote (p179) Stewed fish, meatballs with endives, and other daily specials of home-style cooking.

Pantry (p135) A *gezellig* (cosy, convivial) atmosphere and classic Dutch fare.

Van Dobben (p133) Meaty goodness diner-style.

Contemporary Dutch

Restaurant Elmar (p192) Organic Dutch produce used in stunning flavour combinations.

Wilde Zwijnen (p203) The Oost's rustic gem reaps praise for bold, eclectic seasonal fare.

Gebr Hartering (p104) In a seductive canal-side location, the menu changes daily, but is unfailingly delicious.

Hemelse Modder (p103) North Sea fish followed by a heavenly mousse for dessert.

Moes (p102) Farm-to-fork goodness in De Appel art centre.

Indonesian

Dèsa (p194) Hugely popular for its rijsttafel banquets.

Restaurant Blauw (p181) Feted Indonesian fare in contemporary surrounds.

Tempo Doeloe (p137) High-class rijsttafel without pretense, and one that knows how to fire up the spice.

Surinamese

Tokoman (p101) Crowds queue for the hot-spiced Surinamese sandwiches.

Spang Makandra (p191) Fabulous array of astonishingly cheap dishes served in cosy surrounds.

Roopram Roti (p203) No-frills spot for flaky roti and fiery hot sauce.

Best Bakeries & Sweets

Patisserie Holtkamp (p136) You're in good company, as the gilded, royal coat of arms outside attests.

Lanskroon (p77) One word: *stroopwafel*.

Petit Gâteau (p118) Row upon row of gorgeous mini tarts.

Arti Choc (p177) Original and custom-made chocolate creations.

Van Stapele (p78) Insanely addictive dark-chocolate cookies.

Best Vegetarian

Alchemist Garden (p177) Vegan heaven, serving delicious gluten- and lactose-free dishes.

De Waaghals (p194) The menu emulates a different country each month, but it's always vegie.

Lavinia Good Food (p133) Superb spelt minipizzas, portabello mushroom burgers, and salads.

SLA (p191) Super-chic spot with design-your-own organic salads.

Best Neighbourhood Gems

Volt (p192) Lively locals' local with luscious tapas and Mediterranean mains; in De Pijp.

Lunchcafé Nielsen (p120) Amsterdammers' pick in the Negen Straatjes for breakfasts, sandwiches and cakes.

Éénvistwéévis (p104) Locals fork into fresh seafood from nearby waters; in the Plantage.

Best Views

REM Eiland (p155) There's nothing like this 22m former pirate-radio tower with vistas over the Western Docklands.

Pont 13 (p155) Vintage car ferry moored in the Western Docklands with a superb Mediterranean-inspired menu.

Hotel de Goudfazant (p80) Watch river boats while dining on punk French fare in Amsterdam-Noord.

Best Brunch

Bakers & Roasters (p193) Banana nutbread French toast and Bloody Marys at Amsterdam's brunch specialist.

Worst Wijncafe (p157) Locals pile in for a meaty Sunday brunch in the Western Islands.

Scandinavian Embassy (p193) Goat's milk yoghurt, salmon on Danish rye bread, and more dishes from northern lands.

CT Coffee & Coconuts (p193) Soaring art-deco space for coconut-buckwheat pancakes, eggs and avocado toast.

Little Collins (p193) Hip little hang-out with extraordinarily good, globe-spanning brunches.

Best *Frites*

Vleminckx (p77) To slather your golden potatoes in mayonnaise, curry or one of the myriad other sauces?

Wil Graanstra Friteshuis (p121) This family-run stand has served cones of fries by Anne Frank's house for 60 years.

Frites uit Zuyd (p190) Munch crisp *frites* on the benches out front.

Best Ice Cream

IJsmolen (p104) Lick *stroopwafel*, *speculaas* and other uniquely Dutch flavours by De Gooyer windmill.

Banketbakkerij Van der Linde (p77) The creamiest vanilla you'll ever lay lips on.

Monte Pelmo (p152) Inventive flavours draw loads of locals.

Best Sandwiches

Vinnies Deli (p118) Puts inventive combinations like smoked fish and rhubarb chutney between bread slices.

Rob Wigboldus Vishandel (p77) Great spot to get your herring on.

Loekie (p135) Choose from the lengthy menu of lip-smacking ingredients.

Broodje Bert (p78) It's tough to beat house-special lamb meatballs.

Maoz (p78) For all of your late-night falafel sandwich needs.

Best Pizza

Pazzi (p151) Perfectly charred crust cradles fresh mozzarella.

Yam Yam (p154) Many Amsterdammers swear this contemporary trattoria makes the city's best pizza.

Deegrollers (p177) Cordial neighbourhood spot for wood-fired pies.

Lo Stivale d'Oro (p137) The Italian owner fires up a mighty fine disc of goodness.

YADID LEVY / GETTY IMAGES ©

Drinking & Nightlife

Amsterdam is one of the wildest nightlife cities in Europe and the world, and the testosterone-fuelled stag parties of young chaps roaming the Red Light District know exactly what they're doing here. Yet you can easily avoid the hardcore party scene if you choose to: Amsterdam remains a café *(pub) society where the pursuit of pleasure centres on cosiness and charm.*

Café Papeneiland (p159)

Cafés

Cafés When the Dutch say *café* they mean a pub, and there are more than 1000 of them in Amsterdam. In a city that values socialising and conversation more than the art of drinking itself, *cafés* aren't just about consuming alcohol: they're places to hang out for hours of contemplation or camaraderie. Scores of *cafés* have outside seating on *terrassen* (terraces), which are glorious in summer and sometimes covered and heated in winter. Most serve food as well, ranging from snacks and sandwiches to excellent meals.

Brown Cafés Amsterdam is famed for its historic *bruin cafés*. The name comes from the nicotine stains from centuries of use (although recent aspirants slap on brown paint to catch up). Occasionally you'll find sand on the wooden floor to soak up spilt beer. Most importantly, the city's brown *cafés* provide an atmosphere conducive to conversation – and the nirvana of *gezelligheid* (conviviality, cosiness).

Grand Cafés These are spacious, have comfortable furniture and are, well, grand. They all have food menus, some quite elaborate. Despite the name, there's no need to dress up for a visit to a grand *café*.

Theatre Cafés Often similar to grand *cafés*, these are normally attached or adjacent to theatres, serving meals before and drinks after performances. Generally they're good places to catch performers after the show, though they're lovely any time of day.

NEED TO KNOW

Coffeeshop vs *Café*

First things first: *café* culture should not be mistaken for coffeeshop (marijuana-smoking cafe) culture, and there's a *big* difference between a *café* (pub) or *koffiehuis* (espresso bar) and a coffeeshop. A coffeeshop may serve coffee (never alcohol) but its focus is cannabis and hash.

Smoking (any substance) is banned by law in *cafés*.

Opening Hours

- *Cafés* serving breakfast tend to open between 8am and 10am, while others – notably many of the cosy brown *cafés* – are late risers, opening around noon.
- Bars usually open sometime between 5pm and 6pm.
- Coffeeshops generally open around 10am.
- Closing times at all drinking and smoking establishments tend to be late – between midnight and 2am (as late as 3am at weekends).
- Most nightclubs close at 2am or 3am Sunday to Thursday and at 4am or 5am on Friday and Saturday nights. Most places are dead until after midnight on weeknights, or until 1am or 2am on weekends. Looking for an after-party? Head to an after-hours *nachtcafé* (night *café*).

Wi-Fi

The majority of Amsterdam's bars and cafes and some coffeeshops have free wi-fi; you may need to ask for the code.

Amsterdam's Gay & Lesbian Scene

The Netherlands was the first country to legalise same-sex marriage (in 2001), so it's no surprise that Amsterdam's queer scene is one the largest in the world. Local gay and lesbian organisations (p276) can help you tap into the city's scene. Five hubs party hardest:

Warmoesstraat In the Red Light District (between the Dam and Centraal Station) hosts the infamous, kink-filled leather and fetish bars.

TONY BURNS / GETTY IMAGES ©

Above: Red Light District (p74)

Left: Canalside drinking at 't Smalle (p157)

Drinking & Nightlife by Neighbourhood

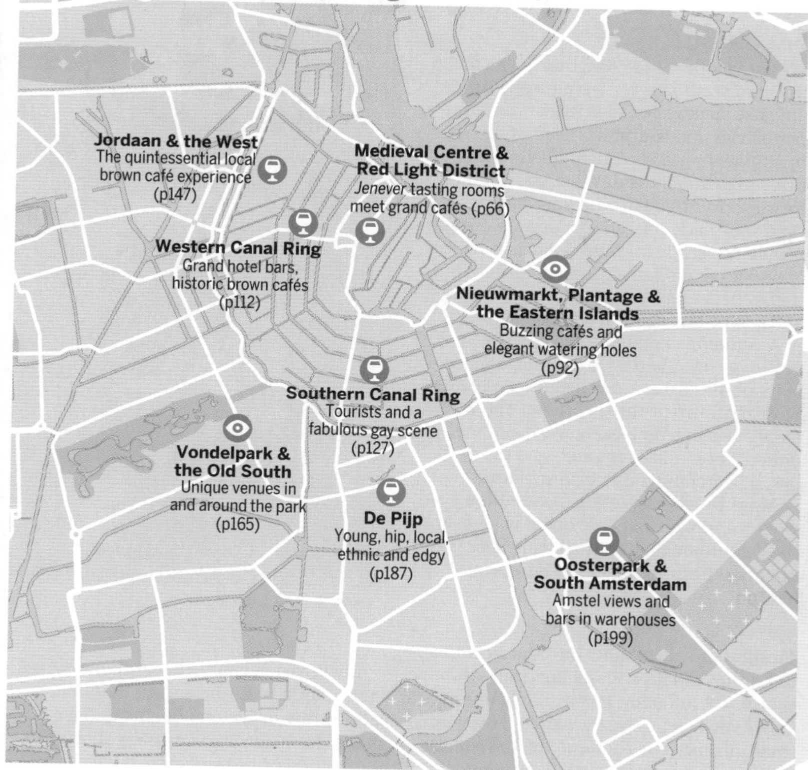

Zeedijk Near Warmoesstraat, crowds spill onto laid-back bar terraces.

Rembrandtplein In the Southern Canal Ring (p141), this area has traditional pubs and brown *cafés*, some with a campy bent, and several popular lesbian hangouts.

Leidseplein A smattering of trendy venues along Kerkstraat.

Reguliersdwarsstraat Draws the beautiful crowd.

Drinks

BEER

In stiff competition with a few of their European cohorts – the Belgians, Germans, Irish and Czechs – the Dutch take their beer very seriously (although they drink less per capita than any of them).

Lager beer is the staple, served cool and topped by a two-finger-thick head of froth to trap the flavour. *Een bier, een pils* or *een vaasje* will get you a normal glass of beer; *een kleintje pils* is a small glass and *een fluitje* is a small, thin, Cologne-style glass. Many places also serve *een grote pils* (half-litre mugs) to please tourists, but it goes flat if you don't drink quickly.

Local brands include Heineken, Amstel, Grolsch, Oranjeboom, Dommelsch and Bavaria (which, despite its name, isn't German but Dutch). Stronger Belgian beers, such as Duvel and Westmalle Triple, are also very popular. *Witbier* (white beer) is a cloudy blonde beer drunk in summer with a slice of lemon. Dark, sweet *bokbier* comes out in the autumn.

Amsterdam's craft beer scene has exploded in the last couple of years. Alongside long-standing microbreweries like Brouwerij 't IJ and Brouwerij de Prael, whose beers you'll find around town as well as at the breweries, are new ones such as Brouwerij Troost and Butcher's Tears. You'll also find craft-beer specialist bars and/or shops like Craft & Draft and the Beer Tree.

WINE & SPIRITS

It's not just beer here: the Dutch also make the hard stuff. *Jenever* (ye-*nay*-ver; Dutch gin; also spelt *genever*) is made from juniper berries and is drunk chilled. It arrives in a tulip-shaped shot glass filled to the brim – tradition dictates that you bend forward over the bar, with your hands behind your back, and take a deep sip. Most people prefer *jonge* (young) *jenever*, which is smooth and relatively easy to drink; *oude* (old) *jenever* has a strong juniper flavour and can be an acquired taste.

A common combination, known as a *kopstoot* (head butt), is a glass of *jenever* with a beer chaser – few people can handle more than two or three of these. There are plenty of indigenous liqueurs, including *advocaat* (a kind of eggnog) and the herb-based Beerenburg, a Frisian schnapps.

More Dutch people drink wine than ever before, and wine bars are opening all over the city, although almost all wine here is imported from elsewhere in Europe and beyond.

Jenever (Dutch gin) and cheese

COFFEE

Amsterdam's merchants introduced coffee to Europe and it's still the hot drink of choice. Traditionally, if you simply order *koffie* you'll get a sizeable cup of java with a small, airline-style container of *koffiemelk*, similar to unsweetened condensed milk. Caffe latte–like *koffie verkeerd* ('wrong coffee') comes in a bigger cup or mug with plenty of real milk.

Roasteries and micro-roasteries are springing up around the city, such as Sweet Cup and Lot Sixty One. Cafe baristas are increasingly using connoisseur styles of drip coffee.

BORREL

Borrel in Dutch means, quite simply, 'drink' – as in a glass of spirits, traditionally *jenever*. But in social parlance, to be invited to *borrel* means to take part in an informal gathering for drinks, conversation and fun. It usually incorporates food too, especially *borrelhapjes* (bar snacks) like *borrelnootjes* (peanuts covered in a crisp, spicy outer shell), and *kroketten* (croquettes) including *bitterballen* (small, round meat croquettes) – the name comes from the tradition of serving them with bitters, namely *jenever*.

Any occasion can be a reason for *borrel*: a birthday, a beautiful sunset that invites patio sitting or the end of a work day (*vrijdagmiddagborrel*, usually shortened to *vrijmibo* or just *vrimibo*, is specifically Friday-afternoon work drinks with colleagues). When you see a group of locals spilling out of a brown *café* onto the street with a glass of beer in hand? That's *borrel*. Grab a beer (or buy someone one) and join in. The famously tolerant and open Dutch rarely mind an addition to the party.

Smoking

MARIJUANA & HASHISH

Despite what you may have heard, cannabis is not *technically* legal in the Netherlands – yet it is widely tolerated. Here's the deal: the possession and purchase of small amounts (5g) of 'soft drugs' (ie marijuana, hashish, space cakes and mushroom-based truffles) is allowed and users won't be prosecuted for smoking or carrying this amount (although authorities do have the right to confiscate it, though this is rare). This means that coffeeshops are actually conducting an illegal business – but again, this is tolerated to a certain extent.

Most cannabis products sold in the Netherlands used to be imported, but today the country has high-grade home produce, so-called *nederwiet*. It's a particularly strong product – the most potent varieties contain 15% tetrahydrocannabinol (THC), the active substance that gets people high (since 2011, anything above 15% is classified as a hard drug and therefore illegal). In a nutshell, Dutch weed will literally blow your mind – perhaps to an extent that isn't altogether pleasant, which is why many native smokers have sworn off the local product. Newbies to smoking pot and hash should exercise caution; even many regular smokers can't stomach the home-grown stuff.

Space cakes and cookies (baked goods made with hash or marijuana) are sold in

COFFEESHOP & SMART SHOP DOS & DON'TS

- Do ask coffeeshop staff for advice on what and how to consume, and heed their advice, even if nothing happens after an hour.
- Don't ask for hard (illegal) drugs.
- Do ask staff for the menu of products on offer. Most shops offer rolling papers, pipes or bongs to use; you can also buy ready-made joints.
- Don't drink alcohol – it's illegal.
- Don't smoke tobacco, whether mixed with marijuana or on its own; it is forbidden in accordance with the Netherlands' laws.
- 'Herbal ecstasy' – usually a mix of herbs, vitamins and caffeine – is sold in smart shops; do ask staff what they recommend, as some varieties can have unpleasant side effects.
- Psilocybin mushrooms (aka magic mushrooms) are now illegal in the Netherlands, but many smart shops sell mushroom truffles, which have a similar effect.

View of Munttoren (Mint Tower) (p134) from Rembrandtplein (p131)

a rather low-key fashion, mainly because tourists often have problems with them. If people are unused to the time they can take to kick in and the effects, they could be in for an intense and long-lasting experience.

THE FUTURE OF AMSTERDAM COFFEESHOPS

Since the decriminalisation of soft drugs in 1976. the 'right to smoke' had never been threatened in Amsterdam until recent years.

In 2011 the government proposed banning foreigners from cafes selling cannabis and requiring Dutch residents to sign up for a one-year *wietpas* ('weed pass') in order to purchase 'soft drugs' at a coffeeshop. Although the top Dutch court declared that such legislation was unlawful, it indicated that restricting tourists and foreigners from entering coffeeshops would not necessarily be considered unconstitutional. The law was passed in 2012, however, Amsterdam's councillors declared their opposition to it – on the grounds of increased crime, street dealing and antisocial behaviour – and coffeeshops have turned a blind eye. If you're travelling further afield, be aware that elsewhere in the Netherlands, a number of regional councils are still trying the *wietpas* system, though some coffeeshops in these areas are currently taking their councils to court so the outcome is uncertain – ask locally what the situation is when you visit.

Despite the 2014 commencement of the Dutch law dictating that coffeeshops must not operate within 250m of primary schools and 350m of secondary schools in Amsterdam, authorities are also against enforcing this, arguing that minors are already forbidden, coffeeshops are monitored and that there are more effective ways to combat youth drug use, such as education.

For now, this means Amsterdam's coffeeshops remain open to anyone (foreigners or locals) aged 18 and above. But the 'coffeeshop issue' remains a wait-and-see situation.

Top: Escape nightclub (p140)

Middle: Old Amsterdam coffeeshop

Bottom: Marijuana for sale at the Grey Area coffeeshop (p123)

Lonely Planet's Top Choices

't Smalle (p157) Amsterdam's most intimate canal-side drinking, with a gorgeous historic interior.

Café Belgique (p81) Belgium's best brews flow from the glinting brass taps.

Amsterdam Roest (p107) Artist collective/bar/urban beach on the site of abandoned shipyards.

Wynand Fockink (p84) This 1679 tasting house pours glorious *jenevers*.

Pllek (p85) Hip bar made out of old shipping containers and flaunting an artificial beach.

SkyLounge (p106) A pinch-yourself, 360-degree city panorama extends from this 11th-floor bar and vast terrace.

Best Brown *Cafés*

Hoppe (p81) An icon of drinking history beloved by journalists, bums and raconteurs.

De Sluyswacht (p105) Swig in the lock-keeper's quarters across from Rembrandt's house.

In 't Aepjen (p84) Candles burn all day long in the time-warped, 500-year-old house.

Café Pieper (p158) Sand covers the floors and antique delft beer mugs hang from the bar here.

Café de Dokter (p81) Amsterdam's teeniest pub wafts old jazz records and pours whiskeys galore.

Eijlders (p138) Stained-glass artists' favourite with a lingering Resistance spirit.

Best Beer

Brouwerij 't IJ (p107) Wonderful independent brewery at the foot of the De Gooyer windmill.

Brouwerij Troost (p195) Watch beer being brewed through glass windows.

Brouwerij Troost Westergas (p160) Slurp all sorts of lovely, frothy house-made suds in the new Westerpark tap room.

Brouwerij De Prael (p84) Socially minded brewery that makes strong organic beers.

Craft & Draft (p181) Check the blackboard for each day's 40 craft beers on tap.

Best Coffeeshops

Dampkring (p82) Hollywood made the hobbit-like decor and Cannabis Cup–winning product famous.

Abraxas (p82) A haven of mellow music, comfy sofas and milkshakes spread over three floors.

Greenhouse (p86) Psychedelic mosaics and stained glass plus a big menu for munchies.

La Tertulia (p159) Cool Van Gogh murals mark this quiet spot on the Prinsengracht.

Best Cocktail Bars

Canvas (p204) Edgy, artsy bar with great views atop the Volkskrant newspaper building (now a flash hotel).

Twenty Third Bar (p196) Aerial 23rd-floor views, sublime champagne cocktails and two-Michelin-star bar snacks.

Door 74 (p139) Speakeasy-style bar mixing some of Amsterdam's wildest cocktails.

Franklin (p181) Creative concoctions include a 'Picnic at Vondel'.

Lion Noir (p140) Ethereal designer cocktail bar.

Best Gay & Lesbian Hangouts

't Mandje (p84) Amsterdam's oldest gay bar is a trinket-covered beauty.

Café de Barderij (p86) Gay regulars and tourists mingle over canal views and Zeedijk revelry.

Getto (p86) A younger crowd piles in for cheap food and Red Light District people watching.

Montmartre (p141) Legendary bar where Dutch ballads and old top-40 hits tear the roof off.

Vivelavie (p141) Flirty lesbian bar with a buzzing terrace and dancing.

Best Coffee

Lot Sixty One (p181) Red-hot Amsterdam roastery.

Scandinavian Embassy (p193) Phenomenal coffee sourced from Scandinavian micro-roasteries.

Sweet Cup (p138) Micro-roastery with five espresso styles and five slow brews.

Koffiehuis De Hoek (p123) Charming old-fashioned coffee-house experience.

Screaming Beans (p122) Has its own barista academy.

Best Wine Bars

Worst Wijncafe (p157) Chequerboard-tiled wine bar with superb sausage tapas dishes.

Glouglou (p196) All-natural, by-the-glass wines.

Vyne (p122) Slick wine bar with blonde-wood surrounds.

Pata Negra (p138) Wonderfully rustic Spanish-style bodega.

Entertainment

Amsterdam supports a flourishing arts scene, with loads of big concert halls, theatres, cinemas and other performance venues filled on a regular basis. Music fans will be in their glory, as there's a fervent subculture for just about every genre, especially jazz, classical and avant-garde beats.

Music

JAZZ

Jazz is extremely popular, from far-out, improvisational stylings to more traditional notes. The grand Bimhuis (p108) is the big game in town, drawing visiting musicians from around the globe, though its vibe is more that of a funky little club. Smaller jazz *cafés* abound and you could easily see a live combo every night of the week.

CLASSICAL

Amsterdam's classical-music scene, with top international orchestras, conductors and soloists crowding the agenda, is the envy of many European cities. Choose between the flawless Concertgebouw (p185) or dramatic Muziekgebouw aan 't IJ (p108) for the main shows.

ROCK & DANCE MUSIC

Amsterdam's dance-music scene thrives, with DJs catering to all tastes. Many clubs also host live rock bands. Huge touring names often play smallish venues such as the Melkweg (p143) and Paradiso (p143); it's a real treat to catch one of your favourites here.

Comedy & Theatre

Given that the Dutch are fine linguists and have a keen sense of humour, it's natural that English-language comedy would thrive in Amsterdam, especially around the Jordaan. Local theatre tends toward the edgy and experimental.

Cinema

Go to the movies on holiday? Actually, Amsterdam's weather is fickle, and let's face it, even art lovers can overdose on museums. Luckily this town is a cinephile's mecca, with oodles of art-house cinemas.

Entertainment by Neighbourhood

- **Medieval Centre & Red Light District** (p66) Several young rock/DJ clubs thrash throughout the 'hood, while avant-garde theatres line Nes.
- **Nieuwmarkt, Plantage & Eastern Islands** (p92)A good place to get your classical fix, especially at the Muziekgebouw aan 't IJ, Bimhuis and Conservatorium.
- **Western Canal Ring** (p112) Not many venues besides Felix Meritis, an oldie but a goodie.
- **Southern Canal Ring** (p127) Amsterdam's top spot for clubs, live-music venues and jazz *cafés*, all around Leidseplein.
- **Jordaan & the West** (p147) Venues for comedy, blues and cult films, plus the Westergasfabriek complex.
- **Vondelpark & the Old South** (p165) The world-renowned Concertgebouw struts its stuff, along with free theatre in the park and an alternative scene at the squats-turned-culture-centres.
- **De Pijp** (p187) Vibrant, buzzy little music *cafés* hold court here.
- **Oosterpark & South Amsterdam** (p199) Mega-venues and Amsterdam's beloved football team entertain in the south.

Lonely Planet's Top Choices

Melkweg (p143) Housed in a former dairy, it's a galaxy of diverse music, cinema and theatre.

Muziekgebouw aan 't IJ (p108) Acoustically and visually stunning performing-arts venue on the IJ.

Westergasfabriek (p161) Options abound in this postindustrial former-gasworks-turned-cultural-complex.

Felix Meritis (p123) It's more than 225 years old, but this arts centre is all about modern, experimental theatre and music.

Paradiso (p143) One-time church that preaches a gospel of rock and roll.

Best Classical & Opera

Concertgebouw (p185) World-renowned concert hall with superb acoustics.

Conservatorium van Amsterdam (p108) Catch recitals by students at Amsterdam's snazzy conservatory of music.

Orgelpark (p185) Listen to organ music in a lovely restored church on the edge of the Vondelpark.

Best Jazz & Blues

North Sea Jazz Club (p161) Concerts by respected musicians and jam sessions, too.

Bimhuis (p108) The beating jazz heart of the Netherlands, inside the Muziekgebouw aan 't IJ.

Jazz Café Alto (p143) Excellent little club where you're practically onstage with the musicians.

Best Rock

CC Muziekcafé (p197) Weekly and monthly themed music nights – from reggae to soul to rock.

De Nieuwe Anita (p161) Rock out by the stage behind the bookcase-concealed door.

Cave (p144) Basement venue hosting live hard rock and metal.

Best Cinemas

EYE Film Institute (p85) New, old, foreign, domestic: the Netherlands' uber-mod film centre shows quality films of all kinds.

Pathé Tuschinskitheater (p144) Amsterdam's most famous cinema, with a sumptuous art-deco/Amsterdam School interior.

Best Theatre & Comedy

Boom Chicago (p161) Laugh-out-loud improv-style comedy in the Jordaan.

Stadsschouwburg (p143) Large-scale plays, operettas and festivals right on Leidseplein.

Best Free or Low Cost

Openluchttheater (p185) Open-air summertime performances in the Vondelpark.

Muziektheater (p108) Classical freebies fill the air Tuesdays at lunchtime.

Concertgebouw (p185) Wednesday's free lunchtime concerts are often rehearsals for the evening's big show.

Best for Kids

Amsterdams Marionetten Theater (p108) Fairy-tale stage sets and stringed puppets bring operas to life.

Kriterion (p109) This cinema's kids' club screens loads of children's films with paired activities.

NEED TO KNOW

Ticket Shops

- Tickets to just about anything – comedy, dance and concerts – are available for a small surcharge at the **Uitburo** (p143), a ticket shop located in the Stadsschouwburg (City Theatre) on the Leidseplein.
- In addition, the Uitburo's Last Minute Ticket Shop (www.lastminuteticketshop.nl) sells half-price seats on the day of performance. Available shows are announced daily at 10am. You can buy online with a credit card (usually only chip cards work), or in person.
- Last Minute shops are also in the **Centrale Bibliotheek Amsterdam** (p100), and **VVV I Amsterdam Visitor Centre** (p279) at Centraal Station, from 10am.

Resources

- **I Amsterdam** (www.iamsterdam.com) Events listings.
- **Film Ladder** (www.filmladder.nl/amsterdam) Movie listings.
- **A-Mag** Magazine covering the local scene, published every two months and available at the visitor centre, local newsagents and various hotels.

Shopping

During the Golden Age, Amsterdam was the world's warehouse, stuffed with riches from the far corners of the earth. The capital's cupboards are still stocked with all kinds of exotica (just look at that Red Light gear!), but the real pleasure here is finding some odd, tiny shop selling something you wouldn't find anywhere else.

Specialities

The city offers plenty of distinct wares, from cool-cat fashion to tulip bulbs. Whatever your price range, you'll find something to take home. Souvenir shops cluster around Dam in the centre and the Bloemenmarkt (p129) in the Southern Canal Ring.

Dutch fashion Locals have mastered the art of casual style and it streams right out of the no-nonsense side of the national character. The result is hip, practical designs – such as floaty, layered separates and tailored denim (that don't get caught in bike spokes).

Dutch-designed homewares Dutch designers have shown a singular knack for bringing a creative, stylish touch to everyday objects. What started as a few innovators – such as Droog and Moooi – has morphed into a world-renowned industry. Items are colourful and sensible, with vintage and witty twists mixed in. They solve problems you didn't know you had. Once you own a hand towel with a rivet in one corner for hanging, you'll wonder how you ever lived without it!

Antiques and art Stores selling gorgeous antiques pop up all around the city. They're not cheap, but the quality is usually excellent. The Spiegel Quarter offers a long line of shops along Spiegelgracht and Nieuwe Spiegelstraat that attract moneyed browsers. Antiekcentrum Amsterdam (p162) is a knick-knack mini-mall in the Jordaan that's absorbing for those who like peculiar old stuff. On summer Sundays, an outdoor antique market (p110) takes over Nieuwmarkt square.

Delftware The Dutch have been firing up the iconic blue-and-white pottery since the 1600s. Authentic delftware comes only from Royal Delft and many visitors make the easy day-trip to the source. A few shops in Amsterdam sell the real deal, but it's much more common (and affordable) to buy replica pottery at souvenir shops.

Flower bulbs Exotic tulip bulbs and other flower seeds are popular gifts to take home. The Bloemenmarkt (aka Flower Market) in the Southern Canal Ring is ground zero for the colourful goods. Ask the vendors about customs regulations, since bringing bulbs into your home country can be prohibited. Those allowable in the USA are usually marked with a special label, and you should receive a certificate to accompany the bulbs.

Cheese Dutch *kaas* is justifiably famous and makes a great economical souvenir. Gouda and Edam are the most common varieties. Visitors from the USA should be OK bringing back cheese as long it's hard cheese (like the aforementioned types) and it's properly wrapped (vacuum packed is best).

Alcohol *Jenever* (Dutch gin) is a distinctive souvenir. Bols is the main brand, and the House of Bols museum (p174) in the Old South has a shop that not only sells bottles but also cool bartending gear. Shops in the Red Light District sell more, er, colourful bottles of alcohol, such as absinthe in bottles painted à la Van Gogh and tequila in sperm-shaped bottles.

Bongs, pot-leaf-logoed T-shirts and sex toys This is Amsterdam after all, so it's no surprise that these items are legion in Red Light District shops.

Boutique Bonanza

Stumbling across offbeat little boutiques is one of the great joys of shopping in Amsterdam. A teeny store selling only antique eyeglass frames or juggling supplies or doll parts? They're here. The best areas for such finds are at the top of the Jordaan, along Haarlemmerstraat and Haarlemmerdijk, which are lined with hip boutiques and food shops. To the south the Negen Straatjes (Nine Streets) offers a satisfying browse among its pint-sized, one-of-a-kind shops. Staalstraat in Nieuwmarkt is another bountiful vein.

Iconic Places to Shop

De Bijenkorf (p89) is Amsterdam's famed department store, taking pride of place by the Royal Palace on Dam. A lovely array of clothing, toys, household accessories and books spreads over five floors. It's quite welcoming and the cafe on the top floor is a must. Hema (p89) is the Netherlands' equivalent to UK-based Marks & Spencer or US-based Target. The thrifty chain carries a bit of everything – wine, homewares, clothing – and is a great place for reasonably priced Dutch design goods.

Shopping Streets

The busiest shopping streets are Kalverstraat by the Dam and Leidsestraat, which leads into Leidseplein. Both are lined with clothing and department stores, including local retailers Hema and De Bijenkorf.

Near Vondelpark, stylish fashion boutiques line Cornelis Schuytstraat and Willemsparkweg. Close by, PC Hooftstraat queues up Chanel, Diesel, Gucci and other luxury brands along its length.

Bargaining

For a nation of born traders the Dutch don't haggle much, if only because most retailers aren't set up for it. Flea markets, art galleries and antique shops are among the few places where you can try.

Markets

No visit to Amsterdam is complete if you haven't experienced one of its lively outdoor markets.

DAILY MARKETS

Amsterdam's daily markets are open every day except Sunday. Albert Cuypmarkt (p190) in De Pijp is the largest, busiest market, offering food, clothing and everything else. Multi-product Dappermarkt (p201), near Oosterpark, is similar but smaller.

There's bric-a-brac galore at Waterlooplein Flea Market (p109) in Nieuwmarkt. Ten Katemarkt (p182) adjoins the new cultural and design complex De Hallen, with fresh food, flowers and more. The Flower Market, Bloemenmarkt (p129), specialises in bulbs (and kitsch souvenirs); it's located in the Southern Canal Ring and open daily. Old tomes, maps and sheet music are the speciality at Oudemanhuis Book Market (p88) in the centre.

WEEKLY MARKETS

Hit Westermarkt (p164) in the Jordaan on Monday for clothing. Also on Monday

NEED TO KNOW

Opening Hours

- Department stores and large shops: 9am or 10am to 6pm Monday to Saturday, noon to 6pm Sunday.
- Smaller shops: 10am or noon to 6pm Tuesday to Friday; 10am to 5pm Saturday (and Sunday if open at all); from noon or 1pm to 5pm or 6pm Monday (if open at all).
- Many shops stay open late (to 9pm) Thursday.

Taxes

- The Dutch value-added tax (VAT) is 21%; it's reduced to 6% for groceries and books.
- Non-EU residents are entitled to a tax refund on purchases, as long as the store has the proper paperwork and you've spent €50 or more. Request a Tax Refund Cheque when paying.
- At the airport, present your goods, receipts and passport to customs and get your refund cheque stamped. Take it to the Global Refund office in Terminal 3 for cash or credit. The process can take a while, so give yourself ample time.

Cash & Cards

A surprising number of stores do not accept credit cards. Conversely, some shops only accept Dutch PIN debit cards, not credit cards or cash (there will be a sign on the window or door).

in the Jordaan, Noordermarkt (p164) has flea-market wares. On Wednesdays and Saturdays a small group of vendors sells stamps and coins at Postzegelmarkt (p90) in the centre. On Saturday, head to Lindengracht Market (p164) in the Jordaan for food and trinkets, or Boerenmarkt (p110) farmers market in Nieuwmarkt and the Jordaan. On Sunday there's the Antiques Market (p110) on Nieuwmarkt square, or the **Art Market** on the Spui in the centre and on Thorbeckeplein in the Southern Canal Ring.

SHOPPING GLOSSARY

Virtually any sales clerk you meet in Amsterdam will speak English, but to make things quick, here's a short list of words you're likely to encounter:

kleed kamer – changing room

kassa – cashier

kassakorting – discount taken at register

korting – discount, as in '25% korting'

laatste dagen – final days

opruiming, uitverkoop – clearance sale

soldes, sale – sale

tot, t/m – up to, as in 'tot 50% korting'

vanaf, va – literally 'and up', as in '€20 va' (€20 and up); note that this can be a clever ploy in which, for example, a clothing rack marked '€10 va' includes just a few items at that price – the rest can be much higher

Shopping By Neighbourhood

➡ **Medieval Centre & Red Light District** (p88) Red Light's vibrator shops, Spui's bookstores: there's something for everyone!

➡ **Nieuwmarkt, Plantage & Eastern Islands** (p109) Waterlooplein Flea Market is a key draw, along with sweetly eccentric local shops on Staalstraat.

➡ **Western Canal Ring** (p123) The Negen Straatjes hold the mother lode of teensy, quirky speciality shops.

➡ **Southern Canal Ring** (p144) Hunt for art and antiques in the Spiegel quarter, and fashion, music and housewares in the surrounding lanes.

➡ **Jordaan & the West** (p162) Jordaan shops have an artsy, eclectic, homemade feel; Haarlemmerdijk has the newest, coolest boutiques.

➡ **Vondelpark & the Old South** (p184) Outdoors equipment plus stylish boutiques on Cornelis Schuytstraat and Willemsparkweg and ultra-luxe labels on PC Hooftstraat.

➡ **De Pijp** (p197) Beyond Albert Cuypmarkt are quirky shops, galleries, and vintage and designer fashion boutiques.

➡ **Oosterpark & South Amsterdam** (p205) Trawl the ethnically diverse Dappermarkt.

Lonely Planet's Top Choices

Moooi Gallery (p162) Dutch designer Marcel Wanders showcases his and others' extraordinary works.

Pied à Terre (p188) The world's largest travel bookshop will make anyone's feet itch.

Condomerie Het Gulden Vlies (p91) Fun setting with a wild array of condoms for sale.

De Kaaskamer (p124) This 'cheese room' is stacked to the rafters with goodness.

PGC Hajenius (p88) Gilded, art-deco tobacco emporium where the royal family has its humidor.

Best Markets

Albert Cuypmarkt (p190) Europe's largest daily (except Sunday) street market spills over with food, fashion and bargain finds.

Waterlooplein Flea Market (p109) Piles of curios, used footwear and cheap bicycle parts for treasure hunters.

Westermarkt (p164) Bargain-priced clothing and fabrics at 163 stalls.

Lindengracht Market (p164) Wonderfully authentic local affair, with bushels of fresh produce.

IJ Hallen (p85) The monthly flea market at NDSM-werf is Europe's largest.

Best for Books

Mendo (p126) Sleek bookshop specialising in art, design, architecture, fashion and photography.

Oudemanhuis Book Market (p89) Covered alleyway lined with second-hand booksellers.

American Book Center (p88) English-language books of all kinds sprawl across three floors.

Best Fashion

SPRMRKT (p162) A major player in Amsterdam's fashion scene.

Young Designers United (p144) Tomorrow's big names jam the racks here.

By AMFI (p89) Students and alumni of the Amsterdam Fashion Institute sell their wares.

Tenue de Nîmes (p124) Übercool denim wear and local designer fashions.

VLVT (p185) Up-and-coming Dutch-designed women's fashion on chic Cornelis Schuytstraat.

Best Souvenirs

Bloemenmarkt (p129) Bulbs, bulbs and more bulbs fill Amsterdam's 'floating' flower market.

Galleria d'Arte Rinascimento (p162) Royal Delftware ceramics (both antique and new).

Mark Raven Grafiek (p89) Artsy, beyond-the-norm T-shirts and prints of the city.

Museum Shop at the Museumplein (p185) The one-stop shop for all your Rembrandt, Vermeer and Van Gogh items.

Best Dutch-Design Housewares

Droog (p109) The famed collective is known for sly, playful, repurposed and reinvented homewares.

Frozen Fountain (p123) Amsterdam's best-known showcase of Dutch-designed furniture and homewares.

Local Goods Store (p182) Inspired fashion and homewares by Dutch designers inside cultural complex De Hallen.

Hutspot (p197) Funky store giving emerging designers an opportunity to sell their work.

Mobilia (p144) Dutch design is stunningly showcased at this three-storey 'lifestyle studio'.

Best Food & Drink

Hart's Wijnhandel (p146) Historic shop selling tipples, including *jenever*.

Het Oud-Hollandsch Snoepwinkeltje (p162) All kinds of Dutch candies, including sweet and salty *drop* (Dutch liquorice).

Papabubble (p162) Lolly shop that's gallery-like in its sweet, sugary, made-in-front-of-you creations.

Beer Tree (p185) Craft beers from over 25 different countries.

Best Antiques & Vintage

Antiekcentrum Amsterdam (p162) Quirky indoor mall with stalls offering anything from 1940s dresses to 1970s Swedish porn.

Marbles Vintage (p109) Awesome selection of classic skirts, dresses and coats.

Gastronomie Nostalgie (p89) Beautiful old china, goblets, candlesticks and other tableware from far-flung auctions.

Explore Amsterdam

AMSTERDAM'S TOP SIGHTS

Neighbourhoods at a Glance

❶ Medieval Centre & Red Light District p66

Amsterdam's oldest quarter is remarkably preserved, looking much as it did in its Golden Age heyday. It's the busiest part of town for visitors. Some come to see the Royal Palace and Oude Kerk. Others barely get out of the train station before hitting the coffeeshops and Red Light District.

❷ Nieuwmarkt, Plantage & the Eastern Islands p92

Nieuwmarkt holds the keys to the Rembrandthuis – the master painter's studio – as well as to centuries-old synagogues, diamond factories and the daily Waterlooplein Flea Market in the old Jewish quarter. Beside it, the leafy Plantage hosts a sprawling zoo as well as a beery windmill. It segues into the

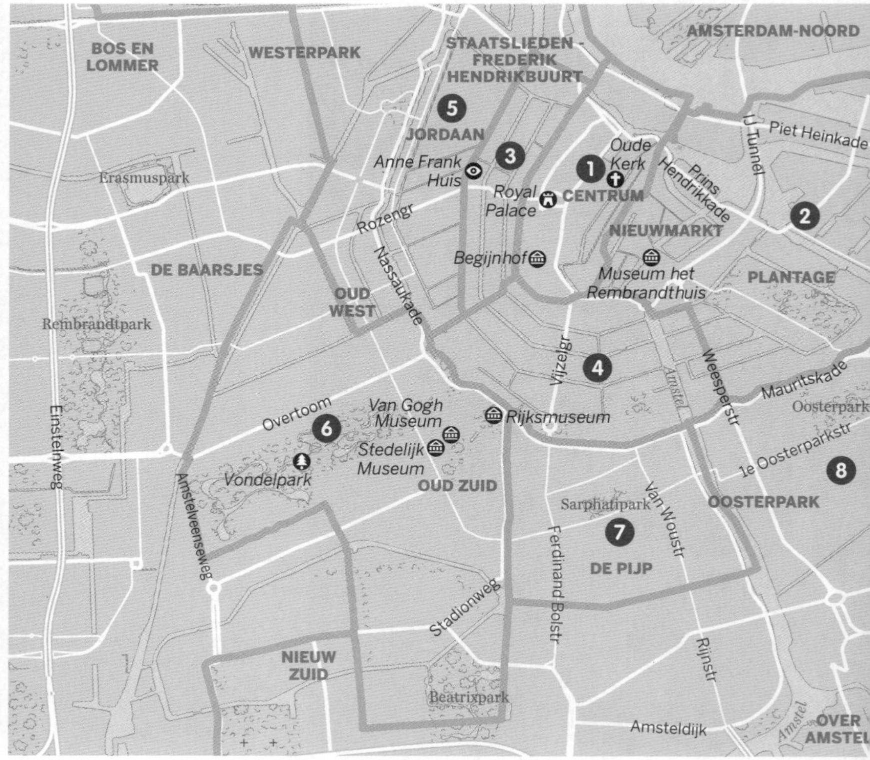

Eastern Islands, old warehouse hubs that have morphed into the cutting edge of Dutch architecture.

❸ Western Canal Ring p112

One of Amsterdam's most gorgeous areas. Grand old mansions and oddball little speciality shops line the glinting waterways. Roaming around them can cause days to vanish. But most people come here for a singular reason: to visit Anne Frank's house and see the famous diary.

❹ Southern Canal Ring p127

Two clubby nightlife districts anchor the Southern Canal Ring: Leidseplein and Rembrandtplein. Both are neon-lit, one-stop shops for partygoers. In between lie several intriguing museums – including the art blockbuster Hermitage Amsterdam – as well as the flower market, terrific restaurants, ritzy cafes and romantic canal views that'll make your camera flash.

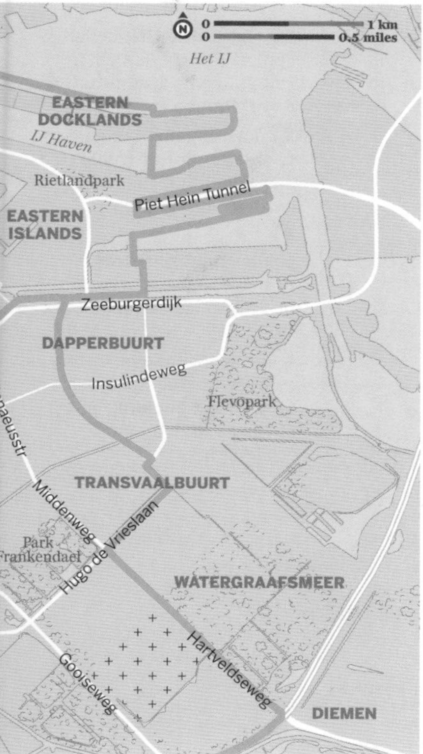

❺ Jordaan & the West p147

A former workers' quarter, the Jordaan teems with cosy pubs, galleries and markets squashed into a grid of tiny lanes. It's short on conventional sights, but there's no better place to lose yourself for an afternoon stroll. It abuts the West, industrial badland that has transformed into an avant-garde cultural hub.

❻ Vondelpark & the Old South p165

Vondelpark is the city's bucolic playground where joggers, picnickers, dope smokers, accordion players and children all cheerfully coexist. It's a great place to experience a freewheeling slice of local life (and practise your cycling). Eclectic eat streets unfurl around the park's edges. Next door, the Old South holds the top-draw Van Gogh, Stedelijk and Rijksmuseum collections. It's one of Amsterdam's richest neighbourhoods, with the high-end shops to prove it.

❼ De Pijp p187

Ethnic meets trendy in De Pijp, a gentrified area that mixes labourers, intellectuals, new immigrants, prostitutes and young urbanites. Marvel at the scene at colourful Albert Cuypmarkt and the eateries and free-spirited *cafés* (pubs) that surround it. The creative district is also a hotbed of pop-up restaurants and businesses.

❽ Oosterpark & South Amsterdam p199

Oosterpark is a culturally diverse neighbourhood, with Moroccan and Turkish enclaves. It's starting to get its groove on as several new posh but economical hotels open in the area. South Amsterdam extends well beyond, offering wild art, lush greenery and goats in the forest.

Medieval Centre & Red Light District

MEDIEVAL CENTRE | RED LIGHT DISTRICT

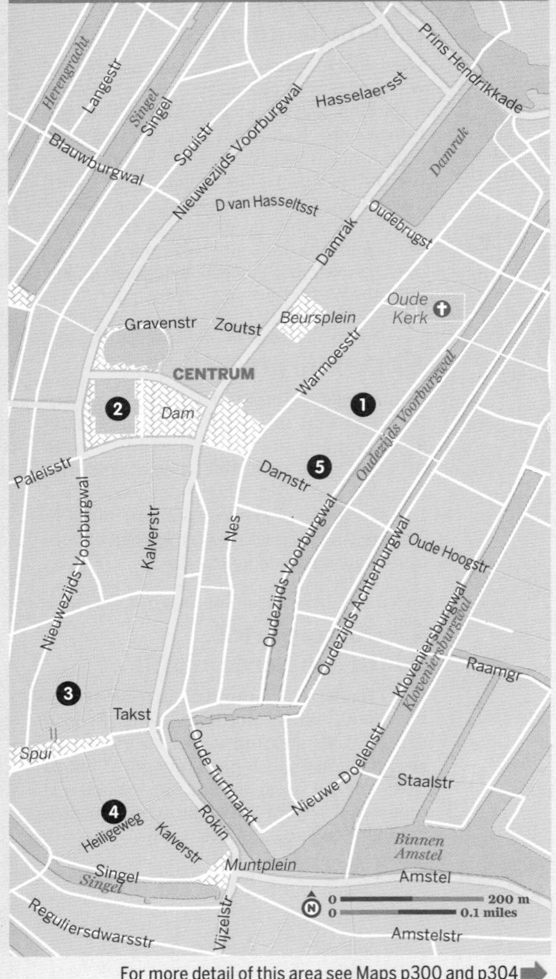

For more detail of this area see Maps p300 and p304

Neighbourhood Top Five

❶ Wandering through the **Red Light District** (p74), which will make your jaw drop, even if near-naked women beckoning from backlit windows is the oldest Amsterdam cliché.

❷ Ogling the chandeliered opulence and taking a Dutch history lesson in the **Royal Palace** (p68).

❸ Pushing open the door to the **Begijnhof** (p69) and beholding the hidden gardens and churches.

❹ Biting into a crisp golden spud slathered in mayonnaise, curry or peanut sauce at **Vleminckx** (p77).

❺ Bowling up to a 17th-century tasting house such as **Wynand Fockink** (p84), to knock back a *jenever* (Dutch gin).

Explore Medieval Centre & Red Light District

Amsterdam's heart beats in its medieval core, as well as in the centuries-old Red Light District. All visitors end up here at some point. Centraal Station is the main landmark – indeed, it is the first thing most visitors see as they arrive by train from the airport or elsewhere in Europe. Damrak slices south from the station to the Dam – Amsterdam's central square and home to the Royal Palace.

A tourist-heavy crowd packs the neighbourhood day and night. While there are several intriguing sights, the big-ticket museums lie elsewhere. The main thing to do here is wander. The compact area is laced with atmospheric lanes, and 17th-century tasting rooms, brown *cafés*, hidden courtyards and wee speciality shops are the prizes for those who venture off the main drags.

Far from being a no-go area, the Red-Light District has some historic bars, as well as the stunning Oude Kerk, the city's oldest church. You'll probably find yourself on Warmoesstraat and Zeedijk while you're here, both commercial thoroughfares full of shops and restaurants.

The charming thing about Amsterdam's core is its remarkable state of preservation. The overall layout has changed little since the 17th century. The happy result? The district has the air of a living museum and certain vistas look like they belong in a Golden Age landscape. You could easily spend your entire trip here, especially when factoring in the quick-ferry-ride-away northern region, so remember: there are more neighbourhoods beyond.

Local Life

➡ **Café Hangouts** *Cafés* and bookstores ring the Spui (p71), a favoured haunt of academics and journalists.

➡ **Dam Bikes** A fair, a protest, a speech by the monarch – there's always something drawing people to Amsterdam's main square (p71), evident by the sea of bicycles locked up in the middle.

➡ **Go North** Amsterdam-Noord (p85) is a hot spot, with hip cafes, cultural centres and hotels popping up one after the other.

Getting There & Away

➡ **Tram** The majority of the city's 15 tram lines go through the neighbourhood en route to Centraal Station. Useful lines include trams 1, 2, 5, 13 and 17, which travel to the station's west side, and trams 4, 9, 16 and 24, which travel to the east side.

➡ **Boat** Free ferries run to NDSM-werf and elsewhere in Amsterdam-Noord, departing from the piers behind Centraal Station.

Lonely Planet's Top Tip

You're at the local tasting house, and you've ordered a *jenever*. It arrives filled to the brim. You can't pick it up without spilling it. What to do? Bend forward over the bar, with your hands behind your back, and take a deep sip. That's what tradition dictates.

Best Places to Eat

➡ Gartine (p76)
➡ De Laatste Kruimel (p77)
➡ Vleminckx (p77)
➡ Thais Snackbar Bird (p80)
➡ Blauw aan de Wal (p81)

For reviews, see p76.

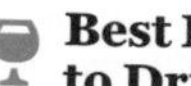

Best Places to Drink

➡ Wynand Fockink (p84)
➡ Hoppe (p81)
➡ In 't Aepjen (p84)
➡ Café Belgique (p81)
➡ Café de Dokter (p81)

For reviews, see p81.

Best Places to Shop

➡ Condomerie Het Gulden Vlies (p91)
➡ American Book Center (p88)
➡ PGC Hajenius (p89)
➡ Oudemanhuis Book Market (p89)
➡ Kokopelli (p91)

For reviews, see p88.

MARIA SWÄRD / GETTY IMAGES ©

TOP SIGHT
ROYAL PALACE (KONINKLIJK PALEIS)

Welcome to the King's house. If he's away, you're welcome to come in and wander around. Today's Royal Palace began life as a glorified town hall and was completed in 1665. The architect, Jacob van Campen, spared no expense to display Amsterdam's wealth in a way that rivalled the grandest European buildings of the day. The result is opulence on a big scale.

Pick up a free audio tour at the desk after you enter; it will explain everything you see in vivid detail. Most of the palace's rooms spread over the 1st floor, which is awash with chandeliers (51 shiners in total), damasks, gilded clocks, and rich paintings by Ferdinand Bol and Jacob de Wit. The great *burgerzaal* (citizens' hall) that occupies the heart of the building was envisioned as a schematic of the world, with Amsterdam as its centre. Check out the maps inlaid in the floor; they show the eastern and western hemispheres, with a 1654 celestial map plopped in the middle.

In 1808 the building became the palace of King Louis, Napoleon Bonaparte's brother. In a classic slip-up in the new lingo, French-born Louis told his subjects here that he was the 'rabbit *(konijn)* of Holland', when he actually meant 'king' *(konink)*. Napoleon dismissed him two years later. Louis left behind about 1000 pieces of Empire-style furniture and decorative artworks. As a result, the palace now holds one of the world's largest collections from the period.

Officially King Willem-Alexander lives here and pays a symbolic rent, though he really resides in Den Haag. The palace is still used for state functions and often closes for such events, especially during April, May, November and December. The website posts the schedule.

DON'T MISS

- Chandeliers (all 51 of them)
- The *burgerzaal*
- Paintings by Ferdinand Bol and Jacob de Wit
- Empire-style decor

PRACTICALITIES

- Koninklijk Paleis
- Map p304
- ☎620 40 60
- www.paleisamsterdam.nl
- The Dam
- adult/child €10/free
- ⏲10am-5pm
- 🚊4/9/16/24 Dam

TOP SIGHT
BEGIJNHOF

It feels like something out of a story book. You walk up to the unassuming door, push it open and voilà – a hidden courtyard of tiny houses and gardens opens up before you. The 14th-century Begijnhof is not a secret these days, but somehow it remains a surreal oasis of peace in the city's midst.

The Beguines were a Catholic order of unmarried or widowed women who lived a religious life without taking monastic vows. The Begijnhof was their convent of sorts. The last true Beguine died in 1971.

Two churches hide in the *hof* (courtyard). The **Begijnhof Kapel** (Map p304) (1671) is a 'clandestine' chapel where the Beguines were forced to worship after the Calvinists took away their Gothic church. Go through the dog-leg entrance to find marble columns, stained-glass windows and murals commemorating the Miracle of Amsterdam (in short: in 1345 the final sacrament was administered to a dying man, but he was unable to keep down the communion wafer and – there's no way to put this delicately – vomited it up. Here's the miracle part: when the vomit was thrown on the fire, the wafer would not burn. Yes, it's all depicted in wall paintings).

The other church is known as the **Engelse Kerk** (English Church; Map p304), built around 1392. It was eventually rented out to the local community of English and Scottish Presbyterian refugees – including the Pilgrim Fathers – and it still serves as the city's Presbyterian church. Look for pulpit panels by Piet Mondrian, in a figurative phase. Note that as this church is still in frequent use, it's sometimes closed to visitors.

Another sight to see is the **Houten Huis** (Wooden House; Map p304) at No 34. It dates from around 1465, making it the oldest preserved wooden house in the Netherlands.

DON'T MISS

- Taking a quiet seat in the garden
- Begijnhof Kapel
- Engelse Kerk
- Wooden House at No 34
- Miracle of Amsterdam paintings

PRACTICALITIES

- Map p304
- ☎622 19 18
- www.begijnhofamsterdam.nl
- off Gedempte Begijnensloot
- admission free
- ⏲9am-5pm
- 🚊1/2/5 Spui

GEORGE PACHANTOURIS / GETTY IMAGES ©

TOP SIGHT
OUDE KERK (OLD CHURCH)

The Oude Kerk is Amsterdam's oldest building, dating back to around 1306. The Gothic-style structure holds the city's oldest church bell (from 1450), a stunning Müller organ (1724), and 15th-century choir stalls with carvings that are far naughtier than you'd expect in a house of worship.

The church was built to honour the city's patron saint, St Nicholas (the inspiration for red-suited Saint Nick). Many famous Amsterdammers are buried under the worn tombstones set in the floor, including Rembrandt's wife, Saskia van Uylenburgh. Some 10,000 citizens in all lie beneath the church. Ask for a map when you enter. The church holds Sunday services at 11am, but generally it hosts intriguing art exhibitions. Carillon concerts, often on Tuesday and Thursday afternoons, also draw locals. Those who don't mind climbing stairs can go up on a guided tour of the **tower** (Map p300; www.westertorenamsterdam.nl; per person €7.50; ⏲1-5.30pm Mon-Sat Apr-Sep; 🚋4/9/16/24 Dam).

The church embodies a huge moral contradiction, as it's in full view of the Red Light District, with passers-by getting chatted up by ladies in windows a stone's throw from the holy walls. Outside on Oudekerksplein is the **statue of Belle** (Map p300), erected in 2007 as a nod to sex-industry workers worldwide. The cobblestones nearby (by the church's main entrance) contain another bold statement: a **golden torso** of a naked woman held by a padlocked hand. The torso mysteriously appeared one day, was removed by police and then put back as most people seemed to like it.

The church has been undergoing extensive renovation work in recent years, so don't be surprised if certain bits are off limits when you visit.

DON'T MISS

- Floor tombstones, including that of Rembrandt's wife Saskia
- Choir stall carvings
- Golden Torso
- Surrounding Red Light ambience
- Tower tour

PRACTICALITIES

- Old Church
- Map p300
- ☎625 82 84
- www.oudekerk.nl
- Oudekerksplein
- adult/child €7.50/free
- ⏲10am-6pm Mon-Sat, 1-5:30pm Sun
- 🚋4/9/16/24 Dam

SIGHTS

Medieval Centre

ROYAL PALACE PALACE
See p68.

BEGIJNHOF SQUARE
See p69.

CIVIC GUARD GALLERY GALLERY
Map p304 (Kalverstraat 92; 10am-5pm; 1/2/5 Spui) FREE This cool gallery is part of the Amsterdam Museum – consider it the free 'teaser' – and fills an alleyway next to the museum's entrance. It displays grand posed-group portraits, from medieval guards painted during the Dutch Golden Age (à la Rembrandt's *Night Watch*) to *Modern Civic Guards,* a rendering of Anne Frank, Alfred Heineken and a joint-smoking personification of Amsterdam.

DAM SQUARE
Map p304 (4/9/16/24 Dam) This square is the very spot where Amsterdam was founded around 1270. Today pigeons, tourists, buskers and the occasional Ferris-wheel-boasting fair take over the grounds. It's still a national gathering spot, and if there's a major speech or demonstration it's held here.

Long before it hosted fun and games, the square was split into two sections called Vissersdam, a fish market where the Bijenkorf department store now stands, and Vijgendam, probably named for the figs and other exotic fruits unloaded from ships. Various markets and events have been held here through the ages, including executions – you can still see holes on the front of the Royal Palace where the wooden gallows were affixed.

NATIONAAL MONUMENT MONUMENT
Map p304 (Dam; 4/9/16/24 Dam) The obelisk on the Dam's east side was built in 1956 to commemorate WWII's fallen. Fronted by two lions, its pedestal has a number of symbolic statues: four males (war), a woman with child (peace) and men with dogs (resistance). The 12 urns at the rear hold earth from war cemeteries of the 11 provinces and the Dutch East Indies. The war dead are still honoured here at a ceremony every 4 May.

SEXMUSEUM AMSTERDAM MUSEUM
Map p300 (www.sexmuseumamsterdam.nl; Damrak 18; admission €4; 9.30am-11.30pm; 1/2/5/13/17 Centraal Station) The Sexmuseum is good for a giggle. You'll find replicas of pornographic Pompeian plates, erotic 14th-century Viennese bronzes, some of the world's earliest nude photographs, an automated farting flasher in a trench coat, and a music box that plays 'Edelweiss' and purports to show a couple in flagrante delicto. It's sillier and more fun than other erotic museums in the Red Light District.

Minimum age for entry is 16.

MADAME TUSSAUDS AMSTERDAM MUSEUM
Map p304 (www.madametussauds.nl; Dam 20; adult/child €22.50/18.50; 9am-9pm Jul & Aug, 10am-7pm Sep-Jun; ; 4/9/16/24 Dam) Sure, Madame Tussauds wax museum is overpriced and cheesy, but its focus on local culture makes it fun: 'meet' the Dutch royals, politicians, painters and pop stars, along with global celebs (Bieber!). Kids love it. Buying tickets online will save you a few euros and get you into the fast-track queue. Going after 3pm also nets discounts.

SPUI SQUARE
Map p304 (1/2/5 Spui) Inviting *cafés* and brainy bookstores ring the Spui, a favoured haunt of academics, students and journalists. On Fridays a book market takes over the square; on Sundays it's an art market. And just so you know, it's pronounced 'spow' (rhymes with 'now').

BEURS VAN BERLAGE HISTORIC BUILDING
Map p300 (530 41 41; www.beursvanberlage.nl; Damrak 243; 1/2/5/13/17 Centraal Station) Master architect and ardent socialist HP Berlage (1856–1934) built Amsterdam's financial exchange in 1903. He filled the temple of capitalism with decorations that venerate labour – look inside the *café* to see tile murals of the well-muscled proletariat of the past, present and future. Within two decades trading had outgrown the building and moved elsewhere. The building now hosts conferences and art exhibitions.

CENTRAAL STATION LANDMARK
Map p300 (Stationsplein; 4/9/16/24 Centraal Station) Beyond being a transport hub, Centraal Station is a sight in itself. The turreted marvel dates from 1889. One of the architects, PJ Cuypers, also designed the Rijksmuseum, and you can see the similarities

in the faux-Gothic towers, the fine red brick and the abundant reliefs (for sailing, trade and industry).

Built on an artificial island, the station was designed as a neo-Renaissance 'curtain', a controversial plan that effectively cut off Amsterdam from the IJ River. The garage in the right-hand wing was built to shelter the Dutch royal carriage, but it's rarely there (read: never). The area around the station always has loads of construction going on.

DAMRAK WATERFRONT

Map p300 (🚊1/2/5/13/17 Centraal Station) The Damrak is the original mouth of the Amstel river – *rak* being a reach, or straight stretch of water. The river flowed from a lock in the Dam into the IJ. In the 19th century the canal was filled in, except for the canal-boat docks on the waterway's west side. The gabled houses backing onto the water are among the town's most picturesque.

Damrak is also the name of the abutting street, which is like a giant stretch of flypaper, with cheap tourist hotels, fast-food restaurants and souvenir shops ready to catch visitors arriving at Centraal Station.

ROKIN AREA

Map p304 (🚊4/9/16/24 Rokin) South of the Dam, this street is part of the route most visitors take from Centraal Station into town, the name being a corruption of *rak-in*, or inward reach. In the early 16th century the northern part was the site of the first Amsterdam stock exchange, which played a big part in spinning Golden Age riches.

The Rokin is now in the grip of the underground construction of a new metro line, which has brought forth a number of archaeological finds from the Amstel's old river bed.

ST NICOLAASKERK CHURCH

Map p300 (www.nicolaas-parochie.nl; Prins Hendrikkade 73; ⌚noon-3pm Mon & Sat, 11am-4pm Tue-Fri; 🚊4/9/16/24 Centraal Station) In plain view from Centraal Station, the magnificent cupola and neo-Renaissance towers belong to the city's main Catholic church, the first built after Catholic worship became legal again in the 19th century. St Nicholas is the patron saint of seafarers, so the church became an important symbol for Amsterdam.

The interior is notable for its high altar, the theatrical crown of Emperor Maximilian I and depictions of the Stations of the Cross, on which tireless painter Jan Dunselman laboured for 40 years. Worship services take place daily at 12.30pm, except on Sunday (10.30am and 1pm).

SCHREIERSTOREN HISTORIC BUILDING

Map p300 (www.schreierstoren.nl; Prins Hendrikkade 94-95; 🚊4/9/16/24 Centraal Station) Built around 1480 as part of the city's defenses, this tower is where Henry Hudson set sail for the New World in 1609; a plaque outside marks the spot. It's called the 'wailing tower' in lore – where women waved farewell to sailors' ships – but the name actually comes from the word 'sharp' (for how the corner jutted into the bay).

Step into the cozy VOC Café for a look inside the tower. The canal-side terrace is a dandy place for a drink.

RONDE LUTHERSE KERK CHURCH

Map p300 (Round Lutheran Church; Singel 11; ⌚hours vary; 🚊1/2/5/13/17 Nieuwezijds Kolk) This domed church, built from 1668 to 1671, has the curious distinction of being the only round Protestant church in the country. Falling attendances forced its closure in 1936. Ironically, the old church on the Spui, which this was designed to replace, is still in use.

NARROW HOUSE BUILDING

Map p300 (Singel 7; 🚊1/2/5/13/17 Nieuwezijds Kolk) It's often said that this house – which appears to be no wider than its door – is the narrowest abode in the city. But don't be deceived. The side facing the canal is actually the rear entrance of a house of normal proportions.

KALVERSTRAAT AREA

Map p304 (🚊4/9/16/24 Dam) You're sure to end up on this crowded street at some point, so we might as well mention it. Named after the livestock markets held here in the 17th century, Kalverstraat is now a place where shoppers lather themselves into a fever pitch over the latest sales. (The Dutch Monopoly game has Kalverstraat as its most expensive street.)

PAPAGAAI CHURCH

Map p304 (Kalverstraat 58; ⌚10am-4pm; 🚊4/9/16/24 Dam) An unexpected oasis in the sea of consumerism on Kalverstraat, the curious Petrus en Pauluskerk, aka Papagaai, is a Catholic church from the 17th century that was a clandestine house of worship. Note the parrot over the door that gave the church its funny name. The slogan you'll see upon entering: '15 minutes for God'.

TORTURE MUSEUM MUSEUM

Map p304 (www.torturemuseum.nl; Singel 449; adult/child €7.50/4; ⏲10am-11pm; 🚊1/2/5 Koningsplein) It's dilapidated and so dimly lit inside you can barely read the placards, but fans of kitsch and oddball lore will enjoy learning about devices like the Flute of Shame for bad musicians (the finger screws tighten), the Neck Violin for quarreling women (a shackle locked the two face-to-face), branding tongs, skull crackers, a guillotine and the Iron Maiden of Nuremberg (use your imagination).

The museum displays each torture tool and describes (in multiple languages) how it works. Graphic engravings show the instruments in action. The building lies across the canal from the flower market.

HEILIGEWEG AREA

Map p304 (🚊1/2/5 Koningsplein) The Heiligeweg (Holy Way) was once part of a route that pilgrims took to the spot where the Miracle of Amsterdam occurred. Halfway along, and directly opposite Voetboogstraat, you'll see the **Rasphuis Gate** (Map p304), which led to a correctional institute in medieval times. The pedestal bears the sculpture of a woman with two criminals chained at her side, under the Latin word *castigatio* (punishment).

ALLARD PIERSON MUSEUM MUSEUM

Map p304 (www.allardpiersonmuseum.nl; Oude Turfmarkt 127; adult/child €10/5; ⏲10am-5pm Tue-Fri, 1-5pm Sat & Sun; 🚊4/9/14/16/24 Spui/Rokin) Run by the University of Amsterdam, this museum boasts one of the world's richest archaeological collections. You'll find an actual mummy, vases from ancient Greece and Mesopotamia, a very cool wagon from the royal tombs at Salamis (Cyprus), and galleries full of other items providing insight into daily life in ancient times.

Each section is explained in a detailed overview via English signage, although most individual items are labelled in Dutch only. It may not be in the same league as the British Museum or the Louvre, but the manageable scale of this museum makes it far more accessible.

UNIVERSITY LIBRARY BUILDING

Map p304 (www.uba.uva.nl; Singel 421-425; 🚊1/2/5 Koningsplein) Today's library is a concrete hulk, not nearly the beautiful building you'd expect from such a historic site,

TOP SIGHT
AMSTERDAM MUSEUM

Amsterdam's history museum is a spiffy place to learn about what makes the city tick. Start with the multimedia DNA exhibit, which breaks down Amsterdam's 1000-year history into seven whiz-bang time periods. At the Revolt Against the King and Church display, you can even 'dress' as a civic guard (ruffled collar!) and have a photo taken; it goes to the museum's Flickr page.

Afterward, plunge into the maze-like lower floors to see troves of religious artefacts, porcelains and paintings. Bonus points for finding Rembrandt's macabre *Anatomy Lesson of Dr Deijman*, showing the good physician cutting into a corpse's brain. There are also displays on the world wars, the spread of bicycle use and a recreation of the original Café 't Mandje, a touchstone in the gay-rights movement.

The museum building used to be Amsterdam's civic orphanage. While you're in the courtyard, note the cupboards in which the orphans stored their possessions (now filled with art). And don't forget to peek in the free **Civic Guard Gallery** (p71) in the arcade next door, lined with grand Golden Age paintings.

The museum is a good choice during soggy weather, as there's rarely a queue that requires you to wait outside, as at most other venues.

DON'T MISS

- *Anatomy Lesson of Dr Deijman*
- Café 't Mandje
- Civic Guard paintings
- Orphan cupboards

PRACTICALITIES

- Map p304
- ☎523 18 22
- www.amsterdammuseum.nl
- Kalverstraat 92
- adult/child €12/6
- ⏲10am-5pm
- 🚊1/2/5 Spui

but its background is fascinating. Citizen militias used to meet here: the 'hand-bow' *(handboog)* militia in No 421, and the 'foot-bow' *(voetboog)* militia in No 425, which also served as headquarters for the Dutch West India Company.

Now you know where the names of the nearby streets Handboogstraat and Voetboogstraat come from. Their firing ranges at the back reached to Kalverstraat.

Red Light District

OUDE KERK CHURCH

See p70.

PROSTITUTION INFORMATION CENTRE LIBRARY

Map p300 (PIC; ☎420 73 28; www.pic-amsterdam.com; Enge Kerksteeg 3; ⏲10am-5pm Wed-Fri, to 7pm Sat; 🚋4/9/16/24 Dam) FREE Established by a former prostitute, the PIC provides frank information about the industry to sex workers, their customers and curious tourists. The small on-site shop sells enlightening reading material and souvenirs, and the centre runs an excellent hour-long **walking tour** (5pm Saturday, €15 per person, no reservations needed), which takes you around the neighbourhood and into a prostitute's working room.

In summer the group adds an extra tour on Wednesdays at 6.30pm. You can also peruse the centre's small library (aka 'sex work study centre') and have a snack (cake, coffee) in the lunchroom. Proceeds go to the centre.

TROMPETTERSTEEG AREA

Map p300 (🚋4/9/16/24 Dam) An intriguing place to view the Red Light action is Trompettersteeg, a teeny alley where the women in the windows charge some of the highest prices. Claustrophobes beware: it's only 1m wide, but it's plenty busy. Look for the entrance in the block south of the Oude Kerk.

MILK GALLERY

Map p300 (www.milkamsterdam.com; Dollebegijnensteeg 5; ⏲hours vary; 🚋4/9/16/24 Dam) FREE This cool exhibition space fosters experimental art and sculptural work that fits in with its Red Light District surroundings. It's also a performance space for fringe-type shows. MILK has moved several times within the area – it jumps around between vacated Red Light windows – and it will likely do so again, so check the website before heading out.

TOP SIGHT NIEUWE KERK

Don't let the 'New Church' name fool you – the structure dates from 1408 (though it *is* a good century fresher than its neighbour, the Oude Kerk). Located smack on the Dam, this basilica is the historic stage of Dutch coronations and royal weddings. The stained glass over the main entrance recalls Queen Wilhelmina, who ascended the throne in 1898, aged 18. Other than such ceremonies, the building no longer functions as a church, but rather as a hall for multimedia exhibitions and organ concerts.

The interior is plain, but several key furnishings – the magnificent oak chancel, the bronze choir screen and the massive gilded organ (1645) – justify a look. Naval hero Admiral Michiel de Ruyter, as well as poets Joost van den Vondel and Pieter Corneliszoon Hooft, are among the luminaries buried here.

It's possible to walk in and take a free peek, but you'll have to pay the admission to get up close. Pick up a 'welcome' brochure at the entrance, which maps out the highlights. Opening times and admission fees can vary, depending on what's going on.

DON'T MISS

- The window for Queen Wilhelmina's inauguration
- Main organ
- Monuments to de Ruyter, Van den Vondel and Hooft
- Oak chancel

PRACTICALITIES

- New Church
- Map p300
- ☎638 69 09
- www.nieuwekerk.nl
- The Dam
- admission €8-16
- ⏲10am-5pm
- 🚋1/2/4/5/9/16/24 Dam

ZEEDIJK
AREA

Map p300 (4/9/16/24 Centraal Station) This is one of Amsterdam's oldest streets. Initially a shipping district, it was a respectable place to be until the 17th century. Then the rich folk moved away to the Herengracht, and the Zeedijk turned to come-hither entertainment for sailors. It has cleaned up again over the past decade or so. It's now the core of Amsterdam's Chinatown and sports lively cafes, bars and eateries.

You'll find a very mixed crowd of visitors bumping over the storied cobblestones.

GUAN YIN SHRINE
BUDDHIST TEMPLE

Map p300 (Fo Guang Shan He Hua Temple; www.ibps.nl; Zeedijk 106-118; noon-5pm Tue-Sat, 10am-5pm Sun; 4/9/16/24 Dam) Europe's first Chinese Imperial–style Buddhist temple (2000) is dedicated to Guan Yin, the Buddhist goddess of mercy. Make a donation, light an incense stick and ponder the thousand eyes and hands of the Bodhisattva statue.

The ornate 'mountain gate' – an intriguing concept in the narrow confines of the Zeedijk – refers to the traditional setting of Buddhist monasteries. The middle section set back from the street was designed along principles of feng shui.

CANNABIS COLLEGE
CULTURAL CENTRE

Map p304 (423 44 20; www.cannabiscollege.com; Oudezijds Achterburgwal 124; 11am-7pm; 4/9/16/24 Dam) This nonprofit centre offers visitors tips and tricks for having a positive smoking experience, as well as provides the lowdown on local cannabis laws. Browse displays, try out a vaporiser (€3; bring your own smoking material) or view marijuana plants growing sky-high in the basement garden (€3; photos permitted).

Staff can provide maps and advice on where to find coffeeshops that sell organic weed and shops that are good for newbies. T-shirts, stickers, postcards and a few other trinkets with the logo are for sale, too.

HASH, MARIJUANA & HEMP MUSEUM
MUSEUM

Map p304 (624 89 26; www.hashmuseum.com; Oudezijds Achterburgwal 148; admission €9; 10am-10pm; 4/9/16/24 Dam) Simple exhibits cover dope botany and the relationship between cannabis and religion. Highlights include an impressive pipe collection, an interactive vaporiser exhibit and a kiosk where you can create an e-postcard of yourself in a marijuana field. Admission also includes the **Hemp Gallery** (Map p304; Oudezijds Achterburgwal 130), filled with hemp art and historical items, in a separate building a few doors north.

The Sensi Seeds company (conveniently attached to the museum) owns the whole thing, so it's no surprise you get to peek at a roomful of growing plants as part of the deal.

RED LIGHT DISTRICT FACTS & FIGURES

- Year prostitution officially legalised in the Netherlands: 2000
- Number of people working as prostitutes in Amsterdam: Between 5000 and 8000 (more than 75% from Eastern Europe)
- Minimum legal age to work as a prostitute in the Netherlands: 21
- Average rent per window: €75 to €150 per eight-hour shift (paid by prostitute), depending on location
- Average price to visit a prostitute: Around €50 for 30 minutes.

RED LIGHT SECRETS MUSEUM OF PROSTITUTION
MUSEUM

Map p300 (662 53 00; www.redlightsecrets.com; Oudezijds Achterburgwal 60h; admission €10; 11am-midnight; 4/9/16/24 Dam) The new prostitution museum is a bit hokey, the kind of place where a tout stands outside and offers discounts if you visit *right now*. But the museum also fills a gap by showing visitors what a Red Light room looks like and answering basic questions about the industry. There are photo opportunities aplenty (ahem, dominatrix room). The venue takes less than an hour to tour.

EROTIC MUSEUM
MUSEUM

Map p300 (www.erotisch-museum.nl; Oudezijds Achterburgwal 54; admission €7; 11am-1am Sun-Thu, to 2am Fri & Sat; 4/9/16/24 Dam) Ho hum. Your usual assortment of bondage exhibits, naughty photos and lewd cartoons. Although this museum has the advantage of location, it's less entertaining, not as well laid out and more expensive when compared with other sex museums in town.

WARMOESSTRAAT
AREA

Map p300 (4/9/16/24 Centraal Station) Amsterdam's earliest canals grew out from the IJ River like the roots of a tree, and

Warmoesstraat was one of the first streets to follow. Its historical pedigree pretty much pales next to its current line-up of leather bars, coffeeshops and fetish shops interspersed with galleries and cool cafes.

W139 GALLERY

Map p300 (www.w139.nl; Warmoesstraat 139; noon-6pm; 4/9/16/24 Dam) FREE Duck into this contemporary arts centre and ponder the multimedia exhibits, which often have an edgy political angle. Check the website for frequent artists talks.

OUDEMANHUISPOORT BUILDING

Map p304 (btwn Oudezijds Achterburgwal & Kloveniersburgwal; 4/9/14/16/24 Spui/Rokin) On Oudezijds Achterburgwal a distinctive gateway with spectacles over the pedestal rises up and marks the entrance to the Oudemanhuispoort, a 17th-century building that was once an almshouse for the elderly. You can't go inside the structure, as it's now part of the University of Amsterdam, but you can wander the leafy courtyard and secondhand book market (p89) that operates in the passageway.

NES AREA

Map p304 (4/9/14/16/24 Spui/Rokin) Beyond the glare of the Red Light District runs this dark, narrow lane, home to theatres for more than 150 years. In 1614 Amsterdam's first bank opened in a pawnshop here, at No 57.

EATING

Medieval Centre

★GARTINE CAFE €

Map p304 (320 41 32; www.gartine.nl; Taksteeg 7; mains €6-12, high tea €16-25; 10am-6pm Wed-Sun; ; 4/9/14/16/24 Spui/Rokin) Gartine is magical, from its covert location in an alley off busy Kalverstraat to its mismatched antique tableware and its sublime breakfast pastries, sandwiches and salads (made from produce grown in its garden plot). The sweet-and-savoury high tea is a scrumptious bonus.

★VLEMINCKX FAST FOOD €

Map p304 (http://vleminckxdesausmeester.nl; Voetboogstraat 31; fries €2.10-4.10, sauces €0.60; noon-7pm Sun & Mon, 11am-7pm Tue, Wed, Fri & Sat, to 8pm Thu; 1/2/5 Koningsplein)

TOP SIGHT
MUSEUM ONS' LIEVE HEER OP SOLDER

It's another one of those 'secret' Amsterdam places. What looks like an ordinary canal house in the Red Light District turns out to have an entire Catholic church stashed inside, with room for 150 worshippers. Ons' Lieve Heer op Solder (Our Dear Lord in the Attic) was founded in the mid-1600s, when local merchant Jan Hartman decided to build a covert church in his house so his son could study to be a priest. At the time, the country's Calvinist rulers had outlawed public worship of Catholicism.

So, as you wander through, you not only get to see the city's richest collection of Catholic art, but also period pieces from 17th-century canal-house life. There is a fantastic labyrinth of staircases, cubbyhole quarters, heavy oak furniture and a porcelain-tiled kitchen. Once upstairs – in the attic, so to speak – you'll see that the church itself is unexpectedly grand, with a marble-columned altar and a painting by Jacob de Wit, a steep gallery and a surprisingly good organ.

The museum completed a multi-year restoration project in late 2015, so the interior now sparkles (and has increased facilities for visitors).

DON'T MISS

- Free audio tour
- The altar
- Kitchen and other 17th-century restored rooms

PRACTICALITIES

- Map p300
- 624 66 04
- www.opsolder.nl
- Oudezijds Voorburgwal 40
- adult/child €9/4.50
- 10am-5pm Mon-Sat, 1-5pm Sun
- 4/9/16/24 Centraal Station

Vleminckx has been frying up *frites* (French fries) since 1887, and doing it at this hole-in-the-wall takeaway shack near the Spui for more than 50 years. The standard is smothered in mayonnaise, though you can also ask for ketchup, peanut sauce or a variety of spicy toppings.

★DE LAATSTE KRUIMEL CAFE €

Map p304 (☎423 04 99; www.delaatstekruimel.nl; Langebrugsteeg 4; mains €2-9; ⏰8am-8pm Mon-Sat, 9am-8pm Sun; 🚋4/9/14/16/24 Spui/Rokin) Hmm, what to look at first: the uber-cute interior decorated with vintage objects from the Noordermarkt and the recycled pallets being used as furniture? Or the glass cases stacked with pies, quiches, breads, cakes and lemon–poppy seed scones. Grandmothers, children, couples on dates and just about everyone else pack the 'Last Crumb' for the fantastic organic sandwiches and treats.

ROB WIGBOLDUS VISHANDEL SANDWICHES €

Map p300 (☎626 33 88; Zoutsteeg 6; sandwiches €2.50-4.50; ⏰9am-5pm Tue-Sat; 🚋4/9/16/24 Dam) A three-table oasis in the midst of surrounding tourist tat, this fish shop in a tiny alley serves excellent herring sandwiches on a choice of crusty white or brown rolls. Don't like fish? Van den Berg's Broodjesbar is next door for other great sandwich options.

VAN DEN BERG'S BROODJESBAR SANDWICHES €

Map p300 (☎622 83 56; www.vandenbergs broodjesbar.nl; Zoutsteeg 4; sandwiches €2-5; ⏰9am-6pm Mon-Sat; 🚋4/9/16/24 Dam) In the sandwich business for more than 30 years, Van den Berg's prepares a variety of options, from a humble cheese-filled roll to *gehakt* (thin meatball slices served warm with killer-hot mustard).

PANNENKOEKENHUIS UPSTAIRS DUTCH €

Map p304 (☎626 56 03; www.upstairspannen koeken.nl; Grimburgwal 2; mains €7-12; ⏰noon-6pm Wed-Sat, to 5pm Sun; 👪; 🚋4/9/14/16/24 Spui/Rokin) Climb some of the steepest stairs in town to reach this small-as-a-stamp restaurant. The lure? Pancakes that are flavoursome, inexpensive and filling. Try the one with bacon, cheese and ginger. It's a two-man show, so service operates at its own pace. Pass the time by admiring all of the teapots hanging from the ceiling. Cash only. Opening hours can be erratic.

GEBR NIEMEIJER CAFE €

Map p300 (☎707 67 52; www.gebroedersniemei jer.nl; Nieuwendijk 35; mains €4-9; ⏰8.30am-6.30pm Tue-Fri, to 5pm Sat, 9am-5pm Sun; 📶; 🚋1/2/5/13/17 Centraal Station) This French bakery is a real find amid Nieuwendijk's head shops. Grab a newspaper and plop down at one of the sturdy wood tables to linger over flaky croissants for breakfast, or fantastic sandwiches made with walnut bread and lamb sausage (or gruyère cheese or fig jam) for lunch.

LANSKROON BAKERY €

Map p304 (☎623 74 43; www.lanskroon.nl; Singel 385; items from €2.25; ⏰8am-5.30pm Mon-Fri, 9am-5.30pm Sat, 10am-5.30pm Sun; 👪; 🚋1/2/5 Spui) Other historic bakeries have prettier fixtures and daintier cakes, but only Lanskroon has such a remarkable *stroopwafel* – crispy, big as a dessert plate and slathered with caramel, honey or a deceptively healthy-tasting fig paste. In winter, locals come for spiced *speculaas* cookies and other holiday treats, and in summer there's thick nut- or fruit-swirled ice cream.

BANKETBAKKERIJ VAN DER LINDE ICE CREAM €

Map p300 (☎624 82 13; Nieuwendijk 183; scoops from €1.10; ⏰1-5pm Mon, 11am-5.45pm Tue-Thu, 9am-5.45pm Fri, 9am-5pm Sat, noon-5pm Sun; 🚋4/9/16/24 Dam) A long line usually snakes out the door of this narrow shop where everyone is queuing for – wait for it – vanilla ice cream. That's the only flavour! Only this vanilla is unlike any other. Imagine licking a delicious sugar cloud, all soft and velvety and almost like whipped cream in texture. Van der Linde has sugar-loaded generations of Amsterdammers.

VILLA ZEEZICHT CAFE €

Map p300 (☎626 74 33; Torensteeg 7; mains €5-12; ⏰9am-10pm; 🚋1/2/5/13/14/17 Dam/Raadhuisstraat) While it serves decent pastas and sandwiches, it's really all just clumsy foreplay for the homemade *appeltaart* (apple pie) main event, a deserved Amsterdam legend. Fork into a mountain of apples dusted in cinnamon, surrounded by warm pastry and fresh cream. In warm weather tables are set up on the bridge over the Singel.

VAN STAPELE BAKERY €

Map p304 (www.vanstapele.com; Heisteeg 4; cookies €2; ⏰noon-6pm Mon, 10am-6pm Tue-Fri, 11am-6pm Sat & Sun; 🚋1/2/5 Spui) Teensy Van

Stapele is a true specialist, baking just one thing and baking it well: chocolate cookies. To be specific, it's a Valrhona dark chocolate cookie on the outside, filled with melted white chocolate inside. The disc of gorgeous sweetness is served soft and warm straight from the oven.

BROODJE BERT — SANDWICHES €

Map p304 (Singel 321; sandwiches €4-7; ⌚8am-5pm; 🚊1/2/5 Spui) Join the locals sitting on wooden chairs in the sun (or on the window seats inside) at this fabulous little sandwich shop in a winning canal-side location. In addition to huge sandwiches, such as marinated grilled chicken or the eponymous house special 'Broodje Bert' (lamb meatballs on Turkish bread), there are burgers and omelettes made to order. Cash only.

MAOZ — MIDDLE EASTERN €

Map p300 (www.maozusa.com; Damrak 40; mains €4-7; ⌚11am-2am; 🖉; 🚊1/2/5/13/17 Centraal Station) This outpost of the local falafel chain provides a dose of cheap, healthy vegetarian food amid the Damrak's waffle shops, *frites* stands and other tourist tat. Get your chickpea balls in a pita or salad box, then add your own toppings from the salad bar. It stays open until the wee hours.

VAN KERKWIJK — INTERNATIONAL €€

Map p304 (www.caferestaurantvankerkwijk.nl; Nes 41; mains €16-24; ⌚11am-1am; 🚊4/9/16/24 Dam) Van Kerkwijk is so low-key you might not notice it, but locals sure know it's there; the small wooden tables are typically packed. They don't take reservations, and there's no menu, so you'll have to wait for the server to tell you what's available that day: perhaps an Indonesian curry, a North African tagine, or various French and Italian meaty classics.

It's quintessentially cosy, with candles burning even during the day – a true, personal-feeling spot in a somewhat generic part of the city.

HAESJE CLAES — DUTCH €€

Map p304 (☎624 99 98; www.haesjeclaes.nl; Spuistraat 273-275; mains €16-26, set menus from €32.50; ⌚noon-10pm; 🚊1/2/5 Spui) Haesje Claes' warm surrounds – a tad touristy, but with lots of dark wood and antique knick-knacks – are just the place to sample comforting pea soup and *stamppot* (mashed pot: potatoes mashed with another vegetable). The fish starter has a great sampling of different Dutch fish.

TOMAZ — FRENCH, DUTCH €€

Map p304 (☎320 64 89; www.tomaz.nl; Begijnensteeg 6-8; mains €15-20; ⌚noon-10pm; 🖉; 🚊1/2/5 Spui) Charming little Tomaz hides near the Begijnhof, and is a fine spot for a light lunch or informal dinner, accompanied by a bottle of wine, of course. A vegetarian special is always available. Linger for a while over a game of chess.

SEAFOOD BAR — SEAFOOD €€

Map p304 (☎233 74 52; www.theseafoodbar.nl; Spui 15; mains €14.50-36.50; ⌚noon-10pm; 🚊1/2/5 Spui) The tables are always crowded with stylish folks clinking wine glasses and slurping oysters. Many tourists find their way here, but who can blame them when slick, well-executed seafood in buzzy environs is the goal? The restaurant can be a good option when other places are booked, as it intentionally saves a third of its seats for walk-in customers. There's another branch near Vondelpark.

D'VIJFF VLIEGHEN — MODERN DUTCH €€€

Map p304 (☎530 40 60; www.vijffvlieghen.nl; Spuistraat 294-302; mains €26-37, set menus from €47; ⌚6-10pm; 🚊1/2/5 Spui) So what if every tourist and business visitor eats here? Sometimes the herd gets it right. The 'Five Flies' is a classic, spread out across five 17th-century canal houses. Oldwood dining rooms are full of character,

RED LIGHT DISTRICT NITTY-GRITTY

➡ Taking photos of the windows is strictly verboten. Your first instinct might be to take a quick snap, but don't do it – out of simple respect, and to avoid having your camera tossed in a canal by the ladies' enforcers.

➡ For their own safety, prostitutes' quarters are equipped with a button that, when pressed, activates a light outside. The police or other protectors show up in a hurry.

➡ The red lights of the Red Light District have been around for a long time; even as early as the 1300s, women carrying red lanterns met sailors near the port. Red light is flattering and, especially when used in combination with black light, it makes teeth sparkle.

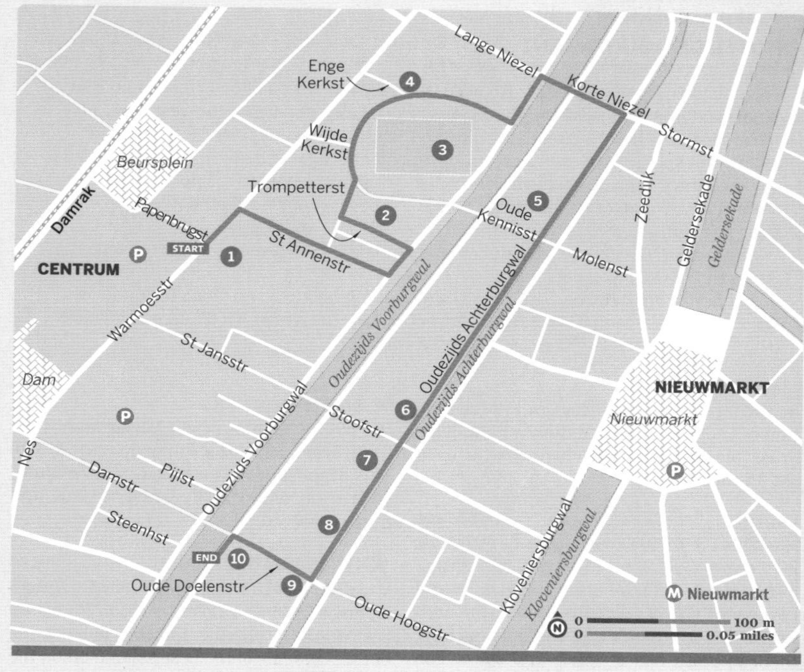

Neighbourhood Walk
Red Light Quickie

START CONDOMERIE HET GULDEN VLIES
END GREENHOUSE
LENGTH 1.25KM; 25 MINUTES

The typical 'quickie', according to Red Light District workers, is 15 minutes, and our walk shouldn't take you much longer.

What better way to set the mood than at **1 Condomerie Het Gulden Vlies** (p91)? Cherry red, hypoallergenic, cartoon character embodiments – the shop is a shrine to condom art, selling all sizes and colours.

It's easy to walk right by the teeny alley **2 Trompettersteeg** (p74). After turning onto Oudezijds Voorburgwal from St Annenstraat, it'll be the second little street you come to en route to the church. Claustrophobes beware: the medieval alley is only 1m wide, and the red-light windows keep it busy.

A contradiction if ever there was one: the 14th-century **3 Oude Kerk** (p70) is Amsterdam's oldest building, but the surrounding square has long been ground-zero for prostitution. Look near the entrance for the 'golden torso' pavement plaque, with a hand groping a breast.

The **4 Prostitution Information Centre** (p74) dispenses forthright facts to sex workers and visitors alike. As you move onwards, observe the separate zones for African, Asian and European women.

Bondage exhibits and dildo bikes 'educate' visitors in the **5 Erotic Museum** (p75). For further browsing, multiple shops around here offer 'nonstop hard porno' and trinkets such as whips, masks and spiked collars.

It's rapid-fire vice as you continue down Oudezijds Achterburgwal: live sex shows at **6 Casa Rosso** (p88), smoky vaporisers at the **7 Cannabis College** (p75), botany lessons at the **8 Hash, Marijuana & Hemp Museum** (p75), and 'Big Bud' at the **9 Sensi Seeds Shop**.

Wind down at surprisingly classy **10 Greenhouse** (p86), a Cannabis Cup–worthy coffeeshop that serves up good food and music. Or choose among the many other coffee joints (pardon the pun!) in the district.

WORTH A DETOUR

HOTEL DE GOUDFAZANT

Located in an isolated stretch of Noord, this **restaurant** (☎636 51 70; www.hotelde goudfazant.nl; Aambeeldstraat 10h; 3-course menu €30; ⏲6pm-1am Tue-Sun; 🚌32, 33 Johan van Hasseltweg)is a pain to get to, so the food better be great. And it is. The restaurant spreads through a cavernous former garage, still raw and industrial, and sticks to the theme by having a Porsche and other cars parked inside. Punk-looking chefs prepare steak tartare, lamb shanks and other French-influenced dishes in the open kitchen.

Staff roll up the garage's big doors in warm weather and you can watch the passing barge traffic while you eat.

Get here from Centraal Station via bus 32 or 33, taking it two stops to Johan van Hasseltweg, and then walk along the street toward the water. It's about a 15-minute trip. There is no hotel, FYI, except in name only.

featuring Delft-blue tiles and works by Rembrandt and Breitner. Some chairs have brass plates for the celebrities who have sat on them.

LUCIUS — SEAFOOD €€€

Map p304 (☎624 18 31; www.lucius.nl; Spuistraat 247; mains €22-30, set menu €39.50; ⏲5pm-midnight; 🚋1/2/5 Spui) Simple, delicious and consistently full, Lucius is known for both its fresh ingredients and for not mucking them up with lots of sauce and spice. The interior, all fish tanks and tiles, is professional, just like the service.

Red Light District

DE BAKKERSWINKEL — CAFE €

Map p300 (☎489 80 00; www.debakkerswinkel.nl; Warmoesstraat 69; mains €8-17; ⏲8am-5.30pm Mon-Wed, to 9pm Thu & Fri, 9am-9pm Sat, to 6pm Sun; 👪; 🚋4/9/16/24 Centraal Station) Family-friendly De Bakkerswinkel offers excellent baked goods (especially scones), sandwiches and soups, and breakfast fare such as quiche, French toast and omelettes, to nibble amid the cute, industrial-meets-farmhouse decor.

KAM YIN — SURINAMESE €

Map p300 (☎625 31 15; www.kamyin.nl; Warmoesstraat 8; mains €7-13; ⏲noon-midnight; 🚋4/9/16/24 Centraal Station) It's nothing much to look at, but this plastic and fluorescent operation dispenses excellent versions of Surinamese standards such as roti and *tjauw min* (thick noodles with assorted meats). Its *broodje pom* (a chicken-casserole sandwich) ranks as one of the city's best.

DE BAKKERSWINKEL — CAFE €

Map p300 (Warmoesstraat 133; sandwiches €6-10; ⏲8am-5.30pm Mon-Fri, to 6pm Sat & Sun) This outpost of the local chain serves sandwiches on wonderfully crusty bread and fresh-squeezed juices for takeaway.

★THAIS SNACKBAR BIRD — THAI €€

Map p300 (☎420 62 89; www.thai-bird.nl; Zeedijk 77; mains €9-16; ⏲2-10pm; 🚋4/9/16/24 Centraal Station) Don't tell the Chinese neighbours, but this is some of the best Asian food on the Zeedijk – the cooks, wedged in a tiny kitchen, don't skimp on lemongrass, fish sauce or chilli. The resulting curries and basil-laden meat and seafood dishes will knock your socks off.

There's a bit more room to spread out in the (slightly pricier) restaurant across the street (No 72).

'SKEK — CAFE €€

Map p300 (☎427 05 51; www.skek.nl; Zeedijk 4-8; sandwiches €4-7, mains €12-14; ⏲4-10pm Mon, noon-10pm Tue-Sun; 📶; 🚋4/9/16/24 Centraal Station) Run by students for students (flashing your ID gets you 25% off), this friendly cafe-bar is an excellent place to get fat sandwiches on thick slices of multigrain bread, and healthy main dishes with chicken, fish or pasta. Bands occasionally perform at night (the bar stays open to 1am weekdays, and 3am on weekends).

DWAZE ZAKEN — CAFE €€

Map p300 (☎612 41 75; www.dwazezaken.nl; Prins Hendrikkade 50; sandwiches €7-8, mains €17-20; ⏲9am-midnight Mon-Sat, to 5.30pm Sun; 🚋4/9/16/24 Centraal Station) A refuge from red-light madness, this mosaic-trimmed corner cafe has big windows and a menu of spicy sandwiches, vegie-rich soups and creative fondue. A fine selection of beer (with an emphasis on Belgian elixirs) helps wash it down. Jazzy live music adds to the vibe on Mondays, when there are €7 dinners as well.

HOFJE VAN WIJS CAFE €€

Map p300 (☎624 04 36; www.hofjevanwijs.nl; Zeedijk 43; mains €9-16; ⏰noon-10pm Tue-Sun; 🚋4/9/16/24 Centraal Station) The 200-year-old coffee and tea vendor Wijs & Zonen (the monarch's purveyor) maintains this pretty courtyard cafe. It serves Dutch stews, fondue and a couple of fish dishes, plus local beers and liqueurs. But what you're really here for are the yummy cakes.

NAM KEE CHINESE €€

Map p300 (☎624 34 70; www.namkee.net; Zeedijk 111-113; mains €11-20; ⏰noon-11pm; 🚋4/9/16/24 Dam) It won't win any design awards, but year in, year out, Nam Kee is the most popular Chinese spot in town. The steamed oysters and black bean sauce are legendary. If you want to avoid the fluorescent-light ambience, try Nam Kee's nearby branch (p103) in Nieuwmarkt, which is fancier.

BLAUW AAN DE WAL INTERNATIONAL €€€

Map p304 (☎330 2257; www.blauwaandewal.com; Oudezijds Achterburgwal 99; 3-/4-course menu €55/67.50; ⏰6-11.30pm Tue-Sat; 🚋4/9/16/24 Dam) Definitely a rose among thorns: a long, often graffiti-covered hallway in the middle of the Red Light District leads to this Garden of Eden. Originally a 17th-century herb warehouse, the whitewashed, exposed-brick, multilevel space still features old steel weights and measures, plus friendly, knowledgeable service and refined French- and Italian-inspired cooking. In summer grab a table in the romantic garden.

ANNA MODERN DUTCH €€€

Map p300 (☎428 11 11; www.restaurantanna.nl; Warmoesstraat 111; mains €19-26, 4-course menu €47.50; ⏰6-10.30pm Mon-Sat; 🚋4/9/16/24 Dam) It's quite a contrast: Anna's sleek line of white-clothed tables topped by plates of curry-sauced monkfish and truffle-and-veal risotto, while steps away the world's oldest profession is in full swing. The restaurant sits right by the Oude Kerk and the active Red Light windows surrounding it. A robust list of organic and global wines complements the brilliantly executed fare.

DRINKING & NIGHTLIFE

Medieval Centre

★HOPPE BROWN CAFÉ

Map p304 (www.cafehoppe.com; Spui 18-20; ⏰8am-1am; 🚋1/2/5 Spui) Gritty Hoppe has been filling glasses for more than 340 years. Journalists, barflies, socialites and raconteurs toss back brews amid the ancient wood panelling. Most months the energetic crowd spews out from the dark interior and onto the Spui. Note Hoppe has two parts: the brown *café* and a modern pub with a terrace, located next door (to the left).

★CAFÉ BELGIQUE BEER CAFÉ

Map p300 (www.cafe-belgique.nl; Gravenstraat 2; ⏰3pm-1am; 🚋4/9/16/24 Dam) Pull up a stool at the carved wooden bar and pick from the glinting brass taps. It's all about Belgian beers here, as you may have surmised. Eight flow from the spouts, and 30 or so more are available in bottles. The ambience is quintessential *gezellig* (convivial, cosy) and draws lots of chilled-out locals. There's live music and DJs some nights.

★CAFÉ DE DOKTER BROWN CAFÉ

Map p304 (☎626 44 27; www.cafe-de-dokter.nl; Rozenboomsteeg 4; ⏰4am-1am Tue-Sat; 🚋1/2/5 Spui) Very atmospheric and slightly spooky, Café de Dokter is said to be Amsterdam's smallest pub. Candles flicker on the tables, music from old jazz records drifts in the background, and a couple of centuries of dust drapes over the chandeliers and birdcage hanging from the ceiling. Whiskys and smoked beef sausage are the specialities, but good beers flow, too.

A surgeon opened the bar in 1798, hence the name. His descendents still run it.

IN DE WILDEMAN BEER CAFÉ

Map p300 (www.indewildeman.nl; Kolksteeg 3; ⏰noon-1am Mon-Thu, to 2am Fri & Sat; 🚋1/2/5/13/17 Centraal Station) This former distillery house has been transformed into a low-key beer *café* with more than 250 bottled beers and 18 varieties on tap. Locals rave about the choice of Trappist ales, and the huge selection from the Netherlands and Belgium. The bar doesn't blast any music, so it's a first-rate spot to chat while sipping.

DAMPKRING COFFEESHOP

Map p304 (www.dampkring-coffeeshop-amsterdam.nl; Handboogstraat 29; ⏲10am-1am; 📶; 🚋1/2/5 Koningsplein) With an interior that resembles a larger-than-life lava lamp, Dampkring is a consistent Cannabis Cup winner, and known for having the most comprehensive menu in town (including details about smell, taste and effect). Its name references the ring of the earth's atmosphere where smaller items combust.

CAFÉ DE JAREN GRAND CAFÉ

Map p304 (www.cafedejaren.nl; Nieuwe Doelenstraat 20; ⏲9.30am-1am Sun-Thu, to 2am Fri & Sat; 🚋4/9/14/16/24 Muntplein) Watch the Amstel flow by from the balcony and waterside terraces of this soaring, bright and *very* grand *café*. The reading table has loads of foreign publications for whiling away hours over beers. If you're feeling peckish, hit the fabulous buffet salad bar (a rarity in Amsterdam).

PILSENER CLUB BROWN CAFÉ

Map p304 (☎623 17 77; Begijnensteeg 4; ⏲noon-1am Mon-Thu, to 2am Fri & Sat; 🚋1/2/5 Spui) Also known as Engelse Reet (ask the bartender for a translation), this small, narrow and ramshackle place doesn't allow you to do anything but drink and talk, which is what a 'real' brown *café* is all about. It opened in 1893 and has hardly changed since. Little name plates mark the seats of the bar's regulars through the years.

DE ZWART BROWN CAFÉ

Map p304 (☎624 65 11; Spuistraat 334; ⏲9am-1am Mon-Sat, 11am-1am Sun; 🚋1/2/5 Spui) 'Not everyone has knowledge of beer, but those who have it drink it here' is the translation of the slogan on a panel above this atmospheric bar, which has an original tiled floor from 1921. Just across the alley from age-old Hoppe, De Zwart gets a different (though amicable) crowd of left-wing journalists and writers, as well as local-government people.

BIERCAFÉ GOLLEM BEER CAFÉ

Map p304 (www.cafegollem.nl; Raamsteeg 4; ⏲4pm-1am Mon-Thu, noon-3am Fri & Sat, to 1am Sun; 🚋1/2/5 Spui) The pioneer of Amsterdam's beer *cafés* is a minuscule space covered all over in beer paraphernalia. The 14 beers on tap and 200 in the bottle (mostly from Belgium) attract lots of connoisseurs. The bartenders are happy to advise.

DE DRIE FLESCHJES TASTING HOUSE

Map p300 (☎624 84 43; www.dedriefleschjes.nl; Gravenstraat 18; ⏲2-8.30pm Mon-Sat, 3-7pm Sun; 🚋4/9/16/24 Dam) Behind the Nieuwe Kerk, the distiller Bootz' tasting room dates from 1650. It specialises in liqueurs (although you can also get superb *jenever*) – the macaroon variety is quite nice. Take a peek at the collection of *kalkoentjes,* small bottles with hand-painted portraits of former mayors. Get an order of the famous meatballs to accompany your drinks.

LUXEMBOURG GRAND CAFÉ

Map p304 (www.luxembourg.nl; Spui 24; ⏲8am-midnight Mon-Fri, 9am-midnight Sat & Sun; 🚋1/2/5 Spui) Join gaggles of glam locals and tourists at this permanently busy *café*. Grab a paper from the reading table, procure a sunny seat on the terrace, order the 'Holland' snack platter (bread, cured meats, Dutch cheese and deep-fried croquettes) and watch the world go by. Inside are parquet floors, a marble bar and an art-deco stained-glass skylight.

ABRAXAS COFFEESHOP

Map p304 (www.abraxas.tv; Jonge Roelensteeg 12; ⏲10am-1am; 📶; 🚋1/2/5/14 Dam/Paleisstraat) It's young stoner heaven: mellow music, comfy sofas, thick milkshakes and rooms with different energy levels spread across three floors. The considerate staff make it a great place for coffeeshop newbies (though the fairy-tale artwork can get a bit intense).

GRAND CAFE-RESTAURANT 1E KLAS GRAND CAFÉ

Map p300 (www.restaurant1eklas.nl; Stationsplein 15, platform 2b; ⏲8:30am-10pm; 🚋4/9/16/24 Centraal Station) This distinguished *café* in Centraal Station (upstairs by platform 2b) used to be the waiting room for first-class passengers, hence the name. It's a nice spot if you're waiting for a train, or even just to hang out in the afternoon for *bitterballen* (croquettes) and a Belgian beer while reading the newspapers. A white parrot named Elvis keeps you company by the bar.

There's also a same-named pub next door, though the *café* has more personality. Prices aren't bad considering the location.

CAFÉ HET SCHUIM BAR

Map p304 (☎638 93 57; Spuistraat 189; ⏲noon-1am Mon-Thu, to 3am Fri & Sat, 1pm-1am Sun; 🚋1/2/5/14 Dam/Paleisstraat) *Schuim* means 'foam' (on beer) and this grungy, arty bar is extraordinarily popular with beer-swilling locals – it gets packed any time of day or night. It offers great people-watching. The eye-catching murals amuse, as well.

BEURS VAN BERLAGE CAFÉ GRAND CAFÉ

Map p300 (☎638 39 14; Beursplein 1; ⏰10am-6pm Mon-Sat, 11am-6pm Sun; 🚋1/2/5/13/17 Nieuwezijds Kolk) The *café* in this landmark building is a cool place to pop in for a beer or coffee so you can ogle the stunning 1903 murals by Jan Toorop representing the past, present and future. On nice days tables spill out into the adjoining plaza and fill with locals.

TARA PUB

Map p304 (www.thetara.com; Rokin 85-89; ⏰10am-1am) This expat meeting place combines folkie Irish with Amsterdam chic. In its maze of rooms (the one-time home of German expressionist Max Beckmann) you'll find warm fireplaces, a cool bar, gorgeous wall carvings, and seats salvaged from an old Irish church. Catch frequent musical happenings and sports on the telly. Meals include a full English breakfast, and burgers.

CAFÉ THE MINDS BAR

Map p304 (www.theminds.nl; Spuistraat 245; ⏰9pm-3am Sun-Thu, to 4am Fri & Sat; 🚋1/2/5 Spui) Don't let the word *café* in the name fool you – this is a hard-core (but very friendly) punk bar where the beer's cheap, the music's loud and the party's rockin'. It's smack in the middle of a little strip of the Spui that's home to a few squats and plenty of graffiti.

OPORTO BROWN CAFÉ

Map p300 (☎638 07 02; Zoutsteeg 1; ⏰11am-1am; 🚋4/9/16/24 Dam) This tiny brown *café* is worth visiting just for the inlaid woodwork behind the bar (check out the Zodiac signs). Its wrought-iron-and-parchment lighting fixtures are said to have been the same for 60 years.

CAFÉ VAN ZUYLEN BROWN CAFÉ

Map p300 (☎639 10 55; Torensteeg 4; ⏰10am-1am Sun-Thu, to 3am Fri & Sat; 🚋1/2/5/13/14/17 Dam/Raadhuisstraat) Although the terrace is one of the prettiest spots for a drink on the Singel, the interior – with its cosy rooms featuring lots of wood and old leather banquettes – is just as appealing in the cooler months.

TWEEDE KAMER COFFEESHOP

Map p304 (☎422 22 36; Heisteeg 6; ⏰10am-1am; 🚋1/2/5 Spui) The teeny, wood-panelled, original location of the Dampkring chain of coffeeshops feels more like a brown *café* than a coffeeshop. But weed there is, and the selection is vast (the chain is known for its detailed, informative menus). The Sativa is highly recommended for a special happy high. It's mostly locals creating the billows of smoke that spill out the door.

> LOCAL KNOWLEDGE
>
> **TOP SPOTS FOR LOCAL SNACKS**
>
> The Centre is a great neighbourhood to sample some of Amsterdam's famed local specialities.
>
> **Vleminckx** (p76) *Frites* with mayo.
>
> **Rob Wigboldus Vishandel** (p77) Herring sandwich.
>
> **Lanskroon** (p77) Gooey, caramel-y *stroopwafel* (syrup waffle).
>
> **Pannenkoekenhuis Upstairs** (p77) Pancakes, sweet or savoury.
>
> **Banketbakkerij Van der Linde** (p77) Unbelievably delicious vanilla ice cream.

DUTCH FLOWERS COFFEESHOP

Map p304 (☎624 76 24; Singel 387; ⏰10am-11pm Sun-Thu, to 1am Fri & Sat; 🚋1/2/5 Spui) Were it not for this shop's main wares, you'd be hard pressed to distinguish it from a brown *café*, with the game on TV and a lovely view of the Singel. It means that you needn't slum it with the college kids in order to enjoy a toke.

CAFÉ DANTE GRAND CAFÉ

Map p304 (☎638 88 39; www.amsterdamdante.com; Spuistraat 320; ⏰11am-1am Mon-Thu, to 3am Fri, 10am-3am Sat, to 1am Sun; 📶; 🚋1/2/5 Spui) This huge art-deco space is quiet as auntie's back garden during the day, but after 5pm weeknights it transforms into a lively bar for the downtown business crowd. Plus, you get your choice of outside views: the busy Spui out front or the lovely Singel out back.

PRIK GAY

Map p300 (www.prikamsterdam.nl; Spuistraat 109; ⏰4pm-1am Sun-Thu, to 3am Fri & Sat; 🚋1/2/5/13/14/17 Dam/Raadhuisstraat) 'Lovely liquids and twisted tunes' is the motto of this peppy retro bar with an 'I've just redone my loft' clientele of 20- to 30-year-olds. Live DJs spin pop, house and dance tunes.

COFFEESHOP RUSLAND COFFEESHOP

Map p304 (www.coffeeshop-rusland-amsterdam.com; Rusland 16; ⌚8am-12.30am; 🚊4/9/14/16/24 Spui/Rokin) Rusland means 'Russia' in Dutch, so it's no surprise there's a different vibe to this coffeeshop. It's a young, mod group – including many expats from the mother country – puffing, sipping tea (more than 40 types are available) and playing the occasional game of chess. It's off the usual tourist path.

CUCKOO'S NEST GAY

Map p300 (www.cuckoosnest.nl; Nieuwezijds Kolk 6; ⌚1pm-1am Sun-Thu, to 2am Fri & Sat; 🚊1/2/5/13/17 Centraal Station) A fetish-oriented clientele crowds into this busy bar, which has one of the largest 'playrooms' in Europe. You could spend a whole night exploring the labyrinth of cubicles and glory holes.

WEB GAY

Map p300 (www.thewebamsterdam.com; St Jacobsstraat 6; ⌚1pm-1am Sun-Thu, to 2am Fri & Sat; 🚊1/2/5/13/17 Centraal Station) Web is a well-established leather bar with darkrooms and a sling room for the more adventurous. Sundays are popular, adding DJs to the mix.

Red Light District

★WYNAND FOCKINK TASTING HOUSE

Map p304 (www.wynand-fockink.nl; Pijlsteeg 31; ⌚3-9pm; 🚊4/9/16/24 Dam) This small tasting house (dating from 1679) serves scores of *jenever* and liqueurs in an arcade behind Grand Hotel Krasnapolsky. Although there are no seats or stools, it's an intimate place to knock back a shot glass or two. Guides give an English-language tour of the distillery and tastings (six samples) on weekends at 3pm, 4.30pm, 6pm and 7.30pm (€17.50, reservations not required).

If you're stuck trying to decide on a flavour, try the house speciality *boswandeling* (secret of the forest), a vivacious combination of young *jenever,* herb bitters and orange liqueur – the mix tastes like cloves.

★IN 'T AEPJEN BROWN CAFÉ

Map p300 (Zeedijk 1; ⌚noon-1am Mon-Thu, to 3am Fri & Sat; 🚊4/9/16/24 Centraal Station) Candles burn even during the day at this bar based in a mid-16th-century house, which is one of two remaining wooden buildings in the city. The name allegedly comes from the bar's role in the 16th and 17th centuries as a crash pad for sailors from the Far East, who often toted *aapjes* (monkeys) with them.

Vintage jazz on the stereo enhances the time-warp feel. The place is stuffed with advertising signs and plenty of locals.

★IN DE OLOFSPOORT TASTING HOUSE

Map p300 (☎624 39 18; www.olofspoort.com; Nieuwebrugsteeg 13; ⌚4pm-12.30am Tue-Thu, 3pm-1.30am Fri & Sat, 3-10pm Sun; 🚊4/9/16/24 Centraal Station) The door of this brown *café*–tasting room was once the city gate. A crew of regulars has *jenever* bottles stocked just for them. Check out the jaw-dropping selection behind the back-room bar. Occasional singalongs add to the atmosphere.

'T MANDJE GAY

Map p300 (www.cafetmandje.nl; Zeedijk 63; ⌚5pm-1am Tue-Thu, 4pm-1am Fri, 3pm-1am Sat & Sun; 🚊4/9/16/24 Centraal Station) Amsterdam's oldest gay bar opened in 1927, then shut in 1982, when the Zeedijk grew too seedy. But its trinket-covered interior was lovingly dusted every week until it reopened in 2008. The bartenders can tell you stories about the bar's brassy lesbian founder. It's one of the most *gezellig* places in the centre, gay or straight.

BROUWERIJ DE PRAEL BEER CAFÉ

Map p300 (☎408 44 69; www.deprael.nl; Oudezijds Armsteeg 26; ⌚noon-midnight Mon-Wed, to 1am Thu-Sat, to 11pm Sun; 🚊4/9/16/24 Centraal Station) Sample organic beers (Scotch ale, IPA, barleywine and many more varieties) at the multilevel tasting room of socially minded De Prael brewery, known for employing people with a history of mental illness. A mostly younger crowd hoists suds and forks into well-priced stews and other Dutch standards at the comfy couches and big wood tables strewn about. There's often live music.

To see the brewery itself, head around the corner to Oudezijds Voorburgwal 30. Tours (€7.50) are offered every hour between 1pm and 5pm Tuesday to Saturday (from 2pm Sunday) and include one beer. De Prael also makes liqueurs that you can taste at the brewery's shop.

TONTON CLUB BAR

Map p300 (www.tontonclub.nl; St Annendwarsstraat 6; ⌚4pm-midnight Mon & Tue, noon-midnight Wed-Sun; 🚊4/9/16/24 Centraal Station) It's a simple concept: craft beer plus arcade games in a neon-bathed room in the Red Light District. Play a little Simpsons pinball, Pac-Man or Mortal Kombat, then brag about

WORTH A DETOUR

AMSTERDAM-NOORD

The avant-garde thrives in Noord, the vast community across the IJ River from downtown Amsterdam. This northern part of the city has shot up recently to become one of Amsterdam's hippest areas. Free ferries depart from behind Centraal Station and glide to the hot spots.

EYE Film Institute & Around

Some of the most impressive places are a mere five-minute boat ride away. Take the 'Buiksloterweg' ferry – which runs 24 hours a day – to reach the following:

EYE Film Institute (☎589 14 00; www.eyefilm.nl; IJpromenade 1; ⊙10am-7pm Sat-Thu, to 9pm Fri) Inside the mod building, movies from the 40,000-title archive screen in four theatres, sometimes with live music. Exhibits (admission €9 to €15) of costumes, digital art and other cinephile amusements run in conjunction with what's playing. A view-tastic bar-restaurant adds to the hep-cat feel. Head to the basement for groovy free displays, including pods where you can sit and watch classic Dutch- and English-language films, and a green screen that injects you into a cartoon.

Tolhuistuin (www.tolhuistuin.nl; IJpromenade 2) This nifty cultural centre hosts African dance troupes, grime DJs and much more on its garden stage under twinkling lights. On sunny days locals pitch up to the bright-coloured picnic tables and bean-bag pillows at the venue's cafe (open 10am until late daily) to while away the day. It's steps away from the ferry dock.

A'DAM Tower (www.adamtoren.nl; Overhoeksplein 1) The 22-storey building next to the EYE Film Institute used to be Royal Dutch Shell oil company offices. As of spring 2016, it's a hip hub for electronic dance music businesses. An observatory (with a giant swing for daredevils) crowns the building. There are also two dance clubs (one up high, and one in the basement) and a revolving restaurant on the 19th floor.

Cycling trips This part of Amsterdam-Noord is also great for cycling. After you depart the ferry, pedal north along the Noordhollands Kanaal. Within a few kilometres you're in the countryside and the landscape morphs to windmills, cows and wee farming communities. You can buy cycling maps at the visitor centre by Centraal Station. Many bike rental companies also sell maps, as well as offer guided tours that cover this very area.

NDSM-werf

NDSM-werf is a derelict shipyard turned edgy arts community, 15 minutes upriver. It wafts a post-apocalyptic vibe: an old submarine slumps in the harbour, abandoned trams rust by the water's edge and graffiti splashes across almost every surface. To get here, take the NDSM-werf ferry. It runs between 7am (9am on weekends) and midnight, departing Centraal Station at 15 minutes and 45 minutes past the hour. The ride takes about 15 minutes. Top spots to check out:

Pllek (www.pllek.nl; TT Neveritaweg 59; ⊙9.30am-1am Sun-Thu, to 3am Fri & Sat; ⛴NDSM-werf) Made out of old shipping containers and sporting an artificial sandy beach in front, this *café* is a terrific spot for a waterfront beer or glass of wine. Locals flock here for events, too: alfresco film screenings on Tuesday nights in summer, weekend yoga classes and dance parties under the giant disco ball.

Café Noorderlicht (www.noorderlichtcafe.nl; NDSM-plein 102; mains €17-19; ⊙11am-10pm, closed Mon in winter; ⛴NDSM-werf) Set in a flag-draped greenhouse, Noorderlicht provides food, drinks and a hippie ambience.

Faralda Crane Hotel (p228) This wild hotel has three rooms set at dizzying heights in a repurposed industrial crane. If you can't get a room, you can always bungee jump off the top (€85).

IJ Hallen (www.ij-hallen.nl; Tt Neveritaweg 15; admission €5; ⊙9am-4.30pm Sat & Sun monthly; ⛴NDSM-werf) This whopping flea market – supposedly the largest of its kind in Europe – sprawls through two vast warehouses. It happens monthly; check the website for the schedule.

your high score to all the gamers in the room. Hot dogs are available for sustenance.

CAFÉ DE BARDERIJ BAR

Map p300 (Zeedijk 14; ⏲4pm-1am; 🚊4/9/16/24 Centraal Station) This super-friendly, candlelit bar draws a mixture of local gay regulars and tourists. It has killer views of the canal out back and Zeedijk in front. The crowd skews a bit older, the soundtrack toward fun pop music.

KAPITEIN ZEPPO'S BAR

Map p304 (☎624 20 57; www.zeppos.nl; Gebed Zonder End 5; ⏲noon-1am Sun-Thu, to 3am Fri & Sat; 🚊4/9/14/16/24 Spui/Rokin) Tucked down an alleyway off Grimburgwal, this site has assumed many guises throughout the centuries: a cloister during the 15th, a horse-carriage storehouse in the 17th and a cigar factory in the 19th. The *café* has a bohemian feel, whether you're at the tile-top, candlelit tables or in the garden with its twinkling lights. It's a soulful little spot for a drink.

Between October and April there's live music on Sundays from 4pm (cover groups and big bands).

WINSTON KINGDOM CLUB

Map p300 (www.winston.nl; Warmoesstraat 127, Hotel Winston; ⏲9pm-4am Sun-Thu, to 5am Fri & Sat; 🚊4/9/16/24 Dam) This is a club that even nonclubbers will love for its indie-alternative music beats, smiling DJs and solid, stiff drinks. No matter what's on – from 'dubstep mayhem' to Thailand-style full-moon parties – the scene can get pretty wild in this good-time little space.

GREENHOUSE COFFEESHOP

Map p304 (www.greenhouse.org; Oudezijds Voorburgwal 191; ⏲9am-1am; 📶; 🚊4/9/16/24 Dam) This is one of the most popular coffeeshops in town. Smokers love the funky music, multicoloured mosaics, psychedelic stained-glass windows and high-quality weed. It also serves breakfast, lunch and dinner to suit all levels of the munchies. It's mostly a young, backpacking crowd partaking of the wares.

GETTO GAY & LESBIAN

Map p300 (www.getto.nl; Warmoesstraat 51; ⏲4.30pm-1am Tue-Thu, to 2am Fri & Sat, to midnight Sun; 🚊4/9/16/24 Centraal Station) This groovy, long restaurant-bar is loved for its open, welcoming attitude, great people-watching from the front and a rear lounge where you can chill. It's a haven for the younger gay and lesbian crowd and anyone who wants a little bohemian subculture in the Red Light District's midst. The food (burgers, vegetarian samosas, deer and mushroom stew etc) is good and cheap, too.

PROEFLOKAAL DE OOIEVAAR TASTING HOUSE

Map p300 (www.proeflokaaldeooievaar.nl; St Olofspoort 1; ⏲noon-1am; 📶; 🚊4/9/16/24 Centraal Station) Not much bigger than a vat of *jenever*, this magnificent little tasting house has been going since 1782. On offer are spirits of the De Ooievaar distillery, still located in the Jordaan. The house was built leaning over and its angle is not a result of subsidence, as many people wrongly assume, even before a shot of Old Dutch.

QUARTIER PUTAIN COFFEE

Map p300 (☎895 01 62; www.quartierputain.nl; Oudekerksplein 4; ⏲8am-6pm Mon-Fri, 10am-6pm Sat & Sun; 🚊4/9/16/24 Dam) This cafe amid Red Light windows by the Oude Kerk

PUT OUT THE RED LIGHT?

Since 2007 city officials have been reducing the number of Red Light windows in an effort to clean up the district. They claim it's not about morals, but about crime: pimps, traffickers and money launderers have entered the scene and set the neighbourhood on a downward spiral. Opponents point to a growing conservatism and say the government is using crime as an excuse, because it doesn't like Amsterdam's reputation for sin.

As the window tally decreases, fashion studios, art galleries and trendy cafes rise up to reclaim the deserted spaces, thanks to a program of low-cost rent and other business incentives. It's called Project 1012, after the area's postal code.

To date, more than a fifth of the 482 windows have been shut down. In 2015 scores of prostitutes and their supporters took to the streets to protest the closures. Supposedly the city is rethinking its plan to buy back many more of the windows. Keep an eye on this space to see what happens next...

is a fine place to have an espresso, listen to soothing music and watch the wild scene unfolding all around.

MOLLY MALONE'S IRISH PUB

Map p300 (☎624 11 50; Oudezijds Kolk 9; ⊙noon-1am Mon-Thu, to 3am Fri, 11am-3am Sat, to 1am Sun) Regularly packed with Irish folk, this dark, woody pub holds spontaneous folk-music sessions. Bring your own guitar and let loose with the other Irish-folk fans. The mainly Irish pub grub is decent, and there are specials (ie burger and a pint, curry and a pint etc) on various weeknights.

BUBBLES & WINES CHAMPAGNE BAR WINE BAR

Map p304 (☎422 33 18; www.bubblesandwines.com; Nes 37; ⊙3.30pm-1am Mon-Sat, 2-9pm Sun; 4/9/16/24 Dam) Ignore the silly name; this stylish wine bar is a gem. There are more than 50 quality wines by the glass, tasting flights (several different wines to try) and the city's most scrumptious bar food: caviar blinis, cheese plates and, our favourite, 'bee stings' (parmesan drizzled with white-truffle-infused honey).

QUEEN'S HEAD GAY

Map p300 (www.queenshead.nl; Zeedijk 20; ⊙4pm-1am Sun-Thu, to 3am Fri & Sat; 4/9/16/24 Centraal Station) This beautifully decorated, old-world-style *café* was once run by legendary drag queen Dusty. The place has toned down a bit and the crowd is now mixed, with gay and straight patrons sipping beer in the warm, red-velvet and dark-wood interior. The back offers a terrific canal view. Drag bingo nights and club DJ nights are among the weekly events.

EAGLE GAY

Map p300 (www.theeagleamsterdam.com; Warmoesstraat 90; ⊙10pm-4am Sun-Thu, to 5am Fri & Sat; 4/9/16/24 Centraal Station) The Eagle is a classic. The men-only, leather-denim bar has been around for more than 35 years, offering three levels of action, including basement darkrooms and a house-music-thumping, laser-light-swirling dance floor. Queues can be lengthy on weekends.

BRASSERIE HARKEMA BAR

Map p304 (☎428 22 22; www.brasserieharkema.nl; Nes 67; ⊙noon-1am; ; 4/9/16/24 Spui/Rokin) At the rear of the Frascati theatre, technicolour-walled Brasserie Harkema gets crammed with a young crowd having a pre-theatre meal or post-theatre glass of wine from the lengthy European list.

LOCAL KNOWLEDGE

PUB EGGS

Look closely behind the bar at many brown *cafés* and pubs, and you might see a rack of hard-boiled eggs. They're an age-old tradition – a snack meant to provide energy to drinkers. Ask the barkeep if you're in need. The eggs are usually free. **Brouwerij De Prael** (p84) and **Proeflokaal de Ooievaar** (p86) are two such places to fuel up.

DE BUURVROUW BAR

Map p304 (www.debuurvrouw.nl; St Pieterspoortsteeg 29; ⊙10pm-3am Mon-Thu, to 4am Fri & Sat) This grungy late-night bar is where you inevitably end up when there's nowhere else to go. Take it easy because someone's watching: above the entrance is a painting of *De Buurvrouw* (the woman next door). And yes, everyone *is* probably as drunk as you are.

DURTY NELLY'S IRISH PUB

Map p300 (www.durtynellys.nl; Warmoesstraat 117; ⊙9am-1am Sun-Thu, to 3am Fri & Sat; ; 4/9/16/24 Centraal Station) Huge, dark and always busy, Nelly's attracts foreign visitors from the cheap lodgings in the area (including the attached Durty Nelly's hostel) with a fun atmosphere, drinks, darts and pool. It serves a decent Irish breakfast all day.

WAREHOUSE AMSTERDAM GAY

Map p300 (www.warehouse-amsterdam.com; Warmoesstraat 96; ⊙11pm-4am Thu & Sun, to 5am Fri & Sat; 4/9/16/24 Centraal Station) It's mostly men dancing to the international array of hardcore DJs, but women are equally welcome.

☆ ENTERTAINMENT

BITTERZOET LIVE MUSIC

Map p300 (www.bitterzoet.com; Spuistraat 2; ⊙8pm-late; 1/2/5/13/17 Nieuwezijds Kolk) Always full, always changing, this is one of the friendliest venues in town. One night it might be full of skater dudes; the next, relaxed 30-somethings. Music (sometimes live, sometimes a DJ) can be funk, roots, drum'n'bass, Latin, Afro-beat, old-school jazz or hip-hop groove.

CASA ROSSO LIVE PERFORMANCE

Map p304 (www.casarosso.nl; Oudezijds Achterburgwal 106-108; admission with/without drinks €50/40; 7pm-2am; 4/9/16/24 Dam) It might be stretching it to describe a live sex show as 'classy,' but this theatre is clean and comfortable and always packed with couples and hen's-night parties. Acts can be male, female, both or lesbian (although not gay...sorry boys!). Performers demonstrate everything from positions of the Kama Sutra to pole dances and incredible tricks with lit candles.

FRASCATI THEATRE

Map p304 (626 68 66; www.frascatitheater.nl; Nes 63; closed Aug; 4/9/14/16/24 Spui/Rokin) This experimental theatre is a draw for young Dutch directors, choreographers and producers. Expect multicultural dance and music performances, as well as hip hop, rap and breakdancing. Check the website for upcoming events.

Frascati also hosts a theatre, dance, art and music festival, Breakin'Walls, in both November (main festival) and April (mini-festival).

DE BRAKKE GROND THEATRE

Map p304 (626 68 66; www.brakkegrond.nl; Nes 45, Flemish Cultural Centre; 4/9/14/16/24 Spui/Rokin) De Brakke Grond sponsors a fantastic array of music, experimental video, modern dance and exciting young theatre at its nifty performance hall. Visit the website to find out about upcoming events.

SHOPPING

Medieval Centre

★AMERICAN BOOK CENTER BOOKS

Map p304 (ABC; www.abc.nl; Spui 12; noon-8pm Mon, 10am-8pm Tue-Sat, 11am-6.30pm Sun; 1/2/5 Spui) This excellent three-storey shop is the biggest source of English-language books in Amsterdam. Its greatest strengths are in the artsy ground-floor department, but on the upper floors there's fiction and oodles of special-interest titles, plus a good travel section. It also stocks foreign periodicals such as the *New York Times*. Top-notch postcards, too!

PGC HAJENIUS GIFTS

Map p304 (www.hajenius.com; Rokin 96; noon-6pm Mon, 9.30am-6pm Tue-Sat, noon-5pm Sun; 4/9/14/16/24 Spui/Rokin) Even if you're not a cigar connoisseur, this tobacco emporium is worth a browse. Inside is all art-deco stained glass, gilt trim and soaring ceilings. Regular customers, including members of the royal family, have private humidors here. You can sample your Cuban stogie and other exotic purchases in the handsome smoking lounge.

OUDEMANHUIS BOOK MARKET BOOKS

Map p304 (Oudemanhuispoort; 11am-4pm Mon-Sat; 4/9/14/16/24 Spui/Rokin) Second-

LOCAL KNOWLEDGE

SMART SHOPS, MUSHROOMS & TRUFFLES

Smart shops – which deal in organic uppers and natural hallucinogens – have long been known for selling 'magic' mushrooms. But in 2008, the government banned them after a high-profile incident in which a tourist died. Nearly 200 varieties of fungus then went on the forbidden list – though conspicuously missing was the magic truffle. Truffles are what smart shops now sell.

Difference between magic mushrooms and truffles Truffles come from a different part of the plant, but they contain the same active ingredient – psilocybin – as mushrooms. Those in the know say a truffle trip is a little more like a body high than a visual experience, though this can vary.

Tips for having a safe and pleasant experience When you're at the smart shop, ask staff questions about dosage and effects. If you aren't satisfied with the answers, go to another shop. Once you've purchased the truffles, have the experience in an outdoor space. Avoid bars and other enclosed areas. Don't drink alcohol during your trip and don't mix truffles with other drugs. The effects normally last for four to six hours.

hand books weigh down the tables in the atmospheric covered alleyway between Oudezijds Achterburgwal and Kloveniersburgwal, where you'll rub tweed-patched elbows with University of Amsterdam professors thumbing through volumes of Marx, Aristotle and other classics. Old posters, maps and sheet music are for sale, too. Most tomes are in Dutch, though you'll find a few in English mixed in.

DE BIJENKORF DEPARTMENT STORE
Map p304 (www.debijenkorf.nl; Dam 1; ⏲11am-8pm Sun & Mon, 10am-8pm Tue & Wed, to 9pm Thu & Fri, 9.30am-8pm Sat; 🚋4/9/16/24 Dam) The city's most fashionable department store is in the highest-profile location, facing the Royal Palace. Design-conscious shoppers will enjoy the well-chosen clothing, toys, household accessories and books. It's a good place to stop in to use the bathrooms, which are free. The very snazzy cafe on the 5th floor has a terrace with steeple views.

HEMA DEPARTMENT STORE
Map p300 (www.hema.nl; Nieuwendijk 174; ⏲9am-7pm Mon-Fri, to 6pm Sat, noon-6pm Sun; 🚋4/9/16/24 Dam) What used to be the nation's equivalent of Marks & Spencer, Woolworths or Target now attracts as many design aficionados as bargain hunters. Expect low prices, reliable quality and a wide range of products, including good-value wines and delicatessen goods.

GASTRONOMIE NOSTALGIE HOMEWARES
Map p304 (www.gastronomienostalgie.nl; 304 Nieuwezijds Voorburgwal; ⏲11am-5pm; 🚋1/2/5 Spui) The owner scours auctions in Paris and other cities for the gorgeous china plates, crystal goblets, silver candlesticks and other antique homewares spilling out of this jam-packed shop. Ring the brass bell to get in, then prepare to browse for a good long while.

BY POPULAR DEMAND GIFTS
Map p304 (☎624 52 31; Raadhuisstraat 2; ⏲10am-7pm Mon-Sat, 11am-7pm Sun; 🚋4/9/16/24 Dam) Stop in this large, sunny shop for nifty gift-y items. Cool cards, gadgets and hip lamps and other home decor stock the shelves. Many items are pocket-sized, so travelers can find original, easy-to-transport souvenirs. The wares are infinitely browsable.

MAGIC MUSHROOM GALLERY SMART SHOP
Map p304 (www.magicmushroom.com; Spuistraat 249; ⏲10am-10pm; 🚋1/2/5 Spui) This outlet of the local chain has an excellent choice of truffles, pipes and bongs. Feel free to wobble the garden swing while you nurse a smart drink, or check out the trippy mood lighting while you wait for the herbal ecstasy to kick in. Even non-'shroomers will appreciate the 3D shark playing cards, mushroom banks and other novelty toys for sale.

MARK RAVEN GRAFIEK SOUVENIRS
Map p300 (www.markraven.nl; Nieuwezijds Voorburgwal 174; ⏲10.30am-6pm; 🚋1/2/5/13/14/17 Dam/Raadhuisstraat) Artist Raven's distinctive vision of Amsterdam is available as posters and on T-shirts – they make genuinely tasteful souvenirs.

BY AMFI FASHION
Map p304 (www.byamfi.nl; Spui 23; ⏲1-6pm Tue, Wed & Fri, to 9pm Thu, noon-6pm Sat; 🚋1/2/5 Spui) Students, teachers and alumni of the Amsterdam Fashion Institute show and sell their wares at this small shop. It's mostly clothing and decor wildly inventive in style, but sure to be one of a kind.

ANDRIES DE JONG BV GIFTS
Map p304 (www.andriesdejong.nl; Muntplein 8; ⏲10am-6pm Mon-Sat; 🚋4/9/14/16/24 Muntplein) When seafarers need ship fittings, rope or brass lamps, they sail to Andries de Jong. Traditional clocks, bells, boats in bottles and other quaint maritime gifts fill the crowded shelves among the workers' items. It's perhaps best known as a supplier of strong, vividly coloured flags.

VROLIJK BOOKS
Map p304 (www.vrolijk.nu; Paleisstraat 135; ⏲11am-6pm Mon-Sat, noon-6pm Sun; 🚋1/2/5/14 Dam/Paleisstraat) The Netherlands' largest gay and lesbian bookshop carries the major magazines as well as novels, guidebooks and postcards. Upstairs you'll find art, poetry and DVDs.

FEMALE & PARTNERS ACCESSORIES
Map p300 (www.femaleandpartners.nl; Spuistraat 100; ⏲1-6.30pm Sun & Mon, 11am-6.30pm Tue-Sat; 🚋4/9/16/24 Dam) Everything you need for your inner dominatrix...or the one who's waiting for you at home. Female & Partners is filled with clothing, undies, leather and toys for women and those who love them.

DE BIERKONING DRINK
Map p304 (www.bierkoning.nl; Paleisstraat 125; ⏲11am-7pm Mon-Sat, 1-6pm Sun; 🚋1/2/5/14

Dam/Paleisstraat) Come here for beer – it stocks some 1500 varieties (with an emphasis on Belgian, German, British and, of course, Dutch brews), the largest beer-glass selection around, beer-logoed T-shirts and beer guidebooks to the region. It also carries a small selection of wines.

RUSH HOUR RECORDS MUSIC

Map p300 (www.rushhour.nl; Spuistraat 98; ⊙1-7pm Mon, 11am-7pm Tue, Wed, Fri & Sat, to 9pm Thu, 1-6pm Sun; 🚋4/9/16/24 Dam) House and techno are the main genres on offer, but funk, jazz, dubstep, electronica and disco fill the bins, too. Artists and DJs are your fellow crate diggers. This is an excellent spot to find out what's going on in the underground dance music scene.

LAUNDRY INDUSTRY CLOTHING

Map p304 (www.laundryindustry.com; St Luciensteeg 18; ⊙10am-6pm Mon-Sat, noon-6pm Sun; 🚋4/9/14/16/24 Spui/Rokin) Hip, urban types head here for well-cut, well-designed women's and men's clothes by this Dutch design house. Shoes, jewellery and designer knick-knacks are also for sale. There's a coffee bar for sustenance.

ATHENAEUM BOOKS

Map p304 (www.athenaeum.nl; Spui 14-16; ⊙11am-7pm Mon, 9.30am-7pm Tue-Sat, noon-5.30pm Sun; 🚋1/2/5 Spui) Amsterdam's savviest bookshop is a bit of an intellectual and style hub. Its adjoining newsagency has a selection of cutting-edge international magazines, newspapers and guidebooks.

TIBETWINKEL GIFTS

Map p304 (www.tibetwinkel.nl; Spuistraat 185a; ⊙1-6pm Mon-Fri, to 5pm Sat & Sun; 🚋1/2/5/14 Dam/Paleisstraat) Volunteers staff this tiny shop that sells fair-trade items from Tibet, including incense, prayer flags, yak-bone jewellery and spinning prayer wheels. Proceeds go to a non-profit group that supports Tibet's independence 'through peaceful actions'.

CONCRETE ART, CLOTHING

Map p304 (www.concrete.nl; Spuistraat 250; ⊙noon-7pm Mon-Sat, 1-6pm Sun; 🚋1/2/5 Spui) Concrete is a well-known local design house in Amsterdam. This venue is part exhibition space, showing rotating exhibitions of adventurous photography, graphics and illustrations, and part cool clothes store, boasting racks of zany T-shirts, jeans and trendy trainers (all pricey).

CHILLS & THRILLS SMART SHOP

Map p300 (www.chillsandthrills.com; Nieuwendijk 17; ⊙10am-8pm Sun-Thu, to 10pm Fri & Sat; 🚋1/2/5/13/17 Centraal Station) Always packed with tourists straining to hear each other over thumping techno music, busy Chills & Thrills sells truffles, herbal trips, E-testing kits, psychoactive cacti, amino-acid and vitamin drinks, novelty bongs and life-sized alien sculptures.

VROOM & DREESMANN DEPARTMENT STORE

Map p304 (V&D; www.vd.nl; Kalverstraat 201; ⊙11am-6.30pm Mon, 10am-6.30pm Tue-Sat, noon-6pm Sun; 🚋4/9/14/16/24 Muntplein) This midrange national chain is popular for its clothing and cosmetics. Its fabulous cafeteria, La Place, serves well-priced, freshly prepared salads, hot dishes and pastries.

INNERSPACE SMART SHOP

Map p300 (www.innerspace.nl; Spuistraat 108; ⊙11am-10pm Mon-Sat, noon-10pm Sun; 🚋1/2/5/13/14/17 Dam/Raadhuisstraat) Known for good service and information, this big shop started as a supplier to large parties; it now sells truffles, herbal ecstasy, psychoactive plants and kratom (kind of like opium). True to its origins, it's also a good place for party info and tickets.

3-D HOLOGRAMMEN/ PRINTED IN SPACE JEWELLERY

Map p304 (www.3-dhologrammen.com; Grimburgwal 2; ⊙1-6pm Sun & Mon, noon-6pm Tue-Fri; 🚋4/9/14/16/24 Spui/Rokin) This fascinating (and trippy) collection of holographic pictures, jewellery and stickers will delight all ages. You can even get a hologram custom-made of yourself. The shop also offers 3-D printed bracelets, vases, lamps and other items.

HANS APPENZELLER JEWELLERY

Map p304 (www.appenzeller.nl; Grimburgwal 1; ⊙11am-5.30pm Tue-Sat; 🚋4/9/14/16/24 Spui/Rokin) Appenzeller is one of Amsterdam's leading designers in gold and stone, known for the simplicity and strength of his designs. If his sparse work is not to your taste, along the same street is a row of jewellery shops of all kinds.

POSTZEGELMARKT MARKET

Map p304 (Stamp & Coin Market; Nieuwezijds Voorburgwal 280; ⊙10am-4pm Wed & Sat; 🚋1/2/5 Spui) This little streetside market sells stamps, coins and medals.

MARKS & SPENCER FOOD

Map p304 (www.marksandspencer.com; Kalverstraat 226; ⏲10am-8.30pm Mon-Sat, 11am-8.30pm Sun; 🚋4/9/14/16/24 Muntplein) Britain's iconic retailer has a little supermarket on Kalverstraat, a prime place to get your genuine clotted cream, chocolate-covered Digestives, bangers, steak and kidney pie, and true cheddar cheese. There's also a little e-boutique with a smattering of clothing brands.

MAGNA PLAZA SHOPPING CENTRE

Map p300 (www.magnaplaza.nl; Nieuwezijds Voorburgwal 182; ⏲11am-7pm Mon, 10am-7pm Tue-Sat, noon-7pm Sun; 🚋1/2/5/13/14/17 Dam/Raadhuis straat) This grand 19th-century landmark building, once the main post office, is now home to an upmarket shopping mall with more than 40 shops stocking fashion, gifts and jewellery – everything from Mango and Sissy Boy to a cashmere shop.

KALVERTOREN SHOPPING CENTRE SHOPPING CENTRE

Map p304 (www.kalvertoren.nl; Kalverstraat 212-220; ⏲11am-6.30pm Mon, 10am-6.30pm Tue-Sat, noon-6.30pm Sun; 🚋4/9/14/16/24 Muntplein) This popular, modern shopping centre contains a Vroom & Dreesmann, a small Hema, and big-brand fashion stores such as Replay, Quiksilver, Levi's, Timberland and DKNY.

Red Light District

★CONDOMERIE HET GULDEN VLIES GIFTS

Map p300 (www.condomerie.com; Warmoes straat 141; ⏲11am-6pm Mon-Sat, 1-5pm Sun; 🚋4/9/14/16/24 Dam) Perfectly positioned for the Red Light District, this boutique sells condoms in every imaginable size, colour, flavour and design (horned devils, marijuana leaves, Delftware tiles…), along with lubricants and saucy gifts.

KOKOPELLI SMART SHOP

Map p300 (www.kokopelli.nl; Warmoesstraat 12; ⏲11am-10pm; 🚋4/9/16/24 Centraal Station) Were it not for its trade in 'magic truffles' (similar to the now-outlawed psilocybin mushrooms, aka 'magic mushrooms') you might swear this large, beautiful space was a fashionable clothing or homewares store. There's a coffee and juice bar and a chill-out lounge area overlooking Damrak.

NANA ACCESSORIES

Map p300 (www.happy-shops.com; Warmoesstraat 62; ⏲11am-midnight; 🚋4/9/16/24 Centraal Station) The 'most vibrating shop in town' is actually pretty classy. Choose from a massive assortment of devices that can battery-power your happiness.

MR B ACCESSORIES

Map p300 (www.misterb.com; Warmoesstraat 89; ⏲10.30am-7pm Mon-Wed & Fri, to 9pm Thu, 11am-6pm Sat, 1-6pm Sun; 🚋4/9/16/24 Dam) *Kinky*! The tamer wares at this renowned Red Light District shop include leather and rubber suits, hoods and bondage equipment, all made to measure if you want. Horny toys add a playful (and somewhat scary) element.

ROB ACCESSORIES

Map p300 (www.rob.eu; Warmoesstraat 71; ⏲11am-7pm Mon-Sat, 1-6pm Sun; 🚋4/9/16/24 Centraal Station) RoB sells anything and everything for one's bondage and rough-sex fantasy: army gear, leather and rubber are just the start. Items ranging from the 'Adonis pouch' to the 'black stretchy ring' stock the shelves.

RED LIGHT RECORDS MUSIC

Map p300 (Oudekerksplein 26; ⏲noon-6pm Mon & Sat, to 7pm Tue-Fri; 🚋4/9/16/24 Dam) This shop sits in a former Red Light window. Ring the doorbell to get buzzed in (it's tucked in a courtyard off the street), then you can join the DJs flicking through stacks of spacey Euro-disco, house and funk music. Headphone stations let you listen before you buy. The underground Red Light Radio station operates from a window across the way.

WONDERWOOD HOMEWARES

Map p304 (www.wonderwood.nl; Rusland 3; ⏲noon-6pm Wed-Sat & by appointment) As much a museum as a shop, here you can ogle the sensuous, delicate, moulded-plywood creations of George Nelson, Marcel Breuer and more – some of the vintage furniture pieces are for sale and some are available in reissue (ie old designs remade). If furniture is impractical, smaller art objects (made of wood, naturally) are also available.

MCCARTHY'S DRINK

Map p300 (Zeedijk 27a; ⏲noon-10pm Wed-Mon) McCarthy's is a run-of-the-mill liquor shop, but it has good prices on absinthe in decorative bottles.

Nieuwmarkt, Plantage & the Eastern Islands

NIEUWMARKT | PLANTAGE | EASTERN ISLANDS

Neighbourhood Top Five

❶ Viewing Rembrandt's studio at the **Museum het Rembrandthuis** (p94), where you can see his brushes, sketches and cabinet stuffed with seashells and Roman busts.

❷ Downing a Dommelsch beer in the old lock-keeper's house at **De Sluyswacht** (p105).

❸ Fathoming the history of Dutch seafaring through the extensive maritime collection at the **Het Scheepvaartmuseum** (p98).

❹ Catching live classical music or jazz at the acoustically and visually stunning **Muziekgebouw aan 't IJ** (p108).

❺ Browsing the **Waterlooplein Flea Market** (p109), filled with bric-a-brac from porcelain teapots to Buddha statues.

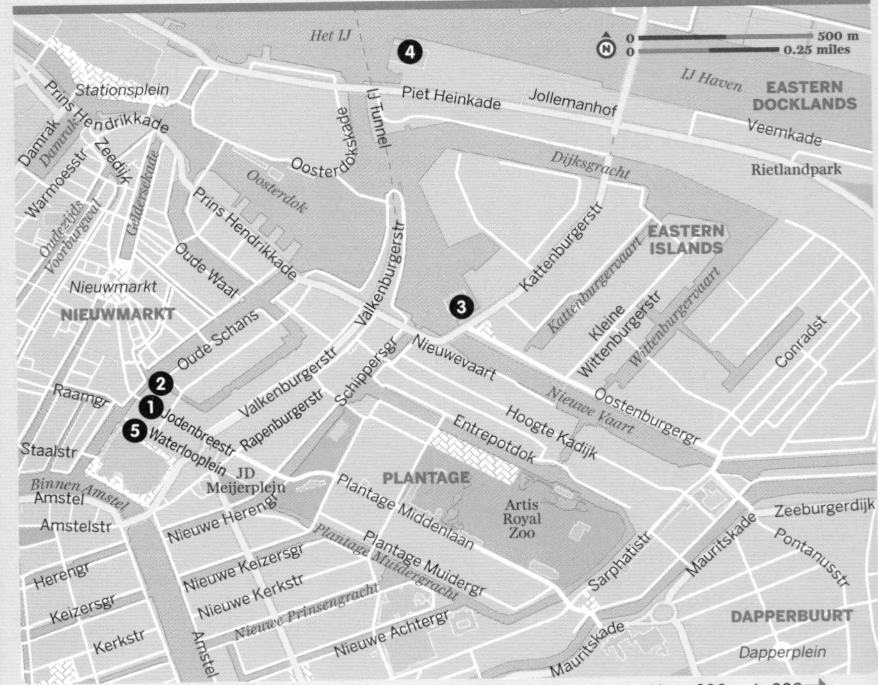

For more detail of this area see Map p306 and p308 ➡

Explore Nieuwmarkt, Plantage & the Eastern Islands

Centred on its namesake square, Nieuwmarkt (New Market) is a district as historic as anything you'll find in Amsterdam. Rembrandt painted canalscapes in Nieuwmarkt, and Jewish merchants generated a fair share of the city's wealth with diamonds and other ventures here.

The neighbourhood's top sight is Museum het Rembrandthuis, the master's impressive home/studio. In the old Jewish quarter is an excellent museum and a synagogue. The famed Gassan Diamond factory is also here, offering free tours.

East of Nieuwmarkt, the leafy district known as Plantage (Plantation) is a lovely place to stroll and admire the 19th-century architecture.

Further east, the former shipyard and warehouse district of the Eastern Islands (Oostelijke Eilanden) and their Eastern Docklands (Oostelijk Havengebied) is a must for cutting-edge Dutch architecture. Explore traditional sights like the Het Scheepvaartmuseum, as well as mod designs such as the sparkling performance halls of the Muziekgebouw aan 't IJ, and swooping views from NEMO's roof.

Local Life

- **Plaza Life** The *cafés* (pubs, bars) ringing Nieuwmarkt square buzz in the afternoon and evening. When the weather cooperates, everyone sits outside in the shadow of the turreted Waag (p95).
- **Shopping Life** Fill your bag with juggling balls, chilli-spiced chocolates or old posters at the neighbourhood favourites along Staalstraat. Then plunge into the Saturday Boerenmarkt (p110) at Nieuwmarkt square.
- **Snack Life** Follow the crowd for a spicy bite of Suriname at Tokoman (p101), famed for its *broodje pom* (chicken-and-tuber-mash sandwich).

Getting There & Away

- **Tram** Trams 9 and 14 go to Waterlooplein and the Jewish sights, as well as Plantage; there are no trams to Nieuwmarkt square, but it's a short walk from Waterlooplein. Tram 10 goes to the Eastern Islands and Eastern Docklands. Tram 26 travels along the IJ waterfront.
- **Metro** There are stops at Waterlooplein and Nieuwmarkt.
- **Bus** Buses 22 and 48 are useful for areas of the Eastern Islands and Eastern Docklands that the tram doesn't reach.

Lonely Planet's Top Tip

Nieuwmarkt has heaps of intriguing architecture, from the imposing Scheepvaarthuis (a classic example of the Amsterdam School style) to the mishmash Stopera. Unique buildings cluster near where Kloveniersburgwal and Oude Hoogstraat intersect, including Amsterdam's narrowest house and the Oostindisch Huis, office of the 17-century, world-dominating Dutch East India Company. Keep an eye out as you wander the neighbourhood.

Best Places to Eat

- Greetje (p105)
- Gebr Hartering (p104)
- Sterk Staaltje (p101)
- Tokoman (p101)
- Moes (p102)

For reviews, see p101.

Best Places to Drink

- De Sluyswacht (p105)
- Amsterdam Roest (p107)
- Brouwerij 't IJ (p107)
- SkyLounge (p106)
- Hannekes Boom (p107)

For reviews, see p105

Best Places to Shop

- Droog (p109)
- Waterlooplein Flea Market (p109)
- Pols Potten (p111)
- Knuffels (p109)
- Frank's Smokehouse (p110)

For reviews, see p109.

TOP SIGHT
MUSEUM HET REMBRANDTHUIS

You almost expect to find the master himself at Museum het Rembrandthuis, set in the three-storey canal house where Rembrandt van Rijn lived and ran the Netherlands' largest painting studio between 1639 and 1658. He bought the abode at the height of his career, when he was awarded the prestigious *Night Watch* commission. The atmospheric, tchotchke-packed interior gives a real feel for how Rembrandt painted his days away. Ask for a free audio guide, available downstairs past the entrance desk.

The house dates from 1606. Rembrandt bought it for a fortune in 1639, made possible by his wealthy wife, Saskia van Uylenburgh. On the ground floor you'll see Rembrandt's living room/bedroom and the anteroom where he entertained clients.

Climb the narrow staircase and you'll come to Rembrandt's light-filled studio, laid out as though he's just nipped down to the kitchen for a bite to eat. Artists give demonstrations here on how Rembrandt sourced and mixed paints. Across the hall is Rembrandt's 'cabinet', a mind-blowing room crammed with the curiosities he collected: seashells, glassware, Roman busts and stuffed alligators.

The top floor is devoted to Rembrandt's famous etchings. The museum has a near-complete collection of them (about 250), although they're not all on display at once. Demonstrators crank up an oak press to show etching techniques several times daily.

The house ultimately caused Rembrandt's financial downfall. He was unable to pay off the mortgage, and in 1656 the household effects, artworks and curiosities were sold to compensate his creditors. It's thanks to the debt collector's itemised list that the museum has been able to reproduce the interior so authentically. Rembrandt lived the rest of his years in cheaper digs in the Jordaan.

DON'T MISS...

- Free audio tour
- The paint-filled studio
- The cabinet stuffed with exotica
- Etching collection
- Etching demonstrations

PRACTICALITIES

- Rembrandt House Museum
- Map p306
- ☎520 04 00
- Jodenbreestraat 4
- adult/child €12.50/4
- ⌚10am-6pm
- 🚊9/14 Waterlooplein

SIGHTS

Nieuwmarkt

SCHEEPVAARTHUIS ARCHITECTURE

Map p306 (Shipping House; Prins Hendrikkade 108; 4/9/16/24 Centraal Station) Now the luxury Grand Hotel Amrath, the grand 1916-built Scheepvaarthuis was the first true example of Amsterdam School architecture. The exterior resembles a ship's bow and is encrusted in elaborate nautical detailing; look for figures of Neptune, his wife and four females that represent the compass points. Step inside to admire stained glass, gorgeous light fixtures and the art-deco-ish central stairwell.

DE APPEL ARTS CENTRE

Map p306 (625 56 51; www.deappel.nl; Prins Hendrikkade 142; adult/child €7/4.50; 11am-6pm Tue-Sun; 4/9/16/24 Centraal Station) See what's on at this spiffy contemporary-arts centre. The curators have a knack for tapping young international talent and supplementing exhibitions with lectures, film screenings and performances. Admission includes a 45-minute tour departing hourly. Moes (p102), the bar-restaurant in the centre's basement, rocks a local crowd of young hipsters.

MONTELBAANSTOREN HISTORIC BUILDING

Map p306 (Montelbaan Tower; Oude Schans 2; 4/9/16/24 Centraal Station) The lower part of this striking tower was built to strengthen Amsterdam's eastern defences in 1512. Positioned on the old city wall, it gave sentries a good view of suspicious characters on the wharves along Oude Schans. The octagonal base and open wooden steeple were added in 1606 to dampen the bells on the clock after the neighbours complained. Just a few years later the tower began to list under the combined weight, but residents attached cables and pulled it upright.

The elegant tower has two sets of bellworks, four clock faces and a nautical vane like the one on top of the Oude Kerk.

WAAG HISTORIC BUILDING

Map p306 (www.indewaag.nl; Nieuwmarkt 4; MNieuwmarkt) The multi-turreted Waag dates from 1488, when it was part of the city's fortifications. From the 17th century onward it was Amsterdam's main weigh house, and later a spot for public executions. A bar-restaurant (open 9am-1am) occupies it today. Out the front, Nieuwmarkt square hosts a variety of events, including a Saturday farmers market and a Sunday antiques market.

In its early days the Waag looked more like a castle, fronted by a moat-like canal and built into the old city walls. By the 17th century it was home to various guilds. The surgeons' guild, which occupied the upper floor, commissioned Rembrandt's famous *The Anatomy Lesson of Dr Tulp* (displayed in the Mauritshuis museum in Den Haag). The masons' guild was based in the tower facing the Zeedijk; note the superfine brickwork.

OOSTINDISCH HUIS ARCHITECTURE

Map p306 (East Indies House; Oude Hoogstraat 24; MNieuwmarkt) This is the former office of the mighty Dutch East India Company (VOC), the globe's first multinational corporation. The sweeping complex, built between 1551 and 1643, was attributed in part to Hendrick de Keyser, the busy city architect. The VOC sailed into rough waters and was dissolved in 1798. You could easily walk straight past, as there's no sign or plaque to identify it (it's now owned by the University of Amsterdam).

TRIPPENHUIS ARCHITECTURE

Map p306 (Kloveniersburgwal 29; MNieuwmarkt) After making their fortune in arms-dealing, the Trip brothers commissioned a young Dutch architect, Justus Vingboons, to build the Trippenhuis in 1660. It's a greystone mansion with eight Corinthian columns across two houses, one for each brother. In a nod to their ignoble profession, the chimneys are shaped like mortars. It's closed to the public, but worth checking out from the street.

ZUIDERKERK CHURCH

Map p306 (http://zuiderkerkamsterdam.nl; Zuiderkerkhof 72; MNieuwmarkt) Famed Dutch Renaissance architect Hendrick de Keyser built the 'Southern Church' in 1611. This was the first custom-built Protestant church in Amsterdam – still Catholic in design but with no choir. The final church service was held here in 1929. During the 'Hunger Winter' of WWII it served as a morgue.

The interior is now used for private events, but you can tour the tower once it reopens after renovations in 2017 for a sky-high city view.

TOP SIGHT
JOODS HISTORISCH MUSEUM

Impressive in scale and scope, the Jewish Historical Museum is housed in a beautifully restored complex of four Ashkenazic synagogues from the 17th and 18th centuries. The enormous Great Synagogue is home to two exhibitions: the 'History of the Jews in the Netherlands, 1600–1890' and 'Religion', about Judaism and Jewish traditions. Exhibits start with the pillars of Jewish identity and gradually give way to an engaging portrait of Jewish life in the city, with profiles of key figures and displays of religious items.

Even more enlightening is the New Synagogue and its 'History of Jews in the Netherlands, 1900–Present Day'. The WWII exhibits cover how 25,000 Dutch Jews went into hiding (18,000 survived) and what life was like after the war as they tried to repatriate.

The complex also has a Children's Museum set up as a Jewish home. Kids can bake challah bread in the kitchen and play tunes in the music room while learning about Jewish traditions.

The free, English-language audio tour that guides you through the collection is excellent, as is the bright cafe serving kosher dishes. Tickets also include admission to the **Portuguese-Israelite Synagogue** (p96).

DON'T MISS

- WWII exhibits
- Children's Museum
- Free audio tour
- Kosher cafe
- Rotating art and photography exhibits

PRACTICALITIES

- Jewish Historical Museum
- Map p306
- ☎531 03 80
- www.jhm.nl
- Nieuwe Amstelstraat 1
- adult/child €15/7.50
- ⏰11am-5pm
- 🚋9/14 Mr Visserplein

PINTOHUIS — ARCHITECTURE

Map p306 (Openbare Bibliotheek; www.huisdepinto.nl; St Antoniesbreestraat 69; ⏰12.30-5.30pm Tue-Fri, noon-4.30pm Sat; Ⓜ Nieuwmarkt) St Antoniesbreestraat was once a busy street, but it lost many of its old buildings during the metro's construction. One of the originals still standing is the Pintohuis, once owned by a wealthy Sephardic Jew, Isaac de Pinto, who had it remodelled with Italianate pilasters in the 1680s. It's now a *bibliotheek* (library) – pop inside to admire the beautiful ceiling frescoes.

MUSEUM HET REMBRANDTHUIS — MUSEUM

See p94.

GASSAN DIAMONDS — FACTORY

Map p306 (www.gassan.com; Nieuwe Uilenburgerstraat 173-175; ⏰9am-5pm; 🚋9/14 Waterlooplein) FREE At this vast workshop, you'll get a quick primer in assessing the gems for quality, and see diamond cutters and polishers in action. The one-hour tour is the best of its kind in town.

The factory sits on Uilenburg, one of the rectangular islands reclaimed in the 1580s during a sudden influx of Sephardic Jews from Spain and Portugal. In the 1880s Gassan became the first diamond factory to use steam power.

PORTUGUESE-ISRAELITE SYNAGOGUE — SYNAGOGUE

Map p306 (www.portugesesynagoge.nl; Mr Visserplein 3; adult/child €15/7.50; ⏰10am-5pm Sun-Thu, to 4pm Fri, closed Sat Mar-Oct, reduced hrs Nov-Feb; 🚋9/14 Mr Visserplein) This was the largest synagogue in Europe when it was completed in 1675, and it's still in use today. The interior features massive pillars and some two dozen brass candelabra. The large library belonging to the Ets Haim seminary is one of the oldest and most important Jewish book collections in Europe. Outside (near the entrance) take the stairs underground to the treasure chambers to see 16th-century manuscripts and gold-threaded tapestries.

Admission tickets also provide entry to the Joods Historisch Museum (p96).

The synagogue's architect, Elias Bouman, was inspired by the Temple of Solomon but the building's classical lines are typical of the Dutch capital. It was restored after WWII.

STOPERA BUILDING

Map p306 (☎625 54 55; www.operaballet.nl; Waterlooplein 22; 🚋9/14 Waterlooplein) This odd, mod building houses both the *stadhuis* (town hall) and the opera hall, aka Muziektheater (p108), hence the name 'Stopera'. It opened in 1986. For a peek behind the scenes, take a guided tour (adult/child €6/5) on Saturdays at 12.15pm. The arcade between the town hall and the theatre has an intriguing display on NAP (p98), Amsterdam's sea level measurements.

Free lunchtime concerts usually take place from 12.30pm to 1pm on Tuesdays from September to May; doors open at 12.15pm.

Plantage

Plantage became a green recreation area during the 17th century. City planners reclaimed the land on the eastern side of the Amstel in a bid to capitalise on the city's flourishing overseas trade. This 'fourth city extension' did not take off, however, and in 1682, the area was converted into garden plots. By the 19th century construction boomed, and it became an entertainment district. Its darkest hour came during WWII when its large Jewish community was detained and deported from here.

HORTUS BOTANICUS GARDENS

Map p308 (Botanical Garden; www.dehortus.nl; Plantage Middenlaan 2a; adult/child €8.50/4.50; ⏲10am-5pm daily, to 7pm Sun Jul & Aug; 🚋9/14 Mr Visserplein) Established in 1638, this venerable garden became a repository for tropical seeds and plants brought in (read: smuggled out of other countries) by Dutch trading ships. From here, coffee, pineapple, cinnamon and palm-oil plants were distributed throughout the world. The 4000-plus species are kept in wonderful structures, including the colonial-era seed house and a three-climate glasshouse.

The butterfly house is a hit with kids in particular. Free one-hour guided tours take place at 2pm on Sunday year-round – pick up a ticket from the entrance and give it to the guide. On Sunday afternoons in July and August from 4pm, you can listen to Latin, jazz, tango, pop music or blues in idyllic tropical surrounds.

WERTHEIMPARK PARK

Map p308 (Plantage Parklaan; ⏲7am-9pm; 🚋9/14 Mr Visserplein) Opposite the Hortus Botanicus, this park is a brilliant, willow-shaded spot for lazing by the Nieuwe Herengracht. Its most significant feature is the **Auschwitz Memorial**, designed by Dutch writer Jan Wolkers: a panel of broken mirrors installed in the ground reflects the sky.

HOLLANDSCHE SCHOUWBURG MEMORIAL

Map p308 (Holland Theatre; ☎531 03 10; www.hollandscheschouwburg.nl; Plantage Middenlaan 24; suggested donation €3; ⏲11am-5pm; 🚋9/14 Plantage Kerklaan) This historic theatre – first known as the Artis Theatre after its inception in 1892 – quickly became a hub of cultural life in Amsterdam, staging major dramas and operettas. In WWII the occupying Germans turned it into a Jewish theatre, then, tragically, a detention centre for Jews held for deportation.

Up to 80,000 Jews passed through here on their way to the death camps. Glass panels are engraved with the names of all Jewish families deported, and upstairs is a modest exhibit hall with photos and artefacts of Jewish life before and during the war.

MUIDERPOORT GATE

Map p308 (Alexanderplein; 🚋9 Alexanderplein) This grand, classical arch was built in 1770 as a gateway to the city. On the south side you'll see the Amsterdam emblem of three St Andreas' crosses, while on the other side there's a cog ship emblem, which appeared on Amsterdam's coat of arms in medieval times.

In 1811 Napoleon rode triumphantly through the gate with his royal entourage, and promptly demanded food for his ragged troops.

LOCAL KNOWLEDGE

DOCKWORKER STATUE

Dockworker Statue (Map p306) Beside the **Portuguese-Israelite Synagogue** (p96), in triangular JD Meijerplein, Mari Andriessen's *Dockworker* statue (1952) commemorates the general strike that began among dockworkers on 25 February 1941 to protest against the treatment of Jews. The first deportation round-up had occurred here a few days earlier.

The anniversary of the strike is still an occasion for wreath-laying, but has become a low-key affair with the demise of the Dutch Communist Party.

NAP: AMSTERDAM'S SEA LEVEL MEASUREMENT

It is widely known that Amsterdam (and indeed more than half of the Netherlands) lies a couple of metres below sea level, but when's the last time you heard anyone ask 'which sea level'? In fact, sea levels vary around the globe and even around the Netherlands. The average level of the former Zuiderzee, in the lee of Friesland, was slightly lower than that of the North Sea along the Netherlands' exposed west coast.

The fascinating display at **NAP Visitors Centre** (Map p306; www.normaalamsterdampeil.nl; Amstel 1; admission €1; ⌚9am-6pm Mon-Fri; 🚊9/14 Waterlooplein) shows the ins and outs of Normaal Amsterdams Peil (NAP; Normal Amsterdam Level). Established in the 17th century as the average high-water mark of the Zuiderzee, it still forms the zero reference for elevation countrywide and is now used throughout the European Union as the European Vertical Reference System (EVRS).

Water columns here represent different sea levels, as well as disastrous flood levels in 1953 (4.55m above NAP).Information sheets and a touch-screen explain the details.

DE GOOYER WINDMILL WINDMILL

Map p308 (Funenkade 5; 🚊10 Hoogte Kadijk) This 18th-century grain mill is the sole survivor of five windmills that once stood in this part of town. It was moved to its current spot in 1814. The mill was fully renovated in 1925 and is now a private home. The public baths alongside the windmill were converted into Brouwerij 't IJ (p107) in 1985.

WERFMUSEUM 'T KROMHOUT MUSEUM

Map p308 (☎627 67 77; www.machinekamer.nl; Hoogte Kadijk 147; adult/child €5/free; ⌚10am-3pm Tue; 🚊10 Hoogte Kadijk) Boats are still repaired at the 18th-century wharf on the outer side of the dyke. The eastern hall is a museum devoted to shipbuilding and to the indestructible marine engines that were designed and built here. Anyone with an interest in marine engineering will love the place; others will probably want to move on. Signage is primarily in Dutch only.

ARCHITECTURAL EXPLORATIONS

For a deeper insight into this multifaceted area, architectural historian Alex Hendriksen runs a series of highly recommended walking, cycling and boat tours of Nieuwmarkt and the IJ with **Architectuur Tours** (Map p306; ☎06 3014 0945; www.architectuurtoursamsterdam.nl; Dijkstraat 55; tours €12.50-25; Ⓜ Nieuwmarkt) that peel away the layers of development to help you understand how a place has arrived at its current appearance. Schedules for English-language tours and departure points are posted online.

ENTREPOTDOK ARCHITECTURE

Map p308 (🚊9/14 Plantage Kerklaan) The area northeast of the Plantage was the stomping ground of the Dutch East India Company (VOC), which grew rich on sea trade in the 17th century. The VOC owned this 500m row of warehouses – the largest storage depot in Europe at the time – located in a customs-free zone.

Some of the original facades have been preserved, and the facility has been converted into desirable offices, apartments and appealing dockside cafes, with tables perfect for lazing away an afternoon at the water's edge.

KADIJKSPLEIN SQUARE

Map p308 (Kadijksplein; 🚊22/48 Kadijksplein) Flanked by *café* (pub-bar) terraces, this tranquil square has twin views of 17th-century canals and cruise ships docking at the Docklands.

Eastern Islands

Visitors often overlook the Eastern Islands, thinking that the area is too far out of the centre, when it's actually less than a 10-minute bike or tram ride. If you're remotely into boats, maritime history or modern architecture, you'll want to spend some time here.

HET SCHEEPVAARTMUSEUM MUSEUM

Map p308 (Maritime Museum; ☎523 22 22; www.scheepvaartmuseum.nl; Kattenburgerplein 1; adult/child €15/7.50; ⌚9am-5pm; 🚌22/48

TOP SIGHT
VERZETSMUSEUM

The Verzetsmuseum (Dutch Resistance Museum) shows, in no uncertain terms, how much courage it takes to actively resist an adversary so ruthless that you can't trust neighbours, friends or even family.

Start by ascending the spiral staircase to the mezzanine to watch the introductory film (available in multiple languages), then head anticlockwise around the main floor. Beginning with the build-up to WWII in the 1930s, the chronologically arranged exhibits give a powerful insight into the difficulties faced by those who fought the propaganda-steeped German occupation from within – as well as the minority who went along with the Nazis. Topics include the concepts of active and passive resistance, how the illegal resistance press operated, how 300,000 people were kept in hiding and how all this could be funded. Beneath the mezzanine an exhibit covers the Dutch role in the war in the Pacific, particularly in relation to Indonesian independence from the Netherlands. Labels are in Dutch and English.

Included in admission, the new **Verzetsmuseum Junior** relates the stories of four Dutch children, putting the resistance into context for kids. Next door, the museum's cafe is a perfect sanctum for a post-museum discussion of Resistance politics over coffee.

DON'T MISS

- The introductory film
- The Resistance press exhibits
- The Pacific exhibit

PRACTICALITIES

- Dutch Resistance Museum
- Map p308
- ☎620 25 35
- www.verzetsmuseum.org
- Plantage Kerklaan 61
- adult/child €10/5
- ⏲10am-5pm Tue-Fri, from 11am Sat-Mon
- 🚋9/14 Plantage Kerklaan

TOP SIGHT
ARTIS ROYAL ZOO

Set amid ponds, statues, and leafy, winding pathways, the Artis Royal Zoo is mainland Europe's oldest zoo, with room to observe and reflect on the wildness and grandness of the animal kingdom.

In addition to the expected zoo attractions – big cats, apes and elephants – a highlight is the African savannah. Another must-see is the aquarium, a graceful purpose-built hall with a rainforest, a tropical coral reef and a cross-section of an Amsterdam canal. All-up there are 900 different animal species and 200 species of trees.

Its newest attraction is the **Micropia** (Map p308; www.micropia.nl; Artisplein, Plantage Kerklaan 38-40; adult/child €14/12, incl Artis Royal Zoo €27/23; ⏲9am-6pm Sun-Wed, to 8pm Thu-Sat; 🚋9/14 Artis) museum, the world's first microbe museum, where you can learn how many of these invisible-to-the-eye lifeforms – the planet's smallest – inhabit the human body and what can be learnt from them (how plant matter can be broken down into different substances such as food and fuel, for instance).

Locals as well as tourists visit to stroll the paths laid out through the former Plantage gardens. The grounds are packed with heritage-listed 19th-century buildings and monuments. There are several cafes onsite.

DON'T MISS

- Micropia museum
- The aquarium
- The lion habitat
- The African savannah

PRACTICALITIES

- Map p308
- ☎523 34 00
- www.artis.nl
- Plantage Kerklaan 38-40
- adult/child €19.95/16.50, incl Micropia €27/23
- ⏲9am-6pm Mar-Oct, to 5pm Nov-Feb

Kattenburgerplein) An immense, 17th-century admiralty building houses one of the world's most extensive collections of maritime memorabilia. Early shipping routes, naval combat, fishing and whaling are all detailed, and there are some 500 models of boats and ships. A full-scale replica of the Dutch East India Company's 700-tonne *Amsterdam*, one of the largest ships of the fleet, is moored outside.

ARCAM ARCHITECTURE

Map p308 (Stichting Architectuurcentrum Amsterdam; ☎620 48 78; www.arcam.nl; Prins Hendrikkade 600; ⊙1-5pm Tue-Sat; 22/48 Kadijksplein) FREE This showpiece building of the Amsterdam Architecture Foundation is a one-stop shop for all your architectural needs. Expert staff are on hand to interpret the fascinating changing exhibits, and you can find books, guide maps and suggestions for tours on foot, by bike and by public transport.

NEMO MUSEUM

Map p308 (☎531 32 33; www.e-nemo.nl; Oosterdok 2; admission €15, roof terrace free; ⊙10am-5.30pm, closed Mon Sep-Mar; 22/48 IJ-Tunnel) Perched atop the entrance to the IJ Tunnel is the science and technology museum, NEMO. The dramatic, green-copper building rises from the waterfront like a ship setting sail. Its hands-on exhibits (with English explanations) are winners with kids and adults: drawing with a laser, 'anti-gravity' trick mirrors and a 'lab' for answering such questions as 'How black is black?' and 'How do you make cheese?'.

NEMO's stepped, decklike roof is the city's largest summer terrace with panoramic views.

Italian architect Renzo Piano conceived the design as the inverse of the IJ tunnel below. Inside, Piano's design reflects a 'noble factory', with exposed wiring and pipes.

ON YOUR BIKE IN NIEUWMARKT, PLANTAGE & THE EASTERN ISLANDS

The central Waterlooplein outlet of **MacBike** (Map p306; ☎428 70 05; www.macbike.nl; Waterlooplein 199; bike rental per 3/24hr from €7.50/9.75; ⊙9am-5.45pm; M Waterlooplein) is a handy spot to pick up a set of wheels to explore.

MUZIEKGEBOUW AAN 'T IJ ARCHITECTURE

Map p308 (www.muziekgebouw.nl; Piet Heinkade 1; 26 Muziekgebouw) Even if you don't catch a performance (p108) here, the magnificent 'Music Building on the IJ' is a visual treat. The complex – with the main hall for varying shows and the smaller Bimhuis (p108) for jazz – was designed by the Danish firm 3xNielsen. Some 20 years in the making, it opened in 2005.

On the upper floor you'll find the computerised 'sound garden', a perfect diversion for children. You can visit the concert hall during box-office opening hours (noon to 6pm Monday to Saturday), or during performances.

With huge windows overlooking the IJ, the venue's excellent Zouthaven (p104) restaurant specialises in seafood.

CENTRALE BIBLIOTHEEK AMSTERDAM LIBRARY

Map p306 (Amsterdam Central Library; ☎523 09 00; www.oba.nl; Oosterdokskade 143; ⊙10am-10pm; 4/9/16/24/26 Centraal) FREE This symmetrical, nine-storey 'tower of knowledge' (its self-appointed nickname) is the country's largest library. Unveiled in 2007, it has claimed a commanding spot in Amsterdam's increasingly modern landscape. Inviting chairs and couches are scattered around every floor, as are loads of free internet terminals (there's also free wi-fi). Panoramic city views unfold from the top-floor cafe.

PERSMUSEUM MUSEUM

(☎692 88 10; www.persmuseum.nl; Zeeburgerkade 10; adult/child €4.50/3.25; ⊙10am-5pm Tue-Fri, from noon Sun; 22 Veelaan) Preserving Dutch journalism history, the press museum is much more interesting to non-Dutch speakers than it may sound. It's housed in sleek premises and has a large collection of historic newspapers (going all the way back to 1600), political and editorial cartoons and press photos, and a great stock of amusing old publicity posters.

WHALE ARCHITECTURE

Map p308 (Ertskade; 10 JF Van Hengelstraat) Built between 1998 and 2000 by Dutch architect Frits van Dongen, this energy-efficient, zinc-clad apartment block has two raised corners to allow more natural light inside, resulting in its unique whale-like shape (best appreciated from Levantkade on KNSM Eiland).

WORTH A DETOUR

IJBURG

From the Eastern Islands, it's less than 10 minutes by tram 26 to Amsterdam's newest neighbourhood, IJburg. Construction by the city of Amsterdam first started on these three artificial islands – Steigereiland, Haveneiland and Rieteilanden – in the IJmeer lake in 1996 to ease Amsterdam's housing shortage. The first IJburg residents arrived in 2002 and building still continues to reach its ultimate goal of 18,000 residences and 45,000 citizens, but it's already coming into its own as a visitor destination.

Checking out striking modern architecture aside, IJburg is a hotspot for windsurfing. At the eastern end of IJburg's beach, Blijburg Aan Zee, **Surfcenter IJburg** (www.surfcenterijburg.nl; Berthaanstrakade; windsurfer/wetsuit rental per hr €17/5; 3-9pm Wed & Fri, 11am-6.30pm Sat & Sun Apr-Oct; 26 IJburg) rents windsurfers from its shipping container.

The neighbourhood is also home to some superb restaurants and bars. Organic produce is prioritised by the passionate Italian chefs at **Restaurant Bloem** (416 06 77; www.bloemopijburg.nl; IJburglaan 1289; mains €16-24; 5.30-10pm; 26 IJburg), with a breezy beach-style decor that belies its exceptional food. The menu changes daily but might include house-made linguine with clams, chilli and parsley or fresh tuna grilled with white asparagus and served with green-bean salsa, as well as authentic wood-fired pizzas. Cash only.

Fittingly named for the Normaal Amsterdams Peil, or **Normal Amsterdam Level** (p98), sea-level benchmark, harbourside restaurant **NAP** (www.napamsterdam.nl; Krijn Taconiskade 124; mains €15.50-31.50, tapas €6.50-10; 11am-10pm; ; 26 IJburg) has a terrace overlooking IJburg's boat-filled marina and a chic semi-industrial interior. Tapas spans crostini with carpaccio to spicy head-on prawns and oysters with vinaigrette, while mains include chanterelle risotto and seared sea bass with tomato salsa.

Timber benches with funky red cushions line the pavement of **Dok 48** (www.dok48.nl; Krijn Taconiskade 328-330; 11am-midnight Tue-Sun; ; 26 IJburg), which also has a table- and chair-filled summer terrace right on the marina that's idyllic for watching the boats docking and setting sail. There's a good range of specialist beers, as well as wines and bubbles by the glass and top-notch food, too. DJs regularly spin at weekends.

IJburg also makes a great jumping-off point for visiting **Muiden** (p102) and its medieval castle, the Muiderslot, and fortress island, Pampus.

EATING

Nieuwmarkt

★STERK STAALTJE DELI €

Map p306 (http://sterkstaaltje.com; Staalstraat 12; dishes €4-7.60; 8am-7pm Mon-Fri, 8am-6pm Sat, 11am-5pm Sun; 4/9/14/16/24 Muntplein) From the fruit stacked up in crates on the pavement, Sterk Staaltje looks like an unassuming greengrocer's, but inside it's a veritable treasure chest of ready-to-eat treats: teriyaki meatballs, feta and sundried tomato quiche, pumpkin-stuffed wraps, a soup of the day, and fantastic sandwiches (roast beef, horseradish and rocket; marinated chicken with guacamole and sour cream) plus salads and pastas.

★TOKOMAN SURINAMESE €

Map p306 (Waterlooplein 327; sandwiches €3-4.50, dishes €6.50-12.50; 11am-8pm Mon-Sat; 9/14 Waterlooplein) Queue with the folks getting their Surinamese spice on at Tokoman. It makes a sensational *broodje pom* (a sandwich filled with a tasty mash of chicken and a starchy Surinamese tuber). You'll want the *zuur* (pickled-cabbage relish) and *peper* (chilli) on it, plus a cold can of coconut water to wash it down.

A second, newer **branch** (Map p306; Zeedijk 136; sandwiches €3-4.50, dishes €6.50-12.50; 11am-9.30pm Mon-Sat; 9/14 Waterlooplein)

WORTH A DETOUR

MUIDEN

Muiden is an unhurried historical town renowned for its red-brick castle, the Muiderslot. Life otherwise focuses on the busy central lock that funnels scores of pleasure boats out into the vast IJsselmeer.

Built in 1280 by Count Floris V, son of Willem II, exceptionally preserved moated fortress **Muiderslot** (Muiden Castle; www.muiderslot.nl; Herengracht 1; adult/child €13.50/9; ⌚10am-5pm Mon-Fri, from noon Sat & Sun Apr-Oct, noon-5pm Sat & Sun Nov-Mar) is equipped with round towers, a French innovation. The count was a champion of the poor and a French sympathiser, two factors that were bound to spell trouble; Floris was imprisoned in 1296 and murdered while trying to flee. Today it's the Netherlands' most visited castle. The interior can be seen only on 30-minute guided tours. The **I Amsterdam Card** (p273) is valid here.

Off the coast lies a derelict fort on the island of **Pampus** (www.pampus.nl; adult/child ferry & tour €20/11; ⌚9am-5pm Tue-Sun Apr-Oct). This massive 19th-century bunker was a key member of a ring of 42 fortresses built to defend Amsterdam and is great fun to explore. Rescued from disrepair by Unesco, it's now a World Heritage Site. Ferries to Pampus depart from Muiderslot port on a varying schedule in season. Usually there's at least one morning departure which allows a couple of hours to prowl the fort before a mid-afternoon return.

In warm weather the clientele of little bar **Café Ome Ko** (www.cafeomekomuiden.nl; cnr Herengracht & Naardenstraat; ⌚8am-2am Sun-Thu, to 3am Fri & Sat) with big green-striped awnings turns the street outside into one big party. When there's no party on, it's a perfect spot to watch the comings and goings through the busy lock right outside. It serves lunchtime sandwiches and classic Dutch bar snacks (croquettes et al).

Muiden is easily reached from **IJburg** (p101), either via a signposted 7km cycle route (you can also walk it in around 1½ hours), or by boat. **Veerdienst** (www.veerdienstamsterdam.nl; Krijn Taconiskade 124; adult/child ferry & tour of either Pampas or Muiderslot €20/15; ⌚11am Tue-Fri, 11am & 1.30pm Sat & Sun Apr-Oct) ferries departing from IJburg include a tour of either Pampus or Muiderslot. Bicycles travel for free.

Alternatively, buses 320, 322 and 327 link Amsterdam's Amstel station (20 minutes, twice hourly) with Muiden. The castle is then a 1km walk.

in the neighbourhood has proved equally popular.

TOKO JOYCE — INDONESIAN €

Map p306 (www.tokojoyce.nl; Nieuwmarkt 38; dishes €6.50-10.50; ⌚4-8pm Mon, from 11am Tue-Sat, from 1pm Sun; Ⓜ Nieuwmarkt) Pick and mix a platter of Indonesian-Surinamese food from the glass case. The 'lunch box' (you choose noodles or rice, plus two spicy, coconutty toppings) is good value. To finish, get a wedge of *spekkoek* (moist, layered gingerbread). Take your meal upstairs to the handful of tables, or head outside where canal-side benches beckon a few steps from the door.

TISFRIS — CAFE €

Map p306 (www.tisfris.nl; St Antoniebreestraat 142; dishes €5-14; ⌚9am-7pm; 🚋9/14 Waterlooplein) Tables splash out of mosaic-trimmed TisFris and over the canal, almost to Rembrandt huis' door. Pull up a chair and ask about the sandwich of the day, or go for one of the staples like smoked mackerel with horseradish and beetroot salsa, or Dutch meatballs with mustard mayo on a choice of wholemeal, white and wholegrain bread.

★MOES — MODERN DUTCH €€

Map p306 (☎623 54 77; www.totmoes.nl; Prins Hendrikkade 142; mains €11.50-19.50; ⌚5-11pm Tue-Fri, 11am-11pm Sat, 11am-6pm Sun; 🖉; 🚋4/9/16/24 Centraal Station) 🌿 The bar-restaurant in the basement of De Appel arts centre (p95) has a farm-to-fork credo. There's always a fish of the day and a daily vegetarian special made with local ingredients. Mains vary, but might include kohlrabi ravioli with peas and mint, or slow-cooked pork neck with borlotti beans. A fine selection of organic wines and ciders adds to the scrumptiousness.

Every first Monday of the month is 'meatless Monday' when the whole menu goes vegetarian. Ask about hands-on lunches and dinners at farms around Amsterdam, which Moes sometimes arranges, where you help prepare meals yourself.

HEMELSE MODDER MODERN DUTCH €€

Map p306 (624 32 03; www.hemelsemodder.nl; Oude Waal 11; mains €20, 3-course menu €35; 6-11pm; Nieuwmarkt) Celery-green walls and blond-wood tables are the backdrop for equally light and unpretentious food, which emphasises North Sea fish and farm-fresh produce in dishes like roast guinea fowl with porcini and morel sauce, followed by desserts like luscious berry pudding and namesake *hemelse modder* (heavenly mud) dark- and white-chocolate mousse. The back terrace makes for lovely al fresco dining.

FRENZI MEDITERRANEAN €€

Map p306 (423 51 12; www.frenzi-restaurant.nl; Zwanenburgwal 232; mains lunch €7-14, dinner €14.50-18.50, tapas €4.50-6; 11am-10pm; 4/9/14/16/24 Muntplein) Stunning tapas at this casual spot will sate your hunger – Manchego cheese and fig compote; marinated sardines; portobello mushrooms with melted gorgonzola – but save room for mains like pan-fried cod with fennel mash, pumpkin gnocchi with wilted spinach, and leg of lamb with roast asparagus. It stocks 110 types of grappa; live jazz plays on Saturdays at 3pm.

LATEI CAFE €€

Map p306 (www.latei.net; Zeedijk 143; lunch dishes €3.75-6.50, dinner mains €6-16; 8am-6pm Mon-Wed, to 10pm Thu & Fri, 9am-10pm Sat, 11am-6pm Sun; ; Nieuwmarkt) Young locals throng groovy Latei, where you can buy the lamps (or any of the vintage decor) right off the wall. The split-level cafe does unusual dinners Thursday through Saturday, often an Ethiopian, Indian or Indonesian dish by the local 'cooking collective'. Otherwise it serves sandwiches, apple pie and *koffie verkeerd* (milky coffee). A cat named Elvis roams the premises.

CAFÉ BERN SWISS €€

Map p306 (622 00 34; www.cafebern.com; Nieuwmarkt 9; mains €12-18; kitchen 6-11pm Sep-Jun; Nieuwmarkt) Indulge in a fondue frenzy at this delightfully well-worn cafe overlooking the Waag. People have been flocking here for more than 30 years for the gruyère fondue and the *entrecôte* (steak). Note: it's closed for a large part of the summer, when steamy weather lessens the hot-cheese demand. Reservations advised.

NYONYA ASIAN €€

Map p306 (www.nyonya-malaysia-restaurant.com; Kloveniersburgwal 38; mains €9.50-19; 1-9pm; Nieuwmarkt) Humble little Nyonya makes a mean bowl of *laksa* (spicy noodle soup), a complex *rendang* curry (spicy and coconutty) with beef, chicken or prawns, and several other Malaysian specialities including *nasi goreng* (fried rice). There's no alcohol, but you can sip milky tea or Sarsae (a Chinese root beer).

POCO LOCO CAFE €€

Map p306 (Nieuwmarkt 24; mains lunch €4.50-12, dinner €12-17; kitchen 9am-10.30pm; ; Nieuwmarkt) Poco Loco stacks up beyond-the-norm sandwiches for lunch like marinated chicken with jalapeños, sour cream and guacamole or ground-beef meatballs with satay sauce, and concocts tapas with a Dutch twist for dinner such as prawn skewers. The retro interior is cool if terrace seating overlooking Nieuwmarkt is unavailable.

NAM KEE CHINESE €€

Map p306 (638 28 48; www.namkee.net; Geldersekade 117; mains €12-22; 4pm-midnight Mon-Fri, 2.30pm-midnight Sat, 2.30-11pm Sun; ; Nieuwmarkt) This is the more stylish branch of Amsterdam's Chinese icon; the best-known Nam Kee (p81) is in the Medieval Centre.

LASTAGE FRENCH €€€

Map p306 (737 08 11; www.restaurantlastage.nl; Geldersekade 29; 3-/4-/5-/6-course menus from €43/53/63/73; 6.30-10pm Tue-Sun; 4/9/16/24 Centraal Station) Small, cosy Lastage is a rose among thorns at the Red Light District's seedy edge. The changing menu might start with, say, aspic of lobster and smoked herring, followed by sweetbread and quail terrine, cod with smoked eel and potato gnocchi, and dark-chocolate and blueberry lava cake. It's all beautifully presented, and the elegant wine list matches to a tee.

Plantage

IJSMOLEN ICE CREAM €

Map p308 (Zeeburgerstraat 2; 1/2/4 scoops €1.50/2.75/4.75; noon-9pm; 10 Hoogte Kadijk) Homemade ice cream at this spot near the De Gooyer windmill comes in

Dutch flavours like *stroopwafel* (classic caramel syrup–filled wafers) and *speculaas* (spicy Christmas biscuits) as well as mango and mint; *stracciatella* (vanilla with shredded chocolate); watermelon; and lemon cheesecake. On hot days it stays open to 10pm.

CAFÉ KADIJK INDONESIAN €€

Map p308 (06 1774 4441; www.cafekadijk.nl; Kadijksplein 5; mains €14.50-19.50; 5-10pm; 22/48 Kadijksplein) This sunny, split-level *café* looks like it can serve no more than coffee from its tiny kitchen, but in fact it does very decent Indonesian food, including a mini version of the normally gigantic rijsttafel (Indonesian banquet). No credit cards.

CAFÉ SMITH EN VOOGT CAFE €€

Map p308 (www.cafesmitenvoogt.nl; Plantage Parklaan 10; mains lunch €4-7.50, dinner €10-18.50; kitchen 10am-9.30pm; ; 9/14 Plantage Kerklaan) Equal parts refined and relaxed, this high-ceilinged, high-spirited cafe is an ideal spot to stop for lunch or a coffee when visiting the adjacent Wertheimpark (p97). Lovely salads and sandwiches are complemented by a handful of dinner choices like baked aubergine with goat's cheese, and duck breast with black-bean sauce.

KOFFIEHUIS VAN DEN VOLKSBOND INTERNATIONAL €€

Map p308 (www.koffiehuisvandenvolksbond.nl; Kadijksplein 4; mains €16-20; 6-10pm; ; 22/48 Kadijksplein) This laid-back place began life as a charitable coffeehouse for dockworkers and it still has a fashionably grungy vibe – wood floors, tarnished chandeliers, a giant red-rose mural and antique bath tub. Creative comfort food spans dishes like gorgonzola and broccoli quiche, roast guinea fowl with lemon sauce, and cold mango soup with coconut ice cream for dessert. No credit cards.

Eastern Islands

★GEBR HARTERING MODERN DUTCH €€

Map p306 (421 06 99; www.gebr-hartering.nl; Peperstraat 10; 4-/7-course menu €40/65 Tue, Wed & Sun, 6-/9-course menu €50/75 Thu-Sat; 6-10.30pm Tue-Sun; 32/33 Prins Hendrikkade) At this jewel of a restaurant founded by two brothers, the menu changes daily so you never know what you'll be tasting, but dishes are unfailingly delicious and exquisitely presented. The wine list is succinct and the timber dining room and canal-side location impossibly romantic.

DE PLANTAGE MODERN EUROPEAN €€

Map p308 (760 68 00; http://caferestaurantdeplantage.nl; Plantage Kerklaan 36; mains lunch €7.50-21.50, dinner €17.50-21.50; 9am-10pm; 9/14 Plantage Kerklaan) A beautiful 1870-built, 1900-expanded former greenhouse with wrought-iron struts and glass-paned windows houses this restaurant by the Artis Royal Zoo's gates. Creative dishes include sea wolf with roasted carrots, lavender and Beluga lentils; lamb's tongue stew with turnip and artichokes; and almond cake with raspberry compote and almond ice cream. Tables scatter beneath trees strung with fairy lights in summer.

ZOUTHAVEN SEAFOOD €€

Map p308 (788 20 90; www.zouthaven.nl; Piet Heinkade 1, Muziekgebouw aan 't IJ; mains lunch €7.50-14.50, dinner €20-26.50; 11.30am-10pm; 26 Muziekgebouw) The Muziekgebouw aan 't IJ's flash dining space is hard to beat for location and views. Several storeys of glass and a sweeping terrace give you an IJ's-eye perspective, and the food, such as a haddock and Zeeland mussels terrine or herb-crusted salmon, is superb. The seafood is sustainably caught or raised.

ÉÉNVISTWÉÉVIS SEAFOOD €€

Map p308 (623 28 94; www.eenvistweevis.nl; Schippersgracht 6; mains €17.50-24.50; 6-10pm Tue-Sat; 22/48 Kadijksplein) This unassuming local favourite, with a shell-and-chandelier interior, has a short, handwritten menu utilising whatever's fresh from the sea, such as gazpacho with fried prawns, sole in butter, or turbot with samphire and hollandaise sauce, as well as great oysters.

GARE DE L'EST INTERNATIONAL €€

Map p308 (463 06 20; www.garedelest.nl; Cruquiusweg 9; 4-course menu €33; 6-10pm; 22 Het Funen) You won't know what to expect from the four courses on the surprise menu until they arrive, but dietary requirements (including vegetarianism) can be accommodated. Portuguese tiles and glowing Middle Eastern lamps adorn the interior of the charming 1901 building, but in warm weather the best seats are in the courtyard.

DE WERELDBOL INTERNATIONAL €€

Map p308 (☎362 87 25; www.dewereldbol.nl; Piraeusplein 59; mains lunch €7.50-16, dinner €17.50-20.50, 3-course menu €35; ⊙noon-9pm Tue-Sun; 🚊10 Azartplein) A passionate and personable owner-chef, an ever-changing menu and an idyllic view of boats bobbing on the water make this small, dark-wood restaurant a fine place to stop for lunchtime soups, salads and sandwiches, or end a day of sightseeing in the area dining on dishes like sea bass with squid-ink spaghetti and banana bread with homemade banana ice cream.

SEA PALACE CHINESE €€

Map p306 (☎626 47 77; www.seapalace.nl; Oosterdokskade 8; mains €17-38, dim sum €4-8.50; ⊙noon-11pm; 🚊4/9/16/24/26 Centraal) It's a funny thing about floating Chinese restaurants: they look like tourist traps but so often serve superb food. The Sea Palace's three floors are busy with locals and visitors who aren't only here for the great views of the city from across the IJ. Try the incredible array of dim sum or the fiery hot pot. Reservations recommended.

KOMPASZAAL CAFE €€

Map p308 (☎419 95 96; www.kompaszaal.nl; KNSM-laan 311; mains lunch €6-13.50, dinner €15-21, high tea €17.50; ⊙kitchen 10am-5pm Wed, 10am-10pm Thu & Fri, 11am-10pm Sat & Sun; 📶; 🚊10 Azartplein) Set in the century-old Royal Dutch Steamboat Company (KNSM in Dutch) arrivals hall, this airy cafe has a breezy menu of dishes like lemon sole with artichokes and lavender butter, and roast *poussin* (young chicken) with aioli and Turkish *pilav* (buttery rice cooked in seasoned broth). Equally captivating are the groovy green tiles and the water view from the balcony.

Regular 1950s swing, jazz, tango and salsa events take place on Friday nights.

INSTOCK INTERNATIONAL €€

Map p308 (www.instock.nl; Czaar Peterstraat 21; dishes €4-10, 3-course dinner menu €26; ⊙9am-10pm Sun-Wed, to 11pm Thu-Sat; 🔌; 🚊10 Eerste Coehoornstraat) 🌿 Instock's raison d'être is reducing food waste. Its electric 'food rescue car' visits shops such as grocery chain Albert Heijn, Hilton Meats, fishmonger Jan van As, and Heineken to collect products that are still in date but would otherwise be thrown out and transform them into delicious three-course meals (including a daily vegetarian option). Ingredients depending, prices can vary slightly.

★GREETJE CONTEMPORARY DUTCH €€€

Map p308 (☎779 74 50; www.restaurantgreetje.nl; Peperstraat 23-25; mains €23-27; ⊙6-10pm Sun-Fri, to 11pm Sat; 🚌22/34/35/48 Prins Hendrikkade) 🌿 Using market-fresh organic produce, Greetje resurrects and re-creates traditional Dutch recipes like pickled beef, braised veal with apricots and leek *stamppot* (traditional mashed potatoes and vegetables), and pork belly with Dutch mustard sauce. A good place to start is the two-person Big Beginning (per person €15), with a sampling of hot and cold starters.

If you can't decide on dessert (which, with dishes like lemon buttermilk pudding with blackberry sauce, or crème brûlée with sweet wood extract and liquorice ice cream, is understandable), go for the Grand Finale (for two people; per person €14) to share all six.

DRINKING & NIGHTLIFE

Don't miss a tour or at least a beer at the Brouwerij 't IJ (p107) microbrewery adjacent to the De Gooyer Windmill.

Nieuwmarkt

★DE SLUYSWACHT BROWN CAFE

Map p306 (www.sluyswacht.nl; Jodenbreestraat 1; ⊙12.30pm-1am Mon-Thu, to 3am Fri & Sat, to 7pm Sun; 🚊9/14 Waterlooplein) Built in 1695 and listing like a ship in a high wind, this tiny black building was once a lock-keeper's house on the Oude Schans. Today the canal-side terrace with gorgeous views of the Montelbaanstoren is one of the most idyllic spots in town to relax with a Dutch beer (Dommelsch is the house speciality).

CAFÉ DE DOELEN BROWN CAFE

Map p306 (Kloveniersburgwal 125; ⊙9am-1am Mon-Thu, 9am-3am Fri & Sat, 10am-1am Sun; 🚊4/9/14/16/24 Muntplein) Set on a busy canal-side crossroad between the Amstel and the Red Light District, De Doelen dates back to 1895 and looks it: there's a carved wooden goat's head, stained-glass lamps and sand on the floor. In fine weather the tables spill across the street for picture-perfect canal views.

CAFE DE ENGELBEWAARDER BROWN CAFE

Map p306 (www.cafe-de-engelbewaarder.nl; Kloveniersburgwal 59; ⏱10am-1am Mon-Fri, 10am-3am Fri & Sat, noon-1am Sun; Ⓜ Nieuwmarkt) Jazz fans will want to settle in at this little *café* on Sunday afternoon from 4.30pm September to June for an open session that has earned quite a following. The rest of the time, it's a tranquil place to sip a beer (there are 15 on tap) by the sunny windows.

CAFE CUBA COCKTAIL BAR

Map p306 (www.cafecuba.nl; Nieuwmarkt 3; ⏱1pm-1am Mon-Thu, 11am-3am Fri & Sat, 11am-1am Sun; Ⓜ Nieuwmarkt) If a brown *café* was beamed to the Caribbean, it would probably have Cafe Cuba's air of faded elegance. It's an atmospheric spot to slouch behind a table with names etched into it and quaff cocktails like mai tais, planter's punch and the legendary mojito. The walls are decorated with photos of Hemingway and old rum advertising posters.

DE BEKEERDE SUSTER BREWERY

Map p306 (www.debekeerdesuster.nl; Kloveniersburgwal 6-8; ⏱noon-1am Mon-Thu, to 2am Fri & Sat, to midnight Sun; Ⓜ Nieuwmarkt) It's got the brew tanks, it's got the beautiful hardwood interior, it's even got the history – a 16th-century brewery-cloister run by nuns. Stop in for pub grub to go with the house suds, or hoist a glass to start an evening on Nieuwmarkt. A tasting tray of four beers costs €9.

BLUEBIRD COFFEESHOP

Map p306 (Sint Antoniesbreestraat 71; ⏱9.30am-1am; Ⓜ Nieuwmarkt) Away from Nieuwmarkt's main cluster of coffeeshops, Bluebird has a less touristy, more local vibe. The multiroom space has beautiful murals and local artists' paintings, lounge with leather chairs, non-alcoholic bar and kitchen serving superior snacks such as freshly made pancakes. It's especially well known for its hashish, including varieties not available elsewhere in Amsterdam.

GOA COFFEESHOP

Map p306 (Kloveniersburgwal 42; ⏱10am-1am; 📶; Ⓜ Nieuwmarkt) Chilled-out Goa's facade opens completely to the street so not only do you get good ventilation, you also get to watch the passing parade along the Kloveniersburgwal, accompanied by a quality hip-hop soundtrack.

LOKAAL 'T LOOSJE BROWN CAFE

Map p306 (www.loosje.nl; Nieuwmarkt 32-34; ⏱8.30am-1am Sun-Thu, to 3am Fri & Sat; Ⓜ Nieuwmarkt) With its beautiful, etched-glass windows and tile tableaux on the walls, this is one of the oldest and prettiest *cafés* in the Nieuwmarkt area. It attracts a vibrant mix of students, locals and visitors. Wicker chairs spill onto the herringbone pavement terrace out front in fine weather.

AMSTELHOECK GRAND CAFE

Map p306 (www.amstelhoeck.nl; Amstel 1; ⏱9am-1am Mon-Thu, 9am-3am Fri, 10am-3am Sat, 10am-1am Sun; 🚋9/14 Waterlooplein) Located in the Stopera building, Amstelhoeck doesn't have the history of some of the other *cafés* in town, but that doesn't make it any less appealing. The great Amstel-side terrace is always busy in summer.

GREEN PLACE COFFEESHOP

Map p306 (www.thegreenplace.nl; Kloveniersburgwal 4; ⏱10am-1am; Ⓜ Nieuwmarkt) The staff at the Cannabis College recommend Green Place for its good selection, good quality product and fair prices. Cash only.

🍷 Plantage

★SKYLOUNGE COCKTAIL BAR

Map p308 (http://doubletree3.hilton.com; Oosterdoksstraat 4; ⏱11am-1am Sun-Thu, to 3am Fri & Sat; 🚋1/2/4/5/9/14/16/24 Centraal Station) An unrivalled 360-degree panorama of Amsterdam extends from the glass-walled SkyLounge on the 11th floor of the DoubleTree Amsterdam Centraal Station hotel – and just gets better when you head out to its vast, sofa-strewn SkyTerrace, with an outdoor bar. Deliberate over more than 500 different cocktails; DJs regularly hit the decks.

DE GROENE OLIFANT BROWN CAFE

Map p308 (www.degroeneolifant.nl; Sarphatistraat 510; 11am-1am Sun-Thu, to 2am Fri & Sat; 🚋9 Alexanderplein) Steeped in Victorian-era opulence with intricate woodwork, the Green Elephant transports you back in time. Sit at the circa-1880 bar with the locals and admire the art-deco glass, or retreat to the lofted dining room for dinner like the the elegant residents of yesteryear's Plantage.

CAFÉ SCHARREBIER BROWN CAFE

Map p308 (http://scharrebier.nl; Rapenburgerplein 1; ⏱11am-1am Sun-Thu, to 3am Fri & Sat;

BROUWERIJ 'T IJ

Beneath the creaking sails of the 1725-built De Gooyer windmill, **Brouwerij 't IJ** (Map p308; www.brouwerijhetij.nl; Funenkade 7; ⌚brewery 2-8pm, English tour 3.30pm Fri-Sun; 🚋10 Hoogte Kadijk), Amsterdam's leading organic microbrewery, produces delicious (and often very potent) standard, seasonal and limited-edition brews. Pop in for a beer in the tiled tasting room, lined by an amazing bottle collection, or on the plane tree–shaded terrace. A beer is included in the 30-minute brewery tour (€4.50).

Put your name down at the bar on the day for a brewery tour; it's not possible to pre-book.

🚋22 Kadijksplein) Overlooking the lock, the terrace at this snug little brown *café* is an inviting spot for a beer or *jenever*. (*Scharrebier*, incidentally, was beer mixed with water to make it more affordable.)

CAFÉ ORLOFF — BAR

Map p308 (www.orloff.nl; Kadijksplein 11; ⌚8am-1am Mon-Thu, 8am-2am Fri, 10am-2am Sat, 10am-1am Sun; 📶; 🚋22/48 Kadijksplein) On the picturesque Kadijksplein, Orloff's sprawling terrace, shaded by a red awning, is one of the most tranquil in town. Inside, there's a magazine-strewn communal table.

CAFÉ KOOSJE — BROWN CAFE

Map p308 (http://koosjeamsterdam.nl; Plantage Middenlaan 37; ⌚9am-1am Sun-Thu, to 3am Fri & Sat; 🚋9/14 Plantage Kerklaan) If the three catchwords for real estate are location, location and location, then Koosje – situated between the Artis Royal Zoo and the Hollandsche Schouwburg – has got a lock on the market. Perch at the window or on the terrace to soak up the street corner's vibrant atmosphere.

Eastern Islands

★AMSTERDAM ROEST — BEER GARDEN

Map p308 (www.amsterdamroest.nl; Jacob Bontiusplaats 1; ⌚11am-1am Sun-Thu, to 3pm Fri & Sat; 🚋22 Wittenburgergracht) Derelict shipyards have been transformed into a super-cool artist collective/bar/restaurant, Amsterdam Roest (Dutch for 'Rust'), with a canal-facing terrace, huge backyard beneath towering blue cranes and an industrial warehouse interior. Regular events held here include films, live music, festivals, fashion shows and markets; there's a sandy urban beach in summer and toasty bonfires in winter.

It's hard to find; the most direct approach is to go along Oostenburgervoorstraat and cross the bridge at the northern end – it's 150m ahead on your left (look for the red double-decker London bus).

★HANNEKES BOOM — BEER GARDEN

Map p308 (www.hannekesboom.nl; Dijksgracht 4; ⌚10am-1am Sun-Thu, to 3am Fri & Sat; 🚋26 Muziekgebouw) Just across the water from NEMO, yet a local secret, this laidback waterside *café* built from recycled materials has a beer garden that really feels like a garden, with timber benches, picnic tables and summer barbecues. Mellow live music such as jazz or singer-songwriters takes place from 3.30pm on Sundays.

The site dates back to 1662, when it was a guard post monitoring maritime traffic into the city.

HPS — COCKTAIL BAR

Map p308 (☎06 2528 3620; www.hpsamsterdam.com; Rapenburg 18; ⌚6pm-1am Sun-Thu, to 3am Fri & Sat; 🚋32/33 Prins Hendrikkade) Adorned with chandeliers and chesterfields, speakeasy-style cocktail bar HPS (for Hiding in Plain Sight) is tiny so it's worth booking ahead on weekends. The menu changes seasonally but offers up concoctions like La Vie en Rose (tequila, lemon and rose petals) and Beetlejuice (tequila, jalapeño-infused Cointreau, fresh beetroot juice and balsamic). A Gypsy swing band plays on Thursdays at 8pm.

KHL — BAR

Map p308 (http://khl.nl; Oostelijke Handelskade 44; ⌚noon-midnight Tue-Sun; 🚋26 Rietlandpark) Set in a historic 1917 brick former warehouse with stunning tile work, KHL opens to a terrace that makes a superb spot for a glass of wine sourced from small vineyards. Regular live music ranges from Latin to pop and *klezmer* (traditional Jewish music).

KANIS & MEILAND — BAR

Map p308 (www.kanisenmeiland.nl; Levantkade 127; ⌚8.30am-1am Mon-Fri, 10am-1am Sat & Sun;

LOCAL KNOWLEDGE

GROENBURGWAL

Step out onto the white drawbridge that crosses the Groenburgwal and look north toward the Zuiderkerk for one of Amsterdam's prettiest canal views. Impressionist Claude Monet certainly took a shining to it, and painted it in 1874 as *The Zuiderkerk (South Church) at Amsterdam: Looking up the Groenburgwal*.

; 10 Azartplein) A favourite among the 'islanders', this cavernous spot has an inviting wooden reading table, tall windows facing the 'mainland' and a quiet terrace directly on the water.

MEZRAB CLUB

Map p308 (419 33 68; www.mezrab.nl; Veemkade 576; 8pm-1am Sun-Thu, to 3am Fri & Sat; 26 Kattenburgerstraat) Well known for its hilariously fun hard-rock karaoke as well as its alternative dance nights, regular indie rock, jazz, world music and other live music gigs, this harbourside venue (formerly Café Pakhuis Wilhelmina) is low-key clubbing at its best. It also hosts storytelling sessions in English and Dutch on the last Thursday of the month. Hours can vary. Cash only.

ENTERTAINMENT

MUZIEKGEBOUW AAN 'T IJ CONCERT VENUE

Map p308 (tickets 788 20 00; www.muziekgebouw.nl; Piet Heinkade 1; tickets free-€37; box office noon-6pm Mon-Sat & 90min before performance; 26 Muziekgebouw) Behind this multidisciplinary performing-arts venue's hi-tech exterior, the dramatically lit main hall has a flexible stage layout and great acoustics. Its jazz stage, Bimhuis, is more intimate. Under-30s can get €10 tickets at the box office 30 minutes before show time. Everyone else should try the **Last Minute Ticket Shop** (www.lastminuteticketshop.nl) for discounts.

BIMHUIS JAZZ

Map p308 (788 21 88; http://bimhuis.nl; Piet Heinkade 3; tickets free-€28; closed Aug; 26 Muziekgebouw) Bimhuis is the beating jazz heart of the Netherlands, and its stylish digs at the Muziekgebouw aan 't IJ draw international jazz greats.

MUZIEKTHEATER CLASSICAL MUSIC

Map p306 (625 54 55; www.operaballet.nl; Waterlooplein 22; box office noon-6pm Mon-Fr, to 3pm Sat & Sun or until performance Sep-Jul; 9/14 Waterlooplein) The Muziektheater is home to the Netherlands Opera and the National Ballet. Big-name performers and international dance troupes also take the stage here. Visitors aged under 30 can get tickets for €10 to €15 by showing up 90 minutes before show time. Free classical concerts (12.30pm to 1pm) are held most Tuesdays from September to May in its Boekmanzaal.

AMSTERDAMS MARIONETTEN THEATER THEATRE

Map p306 (620 80 27; www.marionettentheater.nl; Nieuwe Jonkerstraat 8; adult/child €15/7.50; M Nieuwmarkt) In a former blacksmith's shop, the marionette theatre has a limited repertoire (mainly Mozart operas such as *The Magic Flute*), but kids and adults alike are enthralled by the fairytale stage sets, period costumes and beautiful singing voices that bring the diminutive cast to life. From June to August the theatre performs only for groups; check the website for a schedule.

CONSERVATORIUM VAN AMSTERDAM CLASSICAL MUSIC

Map p308 (527 78 37; www.ahk.nl/conservatorium; Oosterdokskade 151; 4/9/16/24 Centraal Station) Catch a classical recital by students at the Netherlands' largest conservatory of music. It's in a snazzy contemporary building with state-of-the-art acoustics, endless glass walls and light-flooded interiors.

BETHANIËNKLOOSTER CLASSICAL MUSIC

Map p306 (625 00 78; www.bethanienklooster.nl; Barndesteeg 6b; Sep-Jul; M Nieuwmarkt) This former monastery near Nieuwmarkt has a glorious ballroom, and is a superb place to take in exceptional chamber music. Jazz fills the vaulted basement cellar. Concert schedules are posted online.

KRITERION CINEMA

Map p308 (623 17 08; www.kriterion.nl; Roetersstraat 170; tickets from €5; 10.30am-1am Mon-Thu, 10.30am-3am Fri, 12.30pm-3am Sat, 12.30pm-1am Sun; 7/10 Weesperplein) Student-run since 1945, this cinema and *café* has a great array of premieres, themed parties, classics, kids' flicks and more. It also hosts several film festivals throughout the year.

SKINNY HOUSES

Amsterdam is chock-full of slender homes because property used to be taxed on frontage. So the narrower your facade, the less you paid.

Witness the narrow house at **Oude Hoogstraat 22** (Map p306; Ⓜ Nieuwmarkt). It's 2.02m wide, 6m deep and several storeys tall, occupying a mere 12 sq metres per storey. This could well be the tiniest (self-contained) house in Europe.

Nearby, the **Kleine Trippenhuis** (Map p306; Kloveniersburgwal 26; Ⓜ Nieuw markt) is 2.44m wide. It stands opposite the **mansion** (p95) once owned by the wealthy Trip Brothers and, so the story goes, their coachman exclaimed: 'If only I could have a house as wide as my masters' door!' Webers fetish shop now occupies the skinny building.

SHOPPING

Nieuwmarkt

★DROOG — DESIGN, HOMEWARES

Map p306 (www.droog.com; Staalstraat 7; 11am-6pm Tue-Sun; 4/9/14/16/24 Muntplein) Droog means 'dry' in Dutch, and this slick local design house's products are strong on dry wit. You'll find all kinds of smart items you never knew you needed, like super-powerful suction cups. Also here is a gallery space, whimsical blue-and-white cafe, and fairytale-inspired courtyard garden that Alice in Wonderland would love, as well as a top-floor apartment (double €275).

★WATERLOOPLEIN FLEA MARKET — MARKET

Map p306 (www.waterloopleinmarkt.nl; Waterlooplein; 9am-6pm Mon-Sat; 9/14 Waterlooplein) Covering the square once known as Vlooienburg (Flea Town), the Waterlooplein Flea Market draws bargain hunters seeking everything from antique knick-knacks to designer knock-offs. The street market started in 1880 when Jewish traders living in the neighbourhood began selling their wares here.

Food vendors waft falafel sandwiches, *frites* and other quick bites around the market's periphery.

KNUFFELS — TOYS, SHOES

Map p306 (www.knuffels.com; St Antoniesbreestraat 39-51; 10am-6pm Mon-Sat, from 11am Sun; ; Ⓜ Nieuwmarkt) Kids will be drawn to the bobbing mobiles hanging from the ceiling of this busy corner shop, as wells as the *knuffels* (soft cuddly toys), puppets, teddies and jigsaw puzzles. As a bonus, there's a clog shop downstairs with wooden shoes galore.

JOE'S VLIEGERWINKEL — KITES

Map p306 (www.joesvliegerwinkel.nl; Nieuwe Hoogstraat 19; noon-6pm Tue-Fri, to 5pm Sat; ; Ⓜ Nieuwmarkt) Whether you're after a kite for the kids, you're looking for something more exotic, or just want to have fun in one of the city's parks, head to this specialised kite shop. You can also buy build-it-yourself kits.

HET FORT VAN SJAKOO — BOOKS

Map p306 (625 89 79; www.sjakoo.nl; Jodenbreestraat 24; 11am-6pm Mon-Fri, to 5pm Sat; 9/14 Waterlooplein) Get the lowdown on the squat scene, plus locally produced zines and Trotsky translations, at this lefty bookshop, which has been in operation since 1977.

HENXS — CLOTHING

Map p306 (www.henxs.com; St Antoniesbreestraat 136-138; 11am-6pm Mon-Fri, to 5pm Sat; Ⓜ Nieuwmarkt) The two tiny floors of this indie clothes store are crammed with fave labels of skaters and graffiti artists, such as Hardcore, Bombers Best, Evisu and G-Star. Graffiti supplies and edgy accessories are available in Henxs' space next door.

JUGGLE — CIRCUS SUPPLIES

Map p306 (www.juggle-store.com; Staalstraat 3; noon-5.30pm Tue-Sat; 4/9/14/16/24 Muntplein) Wee Juggle puts more than mere balls in the air: it also sells circus supplies, from unicycles to fire hoops to magic tricks.

MARBLES VINTAGE — CLOTHING

Map p306 (Staalstraat 30; 11am-7pm; 4/9/14/16/24 Muntplein) Pretty, feminine and reasonably priced, Marbles offers a wonderfully curated selection of vintage skirts, dresses, coats, shoes, boots and jewellery. Items are sorted by colour and type. Clothes hounds can launch from here into several other hip new and used clothing stores on the same block. There are branches in Jordaan and De Pijp.

FILMANTIQUARIAAT CINE QUA NON ART, BOOKS

Map p306 (http://cinequanonline.com; Staalstraat 14; ⌚1-7pm; 🚊4/9/14/16/24 Muntplein) An encyclopedic collection of film posters, arthouse DVDs and books on films fills this dusty, crammed space. Amazingly, if you ask for something specific, the staff will know exactly where it is in the organised chaos.

PUCCINI BOMBONI CHOCOLATE

Map p306 (www.puccinibomboni.com; Staalstraat 17; ⌚noon-6pm Sun & Mon, from 9am Tue-Sat; 🚊4/9/14/16/24 Muntplein) It's pretty much impossible to walk by and resist the smell. Puccini fills its large, handmade chocolate bonbons with rich and distinctive flavours like anise, tamarind or calvados. There is another branch at Singel 184. Note: these shops have been known to close in warm weather – for the sake of the chocolates, of course.

HET HANZE HUIS AMSTERDAM FOOD

Map p306 (www.hethanzehuis.nl; Staalstraat 20; ⌚1-6pm Mon, 10am-6pm Tue, Wed & Fri, 10am-8pm Thu, 9.30am-5pm Sat; 🚊4/9/14/16/24 Muntplein) This shop stocks wares from Amsterdam's old trading partners from the 12th through 16th centuries, including Copenhagen, Bruges, Hamburg, Riga and Tallinn (members of the once-powerful Hanseatic League). It also only uses suppliers who've been manufacturing from traditional recipes from 1800 onward. The result? You'll find unique coffee, tea, marzipan, wine and honey on the shelves.

'T KLOMPENHUISJE SHOES

Map p306 (www.klompenhuisje.nl; Nieuwe Hoogstraat 9a; ⌚10am-6pm Mon-Sat; Ⓜ Nieuwmarkt) This children's clog shop has the traditional shoes in a rainbow of hues. It sells cute galoshes (and matching raincoats) and other kids' footwear, too.

JACOB HOOY & CO ALTERNATIVE MEDICINE

Map p306 (www.jacobhooy.nl; Kloveniersburgwal 12; ⌚1-6pm Mon, 10am-6pm Tue-Fri, 10am-5pm Sat; Ⓜ Nieuwmarkt) This charming chemist's shop – with its walls of massive wooden drawers – has been selling medicinal herbs, homeopathic remedies and natural cosmetics since 1743.

BOOK EXCHANGE BOOKS

Map p306 (www.bookexchange.nl; Kloveniersburgwal 58; ⌚10am-6pm Mon-Sat, 11.30am-4pm Sun; Ⓜ Nieuwmarkt) This rabbit warren specialises in secondhand English books, with temptingly priced literary titles as well as volumes on the social sciences and more. It's near the university.

WEBERS EROTICA

Map p306 (www.webersholland.nl; Kloveniersburgwal 26; ⌚1-7pm; Ⓜ Nieuwmarkt) Indulge in top-end versions of every kind of fetishwear imaginable (and unimaginable).

BOERENMARKT MARKET

Map p306 (Farmers Market; Nieuwmarkt; ⌚9am-4pm Sat; Ⓜ Nieuwmarkt) 🍃 Stalls selling organic foods and produce draw crowds on Saturdays.

ANTIQUES MARKET MARKET

Map p306 (Nieuwmarkt; ⌚9am-5pm Sun May-Sep; Ⓜ Nieuwmarkt) Treasure hunters will find lots of old books and bric-a-brac to peruse.

HEAD SHOP SMART SHOP

Map p306 (www.headshop.nl; Kloveniersburgwal 39; ⌚11am-6pm Mon-Fri, 11am-7pm Sat, noon-7 Sun; Ⓜ Nieuwmarkt) Established back during the flower power era in 1968, this corner building houses Amsterdam's oldest smart shop. It stocks a mind-boggling array of magic truffles, herbs, seeds, vaporisers and water pipes as well as hippie staples like incense, crystals, paper lanterns and tie-dye clothes.

Plantage

FRANK'S SMOKEHOUSE FOOD & DRINK

Map p308 (www.smokehouse.nl; Wittenburgergracht 303; ⌚9am-4pm Mon, to 6pm Tue-Fri, to 5pm Sat; 🚌22 Wittenburgergracht) Frank is a prime supplier to Amsterdam's restaurants, and his excellent Alaskan salmon, halibut and yellowfin tuna can be vacuum-packed for travelling (customs regulations permitting). He also sells stunning sandwiches (smoked halibut with pumpkin relish; king crab; wild boar and cranberry chutney).

DATEMA AMSTERDAM BOOKS, MAPS

Map p308 (☎427 77 27; www.datema-amsterdam.nl; Prins Hendrikkade 176/50; ⌚10am-6pm Tue-Fri, to 5pm Sat; 🚌22 Kadijksplein) Anyone with a passion for boats will enjoy browsing through the navigation charts and nautical books at this specialist maritime bookshop. If you're setting sail in the Netherlands, its personalised advice is indispensable.

Eastern Islands

★LOODS 6 — SHOPPING CENTRE

Map p308 (www.loods6.nl; KNSM-laan 143; 10 Azartplein) This isn't a shopping centre of the mall variety, but rather a string of shops in a 1900-built former Royal Dutch Steam Company (KNSM) customs warehouse and passenger terminal. Noteworthy shops include children's wear designer Imps & Elfs, and Dutch-designed pottery and homewares at Pols Potten, as well as art galleries and fashion.

★POLS POTTEN — HOMEWARES

Map p308 (419 35 41; www.polspotten.nl; KNSM-laan 39, Loods 6; 10am-6pm Tue-Sat, noon-5pm Sun; 10 Azartplein) How do new residents in this style-conscious district furnish their new apartments? They head straight to this large interior-design shop, which has some particularly stunning ceramic work.

IMPS & ELFS — CHILDREN

Map p308 (www.imps-elfs.com; KNSM-Laan 297, Loods 6; 10am-6pm Tue-Sat, noon-5pm Sun; 10 Azartplein) Clothes made by Dutch design company Imps & Elfs put the focus on the comfort and fit for the child, and are socially responsible (using fair-trade practices) and environmentally friendly (using all-organic fabrics). This huge store is packed with its own designs as well as those from similarly-minded companies like Parisian Finger in the Nose clothing and Janod wooden toys.

DE ODE — SPECIALITY SHOP

Map p308 (419 08 82; www.ode-uitvaartbegeleiding.nl; Levantkade 51; by appointment; 10 Azartplein) Dutch design extends to the end with creative caskets at this one-of-a-kind coffin shop. It's open by appointment only, but a couple of designs are always on display in the window.

LOCAL KNOWLEDGE

ALL ABOUT DIAMONDS

Two diamond factories in town offer free guided tours. **Gassan Diamonds** (p96) offers the slicker version. **Coster Diamonds** (p174) has a convenient location at the Museumplein. You'll see lots of gems, and workers shining them, at both places.

For those in the market to buy, note that diamonds aren't necessarily cheaper in Amsterdam than elsewhere, but between the tours and extensive descriptions and factory offers, you'll know what you're buying.

And a bit of local diamond trivia: Amsterdam has been a diamond centre since Sephardic Jews introduced the cutting industry in the 1580s. The Cullinan, the largest diamond ever found (3106 carats), was split into more than 100 stones here in 1908, after which the master cutter spent three months recovering from stress.

SPORTS & ACTIVITIES

TUNFUN — PLAYGROUND

Map p306 (www.tunfun.nl; Mr Visserplein 7; adult/child free/€8.50; 10am-6pm, last entry 5pm; ; 9/14 Mr Visserplein) This cool indoor playground is located in a former traffic underpass. Kids can build, climb, roll, draw, jump on trampolines and play on a soccer pitch. There's even a children's disco – this is Amsterdam! – and a cafe serving *poffertjes* (small pancakes). Kids must be accompanied by an adult. It gets busy when the weather's bad.

The entrance is located opposite the Portuguese-Israelite Synagogue; look for the two green arches and stairs leading down.

GLOWGOLF — MINIGOLF

Map p308 (737 18 09; glowgolf.nl; Prins Hendrikkade 194, Noah's Arq; adult/child €8.50/7.50, 3D glasses €1.25; noon-8pm Sun-Wed, to 10pm Thu, to 3am Fri & Sat; 22 Kadijksplein) From the street Noah's Arq looks like a normal pub but down in the basement it harbours this trippy-and-then-some minigolf course. The 15 psychedelically coloured holes are played under black light, making them glow luridly in the dark (and making you feel like you're inside a giant pinball machine). Definitely get the 3D glasses to max out the surreal experience.

Western Canal Ring

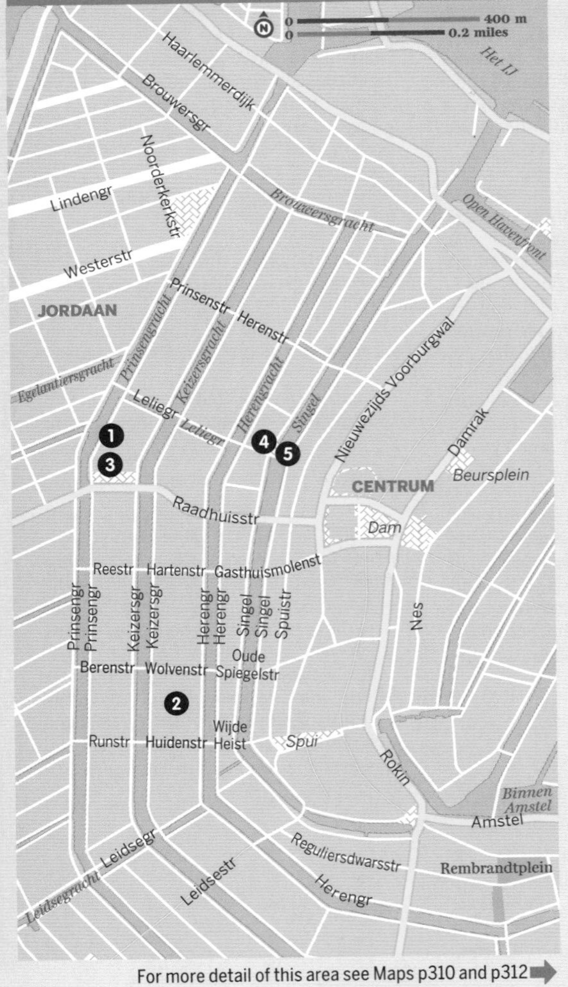

For more detail of this area see Maps p310 and p312

Neighbourhood Top Five

❶ Contemplating the amazing life and tragic death of the most famous Dutch girl in history at the poignant **Anne Frank Huis** (p114), where she and her family hid from the Nazis.

❷ Browsing the speciality shops along the compact and captivating **Negen Straatjes** (p125).

❸ Scaling the bell tower of the mighty **Westerkerk** (p116) and seeing the Netherlands' largest nave.

❹ Learning to distinguish an aged Gouda from a young *boerenkaas* at the **Reypenaer Cheese Tasting** (p126).

❺ Exploring the neighbourhood's standout **canals** on a Western Canal Ring walking tour (p119).

Explore Western Canal Ring

This whole area is a Unesco World Heritage site and you could spend a full day admiring the architecture down one canal alone. And although the neighbourhood is loaded with high-profile sights, half the charm here is simply soaking up the atmosphere: from the street, from a boat, from a backyard garden, from a rooftop balcony, or from the terrace of a canal-side cafe.

Begin your first day at the neighbourhood's northern end around the hip Haarlemmerbuurt shopping district and work your way toward the south, weaving in and out of the lanes and canals to visit the Multatuli Museum, admire the architecture of the Huis Met de Hoofden and pay homage to the Homomonument and the Westerkerk until you wind up at Anne Frank Huis in the early evening, when the crowds are thinnest.

On your second day, start with some of Amsterdam's most enjoyable shopping along the Negen Straatjes (Nine Streets) in the neighbourhood's south. This tic-tac-toe board of *straatjes* (small streets) is full of quirky little boutiques stocking antiques, vintage fashions, homewares and one-off speciality shops dedicated to everything from toothbrushes to antique eye wear. The area is peppered with informal drinking and dining venues that spill out into the streets in warmer weather.

Tear yourself away to check out the Bijbels Museum, the canal-house museum Het Grachtenhuis and the Huis Marseille photography museum, before finishing up at the Prinsengracht's bars, cafes and restaurants.

Local Life

➡ **Ad Life** Glance through the windows of the advertising agencies and design firms lining the Singel and Herengracht canals – the arty designer interiors may cause serious job envy.

➡ **Food and Fashion** The Haarlemmerbuurt, incorporating Haarlemmerstraat, is a hotspot for restaurants, gourmet provisions and kitchen shops, interspersed with hip fashion boutiques.

➡ **Snack Time** Join the locals queuing for fries slathered in mayonnaise or spicier sauces at Wil Graanstra Friteshuis (p121).

Getting There & Away

➡ **Trams** Trams 13, 14 and 17 have stops near the main attractions, and any tram or bus that stops near the Dam is just a short walk away.

Lonely Planet's Top Tip

In the spring and summer, take advantage of the later evening hours of the Anne Frank Huis. Go for an early dinner at one of the many excellent nearby cafes, and then spend the rest of the evening hours in Amsterdam's most moving sight – with fewer crowds and plenty of time to contemplate this remarkable Dutch girl's life and legacy.

Best Places to Eat

- De Belhamel (p120)
- Bistro Bij ons (p120)
- Letting (p118)
- Vinnies Deli (p118)
- Singel 404 (p118)

For reviews, see p118.

Best Places to Drink

- 't Arendsnest (p121)
- Café Tabac (p121)
- Café de Vergulde Gaper (p121)
- Café Het Molenpad (p121)
- De Doffer (p122)

For reviews, see p121.

Best Places to Shop

- Frozen Fountain (p123)
- Tenue de Nîmes (p124)
- I Love Vintage (p124)
- De Kaaskamer (p124)
- Denham the Jeanmaker (p124)

For reviews, see p123.

TOP SIGHT
ANNE FRANK HUIS

It is one of the 20th century's most compelling stories, told by its protagonist: a young Jewish girl forced into hiding with her family and their friends to escape deportation by the Nazis. The house they used as a hideaway should be a highlight of any visit to Amsterdam; indeed, it attracts more than one million visitors a year.

DON'T MISS

- Anne's red-plaid diary
- Anne's bedroom
- WWII news reels
- Peter van Pels' room
- Video of Anne's schoolmate Hanneli Gosler

PRACTICALITIES

- Map p310
- ☎556 71 00
- www.annefrank.org
- Prinsengracht 267
- adult/child €9/4.50
- 9am-7/10pm, hours vary seasonally
- 13/14/17 Westermarkt

Background

Stepping through the bookcase that swings open to reveal the 'Secret Annexe' and going up the steep stairs into the living quarters – where the family lived for more than two years – is to step back into a time that seems both distant and tragically real.

It seems impossible now, but it's true: it took the German army just five days to occupy all of the Netherlands, along with Belgium and much of France. And once Hitler's forces had swept across the country, many Jews – like Anne Frank and her family – eventually went into hiding. Anne's diary describes how restrictions were gradually imposed on Dutch Jews: from being forbidden to ride streetcars to being forced to turn in their bicycles and not being allowed to visit Christian friends.

The Franks moved into the upper floors of the specially prepared rear of the building, along with another couple, the Van Pels (called the Van Daans in Anne's diary), and their son Peter. Four months later Fritz Pfeffer (called Mr Dussel in the diary) joined the household. Here they survived until they were betrayed to the Gestapo in August 1944.

Ground Floor

After several renovations, the house itself is now contained within a modern, square shell that attempts to retain the original feel of the building (it was used during WWII as offices and a warehouse).

On this floor, be sure to watch the multilingual news reels of WWII footage narrated using segments of Anne's diary: it inextricably links the rise of Hitler with the Frank family's personal saga.

Offices

View the former offices of Victor Kugler, Otto Frank's business partner; his identity card and the film magazines he bought for Anne are on display. The other office area belonged to Miep Gies, Bep Voskuijl and Johannes Kleiman, two women and a man who worked in the office by day and provided food, clothing, school supplies and other goods – often purchased on the black market or with ration cards – for the eight residents of the Secret Annexe. You can see some of their personal documents here.

Secret Annexe

While the lower levels are painstakingly curated in a way that presents history with interactive modern technology, the former living quarters of the Frank family in the *Achterhuis* (rear house) retain their stark, haunting austerity. It's as if visitors are stepping back into 1942. Notice how windows of the annexe were blacked out to prevent suspicion among people who might see it from surrounding houses (blackouts were common practice to disorient bombers at night).

Take a moment to observe the ingenious set-up of the Secret Annexe as you walk through. You then enter two floors of the dark and airless space where the Franks and their friends observed complete silence during the daytime, outgrew their clothes and read Dickens, before being mysteriously betrayed and sent to their deaths.

Anne's Bedroom

As you enter Anne's small, simple bedroom, which she shared with Fritz Pfeffer, you can still sense the remnants of a young girl's dreams: the physical evidence of her interests and longings is on the wall with her photos of Hollywood stars and postcards of the Dutch royal family.

The Diary

More haunting exhibits and videos await after you return to the front house – including Anne's red-plaid diary itself, sitting alone in its glass case. Watch the video of Anne's old schoolmate Hanneli Gosler, who describes encountering Anne at Bergen-Belsen.

AVOIDING THE QUEUE

Buy a timed-entry ticket in advance to skip the queue. Prebook via the museum's website (€0.50 surcharge). It's possible to buy a ticket at the main entrance, but queues can easily be an hour-plus wait.

The Franks were among the last Jews to be deported and Anne died in the Bergen-Belsen concentration camp in March 1945, only weeks before it was liberated. Otto was the only member of the family to survive, and after the war he published Anne's diary, which was found among the litter in the annexe (the furniture had been carted away by the Nazis).

SIGHTS & ACTIVITIES

ANNE FRANK HUIS — MUSEUM

See p114.

WESTERKERK — CHURCH

Map p310 (Western Church; ☎624 77 66; www.westerkerk.nl; Prinsengracht 281; ⊙10am-3pm Mon-Sat; 13/14/17 Westermarkt) The main gathering place for Amsterdam's Dutch Reformed community, this church was built for rich Protestants to a 1620 design by Hendrick de Keyser. The nave is the largest in the Netherlands and is covered by a wooden barrel vault. The huge main organ dates from 1686, with panels decorated with instruments and biblical scenes. Rembrandt (1606–69), who died bankrupt at nearby Rozengracht, was buried in a pauper's grave somewhere in the church.

Carillon recitals take place on Fridays at 1pm (though check the schedule posted by the entrance, as this can vary); best listening is from the nearby Bloemgracht. The bells also chime mechanically every 15 minutes.

WESTERKERK BELL TOWER — TOWER

Map p310 (www.westertorenamsterdam.nl; Prinsengracht 281; tours per person €7.50; ⊙10am-7.30pm Mon-Sat Apr-Oct) The Westerkerk's bell tower is famously topped by the blue imperial crown that Habsburg emperor Maximilian I bestowed to the city for its coat of arms in 1489. The climb up the stairs of the 85m tower can be strenuous and claustrophobic, but the guide takes breaks on the landings while describing the bells. Tours depart every half hour. Children under six aren't permitted.

HOMOMONUMENT — MONUMENT

Map p310 (cnr Keizersgracht & Raadhuisstraat; 13/14/17 Westermarkt) Behind the Westerkerk, this 1987 cluster of three 10m x 10m x 10m granite triangles recalls persecution by the Nazis, who forced gay men to wear a pink triangle patch. One of the triangles steps down into the Keizersgracht and is said to represent a jetty from which gay men were sent to the concentration camps.

Others interpret the step-up from the canal as a symbol of rising hope. Note the monuments are flush to the ground, and can be easy to miss at first glance.

HET GRACHTENHUIS — MUSEUM

Map p312 (Canal House; ☎421 16 56; www.hetgrachtenhuis.nl; Herengracht 386; adult/child €12/6; ⊙10am-5pm Tue-Sun; 1/2/5 Koningsplein) If you're the kind of person who walks through the Canal Ring and marvels over what a feat of engineering it is, you won't want to miss the Canal House, which explains how the canals and houses that line them were built. The museum uses holograms, videos, models, cartoons and other innovative ways to tell the story.

Unlike most Amsterdam museums, you can't simply wander through. Small groups go in together to experience the multimedia exhibits. It takes about an hour, and you'll come out knowing why Amsterdam's houses tilt. Tickets are cheaper when purchased online.

HUIS MARSEILLE — MUSEUM

Map p312 (☎531 89 89; www.huismarseille.nl; Keizersgracht 401; adult/child €8/free; ⊙11am-6pm Tue-Sun; 1/2/5 Keizersgracht) This well-curated photography museum stages large-scale, temporary exhibitions, drawing from its own collection as well as hosting travelling shows. Themes might include portraiture, nature or regional photography, spread out over several floors and in a 'summer house' behind the main house.

Huis Marseille is also located in a noteworthy building. The name refers to its original owner in 1665, a French merchant, and the original structure has remained largely intact. It retains some antique touches including the 18th-century fountain in the library, and a painting of Apollo, Minerva and the muses in the garden room.

BIJBELS MUSEUM — MUSEUM

Map p312 (Bible Museum; www.bijbelsmuseum.nl; Herengracht 366-368; adult/child €8/4; ⊙11am-5pm Tue-Sun; 1/2/5 Spui) This place first gained notoriety thanks to a dedicated minister, Leendert Schouten, who built a scale model of the Jewish Tabernacle described in Exodus. Now on the museum's 3rd floor, the model is said to have attracted thousands of visitors even before it was completed in 1851.

A collection of Dutch Bibles includes a Delft Bible printed in 1477. On the ground floor you can sniff scents mentioned in the Good Book and stroll through a garden of biblical trees. Exhibits on the lower floors also show paintings, furniture and other objects from the wealthy merchant family that built and lived in this 1622 canal house for nearly two centuries.

HERENGRACHT

Dug out during the 17th century Golden Age, the Herengracht (Gentlemen's Canal) takes its name from the wealthy landowners who built properties here. Notice how some buildings lean forward and have hoists in the gables. Given the narrowness of interior staircases, people used these hoists to haul large goods to upper floors.

Just north of the Herengracht, near the intersection of the Brouwersgracht, you'll find the Herenmarkt, a small square that is home to the historic 17th-century **West-Indisch Huis** (p117), the former headquarters of the Dutch West India Company.

The Herengracht is at its grandest along the **Golden Bend** (p129) in the Southern Canal Ring.

POEZENBOOT — CAT SANCTUARY

Map p310 (Cat Boat; ☎625 87 94; www.depoezenboot.nl; Singel 38; admission by donation; ⏰1-3pm Mon, Tue & Thu-Sat; 🚊1/2/5/13/17 Nieuwezijds Kolk) This boat on the Singel is a must for cat lovers. It was founded in 1966 by an eccentric woman who became legendary for looking after several hundred stray cats at a time. The boat has since been taken over by a foundation and holds some 50 kitties in proper pens. Fifteen are permanent residents, and the rest are ready to be adopted (after being neutered and implanted with an identifying computer chip, as per Dutch law).

MULTATULI MUSEUM — MUSEUM

Map p310 (www.multatuli-museum.nl; Korsjespoortsteeg 20; ⏰10am-5pm Tue, 2-5pm Thu & Fri, noon-5pm Sat & Sun Jul & Aug, 10am-5pm Tue, noon-5pm Sat & Sun Sep-Jun; 🚊1/2/5/13/17 Nieuwezijds Kolk) FREE Better known by the pen name Multatuli – Latin for 'I have suffered greatly' – novelist Eduard Douwes Dekker was best known for *Max Havelaar* (1860), a novel about corrupt colonialists in the Dutch East Indies. This small but fascinating museum-home chronicles his life and works, and shows furniture and artefacts from his period in Indonesia.

Dekker himself worked in colonial administration in Batavia (now Jakarta), and the book made him something of a social conscience for the Netherlands.

WEST-INDISCH HUIS — HISTORIC BUILDING

Map p310 (West Indies House; Herenmarkt 97; 🚊1/2/5/13/17 Centraal Station) Built in 1617 as a meat market and militia barracks, this historic building was rented by the Dutch West India Company (Geoctroyeerde Westindische Compagnie; GWC) as its headquarters in 1623. It was here that the GWC's governors signed off on the construction of a fort on the island of Manhattan in 1625, establishing New Amsterdam (now New York City).

The booty of Admiral Piet Heyn, the great naval hero, was stored here in 1628 after his men captured the Spanish silver fleet off the coast of Cuba.

Today this landmark on the Herenmarkt is used as a conference venue and houses offices including the John Adams Institute, which fosters cultural ties between the USA and the Netherlands. You can enter the courtyard to see the **statue of Peter Stuyvesant** (c 1612–1672), the colony of New Netherland's final Dutch Director-General until its British acquisition.

The Oost-Indisch Huis (p95), the headquarters of the Dutch East India Company (Vereenigde Oostindische Compagnie; VOC) is in Nieuwmarkt.

DE RODE HOED — CULTURAL CENTRE

Map p310 (The Red Hat; www.rodehoed.nl; Keizersgracht 102; ⏰8.30am-5.30pm, except during special events; 🚊13/14/17 Westermarkt) FREE Occupying three glorious 17th-century canal houses, this cultural centre offers lectures by world-renowned authors and debates on the topics of the day, sometimes in English. Even if nothing is on it's worth a visit to view the three-storey main auditorium, which was once the largest clandestine church in the Netherlands.

The centre was named for the hat shop once located here (spot the tile on the facade that identified it).

HUIS MET DE HOOFDEN — HISTORIC BUILDING

Map p310 (House with the Heads; www.huismetdehoofden.nl; Keizersgracht 123; ⏰10am-5pm Tue-Fri; 🚊13/14/17 Westermarkt) FREE A whimsical example of Dutch Renaissance style, this 1622 canal house has a beautiful step gable with six heads at door level representing the classical muses. The building was recently renovated, and it's now open to the public as a 'centre for free and contrarian thinking,' with a library focused on Western spiritual and philosophical texts, plus exhibitions, concerts and debates.

FYI, the famous heads out front are images of Apollo, Diana, Ceres, Bacchus, Minerva and Mercury. Renowned architect Hendrick de Keyser and his son Pieter designed the building.

VAN BRIENENHOFJE
SQUARE

Map p310 (Prinsengracht 85-133; ⊙6am-6pm Mon-Fri, to 2pm Sat; 🚊1/2/5/13/17 Nieuwezijds Kolk) FREE This charming courtyard (aka *hofje*) was named in the late 18th century for Jan van Brienen, who bought the Star Brewery located here, one of 13 breweries in town at the time. (The place is still called De Star Hofje by many.)

It was turned into an almshouse for older residents, who had a clear division of labour: the women cleaned house for the single men, who in turn toted water buckets from the outside pump (topped by a curious lantern). Hours can vary.

EATING

The Western Canal Ring may not have the multicultural dining diversity of other parts of town, but bear in mind that the Jordaan is only a hop, skip and a jump away. The Negen Straatjes (p125) are filled with cute cafes and small restaurants to match their lovely boutiques.

LETTING
DUTCH €

Map p310 (www.letting.nl; Prinsenstraat 3; mains €7-13; ⊙8.30am-5pm Mon & Thu-Sat, to 3pm Wed, 9am-5pm Sun; ✍; 🚊13/14/17 Westermarkt) Start your day in traditional Dutch style with authentic breakfast dishes such as *wentelteefjes* (sugar bread dipped in egg and cinnamon), *uitsmijter rosbief* (eggs served sunny side up, with cheese and roast beef) and scrambled eggs with smoked halibut. At lunch choose from soups and sandwiches. Or book ahead for royal high tea (€25), accompanied by champagne.

VINNIES DELI
CAFE €

Map p310 (www.vinniesdeli.nl; Haarlemmerstraat 46; mains €7.50-12.50; ⊙7.30am-6pm Mon-Fri, 9am-6pm Sat, 9.30am-6pm Sun; ✍ 👪; 🚊1/2/5/13/17 Centraal Station) Organic fare at this trendy spot spans sandwiches such as black bean hummus and sweet peppers, eggplant with buttermilk sauce and pomegranate, and smoked mackerel with rhubarb chutney. Cakes, such as beetroot-topped cheesecake, are equally creative. Self-caterers can pick up the products used in its dishes from the deli.

If you're imagining the designer furniture in your lounge room, you're in luck: all of the pieces are for sale.

SINGEL 404
CAFE €

Map p312 (☎428 01 54; Singel 404; dishes €5-9; ⊙10.30am-7pm; ✍; 🚊1/2/5 Spui) It's easy to miss this tucked-away spot, despite its location near the bustling Spui (look for the cobalt-blue awning). Sure, the menu is as simple as can be – smoked salmon sandwiches, pumpkin soup, honey-mint lemonade – but the prices are rock bottom, portions are generous and the quality is superb.

PANCAKES!
DUTCH €

Map p312 (☎528 97 97; www.pancakesamsterdam.com; Berenstraat 38; pancakes €9.50-12.50; ⊙9am-7pm; 📶✍👪; 🚊13/14/17 Westermarkt) OK, so maybe it's mostly tourists who grace the blue-tile tables at snug little Pancakes!, but who can blame them? The signature dish rocks, whether it's sweet (apple, nuts and cinnamon) or savory (ham, chicory and Camembert). The batter is made with flour sourced from a local mill. Gluten-free pancakes are also available.

PETIT GÂTEAU
BAKERY €

Map p310 (☎737 15 85; www.petitgateau.nl; Haarlemmerstraat 80; tarts from €2.50; 🚊18/21/22 Buiten Brouwersstraat) The Paris-trained chef makes around 100 types of mini tarts – everything from hazelnut chocolate to caramel toffee and strawberry almond – all lined up in irresistible rows and sending out their siren song from the glass case. Staff use the big industrial kitchen for frequent baking workshops, so you can learn to do it yourself. Petit Gâteau has another outpost at De Hallen (p182).

STROOPWAFEL HEAVEN
BAKERY €

Map p310 (www.stroopwafelheaven.com; Westermarkt 7h; *stroopwafel* €2; ⊙10am-6pm; 🚊13/14/17 Westermarkt) Yes, it's touristy, and locals may argue that there better *stroopwafels* in town (like at the Albert Cuypmarkt), but this little shop makes a perfectly fine treat. The free upstairs

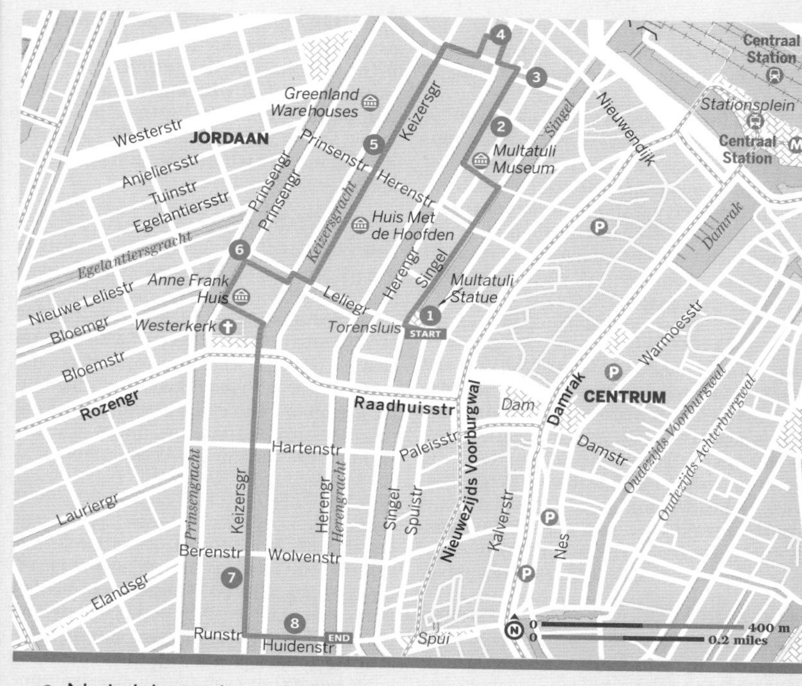

Neighbourhood Walk
Western Canal Ring

START SINGEL, TORENSLUIS
END NEGEN STRAATJES
LENGTH 3KM; 1¼ HOURS

Get to know the Western Canal Ring's 17th-century beauties during this walk.

Originally a moat that defended Amsterdam's outer limits, the 1 **Singel** is the first canal west of the centre. Torensluis, Amsterdam's oldest bridge (built in the mid-1600s), crosses it. Before you do, too, stop to admire the Multatuli statue; the Dutch literary giant's museum is a few blocks north.

Next up is the 2 **Herengracht** (Gentlemen's Canal), named for the rich merchants and powerful regents who clustered here to build their manors. Nearly 400 years later, it remains some of Amsterdam's choicest real estate.

The Herengracht soon intersects with the pretty 3 **Brouwersgracht** (Brewer's Canal), which took its name from the many suds makers located here in the 16th and 17th centuries. To the north is Herenmarkt, home to the 17th-century 4 **West-Indisch Huis** (p117), where the Dutch West India Company's governors authorised the establishment of New Amsterdam (now New York City).

Turning south, cross the Brouwersgracht into the 5 **Keizersgracht** (Emperor's Canal). You'll soon spot the imposing, red-shuttered Greenland Warehouses, which used to store whale oil, and, further on, the Huis Met de Hoofden, with its carvings of Apollo, Ceres and Diana. At peaceful Leliegracht, turn west onto 6 **Prinsengracht**. You'll pass the Anne Frank Huis and the soaring towers of the Westerkerk. Back on Keizersgracht, you can't miss the quirky 7 **Felix Meritis** (p123), a one-time Enlightenment society venue turned alternative theatre. Since you're probably hungry, thirsty or both by this point, head to one of the fetching little cafes lining the nearby 8 **Negen Straatjes** (p125).

'museum' has photos and tablets on the walls explaining the history of the *stroopwafel,* and videos showing how it's made.

STUBBE'S HARING SANDWICHES €

Map p310 (Singel Haarlingersluis; sandwiches $4-7; ⏲11am-7pm; 🚋1/2/5/13/17 Centraal Station) Stubbe's open-air fish stall has been providing pickled herring to Amsterdammers for a century. You can eat it straight up or on a sandwich roll. Just be sure to sprinkle it with diced onion first. It's a hop and a skip from Centraal Station.

LUNCHCAFÉ NIELSEN CAFE €

Map p312 (☎330 60 06; Berenstraat 19; mains €5-11; ⏲8am-4pm Tue-Fri, to 6pm Sat, 9am-5pm Sun; ✎; 🚋13/14/17 Westermarkt) Looking for a locals' favourite in the Negen Straatjes? This bright, airy cafe is an institution, thanks to good value for money, fast and friendly service, Illy coffee, and great food that spans hearty breakfasts, quiches, salads, sandwiches, and fresh lemon- and apple cakes that disappear as quickly as they're put out.

PANCAKE BAKERY DUTCH €

Map p310 (☎625 13 33; www.pancake.nl; Prinsengracht 191; mains €9-15; ⏲9am-9.30pm; 👪; 🚋13/14/17 Westermarkt) This basement restaurant in a restored warehouse features a dizzying 79 varieties of pancakes, from sweet (chocolate, banana or peach) to savoury (the 'Canadian', topped with bacon, cheese and barbecue sauce, or the 'Norwegian' with smoked salmon, cream cheese and sour cream).

★DE BELHAMEL FRENCH €€

Map p310 (☎622 10 95; www.belhamel.nl; Brouwersgracht 60; mains lunch €15-24.50, dinner €22.50-26.50; ⏲noon-4pm & 6-11pm; 🚋1/2/5/13/17 Centraal Station) In warm weather the canal-side tables at the head of the Herengracht are an aphrodisiac, and the sumptuous art-nouveau interior provides the perfect backdrop for superb French- and Italian-inspired dishes such as truffle-parsley-stuffed guinea fowl with polenta, a rack of lamb with aubergine biscuit and pepper coulis, or honey- and mustard-marinated veal.

BISTRO BIJ ONS DUTCH €€

Map p310 (☎627 90 16; www.bistrobijons.nl; Prinsengracht 287; mains €13.50-19; ⏲10am-10pm Tue-Sun; 👪; 🚋13/14/17 Westermarkt) If you're not in town visiting your Dutch *oma* (grandma), try the honest-to-goodness cooking at this charming retro bistro instead. Classics include *stamppot* (potatoes mashed with another vegetable) with sausage, *raasdonders* (split peas with bacon, onion and pickles) and *poffertjes* (small pancakes with butter and powdered sugar).

CAFÉ RESTAURANT VAN PUFFELEN CAFE €€

Map p312 (☎624 62 70; www.restaurantvanpuffelen.com; Prinsengracht 377; mains €15-20.50; ⏲4pm-1am Mon-Thu, noon-1am Fri-Sun; ✎; 🚋13/14/17 Westermarkt) Scallops with lemon cream and basil, chickpea tofu curry, and ravioli filled with asparagus and sage butter are among the ever-changing dishes at this large cafe-restaurant. Its nooks and crannies are enticing for a cosy drink.

VAN HARTE INTERNATIONAL €€

Map p310 (☎625 85 00; www.vanharte.com; Hartenstraat 24; 3-course dinner menu €25; ⏲10am-6pm Sun & Mon, to 11pm Tue-Thu, to midnight Fri & Sat; 🚋13/14/17 Westermarkt) Behind floor-to-ceiling glass windows, a glistening mosaic-tiled bar and massive murals make Van Harte look like an ultrachic drinking spot, but it's an even better place to dine, with an evening menu spanning brie and truffle dim sum with beetroot salad, roasted duck breast on lentils with duck-liver sauce, or skin-baked cod with fennel and *beurre blanc.*

STOUT INTERNATIONAL €€

Map p310 (☎616 36 64; www.restaurantstout.nl; Haarlemmerstraat 73; mains €19-24, shared platters per person €29.50; ⏲10am-1am Sun-Thu, to 3am Fri & Sat; ✎; 🚋1/2/5/13/17 Centraal Station) In warm weather, sit on the benches outside this airy, contemporary cafe to watch the world go by. Indoors, you can share platters and individual dishes such as polenta with pumpkin cream sauce, or wild duck with gingerbread. It's a handy spot if you're looking for a late-night meal.

CASA PERÚ PERUVIAN €€

Map p312 (☎620 37 49; www.casaperu.nl; Leidsegracht 68; mains €18-22; ⏲noon-11pm Apr-Sep, 5.30-11pm Oct-Mar; 📶; 🚋1/2/5 Prinsengracht) There's nothing quite like enjoying a *chupe de camarones* (fisherman's soup) or *lomo saltado* (beef with onion, tomato and French fries) while looking out over the Leidsegracht and the Prinsengracht at this bright, busy spot – the Netherlands' only dedicated Peruvian restaurant.

DE STRUISVOGEL FRENCH €€

Map p312 (☎423 38 17; www.restaurantdestruisvogel.nl; Keizersgracht 312; 3-course menu €26.50; ⏰6pm-midnight Mon-Fri, 5pm-midnight Sat & Sun; 🚋13/14/17 Westermarkt) This former kitchen to some large canal houses is in the basement and offers good value. It doesn't serve the bird (*struisvogel* means 'ostrich'), but it does have a nightly rotating menu with French-inspired choices such as veal tongue stewed in white wine followed by red mullet in prawn bisque and crème caramel for dessert. Book ahead.

SPANJER EN VAN TWIST CAFE €€

Map p310 (☎639 01 09; www.spanjerenvantwist.nl; Leliegracht 60; mains €15-20; ⏰10am-10pm; 🚋13/14/17 Westermarkt) Spanjer en van Twist's tables on the Leliegracht are great for watching the boats cruise by. The eclectic, changing lunch and dinner menu is good – say shrimp croquettes on pumpkin bread, Moroccan *tajine* (stew) with vegetables, or traditional Dutch soup with smoked sausage – but a highlight is the divine apple tart.

KOH-I-NOOR INDIAN €€

Map p310 (☎623 31 33; www.koh-i-noor-restaurant.nl; Westermarkt 29; mains €14-20; ⏰noon-11.30pm; 🌶; 🚋13/14/17 Westermarkt) Tandoori meats, coconutty curries, three-alarm vindaloos and other subcontinent classics fill plates at this long-standing Indian restaurant. A lengthy list of lentil, pea, eggplant and spinach dishes will please vegetarians.

LOCAL KNOWLEDGE

FAVOURITE FRITES

Legions of Amsterdammers swear by the crispy spuds at **Wil Graanstra Friteshuis** (Map p310; ☎624 40 71; Westermarkt 11; frites €2.50-4.50; ⏰noon-7pm Mon-Sat; 🚋13/14/17 Westermarkt) . The family-run business has been frying on the square by the Westerkerk since 1956. Most locals top their cones with mayonnaise, though *oorlog* (a peanut sauce–mayo combo), curry sauce and picalilly (relish) rock the taste buds, too.

DRINKING & NIGHTLIFE

Cafes in this refined district tend to have slick, polished interiors and elaborate menus. More down-to-earth brown *cafés* jam the nearby Jordaan.

★'T ARENDSNEST BEER CAFÉ

Map p310 (www.arendsnest.nl; Herengracht 90; ⏰noon-midnight Sun-Thu, to 2am Fri & Sat; 🚋1/2/5/13/17 Nieuwezijds Kolk) This gorgeous, restyled brown *café*, with its glowing copper *jenever* (Dutch gin) boilers behind the bar, only serves Dutch beer – but with nearly 200 varieties (many from small breweries), including 30 on tap, you'll need to move here to try them all.

CAFÉ TABAC BAR

Map p310 (www.cafetabac.eu; Brouwersgracht 101; ⏰4pm-1am Mon-Thu, to 3am Fri, 10am-3am Sat, to 1am Sun; 📶; 🚋18/21/22 Buiten Brouwersstraat) Is Café Tabac a brown *café*, a designer bar or simply an effortlessly cool place to while away a few blissful hours at the intersection of two of Amsterdam's most stunning canals? The regulars don't seem concerned about definitions, but simply enjoy the views and kicking back beneath the beamed ceilings.

CAFÉ DE VERGULDE GAPER BROWN CAFÉ

Map p310 (www.deverguldegaper.nl; Prinsenstraat 30; ⏰11am-1am Sun-Thu, to 3am Fri & Sat; 📶; 🚋13/14/17 Westermarkt) Decorated with old chemists' bottles and vintage posters, this former pharmacy has amiable staff and a terrace with afternoon sun. It's popular with locals, especially for after-work drinks. The name translates to the 'Golden Gaper', for the open-mouthed bust of a Moor traditionally posted at Dutch apothecaries.

CAFÉ HET MOLENPAD BAR

Map p312 (☎625 96 80; www.cafehetmolenpad.nl; Prinsengracht 653; ⏰noon-1am Sun-Thu, to 3am Fri & Sat; 📶; 🚋1/2/5 Prinsengracht) By day, this gem of a canal-side *café* is full of people poring over newspapers on the terrace. By night the atmosphere turns quietly romantic, with low lamps and candlelight illuminating little tables beneath pressed-tin ceilings.

DE DOFFER BROWN CAFÉ

Map p312 (www.doffer.com; Runstraat 12-14; ⏰11am-3am Sun-Thu, to 4am Fri & Sat; 🚋1/2/5

LOCAL KNOWLEDGE

PRINSENGRACHT

The Herengracht and Keizersgracht might be grander, but locals love to hang out on the Prinsengracht, the liveliest of Amsterdam's inner canals. In summertime you could spend a whole weekend just enjoying its warm-weather charms – exploring the shops and kicking back on its cafe terraces – as boats glide by and houseboats sway in the breeze against the quays. During the chillier months, it's a winter wonderland where you might see skaters take to the iced-over canal.

Spui) Writers, students and artists frequent this popular *café* (with adjoining bar) for affordable food and good conversation. The dining room, with its old Heineken posters, large wooden tables and, occasionally, fresh flowers, is particularly atmospheric at night.

DE ADMIRAAL TASTING HOUSE

Map p312 (www.proeflokaaldeadmiraal.nl; Herengracht 319; 5pm-midnight Mon-Sat; 1/2/5 Spui) The grandest and largest of Amsterdam's tasting houses, De Admiraal is also a restaurant and party venue. Although they pour only their own house brands (16 *jenevers* and 60 liqueurs), it's hard to quibble over the lovely setting and pleasant staff.

SCREAMING BEANS COFFEE

Map p310 (www.screamingbeans.nl; Hartenstraat 12; 8am-5pm Mon-Fri, 9am-5pm Sat, 10am-5pm Sun; 13/14/17 Westermarkt) When energy ebbs during a Negen Straatjes shopping spree, revive at Screaming Beans, where academy-trained baristas serve first-rate cups of caffeine. There's another branch in the neighbourhood at Haarlemmerstraat 68.

WOLVENSTRAAT 23 BAR

Map p312 (320 08 43; Wolvenstraat 23; 9am-1am Sun-Thu, to 3am Fri & Sat; 1/2/5 Spui) This funky bar with no name – there's no sign anywhere – is especially popular with locals, who come for the good wines by the glass, great music and tasty Asian snacks. If this is your kind of place, check out their other bar, Finch (p158), in the Jordaan.

VYNE WINE BAR

Map p312 (www.vyne.nl; Prinsengracht 411; 6pm-midnight Mon-Thu, to 1am Fri, 5pm-1am Sat, 4-11pm Sun; 13/14/17 Westermarkt) With blond timber floors, walls and ceiling, the slickest wine bar in town looks like a stylish sauna (wine bottles notwithstanding). Knowledgeable staff guide you in the right direction, no matter your price point.

BARNEY'S COFFEESHOP

Map p310 (427 94 69; www.barneys.biz; Haarlemmerstraat 102; 7am-1am; 18/21/22 Buiten Brouwersstraat) Decades ago, Barney's got famous on bargain breakfasts all day, along with marijuana. In recent years, the weed has vastly improved, but breakfasts are now across the street in the smoke-friendly, somewhat-slick Barney's Uptown. A vaporiser dots each table at the coffeeshop, and milkshakes quiet hunger pangs until you're ready to dig in at Uptown.

JAY'S JUICES JUICE BAR

Map p310 (www.jaysjuices.nl; Haarlemmerstraat 14; 9am-6pm Mon-Fri, 10am-6pm Sat & Sun; 1/2/5/13/17 Centraal Station) Set yourself up for a day of sightseeing (and/or detox from the night before) at Jay's. There's a huge range of fruit and vegetable juices, and combinations thereof, as well as wheatgrass shots and fresh coconut.

CAFÉ DE PELS BROWN CAFÉ

Map p312 (www.cafedepels.nl; Huidenstraat 25; 10am-1am Sun-Thu, to 3am Fri & Sat; 1/2/5 Spui) This appealingly shabby traditional brown *café* is also a Sunday morning breakfast fave, with plenty of international newspapers to pore over as you sip your *koffie verkeerd* (milky coffee).

IL TRAMEZZINO COFFEE

Map p310 (www.iltramezzinoamsterdam.nl; Haarlemmerstraat 79; 9am-6pm Mon-Sat, 9.30am-5pm Sun; ; 18/21/22 Buiten Brouwersstraat) A perfect Haarlemmerstraat shopping break, this little slice of Milan in Amsterdam, with a white-lacquer and red-cushioned interior, serves steaming espresso from a magnificent chrome contraption imported from Italy.

GREENHOUSE COFFEESHOP

Map p310 (www.greenhouse.org; Haarlemmerstraat 64; 9am-1am; ; 18/21/22 Buiten Brouwersstraat) Yes, that stretch of the floor is glass and there really are koi swimming underfoot in this contemporary coffeeshop lounge. Once you tire of the fish, peer into the microscope to see THC crystals or contemplate one of the pies spinning in the display case.

GREY AREA COFFEESHOP

Map p310 (www.greyarea.nl; Oude Leliestraat 2; ⊙noon-8pm; 🚋1/2/5/13/14/17 Dam/Raadhuisstraat) Owned by a couple of laid-back American guys, this tiny shop introduced the extra-sticky, flavoursome 'Double Bubble Gum' weed to the city's smokers. Organic coffee includes free refills.

PÂTISSERIE POMPADOUR TEAHOUSE

Map p312 (☎623 95 54; www.patisseriepompadour.com; Huidenstraat 12; ⊙10am-6pm Mon-Fri, 9am-5pm Sat, noon-6pm Sun; 🚋1/2/5 Spui) Join society ladies sipping top-notch tea and nibbling homemade Belgian-style chocolates and pastries at this chichi little tearoom in the Negen Straatjes.

KOFFIEHUIS DE HOEK COFFEE

Map p312 (☎625 38 72; Prinsengracht 341; ⊙8am-4.30pm Mon-Fri, 9am-5pm Sat & Sun; 🚋13/14/17 Westermarkt) This *koffiehuis* (espresso bar; not to be confused with a coffeeshop) is one of the best places in the city to get an old-fashioned coffee-house experience in Amsterdam. Come for *lekker* (tasty) cakes, pancakes and sandwiches in a charming, chequered-tablecloth atmosphere.

SIBERIË COFFEESHOP

Map p310 (www.coffeeshopsiberie.nl; Brouwersgracht 11; ⊙11am-11pm Sun-Thu, to midnight Fri & Sat; 📶; 🚋1/2/5/13/17 Nieuwenzidjs Kolk) Popular among locals, Siberië's offerings go beyond marijuana – its owners regularly schedule cultural events such as art exhibits, poetry slams, acoustic concerts, DJ nights and even horoscope readings.

BRIX FOOD 'N' DRINX BAR

Map p312 (☎639 03 51; www.cafebrix.nl; Wolvenstraat 16; ⊙11am-1am Sun-Thu, to 3am Fri & Sat; 🚋1/2/5 Spui) The loungey setting makes this a great place to chill over a cocktail and enjoy nibbles from the starters-only menu, such as raw oysters, beef sashimi and mini Peking duck. There's live evening jazz on Sunday (with established artists) and Monday (with an open stage) from about 9pm.

DULAC GRAND CAFÉ

Map p310 (☎624 42 65; www.restaurantdulac.nl; Haarlemmerstraat 118; ⊙7.30am-1am Sun-Thu, to 3am Fri & Sat; 🚌18/21/22 Buiten Brouwersstraat) This former bank building is outrageously decked out in a kooky, kind of spooky, mixture of styles (art nouveau, Amsterdam School and Turkish, with a few Gothic accents). It has a pool table and an equally eclectic crowd.

ENTERTAINMENT

FELIX MERITIS THEATRE

Map p312 (☎626 23 21; www.felix.meritis.nl; Keizersgracht 324; ⊙box office 9am-7pm; 📶; 🚋1/2/5 Spui) Amsterdam's centre for arts, culture and science puts on innovative modern theatre, music and dance, as well as talks on politics, diversity, art, technology and literature. Its adjoining cafe is exceptional for coffee or cocktails by the huge windows or outside overlooking the canal.

The building was constructed in 1787 by Jacob Otten Husly for Felix Meritis (Latin for 'happiness through achievement'), a society of wealthy residents who promoted the ideals of the Enlightenment through the study of science, arts and commerce. The colonnaded facade served as a model for that of the Concertgebouw.

SHOPPING

You could easily spend all of your shopping time in the Negen Straatjes (p125), but be sure to check out the Haarlemmerbuurt, too.

★FROZEN FOUNTAIN HOMEWARES

Map p312 (www.frozenfountain.nl; Prinsengracht 645; ⊙1-6pm Mon, 10am-6pm Tue-Sat, noon-5pm Sun; 🚋1/2/5 Prinsengracht) The city's best-known showcase of furniture and interior design. Prices are not cheap, but the daring designs are offbeat and very memorable

LOCAL KNOWLEDGE

HAARLEMMERBUURT

Amsterdam's coolest neighbourhood-within-a-neighbourhood (or two – it straddles both the Western Canal Ring and the Jordaan), the Haarlemmerbuurt (www.haarlemmerbuurt-amsterdam.nl) is exploding with restaurants, food shops, designer workshops and funky boutiques. Its website (in Dutch, but easy to navigate) has an interactive map of Haarlemmerstraat and its western extension, Haarlemmerdijk, and details of one-off events.

(designer pen-knives, kitchen gadgets and that birthday gift for the impossible-to-wow friend). Best of all, it's an unpretentious place where you can browse at length without feeling uncomfortable.

TENUE DE NÎMES CLOTHING

Map p310 (www.tenuedenimes.com; Haarlemmerstraat 92-94; ⌚noon-6pm Sun & Mon, 10am-6pm Tue-Sat; 🚌18/21/22 Buiten Brouwersstraat) Ubercool denimwear by legendary brands such as Levi's, Rogue Territory, Pure Blue Japan, Edwin, Naked & Famous, Acne and Rag & Bone are the speciality of this hip boutique. You'll also find hot new fashions including T-shirts, stylishly cut jackets and dresses from local Amsterdam label Amatør.

I LOVE VINTAGE VINTAGE

Map p310 (☎330 19 50; www.ilovevintage.com; Prinsengracht 201; ⌚9.30am-6pm Mon-Sat, noon-5pm Sun; 🚋13/14/17 Westermarkt) A large shop compared to most Amsterdam vintage purveyors, I Love Vintage is known for its terrific selection of dresses and jewellery from the 1920s to 1950s. It also carries retro-style new clothes if pre-worn threads aren't your thing. Prices start at around €20.

DE KAASKAMER FOOD

Map p312 (www.kaaskamer.nl; Runstraat 7; ⌚noon-6pm Mon, 9am-6pm Tue-Fri, to 5pm Sat, noon-5pm Sun; 🚋1/2/5 Spui) The name means 'cheese room' and it is indeed stacked to the rafters with Dutch and organic varieties, as well as olives, tapenades, salads and other picnic ingredients. You can try before you buy, and if it's too much to take home a mondo wheel of Gouda, you can at least procure a cheese and/or meat baguette to take away.

DENHAM THE JEANMAKER MEN'S STORE CLOTHING

Map p312 (www.denhamthejeanmaker.com; Prinsengracht 495; ⌚noon-6pm Sun & Mon, 10am-6pm Tue, Wed, Fri & Sat, to 8pm Thu; 🚋1/2/5 Spui) Next door to Denham's Negen Straatjes studio, this flagship, 'zoned' boutique carries the jeanmaker's menswear lines. Jeans aside, you'll find jackets, knitwear and accessories. Cool vintage touches in-store include an antique haberdashery display case and a vintage scissor collection.

DENHAM THE JEANMAKER WOMEN'S STORE CLOTHING

Map p312 (www.denhamthejeanmaker.com; Runstraat 17; ⌚noon-6pm Sun & Mon, 10am-6pm Tue, Wed, Fri & Sat, to 8pm Thu; 🚋1/2/5 Spui) The upscale jeans maker has a women's store around the corner from the topline men's store and studio.

BOEKIE WOEKIE BOOKS

Map p312 (www.boewoe.home.xs4all.nl; Berenstraat 16; ⌚noon-6pm; 🚋13/14/17 Westermarkt) This artist-run bookstore sells books created by artists. Some tell elegantly illustrated stories; others are riffs on graphic motifs. The merchandise is exquisitely one-of-a-kind.

GAMEKEEPER TOYS

Map p310 (www.gamekeeper.nl; Hartenstraat 14; ⌚10am-6pm Mon-Wed, Fri & Sat, to 8.30pm Thu, 11am-6pm Sun; 🚋13/14/17 Westermarkt) The selection of board games is dizzying, as is the imagination that went into making them. Start with chequers, chess and mah jong, and move on to Cathedral (build a city in the style of the Great Wall of China or the souk in Marrakech) or Rush Hour (help a car get out of traffic).

'Cooperative' games encourage players to play with, not against, each other.

MARLIES DEKKERS CLOTHING

Map p312 (www.marliesdekkers.com; Berenstraat 18; ⌚1-6pm Mon, 11am-6pm Tue-Sat, noon-5pm Sun; 🚋13/14/17 Westermarkt) The preeminent Dutch lingerie designer Marlies Dekkers is known for her subtle hints to bondage, detailed on exquisite undergarments. Summer sees an equally enticing range of swimwear. The shop itself is a sultry bastion of decadence, with handpainted wallpaper and a titillating lounge area with a fireplace.

BRILMUSEUM ACCESSORIES

Map p310 (☎421 24 14; www.brilmuseumamsterdam.nl; Gasthuismolensteeg 7; ⌚11.30am-5.30pm Wed-Fri, to 5pm Sat; 🚋13/14/17 Westermarkt) This spectacles shop is an institution, both for its wares and for its presentation. You can take in the 700-year history of eyeglasses as well as a very 21st-century collection, some of which is pretty outlandish.

DARLING CLOTHING

Map p312 (www.thedarling.nl; Runstraat 4; ⌚1-6pm Mon, 11am-6pm Tue-Sat, noon-6pm Sun; 📶; 🚋1/2/5 Spui) Funky, affordable, locally designed clothes. Whimsical accessories. And cupcakes! Shops like the Darling are why the Negen Straatjes continue to delight and surprise.

SHOPPING THE NEGEN STRAATJES

In a city packed with countless shopping opportunities, each seemingly more alluring than the next, the **Negen Straatjes** (Nine Streets; Map p312; www.de9straatjes.nl; 🚊1/2/5 Spui) represent the very densest concentration of consumer pleasures. These nine little streets are indeed small, each just a block long. The shops are tiny, too, and many are highly specialised. Eyeglasses? Cheese? Toothbrushes? Single-edition art books? Each has its own dedicated boutique.

The streets – from west to east, and north to south: Reestraat, Hartenstraat, Gasthuismolensteeg; Berenstraat, Wolvenstraat, Oude Spiegelstraat; Runstraat, Huidenstraat, Wijde Heisteeg – form a grid bounded by Prinsengracht to the west and Singel to the east.

To help navigate the welter of shops here, pick up a copy of *The Nine Streets* shopping guide, available at many tourist offices and in many of the shops themselves, as well as online. Many shops here are closed entirely on Monday, and sometimes Tuesday, too.

EPISODE — VINTAGE

Map p312 (www.episode.eu; Berenstraat 1; ⏲11am-6pm Mon-Wed, to 8pm Thu, to 7pm Fri, 10am-7pm Sat, noon-6pm Sun; 🚊13/14/17 Westermarkt) Allow plenty of time to browse the seemingly endless racks of 1970s suede coats, folksy peasant blouses, '80s jewellery and big, bright plastic sunglasses across Episode's two floors of fabulous vintage and secondhand gear.

ZIPPER — CLOTHING

Map p312 (www.zipperstore.nl; Huidenstraat 7; ⏲noon-6.30pm Mon, 11am-6.30pm Tue, Wed, Fri & Sat, to 8pm Thu, 1-6.30pm Sun; 🚊1/2/5 Spui) Amsterdam hipsters head here for seriously nostalgic, retro secondhand gear – wacky printed shirts, stovepipe jeans, '40s zoot suits, pork-pie hats and the like.

DE WITTE TANDEN WINKEL — ACCESSORIES

Map p312 (☎623 34 43; www.dewittetandenwinkel.nl; Runstraat 5; ⏲10am-5.30pm Tue-Fri, to 5pm Sat; 🚊1/2/5 Spui) You've got to love shops that are obsessed, and the 'White-Teeth Shop' certainly is – with dental hygiene. There's a huge selection of toothbrushes, toothpastes from around the world, brushing accessories you never knew you needed, and friendly advice.

BEBOB DESIGN — HOMEWARES

Map p310 (☎624 57 63; www.bebob.eu; Herenstraat 8; ⏲1-5pm Sun & Mon, to 6pm Fri & by appointment; 🚊1/2/5/13/17 Nieuwezijds Kolk) Apart from some smaller items such as toasters and perfume bottles, most of the local and international designs here are larger pieces (sofas, chairs, tables, lamps), but it's worth a browse for an insight into the vintage influence on Dutch design.

AMSTERDAM WATCH COMPANY — ACCESSORIES

Map p310 (www.awco.nl; Reestraat 3; ⏲11am-6pm Tue-Fri, to 5pm Sat; 🚊13/14/17 Westermarkt) A small, passionate and highly skilled team of watchmakers restores old watches (post-war to mid-1970s). The company is also the exclusive Amsterdam dealer of such brands as Germany's D Dornblüth and the Dutch Christiaan van der Klaauw, who makes fewer than 200 watches a year.

SCOTCH & SODA — CLOTHING

Map p312 (www.scotch-soda.com; Huidenstraat 3-5; ⏲noon-6pm Sun & Mon, 10am-6pm Tue & Wed, to 9pm Thu, to 7pm Fri & Sat; 🚊1/2/5 Spui) Scotch & Soda's Negen Straatjes store is a prime place to check out the offerings from this Amsterdam fashion label gone global. This branch carries men's and women's styles, including lots of denim. The chic outerwear is guaranteed to keep you looking impossibly cool even during the most tempestuous Dutch weather.

ARCHITECTURA & NATURA — BOOKS

Map p310 (www.architectura.nl; Leliegracht 22; ⏲noon-6pm Mon, 10.30am-6.30pm Tue-Fri, to 5pm Sat, 1-5pm Sun; 🚊13/14/17 Westermarkt) This charming canal-side shop has art, architecture, design, landscape and coffee-table books.

ANTONIA BY YVETTE — SHOES

Map p310 (www.antoniabyyvette.nl; Gasthuismolensteeg 18; ⏲10am-6pm Tue-Fri, 11am-6pm Sat; 🚊13/14/17 Westermarkt) Yvette Riemersma designs and develops shoes and works with Dutch designers. Shoes, boots, sandals and espadrilles run from supremely classy to just plain fun. There's a small section for guys.

EXOTA CLOTHING

Map p310 (www.exota.com; Hartenstraat 13; ⌚noon-6pm Sun & Mon, 11am-7pm Tue-Sat; 🚋13/14/17 Westermarkt) Exota sells its own hip King Louie label plus global brands such as Kookai and French Connection. The shop stocks chic men's and women's designs. Across the street at Hartenstraat 10, the sister shop stocks sportier women's clothes and kids' threads.

MENDO BOOKS

Map p312 (www.mendo.nl; Berenstraat 11; ⌚11am-6pm Mon-Sat, noon-5pm Sun; 🚋13/14/17 Westermarkt) The Mendo graphic design agency runs this smart, black-walled bookshop specialising in books in the creative realm: art, design, architecture, fashion and photography.

NUKUHIVA CLOTHING

Map p310 (www.nukuhiva.nl; Haarlemmerstraat 36; ⌚noon-7pm Mon, 10.30am-7pm Tue-Fri, 10am-6pm Sat, noon-6pm Sun; 🚋1/2/5/13/17 Centraal Station) 🍃 This eco-boutique stocks only ethical and fair-trade clothing and accessories, by brands such as Veja (vegan shoes) and Dutch designer Kuyishi (organic denim).

LAURA DOLS VINTAGE

Map p312 (www.lauradols.nl; Wolvenstraat 7; ⌚11am-6pm Mon-Sat, noon-6pm Sun; 🚋1/2/5 Spui) Compulsive style watchers head to this vintage-clothing store for fur coats, 1920s beaded dresses, lace blouses and '40s movie-star accessories such as hand-stitched leather gloves.

BEADIES JEWELLERY

Map p312 (www.beadies.com; Huidenstraat 6; ⌚10.30am-6pm Mon-Sat, noon-6pm Sun; 🚋1/2/5 Spui) Once the funky jewellery in the window draws you in, you'll find yourself here for hours, selecting gorgeous beads, gems, charms and trinkets to design your own necklaces and bracelets. If you don't want to start from scratch, opt for a variation on Beadies' designs.

HESTER VAN EEGHEN SHOES

Map p310 (www.hestervaneeghen.com; Hartenstraat 1; ⌚noon-6pm Wed-Sat, to 5pm Sun; 🚋13/14/17 Westermarkt) Designed in Amsterdam and handcrafted in Italy from fine leather, internationally renowned Hester van Eeghen's unique shoes are for those who dare to dress their feet dramatically in bright colours, fur, suede, and geometric patterns and prints. Her handbags (available down the street at Hartenstraat 37) are just as attention-grabbing.

VAN RAVENSTEIN CLOTHING

Map p312 (www.van-ravenstein.nl; Keizersgracht 359; ⌚1-6pm Mon, 11am-6pm Tue-Fri, 10.30am-5.30pm Sat; 🚋1/2/5 Spui) Chic men and women shop here for upmarket designers, including Dries van Noten, Ann Demeulemeester, Véronique Leroy and Amsterdam's own avant-garde design duo Viktor & Rolf.

SPORTS & ACTIVITIES

REYPENAER CHEESE TASTING COURSE

Map p310 (☎320 63 33; www.reypenaercheese.com; Singel 182; tastings from €15; ⌚tastings by reservation; 🚋1/2/5/13/14/17 Dam/Raadhuisstraat) Here's your chance to become a *kaas* (cheese) connoisseur. The 100-plus-year-old Dutch cheese maker Reypenaer offers tastings in a rustic classroom under its shop. The hour-long session includes six cheeses – two goat's milk, four cow's milk – from young to old, with wine and port pairings. Staff will guide you through them, helping you appreciate the cheeses' look, smell and taste.

Southern Canal Ring

Neighbourhood Top Five

❶ Catching prestigious exhibitions at the **Hermitage Amsterdam** (p132), put together from the cache of treasures at the original St Petersburg museum.

❷ Enjoying an *ahh*-inducing sunset or starry night by the **Reguliersgracht** (p131), aka the canal of seven bridges.

❸ Exploring the **Museum Van Loon** (p130), Amsterdam's only complete canal house with its back coach house.

❹ Experiencing patrician canal-house life through the eyes of former servants at treasure-packed **Museum Willet-Holthuysen** (p131).

❺ Hitting the cafes, bars, theatres and clubs on and around party central **Leidseplein** (p129).

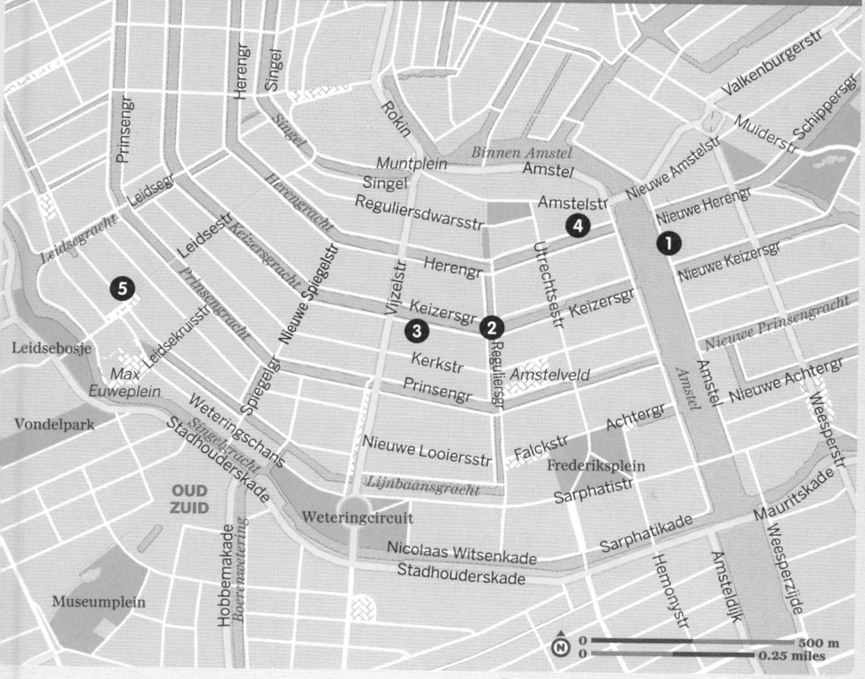

For more detail of this area see Map p318.

Lonely Planet's Top Tip

Don't discount the areas around Leidseplein or Rembrandtplein as simply tourist traps for tour-bus set crowds or cheerfully drunk hooligans on pub crawls (although indeed, they are both). They can be serious (or not-so-serious) fun, with plenty of authentic bars and cafes just waiting to be discovered. To escape the hullabaloo and hang out with the locals, head to happening Utrechtsestraat.

Best Places to Eat

- Restaurant Fyra (p137)
- La Cacerola (p135)
- Buffet van Odette (p135)
- Pantry (p135)
- Tempo Doeloe (p137)

For reviews, see p133.

Best Places to Drink

- Bar Moustache (p138)
- Eijlders (p138)
- De Kroon (p138)
- Sweet Cup (p138)
- Pata Negra (p138)

For reviews, see p138.

Best Entertainment

- Stadsschouwburg (p142)
- Melkweg (p143)
- Paradiso (p143)
- Sugar Factory (p143)
- Koninklijk Theater Carré (p143)

For reviews, see p142.

Explore Southern Canal Ring

Buzzing with activity, the diverse Southern Canal Ring spans the area from the radial Leidsegracht in the west to the Amstel in the east. With museums, restaurants, cafes and shops galore, not to mention miles of gorgeous canal photo-ops, you'll want to give yourself some time here. The neighbourhood is anchored by two key nightlife hubs: Leidseplein and Rembrandtplein, so they're ideal end points for each day's exploration here.

Begin your first day at the flower-filled Bloemenmarkt, then meander past the grand Golden Bend houses before checking out the antique and art shops of Nieuwe Spiegelstraat and the Museum Van Loon, as you make your way to Leidseplein.

On your second day, beat the crowds by getting an early start at the Hermitage Amsterdam. Afterwards, stroll down the Amstel to marvel at the Amstelsluizen locks and the Gijsbert Dommer Huis ('House with the Blood Stains'!). Around the corner is the Museum Willet-Holthuysen.

All that sightseeing is sure to make you hungry, so head to Utrechtsestraat's plethora of quality options. Take in the view of the seven bridges along Reguliersgracht and end the night on lively Rembrandtplein.

Local Life

- **Snack Life** Do as the Dutch royals do and buy beautiful baked goods from Patisserie Holtkamp (p136), fronted by a royal coat of arms.
- **Cafe Life** Off Prinsengracht, tiny Weteringstraat feels like a secret passage; look out for local brown *café* (pub), Café de Wetering (p139).
- **Cocktail Life** The door's unmarked and you'll need to send a text message to get in, but the cocktails at speakeasy Door 74 (p139) are worth it.
- **Jazz Life** Locals pack lovable Jazz Café Alto (p143) every night of the week to catch smooth jazz by local and international musicians.

Getting There & Away

- **Tram** This area is well-served by trams. For the Leidseplein area, take tram 1, 2, 5, 7 or 10. To reach Rembrandtplein, take tram 4, which travels down Utrechtsestraat, or tram 9. Trams 16 and 24 cut through the centre of the neighbourhood down busy Vijzelstraat.

SIGHTS

LEIDSEPLEIN — SQUARE

Map p318 (1/2/5/7/10 Leidseplein) Historic architecture, neon, beer and plenty of tourists – welcome to Leidseplein. A one-stop shop for party-goers, this hyperactive square is a major tram intersection and a litmus test for nightlife. There are countless pubs and clubs, and a smorgasbord of restaurants. Pavement cafes at the northern end are perfect for watching street artists and eccentric passers-by.

On the square's eastern side, farmers would leave their horses and carts at the Leidsepoort (Leiden Gate) before entering town; it was demolished in 1870. The strip of greenery on the other side of the Singelgracht with large chestnut trees is called Leidsebosje (Leiden Wood).

Entertainment venues radiate from its centre, and nearby Kerkstraat pulses with trendy gay establishments. For more intimate (but not necessarily more serene) bars and restaurants, explore the festive streets of Lange Leliedwarsstraat and Korte Leliedwarsstraat, as well as the streets behind the Stadsschouwburg (p142).

MAX EUWE CENTRUM — BUILDING

Map p318 (625 70 17; www.maxeuwe.nl; Max Euweplein 30a-1; noon-4pm Tue-Fri, limited hrs Jul & Aug; 1/2/5/7/10 Leidseplein) FREE Max Euwe (1901–81) was the Netherlands' only world chess champion (in the 1930s) and at this chess centre you'll find a permanent exhibition devoted to the history of the game. You can play against live or digital opponents. The pavement of the square out the front is often crowded with players and onlookers raptly watching games on the outsized chessboard.

AMSTERDAM PIPE MUSEUM — MUSEUM

Map p318 (www.pipemuseum.nl; Prinsengracht 488; adult/child €8/4; museum noon-6pm Wed-Sat, shop 11am-6pm Mon-Sat; 1/2/5 Prinsengracht) Did you know that pipes were first used by Native Americans around 500 BC? It's the starting point of the history of pipes at this unexpectedly fascinating museum, which displays a private collection of objects collected over 40 years from some 60 different countries. Knowledgeable guides take you through the collection's Chinese opium pipes, Turkish water pipes, carved Maori pipes, African ceremonial pipes and much more. The opportunity to explore the beautiful 17th-century canal house is worth the admission price alone.

KRIJTBERG — CHURCH

Map p318 (623 19 23; www.krijtberg.nl; Singel 446; 1-5pm Tue-Thu, Sat & Sun; 1/2/5 Koningsplein) The soaring turrets of this neo-Gothic church are an odd sight in this row of sedate Singel homes. Officially known as the St Franciscus Xaveriuskerk, it replaced a clandestine Jesuit chapel on the same site; these days it's still Jesuit. The lavish paintings and statuary make this one of the most beautiful church interiors in the city.

BLOEMENMARKT — MARKET

Map p318 (Flower Market; Singel, btwn Muntplein & Koningsplein; 8.30am-7pm Mon-Sat, to 7.30pm Sun Apr-Oct, 9am-5.30pm Mon-Sat, 11am-5.30pm Sun Mar-Nov; 1/2/5 Koningsplein) Since 1860 this famous flower market has been located at the spot where nurserymen and women, having sailed up the Amstel from their smallholdings, would moor their barges to sell their wares directly to customers. No longer floating (it's now perched on piles), the market here offers tulips in season and bulbs year-round, as well as clogs, fridge magnets and other kitsch souvenirs.

Hotels almost always have vases available if you want to brighten your room with colourful blooms.

GOLDEN BEND — ARCHITECTURE

Map p318 (Gouden Bocht; Herengracht, btwn Leidsestraat & Vijzelstraat; 1/2/5 Koningsplein) One of the ultimate places to mutter 'if only my family had bought that property way back then', the Golden Bend is about the most prestigious stretch of real estate in Amsterdam, a monument to the Golden Age, when precious goods swelled in cellars of homes already stuffed with valuables. The richest Amsterdammers lived and ruled their affairs from here.

Apart from the Kattenkabinet (p130) museum, the homes are only open on Open Monument Day (Open Monumentendag; second weekend in September).

The earliest mansions date from the 1660s, when the Canal Ring was expanded south. Thanks to some lobbying at city hall, the gables here were twice as wide as the standard Amsterdam model, and the rear gardens were deeper.

TOP SIGHT
MUSEUM VAN LOON

There's no better way to instantly whisk yourself back to 19th-century Amsterdam than by spending an hour or two at this wonderful house museum. The only complete replica of a canal house with its back coach house, where horse-drawn coaches arrived and were stored, the property has a luscious courtyard garden, opulent furniture and countless family portraits that seem to whisper secrets as you pass from room to gorgeous room.

Built in 1672, it was first home to acclaimed painter Ferdinand Bol. By the late 1800s the Van Loons, a prominent patrician family, moved in and have lived here ever since (they still occupy the building's upper floors).

Make sure you take your time soaking up the quiet, calm atmosphere of each room, all of which are notable for the sense of history, wealth and artistry they exude. Among some 150 portraits of the Van Loon family, you'll see important paintings such as *Wedding Portrait* by Jan Miense Molenaer. But the main exhibit is the house itself. Don't miss the intricate wedding-cake plasterwork on the ceilings, and the most fascinating room: the old-fashioned basement kitchen, where cook Leida presided for almost 40 years. Some of the family's favourite recipes are displayed.

DON'T MISS

- The coach house
- The gorgeous brass rococo banisters on the open staircase
- The 19th-century basement kitchen
- The dramatic red bedroom

PRACTICALITIES

- Map p318
- ☎624 52 55
- www.museumvanloon.nl
- Keizersgracht 672
- adult/child €9/5
- ⏲10am-5pm
- 🚊16/24 Keizersgracht

KATTENKABINET MUSEUM

Map p318 (Cats Cabinet; ☎626 90 40; www.kattenkabinet.nl; Herengracht 497; adult/child €7/free; ⏲10am-5pm Mon-Fri, from noon Sat & Sun; 🚊1/2/5 Koningsplein) One Golden Bend house that's open to the public is this offbeat museum, devoted to, of all things, the feline presence in art. It was founded by wealthy financier Bob Meijer in memory of his red tomcat John Pierpont Morgan III. Among the artists, Swiss-born Théophile-Alexandre Steinlen (1859–1923) figures prominently. There's also a small Rembrandt etching (a Madonna and child with a cat and snake) and Picasso's *Le Chat*.

You may get the chance to admire the collection along with the cats that live in the building.

STADSARCHIEF HISTORIC ARCHIVE

Map p318 (Municipal Archives; ☎251 15 11, tour reservations 251 15 10; www.stadsarchief.amsterdam.nl; Vijzelstraat 32; ⏲10am-5pm Tue-Fri, from noon Sat & Sun; 🚊16/24 Keizersgracht) FREE The Amsterdam archives occupy a monumental bank building that dates from 1923. When you step inside, head to the left to the enormous tiled basement vault and displays of archive gems such as the 1942 police report on the theft of Anne Frank's bike. A small cinema at the back shows vintage films about the city.

Tours (adult/child €6/free) run at 2pm on Saturday and Sunday and must be reserved in advance.

Upstairs, a gallery space mounts temporary exhibits (for a small entry fee). Its bookshop, the Stadsboekwinkel (p146), sells city-oriented tomes.

FOAM GALLERY

Map p318 (Fotografiemuseum Amsterdam; www.foam.org; Keizersgracht 609; adult/child €10/free; ⏲10am-6pm Sat-Wed, to 9pm Thu & Fri; 🚊16/24 Keizersgracht) Simple but spacious galleries, some with skylights or grand windows for natural light, create a superb space for changing exhibitions spanning all genres of photography from world-renowned photographers such as Sir Cecil Beaton, Annie Leibovitz and Henri Cartier-Bresson.

GEELVINCK HINLOPEN HUIS MUSEUM

Map p318 (☎639 07 47; www.geelvinck.nl; Keizersgracht 633; adult/child €9/4.50; ⏲11am-5pm Wed-Mon; 🚊16/24 Keizersgracht) To see how

TOP SIGHT
MUSEUM WILLET-HOLTHUYSEN

Built around 1685 for Amsterdam mayor Jacob Hop and redesigned in 1739, this sumptuous residence – now managed by the Amsterdam Museum – is named after the widow who bequeathed the property to the city in the late 19th century. It's now a shining star in Amsterdam's vast constellation of architectural treasures.

As you stroll through the patrician house, you'll be surrounded by the inspiring art, design, and furniture collection of former resident Abraham Willet, including paintings by Jacob de Wit. Also look for the *place de milieu* (centrepiece) that was part of the family's 275-piece Meissen table service, and the intimate French-style garden with sundial – you can also peek at the garden through the iron fence at the Amstelstraat end.

For a fascinating insight into the house through the eyes of the servants, be sure to borrow the notebook from the front desk, with details that make the house (and indeed, an entire era) come alive, such as the tedious, back-breaking ways in which servants went about their domestic tasks, such as roasting the meat and cleaning the windows.

DON'T MISS

- Jacob de Wit paintings
- The French garden
- The notebook
- The Louis XVI–style ground floor

PRACTICALITIES

- Map p318
- 523 18 22
- www.willetholthuysen.nl
- Herengracht 605
- adult/child €8.50/4.25
- 10am-5pm Mon-Fri, from 11am Sat & Sun
- Waterlooplein, 4/9/14 Rembrandtplein

the wealthy lived during the 17th century, visit this opulent 1687-built private mansion and its magnificent classical gardens, which link the former Keizersgracht coach house with the main Herengracht house, and incorporate a herb garden, English garden and French formal garden with Amsterdam's largest private pond. English-speaking guides are on hand to show you the mansion's rooms.

Concerts, many using the estate's period instruments, take place on Sundays at 4.45pm (tickets per adult child from €18/12).

REGULIERSGRACHT CANAL

Map p318 (4/9/14 Rembrandtplein) Amsterdam's prettiest canal was dug in 1658 to link the Herengracht with the canals further south. It was named after an order of monks whose monastery was located nearby. From here you can peer through the arches of at least seven bridges. Many canal boats pass by.

A number of houses along here have intriguing gables, tablets and fancy decorations.

TASSENMUSEUM HENDRIKJE MUSEUM

Map p318 (Museum of Bags & Purses; 524 64 52; www.tassenmuseum.nl; Herengracht 573; adult/child €12.50/7.50; 10am-5pm; 4/9/14 Rembrandtplein) At this handbag museum you'll find half a millennium's worth of arm candy. The largest collection in the Western world (over 5000 bags), it contains everything from a crumpled 16th-century pouch to dainty art deco and design classics by Chanel, Gucci and Versace to Madonna's ivy-strewn 'Evita' bag from the film premiere and an '80s touch-tone phone bag. The 17th-century interiors are stunning.

REMBRANDTPLEIN SQUARE

Map p318 (4/9/14 Rembrandtplein) Originally called Reguliersplein, then Botermarkt, after the butter markets held here until the mid-19th century, this square now takes its name from the **statue** of the painter erected in 1876. Beneath Rembrandt are life-size bronze **sculptures** re-creating his famous painting, the *Night Watch* (you can see the original 2D version in the Rijksmuseum).

Rembrandtplein soon evolved into a nightlife hub as various cafes, restaurants and clubs opened their doors, and remains a cornerstone of Amsterdam nightlife.

On the northern side of the square, De Kroon (p138), opened 1898, is one of the grandest *cafés* in town. Opposite, Café Schiller (p139), dating from 1892, is renowned for its theatrical crowd and fabulous art-deco interior, including leadlight glass windows.

BLAUWBRUG BRIDGE

Map p318 (Blue Bridge; btwn Waterlooplein & Amstelstraat; MWaterlooplein) Built in 1884, one of the city's most striking bridges replaced an old wooden version that had connected these shores of the Amstel since the 17th century. Inspired by the Alexander III bridge in Paris, it features tall, ornate street lamps topped by the imperial crown of Amsterdam, fish sculptures and foundations shaped like the prow of a medieval ship.

MAGERE BRUG BRIDGE

Map p318 (Skinny Bridge; btwn Kerkstraat & Nieuwe Kerkstraat; 4 Prinsengracht) Dating from the 1670s, the iconic nine-arched 'Skinny Bridge' has been rebuilt several times in both concrete and timber. It's still operated by hand and remains photogenic even at night, when 1200 tiny lights make the bridge look like a Christmas decoration. You can spot it in many films, including the 1971 James Bond thriller *Diamonds are Forever*. Stand in the middle and feel it sway under the passing traffic.

AMSTELSLUIZEN ARCHITECTURE

Map p318 (Amstel Locks; Amstel river, near Koninklijk Theater Carré; 4 Prinsengracht) These impressive sluices, or locks, date from 1674 and allowed the canals to be flushed with fresh water from lakes north of the city, rather than saltwater from the IJ, an innovation that made the city more liveable. The locks are regularly shut while fresh water flows in, while the sluices on the western side of the city are left open as the stagnant water is pumped out to sea.

AMSTELKERK CHURCH

Map p318 (520 00 70; www.amstelkerk.net; Amstelveld 10; 9am-5pm Mon-Fri; 4 Prinsengracht) The unique pinewood Amstelkerk was erected in 1668 as a *noodkerk* (makeshift church) under the direction of the city architect, Daniël Stalpaert. The idea was that the congregation would have

TOP SIGHT
HERMITAGE AMSTERDAM

The long-standing ties between Russia and the Netherlands – Tsar Peter the Great learned shipbuilding and Dutch cursing here in 1697 – led to the establishment of an Amsterdam branch of the State Hermitage Museum of St Petersburg. You'll see prestigious collections on loan from the St Petersburg museum's amazing cache of more than three million art objects, such as treasures from the Russian palace or masterworks by Matisse and Picasso. These blockbuster temporary exhibitions change about twice a year and they're as stately (and popular) as you'd expect.

The Hermitage is magnificently housed in the Amstelhof, a 17th-century former almshouse set around a sweeping courtyard. Facing the Amstel river, it offers breathtaking views from the west-side galleries.

No photographs are allowed (but there's a gift shop). Bear in mind, too, that the museum is one of Amsterdam's most popular attractions and waiting times to enter can stretch up to 60 minutes during peak periods. To avoid the worst of the crowds, arrive before 11am. Multilanguage audio guides are available in the entrance hall for €4.

DON'T MISS

- The permanent collection
- The lovely courtyard
- River views from the west-side galleries
- The dazzling temporary exhibitions from St Petersburg

PRACTICALITIES

- Map p318
- 530 74 88
- www.hermitage.nl
- Amstel 51
- adult/child €15/free
- 10am-5pm
- MWaterlooplein, 9/14 Waterlooplein

somewhere to meet while a permanent church arose next to it, but plans for this stone church were abandoned in the 1840s. Its square-shaped interior was updated with neo-Gothic alterations, including a pipe organ.

DE DUIF

CHURCH

Map p318 (The Dove; ☎520 00 90; www.deduif.net; Prinsengracht 756; 🚋4 Prinsengracht) In 1796, shortly after the French-installed government proclaimed freedom of religion, De Duif was the first Catholic church to be built with a public entrance for more than two centuries. Unstable construction meant it had to be demolished; its replacement you see today was built in 1857. These days De Duif is no longer Catholic but Ecumenical, and is also a venue for concerts, opera and private events.

If you're able to peek inside, check out the clay friezes of the Stations of the Cross on the right-hand wall. The pulpit carvings are of St Willebrordus of Utrecht, and the organ is a sight in its own right, reaching up to the vaulted ceiling.

EATING

All roads in Amsterdam seem to lead to Leidseplein, but there are better places to eat – try the adjacent sidestreets or nearby canals. Much the same can be said for Rembrandtplein. Instead of dining here, walk a few steps to Utrechtsestraat, one of the finest restaurant rows in town.

VAN DOBBEN

DUTCH €

Map p318 (☎624 42 00; www.eetsalonvandobben.nl; Korte Reguliersdwarsstraat 5-9; dishes €2.75-8; ⏲10am-9pm Mon-Wed, 10am-1am Thu, 10am-2am Fri & Sat, 10.30am-8pm Sun; 🚋4/9/14 Rembrandtplein) Open since the 1940s, Van Dobben has white-tile walls and white-coated staff who specialise in snappy banter. Traditional meaty Dutch fare is its forte: try the *pekelvlees* (something close to corned beef), or make it a *halfom* (if you're keen on that being mixed with liver).

The *kroketten* (meat croquettes) are up there with the best in town and compulsory after a late-night Rembrandtplein booze-up. There's a second branch in the De Pijp neighbourhood.

LOCAL KNOWLEDGE

HOUSE WITH THE BLOOD STAINS

Look closely at the facade of this sober residence, **Gijsbert Dommer Huis** (Map p318; Amstel 216; 🚋4 Keizersgracht), known locally as the 'House with the Blood Stains'. After losing his fortune, six-time mayor and diplomat Coenraad van Beuningen lost his mind and scribbled graffiti here, allegedly in his own blood, and his unfathomable message – including Hebrew letters and obscure Kabbalah symbols – from the 17th century is still faintly visible.

Well-to-do businessman Gijsbert Dommer commissioned this house from 1671, but it's the mad mayor who is better known today.

BAR HUF

AMERICAN €

Map p318 (http://barhuf.nl; Reguliersdwarsstraat 43; mains €8.50-14.50; ⏲kitchen 4pm-midnight Sun-Thu, to 1am Fri & Sat; 📶; 🚋1/2/5 Koningsplein) You can just drop by for a beer/cocktail but Bar Huf really comes into its own for late-night dining. Five different burgers (eg. Mango Jerry: crab, coleslaw and wasabi mayo; Rocky Balboa: chicken, jalapeños and cheddar), rum- and apple-glazed ribs, macaroni and cheese (made with five cheeses), and lemon meringue pie are all available long after nearby restaurants have closed.

LAVINIA GOOD FOOD

VEGETARIAN €

Map p318 (www.laviniagoodfood.nl; Kerkstraat 176; dishes €4.50-8.50; ⏲8.30am-4pm Mon-Fri, 9.30am-5pm Sat & Sun; 🖉; 🚋16/24 Keizersgracht) Spelt minipizzas, portabello mushroom burgers, salads like pasta or chickpea, and sandwiches with toppings like mango salsa, hummus and guacamole make Lavinia a delicious stop even if you're not vegetarian.

SOUP EN ZO

SOUP BAR €

Map p318 (www.soupenzo.nl; Niewe Spiegelstraat 54; soup €5.40-7; ⏲11am-8pm Mon-Fri, noon-7pm Sat & Sun; 🖉; 🚋7/10 Spiegelgracht) On a chilly day, you can't beat a steaming cup of soup from this little takeaway soup bar. Flavours change every hour but might include potato with roquefort, lentil and minced beef, prunes and pumpkin or spicy spinach and coconut. It now has two other outlets, in Nieuwmarkt and Museumplein, near Vondelpark. Cash only.

Neighbourhood Walk
Southern Canal Ring

START SINGELGRACHT
END AMSTEL RIVER
LENGTH 4KM; TWO HOURS

Set off at the Singelgracht and head north into the nexus of art and antique shops, the 1 **Spiegel Quarter**, along Nieuwe Spiegelstraat. One of Amsterdam's swankiest patches of real estate, the aptly named 2 **Golden Bend** (p129) on Herengracht is awash with classical French flourishes.

Stop by the bustling 3 **Bloemenmarkt** (p129) and from the eastern end you'll see one of Amsterdam's most enduring emblems, the striking 4 **Munttoren (Mint Tower)**. From the tower, head east along the Amstel river to take in the grand 5 **Hotel de l'Europe**, where polished skiffs moor at the terrace restaurant. At the bridge, turn south into tiny Halvemaansteeg (Half-Moon Lane) and the beating heart of the entertainment district around 6 **Rembrandtplein** (p131). As you cross the square, stop to admire the statue of master painter Rembrandt, before making your way to 7 **De Kroon** (p138), one of the most stylish *grand cafés* (bars).

Pass through shady Thorbeckeplein to the Herengracht and snap a postcard-perfect photo of 8 **Reguliersgracht** (p131), aka the canal of the seven bridges. The 9 **house** at Reguliersgracht 34 has an unusual twin entrance and an eagle gable for the original owner, Arent van den Bergh (*arend* is a Dutch word for eagle).

Where the Keizersgracht and Reguliersgracht join up, there's a scene to outdo the mere seven bridges before: here you can count a whopping 10 **15 bridges** as you peer east–west and north–south. A few steps further south you'll come to the 11 **Amstelkerk** (p132), the curious wooden church with a belfry that still looks quite makeshift.

Head east down a quiet section of the Prinsengracht until you reach the shores of the Amstel river. From here you can admire the petite 12 **Magere Brug** (p132) and, beyond the *sluizen* (locks), the neon-lit roof of the 13 **Koninklijk Theater Carré** (p143).

STACH
CAFE €

Map p318 (www.stach-food.nl; Nieuwe Spiegelstraat 52; dishes €7.50-14.50; ⏲8am-10pm Mon-Sat, 9am-9pm Sun; 📶; 🚋7/10 Spiegelgracht) Stach's Southern Canal Ring branch is smaller than its flagship De Pijp premises (p195). But even if you don't score a seat here, it's an equally good option for pastas (like spinach and ricotta ravioli) and amazing sandwiches (such as carpaccio, truffle mayonnaise and rocket, or buffalo mozzarella, basil mayonnaise and tomato) on organic bread to take to a canal-side bench.

LOEKIE
SANDWICHES €

Map p318 (www.loekie.net; Utrechtsestraat 57; sandwiches €5-7.30; ⏲9.30am-5.30pm Mon-Sat; 🚋4 Keizersgracht) This delicatessen piles fresh, delicious ingredients into its takeaway sandwiches, such as smoked beef with egg and salt, or warm goat's cheese with pine nuts and honey. Ask for the English menu if it's not already on the counter.

LITE/DARK
CAFE €

Map p318 (www.litedark.nl; Utrechtsestraat 22; dishes €4-6; ⏲9am-7pm Mon-Fri, from 10am Sat & Sun; 🚋4 Keizersgracht) Somehow this hip, industrial-styled cafe manages to make a convincing case for the health benefits of chocolate (or at least the dark variety), serving chocolate shots and chocolate fondue alongside a huge range of 'lite' smoothies, energy shakes and wheatgrass shots. The short menu includes salads, bagels and sandwiches, as well as choc-dipped fruit.

ON YOUR BIKE IN THE SOUTHERN CANAL RING

MacBike (Map p318; ☎528 76 88; www.macbike.nl; Weteringschans 2; bike rental per 3/24hr from €7.50/9.25; ⏲9am-5.45pm; 🚋1/2/5/7/10 Leidseplein) Rents bikes near Leidseplein.

Mike's Bike Tours (Map p318; ☎622 79 70; www.mikesbiketoursamsterdam.com; Kerkstraat 134; city tours per adult/child from €22/19, countryside from €25/18; ⏲office 9am-6pm Mar-Oct, from 10am Nov-Feb; 🚋16/24 Keizersgracht) Tours depart across the road from the office at Kerkstraat 123. You can also hire bikes (per four/24 hours from €5/10).

★LA CACEROLA
BRAZILIAN €€

Map p318 (☎627 93 97; www.restaurantlacacerola.nl; Weteringstraat 41; mains €21.50-24.50; ⏲6-10.30pm Tue-Sat; 🚋7/10 Spiegelgracht) 🌿 At this rustic, romantic gem, dishes prepared according to traditional methods and Slow Food principals include wild sea bass marinated in lime juice; spiced rack of milk-fed lamb; and house-speciality *churrasco de picanha* (steak barbecued on a charcoal grill and served with spicy pumpkin purée). If you can't decide, go for the chef's surprise four-course menu (€34.50). Service is superb.

★BUFFET VAN ODETTE
CAFE €€

Map p318 (☎423 60 34; www.buffetvanodette.nl; Prinsengracht 598; mains lunch €8-15.50, dinner €15.50-19; ⏲kitchen 10am-10pm; 📶; 🚋7/10 Spiegelgracht) Not a buffet but an airy, white-tiled, sit-down cafe with a beautiful canal-side terrace, where Odette shows how good simple cooking can taste when you start with great ingredients and a dash of creativity. Soups, sandwiches, pastas and quiches are mostly organic with smart little extras like pine nuts or truffle cheese.

PANTRY
DUTCH €€

Map p318 (☎620 09 22; http://thepantry.nl; Leidsekruisstraat 21; mains €13-18, 3-course menus €20-28; ⏲11am-10.30pm; 👪; 🚋1/2/5 Leidseplein) Wood-panelled walls and sepia lighting make this *gezellig* (cosy, convivial) little restaurant an atmospheric place for classic Dutch cooking: *haring met uitjes en zuur* (salted herring with onions and pickles); *zuurkool stamppot* (sauerkraut and potato mash served with a smoked sausage or meatball); *hutspot* ('hotchpotch', with stewed beef, carrots and onions); and *stroopwafelijs* (caramel syrup-filled wafer-like waffles).

RON GASTROBAR ORIENTAL
ASIAN €€

Map p318 (☎223 53 52; www.rongastrobaroriental.nl; Kerkstraat 23; dishes €15; ⏲5.30-11pm; 📶; 🚋1/2/5 Prinsengracht) Ron Blaauw revolutionised dining at Ron Gastrobar (p178) near Vondelpark when he traded his Michelin stars for a one-price menu of tapas-style dishes, and he's recreated the red-hot concept here, this time with an Asian focus. Small plates include dim sum with foie gras, poached chicken with peanut sauce, Wagyu steak tartare, Oriental spare ribs, crispy prawns, and roast Peking duck.

LOCAL KNOWLEDGE

A PATISSERIE FIT FOR A KING

Patisserie Holtkamp (Map p318; www.patisserieholtkamp.nl; Vijzelgracht 15; dishes €2.45-6.50; ⌚8.30am-6pm Mon-Fri, to 5pm Sat, closed late Jul–mid-Aug; 🚋4/7/10/16/24 Weteringcircuit) There's been a bakery on this site since 1886; its gorgeous art-deco interior was added in 1928 by architect Piet Kramer. Look up to spot the gilded royal coat of arms, topped by a crown, attached to the brick facade. The bakery supplies the Dutch royals with sweet and savoury delicacies including *kroketten* (croquets) with fillings including prawns, lobster and veal.

They're also on the menu of some of the city's top restaurants.

IN DE BUURT INTERNATIONAL €€

Map p318 (www.inderbuurt-amsterdam.nl; Lijnbaansgracht 246; mains €14.50-20.50; ⌚kitchen 5-10pm Mon-Thu, from 3pm Fri, from 2pm Sat & Sun; 🚋1/2/5 Leidseplein) A canal-side summer terrace and interior of exposed brick walls and stainless-steel downlights provide a relaxed backdrop for fantastic mini burgers with truffle mayo and roasted cherry tomatoes, cannelloni stuffed with Dutch goats cheese and spinach, and grilled whole sea bream with tarragon oil, but the star of the show is the homemade chocolate- and pecan-brownie with white-chocolate sauce.

ROSE'S CANTINA MEXICAN €€

Map p318 (☎625 97 97; http://rosescantina.com; Reguliersdwarsstraat 38-48; mains €16.50-24; ⌚5.30-10.30pm; 📶; 🚋1/2/5 Koningsplein) Behind a demure black facade Rose's vivid lime-green-painted interior and courtyard are vibrant settings to tuck into fiesty Mexican fare. Starters such as ceviche (raw fish cured in lime juice) are followed by updated versions of Mexican classics like pulled pork or crab tacos, black bean–filled enchiladas with sour cream, and spicy sweet potato empanadas with chipotle mayo and salsa.

DE BLAUWE HOLLANDER DUTCH €€

Map p318 (☎627 05 21; www.deblauwehollander.nl; Leidsekruisstraat 28; mains lunch €4-7.50, dinner €14.50-19.50; ⌚noon-11pm; 🚋1/2/5 Leidseplein) Pancakes and fried eggs on bread are among the quintessential Dutch options for lunch at this red lamp-lit spot, but dinner offerings are much more substantial: homemade cheese croquettes; *stamppot* with pork sausage; a bacon-wrapped meatball with red cabbage; and calf's liver with apple- and potato-mash. Look for the Dutch flag flying out front.

CAFÉ VAN LEEUWEN MODERN EUROPEAN €€

Map p318 (www.cafevanleeuwen.nl; Keizersgracht 711; mains €7.50-19.50; ⌚kitchen 9am-10pm Mon-Fri, 10am-10pm Sat, 11am-9pm Sun; 🚋4 Keizersgracht) You can get a taste of the cooking at this canal-side *café* with snacks at *borrel* (drinks), but with a quality-to-price ratio this good, it's worth staying for a full meal. Top choices include char-grilled tuna steak on warm lentil salad; smoked Dutch sausage with *frites* (fries) and homemade coleslaw; and its house-speciality cheese and crispy bacon Leeuwen burger.

EVERYTHING ON A STICK INTERNATIONAL €€

Map p318 (☎626 18 74; www.eoas.nl; Prinsengracht 478; lunch mains €8.50-15, dinner Thu-Sat adult/child €27/13.50, Tue & Wed €25.50/13.50; ⌚6-11pm Tue-Sun; 👪; 🚋1/2/5 Prinsengracht) Everything at this cool, contemporary restaurant is served, yes, on skewers. Designed for sharing (you get two main sticks and a side per round, for an unlimited number of rounds over two hours), options include seaweed-wrapped prawns, honey and lemon beef, bacon-wrapped scallops in rosemary oil and Dutch spiced chicken. There's a €1 'fine' per uneaten dish. Different and delicious.

BOUCHON DU CENTRE FRENCH, LYONNAIS €€

Map p318 (☎330 11 28; www.bouchonducentreamsterdam.com; Falckstraat 3; mains €15-20; ⌚noon-3pm & 5-8pm Wed-Sat; 🚋4/7/10 Frederiksplein) Classic red-and-white cloths cover the tables at this faithfully re-created Lyonnais *bouchon* (informal, rustic bistro). The daily changing menu of a few dishes only revolves around *bouchon* staples such as *andouillette* (offal sausage) and *quenelles de brochet* (pike dumplings). Don't miss a round of wonderfully gooey St Marcellin cheese and Rhône Valley wines like Beaujolais.

PIET DE LEEUW STEAK €€

Map p318 (☎623 71 81; www.pietdeleeuw.nl; Noorderstraat 11; mains €12.50-21.50; ⌚noon-10.30pm Mon-Fri, from 5pm Sat & Sun; 🚋16/24 Keizersgracht) The building dates from 1900, but it's been a steakhouse and hangout since the 1940s, and the dark and cosy atmosphere has barely changed since. If you don't get your own table, you may make friends at a common table. Good-value steaks come with toppings like onions, mushrooms or bacon, served with salad and piping-hot *frites*.

STACEY'S PENNYWELL CAFE €€

Map p318 (www.staceys.nl; Herengracht 558; mains €9-21.50; ⏲9am-5pm Mon, 9am-10.30pm Tue-Sat, 9.30am-10.30pm Sun; 🚋4 Keizersgracht) Lovely crown mouldings and wrought ironwork chandeliers woo diners up to the second level, a perfect place to curl up on the comfy white-leather chairs to dine on impressive fare like smoked mackerel in green curry or halibut with lime butter and thyme-roasted potatoes. Cocktails are best on the lower level, with pillow-strewn couches overlooking the Herengracht canal.

TASTE OF CULTURE CHINESE €€

Map p318 (☎427 11 36; www.tasteofculture.net; Korte Leliedwarsstraat 139-141; dim sum €3.50-10, mains €13.50-32.50; ⏲5pm-1am Sun-Thu, to 3am Fri & Sat; 🚋1/2/5/7/10 Leidseplein) Freshly prepared regional dishes are enjoyed by a big Chinese clientele. Good options are the razor clams, Peking duck and pancakes, and various stir-fried greens. Added bonus: the kitchen is open late into the night.

PASTINI ITALIAN €€

Map p318 (☎622 17 01; www.pastini.nl; Leidsegracht 29; mains €13.50-23; ⏲6-10pm Mon-Sat; 🚋1/2/5 Keizersgracht) With a *gezellig,* rustic-Renaissance interior and a can't-beat-it location facing two canals, Pastini also wins praise for its pastas – including its signature *tagliatelle gamberi* (Dutch prawns, sweet peppers, spicy chillies, anchovies and garlic) – and exceptionally reasonable prices. A speciality is the three-choice antipasto starter, but save room for *pastina di cioccolata* (dark chocolate tart) for dessert.

BOJO INDONESIAN €€

Map p318 (☎622 74 34; www.bojo.nl; Lange Leliedwarsstraat 49-51; mains €11.50-17.50; ⏲4pm-midnight; 🚋1/2/5 Prinsengracht) After a night on the town, there's nothing like some Indonesian. Bojo is a late-night institution that's surprisingly peaceful, given the location. Clubbers come for sizzling satay, filling fried rice and steaming bowls of noodle soup.

LO STIVALE D'ORO ITALIAN €€

Map p318 (☎638 73 07; www.lostivaledoro.nl; Amstelstraat 49; pizza €7.50-12.50, mains €8-22.50; ⏲5-10.30pm Wed-Mon; 🚋4/9/14 Rembrandtplein) Enjoy awesome pizzas and pastas at this trattoria's chummy tables. Gregarious Italian owner Mario occasionally pulls out his guitar and strums for the crowd.

★RESTAURANT FYRA MODERN EUROPEAN €€€

Map p318 (☎428 36 32; www.restaurantfyra.nl; Noorderstraat 19-23; 3-/4-/5-/6-course menus €36/42.50/47.50/52.50; ⏲6-11pm; 🚋16/24 Weteringcircuit) Many of the vegetables and herbs at this local foodies' favourite are grown in the owner/chef's garden and used in stunning creations like pea and mint soup with local prawns; barbecued tenderloin with potato mousseline; and marinated peaches with Dutch yoghurt, meringue and pomegranate syrup. There's a wonderful selection of artisan cheeses and well-chosen wines.

The setting, inside a traditional brick building framed by French doors, is contemporary and elegant.

TEMPO DOELOE INDONESIAN €€€

Map p318 (☎625 67 18; www.tempodoeloerestaurant.nl; Utrechtsestraat 75; mains €23.50-38.50, rijsttafel & set menus €29-49; ⏲6-11.30pm Mon-Sat; ✍; 🚋4 Prinsengracht) Consistently ranked among Amsterdam's finest Indonesian restaurants, Tempo Doeloe's setting and service are elegant without being overdone. The same applies to the rijsttafel: a ridiculously overblown affair at many places, here it's a fine sampling of the range of flavours found in the country. Warning: dishes marked 'very hot' are indeed like napalm. The wine list is excellent.

SUPPERCLUB MODERN DUTCH €€€

Map p318 (☎638 05 13; www.supperclub.com; Singel 460; 5-course menu €69; ⏲from 8pm; 🚋1/2/5 Koningsplein) If you're looking for a scene, you've found one. Enter the theatrical room, snuggle on the mattresses (here beds take the place of tables and chairs) and snack on victuals as DJs spin house music. Meals are accompanied by provocative and entertaining performance art. If the five-course menu is too much, you can also order à la carte.

HERENGRACHT RESTAURANT & BAR MODERN EUROPEAN €€€

Map p318 (☎616 24 82; www.deherengracht.com; Herengracht 435; mains lunch €9.50-26, dinner €22-26; ⏲kitchen 11am-10.30pm; 🚋1/2/5 Koningsplein) If the canal-side terrace is full, Herengracht not only has a sleek interior but also a beautiful leafy rear courtyard for dining al fresco on starters like buckwheat blinis with pea purée, roast beetroot and Messenklever cheese, mains such as veal loin, liver and sweetbread with onion and bacon sauce, and rhubarb crème brûlée with green-apple sorbet for dessert.

VAN VLAANDEREN FRENCH €€€

Map p318 (☎622 82 92; www.restaurant-vanvlaanderen.nl; Weteringschans 175; mains €24.50-29.50; ⏲noon-3pm & 6-10pm Tue-Fri, 6-10pm Sat; 🚋4/7/10/16/24 Weteringcircuit) One of the best French restaurants in town, Van Vlaanderen has lovely canal views from a raised deck. The fine nuances of dishes, such as smoked duck breast with pan-fried foie gras, roast beef striploin with sweetbread, chicory and truffle jus, and raspberry and elderflower soufflé make all the difference. There are also superb multicourse menus.

DRINKING & NIGHTLIFE

With theatre *cafés* (bars), brown *cafés* (pubs), gay bars, coffeeshops and clubs galore, this area requires a serious strategy. Want to party with other travellers? Head to the bars of Leidseplein. Want to dance? Rembrandtplein's the ticket. Utrechtsestraat is great for local haunts. The gay scene centres on and around Reguliersdwarsstraat.

★BAR MOUSTACHE BAR

Map p318 (www.barmoustache.nl; Utrechtsestraat 141; ⏲8am-1am Mon-Thu, 8am-3am Fri, 9am-3am Sat, 9am-1am Sun; 🚋4 Prinsengracht) With an exposed-brick, minimalist interior designed by Stella Willing, this loft-style cafe-bar has a mix of communal and private tables that fill with hip locals, and a couple of coveted windowsill benches to watch the action along Utrechtsestraat. There's a stunning, pared-down Italian menu and a great drink selection including Italian wines by the glass.

★EIJLDERS BROWN CAFE

Map p318 (www.cafeeijlders.nl; Korte Leliedwarsstraat 47; ⏲4.30pm-1am Mon-Wed, noon-1am Thu & Sun, noon-2am Fri & Sat; 🚋1/2/5/7/10 Leidseplein) During WWII, this beautiful stained-glass brown *café* was a meeting place for artists who refused to toe the cultural line imposed by the Nazis, and the spirit lingers on. It's still an artists' cafe, hosting regular poetry readings (sometimes in English – call to be sure), jam sessions and exhibitions.

★AIR CLUB

Map p318 (www.air.nl; Amstelstraat 16; ⏲Thu-Sun; 🚋4/9/14 Rembrandtplein) One of Amsterdam's 'it' clubs, Air has an environmentally friendly design by Dutch designer Marcel Wanders including a unique tiered dance floor. Bonuses include lockers and refillable cards that preclude fussing with change at the five bars. The awesome sound system attracts cutting-edge DJs spinning everything from disco to house and techno to hip-hop. Hours vary; dress to impress.

DE KROON GRAND CAFE

Map p318 (www.dekroon.nl; Rembrandtplein 17; ⏲4pm-1am Mon-Thu, 4pm-4am Fri, 11am-4am Sat, 11am-1am Sun; 🚋4/9/14 Rembrandtplein) Restored to its original 1898 splendour, De Kroon has high ceilings, velvet chairs, and a beautiful art-deco-tiled staircase up the two floors above Rembrandtplein (there's also a lift). Sit at the atmospheric English-library-themed bar and be mesmerised by the curious display of 19th-century medical and scientific equipment.

SWEET CUP COFFEE

Map p318 (www.sweetcupcafe.com; Lange Leliedwarsstraat 101; ⏲8am-6pm Mon & Wed-Fri, 9am-6pm Sat, 11am-6pm Sun; 🚋1/2/5 Leidseplein) Run by a fun-loving young Dutch couple, this aromatic microroastery supplies coffee to many local cafes, but you can drink it here at the source or pick up a cup to take away, with a choice of five espresso styles and five slow brews. It also sells roasted beans.

PATA NEGRA WINE BAR

Map p318 (www.pata-negra.nl; Utrechtsestraat 124; ⏲noon-1am Sun-Thu, to 3am Fri & Sat; 🚋4 Prinsengracht) The freshly squeezed margaritas are tops at this Spanish tapas bar. Its rustic tiled exterior is matched by a vibrant crowd inside, especially on weekends, downing sangria with garlic-fried shrimps

AMSTERDAM AMERICAN HOTEL

The gorgeous **Amsterdam American Hotel** (Map p318; ☎556 30 00; www.edenamsterdamamericanhotel.com; Leidsekade 97; 🚋1/2/5/7/10 Leidseplein) got its name because the founder of the original hotel, CAA (Cornelis Alidus Anne) Steinigeweg, spent many years in the USA and helped establish a Dutch settlement on Grand Island, New York. Steinigeweg ensured that architect Ed Cuypers adorned the Viennese Renaissance–style building with abundant Americana – life-sized Native American chiefs and their squaws as well as a 4m heraldic eagle over the entrance.

Completed in the early 1880s, less than two decades later it had already become too small and was demolished to make way for the magnificent replacement you see today. Also in Viennese Renaissance style and topped by a belltower, the new **hotel** (p233) opened at the turn of the 20th century; its art-nouveau design is the work of architect Willem Kromhout.

The hotel's **Café Americain**, a heritage-listed showpiece with a beautifully restored art-nouveau interior featuring stained glass, exquisite light fittings and murals, has long been affectionately dubbed 'Amsterdam's living room'.

and grilled sardines (tapas costs €4.50 to €10). It gets packed, and that's half the fun.

DOOR 74 — COCKTAIL BAR

Map p318 (☎06 3404 5122; www.door-74.nl; Reguliersdwarsstraat 74; ⏲8pm-3am Sun-Thu, to 4am Fri & Sat; 🚋9/14 Rembrandtplein) You'll need to leave a voice message or, better yet, send a text for a reservation to gain entry to this cocktail bar behind an unmarked door. Some of Amsterdam's most amazing cocktails are served in a classy, dark-timbered speakeasy atmosphere beneath pressed-tin ceilings. Themed cocktail lists change regularly. Very cool.

CAFÉ SCHILLER — THEATRE CAFE

Map p318 (http://cafeschiller.nl; Rembrandtplein 26; ⏲4pm-1am Mon-Thu, 4pm-2am Fri, 2pm-2am Sat, 2pm-1am Sun; 🚋4/9/14 Rembrandtplein) Most *cafés* would pay a fortune to re-create Schiller's fabulous art-deco interior, but this is original. Walls are lined with portraits of Dutch actors and cabaret artists from the 1920s and '30s. Bar stools and booths are often occupied by pre- and post-theatre goers.

CAFÉ DE WETERING — BROWN CAFE

Map p318 (Weteringstraat 37; ⏲4pm-1am Mon-Thu, 4pm-3am Fri, 3pm-3am Sat, 3pm-1am Sun; 🚋7/10 Spiegelgracht) Bursting with locals of all ages, perennial favourite Café de Wetering is tucked into one of central Amsterdam's hidden streets, not far from the antiques corridor of Nieuwe Spiegelstraat. Perch on the upper level by the fireplace, or at the bar to chat with the wisecracking bartenders. On chilly days, it's an ideal refuge.

BACK TO BLACK — CAFE

Map p318 (www.backtoblackcoffee.nl; Weteringstraat 48; ⏲8am-6pm Mon-Fri, from 10am Sat & Sun; 🚋7/10 Spiegelgracht) If you like the furniture and artworks designed by local artists at this cool corner cafe, you can buy it – it's all for sale. Back to Black sources its Mexican, Ethiopian, Brazilian and Guatemalan coffee from local microroastery Sweet Cup (p138), and serves a small but stellar selection of cakes and pastries.

CAFÉ AMERICAIN — GRAND CAFE

Map p318 (☎556 30 10; www.cafeamericain.nl; Leidsekade 97, Amsterdam American Hotel; ⏲6.30am-10.30pm; 🚋1/2/5/7/10 Leidseplein) Within the Amsterdam American Hotel (p139), this art-nouveau monument, opened in 1902, was a *grand café* (bar) before the concept even existed. Its huge stained-glass windows overlook Leidseplein; there's a lovely terrace. High teas (2pm to 5pm Monday to Saturday; €29.50) and occasional Sunday jazz brunches are especially atmospheric (book ahead).

It also offers 'ice fondue' (€16 per person; minimum of two), where you dip fruit or chocolate in liquid nitrogen.

VAN DYCK BAR — CLUB

Map p318 (www.vandyckbar.com; Korte Leliedwarsstraat 28-32; ⏲10pm-4am Wed, Thu & Sun, to 5am Fri & Sat; 🚋1/2/5/7/10 Leidseplein) Van Dyck brings Ibiza-style clubbing to Amsterdam, with wicked lighting and sound systems and

DJs who know how to pack the dance floor. There's usually no cover before midnight; dress up to get past the door.

ESCAPE CLUB

Map p318 (www.escape.nl; Rembrandtplein 11; ⏲11pm-4am Thu & Sun, to 5am Fri & Sat; 🚊4/9/14 Rembrandtplein) A fixture of Amsterdam nightlife for two decades, this cavernous club is among the city's slickest. Its multispace layout includes the cream of local and international DJs rocking several dance floors, a video-screen-filled studio and an adjoining cafe. Dress up or you may not get in, and bring correct change for the toilets (€0.50).

CAFÉ BRECHT CAFE

Map p318 (www.cafebrecht.nl; Weteringschans 157; noon-1am Sun-Thu, to 3am Fri & Sat; 🚊4/7/10/16/24 Weteringcircuit) Named after the seminal German dramatist and poet, Bertolt Brecht, this may be the only establishment in Amsterdam with German poetry inscribed on the walls. The young and gorgeously rumpled dig the funky, elegant, lounge-room vibe created by mismatched velvet chairs, vintage lamps, and plenty of books and board games.

LION NOIR COCKTAIL BAR

Map p318 (www.lionnoir.nl; Reguliersdwarsstraat 28; ⏲noon-1am Mon-Thu, noon-3am Fri, 6pm-3am Sat, 6pm-1am Sun; 🚊1/2/5 Koningsplein) With a Thijs Murré–designed interior of birdcages, taxidermied birds and plants, Lion Noir lures an A-lister crowd with fine dining, a fabulous terrace, and inspired cocktails like Dutch Garden (lychees, sweet and sour soda, cucumber and *jenever* – Dutch gin), Lionjito (rum, Cointreau, mint, lime, vanilla and organic apple juice) and Flatliner (tequila, sambuca and tabasco).

CAFÉ DE SPUYT BEER CAFE

Map p318 (www.cafedespuyt.nl; Korte Leliedwarsstraat 86; ⏲4pm-3am Mon-Thu, 3pm-4am Fri & Sat, 3pm-3am Sun; 🚊1/2/5/7/10 Leidseplein) Footsteps away from the bustling Leidseplein, the bar staff at this mellow, friendly *café* (bar/pub) will happily guide you through the massive chalkboard menu of more than 100 beers, from Belgian Trappist ales to American Sierra Nevada.

CHICAGO SOCIAL CLUB BAR

Map p318 (☎760 11 71; www.chicagosocialclub.nl; Leidseplein 12; ⏲bar 8pm-4am Sun-Thu, to 5am Fri & Sat, club from 11pm Thu-Sat; 🚊1/2/5/7/10 Leidseplein) Comedy club Boom Chicago (p160) relocated to the Jordaan, but the 1923-founded intimate bar and club on Leidseplein is still going strong, with lots of techno and house, and a cool, unpretentious vibe. The minimum age is 21.

CAFÉ LANGEREIS CAFE

Map p318 (http://cafelangereis.nl; Amstel 202; ⏲11am-3am Sun-Thu, to 4am Fri & Sat; 📶; 🚊4/9/14 Rembrandtplein) Along the Amstel, Café Langereis feels like it's been here forever, in large part because the friendly young owner scoured the city for antique fixtures and furniture to re-create the lived-in vintage feel. Freshly ground coffee, fresh flowers on the tables, an upright piano and a classic rock soundtrack keep things vibrant.

MULLIGANS IRISH PUB

Map p318 (www.mulligans.nl; Amstel 100; ⏲4pm-1am Mon-Thu, 4pm-3am Fri, 2pm-3am Sat, 2pm-1am Sun; 📶; 🚊4/9/14 Rembrandtplein) Amsterdam's most 'authentic' Irish pub, Mulligans has properly poured Guinness and Magners cider on tap and great *craic* (fun), with live Irish trad music most nights from 9pm (no cover charge). Sunday sessions let you participate: BYOI (instrument) and T (talent). On Wednesdays, sing along to Irish tunes in the back room.

UP CLUB

Map p318 (☎623 69 85; www.clubup.nl; Korte Leliedwarsstraat 26; ⏲11pm-4am Thu, to 5am Fri & Sat; 🚊1/2/5/7/10 Leidseplein) You might catch DJs spinning anything from disco, funk, soul, hip hop and deep house to live bands or performance art at this small, quirky club. Occasionally entrance is through De Kring, at Kleine Gartmanplantsoen 7-9; check the website.

A BAR COCKTAIL BAR

Map p318 (☎520 32 45; www.a-bar.nl; Professor Tulpplein 1, InterContinental Amstel Amsterdam; ⏲4pm-1am Mon-Thu, noon-1am Fri & Sat; Ⓜ Weesperplein) The bar at the InterContinental Amstel Amsterdam takes full advantage of its riverside location, opening to a huge sofa-lined terrace. Cocktails such as a Lavender Gin Flip use homemade syrups; it also serves Scandinavian-style bar food. Chilled DJ sessions and live music regularly take place.

WHISKEY CAFÉ L&B WHISKEY BAR

Map p318 (Korte Leliedwarsstraat 92; ⏲8pm-3am Sun-Thu, to 4am Fri & Sat; 🚊1/2/5/7/10 Leidseplein) If whiskey's your poison, skip the beer *cafés* and head straight to this convivial (and usually packed) bar, which stocks 1350 (yes, 1350) different varieties.

NEL BAR

Map p318 (www.nelamstelveld.nl; Amstelveld 12; ⏲10am-1am Sun-Thu, to 3am Fri & Sat; 👪; 🚊4 Prinsengracht) Inside there's a mellow brasserie on one side and a stylish bar on the other, but on a sunny afternoon there's nothing better than sitting under the lush canopy of trees.

NJOY COCKTAIL BAR

Map p318 (www.njoycocktails.com; Korte Leidsedwarsstraat 93; ⏲5pm-3am Sun-Thu, to 4am Fri & Sat; 🚊1/2/5/7/10 Leidseplein) Creative cocktails at this little vixen of a bar are grouped by personality. If you're a 'trendsetter', you might go for a Blazing Mule (fresh ginger and chilli-infused vodka), if you're a 'dreamer', maybe Pandora's Potion (blackberries, mint and vanilla vodka), a 'sparkling star' might try Absolutely Flawless (strawberries, vanilla liqueur, and of course, champagne).

Other personalities span 'Virgin' to 'Connoisseur' and 'Alchemist'. Its chilled-out vibe is a refreshing break from the madness of the street outside; under 23s aren't admitted. Ask about its cocktail-making courses.

OOSTERLING BROWN CAFE

Map p318 (Utrechtsestraat 140; ⏲3pm-midnight Mon-Wed, noon-1am Thu-Sat, 1-8pm Sun; 🚊4 Prinsengracht) Opened in the 1700s as a tea

SOUTHERN CANAL RING GAY & LESBIAN SCENE

For the best gay action in the 'hood, head to Reguliersdwarsstraat and cruise around to see what takes your fancy. Bear in mind that venues on Reguliersdwarsstraat tend to come and go. Keep your eyes open for new bar and club openings.

Amsterdam's other major **hubs** (p49) of gay and lesbian life include Zeedijk and Warmoesstraat in the Red Light District.

Montmartre (Map p318; www.cafemontmartre.nl; Halvemaansteeg 17; ⏲5pm-1am Sun-Thu, to 4am Fri & Sat; 🚊4/9/14 Rembrandtplein) Regarded by many as the best gay bar in the Benelux, and a busy weekend will show why. Patrons sing along (or scream along) to recordings of Dutch ballads and old top-40 hits.

Taboo Bar (Map p318; www.taboobar.nl; Reguliersdwarsstraat 45; ⏲5pm-3am Mon-Thu, 5pm-4am Fri, 4pm-4am Sat, 4pm-3am Sun; 📶; 🚊1/2/5 Koningsplein) Taboo's wicked two-for-one happy hours (6pm to 7pm and midnight to 1am, plus 6pm to 8pm Sunday) guarantee a good time. Wednesday is cocktail night, when cocktails cost just €6 and a drag show and competitions like 'pin the tail on the sailor' take place.

Vivelavie (Map p318; www.vivelavie.net; Amstelstraat 7; ⏲4pm-3am Sun-Thu, 3pm-4am Fri, 1pm-4am Sat; 📶; 🚊4/9/14 Rembrandtplein) Flirty girls, good-natured staff, loud music, large windows and dancing make this one of Amsterdam's most popular lesbian *cafés*. In summer the outdoor terrace buzzes.

The Otherside (Map p318; www.theotherside.nl; Reguliersdwarsstraat 6; ⏲11am-1am; 🚊1/2/5 Koningsplein) House and lounge music make this brilliantly named coffeeshop a hopping and trendy place. It's in the neighbourhood's main gay street and welcomes a mixed gay, lesbian and straight crowd.

Lellebel (Map p318; www.lellebel.nl; Utrechtsestraat 4; ⏲9pm-3am Mon-Wed, 1pm-3am Thu, 1pm-4am Fri & Sat, 3pm-3am Sun; 📶; 🚊4/9/14 Rembrandtplein) This hole in the wall just off Rembrandtplein has karaoke, singing and comedy drag shows that bring out the best in any girl's wardrobe. It can get bitchy, but always in the funniest possible way.

Church (Map p318; www.clubchurch.nl; Kerkstraat 52; ⏲8pm-1am Tue & Wed, 10pm-4am Thu, 10pm-5am Fri & Sat, 4-8pm Sun; 🚊1/2/5 Keizersgracht) This hardcore gay nightclub gives a whole new meaning to the phrase 'I'm going to church'. Unless you come dressed appropriately for the evening (S&M, leather, birthday suits...check the website for events) or with super-hot boys (or happen to be one yourself) you probably won't get in to this high-action cruise spot, but they'll be terribly nice about it.

and coffee outlet for the Dutch East India Company, Oosterling has been run by the same family since 1877 and is one of the very few *cafés* that has an off-licence bottle-shop (liquor-store) permit.

TWO FOR JOY — CAFE

Map p318 (www.twoforjoy.nl; Fredericksplein 29; 7.30am-7pm Mon-Fri, 8am-6pm Sat & Sun; 4 Prinsengracht) This skylit cafe on lush Fredericksplein takes coffee seriously. Choose from French press, lattes and several connoisseur styles of drip coffee (try the high-tech, Japanese-style 'Syphon' method).

BULLDOG — COFFEESHOP, BAR

Map p318 (www.thebulldog.com; Leidseplein 13-17; coffeeshop 9am-1am, bar 10am-1am Mon-Thu, 10am-3am Fri & Sat, 10am-2am Sun; ; 1/2/5/7/10 Leidseplein) Opened in a former police station on April Fool's Day 1985, this brawny, brassy branch of Amsterdam's most famous coffeeshop chain has two sides: one for smoking, one for drinking. Both crowds are pretty much the same: stag parties, backpackers and corporate travellers blowing off steam. It has multiple locations, a hotel, bike rental and even its own energy drink.

DOLPHINS COFFEESHOP — COFFEESHOP

Map p318 (Kerkstraat 39; 10am-1am; ; 1/2/5 Prinsengracht) Painted with huge fishtank-style murals, this surreal space feels like a larger-than-life set for *Finding Nemo*. Upstairs, there's table football and a pool table; you can also get toasties, pastries, tea and juices.

JIMMY WOO — CLUB

Map p318 (626 31 50; www.jimmywoo.com; Korte Leidsedwarsstraat 18; 11pm-4am Thu-Sun; 1/2/5/7/10 Leidseplein) Still a platform for the young and beautiful, venerable Jimmy Woo has fab light-and-sound shows and various club nights that cater for divergent tastes. And really long queues: be patient, or call ahead to get on the list.

SUZY WONG — DESIGNER BAR

Map p318 (www.suzy-wong.nl; Korte Leidsedwarsstraat 45; 6pm-1am Wed, Thu & Sun, to 3am Fri & Sat; 1/2/5/7/10 Leidseplein) With red-velveteen wallpaper and a bamboo garden, Suzy Wong's Victorian-drawing-room-on-speed look packs a visual punch. Join local celebs ordering fresh-fruit mojitos. On Wednesday's mojito nights, they cost just €5.

COFFEESHOP FREE — COFFEESHOP

Map p318 (Reguliersdwarsstraat 70; 10am-1am; 4/9/16/24 Muntplein) Little Coffeeshop Free has been sporting its lazy tiki-bar vibe in the Rembrandtplein area for decades. The South Seas mural inspires a trip to paradise, regardless of the weather outside.

> **LOCAL KNOWLEDGE**
>
> **PHOTOGRAPHING THE SEVEN BRIDGES**
>
> It's easy to focus on the raucous nightlife and forget that one of Amsterdam's most romantic canals flows in the neighbourhood. The **Reguliersgracht** (p131), aka the canal of seven bridges, is especially enchanting by night when its humpbacked arches glow with tiny gold lights.
>
> The best views are from aboard a boat; to get the money shot on land, stand with your back to the Thorbeckeplein and the Herengracht flowing directly in front of you to the left and right. Lean over the bridge and look straight ahead down the Reguliersgracht. Ahhh. Now kiss your sweetie.

ENTERTAINMENT

Much of the Southern Canal Ring's after-dark action gravitates towards two of Amsterdam's busy pleasure centres, Leidseplein and Rembrandtplein. Both are surrounded by a plethora of live-music venues and nightclubs with cutting-edge DJs. On Leidseplein, the grand Stadsschouwburg theatre stages major plays and festivals; smaller theatres and cinemas are scattered throughout the neighbourhood.

STADSSCHOUWBURG — THEATRE

Map p318 (624 23 11; www.stadsschouwburgamsterdam.nl; Leidseplein 26; box office noon-6pm Mon-Sat; 1/2/5/7/10 Leidseplein) In 1894, when this theatre with the grand balcony arcade was completed, public criticism was so fierce that funds for the exterior decorations never materialised. Architect Jan Springer couldn't handle this and promptly retired. The theatre is used for large-scale plays, operettas and festivals. Don't miss the chandeliered splendour of its **Stanislavski** (Map p318; Leidseplein 26, Stadsschouwburg; ⌚10am-1am Sun-Thu, to 3am Fri & Sat; 📶; 🚋1/2/5/7/10 Leidseplein) theatre *café*, and **International Theatre & Film Books** (Map p318; www.theatreandfilmbooks.com; Leidseplein 26, Stadsschouwburg; ⌚noon-6pm Mon, from 11am Tue-Sat; 🚋1/2/5/7/10 Leidseplein) shop.

MELKWEG LIVE MUSIC

Map p318 (www.melkweg.nl; Lijnbaansgracht 234a; ⌚6pm-1am; 🚋1/2/5/7/10 Leidseplein) In a former dairy, the nonprofit 'Milky Way' is a dazzling galaxy of diverse music. One night it's electronica, the next reggae or punk, and next heavy metal. Roots, rock and mellow singer-songwriters all get stage time, too. Check out the website for cutting-edge cinema, theatre and multimedia offerings.

PARADISO LIVE MUSIC

Map p318 (☎622 45 21; www.paradiso.nl; Weteringschans 6; ⌚hours vary; 🚋1/2/5/7/10 Leidseplein) This historic club in a gorgeous old church opened in 1968 as 'Cosmic Relaxation Center Paradiso'. Midweek club nights have low cover charges; the Small Hall upstairs is an intimate venue for up-and-coming bands. The real attraction, of course, is hearing artists like the White Stripes and Lady Gaga rock the Main Hall, wondering if the stained-glass windows might shatter.

SUGAR FACTORY LIVE MUSIC

Map p318 (www.sugarfactory.nl; Lijnbaansgracht 238; ⌚6pm-5am; 🚋1/2/5/7/10 Leidseplein) The vibe at this self-described 'cutting-edge multidisciplinary night theatre' is always welcoming and creative. It's definitely not your average club – most nights start with music, cinema, dance or a spoken-word performance, followed by late-night DJs and dancing. Sunday's Wicked Jazz Sounds party is a sweet one, bringing DJs, musicians, singers and actors together to improvise.

KONINKLIJK THEATER CARRÉ PERFORMING ARTS

Map p318 (☎524 94 52; http://carre.nl; Amstel 115-125; tour adult/child €9.50/6.50; ⌚box office 9am-9pm Mon-Fri, 10am-8pm Sat & Sun, one-hour tour 11am Sat; Ⓜ Weesperplein) This esteemed theatre was built in 1887 by the Carré family, who'd started their career with a horse act at the annual fair. The classical facade is richly decorated with faces of jesters, dancers and theatre folk. It hosts high-calibre musicals, theatre and dance events; its Christmas circus is a seasonal highlight. Saturday-morning tours are in English and Dutch.

The first structure was of wood, but it was eventually rebuilt in concrete because of the fire hazard (early performances for 2000 spectators were lit by gas lamps).

JAZZ CAFÉ ALTO JAZZ

Map p318 (www.jazz-cafe-alto.nl; Korte Leidsedwarsstraat 115; ⌚from 9pm; 🚋1/2/5/7/10 Leidseplein) Serious jazz and blues plays at this respected cafe near Leidseplein. Doors open at 9pm but music starts around 10pm – get here early if you want to snag a seat.

BOURBON STREET JAZZ & BLUES CLUB JAZZ, BLUES

Map p318 (www.bourbonstreet.nl; Leidsekruisstraat 6-8; ⌚10pm-4am Sun-Thu, to 5am Fri & Sat; 🚋1/2/5 Prinsengracht) Catch blues, funk, soul and rock and roll in this intimate venue, with open jam sessions on Mondays when everyone's welcome to take part. Tuesday is soul and reggae, Wednesday blues and rock, Thurday soul and funk, Friday rock, pop and Latin, Saturday pre-rock, and Sunday world, folk and samba. Entry's free before 11pm, when most concerts start.

DE HEEREN VAN AEMSTEL LIVE MUSIC

Map p318 (www.deheerenvanaemstel.nl; Thorbeckeplein 5; ⌚noon-3am Mon-Thu, to 4am Fri & Sat; 🚋4/9/14 Rembrandtplein) Students in particular cram into this *grand-café*-style club to enjoy the roster of live big bands and pop and rock cover bands.

LAST-MINUTE TICKETS

Not sure how to spend the evening? The **Uitburo** (Map p318; ☎624 23 11; www.lastminuteticketshop.nl; Leidseplein 26; ⌚shop noon-6pm, online ticket sales from 10am; 🚋1/2/5/7/10 Leidseplein) sells tickets (with a surcharge), and has a **Last Minute Ticket Shop**, selling same-day half-price seats. They're located in the **Stadsschouwburg** (p142), on the terrace side. Comedy, dance, concerts and even club nights are often available at a significant discount, and are handily marked 'LNP' (language no problem) if understanding Dutch isn't vital.

CAVE LIVE MUSIC

Map p318 (626 89 39; www.thecave.nl; Prinsengracht 472; live music tickets from €5; 8pm-3am Sun-Thu, to 4am Fri & Sat; 1/2/5 Prinsengracht) One for purists, this underground venue (in all senses; it's buried in a basement, hence its name) hosts live hard-rock and metal gigs Thursday to Saturday, and has DJs spinning the same the rest of the week.

CINECENTER CINEMA

Map p318 (www.cinecenter.nl; Lijnbaansgracht 236; 12.30pm-midnight Mon-Sat, from 10.30am Sun; 1/2/5/7/10 Leidseplein) European and American indie and art-house films play in four small screening rooms.

DE UITKIJK CINEMA

Map p318 (www.uitkijk.nl; Prinsengracht 452; 1/2/5 Prinsengracht) This fun art-house stalwart, located in a 1913 canal house is the city's second-oldest surviving cinema. For film buffs who know their Fuller from their Fellini.

PATHÉ TUSCHINSKITHEATER CINEMA

Map p318 (www.pathe.nl; Reguliersbreestraat 26-34; 11.30am-12.30am; 4/9/14 Rembrandtplein) Amsterdam's most famous cinema is worth visiting for its sumptuous art-deco/Amsterdam School interior alone. The *grote zaal* (main auditorium) is the most stunning and generally screens blockbusters; the smaller theatres play art-house and indie films.

DE KLEINE KOMEDIE THEATRE

Map p318 (www.dekleinekomedie.nl; Amstel 56-58; hours vary; 4/9/14 Rembrandtplein) This renowned little theatre, founded in 1786, puts on concerts, dance, comedy and cabaret, sometimes in English.

SHOPPING

From sleek Dutch fashion and design to colourful bouquets and rare Dutch *jenever*, the variety of goods on offer in the Southern Canal Ring is nothing short of staggering. The Nieuwe Spiegelstraat (aka the Spiegel Quarter) is renowned for its antique stores, bric-a-brac collectables, tribal and oriental art, and commercial art galleries.

YOUNG DESIGNERS UNITED CLOTHING

Map p318 (YDU; www.ydu.nl; Keizersgracht 447; 1-6pm Mon, 10am-6pm Tue, Wed, Fri & Sat, 10am-8pm Thu; 1/2/5 Keizersgracht) Racks are rotated regularly at this affordable women's clothing boutique showcasing young designers working in the Netherlands. You might spot durable basics by Agna K, handmade leggings by Leg-Inc; geometric dresses by Fenny Faber; and 'punk rock grunge meets fairytale romance' fashion by Jutka en Riska. Accessorise with YDU's select range of jewellery and bags.

MAISONNL HOMEWARES, CLOTHING

Map p318 (www.maisonnl.com; Utrechtsestraat 118; 1-6pm Mon, 10.30am-6pm Tue-Sat, 1-5pm Sun; 4 Prinsengracht) This gorgeous little concept store looks like a cross between an art gallery and someone's stylish apartment. Artfully displayed products range from tea sets to baby shoes, lamps to shawls, jewellery to leather handbags; there's a clothing rack down the back.

MOBILIA HOMEWARES

Map p318 (www.mobilia.nl; Utrechtsestraat 62; 9.30am-6pm Mon-Sat; 4 Prinsengracht) Dutch and international design is stunningly showcased at this three-storey 'lifestyle studio': sofas, workstations, bookshelves, lighting, cushions, rugs and much more from both emerging and established designers.

CENTRE NEUF CLOTHING

Map p318 (http://centreneuf.com; Utrechtsestraat 120; 1-6pm Mon, 10am-6pm Tue-Sat, 1-5pm Sun; 4 Prinsengracht) Centre Neuf is a favourite with fashion-savvy locals for to-die-for pieces from IRO, Pomandére, YMC, Marc by Marc Jacobs, Athé by Vanessa Bruno, Aaiko, Dante 6 and Avril Gau. Luscious handbags and shoes, too.

SKATEBOARDS AMSTERDAM SPORTS

Map p318 (http://skateboardsamsterdam.nl; Vijzelstraat 77; 1-6pm Sun & Mon, 11am-6pm Tue, Wed, Fri & Sat, 11am-8pm Thu; 16/24 Keizersgracht) Local skater dudes and dudettes shop for cruisers, long boards, shoes, laces, clothing including Spitfire and Skate Mental t-shirts, caps, beanies, bags and backpacks, books and music at this independent boutique.

MARAÑON HANGMATTEN OUTDOORS

Map p318 (www.maranon.net; Singel 488; 10.30am-5.15pm Mon-Fri, 10am-5.30pm Sat,

ART SHOPPING IN THE SOUTHERN CANAL RING

Walls Gallery (Map p318; ☎616 95 97; http://walls.nl; Prinsengracht 737; ⌚noon-6pm Wed-Sun; 🚋1/2/5 Prinsengracht) A former garage now houses this edgy art gallery, which hosts six to eight exhibitions a year and also represents young, up-and-coming art students (meaning prices are reasonable).

Mark Raven Amsterdam Art (Map p318; www.markraven.nl; Leidsestraat 42; ⌚10.30am-6pm; 🚋1/2/5 Keizersgracht) For a souvenir with a difference, visit Dutch artist Mark Raven's gallery where he displays and sells his charming paintings, drawings and sketches of Amsterdam's cityscapes as artworks but also printed on T-shirts, hoodies, posters and coffee mugs.

Lieve Hemel (Map p318; www.lievehemel.nl; Nieuwe Spiegelstraat 3; ⌚noon-6pm Tue-Sat; 🚋16/24 Keizersgracht) You'll find magnificent, contemporary Dutch realist paintings and sculptures at this smart gallery. It shows works by Dutch painters Ben Snijders and Theo Voorzaat, and astounding, lifelike representations of clothing – hewn from wood – by Italian Livio de Marchi.

Jaski (Map p318; www.jaski.nl; Nieuwe Spiegelstraat 27-29; ⌚noon-6pm; 🚋16/24 Keizersgracht) This large commercial gallery sells paintings, prints, ceramics and sculptures by some of the most famous members of the CoBrA (Copenhagen, Brussels, Amsterdam) movement.

Reflex Modern Art Gallery (Map p318; http://reflexamsterdam.com; Weteringschans 79a; ⌚11am-6pm Tue-Sun; 🚋7/10 Spiegelgracht) This prominent gallery, opposite the Rijksmuseum, is filled with contemporary art and photography, including works by members of the CoBrA and Nouveau Réaliste movements.

10.30am-5pm Sun; 🚋1/2/5 Koningsplein) Anyone who loves hanging around should come here and explore Europe's largest selection of hammocks. The colourful creations, made of everything from cotton to pineapple fibres, are made by many producers, from indigenous weavers to large manufacturers. It ships worldwide.

CORA KEMPERMAN — CLOTHING

Map p318 (☎625 12 84; www.corakemperman.nl; Leidsestraat 72; ⌚noon-6pm Sun & Mon, 10am-6pm Tue, Wed, Fri & Sat, 10am-9pm Thu; 🚋1/2/5 Prinsengracht) Kemperman was once a designer with large Dutch fashion houses, but since 1995 she's been working on her own empire – now encompassing nine stores, including three in Belgium. Her well-priced creations feature mainly solid colours, floaty, layered separates and dresses in linen, cotton and wool.

TINKERBELL — CHILDREN

Map p318 (www.tinkerbelltoys.nl; Spiegelgracht 10; ⌚1-6pm Mon, 10am-6pm Tue-Sat, noon-5pm Sun; 🚋7/10 Spiegelgracht) The mechanical bear blowing bubbles outside this shop fascinates kids, as do the intriguing technical and scientific toys inside. You'll also find historical costumes, plush toys and a section for babies.

EDUARD KRAMER — ANTIQUES

Map p318 (www.antique-tileshop.nl; Prinsengracht 807; ⌚11am-6pm Mon, 10am-6pm Tue-Sat, 1-6pm Sun; 🚋7/10 Spiegelgracht) Specialising in antique Dutch tiles, this tiny store is also crammed with lots of other interesting stuff – silver candlesticks, crystal decanters, jewellery and pocket watches.

VLIEGER — STATIONERY

Map p318 (www.vliegerpapier.nl; Amstel 34; ⌚noon-6pm Mon, 9am-6pm Tue-Fri, 11am-5.30pm Sat; 🚋4/9/14 Rembrandtplein) Since 1869 this two-storey shop has been supplying upmarket paper to Amsterdam: Egyptian papyrus, lush handmade papers from Asia and Central America, papers inlaid with flower petals or bamboo and paper with a texture that looks like snake skin. It also sells indestructible, recycled Freitag messenger bags (to safely tote away all that paper on your bike?).

CITYBOEK — ART, BOOKS

Map p318 (☎627 03 49; www.cityboek.nl; Kerkstraat 211; ⌚by appointment; 🚋16/24 Keizersgracht) Skip the commercial souvenir shops and head to this small publishing house for precisely drawn, multicoloured, architecturally faithful prints, books, postcards, posters and placemats of Amsterdam's canal-scapes such as images of the Herengracht or Singel.

STADSBOEKWINKEL BOOKS

Map p318 (www.stadsboekwinkel.nl; Vijzelstraat 32; ⏲10am-5pm Tue-Fri, from noon Sat & Sun; 🚊16/24 Keizersgracht) Run by the city printer, this is the best source for books about Amsterdam's history, urban development, ecology and politics. Most titles are in Dutch (if you don't read it, you can always look at the pictures), but you'll also find some in English. It's in the Stadsarchief (p130) archives building.

GONE WITH THE WIND CHILDREN

Map p318 (www.gonewiththewind.nl; Vijzelstraat 22; ⏲noon-6pm Mon, 10am-6pm Tue-Sat, noon-5pm Sun; 🚊16/24 Keizersgracht) Most of the toys, train sets and games here are made from high-quality wood, as are the shop's speciality, fluttering baby mobiles from around the world. There are also adorable finger puppets, whimsical gifts and jewellery.

HART'S WIJNHANDEL FOOD, DRINK

Map p318 (www.hartswijn.nl; Vijzelgracht 27; ⏲10am-6pm Mon, 9.30am-6pm Tue-Fri, 10am-5pm Sat; 🚊4/7/10/16/24 Weteringcircuit) Listen to classical music as you peruse the large selection of *jenever* and French and Italian wines at this genteel shop. It's been around since 1880 and supplies many a local restaurant with top tipples.

LOOK OUT CLOTHING

Map p318 (http://lookoutmode.nl; Utrechtsestraat 91 & 93; ⏲noon-6pm Mon, from 10am Tue-Sat; 🚊4 Prinsengracht) Searching through the racks at these wonderful neighbouring men's and women's stores is a real delight. Look out for super-stylish labels such as Soho De Luxe, Zenggi, Christian Peau, Fogal and Missoni.

LOCAL KNOWLEDGE

LOUNGING LIZARDS

Slow down alongside the Kleine Gartmanplantsoen park just near Leidseplein to spot 40 lizards nestled in the grass and sunning themselves on the brickwork. Cast in bronze, the surreal life-size reptiles, created by Dutch artist Hans van Houwelingen in 1994, are collectively known as **Blauw Jan** (Map p318; Kleine Gartmanplantsoen; 🚊1/2/5/7/10 Leidseplein). The title comes from an old Amsterdam inn of the same name which, in the 17th and 18th centuries, had a menagerie of exotic animals brought to the port city from faraway lands.

CONCERTO MUSIC

Map p318 (http://concerto.amsterdam; Utrechtsestraat 52-60; ⏲10am-6pm Mon, Wed & Sat, 10am-7pm Thu & Fri, noon-6pm Sun; 🚊4 Prinsengracht) Spread over several buildings, this rambling shop has Amsterdam's best selection of new and secondhand CDs and vinyl in every imaginable genre, from pop to classical, dance to world music and much more. It's often cheap and always interesting, and has good listening facilities.

CARL DENIG OUTDOOR EQUIPMENT

Map p318 (www.carldenig.nl; Weteringschans 113-115; ⏲noon-6pm Mon, 10am-6pm Tue, Wed & Fri, 10am-7pm Thu, 10am-5.30pm Sat; 🚊7/10 Spiegelgracht) Opened in 1912 this is Amsterdam's oldest and best outdoor retailer, though you pay for the quality. There are five floors of packs, tents, hiking and camping accessories, snowboards and skis (not that you'll get much use out of the last two in the Netherlands, but still).

SHIRT SHOP CLOTHING

Map p318 (www.shirtshopamsterdam.com; Reguliersdwarsstraat 64; ⏲1-7pm; 🚊4/9/16/24 Muntplein) On gay Amsterdam's main street, this funky, two-storey shop sells fabulous tight-fitting men's shirts and spurns global, mass-produced products.

HEINEKEN BRAND STORE SOUVENIRS

Map p318 (www.heinekenthecity.nl; Amstelstraat 31; ⏲noon-6pm Mon, from 10am Tue-Sun; 🚊4/9/14 Rembrandtplein) Heineken's multistorey concept store glows cool and green, just like a frosty bottle of the brew itself. Some of the logoed gear is over the top but the decorated beer bottles make groovy souvenirs. A 15-minute shuttle boat ride here is included in Heineken Experience (p189) admission.

EICHHOLTZ DELICATESSEN FOOD, DRINK

Map p318 (http://eichholtzdeli.nl; Leidsestraat 48; ⏲10am-6.30pm Mon, 9am-6.30pm Tue, Wed, Fri & Sat, 9.30am-9pm Thu, noon-6.30pm Sun; 🚊1/2/5 Keizersgracht) Americans missing Hershey's, Brits wanting Hobnobs and Aussies craving Vegemite will find them all – and much more – at this century-plus-old, import-specialist grocers.

Jordaan & the West

JORDAAN | THE WEST

For more detail of this area see Map p313, p314 and p316

Neighbourhood Top Five

❶ Losing yourself in the labyrinth of narrow streets and charming canals while walking through the **Jordaan** (p149), before spending the evening in the neighbourhood's atmospheric brown *cafés* (bars) – nothing is more quintessentially Amsterdam.

❷ Learning about the fascinating history and production of the country's favourite bloom at the **Amsterdam Tulip Museum** (p150).

❸ Listening to rare jazz and classical tunes play on vintage pianolas at the **Pianola Museum** (p149).

❹ Discovering what life is like on the city's waterways at the quaint **Houseboat Museum** (p150).

❺ Pedalling around the unique mash-up of reedy wilderness and old gasworks buildings turned into cafes and theatres in **Westerpark** (p151).

Lonely Planet's Top Tip

Be aware that trams 3 and 10 don't pass by Centraal Station, but take ring routes around the centre instead. If you're heading to areas such as Westerpark and Westergasfabriek from Centraal, a bus is by far your best bet.

Best Places to Eat

- Balthazar's Keuken (p154)
- Marius (p157)
- Restaurant Fraîche (p154)
- Brasserie Blazer (p154)
- Boca's (p151)

For reviews, see p151.

Best Places to Drink

- 't Smalle (p157)
- De Kat in de Wijngaert (p158)
- Cafe Soundgarden (p158)
- Tripel (p158)
- Westergasterras (p160)

For reviews, see p157.

Best Places to Shop

- Moooi Gallery (p162)
- Het Oud-Hollandsch Snoepwinkeltje (p162)
- Noordermarkt (p164)
- Antiekcentrum Amsterdam (p162)
- Back Beat Records (p162)

For reviews, see p162.

Explore Jordaan & the West

Though gentrified today, the Jordaan was a rough, densely populated *volksbuurt* (district for the common people) until the mid-20th century, and that history still shows. You'll discover that this neighbourhood is a curiously enchanting mix of its traditional gritty, hard-drinking, leftist character and its revitalised, trend-conscious sheen.

The area doesn't have many traditional sights, but that's not the point. It's the little things that are appealing here – the narrow lanes, the old facades, the funny little shops. The Jordaan is about taking your time wandering and not worrying if you get lost.

Start the day at the northern end of the Jordaan and crisscross towards the neighbourhood's south, catching the area's museums, architecture and, if you time it right, markets, along the way. Take a coffee break at one of the many canal-side cafes along the Prinsengracht.

On day two, go west. Hop on a bike and wend through the Western Islands before a spin around verdant Westerpark. In the evening, revel in the possibilities that any evening in the Westergasfabriek presents, from an art-house film to jazz or rock and roll.

Local Life

- **Market Life** Morning bliss in the Jordaan means cruising the weekly outdoor markets – Noordermarkt (p164), Lindengracht Market (p164) and Westermarkt (p164) – for mouthwatering food, bargain clothes and funky flea-market treasures.
- **Cultural Life** Locals flock to the former gasworks turned cutting-edge cultural complex, Westergasfabriek (p161).
- **Docklands Life** Two of Amsterdam's most extraordinary bar-restaurants – in a former offshore pirate radio and TV rig, and aboard a moored 1927-built ferry – are just north of the Western Islands in the Western Docklands (p155).

Getting There & Away

- **Tram** Trams 3 and 10 along Marnixstraat skirt the neighbourhood's western edge; trams 13, 14 and 17 along Rozengracht go through its centre.
- **Bus** Buses 18, 21, 22 and 48 provide the quickest access from Centraal to the neighbourhood's north, west and Western Islands.
- **Car** Whatever you do, don't try to drive through the Jordaan's narrow streets. Seriously.

SIGHTS

Jordaan

HAARLEMMERPOORT GATE

Map p314 (Haarlemmerplein; 🚊3 Haarlemmerplein) Once a defensive gateway to the city, the Haarlemmerpoort marked the start of the busy route to Haarlem, which was a major trading route. The structure was finished just in time for King William II's staged entry for his 1840 investiture, hence its little-known official name of Willemspoort (see the plaque inside).

Traffic no longer runs through the gate since a bypass was built over the Westerkanaal. Today this grand archway is home to apartments with an alluring view of the canal and Westerpark beyond.

BROUWERSGRACHT CANAL

Map p314 (🚊3 Haarlemmerplein) Pretty as a Golden Age painting, the Brewers Canal took its name from the many breweries located here in the 16th and 17th centuries. Goods such as leather, coffee, whale oil and spices also were stored and processed here in giant warehouses, such as those with the row of spout gables that still stand at Brouwersgracht 188–194.

The newspaper *Het Parool* dubbed the Brouwersgracht the most beautiful street in Amsterdam. It's a great a place to stroll and to see the waterborne action on King's Day (p23).

NOORDERKERK CHURCH

Map p314 (Northern Church; www.noorderkerk.org; Noordermarkt 48; ⏲10.30am-12.30pm Mon, 11am-1pm Sat; 🚊3/10 Marnixplein) Near the Prinsengracht's northern end, this imposing Calvinist church was completed in 1623 for the 'common' people in the Jordaan. (The upper classes attended the Westerkerk further south.) It was built in the shape of a broad Greek cross (four arms of equal length) around a central pulpit, giving the entire congregation unimpeded access to the word of God.

This design, unusual at the time, would become common for Protestant churches throughout the country.

Sunday services take place at 10am and 6.30pm. Noorderkerk also hosts the well-regarded Saturday afternoon **Nooderkerkconcerten** (Map p314; ☎620 44 15; www.nooderkerkconcerten.nl; tickets from €16; ⏲2pm Sat mid-Sep–mid-Jun) concert series.

PIANOLA MUSEUM MUSEUM

Map p314 (☎627 96 24; www.pianola.nl; Westerstraat 106; adult/child €5/3; ⏲2-5pm Thu-Sun Jul & Aug, Sun only Sep-Jun; 🚊3/10 Marnixplein) This is a very special place, crammed with pianolas from the early 1900s. The museum has around 50 of the instruments, although only a dozen are on display at any given time, as well as some 30,000 music rolls and a player pipe organ. The curator gives an hour-long (or so) guided tour and music demonstrations with great zest.

Every month, except July and August, concerts are held on the player-pianos, featuring anything from Mozart to Fats Waller and rare classical or jazz tunes composed especially for the instrument. More eclectic musical offerings include a popular tango series.

KOCHXBOS GALLERY

Map p314 (☎681 45 67; 1e Anjeliersdwarsstraat 36; ⏲1-6pm Wed-Sat; 🚊3/10 Marnixplein) FREE The art here goes by many names: North European low-brow, pop surrealism, contemporary underground. Whatever the label, the paintings, photos and digital prints are awesomely bright, weird and polychromatic. The welcoming space sits in the converted living room of an apartment.

AMSTERDAM CHEESE MUSEUM MUSEUM

Map p314 (☎331 66 05; www.cheesemuseumamsterdam.com; Prinsengracht 112; ⏲9am-7pm; 🚊13/14/17 Westermarkt) FREE It's a tourist ploy, but a good-humoured one. The main floor is a cheese shop with abundant samples laid out for noshing. The basement floor is the small 'museum' with a handful of exhibits, clothes you can don to look like a Dutch cheesemaker and snap a photo, and the world's most expensive cheese slicer (encrusted with diamonds).

EGELANTIERSGRACHT CANAL

Map p314 (🚊13/14/17 Westermarkt) Many parts of the Jordaan are named after trees and flowers and this canal, lined by lovely houses built for artisans and skilled traders, takes its name from the eglantine rose, or sweet briar.

ELECTRIC LADYLAND MUSEUM

Map p314 (www.electric-lady-land.com; 2e Leliedwarsstraat 5; adult/child €5/free; ⏲1-6pm Tue-Sat; 🚊13/14/17 Westermarkt) The world's first museum of fluorescent art features owner Nick Padalino's psychedelic sculpture work

TOP SIGHT
AMSTERDAM TULIP MUSEUM

Don't be dissuaded – or distracted – by the gift shop overflowing with floral souvenirs at the front of this small museum. And yes, it is small, but the Amsterdam Tulip Museum offers a comprehensive overview of the history of the country's favourite bloom and is a fascinating way to spend half an hour or so, especially before strolling the Southern Canal Ring's 'floating' flower market, the **Bloemenmarkt** (p129).

Through exhibits, timelines and two short films (in English), you'll learn how Ottoman merchants came across the flowers in the Himalayan Steppes and began commercial production in Turkey (the word tulip derives from 'turban' due to the petals' resemblance to the headwear). You'll also find out how fortunes were made and lost during Holland's '**Tulipmania**' in the 17th century, how bulbs were used as food in the war years and discover present-day methods of growing and harvesting the flower. The tulip paintings by 17th-century painter Judith Leijster (or Leyster), a student of Frans Hals, are a highlight; there's also a great collection of tulip vases designed to accommodate separate stems.

DON'T MISS

- The films
- Judith Leijster paintings
- The vase collection

PRACTICALITIES

- Map p314 C6
- ☎421 00 95
- www.amsterdamtulipmuseum.com
- Prinsengracht 112
- adult/child €5/3
- ⏲10am-6pm
- 🚋13/14/17 Westermarkt

on one side and cases of naturally luminescent rocks and manufactured glowing objects (money, government ID cards etc) on the other (his art gallery–shop is upstairs). Jimi Hendrix, the Beatles and other trippy artists play on the stereo while Nick lovingly describes each item in the collection.

BLOEMGRACHT — CANAL

Map p316 (Flower Canal; 🚋13/14/17 Westermarkt) In the 17th-century the 'Herengracht of the Jordaan', as the Bloemgracht was called, was home to paint and sugar factories, and a large number of fine gabled houses. A striking example is **De Drie Hendricken** (Map p316; Bloemgracht 87-91; 🚋3/14/17), built in a sober Renaissance style. The gable stones above the ground floor depict a townsperson, a farmer and a seafarer.

Many artists also lived on Bloemgracht, including Jurriaen Andriessen, whose work is displayed in the Rijksmuseum.

STEDELIJK MUSEUM BUREAU AMSTERDAM — MUSEUM

Map p316 (☎422 04 71; www.smba.nl; Rozenstraat 59; ⏲11am-5pm Wed-Sun; 🚋13/14/17 Westermarkt) FREE Don't blink or you might walk right past this unobtrusive outpost, a 'project space' of the Stedelijk Museum. It's in a former clothing workshop on a quiet block. Exhibits here – from painting and sculpture to new-media and installation pieces – present contemporary artists whose work reflects Amsterdam culture. It's well worth a peek.

Shows change about every two weeks; check ahead to make sure it's not closed while exhibitions are being set up.

HOUSEBOAT MUSEUM — MUSEUM

Map p316 (☎427 07 50; www.houseboatmuseum.nl; Prinsengracht 296k; adult/child €4.50/3.50; ⏲10am-5pm Jul & Aug, Tue-Sun only Mar-Oct, Fri-Sun only Nov-Feb, closed Jan; 🚋13/14/17 Westermarkt) This quirky museum, a 23m-long sailing barge from 1914, offers a good sense of how *gezellig* (cosy) life can be on the water. The actual displays are minimal, but you can watch a presentation on houseboats (some pretty and some ghastly) and inspect the sleeping, living, cooking and dining quarters with all the mod cons.

JOHNNY JORDAANPLEIN — SQUARE

Map p316 (cnr Prinsengracht & Elandsgracht; 🚋13/14/17 Westermarkt) This shady little square is named for Johnny Jordaan (the pseudonym of Johannes Hendricus van Musscher), a popular musician in the mid-1900s who sang the romantic music known as *levenslied* (tears-in-your-beer-style ballads). The colourfully painted hut – a municipal transformer station – proudly displays one of his song lyrics *'Amsterdam, wat bent je mooi'* (Amsterdam, how beautiful you are).

Behind the hut you'll find Johnny and members of the Jordaan musical hall of fame, cast in bronze. On King's Day, this is where many Jordaanians head to rock out to live music.

The West

Amsterdam's west might be off the beaten tourist track but the sights here are only a good 20-minute walk from Centraal Station. Don't miss the former western gasworks, which have been transformed into the Westergasfabriek (p161) cultural complex.

WESTERPARK PARK

Map p313 (Spaarndammerstraat & Zeeheldenbuurt; 3 Haarlemmerplein) Westerpark, which lends the surrounding neighbourhood its name, is a favourite spot for locals to unwind. Families push prams, couples hold hands and teams play cricket in the sweeping green space. When they're finished with the meadows and reedy marshes, people seek out the park's post-industrial buildings that have morphed into cafes, theaters, breweries and other creative spaces. It's a brilliant, eco-urban mash-up, prime for lolling away the day.

MUSEUM HET SCHIP MUSEUM

Map p313 (418 28 85; www.hetschip.nl; Spaarndammerplantsoen 140; admission €7.50; 11am-5pm Tue-Sun; 22 Zaanstraat) Just north of Westerpark over the train tracks, this remarkable 1921-completed housing project is a flagship of the Amsterdam School of architecture. Designed by Michel de Klerk for railway employees and loosely resembling a ship, the triangular block's rocket-like tower links the wings of the complex. Admission is by guided tour (English available).

ON YOUR BIKE IN THE JORDAAN

Bike City (626 37 21; www.bikecity.nl; Bloemgracht 68-70; bike rental per day from €14; 9am-5.30pm; 13/14/17 Westermarkt) These black bikes have no advertising on them, so you can freewheel like a local.

EATING

Jordaan

Restaurants here exude the conviviality that is a hallmark of the Jordaan. Many people gravitate to the eateries along Westerstraat, while the Haarlemmerbuurt offers increasingly trendy options. Or simply wander the narrow backstreets, where the next hot spot may be opening up. Self-caterers shouldn't miss the neighbourhood's markets (p164).

BOCA'S CAFE €

Map p314 (820 37 27; www.bar-bocas.nl; Westerstraat 30; bar snacks €5-8, platters from €16; 10am-1am Mon-Thu, 10am-3am Fri, 9am-3am Sat, 11am-1am Sun; 3/10 Marnixplein) Fronted by a red-and-white-striped awning and white-timber facade, this hip little bar is a perfect place for a drink accompanied by bar snacks. Try the mini lasagnes, burgers, bruschetta and steak tartare, or bigger platters on wooden boards: cheese platters, veggie platters, seafood platters, meat platters, sweet platters. If you can't decide, go for Boca's combination platter.

WINKEL CAFE €

Map p314 (www.winkel43.nl; Noordermarkt 43; mains €4.50-15.50; kitchen 7am-10pm Mon & Sat, from 8am Tue-Fri, from 10am Sun; ; 3/10 Marnixplein) This sprawling, indoor-outdoor space is great for people-watching, popular for coffees and small meals, and out-of-the-park for its tall, cakey apple pie. On market days (Monday and Saturday) there's almost always a queue out the door.

PAZZI PIZZA €

Map p316 (320 28 00; www.pazzislowfood.nl; 1e Looiersdwarsstraat 4; pizzas €8-15; 5-10pm; 7/10/17 Elandsgracht) Seating consists of a single, high banquette and there's one wood-burning oven. But each pizza – dripping with fresh buffalo mozzarella on a perfectly charred crust – is made with serious care. (Which gives you plenty of time to sip a beer and chat with your seatmates.)

ELLIS GOURMET BURGER BURGERS €

Map p316 (www.ellisgourmetburger.com; Prinsengracht 422; burgers €9-13; 11.30am-10pm Sun-Thu, to 11pm Fri & Sat; 1/2/5 Prinsengracht/Leidsestraat) The young and hungry congregate at Ellis to chomp into hefty burgers on the spread-out terrace. The menu goes beyond beef with the Bollywood

WESTERN ISLANDS

In the early 17th century, the wharves and warehouses of the **Western Islands** (Westelijke Eilanden; Map p313; 48 Barentszplein), north of the Jordaan, were abuzz with activity. The Golden Age was taking off, the Dutch still dominated the sea trade and money flowed into this old harbour like beer from a barrel. The wealthy Bicker brothers, both mayors of Amsterdam, even built their own Bickerseiland here to cater for their ships.

Few tourists visit here today, partly because the district is shielded from view by the railway line. Yet it's roughly a 10-minute walk (or five-minute bike ride) from Centraal Station and a wonderful area to explore, with cute drawbridges and handsome old warehouses nestled in quiet lanes. Many addresses have been converted to charming homes and artists' studios. The Prinseneiland (named in honour of the first three Princes of Orange) and Realeneiland (named after the 17th-century merchant Reynier Reael) are the two prettiest isles. The narrow bridge linking them, the **Drieharingenbrug** (Three Herrings Bridge; Map p313; Realengracht; 48 Barentszplein), is a quaint replacement for the pontoon that used to be pulled aside to let ships through.

On Realeneiland's eastern shore, be sure to visit the **Zandhoek** (Map p313; Realeneiland; 48 Barentszplein), a photogenic stretch of waterfront. It's now a modern yacht harbour, but back in the 17th century it was a 'sand market', where ships would purchase bags of the stuff for ballast. The street south of Zandhoek is the Galgenstraat (Gallows St), which on a clear day afforded a look at the executions in Amsterdam-Noord. In those days it was called entertainment.

Burger (marinated chicken, yoghurt-mint sauce and mango chutney) and several meatless options (portabello mushroom, soy burgers). Can't decide? Try the trio of mini burgers. Milkshakes, beer and sparkling wine add to the yum.

PIQNIQ — CAFE €

Map p314 (320 36 69; www.lunchcafepiqniq.nl; Lindengracht 59HS; picnics €8.50-10.50; 9am-5.30pm, closed Wed; 3/10 Marnixplein) Yep, you buy a picnic for your meal here. Mix and match from the changing list of sandwiches (bagel with smoked salmon and cream cheese, ciabatta with hummus), hot items (quiche, soup) and salads. Picnics come with two to four items and a drink. Despite the name, you don't have to take away; there's plenty of seating in the cute, sun-splashed room.

Most items can be made gluten free.

MONTE PELMO — ICE CREAM €

Map p314 (www.montepelmo.nl; 2e Anjeliersdwarsstraat 17; ice cream from €1.50; 1-10pm; 3/10 Marnixplein) Caramel cheesecake, Smurf sorbet, Red Bull and After Eight choc-mint are just some of the inventive flavours concocted by this ice-cream maker founded in 1957. Queues twist out the door in the evening.

FESTINA LENTE — CAFE €

Map p316 (638 14 12; www.cafefestinalente.nl; Looiersgracht 40b; sandwiches €6-8, small plates €4-8; noon-10.30pm Mon & Sun, 10.30am-10.30pm Tue-Sat; ; 7/10/17 Elandsgracht) This canal-side neighbourhood hang out is typical Jordaan *gezelligheid* (cosiness), packed with regulars playing board games, reading poetry and snacking on small-portion Mediterranean dishes and big sandwiches.

RIAZ — SURINAMESE, INDIAN €

Map p316 (683 64 53; www.riaz.nl; Bilderdijkstraat 193; mains €8-15; 1-9pm Mon-Fri, 2-9pm Sun; ; 7/17 Bilderdijkstraat) No-frills Riaz cooks up excellent rotis and an addictive, spicy peanut soup, as well as several Indian vegie dishes (the *saag,* aka spinach, is superb). Note that no alcohol is served and it closes on Saturdays.

DE PIZZA BAKKERS — ITALIAN €

Map p314 (427 41 44; www.depizzabakkers.nl; Haarlemmerdijk 128; mains €9-13; 5-10pm Sun-Thu, to 11pm Fri & Sat; 18/21/22 Buiten Oranjestraat) 'Pizza and Prosecco' is the credo at this arty eatery where you sip the Italian sparkling wine while waiting for delicious wood-fired varieties like pancetta and mascarpone, ham and truffle, or vegetarian with taleggio, aubergine and courgette. Other locations include the Plantage and near the Vondelpark. Cards only; no cash.

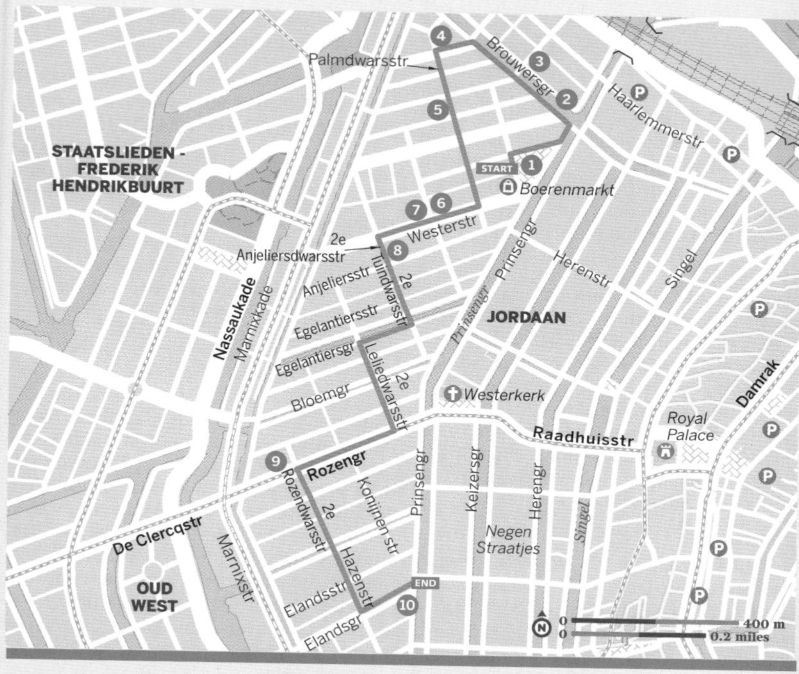

Neighbourhood Walk
Lost in the Jordaan

START NOORDERKERK
END JOHNNY JORDAANPLEIN
LENGTH 2.7KM; ONE HOUR

Begin at the 1 **Noorderkerk** (p149). Out front is the Noordermarkt, site of Amsterdam's most attractive *boerenmarkt* (farmers market), and a flea market.

Make your way north to 2 **Brouwersgracht** (p149). As you move west along this 'Brewers Canal', you'll see the old warehouses 3 **Groene & Grauwe Valk**. At the second drawbridge, turn left into Palmgracht and look out for the red door to the 4 **Rapenhofje** (at 28–38). This little courtyard was home to one of Amsterdam's oldest almshouses (1648).

South along Palmdwarsstraat you'll pass tiny food shops and restaurants frequented by locals. Note the stone tablet of the 5 **white fat pig** over the butcher/deli at 2e Goudsbloemdwarsstraat 26. Soon you'll reach Westerstraat, a main drag of the Jordaan, with the 6 **Pianola Museum** (p149), a weekly clothing market and alluring places for a bite or drink, such as 7 **Café 't Monumentje** (p159). At the 2e Anjeliersdwarsstraat, turn left to enter what locals call the 8 **garden quarter** of ivy-clad lanes and diminutive squares.

Zigzag your way down to Leliedwarsstraat and continue along until you hit busy Rozengracht. Speciality shops sell silk pillows and colourful kitchen wares, among other stock. 9 **Rembrandt's sterfhuis** (death house) is at 184, where the master painter died in 1669 (look upwards for a plaque marking the spot). The part of the Jordaan on 2e Rozendwarsstraat and around is a mad jumble of styles, and though the winch beams may appear decorative, they still see plenty of active duty. Secondhand stores, fancy boutiques and art shops pop up along the way.

Cross over the Lauriergracht, turning left into Elandsgracht. You will find 10 **Johnny Jordaanplein** (p150), a square dedicated to the local hero and singer of schmaltzy tunes such as 'Bij ons in de Jordaan' (With Us in the Jordaan).

BROODJE MOKUM SANDWICHES €

Map p316 (☎623 19 66; www.broodjemokum.nl; Rozengracht 26; sandwiches from €3; ⏲6.30am-6pm Mon-Fri, 8am-5pm Sat; 🚋13/14/17 Westermarkt) This humble, vintage lunch room serves great sandwiches – just point and they'll tell you the price. More so than at most other *broodje* (bread roll) shops, there's room to sit down and spread out on one of the many window-facing seats.

JORDINO SWEETS €

Map p314 (☎420 32 25; www.jordino.nl; Haarlemmerdijk 25; ice cream from €1.50; ⏲1-6.30pm Sun & Mon, from 10am Tue-Sat; 🚌18/21/22 Buiten Oranjestraat) It's the best of both worlds: Jordino makes rich chocolates and velvety ice cream and combines the two by scooping the ice cream atop cones dipped in the house's chocolate or caramel. Of its 80 flavours, 24 (including fruit-based sorbets) are available at any one time.

DUENDE TAPAS €

Map p314 (☎420 66 92; www.cafe-duende.nl; Lindengracht 62; tapas €4-9; ⏲kitchen 5-11pm Mon-Fri, from 4pm Sat & Sun; 🎵; 🚋3/10 Marnixplein) Fiesty house specialities at this long-running tapas *café* include *picantes mejillones* (mussels in spicy tomato sauce) and *pimientos de piquillo con bacalao* (sweet peppers stuffed with cod). The casual buzz in the evenings is enlivened by sultry flamenco performances on many Saturday nights and lessons during the week.

★BALTHAZAR'S KEUKEN MEDITERRANEAN €€

Map p316 (☎420 21 14; www.balthazarskeuken.nl; Elandsgracht 108; 3-course menu €32.50; ⏲6-10.30pm Wed-Sat; 🚋7/10/17 Elandsgracht) In a former blacksmith's forge, with a modern-rustic look, this is consistently one of Amsterdam's top-rated restaurants. Don't expect a wide-ranging menu: the philosophy is basically 'whatever we have on hand', which might mean wild sea bass with mushroom risotto or *confit* of rabbit, but it's invariably delectable. Reservations recommended.

RESTAURANT FRAÎCHE FRENCH €€

Map p314 (☎627 99 32; www.restaurantfraiche.nl; Westerstraat 264; mains €17-22; ⏲6.30-11.30pm Wed-Sat, noon-4pm Sun; 🚋3/10 Marnixplein) Cutting-edge French cuisine at this glass-fronted bistro changes seasonally but might include roast turbot and squid with pickled fennel and smoked carrot purée, or roast duck breast with butterscotch and foie gras sauce. There are various tasting plates too, plus brunch specials.

BRASSERIE BLAZER FRENCH €€

Map p316 (☎620 96 90; www.brasserieblazer.nl; Lijnbaansgracht 190; mains €14.50-23.50; ⏲kitchen noon-11pm; 🚋7/10/17 Elandsgracht) Inside the Antiekcentrum Amsterdam (p162) antique centre and opening out onto a narrow canal, Amsterdam's simplest French brasserie is also its most effortlessly sexy, with well-priced classic dishes – *confit de canard* (preserved duck), rib eye Béarnaise, et al. Try one of the house beers to wash it all down.

MANTOE AFGHANI €€

Map p314 (☎421 63 74; www.restaurantmantoe.nl; 2e Leliedwarsstraat 13; 4-course menu €32; ⏲5-11pm Wed-Sun; 🚋13/14/17 Westermarkt) Settle in for a special meal at Mantoe. An Afghan family runs the small restaurant, which is so snug and friendly it feels like you're eating in someone's home. There is no menu: it's just whatever they cook that day, perhaps steamed dumplings stuffed with minced meat and herbs, or a spicy lamb and rice dish. A good wine list tops it off.

Don't be in a hurry, as the multiple courses take a while.

YAM YAM ITALIAN €€

Map p316 (☎681 50 97; www.yamyam.nl; Frederik Hendrikstraat 88-90; mains €13-16; ⏲5.30-10pm Tue-Sun; 🚋3 Hugo de Grootplein) Ask Amsterdammers to name the city's best pizza and chances are it's this hip, contemporary trattoria. The wood-fired oven turns out thin-crust pizzas such as salami and fennel seed, and the signature Yam Yam (organic smoked ham, mascarpone and truffle sauce). There are mouthwatering pastas and fish- and meat-based mains. Creative desserts include orange-caramel *panna cotta* with balsamic and strawberries.

Reservations recommended.

SEMHAR ETHIOPIAN €€

Map p314 (☎638 16 34; www.semhar.nl; Marnixstraat 259-261; mains €15.50-20; ⏲4-10pm Tue-Sun; 🎵; 🚋10 Bloemgracht) Owner Yohannes gives his customers a warm welcome (as do the heavenly aromas wafting from the kitchen) and is passionate about the quality of his *injera* (slightly sour, spongy pancakes) used to scoop up richly spiced stews and vegetable combos. The most romantic tables are the handful at the back overlooking the canal.

WORTH A DETOUR

WESTERN DOCKLANDS

Just north of the Western Islands, Amsterdam's Western Docklands are home to two utterly unique restaurants – REM Eiland and Pont 13. Both restaurants are a 10-minute walk from the Oostzaanstraat bus stop: from Spaarndammerdijk, turn north onto Archangelweg, then east on Haparandaweg and east again on to Haparandadam and follow it to the end. Alternatively, take a taxi from Centraal Station (around €10 to €15), or hop on a bike (15 minutes).

Towering 22m above the IJ, the vivid red, oil rig–like structure of **REM Eiland** (688 55 01; www.remeiland.com; Haparandadam 45; lunch mains €8-14, dinner mains €18-20, 3-course menu €31; kitchen noon-4pm & 6-10pm; 48 Oostzaanstraat) was built in the 1960s as a pirate radio and TV broadcaster, and now houses an extraordinary restaurant with a 360-degree panorama over the industrial docklands and passing river traffic. Reached by steep metal staircases (or a lift/elevator), the dining rooms open onto wraparound platforms; the rooftop ex-helipad has an outdoor bar.

Casual lunches (gourmet sandwiches et al) segue to bar snacks then dinner mains like lamb with marinated artichokes and port wine sauce or polenta with roasted pumpkin. Reservations recommended, especially for window and platform tables.

With sunny decks at either end and a cavernous interior, **Pont 13** (770 27 22; www.pont13.nl; Haparandadam 50 ; lunch mains €7.50-12.50, dinner mains €16-22.50; noon-10pm; ; 48 Oostzaanstraat), once a vintage 1927 ex-car and passenger ferry that plied the IJ, now serves stunning Mediterranean fare – such as seafood antipasti platters and mains like lasagne with goat cheese or mozzarella-topped burgers – from its open kitchen.

Amazing views of REM Eiland extend across the pier from Pont 13's decks.

MOEDERS DUTCH €€

Map p316 (626 79 57; www.moeders.com; Rozengracht 251; mains €15-19, 3-course menus from €26.50; 5pm-midnight Mon-Fri, from noon Sat & Sun; ; 13/14/17 Marnixstraat) Mum's the word at 'Mothers'. When this welcoming place opened in 1990 customers were asked to bring their own plates and photos of their mums as donations and the decor remains a delightful hotchpotch. So does the food, from pumpkin *stamppot* (potatoes mashed with another vegetable) to seafood and Moroccan dishes. Book ahead.

LA OLIVA BASQUE €€

Map p314 (520 43 16; www.laoliva.nl; Egelantiersstraat 122-124; tapas €10-16, mains €22.50-26.50; noon-10pm Sun-Wed, to 11pm Thu-Sat; 3/10 Marnixplein) Yes, there are perfectly lovely meat and fish mains here, but it's the *pintxos* (tapas from southwestern France/northwestern Spain's Basque region), skewered with wooden sticks and stacked on the gleaming bar, that everyone's raving about. Order some *cava* (Spanish sparkling wine) and deliberate overstuffed figs, mushroom Manchego tartlets and *Pata Negra* ham with pear.

In summer the party spills out into the street.

DE REIGER MODERN DUTCH €€

Map p314 (624 74 26; www.dereigeramsterdam.nl; Nieuwe Leliestraat 34; mains €18.50-23; 5-10:30pm Tue-Sun; 13/14/17 Westermarkt) Assiduously local and very atmospheric, this corner cafe has a quiet front bar and a noisy, more spacious dining section at the back serving a short but stunning menu (venison and stewed pear with honey cinnamon sauce, for instance). No reservations or credit cards.

JAPANESE PANCAKE WORLD JAPANESE €€

Map p314 (320 44 47; www.japanesepancakeworld.com; 2e Egelantiersdwarsstraat 24a; mains €10-20; noon-10pm; 3/10 Marnixplein) At the continent's only shop specialising in *okonomiyaki* (cook as you like), your pancakes come in a hot iron dish with your choice of fillings (meat, seafood, vegies, cheese) topped with flakes of dried fish. There are barely two dozen seats: book ahead to sit at the back counter and watch the chef work his magic.

RAZMATAZ INTERNATIONAL €€

Map p316 (486 84 08; www.razmataz.nl; Hugo de Grootplein 7-15; mains €18-23, 3-course menu €34; 8.30am-1am Mon-Thu, 8.30am-3am Fri, 9am-3am Sat, 11am-1am Sun; 3 Hugo de Grootplein) This place jumps with neighborhood residents. They pile in for drinks in the sun on the cheery terrace and for meals from the inventive French chef. The dishes change, but might include braised rabbit leg with white grapes or salmon marinated in beetroot. The desserts (dreaming of you, hot chocolate cake…) are the pièces de résistance.

HOSTARIA ITALIAN €€

Map p314 (☎626 00 28; 2e Egelantiersdwarsstraat 9; mains €14-22; ⊙6-10pm Tue-Sun; ✎; 🚋3/10 Marnixplein) In a neighbourhood bursting with excellent Italian food, Hostaria holds its own, serving fresh pastas, filling mains and sublime yet simple desserts, accompanied by decently priced wines. Tightly packed tables make it tricky to move about but add to the cosy, convivial atmosphere.

TOSCANINI ITALIAN €€

Map p314 (☎623 28 13; www.restauranttoscanini.nl; Lindengracht 75; mains €15-23; ⊙6-10.30pm Mon-Sat; 👪; 🚋3/10 Marnixplein) Classy Toscanini bakes its own bread, rolls its own pasta and pours Italian wines. The weekly changing dishes that grace the white tablecloths might include seared beef with tarragon, or lamb shoulder stewed with white wine and rosemary. Desserts such as salted caramel *panna cotta* promise to weaken even the fiercest dietary resolves. Book ahead, even on weeknights.

BURGER'S PATIO MEDITERRANEAN €€

Map p314 (☎623 68 54; www.burgerspatio.nl; 2e Tuindwarsstraat 12; mains €15.50-24.50; ⊙6-11pm; 🚋3/10 Marnixplein) Not a hamburger joint, but an easy-going Mediterranean restaurant with a modern interior and namesake patio. A seasonally changing menu features free-range meats and poultry, creative vegie dishes such as sweet-potato pie with falafel and beetroot, and date and hazelnut crumble. Accompaniments such as crudités, aioli and tapenade make the prices seem more reasonable than they already are.

DE PRINS CAFE €€

Map p314 (☎624 93 82; www.deprins.nl; Prinsengracht 124; mains €13-17; ⊙kitchen 10am-10pm; 🚋13/14/17 Westerkerk) On a picturesque stretch of the Prinsengracht, this brown *café* is a wonderful spot for a drink on the canal-side terrace or in the cosy bar. But these days it's best known for its excellent kitchen. Lunch specialities include prawn or meat *bitterballen* (croquettes), while the pick of the dinner menu is a divine four-cheese fondue.

LOCAL KNOWLEDGE

DROP THE LIQUORICE

The Dutch love their lollies, the most famous of which is *drop*, the word for all varieties of liquorice. It may be gummy-soft or tough as leather, shaped like coins or miniature cars, but the most important distinction is between *zoete* (sweet) and *zoute* (salty, also called *salmiak*). The latter is often an alarming surprise, even for avowed fans of the black stuff. But with such a range of textures and additional flavours – mint, honey, laurel – even liquorice sceptics might be converted. **Het Oud-Hollandsch Snoepwinkeltje** (p162) is a good place to do a taste test.

KOEVOET ITALIAN €€

Map p314 (☎624 08 46; Lindenstraat 17; mains €14-26; ⊙6-10pm Tue-Sat; ✎; 🚋3/10 Marnixplein) The congenial Italian owners of Koevoet took over a former cafe on a quiet side street, left the *gezellig* decor untouched and started cooking up their home-country staples such as handmade ravioli. Don't miss its signature, drinkable dessert, *sgroppino limone*: sorbet, vodka and Prosecco whisked at your table and poured into a champagne flute.

CINEMA PARADISO ITALIAN €€

Map p314 (☎623 73 44; www.cinemaparadiso.info; Westerstraat 184-186; mains €15.50-25.50; ⊙6-11pm Wed-Sun; 🚋3/10 Marnixplein) Action! Located in a former movie theatre, this spirited Italian restaurant pays homage to its cinematic roots with black-and-white movie stills, the visages of iconic directors on the walls and a glitterati clientele. Book a booth or table near the open kitchen and enjoy pastas, pizzas, antipasti and stargazing over cocktails.

BORDEWIJK FRENCH, ITALIAN €€€

Map p314 (☎624 38 99; www.bordewijk.nl; Noordermarkt 7; mains €24-30, 3-/4-/5-course menus €39/49/59; ⊙6.30-10.30pm Tue-Sat; 🚌18/21/22 Buiten Oranjestraat) The interior at Bordewijk is so minimal that there's little to do but appreciate the spectacular French/Italian cooking. The chefs aren't afraid to take risks, resulting in dishes such as suckling pig with sausage in puff pastry, quail with foie gras or sea-salt-roasted ribs. Book ahead on weekends.

The West

Those looking for nouveau, scenester eats will strike it rich in the West. For amazing fare in an even more amazing setting, head to the Western Docklands (p155).

WORST WIJNCAFE TAPAS €

Map p313 (☎625 61 67; www.deworst.nl; Barentszstraat 171; tapas €8-15, brunch mains €10; ⊙noon-midnight Tue-Sat, 10am-10pm Sun; 🚌48 Barentszplein) Named for its sausage-skewed tapas dishes (veal tongue white sausage, chorizo, lobster sausage with spinach and asparagus), this chequerboard-tiled wine bar is the more casual sibling of esteemed restaurant Marius (p157) next door. Other dishes include pigs' trotters. There's a fantastic range of mostly French wines by the glass. Sunday brunch is a local event.

DE BAKKERSWINKEL CAFE €

Map p313 (☎688 06 32; www.debakkerswinkel.nl; Polonceaukade 1, Westergasfabriek; dishes €7-14; ⊙8.30am-6pm Mon-Fri, from 10am Sat & Sun; 🚋10 Van Limburg Stirumstraat) The wonderful 'Bakery' has eight branches throughout the city and country, but this one is uniquely situated by the drawbridge in the old regulator's house at the former gasworks, with mezzanine seating, comfy sofas and a great terrace. Quiches, fish terrines, soups and sourdough sandwiches are all good choices, and the carrot cake is unmissable.

RESTAURANT PS INTERNATIONAL €€

Map p313 (☎421 52 18; www.restaurantps.nl; Planciusstraat 49; mains €18-22, 3-course menu €31.50; ⊙6pm-midnight Tue-Sun; 🚋3 Zoutkeetsgracht) Run by an unlikely yet vastly experienced pair – an English chef and a Colombian maître d' – this restaurant in the Western Islands has an army of devoted fans. You can expect reasonable prices, an excellent wine menu and attentive service plus an artsy interior with mosaics of Venetian glass. The set menus change weekly and feature seasonal ingredients.

BOCCONI SANI ITALIAN €€

Map p313 (☎233 64 07; www.bocconisani.nl; Spaarndammerstraat 17; mains €11-17.50; ⊙noon-midnight; 🚌22 Assendelftstraat) Allergy-sensitive eaters flock to Bocconi's mod white room for the many gluten-free pastas it serves. Ravioli, lasagne and tortiglioni shells swaddled in tomato-and-caper sauce hit the sturdy wood tables. The bruschetta comes on spelt bread (which is wheat-free, though not gluten-free). Gluten eaters can fork into a full array of regular pasta dishes. So there's something for everyone!

RAÏNARAÏ ALGERIAN €€

Map p313 (☎486 71 09; www.rainarai.nl; Polonceaukade 40, Westergasfabriek; mains €16.50-23, 3-course menu €38.50; ⊙6-11pm Tue-Sun, lunch by reservation; 🖉; 🚌21 Van Hallstraat) This Algerian restaurant, in an old industrial building in the Westergasfabriek, is decked out with Arabian-style cushions and copper fixtures. The menu changes constantly but might offer seared salmon on chickpea-pumpkin-spiced couscous, or grilled sardines with asparagus, broad beans and tomatoes. There's usually a vegetarian dish of the day, as well.

★MARIUS INTERNATIONAL €€€

Map p313 (☎422 78 80; www.deworst.nl; Barentszstraat 173; 4-course menu €47.50; ⊙6.30-10pm Tue-Sat; 🚌48 Barentszplein) Foodies swoon over pocket-sized Marius, tucked in amid artists' studios in the Western Islands. Chef Kees Elfring shops at local markets, then creates his daily four-course, no-choice menu from what he finds. The result might be grilled prawns with fava bean purée, or beef rib with polenta and ratatouille. Marius also runs the fabulous wine/tapas bar Worst Wijncafe (p157) next door.

DRINKING & NIGHTLIFE

Jordaan

Anyone who seeks an authentic *café* experience 'with the locals' will love the Jordaan.

★'T SMALLE BROWN CAFE

Map p314 (www.t-smalle.nl; Egelantiersgracht 12; ⊙10am-1am Sun-Thu, to 2am Fri & Sat; 🚋13/14/17 Westermarkt) Dating back to 1786 as a *jenever* (Dutch gin) distillery and tasting house, and restored during the 1970s with antique porcelain beer pumps and lead-framed windows, locals' favourite 't Smalle is one of Amsterdam's charming brown *cafés*. Dock your boat right by the pretty stone terrace, which is wonderfully convivial by day and impossibly romantic at night.

It's so gorgeous, so authentic and so Dutch *gezellig* that there's a reproduction of it in Japan.

DE KAT IN DE WIJNGAERT BROWN CAFE

Map p314 (☎620 45 54; www.dekatindewijngaert.nl; Lindengracht 160; ⏰10am-1am Sun-Thu, 10am-3am Fri, 9am-3am Sat; 🚊3/10 Marnixplein) Rivalling 't Smalle for overwhelming *gezelligheid*, this gorgeous bar is the kind of place where one beer soon turns to half a dozen – maybe it's the influence of the old-guard arts types who hang out here. At least you can soak it all up with what many people vote as the best *tosti* (toasted sandwich) in town.

CAFE SOUNDGARDEN BAR

Map p316 (www.cafesoundgarden.nl; Marnixstraat 164-166; ⏰1pm-1am Mon-Thu, 1pm-3am Fri, 3pm-3am Sat, 3pm-1am Sun; 🚊13/14/17 Marnixstraat) In this grungy, all-ages dive bar, the 'Old Masters' are the Ramones and Black Sabbath. Somehow a handful of pool tables, 1980s pinball machines, unkempt DJs and lovably surly bartenders add up to an ineffable magic. Bands occasionally make an appearance, and the waterfront terrace scene is more like an impromptu party in someone's backyard.

All walks of life congregate here: punks, expats, lovey-dovey silver-haired couples. The common denominator isn't fashion, age or politics, it's a diehard love of rock and roll (and booze).

TRIPEL BEER CAFE

Map p316 (☎370 64 21; Lijnbaansgracht 161; ⏰4pm-3am Mon-Fri, from noon Sat & Sun; 📶; 🚊7/10/17 Elandsgracht) With affable bar staff and cosy clutter all around, Tripel feels like a real neighborhood pub. And so it is, located off the tourist path at the Jordaan's edge. The focus is on Belgian beers: around 13 flow from the taps, with 200 more available in bottles. Reserve ahead for roasted chicken and other delicious Belgian dishes (€9.50 to 15.50) from the kitchen.

CAFÉ PIEPER BROWN CAFE

Map p316 (Prinsengracht 424; ⏰noon-1am Mon-Thu, noon-2am Fri & Sat, 2-8pm Sun; 🚊1/2/5 Prinsengracht/Leidsestraat) Small, unassuming and unmistakably old (1665), Café Pieper features stained-glass windows, fresh sand on the floors, antique beer mugs hanging from the bar and a working Belgian beer pump (1875). Sip a Wieckse Witte beer or a terrific cappuccino as you marvel at the claustrophobia of the low-ceilinged bar (after all, people were shorter back in the 17th century – even the Dutch).

TWO FOR JOY COFFEE

Map p314 (☎221 95 52; www.twoforjoy.nl; Haarlemmerdijk 182; ⏰7.30am-7pm Mon-Fri, 8am-6pm Sat & Sun; 🚊3 Haarlemmerplein) Caffeine addicts, welcome to your new home. Two for Joy roasts its own beans and then brews them into Amsterdam's best espresso. Hang out on the vintage couches and lounge chairs, ogle the art on the exposed-brick walls, and enjoy the coffee buzz (perhaps with an egg sandwich). Two For Joy has another outlet in the Southern Canal Ring (p142).

WATERKANT BAR

Map p316 (☎737 11 26; www.waterkantamsterdam.nl; Marnixstraat 246; ⏰11am-1am Sun-Thu, to 3am Fri & Sat; 📶; 🚊7/10/17 Elandsgracht) This rollicking canal-side pub, tucked under an oddball circular parking garage on the Jordaan's outskirts, serves good brews (many local) along with pumpkin rotis and other Surinamese-tinged specialities. For something different, try a watermelon gin and tonic. The terrace buzzes with young locals.

FINCH BAR

Map p314 (☎626 24 61; Noordermarkt 5; ⏰9am-1am Sun-Thu, to 3am Fri & Sat; 🚊3/10 Marnixplein) This funkalicious bar with retro decor (deliberately mismatched yet somehow harmonious) is just the spot to hang out and knock back a few beers after a visit to the market. It attracts an arty-designy clientele and is always packed on the weekends.

PROUST BAR

Map p314 (☎623 91 45; www.proust.nl; Noordermarkt 4; ⏰9am-1am Mon, noon-1am Tue-Thu, noon-3am Fri, 9am-3am Sat, 9am-1am Sun; 🚊3/10 Marnixplein) Stylish Proust is dominated by an amazing chandelier in the shape of a giant revolver that was created by Dutch designer Hans van Bentum. There's a classy menu and scrumptious hot chocolate. It's next door to Finch, another bar for moneyed, creative types; their terraces effectively merge.

CAFÉ P 96 BROWN CAFE

Map p314 (www.p96.nl; Prinsengracht 96; ⏰10am-3am Mon-Fri, from 11am Sat & Sun; 📶; 🚊13/14/17 Westermarkt) If you don't want the night to end, P 96 is an amiable hang out. When most other *cafés* in the Jordaan shut down for the night, this is where everyone ends up, rehashing their evening and striking up conversations with strangers. In summertime head to the terrace across the street aboard a houseboat.

DE TWEE ZWAANTJES
BROWN CAFE

Map p314 (☎625 27 29; www.detweezwaantjes.nl; Prinsengracht 114; ⏰3pm-1am Sun-Thu, to 3am Fri & Sat; 🚋13/14/17 Westermarkt) The small, authentic 'Two Swans' is at its hilarious best on weekend nights, when you can join locals and visitors belting out classics and traditional Dutch tunes in a rollicking, unforgettable cabaret-meets-karaoke evening. The fact that singers are often fuelled by liquid-courage only adds to the spirited fun. Don't be afraid to join in.

CAFÉ DE KOE
BAR

Map p316 (www.cafedekoe.nl; Marnixstraat 381; ⏰4pm-1am Sun-Thu, to 3am Fri & Sat; 🚋1/2/5 Leidseplein) 'The Cow' is loved for its homey *gezellig* atmosphere, with board games, movie nights and free gigs by local DJs and rock bands. A down-to-earth neighbourhood crowd swills beers upstairs by the funky cow mosaic, while diners below gather around worn wooden tables and order good, inexpensive comfort food.

STRUIK
BAR

Map p316 (☎625 48 63; Rozengracht 160; ⏰5pm-1am Mon-Fri, 3pm-3am Sat, 3pm-1am Sun; 🚋13/14/17 Marnixstraat) If you prefer your beer with a background of hip hop, breakbeats and soul, come to this graffitied, split-level corner *café* and hang out with the neighbourhood's hipsters, where everyone lingers drinking and chatting as the candles wear down. Guest chefs whip up good cheap meals on various nights. Cash only.

CAFÉ PAPENEILAND
BROWN CAFE

Map p314 (www.papeneiland.nl; Prinsengracht 2; ⏰10am-1am Sun-Thu, to 3am Fri & Sat; 🚋3/10 Marnixplein) You won't be the only traveller at this *café*, but that doesn't make it any less worthwhile. It's a 1642 gem with Delft-blue tiles and a central stove. The name, 'Papists' Island', goes back to the Reformation, when there was a clandestine Catholic church on the canal's northern side.

Papeneiland was reached via a secret tunnel from the top of the stairs – ask the bar staff to show you the entrance.

CAFÉ 'T MONUMENTJE
BROWN CAFE

Map p314 (☎624 35 41; Westerstraat 120; ⏰8.30am-1am Mon-Thu, 8.30am-3am Fri & Sat, 11am-1am Sun; 🚋3/10 Marnixplein) This slightly scruffy yet lovable *café* with sand on the floor is always heaving with local barflies. It's a good spot for a beer and a snack after shopping at the Westermarkt (p164).

DE TUIN
BROWN CAFE

Map p314 (☎624 45 59; 2e Tuindwarsstraat 13; ⏰10am-1am Mon-Thu, 10am-3am Fri & Sat, 11am-1am Sun; 📶; 🚋3/10 Marnixplein) Always a good place to start the evening – join the youngish clientele enjoying the wide selection of Belgian beers (many on tap), good food and funky soul music. The small terrace has tables made from *amsterdammertjes* (Amsterdam's classic burgundy-brown traffic bollards that separate the pavement from the street).

DE ZOTTE
BEER CAFE

Map p316 (☎626 86 94; Raamstraat 29; ⏰4pm-1am Sun-Thu, to 3am Fri & Sat; 🚋1/2/5 Leidseplein) If you can't make up your mind in this Belgian beer bar, start with the weekly special. Those Trappist monks can brew some deadly ones so you might want to line your stomach with a hearty cheese plate or steak – the kitchen's open between 6.30pm and 9pm.

VESPER BAR
COCKTAIL BAR

Map p314 (☎420 45 92; www.vesperbar.nl; Vinkenstraat 57; ⏰8pm-1am Tue-Thu & Sun, 5pm-3am Fri & Sat; 🚌18/21/22 Buiten Oranjestraat) This luxe cocktail bar gains a certain mystique by its location on a low-key stretch of Jordaanian shops and businesses. Their martinis will coax out your inner James Bond – or Vesper Lynd (the Bond girl from *Casino Royale*).

If you're feeling adventurous, try the Victoria's Secret: ginger liqueur, pear brandy and elderflower with fresh lemon juice and a dash of chili pepper.

CAFÉ THIJSSEN
BAR

Map p314 (☎623 89 94; www.cafethijssen.nl; Brouwersgracht 107; ⏰8am-1am Mon-Thu, 8am-3am Fri, 7.30am-3am Sat, 9am-1am Sun; 🚋3/10 Marnixplein) The glowing dark-wood, art deco–inspired interior with stained-glass windows and big tables is a crowd-puller. It's busy on weekends with groups of neo-Jordaanese young professionals meeting up for a late brunch and staying on until dinner.

LA TERTULIA
COFFEESHOP

Map p316 (☎623 85 03; www.coffeeshoptertulia.com; Prinsengracht 312; ⏰11am-7pm Tue-Sat; 🚋7/10/17 Elandsgracht) A backpackers' favourite, this mother-and-daughter-run coffeeshop has a greenhouse feel. You can sit outside by the Van Gogh–inspired murals, play some board games or contemplate the Jurassic-sized crystals by the counter. Bonus: Tertulia actually has good coffee, made with beans from a Dutch speciality roaster.

CAFÉ DE JORDAAN BAR

Map p316 (☎627 58 63; Elandsgracht 45; ⏰10am-1am Mon-Thu, 10am-3am Fri, noon-3am Sat, 1pm-1am Sun; 🚊7/10/17 Elandsgracht) The epitome of an old-style Jordaan *café*. After midnight crooners link arms and sing along to classic Dutch tunes; the lyrics playing on the TV screens are a hoot. Earlier in the evening it's less vocal and a more relaxed spot for a *biertje* (glass of beer).

DIVINO WIJNBAR WINE BAR

Map p314 (www.wijnbardivino.nl; Boomstraat 41a; ⏰5pm-midnight Mon-Thu, 5pm-2am Fri, 4pm-2am Sat, 4pm-midnight Sun; 🚊3/10 Marnixplein) This wine bar serves only quality Italian wines by the glass and bottle, plus charcuterie and cheese plates. The polished wood bar, flickering candles and lofty corner windows draw you in – though the blankets strewn about the tables and chairs outside are equally inviting.

SAAREIN GAY & LESBIAN

Map p316 (www.saarein.info; Elandsstraat 119; ⏰4pm-1am Tue-Thu, 4pm-2am Fri, noon-2am Sat, 2pm-1am Sun; 🚊7/10/17 Elandsgracht) Dating from the 1600s, this one-time feminist stronghold is still a meeting place for lesbians, although these days gay men are welcome, too. There's a small menu with tapas, soups and specials.

DE TRUT GAY & LESBIAN

Map p316 (☎612 35 24; www.trutfonds.nl; Bilderdijkstraat 165e; ⏰10pm-4am Sun; 🚊7/17 Bilderdijkstraat) In the basement of a former squat, this Sunday-night club is a gay and lesbian institution. Its name means 'the tart' and it comes with an attitude; arrive well before 11pm (the space is fairly small). No cameras and no mobile phones allowed inside.

SPIRIT COFFEESHOP

Map p314 (Westerstraat 121; ⏰noon-1am; 🚊3/10 Marnixplein) Setting this coffeeshop apart from the pack are its half-a-dozen or so state-of-the-art pinball machines, including the Walking Dead, Metallica and AC/DC. You can also shoot pool here. Cash only.

CAFÉ DE LAURIERBOOM PUB

Map p316 (www.laurierboom.nl; Laurierstraat 76; ⏰2.30pm-1am Mon-Thu, 2.30pm-3am Fri, 1pm-3am Sat, 1pm-1am Sun; 📶; 🚊13/14/17 Marnixstraat) The hub of the Jordaan chess circuit is one of its oldest *cafés*, still bearing a stone tablet labelled *tapperij en slijterij* (ask the bartender to explain what this is). Local masters test their wits over a drink; you can also play chess online here or play card or board games.

The West

Off the tourist radar, this up-and-coming area attracts an artsy crowd.

WESTERGASTERRAS BAR

Map p313 (www.westergasterras.nl; Klönneplein 4, Westergasfabriek; ⏰11am-1am Sun-Thu, 11am-3am Fri, 10am-3am Sat, 10am-1am Sun; 🚊10 Van Limburg Stirumstraat) This cool, post-industrial, indoor-outdoor *café* is screamingly popular every day of the week. There's a great range of tapas-style dishes; the massive outdoor terrace, overlooking reed-filled ponds and a weir, is hotly contested on sunny afternoons. The building also holds a popular dance club that lets loose Thursday to Saturday.

BROUWERIJ TROOST WESTERGAS BREWERY

Map p313 (☎737 10 28; www.brouwerijtroostwestergas.nl; Pazzanistraat 27, Westergasfabriek; ⏰4pm-1am Mon-Thu, 4pm-3am Fri, noon-3am Sat, noon-midnight Sun; 📶; 🚊10 Van Limburg Stirumstraat) De Pijp's popular brewery (p195) recently opened an outpost in Westerpark. Take a seat in the cavernous industrial space punctuated by big silver tanks cooking up your saison, blond ale and smoked porter. There's a shop for takeaway, too. Troost doesn't accept cash; credit cards only.

ENTERTAINMENT

Jordaan

BOOM CHICAGO COMEDY

Map p316 (www.boomchicago.nl; Rozengracht 117; 📶; 🚊13/14/17 Marnixstraat) Boom Chicago stages seriously funny improv-style comedy shows in English. They make fun of Dutch culture, American culture and everything that gets in the crosshairs. They take place Wednesday through Sunday in the main theatre. Edgier shows happen in the smaller upstairs theatre. Saturday's late-night show is a low-cost good time.

The bar inside helps fuel the festivities with buckets of ice and beer.

WESTERGASFABRIEK

A stone's throw northwest of the Jordaan, the late-19th century Dutch Renaissance **Westergasfabriek** (Map p313; ☎586 07 10; www.westergasfabriek.nl; Haarlemmerweg 8-10; 🚊3 Haarlemmerplein) complex and adjacent the **Westerpark** (p151) were the city's western gasworks until gas production ceased in 1967. The site was heavily polluted and underwent a major clean-up before it re-emerged as a cultural and recreational park, with lush lawns, a long wading pool, cycleways and sports facilities.

The post-industrial buildings now house creative spaces including advertising agencies and TV production studios, as well as regular festivals and events – including the **Sunday Market** (Map p313; www.sundaymarket.nl; Westergasfabriek; ⏰noon-6pm 1st Sun of month; 🚊10 Van Limburg Stirumstraat), a quality craft and gourmet food soiree that sets up here monthly.

Westergasfabriek's slew of dining, drinking and entertainment options include the following:

- **De Bakkerswinkel** (p157) Split-level cafe inside the gasworks' former regulator's house.
- **Raïnaraï** (p157) Algerian cuisine amid exotic decor.
- **Westergasterras** (p160) One of the hottest terraces in Amsterdam.
- **Brouwerij Troost Westergas** (p160) Brewery for hop heads and cool cats.
- **North Sea Jazz Club** Swingin' live jazz.
- **Het Ketelhuis** Art-house cinema.
- **Pacific Parc** Indie gigs and DJ sets.

DE NIEUWE ANITA — LIVE MUSIC

Map p316 (www.denieuweanita.nl; Frederik Hendrikstraat 111; 🚊3 Hugo de Grootplein) This living-room venue expanded for noise rockers has a great *café*. Behind the bookcase-concealed door, in the back, the main room has a stage and screens cult movies on Mondays. DJs and vaudeville-type acts are also on the eclectic agenda. Entrance fees range from €3 to €7.

MOVIES — CINEMA

Map p314 (☎638 60 16; www.themovies.nl; Haarlemmerdijk 161; 🚊3 Haarlemmerplein) This *gezellig* art-deco cinema (the oldest in Amsterdam, dating from 1912) screens indie films alongside mainstream flicks. From Sunday to Thursday you can treat yourself to a meal in the restaurant (open 5.30pm to 10pm) or have a pre-movie tipple at its inviting *café*-bar.

MALOE MELO — BLUES

Map p316 (☎420 45 92; www.maloemelo.com; Lijnbaansgracht 163; ⏰9pm-3am Sun-Thu, to 4am Fri & Sat; 🚊7/10/17 Elandsgracht) This is the free-wheeling, fun-loving altar of Amsterdam's tiny blues scene. Music ranges from garage and Irish punk to Texas blues and rockabilly. The cover charge is usually around €5.

☆ The West

NORTH SEA JAZZ CLUB — JAZZ

Map p313 (☎722 09 81; www.northseajazzclub.com; Pazzanistraat 1, Westergasfabriek; 🚊10 Van Limburg Stirumstraat) Respected jazz musicians (and several big names) play at this welcoming venue. Many shows are free: up-and-coming performers let loose during 'Summer Sessions' on Wednesdays and Thursdays from 6.30pm to 9.30pm; and modern and electronic musicians play 'Late Night Live' shows on Saturdays (around 11.30pm).

A welcoming pizza restaurant is attached. Three-course menus are available during the headliner concerts (€37.50); the cheapest tickets are standing only.

PACIFIC PARC — LIVE MUSIC

Map p313 (☎488 77 78; www.pacificparc.nl; Polonceaukade 23, Westergasfabriek; 🚊10 Van Limburg Stirumstraat) In a faux-tropical setting Pacific Parc is home to live music, DJ sets and plenty of rock and roll spirit to go along with the potent drinks and hearty food. The sprawling, picnic-table-dotted terrace and cafe open at 11am daily.

HET KETELHUIS — CINEMA

Map p313 (☎684 00 90; www.ketelhuis.nl; Pazzanistraat 4, Westergasfabriek; 🚊10 Van Limburg

PUZZLE ROOMS

Puzzle rooms have taken Amsterdam by storm. Unfamiliar with the concept? It's when you and a group of friends are locked in a room, and together you must solve puzzles and crack codes to get out. Some of the rooms are quite high-tech. **Boom Chicago** (p160) has one called **Escape Through Time** (http://escapethroughtime.nl) that uses live actors and allows you to immerse into WWII Amsterdam. You can do it in English or Dutch. **Sherlocked** (www.sherlocked.nl) is another popular puzzle room; it takes place at the **Beurs van Berlage** (p71) in the centre.

Stirumstraat) The three screening rooms at this art-house cinema have a chic post-industrial vibe and comfy seats. There's also a cosy *café* for pre- or post-show drinks and nibbles.

SHOPPING

Shops here have an artsy, eclectic, home-made feel. The area around Elandsgracht is the place for antiques and art, as well as speciality shops covering everything from hats to cats. Straddling the Jordaan and Western Canal Ring, the Haarlemmerbuurt, incorporating hip Haarlemmerdijk in the northern Jordaan, is teeming with trendy boutiques. The Jordaan also has some fabulous food and flea markets (p164).

★MOOOI GALLERY HOMEWARES

Map p314 (☎528 77 60; www.moooi.com; Westerstraat 187; ⏲10am-6pm Tue-Sat; 🚋3/10 Marnixplein) Founded by Marcel Wanders, this is Dutch design at its most over-the-top, from the life-sized black horse lamp to the 'blow away vase' (a whimsical twist on the classic delft vase) and the 'killing of the piggy bank' ceramic pig (with a gold hammer).

HET OUD-HOLLANDSCH SNOEPWINKELTJE FOOD

Map p314 (☎420 73 90; www.snoepwinkeltje.com; Egelantiersdwarsstraat 2; ⏲11am-6.30pm Tue-Sat; 🚋3/10 Marnixplein) This corner shop is lined with jar after apothecary jar of Dutch penny sweets with flavours from chocolate to coffee, all manner of fruit and the salty Dutch liquorice known as *drop*. It also stocks diabetic-friendly sweets.

ANTIEKCENTRUM AMSTERDAM ANTIQUES

Map p316 (Amsterdam Antique Centre; www.antiekcentrumamsterdam.nl; Elandsgracht 109; ⏲11am-6pm Mon & Wed-Fri, to 5pm Sat & Sun; 🚋7/10/17 Elandsgracht) Anyone with an affinity for odd antiques and bric-a-brac may enter this knick-knack mini-mall and never come out. Spanning 1750 sq metres, there are 72 stalls, plus a handful of larger shops, displays and a private dealers' table market on Wednesday, Saturday and Sunday. You're just as likely to find 1940s silk dresses as you are 1970s Swedish porn.

BACK BEAT RECORDS MUSIC

Map p314 (☎627 16 57; www.backbeat.nl; Egelantiersstraat 19; ⏲11am-6pm Mon-Sat; 🚋13/14/17 Westermarkt) Back Beat has been selling jazz, soul and funk music for close to three decades. Whether you're looking for Sly and the Family Stone vinyl, a Chet Baker box set or a Charles Earland Hammond organ CD, this little shop has it covered. The owner is a font of local jazz lore.

GALLERIA D'ARTE RINASCIMENTO ART, ANTIQUES

Map p314 (☎622 75 09; www.delft-art-gallery.com; Prinsengracht 170; ⏲9am-6pm; 🚋13/14/17 Westermarkt) This pretty shop sells Royal Delftware ceramics (both antique and new), all manner of vases, platters, brooches, Christmas ornaments and intriguing 19th-century wall tiles and plaques.

SPRMRKT CLOTHING

Map p316 (☎330 56 01; www.sprmrkt.nl; Rozengracht 191-193; ⏲noon-6pm Mon, 10am-6pm Tue, Wed & Sat, 10am-7pm Thu & Fri, 1-6pm Sun; 🚋13/14/17 Marnixstraat) Whether you want a supertight pair of Acne jeans, a vintage Thor Larson Pod chair or the latest copy of *Butt* magazine, it's all here at this lofty industrial concept store, a major player in Amsterdam's fashion scene.

PAPABUBBLE FOOD

Map p314 (☎626 26 62; www.papabubble.nl; Haarlemmerdijk 70; ⏲1-6pm Mon & Wed-Fri, from 10am Sat; 🚋3 Haarlemmerplein) This hip lolly shop looks more like a gallery. Pull up a cushion and perch on the stairs to watch the mesmerising process of transforming sugar into gemlike sweets with flavours like pomelo and lavender.

RAW MATERIALS HOMEWARES

Map p316 (www.rawmaterials.nl; Rozengracht 229-233; noon-6pm Mon, 10am-6pm Tue-Sat, noon-5pm Sun; 13/14/17 Marnixstraat) As its name suggests, Raw Materials stocks cool vintage furniture, steel cabinets and pieces made from reclaimed wood as well as a great array of fabrics, soft furnishings, ceramics and glassware that capture the spirit of Dutch design.

KAASHUIS TROMP FOOD

Map p316 (623 00 10; www.kaashuistromp.nl; Elandsgracht 27; 8am-8pm Mon-Fri, to 7pm Sat, to 6pm Sun; 7/10/17 Elandsgracht) Many foodies rank Kaashuis Tromp as the best cheese shop in Amsterdam. Wheels of Gouda, Edam and European cheeses pile high on the shelves. For a fast fix, join the locals queued at the back counter for a takeaway sandwich (€3 to €6), like the goat cheese and fig jam beauty. The shop is part of a small Dutch chain.

TENUE DE NÎMES CLOTHING

Map p316 (www.tenuedenimes.com; Elandsgracht 60; noon-6pm Sun & Mon, from 10am Tue-Sat; 7/10/17 Elandsgracht) The Jordaan branch of the Western Canal Ring (p124) denim specialist stocks groovy new and vintage wares throughout two storeys.

ROCK ARCHIVE ARTS

Map p314 (423 04 89; www.rockarchive.com; Prinsengracht 110; 2-6pm Wed-Fri, noon-6pm Sat & by appointment; 13/14/17 Westermarkt) Limited-edition rock 'n' roll prints of Robert Plant, Debbie Harry, Sting and tons of others are all sold here for relatively small change, in a format of your choice.

A SPACE ODDITY TOYS, BOOKS

Map p316 (www.spaceoddity.nl; Prinsengracht 204; 11am-5.30pm Tue-Fri, 10.15am-5pm Sat; 13/14/17 Westermarkt) This geekalicious shop will sate even the most hardcore *Star Wars* fanatic, DC comics collector or Stanley Kubrick obsessionist. Get lost in the memorabilia, action figures, comics, books and loads of other pop-culture ephemera.

UKE BOUTIQUE MUSIC

Map p316 (753 12 18; www.ukeboutique.nl; Lijnbaansgracht 191; 2-6pm Mon, Thu & Fri, noon-5pm Wed & Sat; 7/10/17 Elandsgracht) This shop just sells one musical instrument: the ukulele. All of its stock is quality checked and adjusted, ready for play; prices start from €35. Ask about uke concerts and lessons.

CATS & THINGS GIFTS

Map p316 (428 30 28; www.catsandthings.nl; Hazenstraat 26; 11.30am-6pm Tue-Fri, to 5pm Sat; 7/10/17 Elandsgracht) If you're a cat lover, or shopping for someone who is, this quirky shop – with its own resident cats – is a must. It stocks every feline-themed gift imaginable (statues, artworks, cat-adorned homewares) and presents for kitty, too (baskets, food, collars and climbers).

LENA CLOTHING

Map p314 (789 17 81; www.lena-library.com; Westerstraat 174H; 10am-7pm Mon, 11am-7pm Wed & Fri, 11am-8pm Thu, 11am-5pm Sat; 3/10 Marnixplein) Here's an inventive concept: a lending library of clothing. Members borrow from the wide array of new and vintage threads. Membership starts at €20 per month.

MECHANISCH SPEELGOED TOYS

Map p314 (638 16 80; Westerstraat 67; 10am-6pm Mon-Fri, to 5pm Sat; 3/10 Marnixplein) This adorable shop is crammed full of nostalgic toys, including snow domes, glow lamps, masks, finger puppets and wind-up toys. And who doesn't need a good rubber chicken every once in a while? Hours can vary.

KITSCH KITCHEN HOMEWARES

Map p316 (622 82 61; www.kitschkitchen.nl; Rozengracht 8-12; 10am-6pm Mon-Sat, noon-5pm Sun; 13/14/17 Westermarkt) You want it flowered, frilly, colourful, over-the-top or just made from plastic? The chances are you'll find it here – Kitsch Kitchen stocks homewares including Mexican tablecloths, pink plastic chandeliers from India, lamps, along with handbags, toys, dolls' dresses, and of course, bouquets of plastic flowers.

LAB 13 CLOTHING

Map p314 (Haarlemmerplein 13; 11am-7pm Sun-Wed & Fri, 11am-9pm Thu, 10am-7pm Sat; 3 Haarlemmerplein) Want a shop where soft T-shirts, handmade bags and jewellery, casual cotton blouses, bath products, floral dresses, spiffy retro pieces and Guatemalan worry dolls coexist? If so, Lab 13 is your spot.

NOU MOE STRIPWINKEL GIFTS

Map p314 (6936345; http://stripwinkelnoumoe.nl; Lindenstraat 1; noon-6pm Mon-Sat, to 8pm Thu; 18/21/22 Buiten Oranjestraat) This tiny

LOCAL KNOWLEDGE

JORDAAN MARKETS

Noordermarkt (Northern Market; Map p314; www.jordaanmarkten.nl; Noordermarkt; ⌚flea market 9am-1pm Mon, farmers market 9am-4pm Sat; 🚋3/10 Marnixplein) A market square since the early 1600s, the plaza in front of the Noorderkerk hosts a couple of lively markets each week. Monday morning's **flea market** has some amazing bargains; Saturday mornings see local shoppers flock to the lush **boerenmarkt** (farmers market) overflowing with organic produce.

There's a great selection of cafes surrounding the square, including **Winkel** (p151) on the southwest corner, home of some of the city's best apple pie.

Lindengracht Market (Map p314; www.jordaanmarkten.nl; Lindengracht; ⌚9am-4pm Sat; 🚋3 Nieuwe Willemsstraat) On Saturdays, the Lindengracht Market is a wonderfully authentic local affair, with bountiful fresh produce, including fresh fish and magnificent cheese stalls, as well as gourmet goods, clothing and homewares. Arrive as early as possible for the best pickings and fewest crowds.

Westermarkt (Map p314; www.jordaanmarkten.nl; Westerstraat; ⌚9am-1pm Mon; 🚋3/10 Marnixplein) Bargain-priced clothing and fabrics are sold at 163 stalls at the Westermarkt (which isn't in fact on Westermarkt but on Westerstraat, just near the Noordermarkt).

corner comics shop features everything from Asterix to Garfield and Tintin. More importantly it sells the merchandise: soft toys, notebooks, stickers, games, coffee mugs and bedroom slippers.

ARNOLD CORNELIS — FOOD

Map p316 (☎625 85 85; www.cornelis.nl; Elandsgracht 78; ⌚8.30am-6pm Mon-Fri, to 5pm Sat; 🚋7/10/17 Elandsgracht) Your dinner hosts will be impressed if you present them with something from this long-standing shop, such as fruitcake, cheesecake, chocolate-stuffed cookies or blue sphere biscuits made with Malaga wine. At lunchtime grab a flaky pastry filled with cheese, meat or vegetables.

'T ZONNETJE — DRINK

Map p314 (☎623 00 58; www.koffietheeenkruiden.nl; Haarlemmerdijk 45; ⌚noon-6pm Mon, 9am-6pm Tue-Sat; 🚋18/21/22 Buiten Oranjestraat) At this charming shop ensconced in a 1642 building, you can find teas from all over the world, as well as coffees, spices and accoutrements.

DISCOSTARS — MUSIC

Map p314 (☎626 17 77; www.discostars-recordstore.nl; Haarlemmerdijk 86; ⌚1-6pm Sun & Mon, from 10am Tue-Sat; 🚋18/21/22 Buiten Oranjestraat) The disco generation will enjoy this repository of the music of yesteryear. If the names Olivia Newton-John, Engelbert Humperdinck, Paul Young, Celia Cruz, Candy Dulfer, Buddy Holly, Yves Montand, Doris Day or Roy Rogers mean anything to you, you'll find lots more to like.

CALLAS 43 — VINTAGE

Map p314 (☎427 37 90; Haarlemmerdijk 43; ⌚noon-6pm Mon-Sat; 🚋18/21/22 Buiten Oranjestraat) Rummage through tightly packed vintage designer garments, creative secondhand finds, good-as-new samples and a large assortment of leather bags (some new, some not) for your next favourite outfit.

CHOCOLÁTL — FOOD & DRINK

Map p316 (☎755 50 47; www.chocolatl.nl; Hazenstraat 25a; ⌚11am-6pm Tue-Sat, 1-5pm Sun; 🚋7/10/17 Elandsgracht) Premium chocolate gifts for the serious chocoholic or connoisseur, including drinking chocolate. Ask about guided 'chocolab' tasting sessions.

JEFFERSON HOTEL — CLOTHING

Map p316 (www.jeffersonhotel.nl; Elandsgracht 57; ⌚noon-6pm Mon, 10am-6pm Tue-Sat, 1-5pm Sun; 🚋7/10/17 Elandsgracht) Not a hotel, although it does resemble a classy lobby, this menswear shop wows with its discerning taste for edgy designers such as Vintage 66 and Girls love DJs. Can't decide between quality shirts and rare denim? Mull it over while sipping a cappuccino at the in-store espresso bar.

CELLARRICH — ACCESSORIES

Map p314 (www.cellarrich.nl; Haarlemmerdijk 98; ⌚1-6pm Tue, 11am-5.30pm Wed & Sat, 11am-6pm Thu & Fri; 🚋3 Haarlemmerplein) Accessorise with colourful, creative, leather wallets, bags and gloves as well as jewellery and scarves. There are beautiful leather-bound notebooks, too.

Vondelpark & the Old South

VONDELPARK | THE OLD SOUTH

Neighbourhood Top Five

❶ Plunging into the Golden Age trove of Dutch Masters paintings, Delft tiles and gilded dollhouses at the **Rijksmuseum** (p167).

❷ Being awestruck by the tortured artist's vivid brushstrokes of yellow sunflowers and purple-blue irises at the **Van Gogh Museum** (p170).

❸ Admiring the abstractions of Mondrian, Matisse and their modern compadres at the **Stedelijk Museum** (p172).

❹ Listening to music soar within the pristine acoustics of the **Concertgebouw** (p185).

❺ Lazing over coffee, searching out sculptures, enjoying a picnic and catching an open-air theatre performance in the **Vondelpark** (p173).

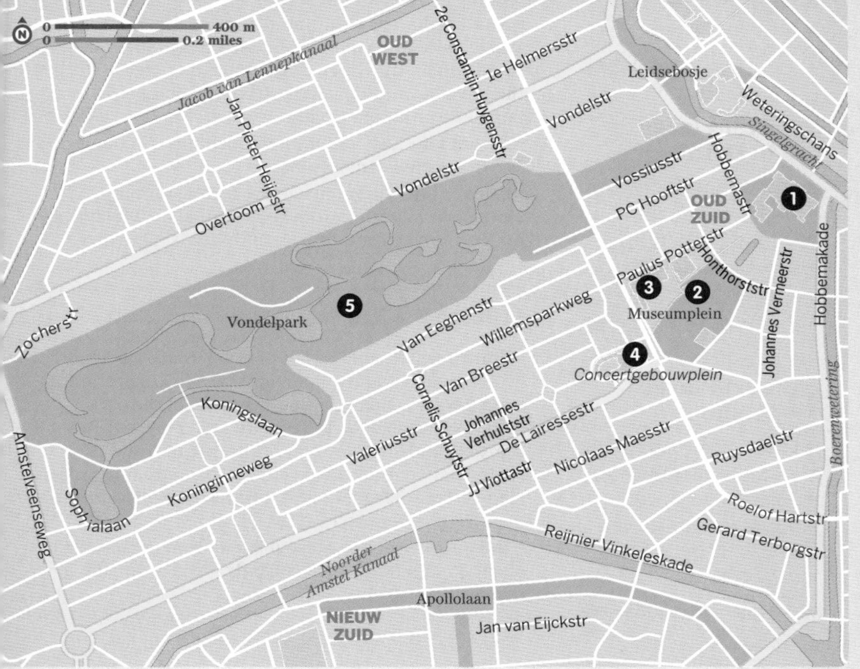

For more detail of this area see Map p322

Lonely Planet's Top Tip

If you've worked up an appetite strolling or cycling through the park, you're spoilt for choice for places to dine along and just off Amstelveenseweg. Running along the western edge of the park, it's a fabulous eat street, with restaurants ranging from vegan to Chinese, Japanese, Indonesian, Indian, Thai, pan-Asian, Dutch, Italian, Brazilian, and American-style steaks, interspersed with stylish wine bars and cosy *cafés* (bars, pubs). Wander along and see what you find.

Best Places to Eat

- Ron Gastrobar (p178)
- Dikke Graaf (p178)
- Foodhallen (p182)
- Adam (p178)
- Braai BBQ Bar (p175)

For reviews, see p175.

Best Places to Drink

- Franklin (p181)
- Craft & Draft (p181)
- Lot Sixty One (p181)
- Café Bédier (p181)
- BarBrå (p181)

For reviews, see p181.

Best Places to Shop

- Local Goods Store (p182)
- Pied à Terre (p185)
- Edha Interieur (p185)
- Van Avezaath Beune (p185)
- VLVT (p185)

For reviews, see p184.

Explore Vondelpark & the Old South

Around the grassy expanse of Museumplein, Amsterdam's top three art museums – the Rijksmuseum, Van Gogh Museum and Stedelijk – are all lined up in a walkable row. You could easily spend a full day here alone. In the evening, the action shifts to the Concertgebouw, the grand music hall built in conjunction with the Rijksmuseum, and genteel *cafés* spring to life.

The Vondelpark itself is more epic for its near-pastoral beauty than for its actual size, and can easily be explored in a few hours.

North of the park around Overtoom, streets burst with eateries and shops for all budgets, while those along leafy Cornelis Schuytstraat to the south are more exclusive. Come dinner time, you'll find plenty of dining options on and around Amstelveenseweg at the park's western end, and in and around the city's new foodhall, Foodhallen, inside the De Hallen cultural complex.

Local Life

- **Cycling** If you need a crash course in the art of Dutch biking away from the traffic-filled streets, Vondelpark is the perfect place to practise spinning your wheels like a local.
- **Skating** Join local in-line skaters setting off from Vondelpark for a two-hour mass skate (p186) every Friday night. In winter, Museumplein's pond looks like the top of a wind-up jewellery box when it becomes a popular ice-skating rink.
- **Street Life** Look out for new openings on booming Jan Pieter Heijestraat (p180).
- **Bunker Life** Buried inside the 1e Constantjin Huygensstraat bridge, the Vondelbunker (p184) hosts underground entertainment and activist activities.

Getting There & Away

- **Tram** Trams 2 and 5 from Centraal Station stop at Museumplein and the main entrance to Vondelpark; tram 2 travels along the southern side of the park along Willemsparkweg. Trams 3 and 12 cross the 1e Constantjin Huygensstraat bridge not far from the park's main entrance, and cross Kinkerstraat near De Hallen. Tram 1 from Centraal travels along Overtoom near the park's western edge.
- **Bus** Bus 197 zips to Museumplein from the airport in about 30 minutes, which is handy if you're staying in the neighbourhood.

TOP SIGHT
RIJKSMUSEUM

The Rijksmuseum is the Netherlands' premier art trove, and no self-respecting visitor to Amsterdam can afford to miss it. The museum was conceived as a repository for several national collections, including art owned by the royal family. Today, Rembrandts, Vermeers, porcelains and countless other treasures crowd its 1.5km of gallery space, which incorporates 80 separate rooms.

The Layout

The museum is spread over four levels, from Floor 0 (where the main atrium is) to Floor 3. The collection is huge. You can see the highlights in a couple of hours, but art buffs will want to allocate much longer.

Pick up a floor plan from the information desk by the entrance. Galleries are well marked; each room displays the gallery's number and theme, which is easy to match to the floor plan.

Floor 2: 1600–1700

Most visitors make a beeline for the Golden Age masterpieces, which are in the Gallery of Honour on Floor 2. It's a bit convoluted to reach. After you go through the ticket gate, head right past the audio tour desk and go up the stairs (the ones by the sign marked 'The Collection'). Walk back to the next set of stairs and ascend – you're following the '1600–1700' signs, though they're not easy to spot. Eventually you'll come to the Great Hall. Push open the glass doors to enter the Gallery of Honour.

Frans Hals

The first room displays several paintings by Frans Hals, who painted with broad brushstrokes and a fluidity that was unique for the time. *The Merry Drinker* (1628–30) shows his style in action. No one knows who the gent with the glass is, but it's clear he's enjoying himself after a hard day's work.

Johannes (Jan) Vermeer

The next room draws crowds to a couple of famed Vermeer works. Check out the *Kitchen Maid* (1660) for Vermeer's noted attention to detail. See the holes in the wall? The nail with shadow? In *Woman in Blue Reading a Letter* (1663) Vermeer uses a different style. He shows only parts of objects, such as the tables and chairs, leaving the viewer to figure out the rest.

Jan Steen

Another Jan hangs across the hall from Vermeer. Jan Steen became renowned for painting chaotic households, such as the one in *The Merry Family* (1668). Everyone is having such a good time in the picture, no one notices the little boy sneaking a taste of wine. Steen's images made quite an impression: in the 18th century the expression 'a Jan Steen household' entered the local lexicon to mean a crazy state of affairs.

Rembrandt

You'll pass through a room of landscape paintings, and then come to a gallery of Rembrandt's works. *The Jewish Bride* (1665), showing a couple's intimate caress, impressed Van Gogh, who declared he would give up a decade of his life just to sit before the painting for a fortnight with only a crust of bread to eat.

DON'T MISS

- Rembrandt's *Night Watch*
- Frans Hals' *The Merry Drinker*
- Vermeer's *Kitchen Maid*
- Delftware pottery
- Special Collections

PRACTICALITIES

- National Museum
- Map p322
- ☎674 70 00
- www.rijksmuseum.nl
- Museumstraat 1
- adult/child €17.50/free
- 9am-5pm
- 2/5 Rijksmuseum

QUEUES & TICKETS

Entrance queues can be long. Friday, Saturday and Sunday are the busiest days. It's least crowded after 3pm. Buy and print your ticket online to save time (there's no surcharge). While you still must wait in the outdoor queue, once inside you can proceed straight into the museum (otherwise you must stand in another queue to pay). Museumkaart owners get the same privilege; I Amsterdam Card holders do not (the card provides a small discount, but not free admission).

Download the museum's free app (there's wi-fi onsite). It offers seven tours through the collection, covering everything from Floor 2 Highlights to Golden Age masterpieces. Each jaunt takes 45 to 90 minutes.

AIRPORT ART

The Rijksmuseum has a free mini-branch at Schiphol airport that hangs 10 to 15 stellar Golden Age paintings. It's located after passport control between the E and F Piers, and is open from 7am to 8pm daily.

Rembrandt's gigantic *Night Watch* (1642) takes pride of place in the subsequent room. It shows the militia led by Frans Banning Cocq. The work is actually titled *Archers under the Command of Captain Frans Banning Cocq*. The *Night Watch* name was bestowed years later, thanks to a layer of grime that gave the impression it was evening. It's since been restored to its original colours. Several other huge civic guard paintings surround it.

Delftware & Dollhouses

Intriguing Golden Age swag fills the rooms on either side of the Gallery of Honour. Delftware was the Dutch attempt to reproduce Chinese porcelain in the late 1600s; gallery 2.22 displays scads of the delicate blue-and-white pottery. Gallery 2.20 is devoted to mind-blowing dollhouses. Merchant's wife Petronella Oortman employed carpenters, glassblowers and silversmiths to make the 700 items inside her dollhouse, using the same materials as they would for full-scale versions.

Floor 3: 1900–2000

The uppermost floor holds a fairly limited collection. It includes avant-garde, childlike paintings by Karel Appel, Constant Nieuwenhuys and their CoBrA compadres (a post WWII movement) and cool furnishings by Dutch designers such as Gerrit Rietveld and Michel de Klerk.

Floor 1: 1700–1900

Highlights on Floor 1 include the *Battle of Waterloo*, the Rijksmuseum's largest painting (in Gallery 1.12). Three Van Gogh paintings hang in Gallery 1.18. Gallery 1.16 recreates a gilded, 18th-century canal-house room.

Floor 0: 1100–1600

This is an awesome floor for lovers of curiosities and less-visited arts. The Special Collections present peculiar tidbits such as locks, keys, magic lanterns, old dresses, goblets and ship models. The Asian Pavilion, a separate structure that's often devoid of crowds, holds first-rate artworks from China, Indonesia, Japan, India, Thailand and Vietnam.

Facade & Gardens

Pierre Cuypers designed the 1885 building. Check out the exterior, which mixes neo-Gothic and Dutch Renaissance styles. The museum's gardens – aka the 'outdoor gallery' – host big-name sculpture exhibitions at least once a year. They're free to stroll, and boast roses, hedges, fountains and a cool greenhouse.

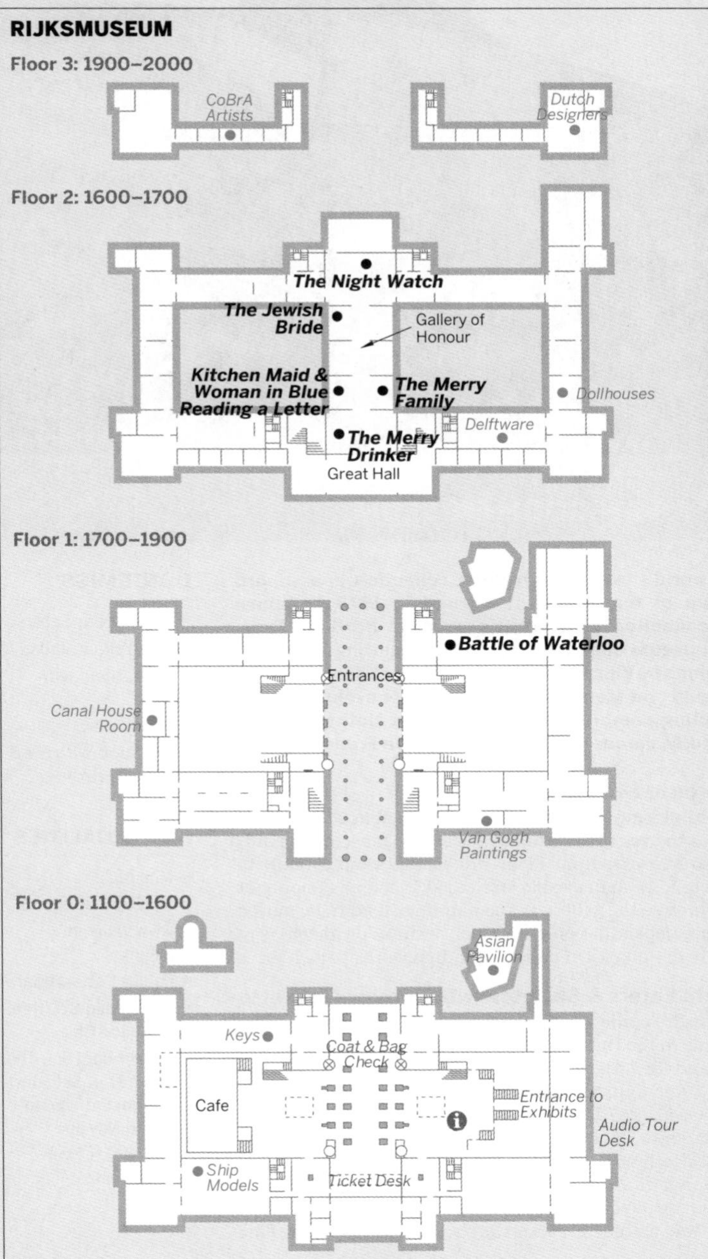
RIJKSMUSEUM
Floor 3: 1900–2000
CoBrA Artists
Dutch Designers
Floor 2: 1600–1700
The Night Watch
The Jewish Bride
Gallery of Honour
Kitchen Maid & Woman in Blue Reading a Letter
The Merry Family
Dollhouses
Delftware
The Merry Drinker
Great Hall
Floor 1: 1700–1900
Battle of Waterloo
Entrances
Canal House Room
Van Gogh Paintings
Floor 0: 1100–1600
Asian Pavilion
Keys
Coat & Bag Check
Cafe
Entrance to Exhibits
Audio Tour Desk
Ship Models
Ticket Desk

TOP SIGHT
VAN GOGH MUSEUM

The world's largest Van Gogh collection is a superb line-up of masterworks. Opened in 1973 to house the collection of Vincent's younger brother, Theo, the museum comprises some 200 paintings and 500 drawings by Vincent and his contemporaries, including Gauguin and Monet. Chart Van Gogh's evolution from depicting sombre countryfolk in the Netherlands to his giddy, colour-swirled landscapes in France.

Museum Setup & Highlights

A dazzling new glass entrance hall opened in 2015, adding 800 sq metres of additional space. The museum spreads over four levels, from Floor 0 (aka the ground floor) to Floor 3. It's a manageable size; allow a couple of hours or so to browse the galleries. The paintings tend to be moved around, depending on the current exhibition theme (say, Van Gogh's images of nature). Seminal works to look for:

Potato Eaters & Skeleton with Burning Cigarette

Van Gogh's earliest works – shadowy and crude – are from his time in the Dutch countryside and in Antwerp between 1883 and 1885. He was particularly obsessed with peasants – *The Potato Eaters* (1885) is his most famous painting from this period. *Still Life with Bible* (1885) shows his religious inclinations. The burnt-out candle is said to represent the recent death of his father, who was a Protestant minister. *Skeleton with Burning Cigarette* (1886) – the print all the stoners are buying in the gift shop – was painted when Van Gogh was a student at Antwerp's Royal Academy of Fine Arts.

DON'T MISS

- *The Potato Eaters*
- *The Yellow House*
- *Wheatfield with Crows*
- *Sunflowers*
- *Skeleton with Burning Cigarette*

PRACTICALITIES

- Map p322
- 570 52 00
- www.vangoghmuseum.nl
- Paulus Potterstraat 7
- adult/child €17/free, audio guide €5
- 9am-6pm Sun-Thu, to 10pm Fri & Sat Jul-Oct, 9am-5pm Sat-Thu, to 10pm Fri Nov-Jun
- 2/3/5/12 Van Baerlestraat

Self-Portraits

In 1886 Van Gogh moved to Paris, where his brother, Theo, was working as an art dealer. Vincent wanted to master the art of portraiture, but was too poor to pay for models. Several self-portraits resulted. You can see his palette begin to brighten as he comes under the influence of the Impressionists in the city.

Sunflowers & The Yellow House

In 1888 Van Gogh left for Arles in Provence to delve into its colourful landscapes. *Sunflowers* (1889) and other blossoms that shimmer with intense Mediterranean light are from this period. So is *The Yellow House* (1888), a rendering of the abode Van Gogh rented in Arles, intending to start an artists' colony with Gaugin. *The Bedroom* (1888) depicts Van Gogh's sleeping quarters at the house. In 1888 Van Gogh sliced off part of his ear.

Wheatfield with Crows

Van Gogh had himself committed to an asylum in St Remy in 1889. While there he painted several landscapes with cypress and olive trees, and went wild with *Irises*. In 1890 he went north to Auvers-sur-Oise. One of his last paintings, *Wheatfield with Crows* (1890), is an ominous work finished shortly before his suicide.

Extras

Intriguing displays enhance what's on the walls. For instance, you might see Van Gogh's actual sketchbook alongside an interactive kiosk that lets you page through a reproduction of the book. The museum has categorised all of Van Gogh's letters online at www.vangoghletters.org. Use the museum's free wi-fi to access them with your smartphone.

Other Artists

Thanks to Theo van Gogh's prescient collecting and that of the museum's curators, you'll also see works by Vincent's contemporaries, including Gauguin, Monet and Henri de Toulouse-Lautrec. In addition, paintings by Van Gogh's precursors, such as Jean-François Millet and Gustave Courbet, pepper the galleries, as do works by artists Van Gogh influenced.

Exhibition Wing

Gerrit Rietveld, the influential Dutch architect, designed the museum's main building. Behind it, reaching toward the Museumplein, is a separate wing (opened in 1999) designed by Kisho Kurokawa and commonly referred to as 'the Mussel'. It hosts temporary exhibitions by big-name artists.

QUEUES & TICKETS

Entrance queues can be long, as only so many visitors are allowed inside at a time. Try waiting until after 3pm. I Amsterdam Card and Holland Pass holders have a separate 'fast' lane for entry, which moves smoothly. E-ticket ticket holders and Museumkaart owners fare the best in their quick-moving lane. E-tickets are available online or at tourist information offices, with no surcharge. They must be printed.

While Van Gogh would come to be regarded as a giant among artists, he sold only one painting during his lifetime *(Red Vineyard at Arles)*. It hangs at Moscow's Pushkin Museum.

FRIDAY NIGHTS

The museum stays open to 10pm on Friday, when it hosts special cultural events and opens a bar downstairs. There's usually live music or a DJ.

The museum's library (Map p322; Museumplein 4; ⏲10am-12.30pm & 1.30-5pm Mon-Fri) FREE has a wealth of reference material – some 35,000 books and articles – for serious study.

TOP SIGHT
STEDELIJK MUSEUM

Amsterdam's weighty modern art museum is among the world's best. The permanent collection includes works by Claude Monet, Pablo Picasso and all the blue chips of the 19th- and 20th-century art world. Displays of textiles, glassworks, posters and cool industrial design pieces add to the engaging scene. Ubercontemporary installations show in its huge recently added wing.

Main Building: Matisse to Wonder Woman

AM Weissman designed the 1895 main building. On the ground floor you'll see all sorts of masterpieces from the 90,000-works collection: Henri Matisse cut-outs, Picasso abstracts, Auguste Rodin sculptures, a vivid collection of paintings by Dutch homeboys Piet Mondrian, Willem de Kooning, Charlie Toorop and Karel Appel, and WWII images by Underground Camera photographer Emmy Andriesse. The Design section – which takes up half of the floor – is particularly awesome, showing inventive jewellery, ceramics, homewares and furniture by masters such as Gerrit Rietveld and Ludwig Mies van der Rohe.

Head upstairs, and the works become more modern, ranging from 1950 to the present. Here you might view anything from a neon sign of fornicating couples to a *Wonder Woman* video installation or maybe a cluster of lava lights. Exhibits change regularly, so you never know what will be on hand, but count on it being offbeat and provocative.

DON'T MISS

- Design collection
- Escalator to the Bathtub
- Piet Mondrian grid paintings
- Henri Matisse paper cut-outs
- Museum highlights tour

PRACTICALITIES

- Map p322
- ☎573 29 11
- www.stedelijk.nl
- Museumplein 10
- adult/child €15/free, audio guide €5
- ⏲10am-6pm Fri-Wed, to 10pm Thu
- 🚋2/3/5/12 Van Baerlestraat

The Bathtub: Mega Mod

The new wing, aka 'the Bathtub' (you'll know why when you see it), is accessed via a trippy, white-lit escalator that doubles as a piece of sound art. Big-name contemporary artists use the galleries here for temporary exhibitions.

That smooth, white tub material, by the way, is called Twaron, a synthetic fiber that's five times as strong as steel and typically used in yacht hulls.

Freebies, Families & Facilities

The Stedelijk doesn't have lengthy queues like its museum neighbours. Admission is free for Museumkaart, I Amsterdam Card and Holland Pass holders. Stop by the front desk when you enter to enquire about free guided tours (Sunday at 2.15pm in Dutch and 3.45pm in English) and gallery talks (typically Thursday, Friday and Sunday). Audio tours (€5) are also available to rent.

The Stedelijk's library (open Tuesday to Saturday from noon to 5pm) is a great resource, with catalogues, books, archive material, art magazines, and art and design documentaries, as well as wi-fi. Admission is free (no museum entrance ticket required).

Kids will find games, drawing materials and other activities in the Family Lab. There's also a special audio tour (€2.50) for young ones.

The cafe on the main floor is a great post-museum refresher. Join the locals sipping from the strong list of wines, both still and sparkling.

TOP SIGHT
VONDELPARK

The urban idyll of Vondelpark is one of Amsterdam's most magical places. On a sunny day, an open-air party atmosphere ensues when tourists, lovers, cyclists, in-line skaters, pram-pushing parents, cartwheeling children, football-kicking teenagers, spliff-sharing friends and champagne-swilling picnickers all come out to play. While the park receives over 10 million visitors per year, it never feels too crowded to enjoy.

Originally known as Nieuwe Park (New Park), these sprawling, English-style gardens, with ponds, lawns, footbridges and winding footpaths, were laid out on marshland by architect Jan David Zocher and opened in 1865. Between 1875 and 1877, Zocher's son, Louis Paul Zocher, expanded the park to its current size of 47 hectares.

In 1867 a **statue** (Map p322) of poet and playwright Joost van den Vondel (1587–1679) was created by sculptor Louis Royer. Amsterdammers began referring to the park as Vondelspark (Vondel's Park), which led to it being renamed. The **rose garden** (Map p322), with some 70 different species, was added in 1936.

About a century after opening, the swampy location meant the park had actually sunk two to three metres. After it was listed as a national monument in the mid-1990s, major renovations incorporated an extensive drainage system and refurbished walking and cycling paths, while retaining its historic appearance.

Near the eastern end, the 19th-century Italian Renaissance-style **Vondelparkpaviljoen** (Vondelpark Pavilion; Map p322) is now a cafe-bar, Vondelpark3. The park also shelters several other cafes, playgrounds, and a wonderful open-air theatre (p184).

Art is strewn throughout the park, with 69 sculptures all up. Among them is Picasso's soaring abstract work *Figure découpée l'Oiseau* (The Bird), better known locally as **The Fish** (Map p322) (1965), which he donated for the park's centenary.

Catch the park's highlights on a walking tour (p176). For bicycle rentals, MacBike (p135) is relatively close to the park's main entrance.

DON'T MISS

- ➡ The rose garden
- ➡ Picasso's *The Fish*
- ➡ The Openluchttheater

PRACTICALITIES

- ➡ Map p322
- ➡ www.vondelpark.nl
- ➡ 🚊2/5 Hobbemastraat

SIGHTS & ACTIVITIES

RIJKSMUSEUM
MUSEUM

See p167.

VAN GOGH MUSEUM
MUSEUM

See p170.

STEDELIJK MUSEUM
MUSEUM

See p172.

MUSEUMPLEIN
SQUARE

Map p322 (2/3/5/12 Van Baerlestraat) The grassy, people-filled square behind the museums entertains with its skateboard ramp, playground, ice-skating pond (in winter) and 2m-high *I Amsterdam* sculpture (a favourite climbing structure/photo op). Locals toss frisbees, couples hold hands, and everyone picnics here when the weather warms up. The space is also used for public concerts and special events.

Museumplein was laid out to host the World Exhibition in 1883, but gained its lasting title only when the Rijksmuseum opened two years later.

One of many facelifts raised a triangle of turf at the southern end, dubbed the 'ass's ear' for its shape; it's now a popular spot for sun worshippers. There's a large supermarket concealed below.

CONCERTGEBOUW
ARCHITECTURE

Map p322 (www.concertgebouw.nl; Concertgebouwplein 10; tour €10; English-language tours 5pm Mon, 6pm Fri & 12.30pm Sun Jul & Aug, 5pm Mon, 1.30pm Wed & 12.30pm Sun Sep-Jun; 3/5/12/16/24 Museumplein) The literal name 'Concert Hall' scarcely does justice to this amazing facility. Architect AL van Gendt designed the Concertgebouw in neo-Renaissance style. Guided tours (75 minutes) show that, in spite of his limited musical knowledge, he gave the two-tiered Grote Zaal (Main Hall) acoustics that are the envy of sound designers worldwide, along with baroque trim, panels inscribed with the names of classical composers, a massive pipe organ and a grand staircase via which conductors and soloists descend to the stage.

DIAMOND MUSEUM
MUSEUM

Map p322 (www.diamantmuseumamsterdam.nl; Paulus Potterstraat 8; adult/child €8.50/6; 9am-5pm; 2/5 Hobbemastraat) Almost all of the exhibits at the small, low-tech Diamond Museum are clever recreations. Those on a budget can save money by going next door to **Coster Diamonds** (Map p322; 305 55 55; www.costerdiamonds.com; Paulus Potterstraat 2; 9am-5pm; 2/5 Hobbemastraat) – the company owns the museum and is attached to it – and taking a free workshop tour, where you can see gem cutters and polishers doing their thing.

Those who do venture into the museum will find exhibits on the history of the trade and the sparkling creations that have adorned the world's rich and powerful. You'll learn how Amsterdam was the globe's diamond trade epicentre for many centuries, where local Jews dominated the cutting and polishing business, and how the trade moved to Antwerp after WWII once Amsterdam lost its Jewish population. Faux royal crowns and jewel-encrusted swords shine in the display cases.

HOUSE OF BOLS
MUSEUM

Map p322 (www.houseofbols.com; Paulus Potterstraat 14; admission incl 1 cocktail €14.50; noon-5.30pm Sun-Thu, to 9pm Fri, to 7pm Sat; 2/5 Hobbemastraat) An hour's self-guided tour

WORTH A DETOUR

REMBRANDTPARK

Rembrandtpark (Orteliuskade 57; 1/17 Surinameplein) The Vondelpark doesn't have a monopoly on sprawling parkland. To its northwest, surrounded by residential buildings, the bucolic Rembrandtpark spreads over 45 leafy (and watery) hectares and is criss-crossed by walking and cycling paths. Unlike the similarly named Southern Canal Ring party square, Rembrandtplein, the Rembrandtpark is little visited by tourists.

Home to abundant wildlife and birdlife, the park is also a favourite with families for its water-play area, climbing pyramid, adventure playground and Amsterdam's oldest petting zoo, **Kinderboerderij de Uylenburg** (618 52 35; www.kinderboerderij-uylenburg.nl; Staalmeesterslaan 420; animal feed per cup €0.50; 10am-5pm; 13 Admiraal Helfrichstraat). In the northwestern corner of the park, the zoo has been here for close to four decades, and kids can interact with donkeys, goats, pigs, sheep, ponies and other friendly critters.

through this *jenever* (Dutch gin) museum includes a confusing sniff test, a distilled history of the Bols company and a cocktail made by one of its formidable bartenders, who train at the academy upstairs. It's kind of cheesy (especially the 'flair booth' where you try out bottle-flipping skills), but fun. On Friday after 5pm admission is €9.50.

VONDELPARK PARK

See p173.

HOLLANDSCHE MANEGE RIDING SCHOOL

Map p322 (☎618 09 42; www.dehollandschemanege.nl; Vondelstraat 140; adult/child €8/4, private riding lessons per 30 min/1hr €37/61; ⏰10am-5pm; 🚋1 1e Constantijn Huygensstraat) Just outside Vondelpark is the neoclassical Hollandsche Manege, an indoor riding school inspired by the famous Spanish Riding School in Vienna. Designed by AL van Gendt and built in 1882, it retains its charming horse-head facade. Take a riding lesson and/or watch the instructors put the horses through their paces during high tea (€24.50) at the elevated cafe.

VONDELKERK HISTORIC BUILDING

Map p322 (www.vondelkerk.nl; Vondelstraat 120d; 🚋1 1e Constantijn Huygensstraat) Architect Pierre Cuypers' favourite church, which he designed and built between 1870 and 1880, suffered from a lack of funds during construction and a fire in 1904. Slated for demolition in 1978, it was saved by a group of architecture enthusiasts. It's a charming steepled church building featuring a fascinating series of shapes with an octagon at its base. The interior (a popular wedding venue) is closed to the public.

EATING

International options abound around Amstelveenseweg and inside De Hallen's Foodhallen (p182). Head to Vondelpark's squats (p184) for organic vegan fare. Several snack vendors line the pavement between the Rijksmuseum and Van Gogh Museum, serving burgers, sandwiches, ice cream and drinks.

★BRAAI BBQ BAR BARBECUE €

(www.braaiamsterdam.nl; Schinkelhavenkade 1; dishes €5-11; ⏰11am-10pm; 🚋1 Overtoomsesluis) A canal-side *haringhuis* (herring stand) has been brilliantly converted into a street-food-style barbecue bar. Snacks span sandwiches such as hummus and grilled veggies or smoked *ossenworst* (raw-beef sausage originating from Amsterdam), a cheese and bacon burger and Braai's speciality – marinated, barbecued ribs (half or full rack). PIN cards are preferred, but it accepts cash. Tables scatter under the trees.

LOCAL KNOWLEDGE

LEIDSEBOSJE'S LITTLE WOODCUTTER

Little Woodcutter (Map p322; Leidsebosje; 🚋1/2/5 Leidseplein) Hidden up in the Leidsebosje parkland's closest tree to the pedestrian crossing on Stadhouderskade (where it intersects with Leidseplein) is a 50cm-high bronze sculpture of a little woodcutter leaning over and sawing a branch with both hands. The sculpture was installed in 1989, but the artist remains anonymous (rumours persist that it was commissioned by then-sovereign Queen Beatrix, but no one knows for sure). The tree has since grown around the little woodcutter and now engulfs his shoes and saw.

CARTER BISTRO €

Map p322 (☎752 68 55; www.barcarter.nl; Valeriusstraat 85; mains €10-12, 3-course dinner menu €32.50; ⏰4-11pm Mon-Fri, 11am-11pm Sat & Sun; 👪; 🚋16 Emmastraat) The kind of local everyone wishes they had in their 'hood, Carter has a split-level dining space with black banquettes, art and photography covering the walls, and a great kitchen turning out dishes such as deep-fried whitebait with wasabi mayo, lobster *bitterballen* (croquettes) with lemon tarragon sauce, a truffle wagyu burger, rib-eye steak with rose-and-pepper sauce, and lemongrass crème brûlée.

Its three-course kids' menu (€16) comes with vegetable chips with tomato mayo, a make-your-own hot dog, and an Oreo milkshake for dessert.

BREAKFAST CLUB CAFE €

Map p322 (www.thebreakfastclub.nl; Bellamystraat 2; dishes €4.50-16; ⏰8am-4pm Mon-Fri, to 5pm Sat & Sun; 🚋17 Ten Katestraat) All-day breakfasts are the speciality of the laid-back Breakfast Club: ricotta flapjacks with honeycomb butter; a full English breakfast with homemade baked beans, bacon, eggs, mushrooms and sausages; buckwheat pancakes with maple

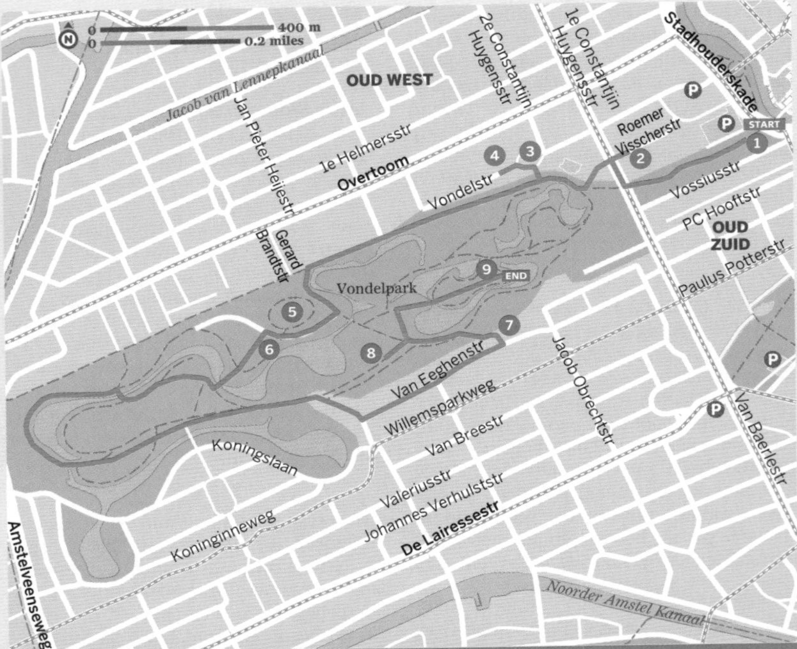

Neighbourhood Walk
Vondelpark

START VONDELPARK MAIN ENTRANCE
END 'T BLAUWE THEEHUIS
LENGTH 4.5KM; 2½ HOURS

While an unstructured stroll through Vondelpark is wonderful, this tour ensures you'll hit the key highlights in and around the park, from a fragrant rose garden to a Moorish manor to art-nouveau treasures.

Enter the park through the 1 **main entrance** and walk straight ahead; climb the stairs on the northern side of the bridge and exit the park along pretty 2 **Roemer Visscherstraat**, where you'll come upon a row of houses built in 1894 in varying styles: English cottage, Dutch Renaissance, onion-domed Russian cathedral, Italian palazzo, Moorish-style Spanish, French Loire Valley chateau and German Romantic.

Head back into the park, picking up the northwest walking loop path and passing the Vondelparkpaviljoen, and exit the park again on Vondelstraat to check out the lovely 3 **Vondelkerk** (p175). Continue west along Vondelstraat to the magnificent riding school, the 4 **Hollandsche Manege** (p175). Return to the park and amble west to the 5 **Joost van den Vondel statue** (p173), which inspired the park's name. Continue round past the statue until you reach the beautiful 6 **rose garden** (p173); it's seldom crowded even in high season.

Cross the footbridge and follow the path to the next footbridge; cross it, too, and follow the path as it loops around the pond and then heads east. Take the second exit to detour down Van Eeghenstraat to see some of the city's most exquisite art-nouveau architecture; the highlight is the ornate 7 **Hotel Atlas** (at number 64). Re-enter the park just west of the hotel and follow the western path. Where the path diverges, take the left-hand fork; Picasso's towering sculpture 8 **The Fish** (p173) is on your right. Return to the fork, walk north and take the right-hand path leading east over a footbridge past the Openluchttheater until you reach the space-agey-looking cafe 9 **'t Blauwe Theehuis** (p183).

syrup; or home-baked croissants and seasonal jam. It also does super-charged smoothies such as beetroot, apple and strawberry, or banana, coconut milk and cocoa powder.

ARTI CHOC SWEETS €

(www.artichoc.nl; Koninginneweg 141; chocolates €1.25-4.50, ice cream per scoop €1.75; ⏲9.30am-6pm Tue-Fri, to 5pm Sat; 🚊2 Valeriusplein) Melt over Arti Choc's homemade pralines and truffles: there are over 50 kinds, including gluten-free, cocoa-free and lactose-free varieties. It can also design and make custom chocolates, including clogs, tulips or Delft-blue tiles. In summer, the shop serves Monte Pelmo (p152) ice cream.

HOLY RAVIOLI ITALIAN €

Map p322 (www.holyravioli.nl; Jan Pieter Heijestraat 88; mains €6.50-12; ⏲1-9pm Sun-Tue, 11am-9pm Wed-Sat; 🚊7/17 Jan Pieter Heijestraat) Pasta-maker Holy Ravioli supplies restaurants around town, but you can get ready-to-eat take-away meals here (or, if you're lucky, snag a seat at its two tables). Delicious ravioli varieties include veal and sage with anchovy butter and wild spinach salad, and goats cheese with orange, rocket and parmesan salad; or try the confit duck, black truffle and forest mushroom lasagne.

MECH MAKE & TAKE SANDWICHES €

Map p322 (www.mech.nl; Willemsparkweg 152; dishes €4.50-7; ⏲8am-5pm Mon-Fri, 9am-5pm Sat; 🚊2 Cornelis Schuytstraat) Jump-start the day with a French double espresso, croissant and freshly squeezed OJ, or stop by for salads and baguettes with fillings such as smoked raw beef sausage with mustard mayo, at this hip, red-brick cafe. The long bench out front is a prime spot to watch the action along Willemsparkweg and Cornelis Schuytstraat.

DEEGROLLERS PIZZA €

Map p322 (☎221 20 98; Jan Pieter Heijestraat 10; pizzas €9-15; ⏲5-10pm; 🚊1 Jan Pieter Heijestraat) In a relaxed industrial-rustic space, a long communal table and a window-facing bench both make sociable perches while dining on pizza straight from the wood-fire oven. Toppings include '5 formaggi' (mozzarella, buffalo mozzarella, *provola,* pecorino and gorgonzola), 'Tartufo' (black truffle, rocket, cherry tomatoes and fresh basil), 'Diavola' (salami, olives, paprika and basil) and 'Carloforte' (tuna, cherry tomatoes and homemade pesto).

IJSBOUTIQUE ICE CREAM €

Map p322 (www.ijsboutique.nl; Johannes Verhulststraat 105; ice cream 1/2/3/4 scoops €1.50/3/4/5; ⏲noon-10pm; 🚊2 Cornelis Schuytstraat) Located in the stylish shopping area near the junction of Cornelis Schuytstraat and Willemsparkweg, IJsboutique has fittingly sophisticated ice-cream flavours like champagne sorbet, salted caramel, strawberry cheesecake, lemon meringue pie and after-dinner mint. If it's not ice-cream weather, order crispy, piping-hot fries (€2.25 to €2.75) from the adjoining **Frietboutique**, which keeps the same hours.

SCALA DELLA PASTA DELI, CAFE €

(www.scaladellapasta.nl; Valeriusstraat 90; dishes €4.50-15.50; ⏲9am-8pm Mon-Sat, 11am-8pm Sun; 🚊Emmastraat) A neighbourhood gathering spot, this greengrocer-style deli-cafe fronted by a striped awning has fantastic sandwich and/or picnic ingredients such as Serrano ham, pastrami, sundried tomatoes, marinated artichokes and Spinata Romana salami, along with pizzas and pastas with toppings such as mascarpone and truffle, mushroom and olive, or gorgonzola, plus heavenly tiramisu and Segafredo coffee. You can also buy wine by the bottle.

ALCHEMIST GARDEN VEGAN €

Map p322 (☎334 33 35; www.alchemistgarden.nl; Overtoom 409; dishes €4-12.50; ⏲8am-10pm Tue-Sat; 📝; 🚊1 Rhijnvis Feithstraat) 🌿 Proving that gluten-, lactose- and glucose-free food can be delicious, this bright, contemporary space serves a vitamin-filled organic menu (raw vegetable pies, sunflower burgers, avocado dumplings and pesto-stuffed portobello mushrooms), plus smoothies, juices and guilt-free treats like raw chocolate cake. Many ingredients are from the owner's own garden. Ask about wild food foraging walks in the Vondelpark.

Tarot readings and hand chakra massages are available.

SAFFRAAN DELI, BISTRO €

Map p322 (www.saffraantraiteur.nl; Jan Pieter Heijestraat 128; dishes €3-12.50; ⏲4-9.30pm Sun-Fri, noon-9.30pm Sat; 🚊1 Jan Pieter Heijestraat) Everything you need for a Vondelpark sunset picnic is here at this chandeliered bareboards deli-bistro: stunning sandwiches (pastrami and sauerkraut with pickles and mustard mayo); burgers (fish with seaweed salad); pastas (squid-ink tagliatelle with crayfish, or ricotta ravioli with spinach and walnuts); mushrooms stuffed with cheese, garlic and spinach; salads (quinoa and pumpkin); soup of the day; and organic wine.

LUNCHROOM WILHELMINA CAFE €

Map p322 (618 97 78; www.lunchroomwilhelmina.nl; 1e Helmersstraat 83a; mains €5-9; 9am-5pm; 1 1e Constantijn Huygensstraat) Lined with framed pictures of Dutch royalty beneath a chandelier, this corner cafe is ideal for a simple lunch (quiches, soups), brunch or *borrel* (drinks).

RENZO'S ITALIAN, DELI €

Map p322 (673 16 73; www.renzosdelicatessen.nl; Van Baerlestraat 67; dishes per 100g €1.50-3.50, sandwiches €5-6; 9am-7pm Mon-Fri, 10am-9pm Sat & Sun; 3/5/12/16/24 Museumplein) Renzo's deli doles out most of its pastas, thickly cut sandwiches and omelettes to take away, but don't be shy about tucking in at the tables on the small mezzanine or mini terrace.

TOASTY CAFE €

Map p322 (www.toasty.nl; Overtoom 437; toasties €3.50-6; 8am-5pm Mon-Fri, 9am-5pm Sat & Sun; ; 1 Rhijnvis Feithstraat) Delicious variations on the humble toasted sandwich here include pastrami and mustard; pear and honey; brie, sundried tomato, rocket and cranberry compote; and a terrific tuna melt, all on a choice of white, brown, multigrain or corn bread.

DE BAKKERSWINKEL BAKERY €

Map p322 (www.debakkerswinkel.com; Roelof Hartstraat 68; dishes €4-11; 7.30am-5pm Tue-Sat, 10am-4pm Sun; ; 3/5/12/24 Roelof Hartplein) This is the original location of the local bakery mini-chain. Order one of the famed scones or a sandwich on wonderfully crusty bread, and take it to the big communal table in the bright lunchroom or the tiny, delightful back garden.

★**RON GASTROBAR** MODERN DUTCH €€

Map p322 (496 19 43; www.rongastrobar.nl; Sophialaan 55; dishes €15, desserts €9; noon-2.30pm & 5.30-10.30pm Mon-Fri, noon-10.30pm Sat & Sun; ; 2 Amstelveenseweg) Ron Blaauw ran his two-Michelin-star restaurant in these stunning designer premises before trading the stars in to transform the space into an egalitarian 'gastrobar', serving around 25 one-flat-price tapas-style dishes such as steak tartare with crispy veal brains, mushroom ravioli with sweet-potato foam, barbecue-smoked bone marrow, Dutch asparagus with lobster-and-champagne sauce, and wagyu burgers – with no minimum order restrictions.

The crafting and flavour combinations remain haute-cuisine standard (the new format was recently awarded a Michelin star in its own right), and are affordable, too.

★**DIKKE GRAAF** MEDITERRANEAN €€

Map p322 (223 77 56; www.dikkegraaf.nl; Wilhelminastraat 153; bar snacks €3.50-15, mains €12.50-22.50; kitchen 3-10pm Wed-Sun; 1 Rhijnvis Feithstraat) Heavenly cooking aromas tip you off to this local secret adorned with copper lamps and black tiling, and opening to a terrace. It's a truly fabulous spot for *borrel* (drinks), with gin cocktails, by-the-glass wines and bar snacks such as oysters, bruschetta, charcuterie and manchego sheep's cheese, and/or heartier, nightly changing meat, fish and pasta dishes.

★**ADAM** GASTRONOMY €€

Map p322 (233 98 52; www.restaurantadam.nl; Overtoom 515; mains €21-24.50, 3-/4-/5-/6-course menus €35/42.50/50/57.50; 6-10.30pm Tue-Sat; 1 Overtoomsesluis) Widely tipped around town for a Michelin star, this chic restaurant serves exquisitely presented gastronomic fare, such as steak tartare with quail's egg, crispy pork belly with celeriac, sea bass with white asparagus, and *côte de bœuf* (on-the-bone rib steak) for two. Dessert is either a cheese platter or a chef's surprise. Paired wines are available for €7.50 per glass.

NARBONNE BISTRO €€

Map p322 (618 32 63; www.narbonne.nl; Bosboom Toussaintstraat 28; tapas €4.50-14, mains €16-23; 5.30-11pm Tue-Sun; 1 1e Constantijn Huygensstraat) A neighbourhood treasure, down-to-earth Narbonne serves main courses such as lamb shank with baked garlic potatoes, but the reason it's locally loved is its tapas, such as smoked mozzarella tortellini, fried manchego sheep's cheese, marinated artichokes, prawns in filo pastry, fresh oysters with lime-and-chive dressing, green-olive tapenade with crusty bread, and grilled beef skewers. Book ahead.

L'ENTRECÔTE ET LES DAMES FRENCH €€

Map p322 (679 88 88; www.entrecote-et-les-dames.nl; Van Baerlestraat 47-49; lunch mains €12.50, 2-course dinner menu €24; noon-3pm & 5.30-10pm; 16/24 Museumplein) With a double-height wall made from wooden drawers and a wrought-iron-balustraded mezzanine seating area, the decor is stunning – but still secondary to the food. The two-course dinner menu offers a meat or fish option, but everyone's here for the entrecôte (premium beef steak). Save room for scrumptious desserts: perhaps chocolate mousse, *tarte au citron* (lemon tart) or *crêpes au Grand Marnier*.

LA FALOTE
DUTCH €€

Map p322 (662 54 54; www.lafalote.nl; Roelof Hartstraat 26; mains €15-23; 2-9pm Mon-Sat; 3/5/12/24 Roelof Hartplein) Wee La Falote, with its chequered tablecloths, focuses on daily changing Dutch home-style dishes such as calf liver, meatballs with endives, or stewed fish with beets and mustard sauce. The prices are a bargain in an otherwise ritzy neighbourhood; and wait till the owner brings out the accordion. Cash only.

VAN 'T SPIT
ROTISSERIE €€

Map p322 (www.vantspit.nl; De Clercqstraat 95; half/whole chicken €10/19.50, sides €3.50-5; kitchen 5pm-midnight; 12/13/14 Willem de Zwijgerlaan) Cut timber logs line the walls at hip, stripped-back Van 't Spit, but they're not just for show – they're the fuel for the wood-fired rotisserie that spit-roasts delicious chicken. Decisions here are limited simply to a half or whole chicken (there are no other mains), and whether you want sides (corn on the cob, fries, salad and homemade coleslaw).

The bar stays open until 1am.

BRASSERIE DE JOFFERS
BRASSERIE €€

Map p322 (673 03 60; www.brasseriedejoffers.nl; Willemsparkweg 163; mains €15.50-21.50, 3-course menu €27.50; 8am-10pm Mon-Sat, 9am-8pm Sun; ; 2 Cornelis Schuytstraat) A timber and curved-glass shopfront, a table-lined terrace and a gorgeous interior with a striped velour banquette entice you into this art-deco brasserie. But what will keep you coming back through the day is the food, from flaky croissants to ricotta-and-sundried-tomato-filled tortellini in walnut and tomato sauce to Portuguese *cataplana* (fish and crustacean stew with rice).

CAFÉ TOUSSAINT
BISTRO €€

Map p322 (685 07 37; www.bosboom-toussaint.nl; Bosboom Toussaintstraat 26; small plates €5-9, mains €15-22; kitchen 10am-11pm; ; 1 1e Constantijn Huygensstraat) On one of Amsterdam's prettiest streets, this casual neighbourhood gem feels like it's straight out of an Edith Piaf song. Come to sip cappuccino under the trees or, in the candlelit evenings, for creative interpretations of old classics – pan-fried mullet with fennel and orange, feta ravioli with peas, mint and almond shavings, and figs in port with vanilla ice cream.

GEORGE BISTRO BISTRO
BISTRO €€

(www.cafegeorge.nl; Valeriusplein 2; mains €11-20; 11.30am-11pm Mon-Fri, 10am-11pm Sat & Sun; 2 Valeriusplein) No, you're not seeing double, there are two Bistros in the name. Signature dishes at buzzing George's include whole charcoal-grilled lobster with garlic butter and lemon, half or whole rotisserie-cooked chicken, and eight different burgers (including halloumi, tuna with wasabi mayo, and smoked bacon and cheese) on toasted brioche buns. Breakfast is served on weekends from 10am to 12.30pm.

ZUS & ZUS
BISTRO €€

Map p322 (616 58 25; www.restaurantzusenzus.nl; Overtoom 548; mains €14.50-17; 6-11pm Mon-Sat; 1 Overtoomsesluis) Zus & Zus (Sister & Sister) is a terrific bet for bistro-style dishes with refreshing twists such as swordfish carpaccio, grilled catfish in anchovy and rosemary sauce, aubergine cannelloni, and Argentinean steak with tomato and olive sauce and roast parsnip, all served in a contemporary red-, orange- and yellow-trimmed dining space. It's fantastic value given the quality; service couldn't be friendlier.

DE ITALIAAN
ITALIAN €€

Map p322 (683 68 54; www.deitaliaan.com; Bosboom Toussaintstraat 29; mains €9.50-21.50; 5.30-10pm; 1 1e Constantijn Huygensstraat) In a hub of restaurants on leafy Bosboom Toussaintstraat, this contemporary two-storey, bare-boards space serves stunning authentic Italian dishes such as Sicilian aubergine stew with ricotta, and cured pork cheek with rigatoni, broad beans and black pepper, as well as magnificent wood-fired pizzas including the house-speciality 'De Italiaan' (gorgonzola, mushrooms, black truffle and rocket).

All of the wines are Italian, spanning vineyards across the country.

LALIBELA
ETHIOPIAN €€

Map p322 (683 83 32; www.lalibela.nl; 1e Helmersstraat 249; mains €10-15; 5-11pm; ; 1 Jan Pieter Heijestraat) Named after the ancient African city, this colourful restaurant just north of Overtoom was the Netherlands' first Ethiopian restaurant and it's still as good as ever. You can drink Ethiopian beer from a half-gourd and eat stews, egg and vegetable dishes using *injera* (slightly sour,

LOCAL KNOWLEDGE

JAN PIETER HEIJESTRAAT

One of the most happening-right-now streets in the 'hood is back-street artery Jan Pieter Heijestraat, which runs south from Kinkerstraat to Overtoom. Hip bars, great local restaurants and out-of-the-box shops continue to pop up here, thanks in large part to the street's proximity to the cultural and design complex **De Hallen** (p182).

Hotspots to watch out for:

- **BarBrå** (p181) House-party-style hang-out with mismatched vintage furniture.
- **Golden Brown Bar** (p183) A JPH trendsetter.
- **Beer Tree** (p185) Craft beer cold in the fridge and on tap to be bottled.
- **Holy Ravioli** (p177) Restaurant supplier that does delicious take-away pastas, too.
- **Deegrollers** (p177) Sociable spot for wood-fired pizza.
- **Saffraan** (p177) Old-school-style deli-bistro.
- **Johnny at the Spot** (p185) Globally sourced edgy fashion and homewares.

spongy pancakes) instead of utensils to a soundtrack of African music.

SEAFOOD BAR — SEAFOOD €€

Map p322 (www.theseafoodbar.nl; Van Baerlestraat 5; mains €14.50-36.50; noon-10pm; ; 2/5 Van Baerlestraat) White-tiled and exposed-brick walls give this seafood specialist a breezy, oceanside feel. Oysters, crabs, lobster and lemon sole are laid out behind glass, and the kitchen turns out freshly cooked fish and chips. No bookings required.

FONDUE & FONDUE — SWISS €€

Map p322 (612 91 04; www.restaurantfondue.nl; Overtoom 415; fondue €16-18.50; kitchen 6-11pm; 1 Rhijnvis Feithstraat) Stylishly refitted with striped herringbone floors and exposed brick, this reasonably priced restaurant serves the most heavenly comfort food to come out of the Alps. Choose from fish (with tuna, salmon and prawns), meat (veal, steak, chicken and pork) or classic cheese fondue (with six different vegetables), all shared between two people. Desserts include a decadent chocolate fondue.

RESTAURANT ELEMENTS — INTERNATIONAL €€

Map p322 (579 17 17; www.heerlijkamsterdam.nl; Roelof Hartstraat 6-8; 4-course menu €24.50; seatings 5.30pm & 7pm Mon-Fri; 3/5/12/24 Roelof Hartplein) Students – the same ones who run the nearby College Hotel (p236) – prepare and serve contemporary international dishes at this mod restaurant. The result is white-glove service at an excellent price. Reserve in advance. No credit cards.

RESTAURANT DE KNIJP — FRENCH €€

Map p322 (671 42 48; http://deknijp.jubels.nl; Van Baerlestraat 134; mains €18-26; 5.30pm-12.30am; 3/5/12/16/24 Museumplein) Fork into French classics – snails in creamy garlic sauce, beef in buttery béarnaise sauce, crème caramel – in this warm, inviting, split-level bistro. De Knijp serves its compact menu of fish and meat dishes later than most places in the neighbourhood. The snug wood tables tend to fill up when there's a show at the nearby Concertgebouw.

SAMA SEBO — INDONESIAN €€

Map p322 (662 81 46; www.samasebo.nl; PC Hooftstraat 27; mains €8, rijsttafel per person lunch/dinner €18/31.50; noon-3pm & 5-10pm Mon-Sat; 2/5 Hobbemastraat) Sama Sebo looks more like a brown *café* than a trip to the South Seas, and that's OK. The rijsttafel (Indonesian banquet) is 17 dishes (four to seven at lunchtime), but you can get individual plates if that's too much.

PASTIS — FRENCH, EUROPEAN €€

Map p322 (616 61 66; www.pastisamsterdam.nl; 1e Constantijn Huygensstraat 15; mains €12.50-23.50; kitchen 4-10.30pm Mon-Fri, 3-10.30pm Sat & Sun; 1 1e Constantijn Huygensstraat) From Pastis' red awning, pavement tables, rustic interior with old French advertising posters, charcuterie including house-made pâté, steak tartare, confit of chicken or beef shoulder with parmesan and truffle *frites* (fries) – as well as its namesake anise-flavoured spirit – you could conceivably think you'd arrived in Provence, but the wines and cheeses (and some mains) are increasingly pan-European.

RESTAURANT BLAUW INDONESIAN €€€

(☎675 50 00; www.restaurantblauw.nl; Amstelveenseweg 158; mains €21.50-27.50, rijsttafel per person €26.50-31.50; ⊙6-10.30pm Mon-Fri, 5-10.30pm Sat & Sun; 🚇2 Amstelveenseweg) The *New York Times* voted Blauw the 'best Indonesian restaurant in the Netherlands' and legions agree, because the large, contemporary dining room is always packed (reserve well ahead). Menu standouts include *ikan pesmol* (fried fish with candlenut sauce) and *ayam singgand* (chicken in semi-spicy coconut sauce with tumeric leaf) and mouthwatering Indonesian desserts.

BLUE PEPPER INDONESIAN €€€

Map p322 (☎489 70 39; www.restaurantbluepepper.com; Nassaukade 366; mains €26, rijsttafel per person €75; ⊙6-10pm; ✍; 🚇7/10 Raamplein) Chef Sonja Pereira serves exquisite Indonesian cuisine in her dramatic blue dining room. The rijsttafel includes specialities from across the islands, such as fish steamed in banana leaves, spicy prawns in fiery red sauce, lamb satay with lime and soy sauce, and soft shell crab with mango and pineapple.

DRINKING & NIGHTLIFE

★FRANKLIN COCKTAIL BAR

(www.barfranklin.nl; Amstelveenseweg 156; ⊙5pm-1am Tue-Thu, to 3am Fri & Sat; 🚇2 Amstelveenseweg) Creative cocktails at this split-level, stained-glass-windowed bar include Picnic at Vondel (lemon-infused gin, summer fruit syrup and chardonnay), Smoke on the Water (*mezcal,* lime syrup and dandelion bitters) and a Porn Star Martini (vanilla-infused vodka, passion fruit purée and Prosecco). Warm evenings see its summer terrace get packed to capacity – arrive early to get a seat.

★CRAFT & DRAFT BEER CAFÉ

Map p322 (www.craftanddraft.nl; Overtoom 417; ⊙bar 2pm-midnight Sun-Thu, to 2am Fri & Sat, shop 2-10pm daily; 🚇1 Rhijnvis Feithstraat) Craft beer fans are spoilt for choice, with no fewer than 40 different beers on tap. A huge blackboard chalks up each day's draught – or draft – offerings, such as Belgian 3 Floyds' Lips of Faith, American Coronado's Stupid Stout and Evil Twin's Yang, British Red Willow's Thoughtless, Swedish Sigtuna's Organic Ale and Danish Mikkeller's Peter, Pale & Mary.

★LOT SIXTY ONE COFFEE

Map p322 (www.lotsixtyonecoffee.com; Kinkerstraat 112; ⊙8am-5pm Mon-Fri, 9am-5pm Sat, 10am-5pm Sun; 🚇3/12 Bilderdijkstraat) 🌿 Look downstairs to the open cellar to see (and better yet, smell) coffee being roasted at this streetwise spot. Beans are sourced from individual ecofriendly farms; varieties include Ethiopian Tchembe, Tanzanian Aranga, Colombian Gerado, Costa Rican Don Mayo, Guatemalan Maravilla and Rwandan Mahembe. All coffees are double shots (unless you specify otherwise); watch Kinkerstraat's passing parade from benches out front.

You can also buy bags of beans to take away.

CAFÉ BÉDIER BROWN CAFÉ

Map p322 (☎662 44 15; Sophialaan 36; ⊙noon-1am Mon-Thu, to 3am Fri, 11am-3am Sat, to 1am Sun; 🚇2 Amstelveenseweg) At the end of the work day, the terrace out the front of Café Bédier is often so crowded it looks like a street party in full swing. Inside, the leather-upholstered wall panels, modular seats and hardwood floors put a 21st-century twist on classic brown *café* decor. Top-notch bar food, too.

BARBRÅ BAR

Map p322 (www.bar-bra.nl; Jan Pieter Heijestraat 137; ⊙4pm-midnight Wed & Thu, 10am-3am Fri & Sat, to 11pm Sun; 🚇1 Jan Pieter Heijestraat) Not, perhaps, what the name might suggest (*brå* means 'good' in Swedish and Norwegian), this cosy hang-out with mismatched, recycled furniture and industrial light fittings feels more like a party in someone's apartment, with comfy vintage sofas, armchairs, and stools around the bar. There's a mini terrace out front, but it's so popular it's usually standing room only out there.

Different chefs cook here each night, offering up an ever-changing menu. A Kung Fu movie night takes place once a month on Tuesdays; check the website for schedules.

CAFÉ SCHINKELHAVEN BROWN CAFÉ

(www.cafeschinkelhaven.nl; Amstelveenseweg 126; ⊙11am-1am Sun-Thu, to 3am Fri & Sat; 📶; 🚇2 Amstelveenseweg) Exiting Vondelpark at the western end, Café Schinkelhaven's candle-topped terrace tables make an irresistible pit stop before heading along Amstelveenseweg in search of dinner. Super-friendly staff make you feel like a regular from the moment you arrive.

DE HALLEN

Disused red-brick 1902-built tram sheds were stunningly converted in 2014 to create the vast, skylit **De Hallen** (Map p322; www.dehallen-amsterdam.nl; Bellamyplein 51; 17 Ten Katestraat), a cultural complex incorporating a food hall, steak restaurant, library, design shops, boutiques, a bike seller/repairer, a cinema and a hotel. Regular events held inside include themed **weekend markets** (such as organic produce or Dutch design); check www.localgoodsmarkets.nl to find out what's happening. A lively street market, Ten Katemarkt, is right outside, running Monday to Saturday.

Foodhallen (Map p322; www.foodhallen.nl; Hannie Dankbaar Passage 3; dishes €5-15; 11am-8pm Sun-Wed, to 9pm Thu-Sat) Inside De Hallen, this glorious international food hall has 21 stands surrounding an airy open-plan eating area. Some are offshoots of popular Amsterdam eateries, such as the **Butcher** (p190) and **Wild Moa Pies** (p192); also look out for Viet View Vietnamese street food, Jabugo Iberico Bar ham, Pink Flamingo pizza, Bulls & Dogs hot dogs, Rough Kitchen ribs and De Ballenbar *bitterballen* (croquettes).

Meat West (Map p322; 218 17 76; www.meatwest.nl; Hannie Dankbaar Passage 3; mains €16.50-28; 6-10pm;) Framed by a soaring floor-to-ceiling glass wall looking through to the Foodhallen food hall inside De Hallen, sit-down restaurant Meat West is a classy place for dry-aged steaks, from 250g to 700g. All are served with herb butter or béarnaise sauce. Flavours like raspberry, white chocolate and salted caramel come together in spectacular desserts.

Local Goods Store (Map p322; www.localgoodsstore.nl; Hannie Dankbaar Passage 39; noon-7pm Tue-Fri & Sun, 11am-7pm Sat) As the name implies, everything at this concept shop inside De Hallen is created by Dutch designers. Look for Woody skateboards, I Made Gin gin production kits, Carhusa purses and handbags, Timbies wooden bow ties, Lucila Kenny hand-dyed scarves and jewellery, and Neef Louis industrial vintage homewares, as well as racks of great Dutch-designed casual men's and women's fashion.

Darling (Map p322; www.thedarlingamsterdam.nl; Hannie Dankbaar Passage 19; 11am-6pm Tue-Sun) Offbeat new and vintage women's clothing, accessories (hats, scarves, jewellery) and shoes are stocked at this little De Hallen boutique. Owner Nadine van der Zee can also custom-alter and upcycle pieces to make them more (or even more) original.

ReCycle (Map p322; 489 70 29; www.recyclefietsen.nl; Hannie Dankbaar Passage 27; 9am-6pm Mon-Wed & Fri, to 9pm Thu, 10am-5pm Sat) In a warehouse-like space in De Hallen, ReCycle sells both new and secondhand bikes, carries out bike repairs, and restores classic two-wheelers – and because a bikeless Amsterdammer would be an oxymoron, there's a free bike-rental service while you wait.

Filmhallen (Map p322; www.filmhallen.nl; Hannie Dankbaar Passage 12; tickets adult/child from €10/7.50; 10am-midnight) Art-house films and new mainstream releases run in both Dutch and English at this cinema inside De Hallen. In the polished-concrete foyer, check out the vintage film-making equipment as well as the retro caravan selling popcorn and other snacks.

Ten Katemarkt (Map p322; www.tenkatemarkt.nl; Ten Katestraat; 9am-5pm Mon-Sat) Right outside De Hallen, this buzzing daily street market has everything you'll find at Amsterdam's bigger, better-known markets – fresh fish, fruit and veggies, fabulous Dutch cheeses, antipasti, nuts, spices, ready-to-eat snacks such as steaming-hot *frites*, fashion, fabrics, homewares and bike locks – but a much more local crowd (and, to date, no kitschy souvenirs like fluffy clogs).

COLD PRESSED JUICERY — JUICE BAR

Map p322 (www.thecoldpressedjuicery.com; Willemsparkweg 8; ⏰7.30am-7pm Mon-Fri, 9am-6pm Sat, 10am-6pm Sun; 🚋2 Cornelis Schuytstraat) Get a nutritious fix with a cold-pressed, oxidant-free, all-natural juice such as Iron Man (carrot, turmeric and lemon) or Glow (pineapple, strawberry, beetroot and ginger). Smoothies include Apple Crumble (apple, buckwheat granola, allspice and almond milk) and the Sinner (banana, caramel, coconut, vanilla, cinnamon and cashew milk). Some 99% of its ingredients are organic and, where viable, locally sourced.

HET GROOT MELKHUIS — CAFE

Map p322 (☎612 96 74; www.grootmelkhuis.nl; Vondelpark 2; ⏰10am-6pm; 📶👪; 🚋1 Jan Pieter Heijestraat) At the edge of the Vondelpark's forest, this huge Swiss-chalet-style timber house appears like something out of a fairytale. The vast drinking and dining forecourt and playground cater to families (and all kid-like guests).

GOLLEM'S PROEFLOKAAL — BEER CAFÉ

Map p322 (www.cafegollem.nl; Overtoom 160-162; ⏰1pm-1am Mon-Thu, noon-3am Fri & Sat, to 1am Sun; 🚋1 1e Constantijn Huygensstraat) Take a day trip to Belgium without leaving the Netherlands. Sip a Kriek (cherry beer) or a Trappist ale amid vintage beer signs and paintings of tippling monks, and soak it up with dishes like Trappist cheese fondue, croquettes and Flemish stew. All up there are 30 beers on tap and over 250 bottled varieties.

'T BLAUWE THEEHUIS — CAFE

Map p322 (www.blauwetheehuis.nl; Vondelpark 5; ⏰9am-10pm; 📶; 🚋2 Jacob Obreachstraat) You might think a flying saucer landed in the park as you approach this wacky structure, but it's simply a fabulous cafe surrounded by greenery. In summer the terrace is packed with seemingly everyone in town enjoying coffee and cake or cocktails and dinner.

WELLING — BROWN CAFÉ

Map p322 (www.cafewelling.nl; Jan Willem Brouwersstraat 32; ⏰4pm-1am Mon-Fri, 3pm-1am Sat & Sun; 🚋3/5/12/16/24 Museumplein) Tucked away behind the Concertgebouw, this is a relaxed spot to sip a frothy, cold *biertje* (glass of beer) and mingle with intellectuals and artists. Don't be surprised if the cafe's friendly cat hops onto your lap. There's often live music such as by jazz musicians after their gigs at the Concertgebouw wrap up.

GOLDEN BROWN BAR — BAR

Map p322 (www.goldenbrownbar.nl; Jan Pieter Heijestraat 146; ⏰11am-1am Sun-Thu, to 3am Fri & Sat; 📶; 🚋1 Jan Pieter Heijestraat) A Jan Pieter Heijestraat pacesetter, this perennially hip, two-level bar attracts a young professional crowd that spills out onto the pavement. In winter, the cream-and-brown interior with its mod woodwork and neon-pink-lit bar offers stylish respite from the chill, especially if you snag a seat on the faux velvet couch.

WILDSCHUT — CAFE

Map p322 (www.cafewildschut.nl; Roelof Hartplein 1; ⏰9am-1am Mon-Fri, 10am-1am Sat & Sun; 🚋3/5/12/24 Roelof Hartplein) This is a real gathering place for the Old South. When the weather's warm, pretty much everyone heads to the terrace for views of the Amsterdam School. When the weather's not great, soak up the atmosphere in the art-deco interior.

TUNES BAR — COCKTAIL BAR

Map p322 (www.conservatoriumhotel.com; Van Baerlestraat 27, Conservatorium Hotel; ⏰12.30pm-1am Mon-Thu, to 2am Fri & Sat, to midnight Sun; 🚋2/3/5/12 Van Baerlestraat) Craving a tangerine-tinged gin and tonic with a side of prawn-filled *bitterballen* (croquettes)? Or a glass of sparkling wine and plate of oysters? Pull up a chair at the see-through bar at Tunes, inside the stunning Conservatorium Hotel. Gin drinks are the speciality, but the overall cocktail list is diverse.

Cigar aficionados can puff in the attached smoking lounge.

☆ ENTERTAINMENT

For alternative entertainment including great live music, check out Vondelpark's squats (p184).

★CONCERTGEBOUW — CLASSICAL MUSIC

Map p322 (☎671 83 45; www.concertgebouw.nl; Concertgebouwplein 10; ⏰box office 1-7pm Mon-Fri, 10am-7pm Sat & Sun; 🚋3/5/12/16/24 Museumplein) Bernard Haitink, former conductor of the venerable Royal Concertgebouw Orchestra, once remarked that the world-famous hall – built in 1888 with near-perfect acoustics – was the orchestra's best instrument. Free half-hour concerts take place every Wednesday at 12.30pm from mid-September to late June; arrive early.

LOCAL KNOWLEDGE

VONDELPARK SQUATS

Vondelpark and its surrounds have strong links to the cultural revolution, when Amsterdam became the *magisch centrum* (magic centre) of Europe. Hippies flocked to Amsterdam during the 1960s and '70s, a housing shortage saw speculators leaving buildings empty and squatting became widespread. The Dutch authorities turned the park into a temporary open-air dormitory. Although the sleeping bags are long gone today, an indie spirit persists.

Buried beneath the park's 1e Constantjin Huygensstraat bridge (you could take the tram straight over it or walk right beneath it and never know it was here) is the hidden **Vondelbunker** (Map p322; www.vondelbunker.nl; Vondelpark 8a; hours vary; 1 1e Constantijn Huygensstraat). A fallout shelter dating from 1947, in 1968 it became Amsterdam's first youth centre and a hotbed of counterculture creativity and activism. If the unmarked black metal doors are open you might catch an underground gig, film or 'activist salon'.

Fringing Vondelpark are several squats that have gone legit and been turned into alternative cultural centres.

OT301 (Map p322; www.ot301.nl; Overtoom 301; 1 Jan Pieter Heijestraat) Graffiti-covered ex-squat OT301, in the former Netherlands Film Academy, hosts an eclectic roster of bands and DJs. There are two bars as well as the friendly vegan restaurant **De Peper** (Map p322; 412 29 54; www.depeper.org; Overtoom 301; mains €7-10; 7-8.30pm Tue, Thu, Fri & Sun; ; 1 Jan Pieter Heijestraat), serving cheap, organic, vegan meals in a lovable dive-bar atmosphere. Sit at the communal table to connect with like-minded folk. Same-day reservations are required; call between 3pm and 6.30pm.

OCCII (671 77 78; www.occii.org; Amstelveenseweg 134; hours vary; ; 2 Amstelveenseweg) Former squat OCCII maintains a thriving alternative scene, and books underground bands, many from Amsterdam. Vegan fare is served at its **Eetcafé MKZ** (679 07 12; www.binnenpr.home.xs4all.nl/mkz.htm; 1e Schinkelstraat 16; mains from €5; from 7pm Tue-Fri; ; 2 Amstelveenseweg), a collectively run, no-frills restaurant. Call between 2.30pm and 6pm to reserve your spot and confirm prices for the changing vegan meals, but be sure to arrive early, as once the food's gone, that's it.

Try the Last Minute Ticket Shop (p143) for half-price seats to all other performances.

Those aged 30 or younger can queue at the box office for €15 tickets 45 minutes prior to shows. All tickets include a free drink in the concert-hall lobby.

OPENLUCHTTHEATER THEATRE

Map p322 (Open-Air Theatre; www.openluchttheater.nl; Vondelpark 5a; May–mid-Sep; ; 1 1e Constantijn Huygensstraat) Each summer the Vondelpark hosts free concerts in its intimate open-air theatre. It's a fantastic experience to share with others. Expect world music, dance, theatre and more. You can make a reservation (€5 per seat) on the website up to two hours in advance of showtime.

ORGELPARK CONCERT HALL

Map p322 (515 81 11; www.orgelpark.nl; Gerard Brandtstraat 26; tickets €12.50-20; 1 Jan Pieter Heijestraat) Not a park, but a renowned stage for organ music, with four big organs in a lovely restored church on the edge of Vondelpark. More than 100 events take place each year, including concerts of classical, jazz and improvised music.

PLAN B POOL HALL

Map p322 (www.planbovertoom.nl; Overtoom 209; 4pm-1am Mon, 2pm-1am Tue-Thu, to 3am Fri, noon-3am Sat, to 1am Sun; 1 Jan Pieter Heijestraat) If your Vondelpark football game's washed out, switch to Plan B and shoot some pool at this friendly hang-out, with 13 pool tables (and two dartboards) and a bar. It also hosts pool comps (beginners 7.30pm Monday, advanced players 7.30pm Thursday) and quiz nights from 7.30pm on Wednesdays.

SHOPPING

The winding paths of Vondelpark must inspire a certain wanderlust, as the nearby streets are full of outdoor and

travel shops. Stylish shops line Cornelis Schuytstraat and Willemsparkweg; check www.cornelisschuytstraat.com for new openings. Nearby, ultraluxe shopping avenue PC Hooftstraat teems with brands that need no introduction: Chanel, Burberry, Hugo Boss, Cartier, Gucci, Armani, Hermès, Tommy Hilfiger and Lacoste, to name just a few.

★PIED À TERRE — BOOKS

Map p322 (☎627 44 55; www.piedaterre.nl; Overtoom 135-137; ⏰1-6pm Mon, 10am-6pm Tue, Wed & Fri, to 9pm Thu, to 5pm Sat; 🚊1 1e Constantijn Huygensstraat) The galleried, sky-lit interior of Europe's largest travel bookshop feels like a Renaissance centre of learning. If it's travel or outdoor-related, it's likely here: gorgeous globes, travel guides in multiple languages (especially English) and over 600,000 maps. Order a coffee and dream up your next trip at the cafe tables.

EDHA INTERIEUR — HOMEWARES

Map p322 (www.edha-interieur.nl; Willemsparkweg 5-9; ⏰10am-6pm Tue-Sat; 🚊2/3/5/12 Van Baerlestraat) You might not end up buying a sofa, kitchen unit or bathroom suite in these three neighbouring 19th-century buildings, but Edha is one of the best places in town to check out cutting-edge Dutch design. Smaller items more suitable to pack in your luggage (or at least ship) include textiles, groovy lights and kitchen gadgets.

VAN AVEZAATH BEUNE — FOOD & DRINK

Map p322 (www.vanavezaath-beune.nl; Johannes Verhulststraat 98; ⏰8am-6pm Mon-Fri, to 5pm Sat; 🚊2 Cornelis Schuytstraat) Counter staff in serious black aprons box up chocolate *amsterdammertjes* (the bollards along city pavements) – a great gift, assuming you can keep from eating them yourself.

VLVT — FASHION

Map p322 (www.vlvt.nl; Cornelis Schuytstraat 22; ⏰noon-6pm Mon, 10am-6pm Tue-Sat, noon-5pm Sun; 🚊2 Cornelis Schuytstraat) Up-and-coming Dutch-designed fashion for women is stocked at this chic, light-filled boutique, including Dutch designers such as ByDanie (renowned stylist-to-the-stars-turned-designer Danie Bles) and Amsterdam-based Anna + Nina, as well as international labels such as Boy London, Lola Cruz, Pinko and Pierre Balmain, basics such as T-shirts, and accessories to make them look fabulous (sunglasses, jewellery, scarves, handbags).

MUSEUM SOUVENIRS

Museum Shop at the Museumplein (Map p322; Hobbemastraat; ⏰shop 10am-6pm, ticket window for museum entrance 8.30am-6pm; 🚊2/5 Hobbemastraat) The Van Gogh Museum and Rijksmuseum jointly operate the Museum Shop at the Museumplein, so you can pick up posters, cards and other art souvenirs from both institutions in one fell swoop (and avoid the museums' entrance queues). While the selection is not as vast as the in-house stores, the shop has enough iconic wares to satisfy most needs.

BEER TREE — DRINK

Map p322 (www.thebeertree.nl; Jan Pieter Heijestraat 148; ⏰noon-10pm Mon-Fri, 11am-10pm Sat & Sun; 🚊1 Jan Pieter Heijestraat) This is the original branch of this ingenious shop, where many of its 250-plus craft beers from over 25 different countries are available cold from the fridge, making them perfect to take to the Vondelpark on a hot day, as well as four rotating beers on tap that can be bottled to take away cold, too.

It now has a second branch in De Pijp (p195).

BUISE — FASHION

Map p322 (www.buise.nl; Cornelis Schuytstraat 12; ⏰12.30-6pm Mon, 10am-6pm Tue-Sat; 🚊2 Cornelis Schuytstraat) Impeccably selected pieces at this beautiful boutique include flatteringly cut jackets by Isabel Marant, shift dresses and stylish sweatshirts by Paul & Joe Sister and geometric prints by Laurence Dolige.

GOOCHEM SPEELGOED — TOYS

Map p322 (www.goochem.amsterdam; 1e Constantijn Huygensstraat 80; ⏰1-6pm Mon, 9.30am-6pm Tue-Sat; 🚊1 1e Constantijn Huygensstraat) A soft-toy, life-size giraffe (well, baby giraffe) stands over a storey high in this delightful toy shop, which has been trading here for over three decades. Toys are arranged by children's age groups; along with cuddly toys, there are musical instruments, dolls, puzzles and more.

JOHNNY AT THE SPOT — FASHION, HOMEWARES

Map p322 (www.johnnyatthespot.com; Jan Pieter Heijestraat 94; ⏰1-6pm Mon, 11am-6pm Tue, Wed & Sat, to 7pm Thu & Fri, 1-5pm Sun; 🚊7/17 Jan Pieter Heijestraat) On up-and-coming Jan Pieter

Heijestraat, multipurpose mega-boutique Johnny at the Spot fills several interconnected buildings with super-stylish men's and women's clothing, shoes and raincoats from all over the globe. Hip homewares include everything from plants and soaps to bowls, vases, crockery and furniture.

BROEKMANS & VAN POPPEL MUSIC

Map p322 (www.broekmans.com; Van Baerlestraat 92-94; ⌚9am-6pm Mon-Fri, to 5pm Sat; 🚋2/3/5/12 Van Baerlestraat) Near the Concertgebouw (surprise!), this is the city's top choice for classical and popular sheet music, as well as music books. Head to the 1st floor for a comprehensive selection from the Middle Ages through to classical and contemporary.

FRIDAY NEXT HOMEWARES

Map p322 (☎612 32 92; www.fridaynext.com; Overtoom 31; ⌚9am-6pm Tue-Fri, 10am-6pm Sat, noon-5pm Sun; 📶; 🚋1 Constanijn Huygensstraat) Not only is this design shop filled with designer furniture and homewares, it runs regular exhibitions and design workshops. A cafe is wedged among the stock.

MANWOOD SHOES

Map p322 (www.manwood.nl; Willemsparkweg 173; ⌚1-6pm Mon, 10am-6pm Tue-Sat, noon-5pm Sun; 🚋2 Cornelis Schuytstraat) Dutch shoemaker Manwood sells stylish men's and women's footwear (boots, lace-ups, heels, ballerina flats, sneakers and slippers) including its own designs. It also stocks other Dutch designs and selected international labels, as well as scarves, belts, hats and bags.

NIKKIE FASHION

Map p322 (www.nikkie.com; Willemsparkweg 175; ⌚noon-6pm Mon, 10am-6pm Tue-Sat, noon-5.30pm Sun; 🚋2 Cornelis Schuytstraat) Amsterdam-based Nikkie Plessen was a familiar face on Dutch television as an actress and presenter, but she's now swapped TV for women's fashion design, establishing two boutiques in town (the other is on nearby luxe avenue PC Hoofstraat) and several others around the Netherlands. Street-smart collections run from graffiti-print separates and bell-bottom jeans to sharp evening wear.

ENNU FASHION

Map p322 (www.ennu.nl; Cornelis Schuytstraat 15; ⌚1-6pm Mon, 10am-6pm Tue-Fri, to 5pm Sat, 1-5pm Sun; 🚋2 Cornelis Schuytstraat) Both men and women can find edgy, up-to-the-minute high fashion in Ennu's smoky grey surrounds. Designer labels stocked here include Ann Demeulemeester, Rick Owens, LGB and If Six Was Nine.

FRETONS SHOES

Map p322 (www.bretoniere.nl; Jacob Obrechtstraat 14; ⌚10.30am-6pm Tue-Fri, to 5pm Sat; 🚋2 Jacob Obrechtstraat) Fretons is shoemaker Fred de la Bretonniere's more relaxed brand, with designs such as chunky sneakers that are comfy, sporty, urban-cool, and pretty much one of a kind.

BEVER OUTDOOR EQUIPMENT

Map p322 (www.bever.nl; Stadhouderskade 4; ⌚11am-7pm Mon, 10am-7pm Tue, Wed, Fri & Sat, to 9pm Thu, noon-6pm Sun; 🚋1/2/5 Leidseplein) One of the Netherlands' leading outdoor-equipment retailers, Bever sells tents, backpacks, sleeping bags et al as well as clothes and footwear for both men and women; its **Women's Outdoor World** (Map p322; ☎412 28 79; www.bever.nl; Overtoom 51-53; ⌚11am-7pm Mon & Wed, 10am-7pm Tue, Fri & Sat, to 9pm Thu, noon-6pm Sun; 🚋1 1e Constantijn Huygensstraat) shop is around the corner.

SPORTS & ACTIVITIES

FRIDAY NIGHT SKATE INLINE SKATING

Map p322 (www.fridaynightskate.com; ⌚8.30pm Fri) FREE Every Friday night (except in rain and snow), Vondelpark is the start of a 20km, two-hour-long mass skate through Amsterdam. It's open to anyone with reasonable skating proficiency (ie knowing how to brake!). Arrive at the meeting point, adjacent to the Vondelparkpaviljoen by 8pm (8.15pm in winter). Check the website for details of skate (and safety gear) rental outlets.

ZUIDERBAD SWIMMING

Map p322 (☎252 13 90; Hobbemastraat 26; admission €3.60; ⌚7am-6pm Mon, to 10pm Tue-Fri, 8am-3.15pm Sat, 10am-3.30pm Sun; 👪; 🚋2/5 Hobbemastraat) If you're looking for something to entertain the kids, consider this pool. The 1912 edifice behind the Rijksmuseum has been restored to its original glory, full of tiles, character and appreciative paddlers.

De Pijp

Neighbourhood Top Five

❶ Feasting your senses on the international free-for-all of fresh produce, cheese, fish, colourful clothing, accessories and quirky Dutch souvenirs at the **Albert Cuypmarkt** (p190), Europe's largest daily street market.

❷ Strolling through **Sarphatipark** (p189), an urban oasis of lawns, statues, ponds and fountains.

❸ Bar hopping between exuberantly friendly neighbourhood watering holes, starting with *borrel* (drinks) at **Boca's** (p196).

❹ Touring the boisterously fun **Heineken Experience** (p189) before boarding its canal boat to the brand store.

❺ Delving into De Pijp's burgeoning brunch scene at specialists like **Bakers & Roasters** (p193).

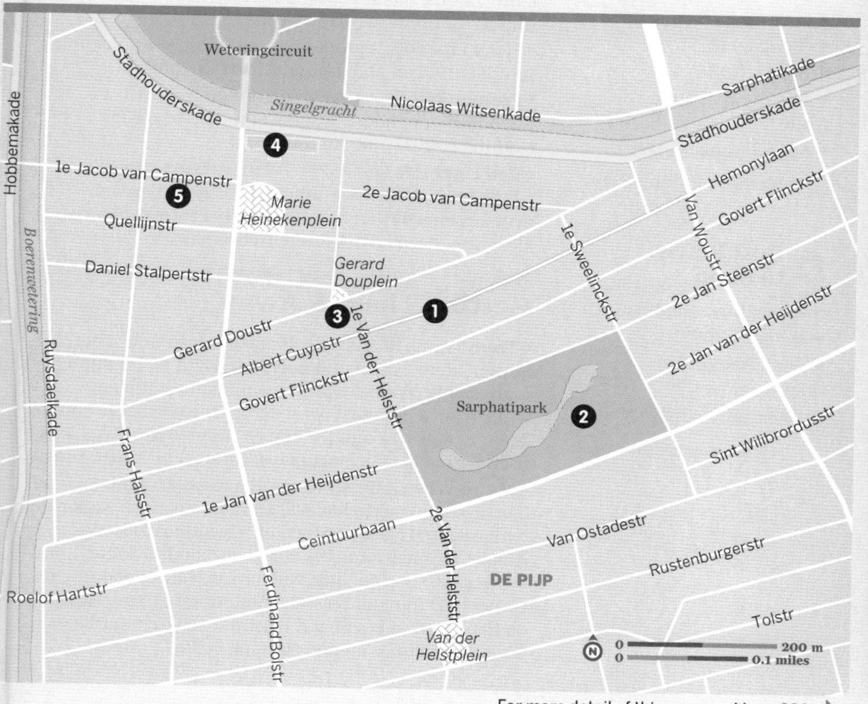

For more detail of this area see Map p326

Lonely Planet's Top Tip

This creative neighbourhood is a hotbed of pop-ups, start-ups and new openings. Backstreets to watch include Frans Halsstraat, 1e Van der Helststraat, 2e Van der Helststraat, Cornelis Troostplein and Ruysdaelkade.

Best Places to Eat

- Fat Dog (p190)
- Bakers & Roasters (p193)
- Ciel Bleu (p195)
- Volt (p192)
- Restaurant Elmar (p192)

For reviews, see p190.

Best Places to Drink

- Brouwerij Troost (p195)
- Glouglou (p196)
- Boca's (p196)
- Café Binnen Buiten (p196)
- Café Sarphaat (p196)

For reviews, see p195.

Best Places to Shop

- Albert Cuypmarkt (p190)
- Hutspot (p197)
- Beer Tree (p195)
- Kolifleur (p197)
- Tiller Galerie (p197)

For reviews, see p197.

Explore De Pijp

De Pijp's village-like character is due in part to the fact that it's an island, connected to the rest of the city by 16 bridges. Its name, 'the Pipe', is thought to reflect its straight, narrow streets that resemble the stems of old clay pipes.

But it's more attributable to its history. The area's 1860s tenement blocks provided cheap housing for newly arrived industrial revolution workers. In the 1960s and '70s many working-class residents left for greener pastures and the government refurbished the tenement blocks for immigrants. Inhabited today by all walks of life, with gentrification continuing apace, this arty, foodie neighbourhood retains a community-oriented bohemian spirit.

Start your day trawling the Albert Cuypmarkt's stalls before strolling peaceful Sarphatipark. Explore the streets' boutiques and speciality shops – and stake out your dinner destination from the overwhelming options – before heading to the Heineken Experience. If you time it for the late afternoon, the tasting at the end provides a built-in happy hour (though of course in fun-loving De Pijp it almost always feels like happy hour).

Local Life

- **Brewery Life** Heineken might not brew in De Pijp any more, but the 'hood has a new craft brewery that does, wonderful Brouwerij Troost (p195).
- **Fishy Life** Locals love to hit up De Pijp's raw herring stands (p197) on and around Albert Cuypmarkt.
- **Fashion Life** The streets surrounding the Albert Cuypmarkt are home to some of the best budget clothing stores (p197) in town.
- **Red Light Life** On De Pijp's western border, there's a little red-light district (minus the stag parties and drunken crowds that frequent its city-centre counterpart) along Ruysdaelkade, opposite Hobbemakade.

Getting There & Away

- **Tram** Trams 16 and 24 roll north–south from Centraal Station along Ferdinand Bolstraat, right by De Pijp's main sights. Tram 4 travels from Rembrandtplein, while tram 3 cuts east–west across the neighbourhood. Tram 12 cuts through De Pijp en route to Vondelpark. (Beware of old transport maps; tram 25 no longer runs.)
- **Metro** When it finally opens, the Noord/Zuidlijn (north–south) metro line will serve De Pijp. The station, with coloured glass designed by Argentinean artist Amalia Pica reflecting the neighbourhood's colours sinking into the building, will have entrances on the corner of Ferdinand Bolstraat and Albert Cuypstraat, and on the corner of Ferdinand Bolstraat and Ceintuurbaan. It's expected to be up-and-running in 2017.

SIGHTS

Apart from the Albert Cuypmarkt (p190) and the Heineken Experience (p189), sights in De Pijp are few. What's really enjoyable here is wandering through the neighbourhood and soaking up the bohemian atmosphere in the bars, cafes and shops.

SARPHATIPARK PARK

Map p326 (Ceintuurbaan; 16/24 Albert Cuypstraat) While the Vondelpark is bigger in size and reputation, this tranquil English-style park delivers an equally potent shot of pastoral summertime relaxation, with far fewer crowds. Named after Samuel Sarphati (1813–66), a Jewish doctor, businessman and urban innovator, the grounds are a mix of ponds, gently rolling meadows and wooded fringes.

In the centre you'll see the **Sarphati memorial** (Map p326; 16/24 Albert Cuypstraat) from 1886, a bombastic temple with a fountain, gargoyles and a bust of the great man himself.

DE DAGERAAD ARCHITECTURE

Map p326 (Dawn Housing Project; Pieter Lodewijk Takstraat; 4 Amstelkade) Following the key Housing Act of 1901, which forced the city to rethink neighbourhood planning and condemn slums, De Dageraad housing estate was developed between 1918 and 1923 for poorer families. One of the most original architects of the expressionist Amsterdam School, Piet Kramer, drew up plans for this idiosyncratic complex in collaboration with Michel de Klerk

HUIS MET DE KABOUTERS ARCHITECTURE

Map p326 (House with the Goblins; Ceintuurbaan 251; 3 Van Woustraat) Look up as you pass Ceintuurbaan 251: on the elaborately carved wooden gables of the 1884 neo-Gothic mansion here you'll see two cheeky lime-green goblin sculptures dressed in red hats and shorts; one is holding a red ball and the other is reaching to catch it. The building was designed by architect AC Boerma; it's thought the sculptures symbolise his client's surname, Van Ballegooijen, which translates in part to 'throwing a ball'. It's been a listed national monument since 1984.

Local legend has it that the ball changes between the goblins' hands in leap years at midnight on February 29.

TOP SIGHT
HEINEKEN EXPERIENCE

Heineken, the Netherlands' world-famous brewery, wants you to know that this is not a museum – it's a multisensory experience. Heineken has been going strong since 1864 and the 'Experience' is an appropriately immodest (read: commercial) celebration of its place in Dutch brewing history.

On the site of the company's old De Pijp brewery, which closed in 1988, the 'Experience' is a rollicking self-guided tour. Allow at least 90 minutes to learn the storied history of the Heineken family, find out how the logo has evolved, and follow the brewing process from water and hops right through to bottling. Along the way you can watch Heineken commercials from around the world, sniff the mash in copper tanks, visit the horse stables and make your own music video. The crowning glory is Brew You – a 4D multimedia exhibit where you 'become' a beer as you get shaken up, heated up, sprayed with water and 'bottled'. True beer connoisseurs will shudder, but it's a lot of fun. Admission includes a 15-minute shuttle boat ride to the **Heineken Brand Store** (p146) near Rembrandtplein.

Prebooking tickets online saves you €2 and allows you to skip the queues.

DON'T MISS

- 'Becoming' a beer through Brew You
- Learning to pour a proper frothy pint, Dutch-style

PRACTICALITIES

- Map p326
- 523 92 22
- www.heinekenexperience.com
- Stadhouderskade 78
- adult/child €18/12.50
- 10.30am-9pm Jul & Aug, to 7.30pm Mon-Thu, to 9pm Fri-Sun Sep-Jun
- 16/24 Stadhouderskade

EATING

Come hungry: anything and everything is fair game on De Pijp's cuisine scene. It's multicultural yet also quintessentially Dutch, with plenty of old brown *cafés* (pubs) churning out hearty lunch specials, and bakeries selling lunchtime *broodjes* (filled bread rolls). Albert Cuypstraat, Ferdinand Bolstraat and Ceintuurbaan are ideal starting points.

★FAT DOG — HOT DOGS €

(www.thefatdog.nl; Ruysdaelkade 251; dishes €4.50-12; 5pm-midnight Mon & Tue, from noon Wed-Sun; 12 Cornelis Troostplein) Überchef Ron Blaauw, of Ron Gastrobar (p178), elevates the humble hot dog to an art form. Ultra-gourmet options include Naughty Bangkok (pickled vegetables, red curry mayo, and dry crispy rice); Vive La France (fried mushrooms, foie gras and truffle mayo); Gangs of New York (sauerkraut, bacon, and smoked-onion marmalade) and Vega Gonzalez (vegetarian sausage, corn, guacamole, sour cream and jalapeño mayo).

FRITES UIT ZUYD — FRITES €

Map p326 (www.fritesuitzuyd.nl; Ceintuurbaan; dishes €3-5.50; noon-10pm Sun & Mon, to 11pm Tue-Thu, to midnight Fri & Sat; 3 Ferdinand Bolstraat) De Pijp's best *frites* (fries) by far are at takeaway shop Frites uit Zuyd, with black-and-white chequerboard tiling on the walls and floors, and at its sleek sit-down restaurant Friterie par Hasard (p192) next door. Crispy, fluffy *frites* are accompanied by traditional pickles, mustard or sauces such as satay, mayo or chilli-spiced sambal. Wooden benches line the pavement out front.

BUTCHER — BURGERS €

Map p326 (470 78 75; www.the-butcher.com; Albert Cuypstraat 129; burgers €6.50-12.50; 11am-late; ; 16/24 Albert Cuypstraat) Burgers at this sizzling spot are cooked right in front of you (behind a glass screen, so you won't get splattered). Mouthwatering choices include 'Silence of the Lamb' (with spices and tahini), the 'Codfather' (beer-battered blue cod and homemade tartare sauce), an Angus beef truffle burger and a veggie version. Ask about its secret cocktail bar.

TOP SIGHT
ALBERT CUYPMARKT

Want to experience Amsterdam at its wonderfully chaotic, multicultural best? Head to Europe's most sprawling daily street market (bar Sunday).

Named after landscape painter Albert Cuyp (1620–91), Albert Cuypmarkt is Amsterdam's largest and busiest market, and is legendary for its huge variety. Scores of aromatic stalls sell Dutch cheese, fish, crustaceans, olives, oils, herbs and spices, and bushels of fresh fruit and vegies. Need some Saturday-night bling or a new smartphone cover? How about a bike lock, hair curling iron, or some flowers for your sweetheart or just to brighten your hotel room? There's also a staggering array of (mostly funky, sometimes junky) clothes and accessories. If you want it, it's likely the Albert Cuypmarkt's got it, and it's probably cheaper than anywhere else.

Don't miss the shops hidden behind the stalls too, selling everything from kitchen gadgets to backpacks and suitcases, bolts of fabric, more bike locks, soaps and shampoos, you name it.

Be sure to sample the cheese (just ask!), from a four-year-old gouda to a creamy *boerenkaas* (farmer's cheese) and indulge in a piping-hot *stroopwafel* (caramel syrup waffle).

DON'T MISS

- Cheese galore
- Only-in-the-Netherlands gifts (furry clog slippers, anyone?)
- *Stroopwafel* to nibble as you go

PRACTICALITIES

- Map p326
- www.albertcuypmarkt.nl
- Albert Cuypstraat, btwn Ferdinand Bolstraat & Van Woustraat
- 9am-5pm Mon-Sat
- 16/24 Albert Cuypstraat

UNITED PANCAKES DUTCH €

Map p326 (www.united-pancakes.nl; 1e Van der Helststraat 57; dishes €3.50-5.50; 10am-6pm Mon-Thu, to 7pm Fri-Sun; 3 2e Van der Helststraat) Many De Pijp success stories prosper by sticking to one speciality and doing it really well, and here it's that Dutch staple, pancakes. Made with organic ingredients, United's pancakes are both sweet (Classic Fantastic: apple, raisin, cinnamon and homemade apple syrup; Berry Nice: blackberries, goji berries, cranberries and spelt syrup) and savoury (Popeye: spinach, goats cheese, walnuts and pear syrup).

It also sells its own range of syrups, sauces and pancake products including its various flours (spelt, gluten-free buckwheat, natural white or multigrain).

BREZEL & BRATWURST GERMAN €

Map p326 (www.brezelenbratwurst.nl; Van der Helstplein 10; dishes €1-8.50; 4-10pm Wed-Sun; 3 2e Van der Helststraat) A brilliant addition to De Pijp's line-up of top-quality cheap eats, Brezel & Bratwurst serves authentic German *Bratwurst* (sausages), either on a bun, as currywurst, or with fries and salad. For something lighter, go for a homemade bio, spelt or natural *Brezel* (pretzel) with traditional dips such as Bavarian *Obatzda*, made with soft cheese, paprika and raw veggies.

SIR HUMMUS MIDDLE EASTERN €

Map p326 (sirhummus.nl; Van der Helstplein 2; dishes €6.8.50; noon-7pm Tue-Fri, to 5pm Sat & Sun; ; 3 2e Van der Helststraat) Sir Hummus is the brainchild of three young Israelis whose passion for the chickpea dip led to a London street market stall and then to this hummus-dedicated cafe. Creamy all-natural, preservative- and additive-free hummus is served with pita bread and salad; SH also does fantastic falafel. You can eat in or take away but arrive early before it sells out.

BOAT RENTAL

Boaty (06 2714 9493; www.boaty.nl; Jozef Israëlskade; boat rental per 3hr from €79; 9am-30min before sunset Apr–mid-Oct; 12 Scheldestraat) Boaty's location on the peaceful Amstelkanaal makes it an ideal launching pad for exploring the waterways before approaching the crowded city-centre canals. Rental includes a map outlining suggested routes; you don't need a boat licence or prior experience. Book ahead online, or phone for same-day reservations. The season can run longer or shorter depending on weather conditions.

ON YOUR BIKE IN DE PIJP

Ajax Bike (Map p326; 06 1568 4831; www.ajaxbike.nl; Gerard Doustraat 153; bike rental per 4/24hr €6.50/8.50; 9.30am-6pm Mon-Sat; 4 Stadhouderskade) rents bargain-priced city bikes, children's bikes, tandems and cargo bikes. It also offers three-hour tours taking in De Pijp, the city and surrounding countryside (€20); contact the company for dates and customised tour options.

SLA SALAD BAR €

Map p326 (www.ilovesla.com; Ceintuurbaan 149; salads €6-11; 11am-9pm; ; 3 2e Van der Helststraat) Amsterdam's fashionistas flock to this super-stylish salad bar for its soups, juices and especially its extensive array of fresh, healthy salads you design yourself. All of the meat, poultry and dairy products, 90% of the vegetables, and the wines are organic. This flagship branch proved so popular over the past few years there are now offshoots all over Amsterdam.

SPANG MAKANDRA SURINAMESE, INDONESIAN €

Map p326 (670 50 81; www.spangmakandra.nl; Gerard Doustraat 39; mains €6.50-10; 11am-10pm Mon-Sat, 1-10pm Sun; 16/24 Albert Cuypstraat) There are just 26 seats at this cosy restaurant and it's a red-hot favourite with students and Surinamese and Indonesian expats, so you'll need to book for dinner. The reward is a fabulous array of dishes like fish soups and satay with spicy sauces at astonishingly cheap prices. Friendly staff are happy to translate the Dutch-only menu.

All the food is halal; no alcohol is served.

GEFLIPT BURGERS €

Map p326 (www.gefliptburgers.nl; Van Woustraat 15; dishes €8-9.50; 11am-9.30pm Sun-Thu, to 10.30pm Fri & Sat; ; 4 Stadhouderskade)

Competition is fierce in this foodie neighbourhood for the best burgers, but Geflipt is a serious contender. In a stripped-back, industrial-chic interior, it serves luscious creations (like Gasconne beef, bacon, golden cheddar, red-onion compote and fried egg) on brioche buns with sauces cooked daily on the premises from locally sourced ingredients. Bonus points for its Amsterdam-brewed Brouwerij 't IJ beers.

TODAY'S — ITALIAN €

Map p326 (☎737 08 70; Saenredamstraat 26; dishes €3-9; ⏰1-8pm Tue-Sat; 🖉; 🚋16/24 Albert Cuypstraat) Tiny and delightful, this deli-cafe functions as an impromptu Italian cultural centre. Charismatic chef Davide creates scrumptious Italian fare from focaccia to pumpkin lasagne, truffle and mushroom ravioli, and sinful tiramisu. Take away, eat in or book a private dinner in the lofted dining room.

TAART VAN M'N TANTE — BAKERY, SWEETS €

Map p326 (☎776 46 00; www.detaart.com; Ferdinand Bolstraat 10; dishes €4-7; ⏰10am-6pm; 👪; 🚋16/24 Stadhouderskade) One of Amsterdam's best-loved cake shops operates from this uber-kitsch parlour, turning out apple pies (Dutch, French or 'tipsy'), pecan pie and wish-you-could-bake-like-this cakes. Hot-pink walls accent cakes dressed like Barbie dolls – or are they Barbies dressed as cakes?

BOULANGERIE 1072 — CAFE €

Map p326 (www.boulangerie1072.nl; Ferdinand Bolstraat 151; dishes €1.50-11; ⏰8am-6pm; 📶; 🚋12 Cornelis Troostplein) Charming Boulangerie 1072 has colourful chairs on the square out front (with blankets when the weather's chilly) and mezzanine seating in the split-level interior. Breakfast choices include oatmeal, soy-and-banana vegan pancakes with Canadian maple syrup; for lunch go for sandwiches like beetroot, goats cheese and Sir Hummus (p191) hummus; smoked salmon, red onion and caviar; and heavenly apple pie.

WILD MOA PIES — PIES €

Map p326 (Van Ostadestraat 147; dishes €3-4; ⏰10am-6.30pm Tue-Sat; 📶🖉; 🚋3 2e Van der Helststraat) Wild Moa is best known for its authentic New Zealand–style meat pies (including NZ lamb) but creative veggie and poultry varieties span Thai chicken to lentil and aubergine, spinach and feta, and pumpkin and paprika.

★VOLT — MEDITERRANEAN €€

Map p326 (☎471 55 44; www.restaurantvolt.nl; Ferdinand Bolstraat 178; mains €14-20, tapas €4-14; ⏰4-10pm; 🚋12 Cornelis Troostplein) Strung with coloured lightbulbs, Volt is a neighbourhood gem for light tapas-style bites (olives and marinated sardines; aioli and tapenade) and more substantial mains (artichoke ravioli with walnuts and rocket; squid stuffed with chorizo and rice; and plaice with mozzarella risotto croquette. Its bar stays open until late, or head across the street to its brown *café* sibling, **Gambrinus** (Map p326; www.gambrinus.nl; Ferdinand Bolstraat 180; ⏰11am-1am Sun-Thu, to 3am Fri & Sat; 📶; 🚋12 Cornelis Troostplein).

★RESTAURANT ELMAR — MODERN DUTCH €€

Map p326 (☎664 66 29; www.restaurantelmar.nl; Van Woustraat 110; mains lunch €7.50-12.50, dinner €19.50-24.50; ⏰noon-3pm & 6-10pm Tue-Sat; 🚋4 Ceintuurbaan) 🍃 Seriously good cooking at this charming little locavore restaurant utilises organic Dutch produce (Flevopolder beef, Texel lamb, Noord-Holland pigs, polder chickens and locally milled flour, along with seasonal fruit and vegetables). Original flavour combinations include ham-wrapped chicken stuffed with liver and sage in marsala jus, and bitter-chocolate mousse with apple compote and iced-coffee foam. There's a delightful courtyard garden.

Multicourse menus are great value.

SPAGHETTERIA — ITALIAN €€

Map p326 (www.spaghetteria-pastabar.nl; Van Woustraat 123; pasta €9-14; ⏰5-10.15pm; 🚋4 Ceintuurbaan) Freshly made pastas at this hip, Italian-run 'pasta bar' come in six daily options that might include ricotta and walnut ravioli; spaghetti with calamari in spicy tomato sauce; squid-ink linguine with pesto and spinach; and ham tortellini in creamy goats-cheese sauce. The huge wooden communal table (and wine) adds to the electric atmosphere. There's another branch near Vondelpark.

FRITERIE PAR HASARD — DUTCH €€

Map p326 (www.cafeparhasard.nl; Ceintuurbaan 113; mains €17.50, 3-course menu €27.50; ⏰noon-10pm Sun-Thu, to 10.30pm Fri & Sat; 🚋3

LOCAL KNOWLEDGE

DE PIJP'S TOP FIVE BRUNCH HOTSPOTS

Bakers & Roasters (Map p326; http://bakersandroasters.com; 1e Jacob van Campenstraat 54; dishes €7.50-15.50; ⌚8.30am-4pm; 16/24 Stadhouderskade) Sumptuous brunch dishes served up at Brazilian/Kiwi-owned Bakers & Roasters include banana nutbread French toast with homemade banana marmalade and crispy bacon; Navajo eggs with pulled pork, avocado, mango salsa and chipotle cream; and a smoked salmon stack with poached eggs, potato cakes and hollandaise. Wash them down with a fiery Bloody Mary. Fantastic pies, cakes and slices, too.

Scandinavian Embassy (Map p326; http://scandinavianembassy.nl; Sarphatipark 34; dishes €4.40-12; ⌚8am-6pm Mon-Fri, 10am-5pm Sat & Sun; 3 2e Van der Helststraat) Oatmeal porridge with blueberries, honey and coconut, served with goat's milk yoghurt; salt-cured salmon on Danish rye with sheep's milk yoghurt; muesli with strawberries; and freshly baked pastries, including cinnamon buns, make this blond-wood-panelled spot a perfect place to start the day. As does its phenomenal coffee sourced from Scandinavian micro-roasteries (including a refreshing cold-brewed coffee with tonic water).

CT Coffee & Coconuts (Map p326; www.ctamsterdam.nl; Ceintuurbaan 282-284; mains €6.50-21.50; ⌚7am-11pm Mon-Fri, from 8am Sat & Sun; ; 3 Ceintuurbaan) A 1920s art-deco cinema has been stunningly transformed into this open-plan, triple-level cathedral-like space (with a giant print of John Lennon at the top). Brunch dishes like coconut, almond and buckwheat pancakes; French-toast brioche with apricots; avocado-slathered toast with *dukkha* (North African spice-and-nut blend) and lemon dressing; scrambled eggs on sourdough with crumbled feta are served to 1pm.

The lunch and dinner menu spans prawn tacos and tempeh burgers to paper-baked cod with roast asparagus and turnips. Any time of day, it's a wonderful space for a homemade cooler (blackberry and sage; honey and lemon), loose-leaf tea from a seasonal menu, coffee or something stronger.

Omelegg (Map p326; www.omelegg.com; Ferdinand Bolstraat 143; dishes €6-10; ⌚7am-4pm Mon-Fri, from 8am Sat & Sun; ; 12 Cornelis Troostplein) In sparing surrounds with polished-concrete floors, wooden furniture and a mural of traditional Dutch windmills on the back wall, this omelette specialist serves a weekly changing version, plus menu regulars like Mariachi (spicy jalapeños, mushrooms and sundried tomatoes), Viking Fisherman (smoked salmon, dill, crème fraîche and lemon zest), and Chilli Hernandez (homemade chilli con carne and cheese).

Other dishes include bacon and eggs and great freshly squeezed OJ.

Little Collins (Map p326; 673 22 93; www.littlecollins.nl; 1e Sweelinckstraat 19; tapas €7.50-18, brunch €5-14; ⌚brunch 10.30am-4pm Wed-Sun, tapas 6-10pm Thu-Sat; 16/24 Albert Cuypstraat) This hip hangout is hopping during brunch, when dishes include Bengali baked eggs with spiced chickpeas and feta, and caramelised banana toast with banana curd. The evening tapas menu is equally inspired: freshly shucked oysters; confit of salmon and pickled beetroot; Korean-style beef with ricepaper crisps; and grilled Stilton with pear and toasted pecans.

Ferdinand Bolstraat) Fronted by a red-and-white chequered awning, low-lit Friterie par Hasard is fêted for its *frites* (fries), served with dishes like ribs in traditional Limburg stew with apple, elderberry and bay-leaf sauce; marinated chicken thighs with satay sauce and pickled cucumber; bavette steak; and beer-battered cod. Its adjacent Frites uit Zuyd (p190) fries up takeaway *frites*.

SURYA

INDIAN €€

Map p326 (www.suryarestaurant.nl; Ceintuurbaan 147; mains €12-20; ⌚5-11pm Tue-Sun; 3 2e Van der Helststraat) Indian restaurants can be surprisingly hit and miss in this multicultural city, making classy Surya an invaluable address for fans of Subcontinental cuisine. Menu standouts include a feisty madras, fire-breathing vindaloo, tandoori tikka dishes, and silky tomato-based *paneer makhni* with soft cottage cheese made fresh on the premises each day. Mains come with papadums, rice and salad.

DÈSA INDONESIAN €€

Map p326 (☎671 09 79; www.restaurantdesa.com; Ceintuurbaan 103; mains €12.50-14.50, rijsttafel €15.20-32; ⏲5-10.30pm; 🚊3 Ferdinand Bolstraat) Named for the Indonesian word for 'village' (apt for this city, but especially this 'hood), Dèsa is wildly popular for its rijsttafel ('rice table') banquets. À la carte options include *serundeng* (spiced fried coconut), *ayam besengek* (chicken cooked in saffron and coconut milk), *sambal goreng telor* (stewed eggs in spicy Balinese sauce), and *pisang goreng* (fried banana) for dessert.

MAMOUCHE MOROCCAN €€

Map p326 (☎670 07 36; www.restaurant-mamouche.nl; Quellijnstraat 104; mains €15.50-23.50; ⏲6-10pm; 🚊16/24 Stadhouderskade) Refined Mamouche's minimalist dining room, with mottled raw plaster walls and slat-beam ceilings, complements its French-accented North African cuisine – a changing selection of *tajine* (Moroccan stew), duck confit with sweet-potato mash and cinnamon, and couscous dishes such as spicy sea bass and saffron butter.

MASTINO PIZZA €€

Map p326 (www.mastinopizza.com; 1e Van der Helststraat 78; pizzas €10-15; ⏲10am-10pm; 🖉; 🚊3 2e Van der Helststraat) Choose from classic flour, spelt or soya for the base, and from topping combinations like Parma (ham, rocket, tomato and buffalo mozzarella), Flower Power (courgette flowers, anchovies, and mozzarella), and Veggie (vegan cheese, artichokes, black olives, cherry tomatoes and basil), then dine in the exposed-brick interior, out on the terrace or take it away.

VAN HOECK INTERNATIONAL €€

Map p326 (☎675 86 68; www.vanhoeck.nl; Frans Halsstraat 28; mains lunch €6.50-12.50, dinner €8.50-16; ⏲noon-10pm; 📶; 🚊16/24 Albert Cuypstraat) On one of De Pijp's loveliest, leafiest backstreets, Van Hoeck has pavement tables, a glassed-in winter garden and gorgeous open-plan interior. Stop by for lunchtime sandwiches, salads, soups and homemade apple pie, or book ahead for evening meals like seared salmon on wilted spinach with lemon and dill sauce, or duck breast with Belgian beer and cherry sauce.

BAZAR AMSTERDAM MIDDLE EASTERN €€

Map p326 (☎675 05 44; http://bazaramsterdam.nl; Albert Cuypstraat 182; mains lunch €5-12.50, dinner €8.50-15.50; ⏲10am-11.30pm Sun-Thu, to 1am Fri & Sat; 🖉👪; 🚊16/24 Albert Cuypstraat) Beneath a golden angel in the middle of the Albert Cuypmarkt, this one-time church has fab-u-lous tile murals and 1001 Arabian lights to complement the Moroccan to Turkish, Lebanese and Iranian cuisine, or just a beer and baklava.

FIRMA PEKELHAARING ITALIAN €€

Map p326 (www.pekelhaaring.nl; Van Woustraat 127-129; mains €12.50-19.50; ⏲10am-10pm; 📶👪; 🚊3/4 Van Woustraat) Sociable touches like the communal table, strewn with magazines and board games to play over dessert, belie the focused attention on fresh Italian flavours at arty, industrial Firma Pekelhaaring. Loads of fun and little pretence.

EN AMSTERDAM JAPANESE €€

Map p326 (☎470 36 66; http://en-amsterdam.nl; Dusartstraat 53; mains €15-27.50, sushi & sashimi plates €18.50-34.50; ⏲5-10.30pm Mon-Sat; 🚊12 Cornelis Troostplein) Secluded in a leafy, residential corner of the neighbourhood, this elegant restaurant serves equally refined Japanese fare: crispy lotus root with prawns; miso chicken with black garlic; *gyoza* dumplings; and sushi and sashimi. There are also premium Wagyu steaks (€39.50), over 30 different types of sake, and three-/five-course menus (€36/58, with sake €64/103).

DE WAAGHALS VEGETARIAN €€

Map p326 (☎679 96 09; www.waaghals.nl; Frans Halsstraat 29; mains €12-19.50; ⏲5-9.30pm; 🖉; 🚊16/24 Stadhouderskade) The popular white-walled 'Daredevil' is stylish enough for non-vegies to re-examine their dining priorities. The menu concentrates on one country each month – say, Thailand or Italy – plus a rotating array of inventive seasonal, organic dishes. Book ahead (it takes online reservations, too).

ZAGROS KURDISH €€

Map p326 (☎670 04 61; www.zagrosrestaurant.nl; Albert Cuypstraat 50; mains €12.50-22.50; ⏲5-11pm Tue-Sat; 🖉; 🚊16/24 Albert Cuypstraat) Delicious Kurdish dishes here include grills and stews (mostly lamb and chicken), salads of cucumber, tomato or onion, and

LOCAL KNOWLEDGE

PICNIC IN THE PARK

Join the locals picnicking on the lawns of lush Sarphatipark when the sun's out. As well as the **Albert Cuypmarkt** (p190), there are some great local places to pick up supplies.

't Kaasboertje (Map p326; Gerard Doustraat 60; ⊙1-5.30pm Mon, 9am-5.30pm Tue-Fri, 9am-4pm Sat; 16/24 Stadhouderskade) Enormous wheels of Gouda line the walls of this enticing cheese shop, and more cheeses fill the glass display cabinet. Crispbreads and crackers are on hand as well as reds, whites and rosés from the Netherlands, Belgium and Germany.

Beer Tree (Map p326; www.thebeertree.nl; 1e Van der Helststraat 53; ⊙noon-10pm; 16/24 Albert Cuypstraat) More than 250 different craft beers from over 25 countries fill this fab space, such as Belgian Abbey Tripel, Scottish BrewDog Dead Pony pale ale, New Zealand Monteith's, and gluten-free Spanish Daura. Many of its beers are kept in fridges and ready to drink, as are four rotating beers on tap, which can be bottled to take away.

The original branch of the **Tree** (p185) is near Vondelpark.

Stach (Map p326; ☎754 26 72; www.stach-food.nl; Van Woustraat 154; ⊙8am-10pm Mon-Sat, from 9am Sun; 4 Lutmastraat) An Aladdin's cave of fresh produce, jams, preserves, teas, coffees, juices and chocolates, this food emporium makes some of the best (and best value) sandwiches around, loaded with gourmet ingredients. If it's not picnic weather, there's a mezzanine dining area inside (dishes €3-14.50). It's expanded around Amsterdam, including a **branch** (p135) in the Southern Canal Ring.

Tjin's (Map p326; 1e Van der Helststraat 64; ⊙10am-7.30pm Mon-Sat; 3 2e Van der Helststraat) Crammed to the rafters with hard-to-find products from North, Central and South America, the Caribbean, Asia and beyond, this international grocers has a cult following for its takeaway Surinamese and Indonesian hot dishes (lamb curry, gado gado, tempeh, and pastries).

starters like hummus and *dumast* (thick, dry yoghurt). Book ahead on weekends.

★CIEL BLEU FRENCH €€€

(☎450 67 87; www.okura.nl; Ferdinand Bolstraat 333, Hotel Okura Amsterdam; mains €60, 7-course menu €110, with paired wines €170; ⊙6.30-10.30pm Mon-Sat, closed late Jul–mid-Aug; 12 Cornelius Trootsplein) Mindblowing, two-Michelin-star creations at this pinnacle of gastronomy change with the seasons, so springtime might see scallops and oysters with vanilla sea salt and gin-and-tonic foam, king crab with salted lemon, beurre blanc ice cream and caviar, or saddle of lamb with star anise. Just as incomparable is the 23rd-floor setting with aerial views north across the city.

If your budget doesn't stretch to dining here, head to the adjacent Twenty Third Bar (p196).

DRINKING & NIGHTLIFE

The neighbourhood that houses the old Heineken brewery is chock-full of places to drink it and much more. In particular, the streets around Gerard Douplein heave with a high-spirited local crowd.

★BROUWERIJ TROOST BREWERY

Map p326 (☎737 10 28; www.brouwerijtroost.nl; Cornelis Troostplein 21; ⊙4pm-1am Mon-Thu, 4pm-3am Fri, 2pm-3am Sat, 2pm-midnight Sun; ; 12 Cornelis Troostplein) Watch beer being brewed in copper vats behind a glass wall at this outstanding craft brewery. Its dozen beers include a summery blonde, smoked porter, strong tripel, and deep-red Imperial IPA; it also distils gin from its beer and serves fantastic bar food including humongous burgers. Troost's popularity (book ahead on weekend evenings) saw its second premises (p160) open in Westergasfabriek.

GLOUGLOU WINE BAR

Map p326 (www.glouglou.nl; 2e Van der Helststraat 3; ⌚4pm-midnight Mon-Fri, from 3pm Sat & Sun; 🚊3 2e Van der Helststraat) Natural, all-organic, additive-free wines are the stock-in-trade of this convivial neighbourhood wine bar in a rustic stained-glass-framed shop, where the party often spills out into the street. More than 40 well-priced French wines are available by the glass; it also sells bottles to drink on site or take away.

BOCA'S BAR

Map p326 (www.bar-bocas.nl; Sarphatipark 4; ⌚10am-1am Mon-Thu, 10am-3am Fri & Sat, 11am-1am Sun; 📶; 🚊3 2e Van der Helststraat) Boca's (Italian for 'mouth') is the ultimate spot for *borrel* (drinks). Mezzanine seating overlooks the cushion-strewn interior but in summer the best seats are on the terrace facing leafy Sarphatipark. Its pared-down wine list (seven by-the-glass choices) goes perfectly with its lavish sharing platters.

CAFÉ BINNEN BUITEN BROWN CAFE

Map p326 (www.cafebinnenbuiten.nl; Ruysdaelkade 115; ⌚11am-1am Sun-Thu, to 3am Fri & Sat; 🚊16/24 Ruysdaelkade) The minute there's a sliver of sunshine, this *café* gets packed. Sure, the food's good and the bar is candlelit and cosy. But what really draws the crowds is simply the best canal-side terrace in De Pijp – an idyllic spot to while away an afternoon.

CAFÉ SARPHAAT BROWN CAFE

Map p326 (☎675 15 65; Ceintuurbaan 157; ⌚9am-1am Sun-Thu, to 3am Fri & Sat; 🚊3/4 Van Woustraat) Grab an outdoor table along Sarphatipark, order a frothy beer and see if you don't feel like a local. This is one of the neighbourhood's most genial spots, with a lovely old bar that makes sipping a *jenever* in broad daylight seem like a good idea. Free live jazz takes place most Sunday afternoons.

CAFÉ BERKHOUT BROWN CAFE

Map p326 (www.cafeberkhout.nl; Stadhouderskade 77; ⌚10am-1am Mon-Thu, to 3am Fri & Sat, 11am-1am Sun; 📶; 🚊16/24 Stadhouderskade) With its dark wood, mirrored and chandelier-rich splendour and shabby elegance, this brown *café* is a natural post–Heineken Experience wind-down spot (it's right across the street). Great food too, especially burgers.

BARÇA DESIGNER BAR

Map p326 (www.barca.nl; Marie Heinekenplein 30-31; ⌚11am-1am Sun-Thu, to 3am Fri & Sat; 🚊16/24 Stadhouderskade) One of the hottest bar-restaurants in the 'hood, this 'Barcelona in Amsterdam' themed bar is the heartbeat of Marie Heinekenplein. Cosy up in the plush-gold and dark-timber interior, or spread out on the terrace.

TWENTY THIRD BAR COCKTAIL BAR

(www.okura.nl; Ferdinand Bolstraat 333, Hotel Okura Amsterdam; ⌚6pm-1am Sun-Thu, to 2am Fri & Sat; 🚊12 Cornelius Trootsplein) Twenty Third Bar has sweeping views to the west and south, a stunning bar-snack menu prepared in the kitchen of Ciel Bleu (p195) (dishes €9 to €18; caviar €36 to €60 per 10g), champagne cocktails and Heineken on tap.

CAFÉ DE GROENE VLINDER BROWN CAFE

Map p326 (www.cafe-de-groene-vlinder.nl; Albert Cuypstraat 130; ⌚10am-1am Sun-Thu, to 3am Fri & Sat; 🚊16/24 Albert Cuypstraat) Right on Albert Cuypstraat, the Green Butterfly strikes just the right balance between hip and *gezellig* (cosy, convivial), making it perfect for a *koffie verkeerd* (milky coffee) in the warm wood interior or a *biertje* (a glass of beer) on the buzzing patio.

CHOCOLATE BAR DESIGNER BAR

Map p326 (www.chocolate-bar.nl; 1e Van der Helststraat 62a; ⌚9am-1am Sun-Thu, to 3am Fri & Sat; 🚊16/24 Albert Cuypstraat) Chocolate isn't the draw here – it's the cool vibe, retro '60s/'70s interior and Euro soundtrack. The candle-lit bar makes it feel like a night out even at noon. On chilly days, curl up with a woolly blanket on the patio. At night, it's a scene; DJs hit the decks from Thursday to Sunday.

PILSVOGEL BROWN CAFE

Map p326 (www.pilsvogel.nl; Gerard Douplein 14; ⌚10am-1am Sun-Thu, to 3am Fri & Sat; 🚊16/24 Albert Cuypstraat) The kitchen dispenses small plates through to full meals but that's really secondary when you're sitting on De Pijp's most festive corner, on one of the neighbourhood's prime people-watching patios.

HET PAARDJE BAR

Map p326 (☎664 35 39; www.cafehetpaardje.nl; Gerard Douplein 1; ⌚10am-midnight Mon-Wed, to 1am Thu, to 2am Fri & Sat, 11am-midnight Sun; 🚊16/24 Albert Cuypstraat) Inside the decor's nothing flash (an updated, blander version of a brown *café*, pretty much), but Het

LOCAL KNOWLEDGE

HOW TO EAT A HERRING

'Hollandse Nieuwe' isn't a fashion trend – it's the fresh catch of super-tasty herring, raked in every June. The Dutch love it, and you'll see vendors selling the salty fish all over town. Although Dutch tradition calls for dangling the herring above your mouth, this isn't the way it's done in Amsterdam. Here the fish is served chopped in chunks and eaten with a toothpick, topped with *uitjes* (chopped onions) and *zuur* (sweet pickles). A *broodje haring* (herring roll) is even handier, as the fluffy white roll holds on the toppings and keeps your fingers fish-fat-free – think of it as an edible napkin.

Paardje has one of best, most sprawling terraces in central De Pijp.

KINGFISHER PUB

Map p326 (www.kingfishercafe.nl; Ferdinand Bolstraat 24; ⏱10am-1am Mon-Thu, to 3am Fri & Sat, noon-1am Sun; 📶; 🚊16/24 Stadhouderskade) With friendly staff and loyal regulars and newly spiffed up with white-and-red walls, Kingfisher is a nucleus of De Pijp's signature feel-good vibe. The communal table welcomes laptops and lunching by day. By happy hour the place is kicking.

KATSU COFFEESHOP

Map p326 (www.katsu.nl; 1e Van der Helststraat 70; ⏱10am-midnight Mon-Thu, 10am-1am Fri & Sat, 11am-midnight Sun; 🚊16/24 Albert Cuypstraat) Like the surrounding neighbourhood, this relaxed coffeeshop brims with colourful characters of all ages and dispositions. When seating on the ground floor and terrace gets tight, head up to the 1st-floor lounge.

ENTERTAINMENT

CC MUZIEKCAFÉ LIVE MUSIC

Map p326 (www.cccafe.nl; Rustenburgerstraat 384; ⏱8pm-1am Sun-Thu, to 3am Fri & Sat; 📶; 🚊12 Cornelis Troostplein) A feel-good little club, CC Muziekcafé is right at home in De Pijp. It dishes up weekly and monthly themed music nights from reggae to soul to rock.

RIALTO CINEMA CINEMA

Map p326 (☎676 87 00; www.rialtofilm.nl; Ceintuurbaan 338; adult/child from €9/7.50; 🚊3 2e Van der Helststraat) This great old cinema near Sarphatipark focuses on premieres, and shows eclectic, art-house fare from around the world (foreign films feature Dutch subtitles). There are three screens and a stylish cafe.

SHOPPING

After you've hit the Albert Cuypmarkt (p190), head to the surrounding streets, which are less crowded and dotted with boutiques and galleries. Look out for eclectic women's fashion and shoes on Van Woustraat, off Ceintruurbaan.

★HUTSPOT CONCEPT STORE

Map p326 (www.hutspotamsterdam.com; Van Woustraat 4; ⏱shop & cafe 10am-7pm Mon-Sat, noon-6pm Sun, bar 5pm-1am Mon-Thu, 4pm-3am Fri & Sat, 4pm-1am Sun; 🚊4 Stadhouderskade) Named after the Dutch dish of boiled and mashed vegies, 'Hotchpotch' was founded by four young guys with a mission to give young entrepreneurs the chance to sell their work. As a result, this concept store is an inspired mishmash of Dutch-designed furniture, furnishings, art, homewares and clothing plus a cool in-store cafe and bar.

KOLIFLEUR VINTAGE

Map p326 (http://kolifleur.nl; Frans Halsstraat 35; ⏱11am-7pm Tue-Sat; 🚊16/24 Albert Cuypstraat) Mint-condition, second-hand designer clothing, jewellery and bags by Dutch designers are the stock-in-trade of funky Kolifleur, along with vintage furniture and homewares.

TILLER GALERIE ART

Map p326 (www.tillergalerie.com; 1e Jacob van Campenstraat 1; ⏱1-7pm Thu & Fri, to 5pm Sat & Sun, by appointment Wed; 🚊16/24 Stadhouderskade) This intimate, friendly gallery has works by George Heidweiller (check out the surreal Amsterdam skyscapes), Peter Donkersloot's portraits of animals and iconic actors like Marlon Brando, and Herman Brood prints.

BRICK LANE FASHION

Map p326 (www.bricklane-amsterdam.nl; Gerard Doustraat 783; ⏱1-6pm Mon, 10.30am-6pm

Tue-Sat, 12.30-5.30pm Sun; 16/24 Albert Cuypstraat) Individual, affordable designs arrive at this London-inspired boutique every couple of weeks, keeping the selection up-to-the-minute.

RAAK CLOTHING

Map p326 (www.raakamsterdam.nl; 1e Van der Helststraat 46; noon-6pm Mon, from 10am Tue-Sat; 16/24 Albert Cuypstraat) Unique casual clothing, bags, jewellery and homewares by Dutch and Scandinavian designers fill Raak's shelves and racks.

RECORD MANIA MUSIC

Map p326 (www.recordmania.nl; Ferdinand Bolstraat 30; noon-6pm Mon-Sat; 16/24 Stadhouderskade) Fantastically old-school, Record Mania stocks vinyl (singles and LPs) and CDs, including rare recordings by artists including Johnny Cash, JJ Kale, Eric Clapton, Def Leppard, the Beatles and the Whalers. The shop, with old posters, stained-glass windows, and records and CDs embedded in the floor, is a treasure in itself.

VAN BEEK ARTS

Map p326 (www.vanbeekart.nl; Stadhouderskade 62-65; 1-6pm Mon, 9am-6pm Tue-Fri, 10am-5pm Sat; 16/24 Stadhouderskade) If you're inspired by Amsterdam's masterpiece-filled galleries, street art and picturesque canalscapes, the De Pijp branch of this venerable Dutch art-supply shop is a great place to pick up canvases, brushes, oils, watercolours, pastels, charcoals and more.

STENELUX GIFTS

Map p326 (662 14 90; 1e Jacob van Campenstraat 2; noon-5pm Thu-Sat; 16/24 Stadhouderskade) Browse Stenelux' delightful collection of gems, minerals, stones and fossils. The fascinating collection from this world and beyond includes meteorites.

NOOR CLOTHING

Map p326 (670 29 16; http://nooramsterdam.nl; Albert Cuypstraat 145; 9.30am-6pm Mon-Sat; 16/24 Albert Cuypstraat) Noor's affordable, modern fashion may make you want to skip the competition on the Albert Cuypmarkt altogether. Don't miss the jam-packed sale rack.

LOCAL KNOWLEDGE

THE NETHERLANDS' LARGEST BAROMETER

Rising 75m above low-rise Amsterdam, the landmark **Hotel Okura Amsterdam** (p236) building is visible from afar, both day and evening. Each night the roof's perimeter is illuminated by LED lights, which change colour depending on the barometer's reading for the following day. Blue lights mean a bright, sunny day is forecast. Green lights mean bad weather is on the way. 'White' (more like a pale pinkish colour and the most common) means the weather will be changeable.

The same lights also change colour on special occasions, such as a verigated rainbow effect for Amsterdam's **Gay Pride Parade** (p24) and New Year's Eve, and, of course, orange for King's Day.

DE EMAILLEKEIZER HOMEWARES

Map p326 (664 18 47; www.emaillekeizer.nl; 1e Sweelinckstraat 15; 10.30am-6pm Mon-Fri, from 10am Sat; 4 Stadhouderskade) This colourful shop brims with enamel treasures, including metal tableware. The Dutch signs, such as the unmistakable 'coffeeshop' signs, make quirky souvenirs.

BLOND GIFTS

Map p326 (www.blond-amsterdam.nl; Gerard Doustraat 69; noon-6pm Mon, 10am-6pm Tue-Fri, 10am-5pm Sat; 16/24 Albert Cuypstraat) The friendly blonde owners glaze plates and dishes in designs that are hilarious, adorable and colourful: ladies lunching, beach scenes, cakes and chocolates. Great gifts for anyone who likes modern kitsch with a sense of humour.

HET IS LIEFDE GIFTS

Map p326 (www.hetisliefde.nl; Gerard Doustraat 65; 11am-6pm Wed-Fri, to 5pm Sat; 16/24 Albert Cuypstraat) Come feel the love in this wedding shop, where all forms of romance and general festivity are celebrated. Keepsakes and ephemera include whimsical cake toppers in boy-girl, boy-boy and girl-girl couplings.

Oosterpark & South Amsterdam

OOSTERPARK | SOUTH AMSTERDAM

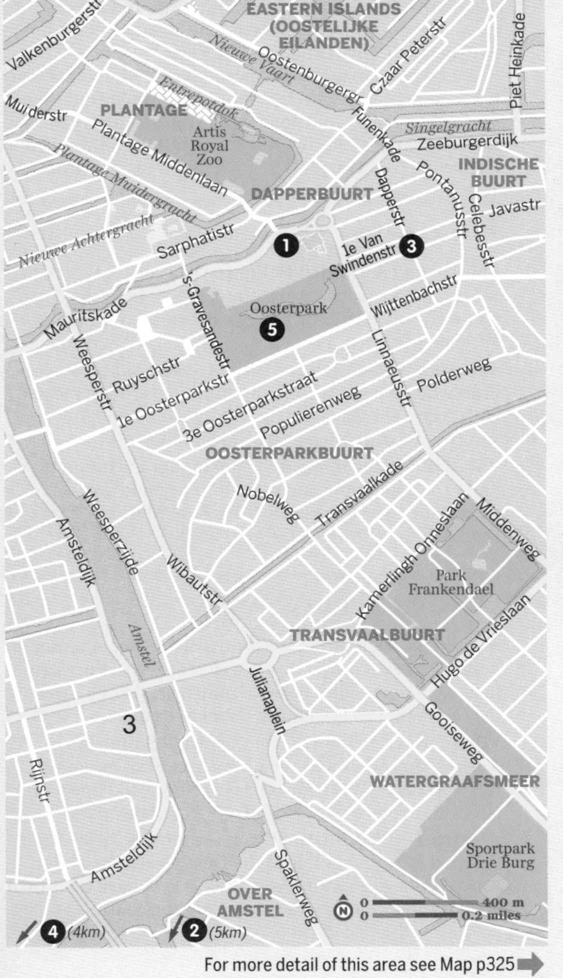

For more detail of this area see Map p325

Neighbourhood Top Five

1. Spending the afternoon yodelling, sitting in a yurt and checking out Dutch colonial booty at the **Tropenmuseum** (p201).
2. Taking a trip through the big, bold, avant-garde paintings of Karel Appel and friends at the **Cobra Museum** (p202).
3. Sniffing out the Turkish pide stall amid multipack sock vendors at the lively **Dappermarkt** (p201).
4. Cycling through **Amsterdamse Bos** (p202) and visiting an organic farm-cafe for fresh goat's-milk ice cream.
5. Seeking out the political monuments and wild parrots of sublime **Oosterpark** (p201).

Lonely Planet's Top Tip

With the Amstel river slicing through the area, Oosterpark and South Amsterdam have no shortage of riverside cafes that remind you of the age-old Dutch bond with water. On gorgeous summer evenings many patrons arrive by boat, settle at a terrace table and watch the freight barges, tugs and rowing teams ply the waters.

Best Places to Eat

- De Kas (p204)
- Wilde Zwijnen (p203)
- Roopram Roti (p203)
- Eetcafe Ibis (p204)

For reviews, see p203.

Best Places to Drink

- De Ysbreeker (p204)
- Distilleerderij 't Nieuwe Diep (p205)
- Canvas (p204)
- Butcher's Tears (p204)
- De Biertuin (p204)

For reviews, see p204.

Best Parks to Visit

- Amsterdamse Bos (p202)
- Amstelpark (p203)
- Oosterpark (p201)
- Park Frankendael (p201)

For reviews, see p201.

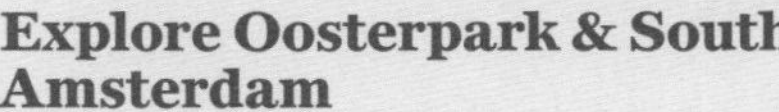

Explore Oosterpark & South Amsterdam

Oosterpark is one of Amsterdam's most culturally diverse neighbourhoods. Unlike De Pijp, it has seen only a small amount of gentrification, though things are starting to pick up.

The best sights are off the everyday tourist path. On the northern fringe you'll find the Tropenmuseum, which gives insights into Dutch colonial activities in the East Indies. The green expanse of Oosterpark itself makes a fine diversion afterwards, with its large pond and several monuments. Fun bars are popping up all around the park.

A walk east from the museum down 1e Van Swindenstraat leads to the street market on Dapperstraat and eventually into Javastraat, a Moroccan and Turkish enclave. Head to the neighbourhood's western edge, home to cool bars Canvas and De Ysbreeker.

Amsterdam extends well beyond here. The sights scatter as you head south, but the things you'll find – wild art, lush greenery and goats in the forest – are worth the trip. Reaching them is pretty straightforward by public transport; count on it taking between 30 and 60 minutes.

Local Life

- **Moroccan & Turkish Delights** On Javastraat (which 1e Van Swindenstraat turns into) old Dutch fish shops and working-class bars sit adjacent to Moroccan and Turkish groceries.
- **Garden Homes** Toward the northwest side of Park Frankendael lies a whole community of garden plots with teeny houses on them. The owners sit out on sunny days with wine and picnic fixings.
- **Market Madness** If you're looking for an authentic place to shop, Dappermarkt is it. If organic fare is more your style, the monthly De Pure Markt in Park Frankendael is where everyone flocks.

Getting There & Away

- **Tram** The 9 goes from the centre to the Tropenmuseum. Trams 10 and 14 swing through the Oosterpark area on their east–west routes as well. Tram 5 heads south from the centre and ends near the Cobra Museum.
- **Bus** Buses 170 and 172 from Centraal Station go to Amsterdamse Bos and the Cobra Museum, but note if you're using a GVB transit pass, it's not valid on these particular routes (you'll need a regional day pass).
- **Metro** The Wibautstraat stop is a stone's throw from the mod bars and hotels at the Oost's southwest edge. Amsterdam ArenA and Amsterdam RAI have their own Metro stops – all easy to reach from the centre.

SIGHTS

Oosterpark

OOSTERPARK PARK

Map p325 (dawn-dusk; ; 9 1e Van Swindenstraat) Oosterpark was laid out in 1891 to accommodate the diamond traders who found their fortunes in the South African mines, and it still has an elegant, rambling feel, complete with regal grey herons swooping around the ponds and wild parrots chattering in the trees.

On the south side, look for two monuments: one commemorates the **abolition of slavery** (Map p325) in the Netherlands in 1863; the other, **De Schreeuw** (The Scream; Map p325325), honours free speech and, more specifically, filmmaker Theo van Gogh, who was murdered here in 2004. Another (living) monument to Van Gogh is the **Spreeksteen** (Map p325), a rock podium marking a 'speakers' corner' established in 2005.

Families will enjoy the playground with a wading pool on the park's north side.

DAPPERMARKT MARKET

Map p325 (www.dappermarkt.nl; Dapperstraat, btwn Mauritskade & Wijttenbachstraat; 9am-5pm Mon-Sat; 3/7 Dapperstraat) The larger Albert Cuypmarkt in De Pijp may the king of street bazaars, but the Dappermarkt is a worthy prince. Reflecting the Oost's diverse immigrant population, it's a whirl of people (Africans, Turks, Dutch), foods (apricots, olives, fish) and goods from sports socks and shimmering fabrics to sunflowers, all sold from stalls lining the street.

PARK FRANKENDAEL PARK

Map p325 (Middenweg 72; 9 Hogeweg) Once part of a posh estate, this lovely, landscaped green space has walking paths, flapping storks, decorative bridges and the remains of follies. It surrounds the historic Frankendael House and De Kas, the restaurant-in-a-greenhouse.

FRANKENDAEL HOUSE HISTORIC BUILDING, GARDENS

Map p325 (www.huizefrankendael.nl; Middenweg 72; gardens dawn-dusk, house noon-5pm Sun; 9 Hugo de Vrieslaan) FREE As early as the 18th century, wealthy Amsterdammers would spend their summers in plush

TOP SIGHT TROPENMUSEUM

Completed in 1926 to house the Royal Institute of the Tropics, and still a leading research institute for tropical hygiene and agriculture, the fascinating Tropenmuseum puts out a whopping collection of colonial artefacts. Galleries are spread around a huge central hall across three floors and present exhibits with insight, imagination and lots of multimedia.

You can watch old Bollywood clips, stroll through a recreated African market and sit inside a life-sized yurt (traditional Central Asian felt hut). The galleries covering former Dutch territory are particularly rich, with gorgeous Indonesian jewellery and enormous Papuan war canoes. 'World of Music' is a splendid exhibit, showing how music and instruments travel throughout the world and remix sounds; enter the Singing School to learn to yodel or throat sing like a Tuvan.

The museum is especially great for kids. The gift shop stocks lots of international goodies. The onsite restaurant serves Indonesian, Indian and other global specialities in a cafeteria-style set-up if you need a bite after all the activity.

DON'T MISS

- 'World of Music' and Singing School
- Papuan war canoes
- Yurt
- Worldly cafe
- Special exhibits

PRACTICALITIES

- Tropics Museum
- Map p325
- 0880 042 800
- www.tropenmuseum.nl
- Linnaeusstraat 2
- adult/child €12.50/8
- 10am-5pm Tue-Sun
- 9/10/14 Alexanderplein

country retreats south of Plantage on a tract of drained land called Watergraafsmeer. The last survivor of the era is Frankendael, an elegant, restored Louis XIV–style mansion. The formal gardens behind the house are open to the public.

Staff hold a free open house every Sunday from noon to 5pm when you can explore the building on your own, or go on a guided tour (in Dutch; it departs at noon). Often there's an art exhibition going on to boot. The **Merkelbach cafe** (Map p325; ☎665 08 80; Middenweg 72; mains €18-25; ⊙8.30am-11pm Tue-Sat, to 6pm Sun & Mon) sits in the adjoining coach house and its patio overlooks the gardens. Be sure to view the house's forecourt with its gushing fountain and statues of Bacchus and Ceres.

South Amsterdam

AMSTERDAMSE BOS — PARK

(Amsterdam Forest; www.amsterdamsebos.nl; Bosbaanweg 5; ⊙park 24hr, visitors centre noon-5pm; 👪; 🚌170, 172) Amsterdamse Bos is a vast tract of lakes, woods and meadows criss-crossed by paths. It's filled with activities and is especially great for kids. You can rent bicycles, visit the goat farm, kayak the waterways, see a play at the open-air theatre, ascend to the treetops in the climbing park or hang out at the cafes and pancake restaurants.

In the densest thickets you can forget you're near a city at all (though, actually, you're right by Schiphol airport). The forest comprises roughly 1000 hectares of green space. A lot of locals use the park, but it rarely feels crowded.

Take bus 170 or 172 from Centraal Station; the trip takes about 40 minutes.

COBRA MUSEUM — MUSEUM

(www.cobra-museum.nl; Sandbergplein 1; adult/child €9.50/6; ⊙11am-5pm Tue-Sun; 🚌170, 172, 🚊5 Binnehof) Formed by artists from Copenhagen, Brussels and Amsterdam after WWII, the CoBrA movement produced semi-abstract works known for their primitive, childlike qualities. This fascinating, canal-side museum holds a trove of boldly coloured, avant-garde paintings, ceramics and statues, including many by Karel Appel, the style's most famous practitioner. Asger Jorn,

AMSTERDAMSE BOS ITINERARY

You can easily spend a half-day in the thick trees and open fields of **Amsterdamse Bos** (p202).

Start at the **visitors centre** (open from noon to 5pm) by the main entrance. Rangers can tell you what sort of activities are happening throughout the park and you can buy a map (€2.50) to get your bearings. The **bicycle rental kiosk** (www.amsterdamse-bosfietsverhuur.nl; rental per 2hr/day €6/9.50; ⊙10am-6pm, closed Mon & Tue in winter; 🚌170, 172) is also by the main entrance. If you plan to explore the park in depth, two wheels are vital. Likewise by the entrance is **Fun Forest** (www.funforest.nl; Bosbaanweg 3; adult/child €24/20; ⊙11am-7pm Jul & Aug, to 6pm Sep & Oct; 👪; 🚌170, 172), a tree-top climbing park geared toward children that uses ropes, ladders and bridges.

From here head west for 2.5km and you'll come to the **open-air theatre** (p205). It stages classic plays (in Dutch) throughout the summer. Nearby at Grote Speelweide you can rent **canoes and kayaks** (€6 per hour) and **pedal boats** (€10 per hour).

About 0.75km south is the park's most delightful attraction. **De Ridammerhoeve** (www.geitenboerderij.nl; ⊙10am-5pm Wed-Mon; 🚌170, 172) FREE is a working organic goat farm where kids can feed bottles of milk to, well, kids (€8 for two bottles). The cafeteria sells goat's-milk ice cream and other dairy products.

There are couple of options for a meal after your park activities. A short distance from the theatre, on the northwest side of the Bosbaan (the long lake used for sculling) is **Boerderij Meerzicht** (www.boerderijmeerzicht.nl; Koenenkade 56; pancakes €6-11; ⊙10am-7pm Tue-Sun Mar-Oct, 10am-6pm Fri-Sun Nov-Feb; 🚌170, 172), an old farmhouse that has been converted into a kid-friendly pancake restaurant. The popular playground beside it lets little ones burn off excess energy. Back by the park entrance, **De Bosbaan Cafe** (www.debosbaan.nl; Bosbaan 4; mains €10-20 ; ⊙10am-9pm; 🚌170, 172) is a lodge-like refuge for coffee or meals. Sit on the terrace to watch the rowers on the lake in front.

Anton Rooskens, Corneille and Constant are among the others. The CoBrA movement was active for just three years (1948–51).

The art is less of a unified whole than a philosophy, inspired by Marxism, of using materials at hand to create paintings, sculpture and even poetry. Changing exhibits by contemporary artists are on show as well.

Buses arrive right by the museum. The tram stop puts you about a kilometre from the museum; follow the 'CoBrA' signs through the mall to reach it.

ELECTRISCHE MUSEUMTRAMLIJN AMSTERDAM MUSEUM

(Tram Museum Amsterdam; 673 75 38; www.museumtramlijn.org; Amstelveenseweg 264; return adult/child €5/3; 11am-5pm Sun mid-Apr–Oct; ; 170 or 172, 16 Haarlemmermeer Station) Beyond the southwestern extremities of Vondelpark, just north of the Olympic Stadium, is the former Haarlemmermeer Station, which houses the tram museum. Historic trams sourced from all over Europe run between here and Amstelveen, making a great outing for kids and adults alike. A return trip takes about 1¼ hours and skirts the large Amsterdamse Bos recreational area.

The tram departs two to three times per hour; see the website for details.

AMSTELPARK PARK

(Europaboulevard; 8am-dusk; ; RAI, 4 RAI) South of the Amsterdam RAI convention centre lies the vast Amstelpark. The park is a paradise for kids, with a petting zoo, minigolf and a playground. In summer a miniature train chugs its way around the park. Other attractions include rose and rhododendron gardens; art exhibitions are held in the Glazen Huis (Glass House), the Orangerie and the Papillon Gallery.

RIEKERMOLEN WINDMILL

(www.molens.nl; RAI, 4 RAI) Just outside Amstelpark's south edge, on the west side of the Amstel river, stands this 1636 windmill. In a field southwest of the mill, you'll find a statue of a sitting Rembrandt, who sketched the windmill here along the riverbank.

DE BIJLMER AREA

(Bijlmer ArenA) Once a crime-ridden public housing area, De Bijlmer today is known for entertainment, shopping and innovative architecture. Hop on the metro to the dramatic Nicholas Grimshaw–designed **Bijlmer station**, opened in 2007. To the west lies Amsterdam ArenA (p205), the Heineken Music Hall (p205) and Ziggo Dome (p205). To the east is the Amsterdamse Poort shopping complex.

When you get off the train, walk toward the Amsterdamse Poort shops. As you continue east you'll pass various glassy office buildings set next to chain stores and exotic little ethnic shops. De Bijlmer holds the city's largest Surinamese population, along with immigrants from west and north Africa.

AMSTERDAM RAI BUILDING

(www.rai.nl; Europaplein 22; RAI, 4 RAI) This exhibition and conference centre (featured, by the way, in Jacques Tati's 1971 film *Trafic*) is the largest such complex in the country. The building opened in 1961 and just keeps expanding for the car, fashion, horse-jumping and 50-odd other shows held here every year.

RAI stands for Rijwiel en Automobiel Industrie, the bicycle and auto trade association that owns much of the complex.

OLYMPIC STADIUM STADIUM

(305 44 00; www.olympischstadion.nl; Olympisch Stadion 21; tours per person €10; 16/24 Olympisch Stadion) The grand Olympic Stadium was designed by Jan Wils, a protégé of architect HP Berlage, and is functionalist in style. The arena was built for the 1928 summer Games and has a soaring tower from which the Olympic flame burned for the first time during competition. Guided tours are available, but must be arranged in advance.

EATING

ROOPRAM ROTI SURINAMESE €

Map p325 (1e Van Swindenstraat 4; mains €4-10; 2-9pm Tue-Sun; 9 1e Van Swindenstraat) There's often a line to the door at this bare-bones Surinamese place, but don't worry – it moves fast. Place your order – lamb roti 'extra' (with egg) and a *barra* (lentil doughnut) at least – at the bar and don't forget the fiery hot sauce. It's some of the flakiest roti you'll find anywhere.

It's super delicious for takeaway or to eat at one of the half-dozen tables.

WILDE ZWIJNEN MODERN DUTCH €€

(463 30 43; www.wildezwijnen.com; Javaplein 23; mains €19-22, 3-/4-course menu €30.50/36.50; 6-10pm Mon-Thu, noon-4pm & 6-10pm Fri-Sun; ; 14 Javaplein) The name means

'wild boar' and if it's the right time of year, you may indeed find it on the menu. The rustic, wood-tabled restaurant serves locally sourced, seasonal fare with bold results. There's usually a vegetarian option and chocolate ganache for dessert. The *eetbar* next door offers small plates for €7 to €12 if you don't want a full-on meal.

It's about 1km east of Oosterpark; get here via 1e Van Swindenstraat, which turns into Javastraat, which runs into Javaplein.

EETCAFE IBIS — ETHIOPIAN €€

Map p325 (☎692 62 67; www.eetcafeibis.com; Weesperzidje 43; mains €12-15; ⏲5-10pm Tue-Sun; ✎; 🚋3 Wibautstraat/Ruyschstraat) African art and textiles decorate Ibis' wee room, a delightful spot to get your hands on (literally, using the spongy Ethiopian *injera* bread) herb-laced vegetable stews and spicy lamb and beef dishes. Ibis sells African beers to go with the authentic food.

★DE KAS — INTERNATIONAL €€€

Map p325 (☎462 45 62; www.restaurantdekas.nl; Kamerlingh Onneslaan 3, Park Frankendael; lunch/dinner menu €39/49.50; ⏲noon-2pm & 6.30-10pm Mon-Fri, 6.30-10pm Sat; ✎; 🚋9 Hogeweg) Admired by gourmets citywide, De Kas has an organic attitude to match its chic glass greenhouse setting – try to visit during a thunderstorm! It grows most of its own herbs and produce right here and the result is incredibly pure flavours with innovative combinations. There's one set menu each day, based on whatever has been freshly harvested. Reserve in advance.

DRINKING & NIGHTLIFE

★DE YSBREEKER — BROWN CAFÉ

Map p325 (www.deysbreeker.nl; Weesperzijde 23; ⏲8am-1am Sun-Thu, to 2am Fri & Sat; 📶; 🚋3 Wibautstraat/Ruyschstraat) The terrace at this *café* on the Amstel is glorious for watching the river lined with houseboats and other vessels gliding by. Inside, stylish drinkers hoist beverages in the plush booths and along the marble bar. It's great for organic and local beers (such as de Prael) and bar snacks such as lamb meatballs.

The building used to be an inn for the men who broke the ice on the Amstel so boats could pass (the art-glass windows in back depict the scene).

CANVAS — BAR

Map p325 (www.canvas7.nl; Wibautstraat 150; ⏲7am-1am Mon-Thu, to 4am Fri, 8am-4am Sat, to 1am Sun; Ⓜ Wibautstraat) Take the elevator to the 7th floor for this bar-club-restaurant atop the mod Volkshotel (located in the former *Volkskrant* newspaper office). Young creatives flock in for terrific views and cocktails in the edgy, urban-cool space. On weekend nights, it morphs into a fresh-beat dance club. Feeling wild? Sneak up to the roof for a dip in one of the hot tubs.

The Wibautstraat metro stop is a stone's throw away; follow signs saying 'Gijsbrecht van Aemstelstraat' as you exit the station.

BUTCHER'S TEARS — BREWERY

(www.butchers-tears.com; Karperweg 45; ⏲4-9pm Wed-Sun; 🚋16 Haarlemmermeerstation) Butcher's Tears' beers have a cult following in Amsterdam. Hop heads like to go straight to the source – the brewery's artsy tap room, tucked down an industrial alley – to get their fix. Six brews flow from the taps, and several more varieties are available in bottles. Look for Far Out (a *saison*) and Misery King (a triple-hopped amber ale).

Check the schedule for bands, films and other entertainment that the brewery hosts.

DE BIERTUIN — BEER GARDEN

Map p325 (www.debiertuin.nl; Linnaeusstraat 29; ⏲11am-1am Sun-Thu, to 3am Fri & Sat; 📶; 🚋9 1e Van Swindenstraat) The name translates to 'the beer garden', and it is indeed the main feature. A young and beautiful crowd packs the beloved terrace (heated when the weather gets chilly). They bite into top-notch burgers and swill from the lengthy beer list (around 12 on tap and 50 more Dutch and Belgian varieties in the bottle). It's a big after-work hangout.

BAR BUKOWSKI — BAR

Map p325 (☎370 16 85; www.barbukowski.nl; Oosterpark 10; ⏲8am-1am Mon-Thu, to 3am Fri, 9am-3am Sat, to 1am Sun; 🚋3/7 Beukenweg) Named after the barfly writer Charles Bukowski, this art-deco cafe is a fine spot to channel the drinking and writing muse. Linger all day over a coffee, Heineken, banana milkshake or jasmine tea. Supplement with a baguette sandwich or *flammkuchen* (Alsatian thin-crust pizza). If you're looking for a stiffer drink, the owners have a cocktail bar next door (open Thursday, Friday and Saturday).

SPARGO BAR

Map p325 (www.cafespargo.nl; Linnaeusstraat 37a; ⌚10am-1am; 🚋9 1e Van Swindenstraat) So you've done Oosterpark – sought out all the monuments and found the wild parrots chattering in the trees – and now you need a drink to replenish? Spargo's buzzy terrace sends out its siren call from across the street. It pours several local Dutch brews, including Brouwerij 't IJ (the windmill-brewery a short distance away). FYI, the cafe's sign looks like 'Spar90'.

ENTERTAINMENT

STUDIO K CINEMA, LIVE MUSIC

(☎692 04 22; www.studio-k.nu; Timorplein 62; ⌚11am-1am Sun-Thu, to 3am Fri & Sat; 📶; 🚋14 Zeeburgerdijk) Sporting two cinemas, a club, a stage for bands and theatre, an eclectic restaurant (serving sandwiches for lunch, and vegetarian-friendly, international-flavoured dishes for dinner) and a huge terrace, the student-run Studio K is your one-stop shop for hip culture in the Oost. Stop in for a coffee and you might wind up staying all night to dance.

You can also rent bicycles at the shop next door.

AMSTERDAM ARENA FOOTBALL

(www.amsterdamarena.nl; Arena Blvd 1; 📶; Ⓜ Bijlmer ArenA) Amsterdam ArenA is a high-tech complex with a retractable roof and seating for 52,000 spectators. Four-times European champion Ajax, the country's most famous football team, play here. Football games usually take place on Saturday evenings and Sunday afternoons from August to May. The arena is about 7km southeast of the centre; the metro will get you there with ease.

Fans can also take a one-hour guided tour of the stadium (adult/child €16/10; discounts available if you book online). There are usually eight tours daily; see the website for the schedule.

AMSTERDAMSE BOS THEATRE THEATRE

(www.bostheater.nl; Bosbaanweg 5; ⌚Jun-early Sep; 🚌170, 172) This large, open-air amphitheatre stages plays (Shakespeare, Brecht, Chekhov) in Dutch. We love it when the actors pause for planes passing overhead.

ZIGGO DOME CONCERT VENUE

(www.ziggodome.nl; De Passage 100; 📶; Ⓜ Bijlmer ArenA) The 17,000-seat, indoor Ziggo Dome hosts big-name concerts. Beyoncé, Madonna and U2 are recent stage takers.

HEINEKEN MUSIC HALL CONCERT VENUE

(www.heineken-music-hall.nl; Arena Blvd 590; Ⓜ Bijlmer ArenA) This midsized venue is praised for its quality acoustics and lighting. Expect rock and pop acts from medium to big names.

LOCAL KNOWLEDGE

DISTILLERY IN THE WOODS

Distilleerderij 't Nieuwe Diep (www.nwediep.nl; Flevopark 13; ⌚3-8pm Tue-Sun Apr-Oct, to 6pm Nov-Mar; 🚋7/14 Soembawastraat) Set in an old pumping station in leafy Flevopark, this little distillery makes around 100 small-batch *jenevers* (Dutch gin), herbal bitters, liqueurs and fruit distillates from organic ingredients according to age-old Dutch recipes. They're delicious, but the coolest part is the setting, which feels very rural and magical, like stumbling onto Hansel and Gretel's cottage in the woods.

The outdoor terrace is on a little lake next to an orchard. To get here, walk east from the tram stop; it's about a 10-minute walk into the park. Cash only.

SHOPPING

DE PURE MARKT MARKET

Map p325 (www.puremarkt.nl; Park Frankendael; ⌚11am-6pm Sun Mar-Oct & Dec; 🚋9 Hogeweg) On the last Sunday of the month De Pure Markt sets up in Park Frankendael (near De Kas restaurant), with artisanal food and craft producers selling sausages, home-grown grapes and much more. Keep an eye out to the market's west for the community of garden plots with wee houses on them.

DE WINKEL VAN NIJNTJE TOYS

(www.dewinkelvannijntje.nl; Scheldestraat 61; ⌚1-6pm Mon, 10am-6pm Tue-Fri, to 5pm Sat, noon-5pm Sun; 👪; 🚋12 Scheldestraat) Dutch illustrator Dick Bruna's most famous character, Miffy (Nijntje in Dutch), is celebrated in toys and kids' merchandise. Items range from pencils and soap bubbles to plush toys, clothing and even Royal Delftware plates.

ERIC FARRELLY / ALAMY STOCK PHOTO ©

1. Cycling (p29)
Do as the locals do and cycle your way around the city.

2. A blooming bicycle
Petal power meets pedal power on this flower-bedecked bike.

3. Bicycle parking
In Amsterdam, bicycles are more common than cars.

4. Vondelpark (p173)
Cycling is one way to explore this popular park, which has an open-air party atmosphere on sunny days.

3

JAN WLODARCZYK / ALAMY STOCK PHOTO ©

Day Trips from Amsterdam

Haarlem p209

Alleys wind among grand 17th-century buildings in this lively city, just a 15-minute hop from Amsterdam.

Leiden p212

Rembrandt's picturesque, canal-woven birthplace is home to the country's oldest and most prestigious university.

Keukenhof Gardens p213

See the world's largest, loveliest flower gardens in bloom during spring.

Delft p217

Delft's Gothic and Renaissance architecture rivals its beautiful Delftware pottery.

Alkmaar p220

Alkmaar's centuries-old cheese market is one of the traditional cheese guilds' last bastions.

Den Haag p221

Masterpieces abound in regal Den Haag's exceptional museums, including the sublime Mauritshuis.

Zaanse Schans p222

Watch windmills twirl and meet the millers at this delightful open-air museum.

Bloemenveiling Aalsmeer p223

Walk above vast, bustling, aromatic flower warehouses and catch the auction action.

Haarlem

Explore

As you stroll from glorious art-nouveau Haarlem Centraal train station (a national monument) to the old centre along Kruisweg and Kruisstraat, past exclusive boutiques, art galleries and antique shops, the city's wealth and elegance soon become apparent. Stop off at the Corrie Ten Boom House to pay homage to one of the Netherlands' most admired Resistance figures before heading to the lively Grote Markt. Just a few blocks south is the Frans Hals Museum. Haarlem was once more important in the art world than Amsterdam, and this incomparable museum possesses one of the country's finest assemblies of Dutch paintings.

Given Haarlem's quick and easy access to Amsterdam, you can easily stay on for sunset drinks, catch live music and enjoy the city's buzzing nightlife.

The Best...

- **Sight** Frans Hals Museum (p210)
- **Place to Eat** Brick (p212)
- **Place to Drink** Jopenkerk (p212)

Top Tip

Try to visit on a Saturday when Haarlem's lively market is in full swing. There's also a market on a Monday, but the Frans Hals Museum is closed.

Getting There & Away

- **Train** Services from Amsterdam's Centraal Station to Haarlem Centraal are frequent (€4.10, 15 minutes, up to eight per hour); the Grote Markt is a 850m walk south of the station. When the trains stop running at night, the N30 night bus links Haarlem Centraal Station to Schiphol airport, Amsterdam.
- **Car** From the ring road west of the city, take the N200, which becomes the A200.

Need to Know

- **Area Code** ☎023
- **Location** 20km west of Amsterdam
- **Tourist Office** (VVV; ☎023-531 73 25; www.haarlemmarketing.nl; Grote Markt 2; ⊙9.30am-5.30pm Mon-Fri, 9.30am-5pm Sat, noon-4pm Sun Apr-Sep, 1-5.30pm Mon, 9.30am-5.30pm Tue-Fri, 10am-5pm Sat Oct-Mar)

SIGHTS

TOWN HALL — HISTORIC BUILDING

(Grote Markt 2) At the western end of the Grote Markt is the florid, 14th-century town hall, which sprouted many extensions including a balcony where judgements from the high court were pronounced. It only opens to the public on Open Monuments Days during the second weekend of September.

GROTE KERK VAN ST BAVO — CHURCH

(www.bavo.nl; Oude Groenmarkt 22; adult/child €2.50/free; ⊙10am-5pm Mon-Sat) Topped by a 50m-high steeple, the Gothic Grote Kerk van St Bavo cathedral contains some fine Renaissance artworks, but the star attraction is its stunning Müller organ – one of the most magnificent in the world, standing 30m high with about 5000 pipes. It was played by Handel and a 10-year-old Mozart. Free hour-long **organ recitals** take place at 8.15pm Tuesday and 4pm Thursday in July and August, and

TRAVEL TIPS

All of these destinations lie within an hour's journey from Amsterdam by train (and, if need be, by connecting tram or bus). If you get an early start, it's possible to 'do' two locations in a day (Alkmaar and Zaanse Schans, for instance) without feeling rushed.

The fast, efficient Dutch railway network makes it a snap to get around. Rather than purchase a *dagkaart* (day pass; €51.40), buy a same-day return ticket from Amsterdam (around €8.20 to €22.40 for the towns in this chapter, depending on the distance), which allows you to hop on and off at multiple stops so long as you complete the journey in a single day.

Cycle paths are everywhere, but there's no need to bring a bike with you – rentals costing around €7.50 to €12 per day are widely available.

Haarlem

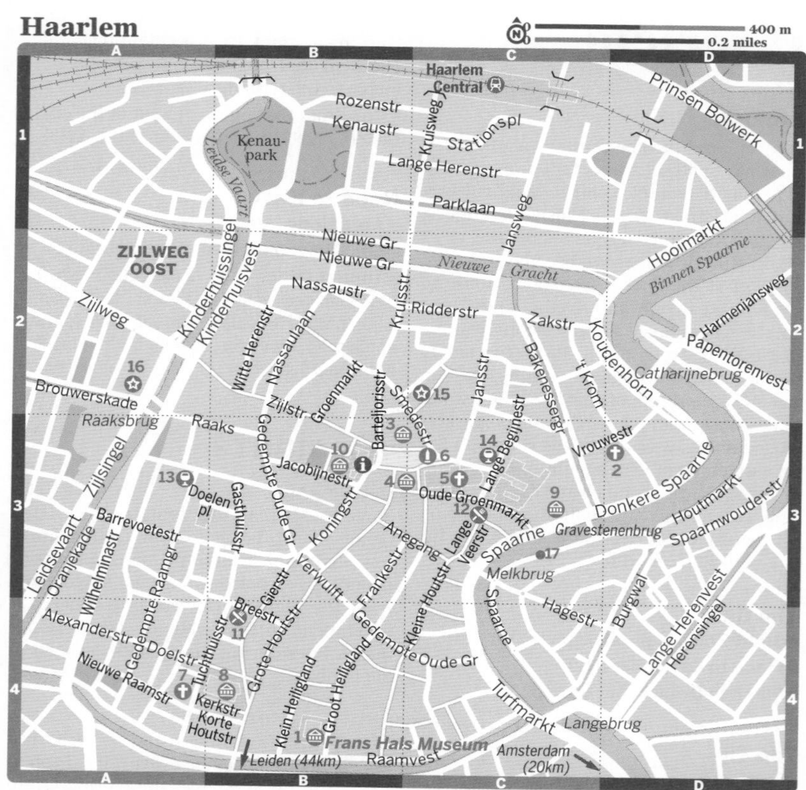

2pm on the last Saturday of the month year-round.

LAURENS COSTER STATUE STATUE

On the square north of the Grote Kerk is the Laurens Coster statue. Haarlemmers believe that Coster has a claim, along with Gutenberg, to be called the inventor of movable type.

DE HALLEN GALLERY

(www.dehallen.nl; Grote Markt 16; adult/child €7.50/free; ⏲11am-5pm Tue-Sat, noon-5pm Sun) Haarlem's modern and contemporary art museum resides within two historic 'halls': the 17th-century Dutch Renaissance **Vleeshal**, a former meat market and the sole place that meat was allowed to be sold in Haarlem from the 17th through to the 19th century, and the neoclassical **Verweyhal** (fish house). Eclectic exhibits rotate every three months and range from Dutch impressionists and CoBrA artists to innovative video, installation art and photography by cutting-edge international artists.

PROVENIERSHUIS HISTORIC BUILDING

(off Grote Houtstraat; ⏲10am-5pm Mon-Sat) FREE Off Grote Houtstraat to the southwest of Grote Markt is one of Haarlem's prettiest buildings, the Proveniershuis. It started life as a *hofje* (almshouse) and became the former headquarters of St Joris Doelen (the Civic Guard of St George).

★FRANS HALS MUSEUM GALLERY

(www.franshalsmuseum.nl; Groot Heiligland 62; adult/child €12.50/free; ⏲11am-5pm Tue-Sat, from noon Sun) A short stroll south of Grote Markt, the Frans Hals Museum is a must for anyone interested in the Dutch Masters. Located in the poorhouse where Hals spent his final years, the collection focuses on the 17th-century Haarlem School; its pride and joy are eight group portraits of the Civic Guard that reveal Hals' exceptional

Haarlem

Top Sights
1 Frans Hals Museum ... B4

Sights
2 Bakenesserkerk ... D3
3 Corrie ten Boom House ... B3
4 De Hallen ... B3
5 Grote Kerk van St Bavo ... C3
6 Laurens Coster Statue ... C3
7 Nieuwe Kerk ... A4
8 Proveniershuis ... B4
9 Teylers Museum ... C3
10 Town Hall ... B3

Eating
11 Brick ... B4
De Haerlemsche Vlaamse ... (see 4)
12 Restaurant Mr & Mrs ... C3

Drinking & Nightlife
13 Jopenkerk ... A3
14 Proeflokaal in den Uiver ... C3

Entertainment
15 Café Stiels ... C2
16 Patronaat ... A2

Sports & Activities
17 Haarlem Canal Tours ... C3

attention to mood and psychological tone. Look out for works by other greats such as Pieter Brueghel the Younger and Jacob van Ruysdael.

Among the museum's other treasures are the works of Hals' teacher, Flemish artist Carel van Mander: stunning illustrations of the human anatomy, all ceiling-high with biblical and mythological references.

TEYLERS MUSEUM MUSEUM
(www.teylersmuseum.nl; Spaarne 16; adult/child €12/2; 10am-5pm Tue-Sat, 11am-5pm Sun) Dating from 1778, Teylers is the country's oldest continuously operating museum. Its array of whiz-bang inventions include an 18th-century electrostatic machine that conjures up visions of mad scientists. The eclectic collection also has paintings from the Dutch and French schools; a magnificent, sky-lighted Ovale Zaal (Oval Room) displays natural-history specimens in elegant glass cases on two levels. Temporary exhibitions regularly take place.

BAKENESSERKERK CHURCH
(cnr Vrouwestraat & Bakenesserstraat) The striking Bakenesserkerk is a late 15th-century church with a lamplit tower of sandstone. The stone was employed here when the Grote Kerk proved too weak to support a heavy steeple – hence the wooden tower. It's closed to the public.

CORRIE TEN BOOM HOUSE HISTORIC BUILDING
(www.corrietenboom.com; Barteljorisstraat 19; admission by donation; 10am-3pm Apr-Oct, 11am-2.30pm Nov-Mar) Also known as 'the hiding place', the Corrie ten Boom House is named for the matriarch of a family that lived in the house during WWII. Using a secret compartment in her bedroom, she hid hundreds of Jews and Dutch resistors until they could be spirited to safety. In 1944 the family was betrayed and sent to concentration camps where three died. Later, Corrie ten Boom toured the world preaching peace. English-language tours take place every 90 minutes.

NIEUWE KERK CHURCH
(Nieuwe Kerksplein; 10am-5pm Mon-Sat) FREE Walk down charming Korte Houtstraat to find the 17th-century Nieuwe Kerk; the ornate tower by Lieven de Key is supported by a rather boxy design by Jacob van Campen.

EATING & DRINKING

DE HAERLEMSCHE VLAAMSE FAST FOOD €
(Spekstraat 3; frites €2.30-4.40; 9am-6.30pm Mon-Fri, 11am-5.30pm Sat, noon-5.30pm Sun) Line up at this local institution for a cone of crispy, golden fries made from fresh potatoes and one of a dozen sauces, including three kinds of mayonnaise.

HAARLEM'S SPANISH INVASION

When the Spanish invaded Haarlem in 1572, thousands of citizens were slaughtered during a seven-month siege. Against the odds, the community recovered quickly. The city then soared into the prosperity of the Golden Age, attracting painters and artists from around Europe.

★BRICK MODERN EUROPEAN €€

(☎023-551 18 70; www.restaurantbrick.nl; Bree-straat 24-26; mains lunch €7.50-10.50, dinner €15.50-21.50; ⌚noon-10pm Tue-Sun) You can watch Brick's chefs creating inspired dishes such as duck and hazelnut ravioli with black truffle and foie-gras sauce, not only from the street-level dining room but also the first-floor space, which has a glass floor directly above the open kitchen. There are pavement tables out front but in summer the best seats are on the roof terrace.

RESTAURANT MR & MRS INTERNATIONAL €€

(☎023-531 59 35; www.restaurantmrandmrs.nl; Lange Veerstraat 4; small plates €9-12, 4-/5-/6-course menu €36/44/52; ⌚5-10pm) Unexpectedly gastronomic cooking at this tiny restaurant is artfully conceived and presented. Small hot and cold plates designed for sharing might include steak tartare with black truffles, baby octopus with mango and jalapeño, mackerel with avocado dressing and caviar, hoisin-marinated steak with foie gras and portobello mushrooms and crème brûlée with whisky meringue. Definitely book ahead.

★JOPENKERK BREWERY

(www.jopenkerk.nl; Gedempte Voldersgracht 2; ⌚brewery & cafe 10am-1am, restaurant 5.30pm-late Tue-Sat) Haarlem's most atmospheric place to drink is this independent brewery inside a stained-glass-windowed, 1910 church. Enjoy brews such as citrusy Hopen, fruity Lente Bier or chocolatey Koyt along with classic Dutch bar snacks (*bitterballen* (round meat croquettes), cheeses) beneath the gleaming copper vats. Or head to the mezzanine for dishes made from locally sourced, seasonal ingredients and Jopenkerk's beers, with pairings available.

PROEFLOKAAL IN DEN UIVER BROWN CAFE

(www.indenuiver.nl; Riviervischmarkt 13; ⌚4pm-1am Mon-Wed, to 2am Thu-Sat, to midnight Sun) One of many atmospheric places overlooking the Grote Markt, this nautical-themed place has shipping knick-knacks and a schooner sailing right over the bar. Live jazz often plays; check the online agenda for dates.

ENTERTAINMENT

CAFÉ STIELS LIVE MUSIC

(www.stiels.nl; Smedestraat 21; ⌚8pm-2am Sun-Wed, to 3am Thu, to 4am Fri & Sat) Bands play jazz and rhythm and blues on the back stage almost every night of the week from 10pm onward to as late as 4am on weekends.

PATRONAAT LIVE MUSIC

(www.patronaat.nl; Zijlsingel 2; ⌚hours vary) Haarlem's top music and dance club attracts bands with banging tunes. Events in this cavernous venue usually start around 9pm.

SPORTS & ACTIVITIES

HAARLEM CANAL TOURS CANAL TOUR

(www.haarlemcanaltours.com; opposite Spaarne 17; tour per person €13.50; ⌚tours 10am-7pm Apr-Sep) Fun 1¼-hour tours in vintage open-top boats depart every 90 minutes.

Leiden

Explore

Vibrant Leiden is one of the Netherlands' great cities.

As you walk south from the striking, hyper-modern Centraal Station, the city's traditional character unfolds. A five-minute stroll takes you to Leiden's historic waterways, the most notable of which are the Oude Rijn and the Nieuwe Rijn. They meet at Hoogstraat to form the Rijn canal.

Leiden is renowned for being Rembrandt's birthplace; the home of the Netherlands' oldest and most illustrious university (Einstein was a regular professor), with a lively 23,000-strong student population; and the place America's pilgrims raised money to lease the leaky *Mayflower* that took them to the New World in 1620.

The city's cache of museums, all within walking distance of each other, are a major draw, as is wandering along the picturesque streetscapes.

KEUKENHOF GARDENS

Keukenhof Gardens (www.keukenhof.nl; Lisse; adult/child €16/8, parking €6; ⏲8am-7.30pm mid-Mar–mid-May, last entry 6pm) One of the Netherlands' top attractions, Keukenhof, 1km west of Lisse, is the world's largest bulb-flower garden. It attracts nearly 800,000 visitors during its eight-week season, which is almost as short-lived as the blooms on the millions of multicoloured tulips, daffodils and hyacinths.

Special buses (€9, every 15 minutes, 30 minutes) link Keukenhof with Amsterdam's Schiphol Airport and Leiden's Centraal Station; combination tickets covering entry and transport are available (adult/child €23.50/12.50). Pre-purchase tickets online to help avoid huge queues.

Kasteel Keukenhof (☎0252-750 690; www.kasteelkeukenhof.nl; Keukenhof-Noord 1; adult/child €12.50/5.50, gardens only €5/2; ⏲8.30am-5pm Mon-Fri, 10.30am-5pm Sat & Sun) Completely restored in 2012, this grand castle across the road from **Keukenhof Gardens** (p213) was built in 1641 by VOC commander Adriaan Muertenszoon Block. Tickets include a compulsory 30-minute guided tour of its lavish interior. It sits on more than 80 hectares of woodland, meadows and flowering gardens. There's a delightful petting zoo where kids can crawl into the pens with the guinea pigs and rabbits, and an adjacent teahouse (both open from 10am to 5pm).

The Best...

➡**Sight** Hortus Botanicus Leiden (p215)

➡**Place to Eat** In den Doofpot (p216)

➡**Place to Drink** Café L'Esperance (p216)

Top Tip

Explore the university precinct, where such historic sights as one of Europe's oldest botanical gardens coexist with Leiden's buzzing student life.

Getting There & Away

➡**Train** Services run from Amsterdam's Centraal Station (€8.80, 35 minutes, six per hour).

➡**Car** Take the A4 from the southwest point of the A10 ring road.

Need to Know

➡**Area Code** ☎071

➡**Location** 45km southwest of Amsterdam

➡**Tourist Office** (☎071-516 60 00; www.visitleiden.nl; Stationsweg 41; ⏲7am-7pm Mon-Fri, 10am-4pm Sat, 11am-3pm Sun)

SIGHTS

★RIJKSMUSEUM VAN OUDHEDEN — MUSEUM

(National Museum of Antiquities; www.rmo.nl; Rapenburg 28; adult/child €9.50/3; ⏲10am-5pm Tue-Sun) This museum has a world-class collection of Greek, Roman and Egyptian artefacts, the pride of which is the extraordinary **Temple of Taffeh**, a gift from former Egyptian president Anwar Sadat to the Netherlands for helping to save ancient Egyptian monuments from flood.

Note: the Egyptian collection is closed until October 2016.

PIETERSKERK — CHURCH

(www.pieterskerk.com; Pieterskerkhof 1; admission €2; ⏲11am-6pm) Crowned by its huge steeple, Pieterskerk is often under restoration – a good thing, as it has been prone to collapse since it was built in the 14th century.

The precinct here is as old Leiden as you'll get and includes the gabled old **Latin School** (Lokhorststraat 16), which – before it became a commercial building – was graced by a pupil named Rembrandt from 1616 to 1620. Across the plaza, look for the **Gravensteen** (Pieterskerkhof 6), which dates to the 13th century and was once a prison. The gallery facing the plaza was where judges watched executions.

Leiden

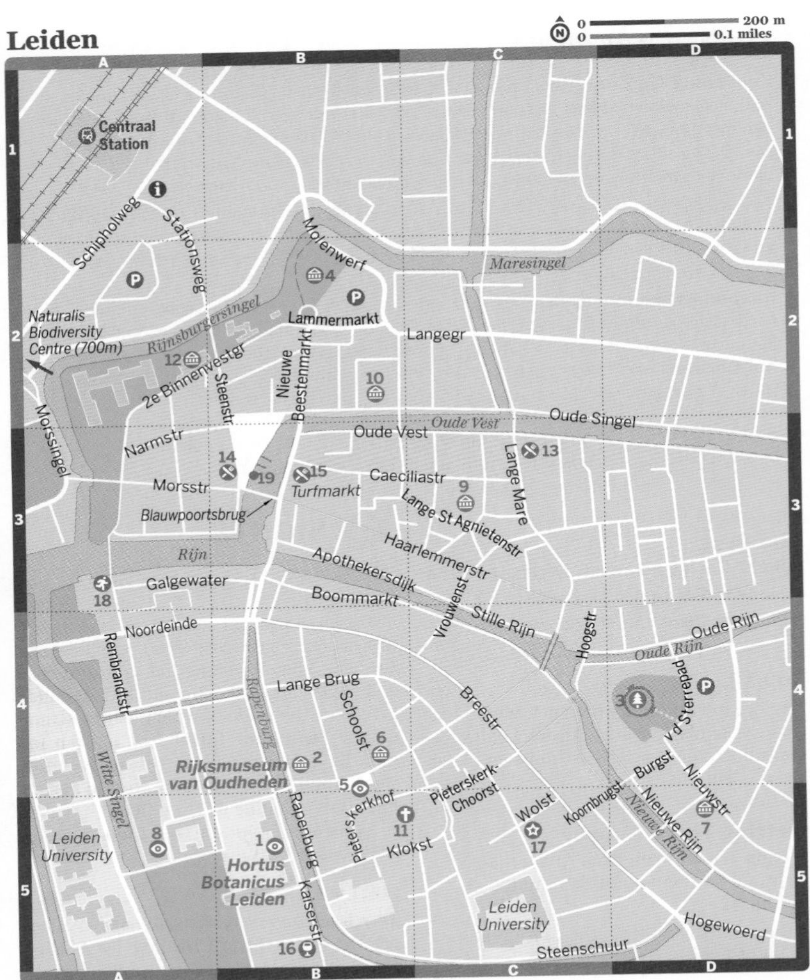

LEIDEN AMERICAN PILGRIM MUSEUM MUSEUM

(☎071-512 24 13; www.leidenamericanpilgrimmuseum.org/index.htm; Beschuitsteeg 9; admission €5; ⊙1-5pm Wed-Sat) The Leiden American Pilgrim Museum is a fascinating restoration of a one-room house occupied around 1610 by the soon-to-be Pilgrims (p216). The house itself dates from 1375 (check out the original 14th-century floor tiles), but the furnishings are from the Pilgrims' period. Curator Jeremy Bangs is an author who has written extensively on the Pilgrims and has a vast knowledge of their Leiden links.

DE BURCHT PARK, MONUMENT

(⊙sunrise-sunset) FREE De Burcht, an 11th-century citadel on an artificial hill, lost its protective functions as the city grew around it. It's now a park with lovely places to view the steeples and rooftops, with a cafe at its base.

LEIDEN UNIVERSITY UNIVERSITY

(www.leiden.edu) The oldest university in the Netherlands was a gift to Leiden from Willem the Silent in 1575 for withstanding two Spanish sieges in 1573 and 1574. The campus comprises an interesting mix

Leiden

Top Sights

1 Hortus Botanicus Leiden B5
2 Rijksmuseum van Oudheden B4

Sights

3 De Burcht D4
4 De Valk B2
5 Gravensteen B4
6 Latin School B4
7 Leiden American Pilgrim Museum D5
8 Leiden University A5
9 Museum Boerhaave C3
10 Museum De Lakenhal B2
11 Pieterskerk B5
12 Rijksmuseum Volkenkunde A2

Eating

13 Brasserie de Engelenbak C3
14 David's Burger B3
15 In den Doofpot B3

Drinking & Nightlife

16 Café L'Esperance B5

Entertainment

17 Café de WW C5

Sports & Activities

18 Botenverhuur 't Galgewater A3
19 Rederij Rembrandt B3

of modern and antique buildings that are scattered around town.

RIJKSMUSEUM VOLKENKUNDE MUSEUM
(National Museum of Ethnology; www.volkenkunde.nl; Steenstraat 1; adult/child €12/6; ⏱10am-5pm Tue-Sun) Cultural achievements by civilisations worldwide are on show at the Museum Volkenkunde. More than 200,000 artefacts span China, South America and Africa, much like Amsterdam's Tropenmuseum. There's a rich Indonesian collection; watch for performances by the museum's gamelan troupe.

★**HORTUS BOTANICUS LEIDEN** GARDENS
(www.hortusleiden.nl; Rapenburg 73; adult/child €7/3; ⏱10am-6pm daily Apr-Oct, to 4pm Tue-Sun Nov-Mar) The lush Hortus Botanicus is one of Europe's oldest botanical gardens (1590; the oldest was created in Padua, Italy, in 1545), and is home to the Netherlands' oldest descendants of the Dutch tulips. It's a wonderful place to relax, with explosions of tropical colour and a fascinating (and steamy) greenhouse.

MUSEUM DE LAKENHAL MUSEUM
(www.lakenhal.nl; Oude Singel 28-32) Leiden's foremost museum, the Lakenhal, displaying works by native son Rembrandt among others, will close its doors between 2016 and 2018 while it undergoes a major renovation and expansion. Check online or with the tourist office for updates.

DE VALK MUSEUM
(The Falcon; ☎071-516 53 53; http://molenmuseumdevalk.nl; 2e Binnenvestgracht 1; adult/child €4/2; ⏱10am-5pm Tue-Sat, 1-5pm Sun) Leiden's landmark windmill museum receives loving care, with constant renovation, and many consider it the best example of its kind. Its arms are free to turn 'whenever possible', when wind conditions are right, and it can still grind grain.

NATURALIS BIODIVERSITY CENTRE MUSEUM
(www.naturalis.nl; Darwinweg 2; adult/child €12/9; ⏱10am-5pm) A stuffed elephant greets you at this large, well-funded collection of all the usual dead critters and, notably, the skullcap of the million-year-old Java Man discovered by Dutch anthropologist Eugène Dubois in 1891. It's 300m west of the town centre.

MUSEUM BOERHAAVE MUSEUM
(www.museumboerhaave.nl; Lange St Agnietenstraat 10; adult/child €9.50/4.50; ⏱10am-5pm Tue-Sun) Leiden University was an early centre for Dutch medical research. This museum displays the often-grisly results (five centuries of pickled organs and surgical tools and skeletons) plus you can have a gander at the anatomical theatre with skeletons in stiff relief.

EATING & DRINKING

DAVID'S BURGER BURGERS €
(www.davidsburger.nl; Steenstraat 57; mains €10-13.50; ⏱5-11pm) Cowhide covers the timber booths, and horseshoes and farm equipment hang on the walls at David's, serving Leiden's best, all-organic burgers

LEIDEN'S PILGRIM LINKS

In 1608 a group of Calvinist Protestants split from the Anglican church and left persecution in Nottinghamshire, England, for a journey that would span decades and thousands of miles. Travelling first to Amsterdam under the leadership of John Robinson, they encountered theological clashes with local Dutch Protestants.

In Leiden they found a more liberal atmosphere, thanks to the university and some like-minded Calvinists who already lived there. They also found company with refugees who had escaped from persecution elsewhere. However, the group's past was to catch up with them. In 1618, James I of England announced he would assume control over the Calvinists living in Leiden. In addition, the local Dutch were becoming less tolerant of religious splinter groups.

The first group of English left Leiden in 1620 for Delfshaven in what is now Rotterdam, where they bought the *Speedwell* with the intention of sailing to the New World. Unfortunately, the leaky *Speedwell* didn't live up to its name; after several attempts to cross the Atlantic, the group gave up and, against their better judgement, sailed into Southampton in England. After repairs to their ship and a thwarted attempt to restart their journey, the group joined the much more seaworthy *Mayflower* in Dartmouth and sailed, as it were, into history as the Pilgrims.

This legendary voyage was actually just one of many involving the Leiden group. It wasn't until 1630 that most had made their way to the American colonies founded in what is today New England. Some 1000 people made the voyages, including a number of Dutch who were considered oddballs for their unusual beliefs.

In Leiden today, traces of the Pilgrims are elusive. The best place to start is the **Leiden American Pilgrim Museum** (p214).

such as the gaucho (beef with grilled pepper, courgette and *chimichurri*), spicy veggie (bean and chipotle-pepper patty with guacamole and cheese), lams (lamb with red-onion relish) and classic (beef with lettuce, tomato and pickles), plus corn on the cob.

BRASSERIE DE ENGELENBAK MODERN DUTCH €€

(☎071-512 54 40; www.deengelenbak.nl; Lange Mare 38; mains lunch €8-19, dinner €17-19, 3-course dinner menu €29; ⏲11am-10pm) In the shadow of the 17th-century octagonal Marekerk, this elegant bistro serves a seasonally changing menu of fresh fare that takes its cues from across the continent. Local organic produce features in many of the dishes. Tables outside enjoy views of the passing crowds. Its adjoining *café* (pub) serves snacks until midnight.

LOT EN DE WALVIS INTERNATIONAL €€

(☎071-763 03 83; www.lotendewalvis.nl; Haven 1; mains €7-19; ⏲9am-10pm) Lot's sun-drenched terrace sits at the water's edge but the reason it's a Leiden hotspot is the outstanding food, from breakfast (French toast with cinnamon sugar; eggs Benedict on sour dough) to lunch (Thai yellow-curry fish burger; smoked mackerel pasta) and dinner (fiery harissa lamb skewers with yoghurt dip; pear-and-hazelnut cake). Book ahead at all times.

★IN DEN DOOFPOT MODERN EUROPEAN €€€

(☎071-512 24 34; www.indendoofpot.nl; Turfmarkt 9; mains €25, 3-/4-course lunch menu €39/45, 4-/5-/6-/8-course dinner menu €55/65/70/80; ⏲noon-3pm & 5-10pm Mon-Fri, 5-10pm Sat) Given the sky-high calibre of chef Patrick Brugman's cooking, In den Doofpot's prices are a veritable steal. Pork belly with smoked eel, grilled lobster with truffle butter and micro-herb salad, organic Dutch beef fillet with Madeira sauce, potatoes and caramelised orange and other intense flavour combinations are all executed with artistic vision. Wines cost €8 per course.

CAFÉ L'ESPERANCE BROWN CAFE

(www.lesperance.nl; Kaiserstraat 1; ⏲3pm-1am Mon-Wed, 11am-1am Thu-Sun) Decked out with wood-panelled walls lined with framed photos, this nostalgic *bruin café* overlooks an evocative bend in the canal, with tables propagating along the pavement outside in summer.

ENTERTAINMENT

CAFÉ DE WW LIVE MUSIC

(www.deww.nl; Wolsteeg 6; ⏲2pm-2am Sun-Wed, to 3am Thu, to 4am Fri & Sat) On Friday and Saturday, live rock in this glossy scarlet bar can expand to an impromptu stage in the alley with crowds trailing up to the main street. On other nights DJs play. Though the emphasis is on the music, there's a great beer selection. Cash only.

SPORTS & ACTIVITIES

REDERIJ REMBRANDT BOAT TOUR

(☎071-513 49 38; www.rederij-rembrandt.nl; Blauwpoortshaven 5; adult/child €10/6.50; ⏲11am, 1.30pm & 2.45pm May-Oct) Leisurely one-hour canal boat tours taken in the channel around the old town centre, accompanied by multilingual commentary (including English).

BOTENVERHUUR 'T GALGEWATER BOAT RENTAL

(☎071-514 97 90; www.botenverhuurleiden.nl; Galgewater 44a; kayak/rowboat/canoe/boat per hour from €6/7/8/50; ⏲noon-10pm Mon-Thu, 11am-10pm Fri-Sun mid-May–mid-Aug, noon-7pm Mon-Thu, 11am-7pm Fri-Sun mid-Apr–mid-May & mid-Aug–early Oct) Rent a kayak, rowboat, canoe or *sloepen* (traditional Dutch powered boat) here to explore Leiden's meandering canals. Minimum *sloepen* rental is two hours (no boat licence required).

SLEEPING

HUYS VAN LEYDEN BOUTIQUE HOTEL €€

(☎071-260 07 00; www.huysvanleyden.nl; Oude Singel 212; d from €134; 📶) Steeped in history, this 1611 canal house has luxurious rooms and amenities including a sauna, roof terrace, and Nespresso machines in each of the five Golden Age–meets-21st-century rooms richly decorated with shimmering fabrics and canopied beds. Its sister property, **De Barones van Leyden** (☎071-260 07 00; www.debaronesvanleyden.nl; Oude Herengracht 22; d from €146; 📶), is, incredibly, even more opulent.

Delft

Explore

Compact and charming, Delft is synonymous with its blue-and-white-painted porcelain. It's *very* popular with visitors strolling its narrow canals, gazing at the remarkable old buildings and meditating on the career of Golden Age painter Johannes Vermeer, who was born and lived here, so getting an early start helps beat the crowds.

After touring Royal Delft's porcelain factory, Koninklijke Porceleyne Fles, pick up a walking tour brochure from the tourist office and explore the city's riches at your own pace. Be sure to allow time for shopping, wining and dining around the Markt.

Although Delft is just an hour from Amsterdam, excellent-value hotels cater to day-trippers who don't want to go home quite just yet.

The Best...

➡**Sight** Vermeer Centrum Delft (p218)

➡**Place to Eat** Brasserie 't Crabbetje (p219)

➡**Place to Drink** Locus Publicus (p220)

Top Tip

It's not all Delftware and Vermeer: take time to wander the streets of one of the Netherlands' prettiest cities, a veritable treasure trove of Gothic and Renaissance architecture.

Getting There & Away

➡**Train** Services between Amsterdam's Centraal Station and Delft are frequent (€12.70, one hour, up to four per hour). Delft's gleaming new train station, opened in 2015, is 700m south of the Markt.

➡**Car** Take the A13/E19, which passes through Den Haag en route to Rotterdam.

Need to Know

➡**Area Code** ☎015

➡**Location** 55km southwest of Amsterdam

➡**Tourist Office** (VVV; ☎015-215 40 51; www.delft.nl; Kerkstraat 3; ⏲10am-4pm Sun & Mon, 10am-5pm Tue-Sat Apr-Oct, noon-4pm Mon, 10am-4pm Tue-Sat, 11am-3pm Sun Nov-Mar)

Delft

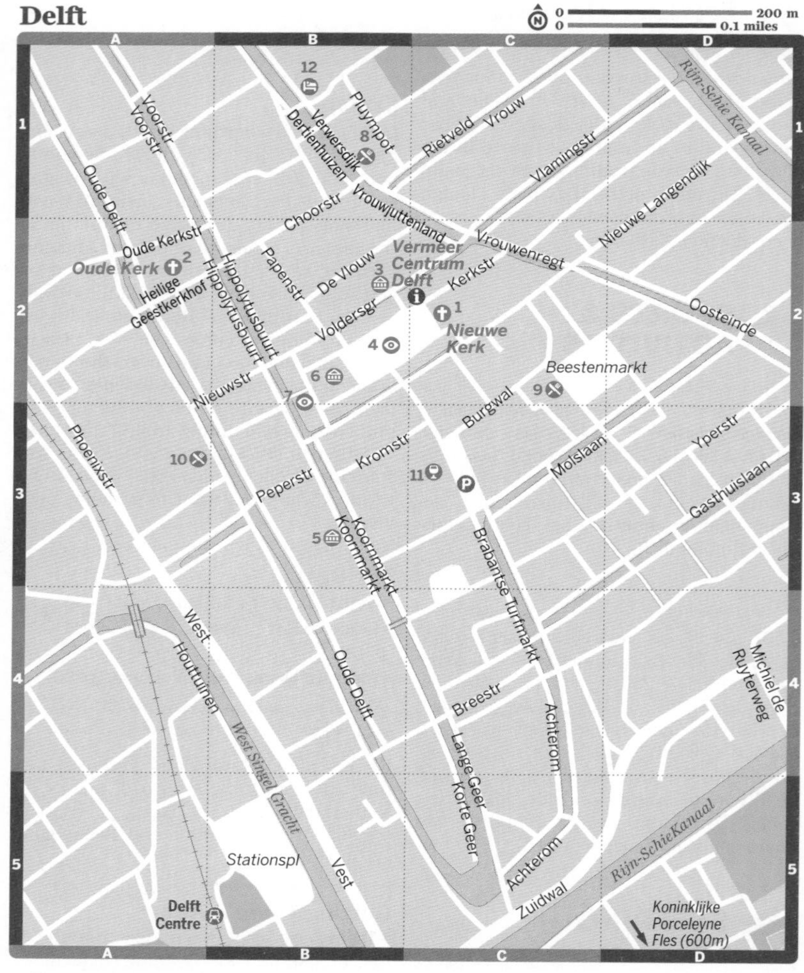

SIGHTS

★VERMEER CENTRUM DELFT MUSEUM

(www.vermeerdelft.nl; Voldersgracht 21; adult/child €8/4; ⏲10am-5pm) As the place where Vermeer was born, lived, and worked, Delft is 'Vermeer Central' to many art-history and old-masters enthusiasts. Along with viewing life-sized images of Vermeer's oeuvre, you can tour a replica of his studio, which reveals the way the artist approached the use of light and colour in his craft. A 'Vermeer's World' exhibit offers insight into his environment and upbringing, while temporary exhibits show how his work continues to inspire other artists.

MARKT SQUARE

The pedestrianised city square is worth a stroll for its pleasant collection of galleries, antiques stores, clothing boutiques and quirky speciality shops.

The **town hall** has an unusual combination of Renaissance construction surrounding a 13th-century tower. Behind it, the **Waag** is a 1536 weigh house; its giant green doors were installed in 1644.

Delft

Top Sights

Sights

Eating

Drinking & Nightlife

Sleeping

★**OUDE KERK** CHURCH

(Old Church; http://oudeennieuwekerkdelft.nl; Heilige Geestkerkhof 25; adult/child incl Nieuwe Kerk €3.75/2.25; 9am-6pm Apr-Oct, 11am-4pm Nov-Mar, closed Sun) The Gothic Oude Kerk, founded in 1246, is a surreal sight: its 75m-high tower leans nearly 2m from the vertical due to subsidence caused by its canal location, hence its nickname Scheve Jan ('Leaning Jan'). One of the tombs inside the church is Vermeer's.

★**NIEUWE KERK** CHURCH

(New Church; http://oudeennieuwekerkdelft.nl; Markt 80; adult/child incl Oude Kerk €3.75/2.25, Nieuwe Kerk tower additional €3.75/2.25; 9am-6pm Mon-Sat Apr-Oct, 11am-4pm Mon-Fri, 10am-5pm Sat Nov-Jan, 10am-5pm Mon-Sat Feb & Mar) Construction on Delft's Nieuwe Kerk began in 1381; it was finally completed in 1655. Amazing views extend from the 108.75m-high tower: after climbing its 376 narrow, spiralling steps you can see as far as Rotterdam and Den Haag on a clear day. It's the resting place of William of Orange (William the Silent), in a mausoleum designed by Hendrick de Keyser.

MUSEUM PAUL TETAR VAN ELVEN MUSEUM

(www.museumpaultetarvanelven.nl; Koornmarkt 67; adult/child €5/free; 1-5pm Tue-Sun) This off-the-radar museum is the former studio and home of 19th-century Dutch artist Paul Tetar van Elven, who lived and worked here from 1864 until 1894, and bequeathed it to the town. The museum features his works including reproductions of notable paintings, along with his collection of antique furniture, oriental porcelain and Delftware. The evocative interior retains its original furnishings and lived-in feel.

★**KONINKLIJKE PORCELEYNE FLES** PORCELAIN FACTORY

(Royal Delft; www.royaldelft.com; Rotterdamseweg 196; factory tour adult/child €12.50/6.25; 9am-5pm mid-Mar–Oct, 9am-5pm Mon-Sat, noon-5pm Sun Nov–mid-Mar) Pottery fans will love Royal Delft, 1km southeast of the centre. Tour tickets include an audiotour which leads you through a painting demonstration, the company museum, and the factory production process. You can also take a workshop (€26.50 to €32) where you get to paint your own piece of Delft blue (tiles, plates and vases). For many, of course, the real thrill begins in the gift shop.

EATING & DRINKING

STADS-KOFFYHUIS CAFE €

(http://stads-koffyhuis.nl; Oude Delft 133; mains €8-16.50; 9am-8pm Mon-Fri, to 6pm Sat) The most coveted seats at this delightful cafe are on the terrace, aboard a barge moored out front. Tuck into award-winning bread rolls, with fillings such as aged artisan Gouda with apple sauce, mustard, fresh figs and walnuts, or house-speciality pancakes, while admiring possibly the best view of the Oude Kerk, just ahead at the end of the canal.

★**BRASSERIE 'T CRABBETJE** SEAFOOD €€

(015-213 8850; www.crabbetjedelft.nl; Verwers-dijk 14; mains €11.50-34.50; 5.30-10pm Wed-Sun;) Seafood is given the gourmet treatment at this cool, sophisticated restaurant, from scallops with leek and lobster reduction to skate wing with hazelnut crumb and *beurre noisette* (warm butter sauce), salmon carpaccio with smoked-eel croquette, and grilled lobster with tomato and truffle oil. Lavish seafood platters for two people cost €83. Desserts are exquisite, too.

SPIJSHUIS DE DIS MODERN DUTCH €€

(015-213 17 82; www.spijshuisdedis.com; Beestenmarkt 36; soups €6-7.50, mains €17-24.50; 5-9.30pm Tue-Sun) Fresh fish and amazing soups served in bread bowls take centre stage at this romantic foodie haven, but meat eaters and vegetarians are well catered for, too. Creative starters include smoked, marinated mackerel on sliced apple with horseradish. Don't skip the Dutch pudding served in a wooden shoe.

LOCUS PUBLICUS BROWN CAFE
(www.locuspublicus.nl; Brabantse Turfmarkt 67; ⌚11am-1am Mon-Thu, 11am-2am Fri & Sat, noon-1am Sun) Cosy little Locus Publicus is filled with cheery locals quaffing their way through the 175-strong beer list. There's great people-watching from the front terrace.

SLEEPING

HOTEL DE PLATAAN BOUTIQUE HOTEL €€
(☎015-212 60 46; www.hoteldeplataan.nl; Doelenplein 10; s/d from €105/115, themed d from €140; 📶) On a pretty canal-side square in the old town, this family-run gem has small but elegant standard rooms and wonderfully opulent theme rooms, including the 'Garden of Eden'; the Eastern-style 'Amber', with a Turkish massage shower; or the desert-island 'Tamarinde'. Modesty alert: many en suites are only partially screened from the room. Rates include breakfast and secure parking.

Alkmaar

Explore

On Friday mornings from April to early September, Alkmaar's canal-ringed centre throngs with tourists eager to catch a glimpse of the city's famous cheese market. It's a genuine spectacle but even if it's not on, the town is an engaging place to visit any time of the week or year.

If you've spent the morning at the cheese market, you'll be understandably hungry. Head to lunch, or make your own Gouda or *boerenkaas* (farmer's cheese) sandwiches from the shops on Magdalenenstraat. During the afternoon, visit the Stedelijk Museum and make your way to the National Beer Museum. Afterwards, stop in for a beer at its historic on-site pub.

The Best...

- **Sight** Kaasmarkt (p220)
- **Place to Eat** Cafe Restaurant De Buren (p222)
- **Place to Drink** De Boom (p222)

Top Tip

While most people come for the cheese, don't miss the wonderful Stedelijk Museum, which houses an impressive collection of Dutch Masters.

Getting There & Away

- **Train** Services run regularly from Amsterdam's Centraal Station (€7.40, 35 minutes, up to four per hour). Alkmaar's canal-bound centre is 1km southeast of the train station.
- **Car** Take the A9 in the west of Amsterdam, which goes directly to Alkmaar.

Need to Know

- **Area Code** ☎072
- **Location** 35km northwest of Amsterdam
- **Tourist Office** (VVV; ☎072-511 42 84; www.vvvalkmaar.nl; Waagplein 2; ⌚10am-4pm Mon-Thu & Sat, 9am-4pm Fri Apr-Sep, 10am-4pm Mon-Sat Oct, 1-4pm Mon, 10am-4pm Tue-Sat Nov-Mar)

SIGHTS

KAASMARKT MARKET
(Cheese Market; Waagplein; ⌚10am-noon Fri Apr–early Sep) On Friday mornings, waxed rounds of *kaas* (cheese) are ceremoniously stacked on the main square. Soon, porters appear in colourful hats (denoting the cheese guild), and dealers in white smocks insert a hollow rod to extract a cheese sample, and sniff and crumble to check fat and moisture content. Once deals are struck, the porters whisk the cheeses on wooden sledges to the old cheese scale. It's primarily for show but as living relics go it's both fascinating and entertaining.

STEDELIJK MUSEUM MUSEUM
(http://stedelijkmuseumalkmaar.nl; Canadaplein 1; adult/child €10/free; ⌚10am-5pm Tue-Sun) The Stedelijk Museum's collection of oil paintings by Dutch Masters, including impressive life-sized portraits of Alkmaar nobles, is alone worth the entry fee. Other works show

DEN HAAG (THE HAGUE)

The Netherlands' third-largest city, Den Haag, is a stately, regal place filled with embassies and mansions, green boulevards and parks, a refined culinary scene, a clutch of fine museums including the magnificent Mauritshuis, and a sybaritic cafe culture.

Officially known as 's-Gravenhage (the Count's Hedge), Den Haag is the Dutch seat of government and home to the royal family. Prior to 1806, Den Haag was the Dutch capital. However, that year, Louis Bonaparte installed his government in Amsterdam. Eight years later, when the French had been ousted, the government returned to Den Haag, but the title of capital remained with Amsterdam.

In the 20th century Den Haag became the home of several international legal entities, including the UN's International Court of Justice.

Frequent trains link Amsterdam Centraal with Den Haag Centraal Station (CS) and Hollands Spoor Train Station (HS), a 1.5km walk south of CS (€11.20, one hour, six per hour). Den Haag is also linked to Delft by tram 1, which takes 30 minutes.

Mauritshuis (www.mauritshuis.nl; Plein 29; adult/child €14/free, combined ticket with Galerij Prins Willem V €17.50; ⌚1-6pm Mon, 10am-6pm Tue, Wed & Fri-Sun, 10am-8pm Thu) For a comprehensive introduction to Dutch and Flemish Art, visit the Mauritshuis, a jewel-box of a museum in an old palace and brand-new wing. Almost every work is a masterpiece, among them Vermeer's *Girl with a Pearl Earring*, Rembrandts including a wistful self-portrait from the year of his death, 1669, and *The Anatomy Lesson of Dr Nicolaes Tulp*. A five-minute walk southwest, the recently restored Galerij Prins Willem V (www.mauritshuis.nl; Buitenhof 35; adult/child €5/2.50, combined ticket with Mauritshuis €17.50; ⌚noon-5pm Tue-Sun) contains 150 old masters (Steen, Rubens, Potter, et al).

Binnenhof The Binnenhof's central courtyard (once used for executions) is surrounded by parliamentary buildings. The splendid 17th-century North Wing is still home to the Upper Chamber of the **Dutch Parliament**. The Lower Chamber formerly met in the ballroom, in the 19th-century wing; it now meets in a modern building on the south side. A highlight of the complex is the restored 13th-century Ridderzaal (Knights' Hall).

To see the buildings you need to join a tour through visitor organisation **ProDemos** (☎070-757 02 00; www.prodemos.nl; Hofweg 1; 45min Ridderzaal tour €5, 90min Ridderzaal & House of Representative tour €8.50, 75min Ridderzaal & Senate tour €8.50, 90min Ridderzaal, House of Representative & Senate tour €10; ⌚office 10am-5pm Mon-Sat, tours by reservation).

Escher in Het Paleis Museum (www.escherinhetpaleis.nl; Lange Voorhout 74; adult/child €9/6.50; ⌚11am-5pm Tue-Sun) The Lange Voorhout Palace was once Queen Emma's winter residence. Now it's home to the work of Dutch graphic artist MC Escher. The permanent exhibition features notes, letters, drafts, photos and fully mature works covering Escher's entire career, from his early realism to the later phantasmagoria. There are some imaginative displays, including a virtual reality reconstruction of Escher's impossible buildings.

the city in post–Golden Age decline; sombre scenes of almswomen caring for the poor recall how the church's role grew as trade declined. Modern works on display include Charley Toorop's odd oil painting of the Alkmaar cheese market; her cheese-bearers with grotesque features remain controversial.

WAAGGEBOUW — HISTORIC BUILDING

(Weigh House; Waagplein 2; ⌚carillon 6.30pm & 7.30pm Thu, 11am & noon Fri, noon & 1pm Sat mid-Apr–mid-Sep) Built as a chapel in the 14th century, the Waaggebouw was pressed into service as a weigh house two centuries later. This handsome building houses the tourist office and the Hollands Kaasmuseum.

The mechanical tower **carillon** springs to life with jousting knights.

HOLLANDS KAASMUSEUM — MUSEUM

(Dutch Cheese Museum; www.kaasmuseum.nl; Waagplein 2; adult/child €3/1.50; ⌚10am-4pm Mon-Sat Apr-Oct, to 4pm Sat Nov-Mar) Housed in the Waaggebouw (p221), the Dutch Cheese Museum has a reverential display of cheese-making utensils, photos and a curious stock of paintings by 16th-century female artists.

NATIONAAL BIERMUSEUM MUSEUM

(www.biermuseum.nl; Houttil 1; adult/child €4/2; ⌚10.30am-4.30pm Mon-Sat Jun-Aug, 1-4pm Mon-Sat Sep-May) Housed in the atmospheric old De Boom brewery, the Nationaal Biermuseum has a decent collection of beer-making equipment and wax dummies showing how the suds were made. The video of Dutch beer commercials since the 1950s will have you in stitches. After your tour, head to the sociable bar.

GROTE KERK CHURCH

(www.grotekerkalkmaar.nl; Kerkplein; ⌚11am-5pm Tue-Sun Jun-Aug, Thu-Sat mid-Apr–May) FREE Alkmaar's Grote Kerk is renowned for its organs. The most famous is the little 'Swallow Organ' (1511) in the north ambulatory. The 17th-century organ built by Jaco van Campen dominates the nave. Organ recitals – which will thrill any fan of 1930s horror movies – take place on Wednesday evenings and at noon on days when the church is open. The pastel stained-glass windows bathe the interior in spring colour.

EATING & DRINKING

Running northwest from the Waagplein cheese marketplace, Magdalenenstraat is lined with cheese shops and bakeries.

DE VLAMINCK FRITES €

(www.devlaminck.nl; Voordam 2; frites from €2.50; ⌚11am-7pm Fri-Wed, to 9.15pm Thu) The fries are superb at this storefront counter, as are the 17 different sauces, including peanut, *sambal oelek* (Indonesian chilli sauce), garlic, and tomato ketchup. Take your paper cone to the benches in front alongside the canal.

CAFE RESTAURANT DE BUREN INTERNATIONAL €€

(www.restaurant-deburen.nl; Mient 37; mains €15.50-26.50; ⌚10am-10pm Mon-Sat, 11am-9pm Sun) Outside tables at this vintage cafe/restaurant stretch along the canal and wrap around to the old fish market. The menu spans the globe, with dishes such as *coq au vin blanc* (chicken thighs in white wine), steak and *frites* with pepper-cognac sauce, pumpkin ravioli, smoked spare ribs with corn on the cob, and feisty Thai curries.

★DE BOOM BROWN CAFE

(http://proeflokaaldeboom.nl; Houttil 1; ⌚2pm-midnight Sun & Mon, 1pm-midnight Tue & Wed, 1pm-2am Thu-Sat) The pub on the ground floor of the Nationaal Biermuseum (p222) lives up to its location. The inside is unchanged since the 1930s – you expect to hear a scratchy 78rpm playing. Outside you can enjoy the fine selection of brews at seats on a moored old canal boat. Live jazz plays on Thursday nights.

SPORTS & ACTIVITIES

GRACHTENRONDVAART ALKMAAR CANAL TOUR

(www.rondvaartalkmaar.nl; Mient; adult/child €6/4.50; ⌚hourly 11am-5pm Apr-Oct) Scenic canal tours with multilingual commentary depart from Mient, near the Waag, and last 45 minutes.

Zaanse Schans

Explore

People come for an hour and stay for several at this working and fully inhabited village, which functions as a kind of open-air windmill gallery on the Zaan river. It's *the* place to see windmills operating, although only a few of the formerly more than 1000 windmills in the area have been restored. While the village has a strong touristy element, the mills are completely authentic and are operated with enthusiasm and love.

Spend your time exploring the six working mills. One sells fat jars of its freshly ground mustard, while the others turn out oils, flour and sawed planks. Most are open for inspection, and it's a delight to clamber about the creaking works while the mills shake in the North Sea breeze.

Top Tip

Hire a bike and pedal from Amsterdam to Zaanse Schans. It only takes about 90 minutes, and the picturesque trip is a highlight of many travellers' holiday.

BLOEMENVEILING AALSMEER

Bloemenveiling Aalsmeer (www.floraholland.com; Legmeerdijk 313; adult/child €6/3.50; ⏲7-11am Mon-Wed & Fri, to 9am Thu) Aalsmeer is home to the world's biggest *bloemenveiling* (flower auction), run by vast flower conglomerate FloraHolland. Get to the viewing gallery before 9am to catch the best action as the flower-laden carts go to Dutch auction, with a huge clock showing the starting price. From the starting bell, the hand drops until a deal is struck.

Take bus 172 from Amsterdam Centraal Station to the Hoofdingang stop (45 minutes, four per hour, from 4.59am). Monday is busiest, Thursday quietest.

The one-million-sq-metre space sees some 90 million flowers and two million plants change hands every day of operation. You can take an aromatic self-guided tour on a 3km-long, wheelchair-accessible elevated walkway above the frenetic warehouse floor, overlooking the choreography of flower-laden forklifts and trolleys. Along the route, signboards with push-button audio recordings interpret the action.

The route also passes windows where you can peek into the auction rooms and see blooms being prepped for display as the carts go to auction. More and more transactions are taking place online, so catch the flower auction while it's still here.

Getting There & Away

➡**Train** Take the train from Amsterdam's Centraal Station towards Alkmaar and get off at Koog-Zaandijk (€3.10, 15 minutes, up to four per hour), then walk 1.5km via the Julianabrug spanning the Zaan river to Zaanse Schans.

➡**Car** Travel to the northwestern side of Amsterdam on the A10 ring road, and take the A8 turn-off. Exit at Zaandijk.

Need to Know

➡**Area Code** ☎075

➡**Location** 10km northwest of Amsterdam

➡Tourist Office (p223)

SIGHTS

ZAANSE SCHANS WINDMILLS WINDMILLS

(www.dezaanseschans.nl; site free, per windmill adult/child €4/2; ⏲windmills 10am-5pm Apr-Nov, hours vary Dec-Mar) The working, inhabited village Zaanse Schans functions as an open-air windmill gallery on the Zaan river. Popular with tourists, its mills are completely authentic and operated with enthusiasm and love. You can explore the windmills at will, seeing the vast moving parts first-hand.

The impressive **Zaans Museum** (☎075-616 28 62; www.zaansmuseum.nl; Schansend 7; adult/child €9/5; ⏲10am-5pm Apr-Nov, hours vary Dec-Mar) shows how wind and water were harnessed.

Trains (€3.10, 17 minutes, four per hour) run from Amsterdam Centraal Station (direction Alkmaar) to Koog Zaandijk, from where it's a well-signposted 1.5km walk.

The mill with paint pigments for sale will delight artists – you can see the actual materials used in producing Renaissance masterpieces turned into powders. Ask to see the storeroom where ground pigments are for sale.

The other buildings have been brought here from all over the country to re-create a 17th-century community. There's an early Albert Heijn market, a cheese maker, and a popular clog factory that turns out wooden shoes as if grinding keys (which has a surprisingly interesting museum). The engaging pewtersmith will explain the story behind dozens of tiny figures while the soft metal sets in the moulds.

Once you've finished exploring the village, take a **boat** (adult/child €5/3; ⏲9am-6pm May-Sep) across the Zaan river. It runs on demand.

Sleeping

In its typically charming way, Amsterdam has loads of hotels in wild and wonderful spaces: inspired architects have breathed new life into old buildings, from converted schools and industrial lofts to entire rows of canal houses joined at the hip. Many lodgings overlook gorgeous waterways or courtyards. But charm doesn't come cheap...

Seasons & Prices

Rates and crowds peak in summer and on weekends at any time of the year. Book well in advance if you're travelling then. Prices are lowest from October to April (excluding Christmas/New Year and Easter).

Hotels

Any hotel with more than 20 rooms is considered large, and most rooms themselves are on the snug side. You'll see a 'star' plaque on the front of every hotel, indicating its rating according to the Benelux Hotel Classification. The stars (from one to five) are determined by the existence of certain facilities, rather than their quality. This means that a two-star hotel may be in better condition than a hotel of higher rank, though admittedly with fewer facilities.

B&Bs & Houseboats

Amsterdam has a scattering of B&Bs, but most don't have exterior signage and access is by reservation only, giving an intimate feel. A couple of particularly cool ones are on houseboats.

Hostels

Jeugdherbergen (youth hostels) are popular in Amsterdam. The Netherlands hostel association goes by the name Stayokay (www.stayokay.com) and is affiliated with Hostelling International (www.hihostels.com). Luxury hostels, aka 'poshtels', are starting to pop up around town, too.

Party & Stoner Hotels

A number of hotels in the budget category welcome party guests as well as pot smokers. By and large they're pretty basic affairs. If in doubt whether smoking marijuana is permitted, ask when you make your reservation. Many hotels have strict no-drugs policies.

Amenities

Wi-fi is nearly universal across the spectrum, but air-conditioning and lifts are not.

BUDGET

Lodgings in the lowest price bracket, other than hostels, are thin on the ground. The better options tend to be spick and span, with furnishings that are, at best, cheap and cheerful. Rates often include breakfast.

MIDRANGE

Most hotels in this category are big on comfort, low on formality and small enough to offer personal attention. Rooms usually have a toilet and shower, a TV and a phone. Not many midrange hotels of more than two storeys have lifts, and their narrow stairwells can take some getting used to, especially with luggage. Rates often include breakfast.

TOP END

Expect lifts (elevators), minibars and room service. At the top end of top end, facilities such as air-conditioning and fitness centres are standard. Breakfast is rarely included.

Lonely Planet's Top Choices

Hoxton Amsterdam (p229) Groovy hipster style at affordable prices.

Collector (p234) Offbeat B&B in the Old South with backyard chickens.

Hotel Fita (p234) Sweet little family-owned hotel a stone's throw from the Museumplein.

Sir Albert Hotel (p236) Diamond factory converted to sparkly design hotel.

ClinkNOORD (p227) Artsy, avant-garde hostel in artsy, avant-garde Amsterdam-Noord.

Best by Budget

€

Cocomama (p232) Red-curtained boutique hostel in a former brothel.

Generator Amsterdam (p230) Posh new hostel with bars overlooking Oosterpark.

Stayokay Amsterdam Stadsdoelen (p231) Bustling backpacker digs near Nieuwmarkt square.

€€

Hotel Brouwer (p227) Eight rooms get artsy in a 17th-century canal house.

Hotel V (p232) Retro-chic hotel facing lush Frederiksplein.

Conscious Hotel Vondelpark (p235) Eco innovations extend to pressed-cardboard benchtops.

€€€

Hotel Okura Amsterdam (p236) Rare-for-Amsterdam views and three Michelin stars in the building.

Toren (p229) Blends 17th-century opulence with a sensual decadence.

College Hotel (p236) Celebrity-favourite boutique run by hotel-school students.

Best Canal Views

Canal House (p230) Gorgeous water views out front and a sofa-strewn garden out back.

Seven Bridges (p232) One of the city's most exquisite little hotels on one of its loveliest canals.

Best Only in Amsterdam

B&B Le Maroxidien (p231) Wonderful houseboat B&B aboard a 1920s freighter.

Xaviera Hollander's Happy House (p235) B&B owned by the famed author and former madam.

Best Design Savvy

Hotel Notting Hill (p233) A lobby wall of vintage suitcases is among designer Wim Hoopman's touches.

Hotel Not Hotel (p234) Design academy students put together rooms that are eye-popping art installations.

Andaz Amsterdam (p230) A wonderland envisioned by iconic Dutch designer Marcel Wanders.

Best for Romantics

Houseboat Ms Luctor (p228) Hide away on your own houseboat, with a breakfast basket delivered to your door.

Seven One Seven (p233) Nine spacious, breathtakingly beautiful rooms that you won't want to leave.

NEED TO KNOW

Price Ranges

Prices quoted are for an en-suite double room in high season (excluding breakfast unless stated otherwise).

€ less than €100

€€ €100 to €180

€€€ more than €180

Reservations

➡ Book as far in advance as possible, especially during summer and for weekend visits.

➡ Many hotels offer discounts via their websites, especially for last-minute bookings.

➡ The I Amsterdam visitor centre can make last-minute bookings, but there is a charge (around €3).

Tipping

Tipping is not expected, though at larger hotels the porter often receives a euro or two, and the room cleaner gets a few euros for a job well done.

Tax

Properties often include the 5% city hotel tax in quoted rates, but ask before booking. If you're paying by credit card, some hotels add a surcharge of up to 5%.

Websites

➡ **Lonely Planet** (www.lonelyplanet.com/amsterdam) Destination information, hotel bookings and more.

➡ **I Amsterdam** (www.iamsterdam.com) City-run portal packed with sightseeing, accommodation and event info.

Where to Stay

Neighbourhood	For	Against
Medieval Centre & Red Light District	In the thick of the action; close to sights, nightlife, theatres and transport	Can be noisy, touristy and seedy; not great value for money
Nieuwmarkt, Plantage & Eastern Islands	Nieuwmarkt is near the action, but with a slightly more laid-back vibe than the Centre. Plantage hotels are amid quiet greenery	Some parts of Nieuwmarkt are close enough to the Red Light District to get rowdy spillover. Plantage lodgings can be a hike from the major sights, requiring a tram or bike ride
Western Canal Ring	Tree-lined canals; oddball boutiques and the Jordaan's cafes are nearby. Within walking distance of Amsterdam's most popular sights	Given all the positives, rooms book out early and can be pricey
Southern Canal Ring	Swanky hotels, not far from the restaurants of Utrechtsestraat and the antique shops of Nieuwe Spiegelstraat	Can be loud, crowded, pricey and touristy – especially around the high-traffic areas of Leidseplein and Rembrandtplein
Jordaan & the West	Cosy cafes, quirky shops and charming village character	Sleeping options are few, due in part to the paucity of big-name sights close by
Vondelpark & the Old South	Genteel, leafy streets; walking distance to Museumplein; small, gracious properties; lots of midrange options and cool design hotels	Not much nightlife in the Old South; prices around Vondelpark can slide toward the high end
De Pijp	Ongoing explosion of dining/drinking cool in the area; located near Museumplein and Southern Canal Ring	Easy walking distance to Museumplein, Vondelpark and Leidseplein, but a hike from the Centre; options are fairly limited
Oosterpark & South Amsterdam	Lower prices due to remote location (which is really just a short tram/metro ride away); quiet area amid locals	Fewer options for dining and drinking

Medieval Centre & Red Light District

★CLINKNOORD HOSTEL €

(☎214 97 30; www.clinkhostels.com; Badhuiskade 3; dm €30-55, d from €100; ; ; Buiksloterweg) Clink is a European designer hostel chain that opened this Amsterdam outpost in summer 2015. While it's a bit off the beaten path in Amsterdam-Noord, it's just a five-minute ferry ride from Centraal Station (the ferry is free and runs 24/7, incidentally). Dorms are done up in minimalist-industrial style, with four to 16 beds and en-suite facilities.

Some rooms are female only, some are co-ed. Breakfast costs €7, or you can self cater using the mod kitchen. The artsy property has an on-site bar that hosts DJs and other performances.

ST CHRISTOPHER'S AT THE WINSTON HOSTEL, HOTEL €

Map p300 (☎6231380; www.winston.nl; Warmoesstraat 129; dm €40-45, s €95, d €124-144; ; 4/9/16/24 Dam) This place hops 24/7 with rock 'n' roll rooms, and a busy club, bar, beer garden and smoking deck downstairs. En-suite dorms sleep up to eight. Most private rooms are 'art' rooms: local artists were given free rein, with super-edgy (entirely stainless steel) to questionably raunchy results. Rates include breakfast (and ear plugs!).

FLYING PIG DOWNTOWN HOSTEL HOSTEL €

Map p300 (☎420 68 22; www.flyingpig.nl; Nieuwendijk 100; dm €36-50; @; 1/2/5/13/17 Centraal Station) Hang out with hundreds of young, dope-smoking backpackers at this very relaxed, massive 250-bed hostel. It's a bit grungy, but no one seems to mind, especially when there's so much fun to be had in the throbbing lobby bar, which has a pool table and occasional DJs. There's also an indoor smoking area, full-service kitchens and a cushion-lined basement nicknamed the 'happy room'. Rates include a continental breakfast.

HOTEL BROUWER HOTEL €€

Map p300 (☎624 63 58; www.hotelbrouwer.nl; Singel 83; s €78-98, d €128-148, tr €160-180; @; 1/2/5/13/17 Nieuwezijds Kolk) A bargain-priced (for Amsterdam) favourite, Brouwer has just eight rooms in a house dating back to 1652. Each chamber is named for a Dutch painter and furnished with simplicity, but all have canal views. There's a mix of Delft-blue tiles and early-20th-century decor, plus a tiny lift. Staff dispense friendly advice. Reserve well in advance. Rates include a hearty breakfast. Cash only.

HOTEL RÉSIDENCE LE COIN APARTMENT €€

Map p304 (☎524 68 00; www.lecoin.nl; Nieuwe Doelenstraat 5; s/f €125/250, d €145-160; ; 4/9/14/16/24 Muntplein) This shiny inn, owned by the University of Amsterdam, offers 42 small, high-class apartments spread over seven historical buildings, all equipped with designer furniture, wood floors and kitchenettes – and all reachable by lift. It's in the thick of things, opposite the popular grand Café de Jaren and just a five-minute stroll to pretty Nieuwmarkt. Wi-fi is free, with decent speed.

HOTEL THE EXCHANGE DESIGN HOTEL €€

Map p300 (☎523 00 89; www.hoteltheexchange.com; Damrak 50; d €100-225; @; 1/2/5/13/17 Centraal Station) The Exchange's 61 rooms have been dressed 'like models' in eye-popping style by students from the Amsterdam Fashion Institute. Anything goes, from oversized button-adorned walls to a Marie Antoinette dress tented over the bed. If you like plain decor, this isn't your place. Rooms range from small and viewless to spacious sanctums, but all have en-suite bathrooms.

Rooms fronting the Damrak can be noisy, but the young and hip guests don't seem to notice.

HOTEL LUXER HOTEL €€

Map p300 (☎330 32 05; www.hotelluxer.nl; Warmoesstraat 11; r €100-190; @; 4/9/16/24 Centraal Station) A pleasant surprise if ever there was one, this smart little number is probably the best option for your money in the thick of the Red Light District. Rooms are small, but well equipped (air-con!), and at night the breakfast area becomes a chic little bar. Breakfast costs €8.

HOTEL HOKSBERGEN HOTEL €€

Map p304 (☎626 60 43; www.hotelhoksbergen.nl; Singel 301; d €100-155; ; 1/2/5 Spui) You sure can't beat Hoksbergen's fantastic canal-side location, and there's a free breakfast buffet, but be warned: even sardines would have trouble squishing into the small rooms (with clean but plain furnishings).

HOTEL DE L'EUROPE HOTEL €€€

Map p304 (☎531 17 77; www.leurope.nl; Nieuwe Doelenstraat 2-8; r from €340; @; 4/9/14/16/24 Muntplein) Owned by the Heineken family, luxury L'Europe mixes classical elements (glass chandeliers, doorkeepers in top hats) with whimsical Dutch design. The 111 rooms are grand, with iPads, canal views, heated floors and white marble bathtubs; wi-fi is free. The on-site cigar lounge and Freddy's Bar, with brass-topped tables and leather chairs, attract a professional crowd.

ART'OTEL AMSTERDAM BOUTIQUE HOTEL €€€
Map p300 (719 72 00; www.artotels.com; Prins Hendrikkade 33; r €289-389; ; 1/2/5/13/17 Centraal Station) Located opposite Centraal Station, this stylish hotel offers 107 rooms with mod decor and original artworks on the wall. To add to the creative theme, there's an open-to-the-public gallery in the basement. The lobby is a swank refuge with a fireplace and library. A free, beyond-the-norm hot breakfast is included.

FARALDA CRANE HOTEL DESIGN HOTEL €€€
(760 61 61; www.faralda.com; NDSM-plein 78; r €435-535; ; NDSM-werf) That vivid red, yellow and gunmetal-grey industrial crane rising up at NDSM-werf? It's a hotel. The three fantasy-world suites perched at varying heights – Free Spirit, Secret and Mystique – are swathed in shimmering fabrics, with freestanding baths, bold objets d'art and vertiginous views. On the crane's rooftop, you can soak in the outdoor hot tub or plunge off (attached to a bungee cord).

Jordaan & the West

CHRISTIAN YOUTH HOSTEL 'THE SHELTER JORDAAN' HOSTEL €
Map p316 (624 47 17; www.shelter.nl; Bloemstraat 179; dm €25-39; @; 10/13/14/17 Marnixstraat) Putting up with the 'no-everything' (drinking, smoking, partying) policy at this small hostel isn't hard, because it's such a gem. Single-sex dorms are quiet and clean, there's a piano, and breakfasts – especially the fluffy pancakes – are great. The cafe serves cheap meals the rest of the day.

INTERNATIONAL BUDGET HOSTEL HOSTEL €
Map p316 (624 27 84; www.internationalbudgethostel.com; Leidsegracht 76; dm €25-45; @; 1/2/5 Prinsengracht/Leidsestraat) So what if it's a bit grungy? Here are the selling points: canal-side location in a former warehouse; close to Leidseplein nightlife; mix of backpackers from around the world; bike rental; and staff who are more pleasant than they need to be. There are eight beds per dorm; two-night minimum stay on weekends.

★**AMSTERDAM WIECHMANN HOTEL** HOTEL €€
Map p316 (626 33 21; www.hotelwiechmann.nl; Prinsengracht 328; s/d from €85/155; @; 7/10/17 Elandsgracht) Lovingly cared-for rooms at this family-run hotel in three canal houses are furnished like an antique shop, with country quilts and chintz, while the lobby knick-knacks have been here for some 75 years. It's an ace location right on the pretty Prinsengracht. Rates include breakfast.

★**HOUSEBOAT MS LUCTOR** B&B €€
Map p313 (06 2268 9506; www.boatbedandbreakfast.nl; Westerdok 103; d from €130; ; 48 Barentszplein) A brimming organic breakfast basket is delivered to you each morning at this self-contained mahogany-panelled 1913 houseboat, moored in a quiet waterway 10 minutes' walk from Centraal Station (five from the Jordaan). Eco initiatives include solar power, two bikes to borrow and a canoe for canal explorations. Minimum stay two nights.

BACKSTAGE HOTEL HOTEL €€
Map p316 (624 40 44; www.backstagehotel.com; Leidsegracht 114; s without bathroom from €65, d with/without bathroom from €100/85; @; 1/2/5 Leidseplein) Seriously fun, this music-themed hotel is a favourite among musicians jamming at nearby Melkweg and Paradiso, as evidenced by the lobby bar's band-signature-covered piano and pool table. Gig posters (many signed) line the corridors, and rooms are done up in neo-retro black and white, with iPod docking stations, and drum kit overhead lights.

Late at night, bands (and their fans) hold court in the lively bar.

HOTEL VAN ONNA HOTEL €€
Map p316 (626 58 01; www.hotelvanonna.nl; Bloemgracht 102-108; s €55-75, d €85-145; @; 10 Bloemgracht) Some of these simple, reasonably priced rooms occupy a lovely 1644 canal house in a gorgeous section of the Jordaan. The bells of the Westerkerk are within earshot, which is either charming or not (in which case get a room in the back). Rates include a continental breakfast.

The two attic rooms are the most atmospheric, with old wooden roof beams and views over the Bloemgracht (Flower Canal), though these, too, can be a bit noisy.

MORGAN & MEES BOUTIQUE HOTEL €€€

Map p316 (233 49 30; www.morganandmees.com; 2e Hugo de Grootstraat 2-6; r €165-300; 3 Hugo de Grootplein) It's all about comfort and cool at this stylish little hotel at the Jordaan's edge. Nine crisp rooms with cushy beds, mod fixtures and big flat-screen TVs sit on top of Morgan & Mees' slick bar and restaurant. The easygoing staff make you feel very much at home, and the off-the-beaten-path location also lends an intimate vibe.

Western Canal Ring

★HOXTON AMSTERDAM DESIGN HOTEL €€

Map p310 (888 55 55; www.thehoxton.com; Herengracht 255; r €120-200; 13/14/17 Westermarkt) Part of a European-based chain known for high style at affordable prices, the Hoxton opened in 2015 to great hipster fanfare. The 111 rooms splash through five canal houses and come in sizes from 'shoebox' to 'roomy'. The breakfast snack, speedy wi-fi, free international calls and low-priced canteen items are nice touches.

The hotel also organizes events with local artists and designers, so you get to meet creative locals.

FREDERIC RENTABIKE APARTMENT €€

Map p310 (624 55 09; www.frederic.nl; Brouwersgracht 78; houseboat from €145; 18/21/22 Brouwersstraat) Frederic offers nicely outfitted houseboats on the Prinsengracht, Brouwersgracht and Bloemgracht that are bona fide floating holiday homes with all mod cons. On land, the company also has various rooms and apartments in central locations. (And yes, bikes, too.)

MAES B&B B&B €€

Map p310 (427 51 65; www.bedandbreakfastamsterdam.com; Herenstraat 26; r €115-155; @; 1/2/5/13/17 Nieuwezijds Kolk) If you were designing a traditional home in the Western Canal Ring, it would probably turn out a lot like this property: oriental carpets, wood floors and exposed brick. It's actually fairly spacious for such an old building, but the kitchen (open all day for guests to use) is definitely *gezellig* (convivial, cosy).

HOTEL CLEMENS AMSTERDAM HOTEL €€

Map p310 (624 60 89; www.clemenshotel.nl; Raadhuisstraat 39; d €135-185; @; 13/14/17 Westermarkt) Very reasonably priced for its near-everything location, the 14 bright rooms at Clemens have rain showers, speedy free wi-fi and air-conditioning. If you don't score a room with a private balcony (some others have window seats or fireplaces), there's a lovely terrace for breakfast (included in the rate). There is no lift/elevator, so be prepared for stairs.

SUNHEAD OF 1617 INN €€

Map p310 (626 18 09; www.sunhead.com; Herengracht 152; r €140-170; @; 13/14/17 Westermarkt) The fabulous and funny Carlos is your host at these two flower-themed suites along some of Amsterdam's prettiest stretches of canal. There's a delightful balance of modern design and traditional Dutch charm. Guests can mingle over free wine and nibbles daily at 5pm.

SEBASTIAN'S BOUTIQUE HOTEL €€

Map p310 (433 23 42; www.hotelsebastians.nl; Keizersgracht 15; d €150-260; @; 13/14/17 Westermarkt) The younger, more affordable sister of Toren, a few blocks along the same picturesque canal. Sebastian's rocks its sibling's brand of dramatic cool, with striking purple and gold colour schemes, big vases and a backlit bar.

TOREN BOUTIQUE HOTEL €€€

Map p310 (622 63 52; www.thetoren.nl; Keizersgracht 164; d with garden/canal view from €290/310; @; 13/14/17 Westermarkt) A title-holder for room size and personal service, the Toren's communal areas mix 17th-century opulence – gilded mirrors, fireplaces and chandeliers – with sensual decadence that whispers Parisian boudoir. Guest rooms are elegantly furnished with modern facilities (including Nespresso coffee machines). It also rents historic boats (from €140 to €345 per hour) for private canal cruises.

DYLAN BOUTIQUE HOTEL €€€

Map p312 (530 20 10; www.dylanamsterdam.com; Keizersgracht 384; d/ste from €350/500; @; 1/2/5 Spui) Exquisite boutique hotel the Dylan occupies an 18th-century Keizersgracht canal house that is set around a topiary-filled courtyard. Bespoke furniture such as silver-leaf and mother-of-pearl drinks cabinets adorn its 40 individually decorated rooms and suites (some duplex). Its Michelin-starred Restaurant Vinkeles also hosts private chef's tables aboard its boat, the *Muze,* as it cruises the canals.

ANDAZ AMSTERDAM DESIGN HOTEL €€€

Map p312 (☎523 12 34; www.amsterdam.prinsengracht.andaz.hyatt.com; Prinsengracht 587; d €375-650; @📶; 🚋1/2/5 Prinsengracht) Visionary Dutch designer Marcel Wanders has transformed Amsterdam's former public library into a fantasy of giant gold and silver cutlery, fish murals, Delftware-inspired carpets, library-book pages writ large on the walls and other flights of imagination. The 122 guest rooms have Geneva sound systems with iPod docks, king-size beds, and complimentary snacks and non-alcoholic drinks. Free bikes to use, too.

CANAL HOUSE BOUTIQUE HOTEL €€€

Map p310 (☎622 51 82; www.canalhouse.nl; Keizersgracht 148; d from €255; ❄📶; 🚋13/14/17 Westermarkt) A large, leafy, sofa-strewn garden is an unexpected find behind these adjoining 17th-century canal houses. Inside, the 23 rooms – in categories ranging from Good and Better to Great and Exceptional – have purple, grey and brown tones, soaring ceilings and king-size beds. There's a clubby cocktail bar; rates include breakfast.

Oosterpark & South Amsterdam

GENERATOR AMSTERDAM HOSTEL €

Map p325 (www.generatorhostels.com; Mauritskade 57; dm €30-50; 🚋9/14 9/10/14 Alexanderplein) Generator continues its push into the upscale hostel market with this design-savvy newbie. Set in a century-old university building right smack by Oosterpark, the property has 566 beds spread out in 168 twin and quad rooms, all with en-suite bathrooms. Guests can socialise in the cafe with terrace overlooking the park, in a bar carved from the old lecture hall or in a basement speakeasy.

STUDENT HOTEL HOTEL €

Map p325 (☎214 99 99; www.thestudenthotel.com; Wibautstraat 129; r from €70; 📶; Ⓜ Wibautstraat) This shiny new property has more than 300 rooms. Students and interns really do stay here, but anyone (any age) can book a room for a night or so. The chambers are small and institutional-looking, but each has an en-suite bathroom, work desk, flatscreen TV and free wi-fi. A gym, game room and bar-restaurant add to the practicality.

The Metro station is a stone's throw away; you can get downtown in 10 minutes.

STAYOKAY AMSTERDAM ZEEBURG HOSTEL €

(☎551 31 90; www.stayokay.com; Timorplein 21; dm €22-42, r from €89; @📶; 🚋14 Zeeburgerdijk) The sibling of Stayokay Vondelpark and Stayokay Stadsdoelen, Zeeburg might be the best of the bunch. It has 508 beds spread over three floors; most of the spick-and-span rooms are four- or six-bed dorms, all with en-suite bathroom and bright orange decor. Hot breakfast is included. Linens are free, but towels cost €4.50. Wi-fi is in the lobby only.

Next door is Studio K, a cool arts centre, cinema and cafe. Dappermarkt and Javaplein – with great restaurants – are a short stroll away. Get here via tram 14 from the Dam, a 15-minute journey.

VOLKSHOTEL HOTEL €€

Map p325 (☎261 21 00; www.volkshotel.nl; Wibautstraat 150; r €90-190; 📶; Ⓜ Wibautstraat) In vintage Amsterdam fashion, squatters took over this former newspaper building, and an art community developed. People started visiting the studios and the improvisational club-restaurant that sprouted. And voilà: it's now transformed into the ubercool, 172-room Volkshotel, complete with rooftop hot tubs and a panoramic lounge. Rooms have a wood-glass-and-concrete raw-industrial look that the under-35 crowd is lapping up.

It's not close to the major sights, but it is right by a Metro stop that will take you to the centre lickety-split.

Nieuwmarkt, Plantage & the Eastern Islands

HOTEL HORTUS HOTEL €

Map p308 (☎625 99 96; www.hotelhortus.com; Plantage Parklaan 8; s €63-70, d €72-80, f €144-160; 📶; 🚋9/14 Plantage Kerklaan) Facing the botanical garden, this well-worn, comfortable 20-room hotel is terrific value for this area and contains a large common area with a pool table and several TVs. There are only two doubles with a shower, and two without; all share toilets, but have a safe and a sink.

STAYOKAY AMSTERDAM STADSDOELEN HOSTEL €

Map p306 (☎624 68 32; www.stayokay.com; Kloveniersburgwal 97; dm €29.50-45, tw/d from €85; @📶; 🚋4/9/14/16/24 Muntplein) Efficient Stadsdoelen is always bustling with backpackers. Staff are friendly and the 11 single-sex and mixed rooms (each with up to 20 beds and free lockers) offer a modicum of privacy. There's a big TV room, a pool table, a laundry, free wi-fi throughout the building and free continental breakfast. Towel rental costs €4.50.

One catch: there are few power points in the dorms, so charge up your phone when you're out and about if you can.

CHRISTIAN YOUTH HOSTEL 'THE SHELTER CITY' HOSTEL €

Map p306 (☎625 32 30; www.shelterhostelamsterdam.com; Barndesteeg 21; dm €19-37.50; @ 📶; Ⓜ Nieuwmarkt) The price is right at this rambling hostel just outside the Red Light District, but only if you can handle a bit of religious zeal and a tough no-drugs-or-alcohol policy. The pros of staying here include large, airy, single-sex dorms, filling free breakfasts, a quiet cafe, and a garden courtyard with a ping-pong table. Towel/padlock rental costs €1/4.

There's a partner hostel in the Jordaan (p228) .

★ B&B LE MAROXIDIEN HOUSEBOAT, B&B €€

Map p306 (☎400 40 06; www.lemaroxidien.com; Prins Hendrikkade 534; d without bathroom €110-120; 📶; 🚋22/32/34/35/48 Prins Hendrikkade) Moored within easy reach of Centraal Station, Kathrin Rduch's wonderful houseboat (a 1920s former freighter) has a guest wing with three exotic cabins – the sky-blue 'Morocco', spacious 'Mexico' and small 'India' – which share two bathrooms and a cosy lounge. Kathrin provides an organic feast each morning for breakfast. There's a minimum two-night stay; children over six are welcome. Cash only.

HOTEL ALLURE HOTEL €€

Map p308 (☎627 27 14; www.hotel-allure.hotelsofamsterdam.net; Sarphatistraat 117; s/d/tr from €89/99/145; 📶; 🚋7/10 Weesperplein) Scarlet drapes and carpets and a vivid red dining room add dramatic flair to this gleaming contemporary hotel. It's within walking distance of the Hermitage Amsterdam and the Artis Royal Zoo.

HOTEL REMBRANDT HOTEL €€

Map p308 (☎627 27 14; www.hotelrembrandt.nl; Plantage Middenlaan 17; s/d/tr/q from €120/135/195/210; 📶; 🚋9/14 Plantage Kerklaan) With its spotless modern rooms, the Rembrandt shines. Most rooms contain pop-art prints of Rembrandt himself, but room 8 is graced with a nearly life-sized mural of *Night Watch*. Breakfast (€10) is served in a wood-panelled room with chandeliers and 17th-century paintings on linen-covered walls. Take care not to let cute resident cat Bink out of the building.

LLOYD HOTEL BOUTIQUE HOTEL €€

Map p308 (☎561 36 07; www.lloydhotel.com; Oostelijke Handelskade 34; r €95-348; @ 📶; 🚋26 Rietlandpark) Now a 'one- to five-star' hotel, the Lloyd was a hotel for migrants back in 1921, and many of the original fixtures remain, alongside contemporary Dutch design. Budget (bathroom down the hall) to top-end (racquetball-court-sized) rooms are so one-of-a-kind (bathtub in the centre, fold-away bathrooms, a giant bed for eight...) they'll even impress travellers who think they've seen it all.

AIRPORT ACCOMMODATION

If you need a bed by the airport, try these reasonably priced hotels:

Citizen M (☎811 70 80; www.citizenmamsterdamairport.com; Plezierweg 2; r €89-179; ❄ @ 📶) A five-minute walk from the terminals, the Starship Enterprise–like rooms are snug, but maximise space to the utmost, with plush, wall-to-wall beds, and shower and toilet pods. Each room includes a lighting control – command central for the lighting (purple, red or white), blinds, flat-screen TV (free on-demand movies), music, temperature and rain shower. Sushi, sake and self-service snacks are for sale in the club-like canteen.

Yotel (☎in UK 020-7100 1100; www.yotel.com; Schiphol Airport Plaza; r per 4hr from €49; @ 📶) Yotel's Japanese-style capsule hotel at Schiphol is a blessing for travellers who need to catch shut-eye. Prices for the standard 7-sq-metre glam cabins are time-based (four-hour minimum) for short layovers. The standards and twins have bunks and fold-up desks, while the premiums contain regular beds; all are stylish, with crisp white bedspreads, free wi-fi and coffee. Located in Lounge 2, near Pier D.

MISC EATDRINKSLEEP BOUTIQUE HOTEL €€€

Map p306 (☎330 62 41; www.misceatdrinksleep.com; Kloveniersburgwal 20; s/d from €155/165; ❄📶; MNieuwmarkt) Steps from Nieuwmarkt square, the Misc's six themed rooms range from 'baroque' (quite romantic) to 'the room of wonders' (a Moroccan escapade); two rooms contain quirky 'bumblebee' ceiling fans. Canal View rooms cost more, but have air-conditioning; the Garden View rooms are equally charming (if smaller, and with fans only). Breakfast is included in the rate.

Bonus: all in-room snacks and nonalcoholic beverages (from the minibar) and coffee (from your own Nespresso machine) are free.

Southern Canal Ring

★COCOMAMA HOSTEL €

Map p318 (☎627 24 54; www.cocomama.nl; Westeinde 18; dm/d/tr from €38/109/146; @📶; 🚋4/25 Stadhouderskade) Amsterdam's first self-proclaimed 'boutique hostel' plays up its salacious past (the building was once home to a high-end brothel) in some themed bunk rooms, while others are more demure, with Delftware or windmill themes. Private rooms (check out the monarchy-themed 'Royal' room) have iPod docking stations and flat-screen TVs.

Amenities are way above typical hostel standard, with en-suite bathrooms, in-room wi-fi, a relaxing back garden, a well-equipped kitchen, a book exchange and a super-comfy lounge for movie nights.

CITY HOTEL HOTEL €

Map p318 (☎627 23 23; www.city-hotel.nl; Utrechtsestraat 2; 1-2 people €69, 3-6 people €99-189, 5-8 people without bathroom €149-239; @📶; 🚋4/9/14 Rembrandtplein) Above the Old Bell pub, practically on Rembrandtplein, is this unexpectedly fabulous budget hotel, run by a friendly family. Rooms sleeping two to six have private bathrooms; larger rooms, sleeping five to eight people, share bathroom facilities; all come with crisp linen. The attic annexe has a wonderful view of town.

HANS BRINKER BUDGET HOTEL HOSTEL €

Map p318 (☎622 06 87; www.hansbrinker.com; Kerkstraat 136; dm €22.50-25.50, d/tr from €73/93; @📶; 🚋1/2/5 Keizersgracht) The lobby is mayhem and spartan rooms have the ambience of a public hospital, but its beds are almost always filled to capacity with boisterous backpackers and groups who pack into the bright and happy bar, the pulsating disco and the inexpensive restaurant. Rooms have private bathrooms and lockers; wi-fi is available in public areas.

SEVEN BRIDGES BOUTIQUE HOTEL €€

Map p318 (☎623 13 29; www.sevenbridgeshotel.nl; Reguliersgracht 31; d €115-220; 📶; 🚋4 Keizersgracht) Sophisticated and intimate, the Seven Bridges is one of the city's most exquisite little hotels on one of its loveliest canals. It has eight tastefully decorated rooms (all incorporating lush oriental rugs and elegant antiques). The urge to sightsee may fade once breakfast (€10), served on fine china, is delivered to your room.

HOTEL ASTERISK BOUTIQUE HOTEL €€

Map p318 (☎626 23 96; www.asteriskhotel.nl; Den Texstraat 16; s/d from €68/104; @📶; 🚋16/24 Wetering Circuit) Some rooms are minuscule, but you'll sleep soundly on the comfy mattresses at this central, family-owned 42-room hotel. Little touches of elegance include crown mouldings, crystal chandeliers and a pretty breakfast room.

HOTEL PRINSENHOF HOTEL €€

Map p318 (☎623 17 72; www.hotelprinsenhof.com; Prinsengracht 810; d/tr from €100/130; 📶; 🚋4 Prinsengracht) This good-value, 18th-century house features lovely canal views and a breakfast room with some Delft-blue tiles. Staff are affable and the rooms are spacious. Recent renovations have meant that all the rooms now have en-suite bathrooms.

HOTEL V BOUTIQUE HOTEL €€

Map p318 (☎662 32 33; www.hotelv.nl; Weteringschans 136; d €101-260; 📶; 🚋4/7/10 Frederiksplein) Facing lush Frederiksplein and footsteps away from Utrechtsestraat, the retro-chic Hotel V offers fantastic value given its style and location. Its 48 artsy rooms are done up in charcoal colours and feature stone-wall bathrooms. Ask for rates for its four-person loft apartment, which has a private entrance and a kitchenette.

HOTEL FREELAND HOTEL €€

Map p318 (☎622 75 11; www.hotelfreeland.com; Marnixstraat 386; s without bathroom from €60, s/d/tr from €70/110/130; 📶; 🚋1/2/5/7/10 Leidseplein) In a prime canal-side location, Freeland has 15 tidy themed rooms (tulips, roses and sunflowers, and a few with Moroccan details). Add in a tasty breakfast and it pretty much kills the Leidseplein competition. It's gay-friendly and all-welcoming.

HOTEL AMSTELZICHT HOTEL €€

Map p318 (☎623 66 93; www.hotelamstelzicht.nl; Amstel 104; d/tr/ste from €119/149/169; 📶; 🚋4/9/14 Rembrandtplein) The view out front is straight from a 17th-century painting, so make sure you get one of the rooms facing the Amstel river and the gabled houses beyond. From the blue tiles in the lobby to the elegant rooms it's smooth and refined.

HOTEL ADOLESCE HOTEL €€

Map p318 (☎626 39 59; www.adolesce.nl; Nieuwe Keizersgracht 26; s/d without bathroom €80/110, s/d €85/130; @📶; 🚋Waterlooplein) Simple rooms are brightened by artistic prints at this little family-owned hotel in an old canal house. You can help yourself all day to coffee, tea and snacks, including fruit. Some, but not all, rooms have wi-fi – ask when you book.

HOTEL KAP HOTEL €€

Map p318 (☎624 59 08; www.kaphotel.nl; Den Texstraat 5b; s/d/tr/q from €75/100/135/160; 📶; 🚋16/24 Weteringcircuit) Affordable rates, breakfast served in an attractive dining room or courtyard, and courteous, gay-friendly owners make up for the plain rooms and lack of lift/elevator at this simple hotel. Wi-fi costs €5 per stay, and bikes are available for hire. A handful of cheaper single and twin rooms with shared bathrooms are available.

AMISTAD HOTEL BOUTIQUE HOTEL €€

Map p318 (☎624 80 74; www.amistad.nl; Kerkstraat 42; s without bathroom from €95, s/d/tr from €125/135/145; @📶; 🚋1/2/5 Keizersgracht) Rooms at this bijou gay hotel are adorned with Philippe Starck chairs, sound systems and laptops. The breakfast room (with ruby-red walls and communal tables) serves until 1pm and becomes a hopping *café* later in the day.

★**SEVEN ONE SEVEN** LUXURY HOTEL €€€

Map p318 (☎427 07 17; www.717hotel.nl; Prinsengracht 717; d €500-650; ❄📶; 🚋1/2/5 Prinsengracht) The nine hyperplush, deliciously appointed rooms at this breathtaking hotel come with that all-too-rare luxury: space. Step into the prodigious Picasso suite – with its soaring ceiling, elongated sofa, and contemporary and antique decorations – and you may never, ever want to leave. Rates include breakfast, afternoon tea, house wine, beer and personalised service.

BANKS MANSION HOTEL €€€

Map p318 (☎420 00 55; www.carlton.nl/banksmansion; Herengracht 519-525; d/ste from €209/389; ❄@📶; 🚋16/24 Keizersgracht) You get far more than a fancy bed here: refreshments are complimentary at the self-service bar in the Frank Lloyd Wright–designed lobby. When you retire to your contemporary room, you'll enjoy a plasma-screen TV, DVD player (with free films), a huge rain shower, and gin, whisky and cognac on the house.

HOTEL NOTTING HILL DESIGN HOTEL €€€

Map p318 (☎523 10 35; www.hotelnottinghill.nl; Westeinde 26; d €214-499; ❄📶; 🚋4 Stadhouderskade) Styled by Dutch designer Wim Hoopman of Hoopman Interior Projects (aptly abbreviated to HIP), this stunning former office block features a wall of vintage suitcases in the lobby, quirky sculptures and outsized contemporary art, and richly patterned wallpaper in the 71 guest rooms. Higher-priced rooms have canal views. It's in a bulls-eye location between Utrechtsestraat and De Pijp.

AMSTERDAM AMERICAN HOTEL HOTEL €€€

Map p318 (☎556 30 00; www.edenamsterdamamericanhotel.com; Leidsekade 97; d from €243; ❄📶; 🚋1/2/5/7/10 Leidseplein) You can't get closer to the action than this ornate, tower-topped landmark on Leidseplein, a short walk to the Museum Quarter. Furnishings are sleek and contemporary; guests have use of a gym with sauna.

Vondelpark & the Old South

VAN GOGH HOSTEL & HOTEL HOSTEL, HOTEL €

Map p322 (☎262 92 00; www.hotelvangogh.nl; Van de Veldestraat 5; dm/d/tr/q from €28/119/149/179; ❄@📶; 🚋2/3/5/12 Van Baerlestraat) No false advertising here: it sits about 14 steps from the Van Gogh Museum, and every room has a Van Gogh mural. The setup puts the 200-bed hostel on one side, the hotel on the other, and the common area for breakfast (€5) between them. The hostel dorms have six to eight beds, en-suite bathroom and flat-screen TV.

The hotel rooms have balconies on the higher floors (ask for one when booking).

STAYOKAY AMSTERDAM VONDELPARK HOSTEL €

Map p322 (☎589 89 96; www.stayokay.com; Zandpad 5; dm €31-48, tw €75-152; 📶; 🚋1 1e Constantijn Huygensstraat) A frisbee's throw from the Vondelpark, this HI-affiliated 536-bed hostel attracts over 75,000 guests a year –

no wonder the lobby feels like a mini-UN. It's the best Stayokay in town, with renovated rooms sporting lockers, private bathrooms and well-spaced bunks. Chill out in the congenial bar-cafe, or shoot some pool.

★HOTEL NOT HOTEL DESIGN HOTEL €€

Map p322 (☎820 45 38; www.hotelnothotel.com; Piri Reisplein 34; d €75-200, without bathroom €82-120; 🚋7 Postjesweg) The name's apt: rooms here are wild, no-holds-barred art installations. You can sleep inside Amsterdam Tram 965 (in a king-size bed), hide behind a secret bookcase, lounge on a private Spanish villa al fresco terrace, escape the daily grind in the Crisis Free Zone framed by Transylvanian-inspired woodcarvings to deter evil spirits, or climb a ladder to a crow's nest.

Students from Eindhoven's Design Academy created the rooms. Kevin Bacon (its bar, named in homage of the actor) mixes rockin' cocktails.

★HOTEL DE HALLEN DESIGN HOTEL €€

Map p322 (☎515 04 53; www.hoteldehallen.com; Bellamyplein 47; d from €145; ❄📶; 🚋17 Ten Katestraat) Within disused tram sheds recently transformed into the De Hallen cultural complex (p182), this stunner has 55 rooms, all with Coco-Mat mattresses, Nespresso coffee machines and minibars. Each of the spacious rooms has an individual industrial design; the vast public spaces include top-notch restaurant Remise47, lounge areas, a bar and a wraparound umbrella-shaded terrace. Breakfast costs €20.

★COLLECTOR B&B €€

Map p322 (☎673 67 79; www.the-collector.nl; De Lairessestraat 46; s/d/tr from €80/95/115; @📶; 🚋5/16/24 Museumplein) This spotless B&B near the Concertgebouw is furnished with museum-style displays of clocks, wooden clogs and ice skates – things the owner, Karel, collects. Each of the three rooms has balcony access and a TV. Karel stocks the kitchen for guests to prepare breakfast at their leisure (the eggs come from his hens in the garden).

The kitchen is open all day if you want to cook your own dinner. There are also a couple of bikes Karel lends out to guests.

★HOTEL FITA HOTEL €€

Map p322 (☎679 09 76; www.fita.nl; Jan Luijkenstraat 37; s/d from €115/149; 📶; 🚋2/3/5/12 Van Baerlestraat) Family-owned Fita, on a quiet street off the Museumplein and PC Hooftstraat, has 15 handsome rooms with nicely appointed bathrooms; a bountiful free breakfast of eggs, pancakes, cheeses and breads; and an lift/elevator. The dynamic young owner keeps the property in mint condition (new furniture, new artwork, fresh paint), and service could not be more attentive.

It's one of the neighbourhood's best-value digs, and tends to book up fast.

CONSCIOUS HOTEL MUSEUM SQUARE BOUTIQUE HOTEL €€

Map p322 (☎671 95 96; www.conscioushotels.com; De Lairessestraat 7; d/f from €90/171; @📶; 🚋5/16/24 Museumplein) 🍃 This is a fantastic place to go green. It starts with the living plant wall in the lobby and the organic breakfast (€10 extra), and continues with the modern rooms – beds made with 100% natural materials, desks constructed from recycled yoghurt containers, and energy-saving plasma TVs. There is a second location near Vondelpark (p235), and a third in the works.

HOTEL AALDERS HOTEL €€

Map p322 (☎662 01 16; www.hotelaalders.nl; Jan Luijkenstraat 13-15; s/d/tr/f from €139/159/219/259; @📶; 🚋2/3/5/12 Van Baerlestraat) There are fancier hotels in town, but family-owned Aalders is homey and well situated near the museums. The 28 rooms are spread among two tall, adjoining buildings and come in varying sizes and styles (some with wood panelling and decorative-glass windows). In the morning, munch free homemade pastries in the chandelier-adorned breakfast room. Aalders also rents out bikes.

HOTEL DE FILOSOOF BOUTIQUE HOTEL €€

Map p322 (☎683 30 13; www.sandton.eu; Anna van den Vondelstraat 6; s/d/tr from €109/119/179; 📶; 🚋1 Jan Pieter Heijestraat) It's easy to clear your mind in rooms named after philosophers. Each room has its own theme representing its namesake, from Thoreau (with a mural of Walden Pond) to Nietzsche (lots of red, representing his book *Morgenröte*, meaning 'The Dawn'). There's an elegant bar, and the tranquil English garden is a pastoral pleasure come summer.

The hotel features in the novel *The Fault in Our Stars* by John Green, though it wasn't used as a filming location in the hugely popular 2014 film adaptation (in the movie, the American Hotel on Leidseplein is used as its stand-in).

CONSCIOUS HOTEL VONDELPARK BOUTIQUE HOTEL €€

Map p322 (☎820 33 33; www.conscioushotels.com; Overtoom 519; d/tr from €90/121.50; 📶; 🚋1 Rhijnvis Feithstraat) 🍃 At the 81-room Vondelpark branch of Europe's first officially eco-certified hotel, enviro-friendly features are both practical and stylish, from a growing wall in the stunning lobby, live plants in the rooms and recycled materials made into artful furnishings (including pressed-cardboard bathroom benchtops) to the organic breakfast buffet (€13.50).

NEIGHBOUR'S MAGNOLIA HOTEL €€

Map p322 (☎676 93 21; www.magnoliahotelamsterdam.com; Willemsparkweg 205; s/d from €69/119; 📶; 🚋2 Emmastraat) Formerly the Zandbergen hotel, the Neighbour's Magnolia stands out like sterling silver in a tray of plastic cutlery. The staff at this peacefully situated hotel go overboard to help; the 21 rooms are done out in soft pink and green pastels, and those at the rear have balconies overlooking a quiet, flower-filled courtyard (and, yes, there's a magnolia tree).

Each room has a fluffy *knuffel* (soft cuddly toy) for company. Excellent value for money.

HOTEL PIET HEIN BOUTIQUE HOTEL €€

Map p322 (☎662 72 05; www.hotelpiethein.com; Vossiusstraat 52-53; s/d/tr €84/103/148; 📶; 🚋2/5 Van Baerlestraat) Overlooking the Vondelpark's fine old arbour, this immaculate hotel offers a startling variety of contemporary rooms (including snug, single 'business' rooms). There's a sublime garden and a relaxing bar.

FLYNT B&B B&B €€

Map p322 (☎618 46 14; www.flyntbedandbreakfast.nl; 1e Helmersstraat 34; d €85-130; @📶; 🚋1 1e Constantijn Huygensstraat) The spacious slate bathrooms make you feel like you're in a mod boutique hotel, but the friendly owner, the cosy breakfast nook (with breakfast goodies available round the clock) and the pet-friendly policy are pure Vondelpark neighbourhood B&B. Each of the rooms are themed (the Cat Room, the Bike Room and the Post Office).

It also arranges apartment rental elsewhere in the city on request.

XAVIERA HOLLANDER'S HAPPY HOUSE B&B €€

(☎673 39 34; www.xavierahollander.com; Stadionweg 17; d from €120; 📶; 🚋5/24 Gerrit van der Veenstraat) The former madam and author of *The Happy Hooker* welcomes guests to her home in the ritzy Beethovenstraat neighbourhood (minimum two-night stay). The two rooms (which share a bathroom) are decked out with erotic photos, red-heart pillows, and books such as her recent *Guide to Mind-Blowing Sex*. There's also a garden hut with its own facilities (bathroom, refrigerator, terrace).

Xaviera's still something of a media star, and if you're lucky enough to meet her during your stay you'll quickly understand her charisma. The B&B is a good 1km south of the Museumplein.

OWL HOTEL HOTEL €€

Map p322 (☎618 94 84; www.owl-hotel.nl; Roemer Visscherstraat 1; s/d from €91/120; 📶; 🚋1 1e Constantijn Huygensstraat) Some guests love this 34-room place so much that they send in owl figurines from all over the world to add to the hotel's collection. Staff are warm and welcoming, and rooms are bright and quiet. The buffet breakfast (included in the rate) is served in a serene, light-filled room overlooking a delightful garden.

POET HOTEL HOTEL €€

Map p322 (☎662 05 26; www.poethotelamsterdam.com; Jan Luijkenstraat 44; d from €100; 📶; 🚋2/5 Hobbemastraat) The big bed pretty much takes up the entire space in each of the Poet's 64 rooms, and the B&W colour scheme is a bit stark, but on the plus side is decent prices for a leafy location a couple of blocks from the museums. It's mostly a younger crowd that stays here. The welcoming bar is filled with photos of old Amsterdam.

★HOTEL VONDEL BOUTIQUE HOTEL €€€

Map p322 (☎612 01 20; www.vondelhotels.com; Vondelstraat 26-30; d €150-250; 📶; 🚋1 1e Constantijn Huygensstraat) Named after the famed Dutch poet Joost van den Vondel (as is the nearby park), this chic hotel has calm, comfortable rooms (lots of plush grey), and a bar opening to decks overlooking the gardens, as well as bike rental and an in-room flower service. Its dramatic, art-lined restaurant, Joost, is excellent; breakfast here costs €19.

CONSERVATORIUM HOTEL DESIGN HOTEL €€€

Map p322 (☎570 00 00; www.conservatoriumhotel.com; Van Baerlestraat 27; d from €460; ❄📶🏊; 🚋2/5 Van Baerlestraat) Opposite the Royal Concertgebouw, this palatial neo-Gothic building was originally a bank, then the city's conservatorium of music. Its most recent incarnation sees it stunningly converted into an eight-storey, 129-room hotel with soaring glass and steel connecting the 19th-century brickwork (especially in the light-filled atrium lounge) and a 1000-sq-metre gym and spa – the largest of Amsterdam's hotels.

Nods to the building's musical history include a light fitting incorporating dozens of suspended violins.

COLLEGE HOTEL BOUTIQUE HOTEL €€€
Map p322 (571 15 11; www.thecollegehotel.com; Roelof Hartstraat 1; d from €178; 3/5/12/24 Roelof Hartplein) Originally a 19th-century school, the College Hotel has fashioned its 40 chambers – with high ceilings, tasteful furnishings and the occasional stained-glass window – from former classrooms. Hospitality-school students now staff the hotel to earn their stripes, while celebs from Brooke Shields to Fatboy Slim enjoy the swanky end product.

The hotel is well situated between the Museum Quarter and De Pijp's sights and cafes (about 1km from both).

PARK HOTEL HOTEL €€€
Map p322 (671 12 22; www.parkhotel.nl; Stadhouderskade 25; d from €169; 1/2/5/7/10 Leidseplein) Design features at this individual hotel include adjustable mood lighting, incense, and stunning George Heidweiller cityscapes on the walls. Downstairs, curl up with a coffee in the 'Living Room' with its changing gallery of modern art. It has a well-equipped fitness room and is within spitting distance of Vondelpark, so there's little excuse to not work out. Minimum two-night stay.

An Asian-inspired breakfast costs €18.50. A rarity for Amsterdam, on-site, undercover parking is available, but costs an eye-watering €65 per 24 hours.

De Pijp

BICYCLE HOTEL AMSTERDAM HOTEL €€
Map p326 (679 34 52; www.bicyclehotel.com; Van Ostadestraat 123; s/d/tr without bathroom from €30/60/120, d/tr/f from €100/150/170; 3 Ferdinand Bolstraat) Run by Marjolein and Clemens, this casual, friendly, green-minded hotel has rooms that are comfy and familiar. It also rents bikes (€8 per day) and serves a killer organic breakfast (included in the rate).

BETWEEN ART & KITSCH B&B B&B €€
Map p326 (679 04 85; www.between-art-and-kitsch.com; Ruysdaelkade 75; s/d from €85/100; 16 Ruysdaelkade) Mondrian once lived here – that's part of the art – while the kitsch includes the crystal chandelier in the baroque room and a smiling brass Buddha. The art-deco room has gorgeous tile work and views of the Rijksmuseum. Husband and wife hosts Ebo and Irene couldn't be friendlier. Note that it's on the third floor, with no lift/elevator.

CAKE UNDER MY PILLOW B&B €€
Map p326 (751 09 36; www.cakeundermypillow.com; 1e Jacob van Campenstraat 66; d with/without bathroom from €160/110; 16/24 Stadhouderskade) Run by the owners of bakery Taart van m'n Tante (p192), this B&B above the cafe (no lift/elevator) has comfy rooms decorated with plates. A two-night minimum stay is required.

★**SIR ALBERT HOTEL** DESIGN HOTEL €€€
Map p326 (305 30 20; www.siralberthotel.com; Albert Cuypstraat 2-6; d from €200; 16/24 Ruysdaelstraat) A 19th-century diamond factory houses this glitzy design hotel. Its 90 creative rooms and suites have soaring ceilings and large windows, with custom-made linens and Illy espresso machines; iPads are available for guest use in the Persian-rug-floored study. Energetic staff are genuine and professional in equal measure.

It's on the same street as the busy Albert Cuypmarkt, but at the peaceful, leafy western end.

HOTEL OKURA AMSTERDAM LUXURY HOTEL €€€
(678 83 00; www.okura.nl; Ferdinand Bolstraat 333; d/ste from €220/415;) Rare-for-Amsterdam amenities that elevate this business-oriented hotel way above the competition include panoramic city views (particularly from higher-priced north-facing rooms), a total of three Michelin stars on the premises (two at top-floor Ciel Bleu (p195), and one at lobby-level Japanese restaurant Yamazato), and an amazing health club with an 18m-long jet-stream swimming pool. Breakfast costs €32.50.

It's locally loved for its social responsibility and donating to the surrounding community. The roof acts as the Netherlands' largest barometer (p198).

Understand Amsterdam

Amsterdam Today

From the famed coffeeshops to the Red Light District, Amsterdam's tolerance is on display wherever you wander. The city counts 180 nationalities living within its borders and most agree: the quality of life here makes other metropolises envious. Dramatic architecture and grand urban projects continue to rise up and transform the cityscape, merging Golden Age charm with hypermodernity. Meanwhile, the stylish, practical Queen steals the spotlight.

Best on Film

Zwartboek (Black Book; directed by Paul Verhoeven; 2006) This action-packed story explores some of the less heroic aspects of the Dutch Resistance in WWII. It launched the international career of today's hottest Dutch actor, Carice van Houten.

The Paradise Suite (directed by Joost van Ginkel; 2015) A Bulgarian woman forced into prostitution, a Swedish piano prodigy, a Serbian war criminal and other troubled characters cross paths in Amsterdam.

Best in Print

The Diary of Anne Frank (Anne Frank; 1952) A moving account of a young girl's thoughts and yearnings while in hiding from the Nazis in Amsterdam. The book has been translated into 60 languages.

After the Silence (Jake Woodhouse, 2014) Noir novel in which Inspector Jap Rykel, an Amsterdam detective, hunts down a murderer in the city's tangled streets. It's book one of a four-part series.

Tolerant Culture

Laid-back. Progressive. Bilingual (sometimes trilingual). Industrious. Aware. International. Amsterdam's locals embody these qualities in spades with their famously tolerant attitudes toward diversity and differences. Perhaps this is why Amsterdam is celebrated for being a consummately easy and relaxed place to travel.

It's an open society in the literal sense. Walk down any street and notice the abundance of curtain-less windows – even in the ritziest neighbourhoods – where families and couples cook, eat, watch TV and play with their children in full view.

As of 2015, the Dutch economy is humming along. But even in the just-prior years when it wasn't, locals still ranked among the world's most contented people, according to the World Happiness Report by Columbia University. The nation placed seventh in the most recent study, thanks to its high quality of life based on freedom to make choices, social supports and other factors.

Sex & Drugs

Amsterdam is famously open-minded when it comes to cannabis use and prostitution. But since 2008 a bit of a tussle has ensued, as the city embarks on a plan to reduce the number of coffeeshops and Red Light District windows. The city says organised crime has entered the scene and must be stopped; opponents say the city simply doesn't like its reputation for sin. The upshot: many spaces in the Red Light area are being converted to galleries, cafes and other more wholesome businesses. The industry certainly won't disappear anytime soon, but it is shrinking markedly.

Growing & Innovating

Amsterdam has had the knack for innovation from the get-go. Just look at the 400-plus-year-old canal ring. City planners built it to drain and reclaim waterlogged land to accommodate the exploding population during the Golden Age. Flash-forward to today and it's a similar story. Amsterdam is running out of room for its growing number of denizens – some 70,000 people joined the city's ranks since 2008 – and urban planners are using visionary architecture to make room for the newcomers.

The shores along the IJ have seen the most action, with swooping modern developments transforming industrial areas such as the Eastern Docklands and Western Docklands (on either side of Centraal Station), as well as Amsterdam-Noord across the water. These are the new 'it' neighbourhoods for eye-popping, sustainably designed housing, offices and public buildings like the EYE Film Institute and A'DAM Tower.

Then there's IJburg, where the city is building 10 artificial islands in the IJmeer lake. Engineers place layer upon layer of sand, and then build housing on the 'islands' that arise. Six islands are now inhabited; construction on the last four begins in 2017.

The innovation extends underground, too, as engineers build the new North-South Metro Line from Amsterdam-Noord to the World Trade Centre in south Amsterdam, tunneling under the IJ and the historic centre en route. The project, which is the cause of the torn-up streets you see around town, should be finished in 2017.

Technology Hub

In 2014, entrepreneurial magazine *Inc.* named Amsterdam as a startup hub to keep an eye on. It is cheaper for running a business than hot spots such as Silicon Valley, Beijing and New York City. It has plenty of English-fluent coders and programmers. It's a creative environment. And there are around 200 startup companies within a four-mile radius of the centre. They're working on projects such as building a canal house and canal bridge by 3D printer, honing bitcoin technology and offering networks where residents can trade surplus green energy with each other.

Queen Máxima

Amsterdammers aren't obsessed with their royal family as in some other cultures. King Willem-Alexander (b 1967) is a modest guy who keeps a relatively low profile. But if locals had to admit to one royal fascination, it would be his wife, Queen Máxima. The stylish, blonde Argentinean, married to the king since 2002, has been known to ride her bike to royal functions and reuse her elegant dresses. Her sensational, wide-brimmed hats always cause a stir. No wonder her approval rating hovers near 80%.

if Amsterdam were 100 people

49 would be Dutch
16 would be from Europe
9 would be from Suriname
9 would be from Morocco
5 would be from Turkey
12 would be from elsewhere

Belief system

(% of population)

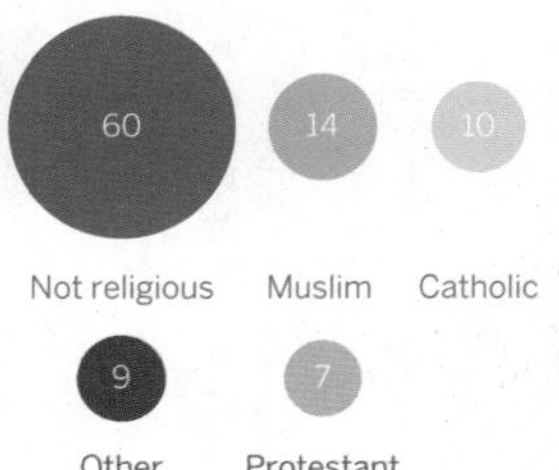

population per sq km

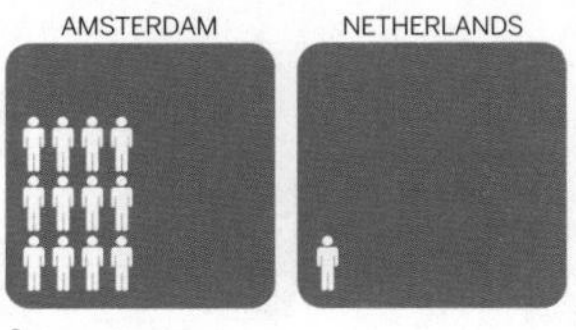

GEORGE TSAFOS / GETTY IMAGES ©

. Hortus Botanicus (p97)
ore than 4000 plant species grow in these otanical gardens.

. House of Bols (p174)
isitors try the 'sniff test' at this *jenever* (Dutch n) museum.

. Vondelpark (p173)
his 47-hectare park is one of Amsterdam's most agical places.

. Winter in Vondelpark (p173)
hildren learn to ice skate at this family-friendly oot.

LONELY PLANET / GETTY IMAGES ©

History

Amsterdam may have spawned one of the world's great trading empires, but this area was once an inhospitable patchwork of lakes, swamps and peat, at or below sea level; its contours shifted with the autumn storms and floods. The oldest archaeological finds here date from Roman times, when the IJ river lay along the northern border of the Roman Empire. Maritime trading, egalitarian attitudes and engineering ingenuity all paved the way for the modern city today.

From the Beginning

The mighty Romans – who had conquered the lands now known as the Netherlands in the 1st century – left behind no colosseums or magnificent tombs. In uncharacteristic style, they left practically no evidence, much less any grand gestures, of settlement. While the swampy, sea-level topography made the construction of grand edifices challenging, the Romans had been known to bypass such challenges before in other regions. In the end, they simply had other more important lands south of the Low Countries to inhabit and rule.

Around 1200, a fishing community known as Aemstelredamme ('the dam built across the Amstel') emerged at what is now the Dam, and the name Amsterdam was coined.

Historical Reads: Non-Fiction

Amsterdam: A History of the World's Most Liberal City (Russell Shorto)

The Embarrassment of Riches (Simon Schama)

Amsterdam: The Brief Life of a City (Geert Mak)

Tulipomania: The Story of the World's Most Coveted Flower (Mike Dash)

Early Trade

Farming was tricky on the marshland and with the sea on the doorstep, early residents turned to fishing. But it was commercial trade that would flourish. While powerful city-states focused on overland trade with Flanders and northern Italy, Amsterdam shrewdly levelled its sights on the maritime routes. The big prizes? The North and Baltic Seas, which were in the backyard of the powerful Hanseatic League, a group of German trading cities.

Ignoring the league's intimidating reputation, Amsterdam's clever *vrijbuiters* (buccaneers) sailed right into the Baltic, their holds full of cloth and salt to exchange for grain and timber. It was nothing short of

TIMELINE

1150–1300

Dams are built to retain the IJ river between the Zuiderzee and Haarlem. A tiny community of herring fishermen settles on the banks of the Amstel river.

1275

Amsterdam is founded after toll-free status is granted to residents along the Amstel. The city gains direct access to the ocean via the Zuiderzee, now the IJsselmeer.

1380

Canals of the present-day Medieval Centre are dug. Amsterdam flourishes, winning control over the sea trade in Scandinavia and later gaining free access to the Baltic.

a coup. By the late 1400s the vast majority of ships sailing to and from the Baltic Sea were based in Amsterdam.

By this time sailors, merchants, artisans and opportunists from the Low Countries (roughly present-day Netherlands, Belgium and Luxembourg) made their living here.

At the time, Amsterdam was unfettered by the key structures of other European societies. With no tradition of Church-sanctioned feudal relationships, no distinction between nobility and serfs, and hardly any taxation, a society of individualism and capitalism took root. The modern idea of Amsterdam – free, open, progressive and flush with opportunity – was born.

Independent Republic

The Protestant Reformation wasn't just a matter of religion; it was also a classic power struggle between the 'new money' (an emerging class of merchants and artisans) and the 'old money' (the land-owning, aristocratic order sanctioned by the established Catholic Church).

The Protestantism that took hold in the Low Countries was its most radically moralistic stream, known as Calvinism. It stressed the might of God and treated humans as sinful creatures whose duty in life was sobriety and hard work. The ascetic Calvinists stood for local decision-making and had a disdain for the top-down hierarchy of the Catholic Church.

Calvinism was key to the struggle for independence from King Philip II of Spain. The hugely unpopular Philip, a fanatically devout Catholic, had acquired the Low Countries in something of a horse trade with Austria. His efforts to introduce the Spanish Inquisition, centralise government and levy taxes enraged his subjects and awoke a sense of national pride.

In 1579 the seven northern provinces, with mighty Amsterdam on their side, declared themselves to be an independent republic, led by William of Orange: the seed that grew into today's royal family. William was famously dubbed 'the Silent' because he wisely refused to enter into religious debate. To this day, he remains the uncontested founder – and father – of the Netherlands.

Golden Age (1580–1700)

In 1588, Den Haag was established as the seat of the Dutch republic, but Amsterdam grew rapidly to become the largest and most influential city in the Netherlands.

By 1600 Dutch ships controlled the sea trade between England, France, Spain and the Baltic, and had a virtual monopoly on North

Historical Reads: Fiction

- *Tulip Fever* (Deborah Moggach)
- *Max Havelaar* (Eduard Douwes Dekker)
- *The Coffee Trader* (David Liss)
- *Rembrandt's Whore* (Sylvie Matton)

The Dutch 'bought' (a concept foreign to North American tribes at the time) the island of Manhattan from the Lenape in 1626 for the equivalent of US$24 worth of beads.

1452

Following the second 15th-century fire to devastate the city, laws decree that brick and tile are the only building materials that can be used in the city.

1519

Spain's Charles V is crowned Holy Roman Emperor. Treaties and dynastic marriages make Amsterdam part of the Spanish empire, with Catholicism the main faith.

1543

Charles V unites the Low Countries (roughly the area covering what is now the Netherlands, Belgium and Luxembourg) and establishes Brussels as the region's capital.

1578

Amsterdam is captured in a bloodless coup. A Dutch Republic made up of seven provinces is declared a year later, led by William the Silent.

Sea fishing and Arctic whaling. Jewish refugees taught Dutch mariners about trade routes, giving rise to the legendary Dutch East India and Dutch West India Companies. For a while, the Dutch ran rings around the fleets of great powers, which were too slow or cumbersome to react. In the absence of an overriding religion, ethnic background or political entity, money reigned supreme.

Two decades on, Dutch traders had gone global, exploring the far corners of the earth, and by the mid-17th century the Dutch had more seagoing merchant vessels than England and France combined. Half of all ships sailing between Europe and Asia belonged to the Dutch, and exotic products – coffee, tea, spices, tobacco, cotton, silk and porcelain – became commodities. Amsterdam became home to Europe's largest shipbuilding industry, and the city was veritably buzzing with prosperity and innovation.

In 1651, England passed the first of several Navigation Acts that posed a serious threat to Dutch trade, leading to several thorny, inconclusive wars on the seas. Competitors sussed out Dutch trade secrets, regrouped and reconquered the sea routes. In 1664 the Dutch lost the colony of New Netherland, including the provincial capital New Amsterdam (now New York City) to the British, in exchange for Suriname in South America (which the Dutch governed until 1954). Louis XIV of France seized the opportunity to invade the Low Countries two decades later, and the period of prosperity known as the Golden Age ended. While the city hardly went into decay or ruin, the embattled economy would take more than a century to regain its full strength.

Amsterdam is the official (constitutional) capital of the Netherlands, but Den Haag is the seat of government and the site of the royal family's residence, Huis ten Bosch. All embassies are located in Den Haag, although some countries also have consulates general in Amsterdam.

Wealthy Decline (1700–1814)

If you can't beat them, pacify them: while the Dutch Republic didn't have the resources to fight France and England head on, it had Amsterdam's money to buy them off and ensure freedom of the seas.

As the costs mounted, Amsterdam went from being a place where everything (profitable) was possible, to a lethargic community where wealth creation was a matter of interest rates. Gone were the daring sea voyages, the achievements in art, science and technology, and the innovations of government and finance. Ports such as London and Hamburg became powerful rivals.

The decline in trade brought poverty, and exceptionally cold winters hampered transport and led to serious food shortages. The winters of 1740 and 1763 were so severe that some residents froze to death.

Amsterdam's support of the American War of Independence (1776) resulted in a British blockade of the Dutch coast, followed by British

1600s

The Golden Age places Amsterdam firmly on the cultural map. While Rembrandt paints in his atelier, the grand inner ring of canals is constructed. The city's population surges to 200,000.

1602

Amsterdam becomes the site of the world's first stock exchange when the offices of the Dutch East India Company trade their own shares.

1618

World's first weekly broadsheet newspaper, the *Courante uyt Italien, Duytslandt, &c.*, is printed in Amsterdam. Catholicism is outlawed, with clandestine worship permitted.

1664

The Dutch infamously lose the colony of New Netherland (now the northeastern US), including New Amsterdam (now New York City), to the British.

conquests of Dutch trading posts around the world, forcing the closure of the Dutch West and East India Companies.

Enter the French: in 1794 French revolutionary troops invaded the Low Countries. In a convenient act of nepotism, the Dutch Republic became a monarchy in 1806, when Napoleon installed his brother Louis Napoleon as king.

After Napoleon's defeat in 1813, Amsterdam's trade with the world recovered only slowly; domination of the seas now belonged to the British.

THE CURIOUS HISTORY OF TULIPMANIA

When it comes to investment frenzy, the Dutch tulip craze of 1636–37 ranks alongside the greatest economic booms and busts in history.

Tulips originated as wildflowers in Central Asia and were first cultivated by the Turks, who filled their courts with these beautiful spring blooms. In the mid-1500s the Habsburg ambassador to Istanbul brought some bulbs back to Vienna, where the imperial botanist, Carolus Clusius, learned how to propagate them. In 1590 Clusius became director of the Hortus Botanicus in Leiden – Europe's oldest botanical garden – and had great success growing and cross-breeding tulips in Holland's cool, damp climate and fertile delta soil.

The more exotic specimens of tulip featured frilly petals and 'flamed' streaks of colour, which attracted the attention of wealthy merchants, who put them in their living rooms and hallways to impress visitors. Trickle-down wealth and savings stoked the taste for exotica in general, and tulip growers arose to service the demand.

A speculative frenzy ensued, and people paid top florin for the finest bulbs, many of which changed hands time and again before they sprouted. Vast profits were made and speculators fell over themselves to outbid each other. Bidding often took place in taverns and was fuelled by alcohol, which no doubt added to the enthusiasm.

Of course, this bonanza couldn't last, and when several bulb traders in Haarlem failed to fetch their expected prices in February 1637, the bottom fell out of the market. Within weeks many of the country's wealthiest merchants went bankrupt and many more people of humbler origins lost everything.

However, love of the unusual tulip endured, and cooler-headed growers perfected their craft. To this day, the Dutch continue to be the world leaders in tulip cultivation and supply most of the bulbs planted in Europe and North America. They also excel with other bulbs such as daffodils, hyacinths and crocuses.

So what happened to the flamed, frilly tulips? They're still produced but have gone out of fashion, and are now known as Rembrandt tulips because of their depiction in so many 17th-century paintings.

Oudezijds Achterburgwal

1688

William III of Orange repels the French with the help of Austria, Spain and Brandenburg. William then invades England, where he and his wife are proclaimed king and queen.

1795

French troops occupy the Netherlands and install the Batavian Republic. The fragmented United Provinces become a centralised state, with Amsterdam as its capital.

1806

The Dutch Republic becomes a monarchy when Napoleon installs his brother Louis Napoleon as king.

New Infrastructure (1814–1918)

In the first half of the 19th century, Amsterdam was a gloomy, uninspiring place. Its harbour had been neglected and the sandbanks in the IJ proved too great a barrier for modern ships. Rotterdam was set to become the country's premier port.

Things began to look up as the country's first railway, between Amsterdam and Haarlem, opened in 1839. Trade with the East Indies was the backbone of Amsterdam's economy, and a canal, later extended to the Rhine, helped the city to benefit from the Industrial Revolution under way in Europe.

Amsterdam again attracted immigrants, and its population doubled in the second half of the 19th century. Speculators hastily erected new housing beyond the Canal Ring – dreary, shoddily built tenement blocks.

The Netherlands remained neutral in WWI, but Amsterdam's trade with the East Indies suffered from naval blockades. Food shortages brought riots, and an attempt to bring the socialist revolution to the Netherlands was put down by loyalist troops.

The Miniaturist (2014), by Jessie Burton, is a historical novel that takes place during the Golden Age and centres on Petronella Oortman, owner of the intricate dollhouse that's now a big draw at the Rijksmuseum. The title character is an enigmatic artist who helps Nella furnish it precisely to scale... and may hold the key to her family's future.

Boom & Depression (1918–40)

After WWI, Amsterdam remained the country's industrial centre. The Dutch Shipbuilding Company operated the world's second-largest wharf and helped carry a large steel and diesel-motor industry. The harbour handled tropical produce that was processed locally, such as tobacco and cocoa (Amsterdam is still the world's biggest centre for cocoa distribution).

The 1920s were boom years. In 1920 KLM (Koninklijke Luchtvaart Maatschappij; Royal Aviation Company) began the world's first regular passenger air service between Amsterdam and London from an airstrip south of the city, and bought many of its planes from Anthony Fokker's factory north of the IJ. There were two huge breweries, a sizeable clothing industry and even a local car factory. The city hosted the Olympic Games in 1928.

The world Depression in the 1930s hit Amsterdam hard. Make-work projects did little to defuse the mounting tensions between socialists, communists and a small but vocal party of Dutch fascists. The city took in 25,000 Jewish refugees fleeing Germany; many were turned back at the border because of the country's neutrality policy.

Hans Brinker, who supposedly stuck his finger in a dyke and saved the Netherlands from a flood, is an American invention and unknown in the Netherlands. He starred in a 19th-century children's book.

1813–14

The French are overthrown and William VI of Orange is crowned as Dutch King William I.

1830

With French help, the southern provinces secede to form the Kingdom of Belgium. The country is not formally recognised by the Dutch government until 1839.

1865–76

In a period of rapid economic and social change, the North Sea Canal is dug, the Dutch railway system is expanded and socialist principles of government are established.

1889

Centraal Station makes its grand debut, and – in an instant – Amsterdam is connected by rail to the rest of Europe.

WWII (1940–45)

The Netherlands tried to remain neutral in WWII, but Germany invaded in May 1940. For the first time in almost 400 years, Amsterdammers experienced war firsthand. Few wanted to believe that things would turn really nasty (the Germans, after all, had trumpeted that the Dutch were of the 'Aryan brotherhood').

In February 1941, dockworkers led a protest strike over the treatment of Jews, commemorated as the 'February Strike'. By then, however, it was already too late.

The official website of the Dutch royal family (www.koninklijkhuis.nl) features minibiographies and virtual tours of the palaces, as well as news.

JEWISH AMSTERDAM

It's hard to overstate the role Jews have played in the evolution of civic and commercial life in Amsterdam. The first documented Jewish presence goes back to the 12th century, but it was their expulsion from Spain and Portugal in the 1580s that brought a large number of Sephardic (Jews of Spanish, Middle Eastern or North African heritage) refugees.

As in much of Europe, Jews in Amsterdam were barred from many professions. Monopolistic guilds kept most trades firmly closed. But some Sephardim were diamond cutters, for which there was no guild. Other Sephardic Jews introduced printing and tobacco processing, or worked in unrestricted trades such as retail, finance, medicine and the garment industry. The majority, however, eked out a meagre living as labourers and small-time traders. They lived in the Nieuwmarkt area, which developed into the Jewish quarter.

Yet Amsterdam's Jews had some human rights unheard of elsewhere in Europe. They were not confined to a ghetto and, with some restrictions, could buy property. Although the Protestant establishment sought to impose restrictions, civic authorities were reluctant to restrict such productive members of society.

The 17th century saw more Jewish refugees arrive, this time Ashkenazim (Jews from Europe outside of Iberia), fleeing pogroms in Central and Eastern Europe. Amsterdam became the largest Jewish centre in Europe – some 10,000 strong by Napoleonic times. The guilds and all remaining restrictions on Jews were abolished during the French occupation, and Amsterdam's Jewish community thrived in the 19th century.

All that came to an end, however, with WWII. The Nazis brought about the near-complete annihilation of Amsterdam's Jewish community. Before the war about 140,000 Jews lived in the Netherlands, of whom about 90,000 lived in Amsterdam (comprising 13% of the city's population). Only about 5500 of Amsterdam's Jews survived the war, barely one in 16, the lowest proportion of anywhere in Western Europe.

Today there are roughly 41,000 to 45,000 Jews in the Netherlands, nearly half of whom live in Amsterdam.

1914–20

The Netherlands remains neutral in WWI. Food shortages cripple the country, leading to strikes, unrest and growing support for the Dutch Communist Party.

1939

The Dutch government establishes Westerbork as an internment camp to house Jewish refugees.

1940

Germany invades the Netherlands. Rotterdam is destroyed by the Luftwaffe, but Amsterdam suffers only minor damage before capitulating.

1944–45

The Allies liberate the southern Netherlands, but the north and west of the country are cut off from supplies. Thousands of Dutch perish in the bitter 'Hunger Winter'.

The Dutch Resistance, set up by an unlikely alliance of Calvinists and communists, only became large-scale when the increasingly desperate Germans began to round up able-bodied men to work in Germany.

Towards the end of the war, the situation in Amsterdam was dire. Coal shipments ceased; many men aged between 17 and 50 had gone into hiding or to work in Germany; public utilities were halted; and the Germans began to plunder anything that could assist their war effort. Thousands of lives were lost to severe cold and famine. Canadian troops finally liberated the city in May 1945 in the final days of the war in Europe.

Postwar Growth (1945–62)

The city's growth resumed after the war, with US aid through the Marshall Plan.

Massive apartment blocks arose in areas annexed west of the city to meet the continuing demand for housing, made more acute by the demographic shift away from extended families. The massive Bijlmermeer housing project (now called De Bijlmer) southeast of the city, begun in the mid-1960s and finished in the 1970s, was built in a similar vein.

Cultural Revolution (1962–82)

John Lennon and Yoko Ono took to bed at the Amsterdam Hilton for a week in 1969, and invited the world's press to join them. Rather than salacious entertainment, however, they offered bromides about world peace.

For nearly a century leading up to the 1960s, Dutch society had become characterised by *verzuiling* (pillarisation), a social order in which each religion and political persuasion achieved the right to do its own thing, with its own institutions. Each persuasion represented a pillar that supported the status quo in a general 'agreement to disagree'. In the 1960s the old divisions were increasingly irrelevant and the pillars came tumbling down, but not the philosophy they spawned.

Amsterdam became Europe's 'Magic Centre': hippies smoked dope on the Dam, camped in Vondelpark and tripped at clubs such as the Melkweg, an abandoned dairy barn. In 1972 the first coffeeshop opened, and in 1976 marijuana was decriminalised to free up police resources for combating hard drugs. With soaring housing prices, squatters began to occupy buildings left empty by speculators. In the process, they helped save several notable historical structures from demolition.

Since 2010, squatting has been illegal, and some former squats have become legitimate cultural centres.

New Consensus (1982–2000)

Twenty years after the cultural revolution began, a new consensus emphasised a decentralised government. Neighbourhood councils were

1976

The Netherlands' drug laws distinguish soft from hard drugs; possession of small amounts of marijuana is decriminalised.

1980

Queen Beatrix's investiture in Amsterdam is disrupted by smoke bombs and riots instigated by squatters reacting against the lack of affordable housing.

2001

The Netherlands becomes the first country in the world to legalise same-sex marriage. Sixteen more nations (and counting) follow suit in the years that follow.

established with the goal of creating a more liveable city, through integration of work, schools and shops within walking or cycling distance; decreased traffic; renovation rather than demolition; friendly neighbourhood police; a practical, nonmoralistic approach towards drugs; and legal recognition of homosexual couples.

By the early 1990s, the families and small manufacturers that had dominated inner-city neighbourhoods in the early 1960s had been replaced by professionals and a service industry of pubs, coffeeshops, restaurants and hotels. The city's success in attracting large foreign businesses resulted in an influx of high-income expats.

Testing Times (2000–Present)

The first decade-and-a-half of the new century have been full of ups and downs for Amsterdam. After smouldering for years, a noisy debate erupted over the Netherlands' policy towards newcomers, which quickly led to a tightening of immigration laws. The limits of tolerance, a core value of Dutch identity, were called into question. Pim Fortuyn, a right-wing politician, declared the country 'full' before he was assassinated in 2002.

Dubbed the 'most famous bleached blond since Marilyn Monroe', parliamentary leader Geert Wilders has been a divisive, controversial politician in the Netherlands, comparing the Koran to *Mein Kampf*, calling for immigrants to be deported and demanding that religious services be conducted only in Dutch.

Social tensions flared in the wake of the Fortuyn murder, and the number of people leaving the country reached a 50-year high, although most departed for economic and family reasons. The mood was edgy, like a cauldron about to boil over.

It finally did in the autumn of 2004, when filmmaker Theo van Gogh – known for his anti-Muslim views – was murdered on an Amsterdam street. The leading political parties in the Netherlands responded with a big shift to the right. In 2006 the government passed a controversial immigration law requiring newcomers – except those from countries with reciprocal arrangements or pre-existing treaties – to have competency in Dutch language and culture before they could get a residency permit. This meant the policy mostly fell on immigrants from non-Western countries. Indeed, immigration from these countries slowed considerably after the law was enacted – but recently it began to tick upward again given the many refugees who have streamed in as they flee conflict in the Middle East. Immigration overall has been on the rise since 2008, thanks to newcomers from Eastern Europe.

In 2008, the Dutch government made waves – both locally and abroad – by announcing its plans to reduce the number of coffeeshops and legal brothels. The legal age of prostitutes was raised from 18 to 21 in 2013, and rules went into effect in 2014 to shut down coffeeshops operating near schools. Amsterdam's authorities are often at odds with the national government when it comes to such policies, especially those involving

2002

Pim Fortuyn, a hard-line politician on immigration and integration, is assassinated. The ruling Dutch parties shift to the right after suffering major losses in the national election.

2004

Activist filmmaker Theo van Gogh, a fierce critic of Islam, is murdered, touching off intense debate over the limits of Dutch multicultural society.

2006

The government passes a law requiring immigrants (except from countries with pre-existing treaties) to have competency in Dutch language and culture in order to get a residency permit.

2008

The city announces Project 1012. The goal is to clean up the Red Light District and close prostitution windows and coffeeshops believed to be controlled by organised crime.

coffeeshops, and the city is loath to enforce the issue. Nonetheless, quite a few coffeeshops have closed over the past few years, as have about one-fifth of the Red Light District's windows.

A budget crisis over austerity measures as a result of the global financial crisis led to the fall of the Dutch government in 2012. Subsequent elections saw Prime Minister Mark Rutte retain the position of de-facto head of government and form a new coalition government with his liberal VVD party and the centre-left Labour party. The latter is the faction of Amsterdam mayor Eberhard van der Laan, who has been in the job since 2010.

King Willem-Alexander and his wife Queen Máxima have three daughters: Princess Catharina-Amalia (the Princess of Orange), Princess Alexia and Princess Ariane.

Perhaps the biggest recent headline was when Queen Beatrix stepped down after 33 years. She abdicated (in the Royal Palace) in favour of her eldest son Willem-Alexander, who became king on 30 April 2013. His investiture took place in the Nieuwe Kerk. He is the first male to accede to the Dutch throne since 1890.

SIGHTS FOR HISTORY BUFFS

- **Amsterdam Museum** (p73) Lift the veil on the city's storied past.
- **Stadsarchief** (p1) Plumb the city's rich archives.
- **Anne Frank Huis** (p114) See the annexe where the Frank family hid, and pages from Anne's poignant diary.
- **Verzetsmuseum** (p99) Learn about Dutch Resistance efforts during WWII.
- **West-Indisch Huis** (p117) Ponder the 17th-century building where the Dutch West India Company's governors authorised establishing New Amsterdam (now New York City).

2009

Amsterdam courts prosecute Dutch parliamentary leader Geert Wilders for 'incitement to hatred and discrimination'. (He is acquitted of all charges in 2011.)

2010

Members of the Dutch government officially apologise to the Jewish community for failing to protect the Jewish population from genocide in WWII.

2013

After a 33-year reign, Queen Beatrix abdicates in favour of her eldest son, Willem-Alexander, who becomes the Netherlands' first king in 123 years.

2015

Scores of prostitutes and their supporters take to the streets to protest the closure of roughly one-fifth of the Red Light District's windows.

Dutch Painting

They don't call them the Dutch Masters for nothing. The line-up includes Rembrandt, Frans Hals and Johannes Vermeer – these iconic artists are some of the world's most revered and celebrated painters. And then, of course, there's Vincent van Gogh, who toiled in ignominy while supported by his loving brother Theo, and 20th-century artists including De Stijl–proponent Piet Mondrian and graphic genius MC Escher. Understanding these quintessential Dutch artists requires a journey back into history.

15th & 16th Centuries

Flemish School

Prior to the late 16th century, when Belgium was still part of the Low Countries, art focused on the Flemish cities of Ghent, Bruges and Antwerp. Paintings of the Flemish School featured biblical and allegorical subject matter popular with the Church, the court and (to a lesser extent) the nobility, who, after all, paid the bills and called the shots.

Among the most famous names of the era are Jan van Eyck (c 1385–1441), the founder of the Flemish School, who was one of the earliest artists to use oils in detailed panel painting; Rogier van der Weyden (1400–64), whose religious portraits showed the personalities of his subjects; and Hieronymus (also known as Jeroen) Bosch (1450–1516), with his macabre allegorical paintings full of religious topics. Pieter Brueghel the Elder (1525–69) used Flemish landscapes and peasant life in his allegorical scenes.

Female painters during the Dutch Golden Age were rare. Judith Leyster (1609–1660) was the only woman registered with the artists' guild during the time. She trained with Frans Hals, and his influence is seen in her fluid portraits. Leyster had her own studio in Haarlem, but once she married she vanished from the scene. The Rijksmuseum has some of her works.

Dutch School

In the northern Low Countries, painters began to develop a style of their own. Although the artists of the day never achieved the level of recognition of their Flemish counterparts, the Dutch School, as it came to be called, was known for favouring realism over allegory. Haarlem, just west of Amsterdam, was the centre of this movement, with artists such as Jan Mostaert (1475–1555), Lucas van Leyden (1494–1533) and Jan van Scorel (1495–1562). Painters in the city of Utrecht were famous for using chiaroscuro (deep contrast of light and shade), a technique associated with the Italian master Caravaggio.

17th Century (Golden Age)

When the Spanish were expelled from the Low Countries, the character of the art market changed. There was no longer the Church to buy artworks and no court to speak of, so art became a business, and artists were forced to survive in a free market – how very Dutch. In place of Church and court emerged a new, bourgeois society of merchants, artisans and shopkeepers who didn't mind spending money to brighten up their houses and workplaces. The key: they had to be pictures the buyers could relate to.

Painters became entrepreneurs in their own right, churning out banal works, copies and masterpieces in factory-like studios. Paintings were mass-produced and sold at markets alongside furniture and chickens. Soon the wealthiest households were covered in paintings from top to bottom. Foreign visitors commented that even bakeries and butcher shops seemed to have a painting or two on the wall. Most painters specialised in one of the main genres of the day.

Rembrandt van Rijn

Great Rembrandt Paintings

Night Watch (1642; Rijksmuseum)

Peter Denies Christ (1660; Rijksmuseum)

Self Portrait (1628; Rijksmuseum)

The 17th century's greatest artist, Rembrandt van Rijn (1606–69), grew up a miller's son in Leiden, but had become an accomplished painter by his early 20s.

In 1631 he went to Amsterdam to run the painting studio of the wealthy art-dealer Hendrick van Uylenburgh. Portraits were the studio's cash cow, and Rembrandt and his staff (or 'pupils') churned out scores of them, including group portraits such as *The Anatomy Lesson of Dr Tulp*. In 1634 he married Van Uylenburgh's niece, Saskia, who often modelled for him.

Rembrandt fell out with his boss, but his wife's capital helped him buy the sumptuous house next door to Van Uylenburgh's studio (the current Museum het Rembrandthuis). There Rembrandt set up his own studio, with staff who worked in a warehouse in the Jordaan. These were happy years: his paintings were a success and his studio became the largest in Holland, though his gruff manner and open agnosticism didn't win him dinner-party invitations from the elite.

Rembrandt became one of the city's biggest art collectors. He was a master manipulator, and not only of images: the painter was also known to have his own pictures bid up at auctions. He often sketched and painted for himself, urging his staff to do likewise. Residents of the surrounding Jewish quarter provided perfect material for his dramatic biblical scenes.

Night Watch

Great Frans Hals Paintings

The Merry Drinker (1628–30; Rijksmuseum)

Wedding Portrait (1622; Rijksmuseum)

Meagre Company (1637; Rijksmuseum)

In 1642, a year after the birth of their son Titus, Saskia died and business went downhill. Although Rembrandt's majestic group portrait *Night Watch* (1642) was hailed by art critics (it's now the Rijksmuseum's prize exhibit), some of the influential people he depicted were not pleased. Each subject had paid 100 guilders, and some were unhappy at being shoved to the background. In response, Rembrandt told them where they could shove their complaints. Suddenly he received far fewer orders.

Rembrandt began an affair with his son's governess, but kicked her out a few years later when he fell for the new maid, Hendrickje Stoffels, who bore him a daughter, Cornelia. The public didn't take kindly to the man's lifestyle and his spiralling debts, and in 1656 Rembrandt went bankrupt. His house and rich art collection were sold and he moved to the Rozengracht in the Jordaan.

Etchings

No longer the darling of the wealthy, Rembrandt continued to paint, draw and etch – his etchings on display in the Museum het Rembrandthuis are some of the finest ever produced. He also received the occasional commission, including the monumental *Conspiracy of Claudius Civilis* (1661) for the city hall, although authorities disliked it and had it removed. In 1662 he completed the *Staalmeesters* (The Syndics) for the drapers' guild and ensured that everybody remained clearly visible, though it ended up being his last group portrait.

Later Works

The works of his later period show that Rembrandt had lost none of his touch. No longer constrained by the wishes of clients, he enjoyed newfound freedom. His works became more unconventional, yet showed an ever-stronger empathy with their subject matter, as in *The Jewish Bride* (1667). The many portraits of his son, Titus, and Hendrickje, and his ever-gloomier self-portraits, are among the most stirring in the history of art.

A plague epidemic between 1663 and 1666 killed one in seven Amsterdammers, including Hendrickje. Titus died in 1668, aged 27 and just married; Rembrandt died a year later, a broken man.

Frans Hals

Another great painter of this period, Frans Hals (c 1582–1666), was born in Antwerp, but lived in Haarlem. He devoted most of his career to portraits, dabbling in occasional genre scenes with dramatic chiaroscuro. His ability to capture his subjects' expressions was equal to Rembrandt's, though he didn't explore their characters as much. Both masters used the same expressive, unpolished brush strokes and their styles went from bright exuberance in their early careers to dark and solemn later on. The 19th-century Impressionists also admired Hals' work. In fact, his *Merry Drinker* (1628–30), in the Rijksmuseum's collection, with its bold brush strokes, could almost have been painted by an Impressionist.

Great Vermeer Paintings

Kitchen Maid (c 1660; Rijksmuseum)

Woman in Blue Reading a Letter (c 1663; Rijksmuseum)

Girl with a Pearl Earring (c 1665; Mauritshuis)

Group Portraits

Hals also specialised in beautiful group portraits, in which the participants were depicted in almost natural poses, unlike the rigid line-ups produced by lesser contemporaries – though he wasn't as cavalier as Rembrandt in subordinating faces to the composition. A good example is the pair of paintings known collectively as *The Regents & the Regentesses of the Old Men's Almshouse* (1664) in the Frans Hals Museum in Haarlem. The museum is a space that Hals knew intimately; he lived in the almshouse.

Vermeer

The grand trio of 17th-century masters is completed by Johannes (also known as Jan) Vermeer (1632–75) of Delft. He produced only 35 meticulously crafted paintings in his career and died poor with 10 children; his baker accepted two paintings from his wife as payment for a debt of more than 600 guilders. Yet Vermeer mastered genre painting like no other artist. His paintings include historical and biblical scenes from his earlier career, his famous *View of Delft* (1661) in the Mauritshuis in Den Haag, and some tender portraits of unknown women, such as the stunningly beautiful *Girl with a Pearl Earring* (c 1665), also hanging in the Mauritshuis.

To comprehend Vermeer's use of perspective, study *The Love Letter* (1670) in the Rijksmuseum.

The Little Street (1658), also in the Rijksmuseum's collection, is Vermeer's only street scene.

Vermeer's work is known for serene light pouring through tall windows. The calm, spiritual effect is enhanced by dark blues, deep reds, warm yellows and supremely balanced composition. Good examples include the Rijksmuseum's *Kitchen Maid* (aka *The Milkmaid*) and *Woman in Blue Reading a Letter*.

Other Golden Age Painters

Around the middle of the century, the focus on mood and subtle play of light began to make way for the splendour of the baroque. Jacob van Ruysdael (c 1628–82) went for dramatic skies, while Albert Cuyp (1620–91) painted Italianate landscapes. Van Ruysdael's pupil Meindert

Hobbema (1638–1709) preferred less heroic, more playful scenes, full of pretty bucolic detail. (Note that Cuyp, Hobbema and Van Ruysdael all have main streets named after them in the Old South and De Pijp districts, and many smaller streets here are named after other Dutch artists.)

Jan Steen was also a tavern keeper, and his depictions of domestic chaos led to the Dutch expression 'a Jan Steen household'.

The genre paintings of Jan Steen (1626–79) show the almost frivolous aspect of baroque. A good example is the animated revelry of *The Merry Family* (1668) in the Rijksmuseum; it shows adults having a good time around the dinner table, oblivious to the children in the foreground pouring themselves a drink.

18th Century

The Golden Age of Dutch painting ended almost as suddenly as it began, when the French invaded the Low Countries in 1672. The economy collapsed and the market for paintings went south with it. Painters who stayed in business concentrated on 'safe' works that repeated earlier successes. In the 18th century they copied French styles, pandering to the fashion for anything French.

The results were competent, but not groundbreaking. Cornelis Troost (1696–1750) was one of the best genre painters, and is sometimes compared to the British artist William Hogarth (1697–1764) for his satirical as well as sensitive portraits of ordinary people; Troost, too, introduced scenes of domestic revelry into his pastels.

Gerard de Lairesse (1641–1711) and Jacob de Wit (1695–1754) specialised in decorating the walls and ceilings of buildings – de Wit's trompe l'œil decorations (painted illusions that look real) in the Bijbels Museum are worth seeing.

Van Gogh Museum's Famous Five

- *Sunflowers (1889)*
- *Wheatfield with Crows (1890)*
- *Self Portrait with Felt Hat (1886–87)*
- *Almond Blossom (1890)*
- *The Bedroom (1888)*

19th Century

The late 18th century and most of the 19th century produced little of note, save for the landscapes and seascapes of Johan Barthold Jongkind (1819–91) and the gritty, almost photographic Amsterdam scenes of George Hendrik Breitner (1857–1923). They appear to have inspired French Impressionists, many of whom visited Amsterdam.

Jongkind and Breitner reinvented 17th-century realism and influenced the Hague School of the last decades of the 19th century. Painters such as Hendrik Mesdag (1831–1915), Jozef Israels (1824–1911) and the three Maris brothers (Jacob, Matthijs and Willem) created landscapes, seascapes and genre works, including Mesdag's impressive *Panorama Mesdag* (1881; located in Den Haag), a gigantic, 360-degree cylindrical painting of the seaside town of Scheveningen viewed from a dune.

Vincent Van Gogh

Without a doubt, the greatest 19th-century Dutch painter was Vincent van Gogh (1853–90), whose convulsive patterns and furious colours were in a world of their own and still defy comfortable categorisation. (A post-Impressionist? A forerunner of expressionism?)

While the Dutch Masters were known for their dark, brooding paintings, it was Van Gogh who created an identity of suffering as an art form, with a morbid style all his own. Even today, he epitomises the epic struggle of the artist: the wrenching poverty; the lack of public acclaim; the reliance upon a patron – in this case, his faithful brother Theo; the mental instability; the untimely death by suicide; and, of course, one of the most iconic images of an artist's self-destruction, the severed ear.

Van Gogh produced an astonishing output of art during his 10-year artistic career, of which 864 paintings and almost 1200 drawings and prints have survived.

The Artist's Legend

Vincent Van Gogh may have been poor – he sold only one painting in his lifetime – but he wasn't old. It's easy to forget from his self-portraits, in which he appears much older (partly the effects of his poverty), that he was only 37 when he died. But his short life continues to influence art to this day.

Born in Zundert in 1853, the Dutch painter lived in Paris with his younger brother Theo, an art dealer, who supported him financially from his modest income. In Paris he became acquainted with seminal artists including Edgar Degas, Camille Pissarro, Henri de Toulouse-Lautrec and Paul Gauguin.

Van Gogh moved south to Arles, Provence, in 1888. Revelling in its intense light and bright colours, he painted sunflowers, irises and other vivid subjects with a burning fervour. He sent paintings to Theo in Paris to sell, and dreamed of founding an artists' colony in Provence, but only Gauguin followed up his invitation. Their differing artistic approaches – Gauguin believed in painting from imagination, Van Gogh painting what he saw – and their artistic temperaments, fuelled by absinthe, came to a head with the argument that led to Van Gogh lopping his ear (which he gave to a prostitute acquaintance) and his subsequent committal in Arles.

In May 1889, Van Gogh voluntarily entered an asylum in St-Rémy de Provence, where he painted prolifically during his one-year, one-week and one-day confinement, including masterpieces like *Irises* and *Starry Night*. While there, Theo sent him a positive French newspaper critique of his work. The following month, Anna Boch, sister of his friend Eugène Boch, bought *The Red Vines* (or *The Red Vineyard;* 1888) for 400 francs (less than €100 today). It now hangs in Moscow's Pushkin Museum.

VAN GOGH

For a moving window into the inner life of Vincent van Gogh, and the extraordinary friendship and artistic connection he shared with his brother Theo, read *Vincent van Gogh: the Letters*. It contains all 902 letters to and from Van Gogh in correspondance with his brother and other confidantes.

Legacy of a Tortured Genius

On 16 May 1890 Van Gogh moved to Auvers-sur-Oise, just outside Paris, to be closer to Theo, but on 27 July that year he shot himself, possibly to avoid further financial burden on his brother, whose wife had just had a baby son, named Vincent, and who was also supporting their ailing mother. Van Gogh died two days later with Theo at his side. Theo subsequently had a breakdown, was also committed, and succumbed to physical illness. He died, aged 33, just six months after Van Gogh.

It would be less than a decade before Van Gogh's talent would start to achieve wide recognition, and by the early 1950s, he had become a household name. In 1990 he broke the record for a single painting (*A Portrait of Doctor Gachet*) at Christie's, which fetched US$82.5 million. Accounting for inflation, it's still one of the highest prices paid at a public auction for art to this day.

Even Van Gogh's last words ring with the kind of excruciating, melancholic beauty that his best paintings express. With Theo at his side, two days after he shot himself in the chest, he's said to have uttered in French '*la tristesse durera toujours*' (the sadness will last forever).

20th Century

De Stijl

De Stijl (The Style), also known as neoplasticism, was a Dutch design movement that aimed to harmonise all the arts by bringing artistic expressions back to their essence. Its advocate was the magazine of the same name, first published in 1917 by Theo van Doesburg (1883–1931). Van Doesburg produced works similar to Piet Mondrian's, though he dispensed with the thick, black lines and later tilted his rectangles at 45 degrees, departures serious enough for Mondrian to call off the friendship.

Throughout the 1920s and 1930s, De Stijl also attracted sculptors, poets, architects and designers. One of these was Gerrit Rietveld (1888–1964), designer of the Van Gogh Museum and several other buildings, but best known internationally for his furniture, such as the *Red Blue Chair* (1918) and his range of uncomfortable zigzag seats that, viewed side-on, formed a 'z' with a backrest.

In 2013, a stunning Arles landscape painting by Van Gogh was found in a Norwegian home. Industrialist Christian Nicolai Mustad bought *Sunset at Montmajour* for his collection in 1908, but banished it to his attic soon after when someone told him it was a fake.

MC Escher

One of the most remarkable graphic artists of the 20th century was Maurits Cornelis Escher (1898–1972). His drawings, lithographs and woodcuts of blatantly impossible images continue to fascinate mathematicians: a waterfall feeds itself; people go up and down a staircase that ends where it starts; a pair of hands draw each other. You can see his work at Escher in het Paleis in Den Haag.

MC Escher's work was greatly influenced by his visit to the Alhambra, the 14th-century Moorish palace in Granada, Spain. The repetitive, interlocking geometric patterns sculpted into the structure's walls and ceilings provided inspiration for his own designs.

CoBrA

After WWII, artists rebelled against artistic conventions and vented their rage in abstract expressionism. In Amsterdam, Karel Appel (1921–2006) and Constant (Constant Nieuwenhuys, 1920–2005) drew on styles pioneered by Paul Klee and Joan Miró, and exploited bright colours and 'uncorrupted' children's art to produce lively works that leapt off the canvas. In Paris in 1945 they met up with the Danish Asger Jorn (1914–73) and the Belgian Corneille (Cornelis van Beverloo, 1922–2010), and together with several other artists and writers formed a group known as CoBrA (Copenhagen, Brussels, Amsterdam). It has been called the last great avant-garde movement.

Their first major exhibition, in the Stedelijk Museum in 1949, aroused a storm of protest (with comments such as 'my child paints like that, too'). Still, the CoBrA artists exerted a strong influence in their respective countries, even after they disbanded in 1951. The Cobra Museum in Amstelveen displays a good range of their works, including colourful ceramics.

MONDRIAN

A major proponent of De Stijl was Piet Mondrian (originally Mondriaan, 1872–1944), who initially painted in the Hague School tradition. After flirting with cubism, he began working with bold rectangular patterns, using only the three primary colours (yellow, blue and red) set against the three neutrals (white, grey and black). He named this style neoplasticism and viewed it as an undistorted expression of reality in pure form and pure colour. His *Composition in Red, Black, Blue, Yellow & Grey* (1920), in the Stedelijk Museum's collection, is an elaborate example.

Mondrian's later works were more stark (or 'pure') and became dynamic again when he moved to New York in 1940. The world's largest collection of his paintings resides in the Gemeentemuseum (Municipal Museum) in his native Den Haag.

Architecture in Amsterdam

It is difficult not to be struck by Amsterdam's well-preserved beauty: the lovely canalscapes depicted in centuries-old paintings remain remarkably unchanged. The city was spared from wartime destruction, and it has been thoughtful about preserving its core from ham-fisted developers. In fact, the enchanting old centre boasts no fewer than 7000 historical monuments, more humpback bridges than Venice and more trees per capita than Paris.

A City Built on Freedom

Above: Oude Kerk (p70)

Unlike many capitals, Amsterdam has few grand edifices to trumpet. There is hardly the space for a Louvre or a Westminster Abbey, which would be out of keeping with Calvinist modesty anyway. But you'll be pressed to find another city with such a wealth of residential architecture, and with an appeal that owes more to understated elegance than to power and pomp.

Amsterdam's beauty was built on freedoms – of trade, religion and aesthetics. Many of its gabled mansions and warehouses were erected by merchants in the Golden Age, with little meddling by city officials. Thus its leading citizens determined the look of the city, in what amounted to an early urban experiment.

Dutch architecture today is one of the country's most successful exports, with names such as Rem Koolhaas and Lars Spuybroek popping up on blueprints from Beijing to Seattle. Back home, rivalry can be intensely local as talents in Amsterdam and Rotterdam jostle for a spot in the architectural pantheon.

Notable Historic Buildings

Oude Kerk (Old Church; Red Light District)

Nieuwe Kerk (New Church; Medieval Centre)

Royal Palace (Medieval Centre)

Amsterdam American Hotel (Southern Canal Ring)

Rijksmuseum (Old South)

Middle Ages

Around the year 1200, Amsterdam was a muddy little trading post on the Amstel river. The soft marshland couldn't support brick, so the earliest houses were made of timber, often with clay and thatched roofs (similar to ones still standing in Amsterdam-Noord today), but even these modest abodes would list into the soggy ground.

Two fires burned down much of the city centre in 1421 and 1452, and wood was sensibly outlawed as a main building material. There was plenty of clay to make brick, but this was too heavy, as was stone.

Engineers solved the problem by driving piles into the peat. Timber gave way to heavier brick, and thatched roofs were replaced by sturdier tile. Eventually brick and sandstone became de rigueur for most structures.

Dutch Renaissance

As the Italian Renaissance filtered north, Dutch architects developed a rich ornamental style that merged the classical and the traditional with their own brand of subtle humour. They inserted mock columns, known as pilasters, into facades and replaced old spout gables with step gables. Sculptures, columns and little obelisks suddenly appeared all over the Canal Ring. Red brick and horizontal bands of white were all the rage, too.

Without a doubt, the best-known talent of this period was Hendrick de Keyser (1565–1621), the city sculptor. He worked with Hendrick Staets, a canal ring planner, and Cornelis Danckerts, the city bricklayer, to produce some of Amsterdam's finest masterpieces, including magnificent canal architecture such as the Bartolotti House. De Keyser also designed several of Amsterdam's churches. His Zuiderkerk (p95), Noorderkerk (p149) and Westerkerk (p116) show off the style of the day with ornate steeples and layouts, and florid details enlivening the walls and roof lines.

One of the city's signature buildings and a Rembrandt favourite, the Montelbaanstoren was built as a defensive tower in 1516. Its octagonal steeple was designed by master architect Hendrick de Keyser in 1606 to house a clock that's still in use today.

Dutch Classicism

During the Golden Age of art in the 17th century, architects such as Jacob van Campen and brothers Philips and Justus Vingboons decided to stick to Greek and Roman classical design, dropping many of De Keyser's playful decorations.

Influenced by Italian architects, the Dutch made facades look like temples and pilasters like columns. All revolved around clever deception. Neck gables with decorative scrolls came into fashion, often crowned by a temple-like roof. Garlands appeared under windows,

Royal Palace (p68)

and red brick, which was prone to crumbling, was hardened with dark paint.

The Vingboons designed the Bijbels Museum (p116) and the fine example at Keizersgracht 319. Don't miss Justus Vingboons' Trippenhuis (p95): it's about as austere as it gets. It was built between 1660 and 1664 for the wealthy Trip brothers, who made their fortune in metals, artillery and ammunition. The most striking hallmarks are up at roof level – chimneys shaped like mortars.

18th-Century 'Louis Styles'

The Gallic-culture craze proved a godsend for architect and designer Daniel Marot, a Huguenot refugee who introduced matching French interiors and exteriors to Amsterdam. Living areas with white stuccoed ceilings were bathed in light that streamed in through sash windows. As the elegant bell gable became a must, many architects opted for the next big thing: a horizontal cornice.

The dignified facades and statuary of the Louis XIV style hung on until about 1750. In rapid succession it was followed by Louis XV style – rococo rocks, swirls and waves – and Louis XVI designs, with pilasters and pillars making a comeback. The late Louis-style Felix Meritis (p123), with its enormous Corinthian half-columns, is an exemplar of the genre.

The most impressive example of Dutch Classicism is Jacob van Campen's town hall (now the Royal Palace). It was the largest town hall in Europe, and was given a precious shell of Bentham sandstone, and a marble interior inspired by the Roman palaces.

19th-Century Neostyles

After the Napoleonic era, the Dutch economy stagnated, merchants closed their pocketbooks and fine architecture ground to a halt. Seen as safe and sellable, neoclassicism held sway until the more prosperous 1860s, when planners again felt free to rediscover the past.

An example of Amsterdam School architecture

The late 19th century was all about the neo-Gothic, harking back to the grand Gothic cathedrals, and the neo-Renaissance. It was around this time that Catholics regained their freedom to worship openly, and built churches like mad in neo-Gothic style.

A leading architect of the period was Pierre Cuypers, known for a skilful design of several neo-Gothic churches. Cuypers also designed two of Amsterdam's most iconic buildings: Centraal Station (p71) and the Rijksmuseum (p167), both of which display Gothic forms and Dutch Renaissance brickwork. A similar melange is CH Peters' General Post Office, now the Magna Plaza (p91).

Around the turn of the century, the neo-Goths suddenly fell out of favour as art nouveau spread its curvy plant-like shapes across Europe. Gorgeous relics of the era include the Amsterdam American Hotel (p139) and the riotous Pathé Tuschinskitheater (p144).

GABLES

Among Amsterdam's great architectural treasures are its magnificent gables – the roof-level facades that adorn the elegant houses along the canals. The gable hid the roof from public view, and helped to identify the house, until the French occupiers introduced house numbers in 1795. Gables then became more of a fashion accessory.

There are four main types of gable: the simple **spout gable**, with diagonal outline and semicircular windows or shutters, that was used mainly for warehouses from the 1580s to the early 1700s; the **step gable**, a late-Gothic design favoured by Dutch Renaissance architects; the **neck gable**, also known as the bottle gable, a durable design introduced in the 1640s; and the **bell gable**, which appeared in the 1660s and became popular in the 18th century.

HOISTS & HOUSES THAT TIP

Many canal houses deliberately tip forward. Given the narrowness of staircases, owners needed an easy way to move large goods and furniture to the upper floors. The solution: a hoist built into the gable, to lift objects up and in through the windows. The tilt allowed loading without bumping into the house front. Some houses even have huge hoist-wheels in the attic with a rope and hook that run through the hoist beam. The forward lean also makes the houses seem larger, which makes it easier to admire the facade and gable – a fortunate coincidence for everyone.

Berlage & the Amsterdam School

The father of modern Dutch architecture was Hendrik Petrus Berlage (1856–1934). He criticised the lavish neostyles and their reliance on the past, instead favouring simplicity and a rational use of materials.

In Berlage's view, residential blocks were a holistic concept rather than a collection of individual homes. Not always popular with city elders, Berlage influenced what became known as the Amsterdamse School (Amsterdam School) and its leading exponents Michel de Klerk, Piet Kramer and Johan van der Mey.

The titans of the Amsterdam School designed buildings of 'Plan South', an ambitious project mapped out by Berlage. It was a productive period: the Beurs van Berlage (p71) displayed the master's ideals to the full, with exposed inner struts and striking but simple brick accents.

Johan van der Mey's remarkable Scheepvaarthuis (p95) was the first building in the Amsterdam School style. It draws on the street layout to reproduce a ship's bow.

De Klerk's Het Schip (p151) and Kramer's De Dageraad (p189) are like fairytale fortresses rendered in a Dutch version of art deco. Their eccentric details are charming, but the 'form over function' ethic meant these places weren't always great to live in.

The Amsterdam School ushered in a new philosophy of city planning, given a boost by the 1928 Olympic Games held in Amsterdam. Humble housing blocks became brick sculptures with curved corners, odd windows and rocket-shaped towers, to the marvel (or disgust) of traditionalists.

Functionalism

As the Amsterdam School flourished, a new generation began to rebel against the movement's impractical and expensive methods. In 1927 they formed a group called 'de 8', influenced by the German Bauhaus school, America's Frank Lloyd Wright and France's Le Corbusier.

Architects such as Ben Merkelbach and Gerrit Rietveld believed that form should follow function and advocated steel, glass and concrete. The Committee of Aesthetics Control didn't agree, however, which is why you'll see little functionalism in the Canal Ring.

After WWII, entire suburbs, such as the sprawling Bijlmermeer in Amsterdam-Zuidoost, were designed along functionalist lines. By the late 1960s, however, resistance had grown against such impersonal, large-scale projects.

Rietveld left Amsterdam the Van Gogh Museum (p170), where the minimalist, open space allows the artist's works to shine.

Must-See Canal Buildings

Bartolotti House (Western Canal Ring)

Entrepotdok (Plantage)

Huis aan de Drie Grachten (Medieval Centre)

Huis met de Hoofden (Western Canal Ring)

DENNIS VAN DE WATER / SHUTTERSTOCK ©

Top: NEMO (p100)
Left: Magna Plaza (p91)

The Whale (p100), designed by De Architekten Cie.

The Present

On the shores of the IJ just east of Centraal Station stands the Oosterdokseiland, a row of landmark buildings that includes the Centrale Bibliotheek Amsterdam (p100) and features a high-density mix of shops, restaurants, offices, apartments and a music conservatorium (p108).

Looking southeast from Centraal Station, you can't miss the green copper snout of NEMO (p100), a science museum designed by Renzo Piano that resembles the prow of a ship. The cubelike glass shell of the Muziekgebouw aan 't IJ (p100) stands not far to the north, on the IJ waterfront. In the Plantage district, a must-see is the huge Entrepotdok (p98). Sprawling half a kilometre along a former loading dock, the crusty shipping warehouses have been recast as desirable apartments, studios and commercial spaces.

Heading east, the Eastern Islands and Eastern Docklands were full of derelict industrial buildings until the 1980s and early '90s, when they got a new lease of life. Borneo, Java and KNSM islands are home to innovative residential projects as well as stylishly repurposed buildings. Striking Docklands' buildings include the residential and commercial complex dubbed the Whale (p100).

Further east is the burgeoning IJburg neighbourhood, on a string of artificial islands some 10km from the city centre. About 45,000 residents are predicted to inhabit the islands by 2025. The curvaceous Enneüs Heerma Brug, dubbed Dolly Parton Bridge by locals, links it to the mainland.

Notable Modern Buildings

NEMO (Eastern Islands)

EYE Film Institute (Amsterdam-Noord)

Muziekgebouw aan 't IJ (Eastern Islands)

The Whale (Eastern Islands)

Centrale Bibliotheek Amsterdam (Eastern Islands)

EYE Film Institute (p85), designed by Delugan Meissl Associated Architects.

Based in Amsterdam, influential architecture firm Concrete has designed projects around the globe, from London's Spice Market to Stuttgart's Mercedes-Benz Museum, Seoul's Hyundai finance outlets and New Jersey's Harborside Plaza skyscrapers. Locally, Concrete designed REM Eiland and the Van Gogh Museum's central hall, among many, many others.

Northwest of Centraal Station and also on the IJ, you'll find the Westerdokseiland, a harbour that has been repurposed. One of the most striking sites in the Western Docklands is the REM Eiland (p155), a 22m-high former pirate-broadcasting rig transformed into a restaurant and bar.

Across the IJ river in Amsterdam-Noord, housing blocks and office towers are springing up on a former industrial estate at the Overhoeks development, where the architectural centrepieces are the EYE Film Institute (p85) and A'DAM Tower (p85).

Exciting projects continue to sweep through the city – watch this space.

ɔog (p109)

Dutch Design

Contemporary Dutch design has a reputation for minimalist, creative approaches to everyday furniture and homewares products, mixed with vintage twists and tongue-in-cheek humour to keep it fresh. In the past two decades or so, what started out as a few innovators has accelerated to become a movement that is putting the Netherlands at the forefront of the industry. Dutch fashion is also reaching far beyond the country's borders, with designs that are vibrant and imaginative, yet practical, too.

The Beginning of a Movement

The Dutch design movement today can be traced back to a handful of designers working in different materials and media around the same time, who started gaining respect at home and abroad.

Providing a key platform was Droog (p109), established in 1993. This design collective works with a community of designers to help produce

Dutch Design Online Resources

Fashion NL (www.fashionnl.com) Blogs, events, shops and designers.

Dutch Design Daily (www.dutchdesigndaily.com) Highlights a new, thought-provoking idea each day.

Dutch Profiles (www.dutchprofiles.com) Local icons explain design concepts in short videos.

their works and sell them to the world, with the partners to make it happen and the connections to facilitate collaborations with big brands.

Signature Droog designs employ surreal wit, such as a chandelier made of 80-plus light bulbs clustered like fish eggs, or an off-centre umbrella, surely inspired by the country's blustery weather.

Design Pioneers

Among the contemporary pioneers was Marcel Wanders, who first drew international acclaim for his iconic Knotted Chair, produced by Droog in 1996. Made from a knotted aramid-and-carbon-fibre thread and resin, Wanders' air drying technique meant it was ultimately shaped by gravity. It's now in the permanent collection of the Museum of Modern Art in New York. In 2001 Wanders founded Moooi (p162) – the name is a play on the Dutch word for 'beautiful', with an additional 'o' symbolising extra beauty and uniqueness. Now a world-leading design label, Moooi also showcases other pioneering designers such as Maarten Baas (best known for his Smoke series of charred timber furniture) and Studio Job (Job Smeets and Nynke Tynagel's neo-Gothic decorative arts).

Other pioneering designers include Droog designer Jurgen Bey, who has strong architectural links, working with interior and public-space design; Hella Jongerius, whose designs include porcelain plates and tiles using new printing techniques; Piet Hein Eek, who works with reclaimed wood; Scholten & Baijings (Stefan Scholten and Carole Baijings), who produce colourful textiles and kitchenware; Hans van Bentum, whose extraordinary giant revolver chandelier can be found in the Jordaan *café*, Proust (p158); and Ineke Hans, whose celebrated recyclable plastic Ahrend 380 chair incorporates a table.

Furniture, product and interior designer Richard Hutten has been involved with Droog since its foundation. Famed for his 'no sign of design' humorous, functional furniture, his works have been exhibited worldwide and are held in the permanent collections of museums including Amsterdam's Stedelijk Museum.

Best Dutch Design Stores

- Droog (Nieuwmarkt)
- Moooi (Jordaan)
- Frozen Fountain (Western Canal Ring)
- Hutspot (De Pijp)
- Mobilia (Southern Canal Ring)
- Raw Materials (Jordaan)
- Edha (Old South)
- Friday Next (Vondelpark)
- Pols Potten (Eastern Islands)
- BeBoB (Western Canal Ring)
- WonderWood (Centre)

Gaining Momentum

The momentum that Wanders, Bey, Hutten and the others generated inspired a new wave of young designers. This second generation focused not just on concept and function, but also on aesthetics. Often starting with traditional influences, their works tend to mix vintage and reclaimed materials, colour and form, resulting in something totally unique. Renowned second-wave makers include Wieki Somers, awarded for designs such as her Merry-go-round Coat Rack and rowboat-shaped Bathboat tub, and Marloes Hoedeman, who designed the interiors of retailer Scotch & Soda and who has more recently dipped into fashion design with her lingerie line, LoveStories.

The Future of Dutch Design

Dutch designers to watch for include Lex Pott, working with raw materials including wood, stone and metal at his studio in the old shipyard at NDSM-werf; Pepe Heykoop, whose recycled objects include his 'Skin Collection' of leftover leather covering modified secondhand pieces; and Mae Engelgeer, a designer who incorporates tufts of colour and texture into towels, rugs and other textiles at her studio in the Eastern Islands.

The waves of intrepid designers have also triggered an explosion of new design stores stocking innovative pieces by established and emerging artists, which continues to feed the industry. Not simply places to

Interior of Andaz Amsterdam (p230)

view the artistic designs, gain inspiration, or even pick up products for your own home or workplace (although they are all that), these accessible galleries frequently incorporate cafes where you can browse design magazines amid the wares (and where, often, even the chair you're sitting on is for sale).

Design & Fashion

Around the same time as the Dutch furniture, product and interior designers were taking flight, so too was a generation of cutting-edge fashion designers.

Veterans of today's contemporary Dutch fashion scene include Cora Kemperman (p145), the label founded by Cora Kemperman and Gloria Kok (who previously worked together at Mac & Maggie), which focuses on well-priced creations – mainly solid colours, floaty, layered separates and dresses in linen, cotton and wool.

The lingerie label Undressed by Marlies Dekkers (p124) was hailed as a new approach in lingerie design; her spin-off lines include Undressed Men, Undressed Secrets (her vintage lingerie collection), Sundressed (beachwear and sunglasses) and Nightdressed (evening wear).

Shoe and accessory designer Hester van Eeghen (p126) creates eye-catching leather shoes and handbags in bright colours, fur, suede, and geometric patterns and prints.

Headed up by Anja Klappe, Agna K (www.agnak.com) teams up with changing young designers to build its classic, well-cut womenswear collections. Eline Starink, who founded her label Amatør (www.amatorcollection.com) in Amsterdam in 2011, creates clothing targeted at young, ambitious businesswomen. Her jackets, suits and dresses are

Best Boutiques for Dutch Fashion

SPRMRKT (Jordaan)

Young Designers United (Southern Canal Ring)

By AMFI (Medieval Centre)

VLVT (Old South)

Nikkie (Old South)

Tenue de Nîmes (Western Canal Ring)

Van Ravenstein (Western Canal Ring)

Centre Neuf (Southern Canal Ring)

sophisticated and cool, fusing stylish colour and materials, but always practical enough to wear while cycling.

Amsterdam fashion house Viktor & Rolf, founded by Viktor Horsting and Rolf Snoeren, is enjoying huge international success. From haute couture to ready-to-wear collections, their range now spans men's and women's apparel, shoes, accessories including eyewear, and fragrances. Collaborations, such as with retail giant H&M, have broadened their appeal.

Dutch retail brands making a global impact include Amsterdam success-story Scotch & Soda (p125), selling its own-label affordable designs for men, women and children, as well as the Amsterdams Blauw denim line and a vintage furniture collection. Amsterdam brand Denham the Jeanmaker (p124) is also making a name for itself in denim wear, both in the city and as far afield as Japan.

Other designers to keep an eye on include Daisy Kroon, who produces brightly coloured, minimally cut womenswear, and Jivika Biervliet, who seeks out and subverts boundaries in her conceptual, wearable menswear lines. Renowned stylist to the stars Danie Bles is earning recognition with ByDanie, her line of bohemian, retro-tinged clothing and accessories for women. Emerging designers Anna + Nina specialise in chic jewellery.

Dutch Design Events

FashionWeek Amsterdam: Twice-yearly runway shows of new season collections

vt wonen&design beurs: Interior design fair with over 300 stalls, held over six days in early October

Elle Festival: Held over a weekend in late October, showcasing emerging Dutch-designed furniture and products

Designer Hotels

Dutch design has now moved beyond furnishings and fashion to become a lifestyle. This is evident at several hotels that have opened in recent years, where design is implicit to the brand.

Take Droog, the trailblazing collective. It expanded its concept to include Hôtel Droog, a complex that houses the Droog store, along with a gallery and cafe, and a guest room (really an apartment, complete with a kitchen and separate bedroom) on the top floor.

Another inspired hotel intersecting the design and fashion spheres is the independent Hotel The Exchange (p227) in Amsterdam's former stock exchange. Created by Otto Nan and Suzanne Oxenaar, who also worked on Amsterdam's Lloyd Hotel (p231), Hotel The Exchange's 61 rooms are dressed 'like models' by young designers from the Amsterdam Fashion Institute. Decor ranges from details such as buttons or embroidery hoops on the walls to eye-popping whole-room concepts such as a gigantic knitted jumper or Rembrandt-esque collar.

Marcel Wanders put his talents to work on the Hyatt's fantastical Andaz Amsterdam (p230), in the city's former public library. Students from Eindhoven's Design Academy let their imaginations run wild creating the rooms at Hotel Not Hotel (p234).

Survival Guide

Transport

ARRIVING IN AMSTERDAM

Most visitors arrive by air at Schiphol International Airport or by train at Centraal Station.

Schiphol is among Europe's busiest airports and has copious air links worldwide, including many on low-cost European airlines. It's the hub of Dutch passenger carrier KLM.

National and international trains arrive at Centraal Station. There are good links with several European cities. The high-speed Thalys runs from Paris (3¼ hours direct, 3¾ hours via Brussels) nearly every hour between 6am and 7pm. **Eurostar** (www.eurostar.com) runs from London (around five hours); it stops in Brussels, where you transfer onward via Thalys. A direct London–Amsterdam route is slated to launch in late 2016, and will cut travel time to four hours. German ICE trains run six times a day between Amsterdam and Cologne (2¾ hours); many continue on to Frankfurt (four hours). For more information on international trains (including ICE), see **NS International** (www.nsinternational.nl).

Eurolines buses connect with all major European capitals. The **Eurolines Ticket Office** (www.eurolines.nl; Rokin 38a; ⌚9am-5pm Mon-Sat; 🚋4/9/14/16/24 Dam) is near the Dam. Bus travel is typically the cheapest way to get to Amsterdam.

Flights, cars and tours can be booked online at lonelyplanet.com/bookings.

Schiphol International Airport

Eighteen kilometres southwest of the city centre, **Schiphol International Airport** (AMS; www.schiphol.nl) has ATMs, currency exchanges, tourist information, car hire, train ticket sales counters, luggage storage, food and free wi-fi. It's easy to reach the city from Schiphol.

Train Trains run to Amsterdam's Centraal Station (€5.10 one way, 17 minutes) 24 hours a day. From 6am to 12.30am they go every 10 minutes or so; hourly in the wee hours. The rail platform is inside the terminal, down the escalator.

Shuttle bus A shuttle van is run by **Connexxion** (www.schipholhotelshuttle.nl; one-way/return €17/27), every 30 minutes from 6am to 9pm, from the airport to several hotels. Look for the Connexxion desk by Arrivals 4.

Bus Bus 197 (€5 one way, 25 minutes) is the quickest way to places by the Museumplein, Leidseplein or Vondelpark. It departs outside the arrivals

CLIMATE CHANGE & TRAVEL

Every form of transport that relies on carbon-based fuel generates CO2, the main cause of human-induced climate change. Modern travel is dependent on aeroplanes, which might use less fuel per kilometre per person than most cars but travel much greater distances. The altitude at which aircraft emit gases (including CO2) and particles also contributes to their climate change impact. Many websites offer 'carbon calculators' that allow people to estimate the carbon emissions generated by their journey and, for those who wish to do so, to offset the impact of the greenhouse gases emitted with contributions to portfolios of climate-friendly initiatives throughout the world. Lonely Planet offsets the carbon footprint of all staff and author travel.

hall door. Buy a ticket from the driver.

Taxi Taxis take 20 to 30 minutes to the centre (longer in rush hour), costing around €47. The taxi stand is just outside the arrivals hall door.

Centraal Station

Centraal Station is in the city centre, with easy transport connections onward. The station has ATMs, currency exchanges, tourist information, restaurants, shops, luggage storage (€10 per day), and national and international train ticket sales. Most accommodation is a short walk or tram ride from the station.

Tram Ten of Amsterdam's 15 tram lines stop at Centraal Station, and then fan out to the rest of the city. For trams 4, 9, 16, 24 and 26, head far to the left (east) when you come out the station's main entrance; look for the 'A' sign. For trams 1, 2, 5, 13 and 17, head to the right (west) and look for the 'B' sign.

Taxi Taxis queue near the front entrance toward the west side. Fares are meter-based. It should be €10 to €15 for destinations in the centre, canal ring or the Jordaan.

TRAIN TRIPS FROM AMSTERDAM

NS (Nederlandse Spoorwegen; www.ns.nl), aka Dutch Railways, runs the nation's rail service. Trains are frequent from Centraal Station and serve domestic destinations such as Haarlem, Leiden and Delft several times per hour, making for easy day trips.
The main service centre to buy tickets for both national and international trains is on the station's west side. The left-luggage lockers are on the east side.

Domestic Tickets

- Tickets can be bought at the NS service desk windows or at ticketing machines. The ticket windows are easiest to use, though there is often a queue.
- Pay with cash, debit or credit card. Visa and MasterCard are accepted, though there is a €0.50 surcharge to use them, and they must have chip-and-PIN technology (which many American cards do not).
- There is a €1 surcharge for buying a single-use disposable ticket. (Locals typically use a personalised, rechargeable plastic chip card, which exempts them from the fee.)
- Visitors can get a non-personalised rechargeable card at NS windows or at GVB public transport offices. It's not that useful unless you'll be travelling a lot by train. It costs €7.50 (non-refundable) and has a €10 minimum balance.
- If you want to use a ticketing machine and pay cash, know that they accept coins only (no paper bills). The machines have instructions in English.
- When choosing between 1st or 2nd class, there's little difference in comfort, but if the train is crowded there are usually more seats in 1st class.
- There are basically two types of domestic train: Intercity (faster, with fewer stops) and Sprinter (slower, stops at each station).
- Check in *and* out with your ticket/card. Tap it against the card reader in the gates or free-standing posts. You'll hear one beep to enter, and two beeps when departing.

International Tickets

- **NS International** (www.nsinternational.nl) has separate windows to buy international tickets. Queues can be long. Upon entering, an agent will give you a numbered ticket. When your number is called, you can proceed to the window.
- Unless you have a credit card with chip-and-PIN technology, you'll need to use cash to buy your ticket on site. There's also a €3.50 to €7.50 booking charge for on-site purchases.
- An alternative is to buy tickets online (where credit cards are accepted), and print your tickets at home or via kiosks at the station. Online purchases do not incur booking fees.
- Be sure to reserve in advance during peak periods.

Bus Station

Buses arrive at **Duivendrecht station** (Stationsplein 3, Duivendrecht), south of the centre, which has an easy metro link to Centraal Station (about a 20-minute trip via metro number 54).

Car

If you're arriving by car, it's best to leave your vehicle in a park-and-ride lot near the edge of town. A nominal parking fee (around €8 per 24 hours) also gets you free public transport tickets. For more info see www.bereikbaar.amsterdam.nl.

GETTING AROUND AMSTERDAM

Central Amsterdam is relatively compact and best seen on foot or by bicycle.

The **GVB** (www.gvb.nl; Stationsplein 10; ⏲7am-9pm Mon-Fri, 8am-9pm Sat & Sun; 🚋1/2/4/5/9/14/16/24 Centraal Station) operates the public transport system, a mix of tram, bus, metro and ferry. Visitors will find trams the most useful option.

The excellent **Journey Planner** (www.9292.nl) calculates routes, costs and travel times, and will get you from door to door, wherever you're going in the city.

Tram

➡ Most public transport within the city is by tram. The vehicles are fast, frequent and ubiquitous, operating between 6am and 12.30am.

➡ On trams with conductors, enter at the rear; you can buy a disposable **OV-chipkaart** (www.ov-chipkaart.nl; 1hr €2.90) or day pass (€7.50) when you board. On trams without conductors (line 5, and some on line 24), buy a ticket from the driver.

➡ When you enter *and* exit, wave your card at the pink machine to 'check in' and 'check out'.

➡ Most tram lines start at Centraal Station and then fan out into the neighbourhoods.

➡ You can pick up tickets, passes and maps at the **GVB Information Office** (www.gvb.nl; Stationsplein 10; ⏲7am-9pm Mon-Fri, 8am-9pm Sat & Sun; 🚋1/2/4/5/9/14/16/24 Centraal Station). It's across the tram tracks from Centraal Station, and attached to the VVV I Amsterdam Visitor Centre.

COMMON TRAM ROUTES

Jordaan & Western Canals	Tram 1, 2, 5, 13
Southern Canal Ring	Tram 1, 2, 5 for Leidseplein; 4, 9 for Rembrandtplein
Vondelpark & the Old South	Tram 1, 2, 5
De Pijp	Tram 16, 24
Nieuwmarkt & Plantage	Tram 9

Metro & Bus

➡ Amsterdam's buses and metro (subway) primarily serve outer districts. Fares are the same as for trams.

➡ *Nachtbussen* (night buses) run after other transport stops (from 1am to 6am, every hour). A ticket costs €4.50.

➡ Note that Connexxion buses (which depart from Centraal Station and are useful to reach sights in South Amsterdam) and the No 197 airport bus are not part of the GVB system. They cost more (around €5).

Bicycle

The vast majority of Amsterdammers get around town on their *fietsen* (bikes). Cycling is a big deal here, we've devoted an entire chapter to the pursuit (p29).

Boat

Canal Bus

The **Canal Bus** (☎217 05 00; www.canal.nl; day pass adult/child €23/11.50; ⏲10am-6pm; 📶; 🚋1/2/5 Leidseplein) offers a unique hop-on, hop-off service among its 16 docks around the city and near the big museums.

Ferry

Free ferries to Amsterdam-Noord depart from piers behind Centraal Station. The ride to Buiksloterweg is the most direct (five minutes) and runs 24 hours; this is how you reach the EYE Film Institute and Tolhuistuin. Another boat runs to NDSM-werf (15 minutes) between 7am and midnight (from 9am weekends). Another goes to IJplein (6.30am to midnight). Bicycles are permitted on all.

Taxi & Rideshare

➡ Taxis are expensive and not very speedy, given Amsterdam's maze of streets.

➡ You don't hail taxis on the road. Instead, find them at stands at Centraal Station, Leidseplein and other busy spots around town. You needn't take the first car in the queue.

➡ Another method is to book a taxi by phone. **Taxicentrale Amsterdam** (TCA; ☎777 77 77; www.tcataxi.nl) is the most reliable company.

➡ Fares are meter-based. The meter starts at €2.95, then it's €2.17 per kilometre thereafter. A ride from Leidseplein to the Dam runs about €12; from

Centraal Station to Jordaan is €10 to €15.

➡ The rideshare company **Uber** (www.uber.com) is also popular in Amsterdam. UberX is the legal, low-cost service that operates citywide.

Car & Motorcycle

We absolutely advise against having a car in Amsterdam, but if you must, read on.

Parking

➡ Pay-and-display applies in the central zone from 9am to midnight Monday to Saturday, and noon to midnight on Sunday.

➡ Costs are around €5/30 per hour/day in most of the city centre and Canal Ring, and around €4/25 in the Jordaan, Old South and around. Prices ease as you move away from the centre.

➡ Parking garages include locations at Damrak, near Leidseplein and under Museumplein and the Stopera, but they're often full and cost more than street parking.

➡ It's best to leave your vehicle in a park-and-ride lot near the edge of town. See www.bereikbaar.amsterdam.nl for details.

Road Rules

➡ Drive on the right-hand side of the road.

➡ Seat belts are required for everyone in a vehicle.

➡ Children under 12 must ride in the back if there's room.

➡ Be alert for bicycles, and if you are trying to turn right, be aware that bikes going straight ahead have priority.

➡ Trams always have right of way.

➡ On roundabouts (traffic circles), approaching vehicles have right of way, unless there are traffic signs indicating otherwise.

➡ The blood-alcohol limit when driving is 0.05%.

Automobile Association

The **ANWB** (www.anwb.nl) is the Netherlands' auto association. Members of auto associations in their home countries (the AAA, CAA etc) can get assistance, free maps, discounts and more.

Rental

Requirements for renting a car in the Netherlands:

➡ Be able to show a valid driving license from your home country.

➡ Be at least 23 years of age (some companies levy a small surcharge – €10 or so – for drivers under 25).

➡ Have a major credit card.

RENTAL AGENTS

Note most cars do *not* have an automatic transmission. If you need this, request it and be prepared for a hefty surcharge.

All the big multinational rental companies are here; many have offices on Overtoom, near Vondelpark. Rates start at around €45 per day, but they change frequently, so call around. Rentals at Schiphol Airport incur a surcharge. Companies include:

Avis (www.avis.nl)

Enterprise (www.enterprise.nl)

Europcar (www.europcar.com)

Hertz (www.hertz.nl)

Sixt (www.sixt.com)

TRAVEL PASSES

➡ Travel passes are extremely handy and provide substantial savings over per-ride ticket purchases.

➡ The GVB offers unlimited-ride passes for one to seven days (€7.50/12/16.50/21/26/29.50/32), valid on trams, some buses and the metro.

➡ Passes are available at the GVB office, **VVV I Amsterdam Visitor Centres** (Map p300; www.iamsterdam.com; Stationsplein 10; ⌚9am-6pm; 🚊4/9/16/24 Centraal Station) and from tram conductors (one- and two-day passes only).

➡ The **I Amsterdam Card** (www.iamsterdam.com; per 24/48/72hr €49/59/69) includes a GVB travel pass in its fee.

➡ A wider-ranging option is the Amsterdam & Region Day Ticket (€13.50), which goes beyond the tram/metro system, adding on night buses, airport buses, Connexxion buses and regional EBS buses that go to towns such as Haarlem, Muiden and Zaanse Schans. The pass is available at the GVB office and at visitor centres.

➡ Just to confuse you, there is yet another choice: the Amsterdam Travel Ticket (per one/two/three days €15/20/25). It's basically a GVB unlimited-ride pass with an airport train ticket added on. Buy it at the airport (at the NS ticket window) or GVB office.

TOURS

For cycling tours, see p29. For an architecture tour, see p98. Favourite walking tours include the following:

Prostitution Information Centre Red Light District Tour (Map p300; www.pic-amsterdam.com; Enge Kerksteeg 3; tours €15; ⏲5pm Sat year-round, plus 6.30pm Wed Jun-Aug; 🚊4/9/16/24 Dam) The nonprofit **Prostitution Information Centre** (PIC; ☎420 73 28; ⏲10am-5pm Wed-Fri, to 7pm Sat) offers fascinating one-hour tours of the Red Light District, where guides explain the details of how the business works and take you into a Red Light room. Profits go to the centre; reservations are not necessary.

Sandeman's New Amsterdam Tours (Map p304; www.newamsterdamtours.com; donations encouraged; ⏲10am, 11.15am & 2.15pm; 🚊4/9/16/24 Dam) Energetic young guides working on a tip-only basis lead a three-hour jaunt past the top sights of the Medieval Centre and Red Light District (with a dip into the Jordaan). Meet at the Nationaal Monument on the Dam, regardless of the weather. The tour is first come, first served; to guarantee a spot you can make a reservation.

Hungry Birds Street Food Tours (☎06 1898 6268; www.hungrybirds.nl; per person €69; ⏲11am Mon-Sat) Guides take you 'off the eaten track' to chow on Dutch and ethnic specialities. Tours visit around 10 spots over four hours in De Pijp, Utrechtsestraat, Rembrandtplein and the Spui, from family-run eateries to street vendors. The price includes all food. The Birds offer a tour by bike as well. Book in advance; the meet-up location is given after you make reservations.

Brews and Tales (Map p300;☎06 2889 7599; www.brewsandtales.com; per person €79; ⏲4pm Wed, Fri & Sat; 🚊4/9/16/24 Centraal Station) This fun guided jaunt through the city centre and the Jordaan takes in five bars over the course of four hours, during which time you'll learn about Amsterdam through its indigenous frothy beverages and meaty bar snacks. The price includes all food and drinks. Departure is from the VVV I Amsterdam Visitor Centre by Centraal Station.

Randy Roy's Redlight Tours (Map p300;☎06 4185 3288; www.randyroysredlighttours.com; tours €15; ⏲8pm Sun-Thu, 8pm & 10pm Fri & Sat, closed Dec-Feb; 🚊1/2/5/13/17 Centraal Station) Fun guides provide in-the-know anecdotes about the city's sex life and celebrity secrets on Randy Roy's lively 1½-hour tour. The jaunt ends at a local bar with a free drink. Meet in front of the Victoria Hotel (Damrak 1-5), opposite Centraal Station, rain or shine. Reserving in advance is a good idea.

Drugs Tour (Map p300; www.drugstour.nl; tours by donation; ⏲6pm Fri; 🚊4/9/16/24 Dam) The illuminating, 1½-hour itinerary looks at Amsterdam's drug culture, both its myths and reality. It includes smart shops, a 'user room' (the tour doesn't go inside) and a look at fake drugs being sold on the street. Tours depart by the Oude Kerk. Reserve in advance. Private tours also can be arranged (€40 per four people) in multiple languages.

Mee in Mokum (Map p304; www.gildeamsterdam.nl; Kalverstraat 92; tours €7.50; ⏲11am & 2pm Tue-Sun; 🚊1/2/5 Spui) Mee in Mokum's low-priced walkabouts are led by senior-citizen volunteers who often have personal recollections to add. The tours can be a bit hit or miss, depending on the guide. They depart from the cafe in the Amsterdam Museum. Reserve at least a day in advance.

Directory A–Z

Customs Regulations

For visitors from EU countries, limits only apply for excessive amounts. Log on to www.douane.nl for details.

Residents of non-EU countries are limited to the following:

Alcohol 1L of spirits, wine or beer.

Coffee 500g of coffee, or 200g of coffee extracts or coffee essences.

Perfume 50mL of perfume and 250mL of eau de toilette.

Tea 100g of tea, or 40g of tea extracts or tea essences.

Tobacco 200 cigarettes, or 250g of tobacco (shag or pipe tobacco), or 100 cigarillos, or 50 cigars.

Discount Cards

Visitors of various professions, including artists, journalists, museum conservators and teachers, may get discounts at some venues if they show accreditation.

Students regularly get a few euros off museum admission; bring ID.

Seniors over 65, and their partners of 60 or older, benefit from reductions on public transport, museum admissions, concerts and more. You may look younger, so bring your passport.

I Amsterdam Card (per 24/48/72 hours €49/59/69) Provides admission to more than 30 museums (though not the Rijksmuseum), a canal cruise, and discounts at shops, entertainment venues and restaurants. Also includes a GVB transit pass. Useful for quick visits to the city. Available at VVV I Amsterdam Visitor Centres and some hotels.

Museumkaart (adult/child €55/27.50, plus for first-time registrants €5) Free and discounted entry to some 400 museums all over the country for one year. Purchase at participating museum ticket counters or at Uitburo ticket shops.

Holland Pass (two/four/six attractions €42/62/82) Similar to the I Amsterdam Card, but without the rush for usage; you can visit sights over a month. Prices are based on the number of attractions, which you pick from tiers (the most popular/expensive sights are gold tier). Also includes a train ticket from the airport to the city, and a canal cruise. Available from GWK Travelex offices and various hotels.

PRIOPASS

Priopass (www.priopass.com) is a new ticketing platform to keep an eye on. Many hotels have started to offer it to their customers. The pass – either a printed piece of paper or an electronic version on your mobile phone – provides fast-track entry to most attractions. It's not a discount card: you pay normal rates for museums and tours. But many visitors like it because it's convenient for queue-jumping, there's no deadline for use (so you don't have to scurry around and see several museums in a day to get your money's worth), and you only end up paying for what you use (ie it's not bundled with transit passes, canal cruises, etc). The pass itself is free; you link it to your credit card and get charged as you go along.

Electricity

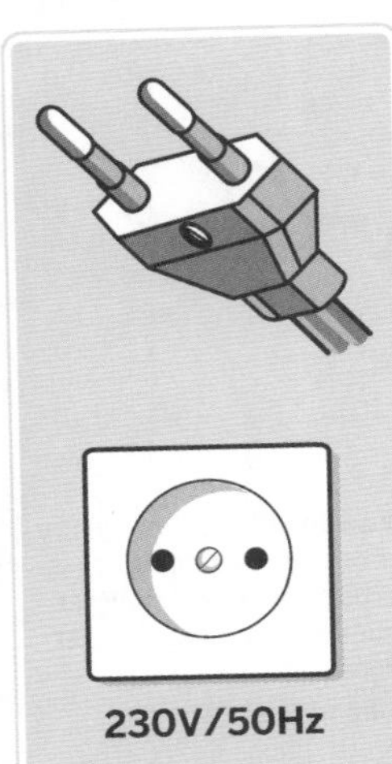

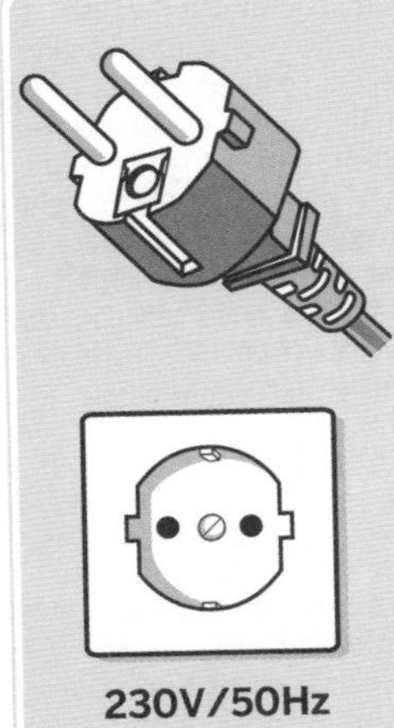

Emergency

Police, fire, ambulance: ☎112

Gay & Lesbian Travellers

The Netherlands was the first country to legalise same-sex marriage (in 2001), so it's no surprise that Amsterdam's gay scene is among the world's largest.

Five hubs of the queer scene party hardest: Warmoesstraat, Zeedijk, Rembrandtplein, Leidseplein and Reguliersdwarsstraat. See p49 for details.

Top festivals include the music-rocking **Milkshake Festival** (www.milkshakefestival.nl) in July, **Amsterdam Gay Pride** (p24) in late July/early August and **Hartjesdagen Zeedijk** (Days of Hearts; www.stichting-hartjesdagen.nl) the third weekend of August.

Resources:

➡ **Gay Amsterdam** (www.gayamsterdam.com) Lists hotels, shops and clubs, and provides maps.

➡ **Pink Point** (Map p310; ☎428 10 70; www.facebook.com/pinkpointamsterdam; Westermarkt; ⏰10.30am-6pm; 🚋13/14/17 Westermarkt) Located behind the Westerkerk, this is part information kiosk, part souvenir shop. It's a good place to pick up gay and lesbian publications, and news about parties, events and social groups.

➡ **Reguliers** (www.reguliers.net) Info on the Reguliersdwarsstraat scene, including current club openings and closings.

➡ **Gay & Lesbian Information and News Center** (www.gaylinc.nl) Lists hotels, restaurants, nightlife and 'sexciting' events around town.

Internet Access

➡ Free wi-fi is common in lodgings across the price spectrum; many places also have a computer on-site for you to use.

➡ Most bars, *cafés* and coffeeshops have free wi-fi. You may need to ask for the code.

➡ Outlets of the public library (Openbare Bibliotheek) usually charge a small fee (€1 per half hour) to use their wi-fi or computer terminals to go online.

➡ For free wi-fi hot spots around the city, check www.wifi-amsterdam.nl.

➡ We've identified listings that have wi-fi (📶) and we've denoted lodgings that offer internet terminals for guest use (@).

Legal Matters

Amsterdam *politie* (police) are pretty relaxed and helpful unless you do something clearly wrong, such as littering or smoking a joint right under their noses.

Police can hold offenders for up to six hours for questioning (plus another six hours if they can't establish your identity, or 24 hours if they consider the matter serious). You won't have the right to a phone call, but they'll notify your consulate. You're presumed innocent until proven guilty.

ID Papers

Anyone over 14 years of age is required by law to carry ID. Foreigners should carry a passport or a photocopy of the relevant data pages; a driver's licence isn't sufficient.

Drugs

➡ Technically, marijuana is illegal. However, possession of soft drugs (eg cannabis) up to 5g is tolerated. Larger amounts are subject to prosecution.

➡ Don't light up in an establishment other than a coffeeshop without checking that it's OK to do so.

➡ Hard drugs are treated as a serious crime.

➡ Never buy drugs of any kind on the street.

Prostitution

Prostitution is legal in the Netherlands. The industry is

protected by law, and prostitutes pay tax. Much of this open policy stems from a desire to undermine the role of pimps and the underworld in the sex industry.

In Amsterdam's Red Light District you have little to fear as the streets are well-policed, but the back alleys are more dubious.

Medical Services

- The Netherlands has reciprocal health arrangements with other EU countries and Australia. If you're an EU citizen, a European Health Insurance Card (EHIC), available from health centres (or, in the UK, post offices), covers you for most medical care. You still might have to pay on the spot, but you should be able to claim it back at home.
- Citizens of other countries are advised to take out travel insurance; medical or dental treatment is less expensive than in North America but still costs enough.
- For minor health concerns, see a local *drogist* (chemist) or *apotheek* (pharmacy, to fill prescriptions).
- For more serious problems, go to the casualty ward of a *ziekenhuis* (hospital).

Referrals

Contact the **Centrale Doktersdienst** (Central Doctors Service; ☎900 15 15; www.doktersdienst.nl; ⏱24hr) for doctor, dentist or pharmacy referrals.

Emergency Rooms

A number of hospitals have 24-hour emergency facilities.

Onze Lieve Vrouwe Gasthuis (☎599 91 11; www.olvg.nl; Oosterpark 9; ⏱24hr; 🚋3/14 Beukenweg) At Oosterpark, near the Tropenmuseum. It's the closest public hospital to the centre of town.

VU Medisch Centrum (☎444 44 44; www.vumc.com; De Boelelaan 1117; ⏱24hr; 🚋16/24 VU Medisch Centrum) Hospital of the Vrije Universiteit (Free University).

Pharmacies

Forget about buying flu tablets and antacids at supermarkets; for anything stronger than toothpaste you'll have to go to a pharmacy.

BENU Apotheek Dam (☎624 43 31; www.dam.benuapotheek.nl; Damstraat 2; ⏱8.30am-5.30pm Mon-Fri, 10am-5pm Sat, noon-5pm Sun; 🚋4/9/16/24/25 Dam) Pharmacy just off the Dam.

Money

The Netherlands uses the euro (€). Denominations of the currency are €5, €10, €20, €50, €100, €200 and €500 notes, and €0.05, €0.10, €0.20, €0.50, €1 and €2 coins (amounts under €1 are called cents).

To check the latest exchange rates, visit www.xe.com.

ATMs

Automatic teller machines can be found outside most banks, at the airport and at Centraal Station. Most accept credit cards such as Visa and MasterCard/Eurocard, as well as cash cards that access the Cirrus and Plus networks. Check with your home bank for service charges before leaving.

ATMs are not hard to find, but they often have queues or run out of cash on weekends.

Cash

A surprising number of businesses do not accept credit cards, so it's wise to have cash on hand.

Changing Money

Generally your best bet for exchanging money is to use **GWK Travelex** (☎0900 05 66; www.gwk.nl), with several branches around town:

GWK Travelex Centraal Station (Stationsplein; ⏱8am-8pm Mon-Sat, 10am-5pm Sun; 🚋4/9/16/24 Centraal Station)

GWK Travelex Leidseplein (Leidseplein 31a; ⏱10.15am-5.15pm Mon-Sat; 🚋1/2/5/7/10 Leidseplein)

GWK Travelex Schiphol Airport (⏱6am-10pm)

Credit Cards

All the major international credit cards are recognised, and most hotels and large stores accept them. But a fair number of shops, restaurants

PRACTICALITIES

Dutch newspapers *De Telegraaf*, the Netherlands' biggest seller; and *Het Parool*, Amsterdam's paper, with the scoop on what's happening around town.

English newspapers *International Herald Tribune* and the *Guardian*, or weeklies such as the *Economist* or *Time*, are widely available on newsstands.

Dutch listings magazines *Uitkrant* and *NL20* are free and you can pick them up around town.

Smoking Amsterdam bans cigarette smoking inside all bars and restaurants, but you're free to light up outdoors on venues' terraces.

and other businesses (including supermarket chain Albert Heijn) do not accept credit cards, or accept only cards with chip-and-PIN technology (which many American cards lack).

Some establishments levy a 5% surcharge (or more) on credit cards to offset the commissions charged by card providers. Always check first.

For a backup plan against the chip-and-PIN issue, consider getting a pre-loaded debit card that has the technology embedded. Many banks provide such cards.

PIN Cards

While in Amsterdam you'll notice people using 'PIN' cards everywhere, from shops to restaurants to cigarette vending machines. These direct-debit cards look like credit or bank cards with little gold-printed circuit chips on them, but they won't be of much use to visitors without a Dutch bank account.

Tipping

Tipping is not essential, as restaurants, hotels, bars etc include a service charge on their bills. A little extra is always welcomed though, and common in certain instances.

Hotel porters	€1–2
Restaurants	5–10% for a cafe snack, 10% or so for a full meal
Taxis	5–10%

Travellers Cheques

Travellers cheques are rare – you'll be hard-pressed to find a bank that will change them for you.

Opening Hours

Hours can vary by season. Our listings depict operating times for peak season (from around May to September). Opening hours often decrease during off-peak months.

Banks 9am–4pm Monday to Friday, some Saturday morning.

Cafés, bars & coffeeshops Open noon (exact hours vary); most close 1am Sunday to Thursday, 3am Friday and Saturday.

Clubs Open around 10pm (exact hours vary); close 4am or 5am Friday and Saturday (a few hours earlier on weekdays).

General office hours 8.30am–5pm Monday to Friday.

Museums 10am-5pm daily, some close Monday.

Restaurants Lunch 11am–2.30pm, dinner 6-10pm.

Shops (large) 9am or 10am to 6pm Monday to Saturday, noon–6pm Sun.

Shops (small) 10am or noon to 6pm Tuesday to Friday, 10am to 5pm Saturday and Sunday, from noon or 1pm to 5pm or 6pm Monday (if open at all). Many shops stay open late (to 9pm) Thursday.

Supermarkets 8am-8pm, though some in the central city stay open until 9pm or 10pm.

Post

The national post office in the Netherlands is privatised and has gone through various name changes. The current operator is **PostNL** (www.postnl.nl). It has closed most city post offices and to mail a letter or package you'll need to go to a postal service shop which may be a supermarket or tobacco shop or something else. Use the website (available in English) to find a location near you. Note that if you're trying to mail a parcel abroad, the staff at the third-party shop may have no idea how to help you.

Public Holidays

Many restaurants and other businesses close for two to six weeks in summer, usually in July or early August.

Banks, schools, offices and most shops close on these days:

Nieuwjaarsdag New Year's Day, 1 January

Goede Vrijdag Good Friday, 25 March 2016, 14 April 2017

Eerste & Tweede Paasdag Easter Sunday and Easter Monday, 27/28 March 2016, 16/17 April 2017

Koningsdag King's Day, 27 April

Bevrijdingsdag Liberation Day, 5 May. It's celebrated officially every five years; the next is in 2020.

Hemelvaartsdag Ascension Day, 5 May 2016, 25 May 2017

Eerste & Tweede Pinksterdag Whit Sunday (Pentecost) and Whit Monday, 15/16 May 2016, 4/5 June 2017

Eerste & Tweede Kerstdag Christmas Day and Boxing Day, 25/26 December

Telephone

The Dutch phone network, **KPN** (www.kpn.com), is efficient, and prices are reasonable by European standards. It's free to make a collect call (*collect gesprek*; domestic ☎0800 01 01, international ☎0800 04 10).

Mobile Phones

The Netherlands uses GSM phones compatible with the rest of Europe and Australia but not with some North American GSM phones. Smartphones such as iPhones will work – but beware of enormous roaming costs, especially for data (buy an international plan from your carrier before you leave home).

Prepaid mobile phones are available at mobile-phone shops, starting from around €35 when on special. You can also buy SIM cards (from €5) for your own GSM mobile phone that will give you a Dutch telephone number. Look for Phone House, T-Mobile and Vodafone shops along Kalverstraat and Rokin.

New prepaid phones generally come with a small amount of call time already stored. To top it up, purchase more minutes at one of the branded stores, news agencies or supermarkets, and follow the instructions. Incoming calls to Dutch mobile phones are generally free to the recipient.

For messaging, a huge percentage of Dutch use **WhatsApp** (www.whatsapp.com).

Phone Codes & Dialling

Phone numbers in the Netherlands are 10 digits long and include a three-digit city code followed by a seven-digit local number. Mobile numbers are also 10 digits; they start with 06 followed by an eight-digit number. Drop the leading 0 on numbers if you're calling from outside the Netherlands.

Netherlands country code ☎31

Amsterdam city code ☎020

Free calls ☎0800

Mobile numbers ☎06

Paid information calls ☎0900, cost varies but are usually between €0.35 and €1.30 per minute.

To call Amsterdam from abroad Dial ☎00 + 31 + 20 + seven-digit local number (drop the leading 0 from the city code).

To call Amsterdam from within the Netherlands Dial ☎020 + seven-digit local number (keep the 0 in the city code).

To call locally within Amsterdam Just dial the seven-digit local number.

To call a Dutch mobile number locally Dial ☎06 + eight-digit local number.

To call internationally from Amsterdam Dial ☎00 + country code + area code + local number (drop the leading 0 from the city code).

Phonecards

➡ For public telephones, cards (for €5, €10 and €20) are available at train station counters, tourist offices, GWK offices and tobacco shops.

➡ KPN's card is the most common but there are plenty of competitors (T-Mobile and Vodafone among them) that usually have better rates.

Time

Amsterdam is in the Central European time zone (the same as Berlin and Paris), GMT/UTC plus one hour. Noon in Amsterdam is 11am in London, 6am in New York, 3am in San Francisco and 9pm in Sydney. For daylight savings time, clocks are put forward one hour at 2am on the last Sunday in March and back again at 3am on the last Sunday in October.

When telling the time, be aware that the Dutch use 'half' to indicate 'half before' the hour. If you say 'half eight' (8.30 in many forms of English), a Dutch person will take this to mean 7.30.

Toilets

Public toilets are not a widespread facility on Dutch streets, apart from the redolent, free-standing public urinals for men in places such as the Red Light District. Many people duck into a *café* or department store. The standard fee for toilet attendants is €0.50.

There's also an app that can help you find the nearest facility. Students at the University of Amsterdam designed **HogeNood** (High Need; www.hogenood.nu) that maps toilets based on your location.

Tourist Information

VVV I Amsterdam Visitor Centre (Map p300; www.iamsterdam.com; Stationsplein 10; ⏲9am-6pm; 🚊4/9/16/24 Centraal Station) Located outside Centraal Station, this office can help with just about anything: it sells the I Amsterdam discount card; theatre and museum tickets; a good city map (€2.50); cycling maps; public transit passes (the GVB transport office is attached); and train tickets to Schiphol Airport. It also books hotel rooms (commission charged). Queues can be long; be sure to take a number when you walk in. VVV is the name for the Netherlands' tourism board, which jointly operates the centre.

VVV I Amsterdam Visitor Centre Schiphol (⏲7am-10pm) Provides hotel bookings, maps and discount cards inside Schiphol International Airport at the Arrivals 2 hall.

Travellers with Disabilities

➡ Travellers with reduced mobility will find Amsterdam moderately equipped to meet their needs.

➡ Most offices and museums have lifts and/or ramps and toilets for the disabled.

➡ Many budget and midrange hotels have limited accessibility, as they are in old buildings with steep stairs and no lifts.

- The city's many cobblestone streets are rough for wheelchairs.
- Restaurants tend to be on ground floors, though 'ground' sometimes includes a few steps.
- Most buses are wheelchair accessible, as are metro stations. Trams are becoming more accessible as new equipment is added. Lines 1, 5, 13, 17 and 26 have lots of elevated stops for wheelchair users. The GVB website denotes which stops are wheelchair accessible.
- Accessible Travel Netherlands publishes a downloadable guide (www.accessibletravelnl.com/blogs/new-city-guide-for-Amsterdam) of restaurants, sights, transport and routes in Amsterdam for those with limited mobility.
- More questions? Check the accessibility guide at **Accessible Amsterdam** (www.toegankelijkamsterdam.nl).

Visas

Tourists from nearly 60 countries – including Australia, Canada, Israel, Japan, New Zealand, Singapore, South Korea, the USA and most of Europe – need only a valid passport to visit the Netherlands for up to three months. EU nationals can enter for three months with just their national identity card or a passport that expired less than five years ago.

Nationals of most other countries need a so-called Schengen visa, valid within the EU member states (except the UK and Ireland), plus Norway and Iceland, for 90 days within a six-month period. Schengen visas are issued by Dutch embassies or consulates overseas and can take a while to process (up to two months). You'll need a passport that's valid until at least three months after your visit, and will have to prove you have sufficient funds for your stay and return journey.

The **Netherlands Foreign Affairs Ministry** (www.government.nl) lists consulates and embassies around the world. Visas and extensions are handled by the **Immigratie en Naturalisatiedienst** (Immigration & Naturalisation Service; www.ind.nl). Study visas must be applied for via your college or university in the Netherlands.

Women Travellers

In terms of safety, Amsterdam is probably as secure as it gets in Europe's major cities. There's little street harassment, even in the Red Light District, although it's best to walk with a friend to minimise unwelcome attention.

Language

Dutch has around 20 million speakers worldwide. As a member of the Germanic language family, Dutch has many similarities with English.

The pronunciation of Dutch is fairly straightforward. It distinguishes between long and short vowels, which can affect the meaning of words, for example, *man* (man) and *maan* (moon). Also note that aw is pronounced as in 'law', eu as the 'u' in 'nurse', ew as the 'ee' in 'see' (with rounded lips), oh as the 'o' in 'note', öy as the 'er y' (without the 'r') in 'her year', and uh as in 'ago'.

The consonants are pretty simple to pronounce too. Note that kh is a throaty sound, similar to the 'ch' in the Scottish *loch*, r is trilled and zh is pronounced as the 's' in 'pleasure'. This said, if you read our coloured pronunciation guides as if they were English, you'll be understood just fine. The stressed syllables are indicated with italics.

Where relevant, both polite and informal options in Dutch are included, indicated with 'pol' and 'inf' respectively.

BASICS

Hello.	*Dag./Hallo.*	dakh/ha·*loh*
Goodbye.	*Dag.*	dakh
Yes./No.	*Ja./Nee.*	yaa/ney
Please.	*Alstublieft.* (pol) *Alsjeblieft.* (inf)	al·stew·*bleeft* a·shuh·*bleeft*
Thank you.	*Dank u/je.* (pol/inf)	dangk ew/yuh
You're welcome.	*Graag gedaan.*	khraakh khuh·*daan*
Excuse me.	*Excuseer mij.*	eks·kew·*zeyr* mey

WANT MORE?

For in-depth language information and handy phrases, check out Lonely Planet's *Dutch Phrasebook*. You'll find it at **shop.lonelyplanet.com**, or you can buy Lonely Planet's iPhone phrasebooks at the Apple App Store.

How are you?
Hoe gaat het met u/jou? (pol/inf) — hoo khaat huht met ew/yaw

Fine. And you?
Goed. — khoot
En met u/jou? (pol/inf) — en met ew/yaw

What's your name?
Hoe heet u/je? (pol/inf) — hoo heyt ew/yuh

My name is ...
Ik heet ... — ik heyt ...

Do you speak English?
Spreekt u Engels? — spreykt ew *eng*·uhls

I don't understand.
Ik begrijp het niet. — ik buh·*khreyp* huht neet

ACCOMMODATION

Do you have a ... room?	*Heeft u een ...?*	heyft ew uhn ...
single	*éénpersoons-kamer*	*eyn*·puhr·sohns·kaa·muhr
double	*tweepersoons-kamer met een dubbel bed*	*twey*·puhr·sohns·kaa·muhr met uhn *du*·buhl bet
twin	*tweepersoons-kamer met lits jumeaux*	*twey*·puhr·sohns·kaa·muhr met lee zhew·*moh*

How much is it per ...?	*Hoeveel kost het per ...?*	hoo·*veyl* kost huht puhr ...
night	*nacht*	nakht
person	*persoon*	puhr·*sohn*

Is breakfast included?
Is het ontbijt inbegrepen? — is huht ont·*beyt* *in*·buh·khrey·puhn

bathroom	*badkamer*	*bat*·kaa·muhr
bed and breakfast	*gasten-kamer*	*khas*·tuhn·kaa·muhr
campsite	*camping*	*kem*·ping
guesthouse	*pension*	pen·*syon*
hotel	*hotel*	hoh·*tel*
window	*raam*	raam
youth hostel	*jeugdherberg*	*yeukht*·her·berkh

DIRECTIONS

Where's the ...?
Waar is ...? — waar is ...

How far is it?
Hoe ver is het? — hoo ver is huht

What's the address?
Wat is het adres? — wat is huht a·*dres*

Can you please write it down?
Kunt u dat alstublieft opschrijven? — kunt ew dat al·stew·*bleeft op*·skhrey·vuhn

Can you show me (on the map)?
Kunt u het mij tonen (op de kaart)? — kunt ew huht mey *toh*·nuhn (op duh kaart)

at the corner	*op de hoek*	op duh hook
at the traffic lights	*bij de verkeers-lichten*	bey duh vuhr·*keyrs*·likh·tuhn
behind	*achter*	*akh*·tuhr
in front of	*voor*	vohr
left	*links*	lingks
near (to)	*dicht bij*	dikht bey
next to	*naast*	naast
opposite	*tegenover*	tey·khuhn·*oh*·vuhr
straight ahead	*rechtdoor*	rekh·*dohr*
right	*rechts*	rekhs

EATING & DRINKING

What would you recommend?
Wat kan u aanbevelen? — wat kan ew *aan*·buh·vey·luhn

What's in that dish?
Wat zit er in dat gerecht? — wat zit uhr in dat khuh·*rekht*

I'd like the menu, please.
Ik wil graag een menu. — ik wil khraakh uhn me·*new*

Delicious!
Heerlijk/Lekker! — *heyr*·luhk/*le*·kuhr

Cheers!
Proost! — prohst

Please bring the bill.
Mag ik de rekening alstublieft? — makh ik duh *rey*·kuh·ning al·stew·*bleeft*

KEY PATTERNS

To get by in Dutch, mix and match these simple patterns with words of your choice:

When's (the next bus)?
Hoe laat gaat (de volgende bus)? — hoo laat khaat (duh *vol*·khun·duh bus)

Where's (the station)?
Waar is (het station)? — waar is (huht sta·*syon*)

I'm looking for (a hotel).
Ik ben op zoek naar (een hotel). — ik ben op zook naar (uhn hoh·*tel*)

Do you have (a map)?
Heeft u (een kaart)? — heyft ew (uhn kaart)

Is there (a toilet)?
Is er (een toilet)? — is uhr (uhn twa·*let*)

I'd like (the menu).
Ik wil graag (een menu). — ik wil khraakh (uhn me·*new*)

I'd like to (hire a car).
Ik wil graag (een auto huren). — ik wil khraakh (uhn *aw*·toh *hew*·ruhn)

Can I (enter)?
Kan ik (binnengaan)? — kan ik (*bi*·nuhn·khaan)

Could you please (help me)?
Kunt u alstublieft (helpen)? — kunt ew al·stew·*bleeft* (*hel*·puhn)

Do I have to (get a visa)?
Moet ik (een visum hebben)? — moot ik (uhn *vee*·zum *he*·buhn)

I'd like to reserve a table for ...	*Ik wil graag een tafel voor ... reserveren.*	ik wil khraakh uhn *taa*·fuhl vohr ... rey·ser·*vey*·ruhn
(two) people	*(twee) personen*	(twey) puhr·*soh*·nuhn
(eight) o'clock	*(acht) uur*	(akht) ewr

I don't eat ...	*Ik eet geen ...*	ik eyt kheyn ...
eggs	*eieren*	*ey*·yuh·ruhn
fish	*vis*	vis
(red) meat	*(rood) vlees*	(roht) vleys
nuts	*noten*	*noh*·tuhn

Key Words

bar	*bar*	bar
bottle	*fles*	fles
breakfast	*ontbijt*	ont·*beyt*
cafe	*café*	ka·*fey*
cold	*koud*	kawt
dinner	*avondmaal*	*aa*·vont·maal

drink list	*drankkaart*	*drang*·kaart
fork	*vork*	vork
glass	*glas*	khlas
grocery store	*kruidenier*	kröy·duh·*neer*
hot	*heet*	heyt
knife	*mes*	mes
lunch	*middagmaal*	*mi*·dakh·maal
market	*markt*	markt
menu	*menu*	me·*new*
plate	*bord*	bort
pub	*kroeg*	krookh
restaurant	*restaurant*	res·toh·*rant*
spicy	*pikant*	pee·*kant*
spoon	*lepel*	*ley*·puhl
vegetarian (food)	*vegetarisch*	vey·khey·*taa*·ris
with/without	*met/zonder*	met/*zon*·duhr

Meat & Fish

beef	*rundvlees*	*runt*·vleys
chicken	*kip*	kip
duck	*eend*	eynt
fish	*vis*	vis
herring	*haring*	*haa*·ring
lamb	*lamsvlees*	*lams*·vleys
lobster	*kreeft*	kreyft
meat	*vlees*	vleys
mussels	*mosselen*	*mo*·suh·luhn
oysters	*oester*	*oos*·tuhr
pork	*varkensvlees*	*var*·kuhns·vleys
prawn	*steurgarnaal*	*steur*·khar·naal
salmon	*zalm*	zalm
scallops	*kammosselen*	*ka*·mo·suh·luhn
shrimps	*garnalen*	khar·*naa*·luhn
squid	*inktvis*	*ingkt*·vis
trout	*forel*	fo·*rel*
tuna	*tonijn*	toh·*neyn*
turkey	*kalkoen*	kal·*koon*
veal	*kalfsvlees*	*kalfs*·vleys

QUESTION WORDS

How?	*Hoe?*	hoo
What?	*Wat?*	wat
When?	*Wanneer?*	wa·*neyr*
Where?	*Waar?*	waar
Who?	*Wie?*	wee
Why?	*Waarom?*	*waa*·rom

Fruit & Vegetables

apple	*appel*	*a*·puhl
banana	*banaan*	ba·*naan*
beans	*bonen*	*boh*·nuhm
berries	*bessen*	*be*·suhn
cabbage	*kool*	kohl
capsicum	*paprika*	*pa*·pree·ka
carrot	*wortel*	*wor*·tuhl
cauliflower	*bloemkool*	*bloom*·kohl
cucumber	*komkommer*	kom·*ko*·muhr
fruit	*fruit*	fröyt
grapes	*druiven*	*dröy*·vuhn
lemon	*citroen*	see·*troon*
lentils	*linzen*	*lin*·zuhn
mushrooms	*paddestoelen*	*pa*·duh·stoo·luhn
nuts	*noten*	*noh*·tuhn
onions	*uien*	*öy*·yuhn
orange	*sinaasappel*	see·*naas*·a·puhl
peach	*perzik*	*per*·zik
peas	*erwtjes*	*erw*·chus
pineapple	*ananas*	*a*·na·nas
plums	*pruimen*	*pröy*·muhn
potatoes	*aardappels*	*aart*·a·puhls
spinach	*spinazie*	spee·*naa*·zee
tomatoes	*tomaten*	toh·*maa*·tuhn
vegetables	*groenten*	*khroon*·tuhn

Other

bread	*brood*	broht
butter	*boter*	*boh*·tuhr
cheese	*kaas*	kaas
eggs	*eieren*	*ey*·yuh·ruhn
honey	*honing*	*hoh*·ning
ice	*ijs*	eys
jam	*jam*	zhem
noodles	*noedels*	*noo*·duhls
oil	*olie*	*oh*·lee
pastry	*gebak*	khuh·*bak*
pepper	*peper*	*pey*·puhr
rice	*rijst*	reyst
salt	*zout*	zawt
soup	*soep*	soop
soy sauce	*sojasaus*	*soh*·ya·saws
sugar	*suiker*	*söy*·kuhr
vinegar	*azijn*	a·*zeyn*

Drinks

beer	*bier*	beer
coffee	*koffie*	*ko*·fee
juice	*sap*	sap
milk	*melk*	melk
red wine	*rode wijn*	*roh*·duh weyn
soft drink	*frisdrank*	*fris*·drangk
tea	*thee*	tey
water	*water*	*waa*·tuhr
white wine	*witte wijn*	*wi*·tuh weyn

EMERGENCIES

Help!
Help! — help

Leave me alone!
Laat me met rust! — laat muh met rust

Call a doctor!
Bel een dokter! — bel uhn *dok*·tuhr

Call the police!
Bel de politie! — bel duh poh·*leet*·see

There's been an accident.
Er is een ongeluk gebeurd. — uhr is uhn *on*·khuh·luk khuh·*beurt*

I'm lost.
Ik ben verdwaald. — ik ben vuhr·*dwaalt*

I'm sick.
Ik ben ziek. — ik ben zeek

It hurts here.
Hier doet het pijn. — heer doot huht peyn

Where are the toilets?
Waar zijn de toiletten? — waar zeyn duh twa·*le*·tuhn

I'm allergic to (antibiotics).
Ik ben allergisch voor (antibiotica). — ik ben a·*ler*·khees vohr (an·tee·bee·*yoh*·tee·ka)

SHOPPING & SERVICES

I'd like to buy ...
Ik wil graag ... kopen. — ik wil khraakh ... *koh*·puhn

I'm just looking.
Ik kijk alleen maar. — ik keyk a·*leyn* maar

Can I look at it?
Kan ik het even zien? — kan ik huht *ey*·vuhn zeen

Do you have any others?
Heeft u nog andere? — heyft ew nokh *an*·duh·ruh

How much is it?
Hoeveel kost het? — hoo·*veyl* kost huht

That's too expensive.
Dat is te duur. — dat is tuh dewr

Can you lower the price?
Kunt u wat van de prijs afdoen? — kunt ew wat van duh preys *af*·doon

SIGNS

Ingang	Entrance
Uitgang	Exit
Open	Open
Gesloten	Closed
Inlichtingen	Information
Verboden	Prohibited
Toiletten	Toilets
Heren	Men
Dames	Women

There's a mistake in the bill.
Er zit een fout in de rekening. — uhr zit uhn fawt in duh *rey*·kuh·ning

ATM	*pin-automaat*	*pin*·aw·toh·maat
foreign exchange	*wisselkantoor*	*wi*·suhl·kan·tohr
post office	*postkantoor*	*post*·kan·tohr
shopping centre	*winkel-centrum*	*wing*·kuhl·sen·trum
tourist office	*VVV*	vey·vey·*vey*

TIME & DATES

What time is it?
Hoe laat is het? — hoo laat is huht

It's (10) o'clock.
Het is (tien) uur. — huht is (teen) ewr

Half past (10).
Half (elf). (lit: half eleven) — half (elf)

am (morning)	*'s ochtends*	*sokh*·tuhns
pm (afternoon)	*'s middags*	*smi*·dakhs
pm (evening)	*'s avonds*	*saa*·vonts

yesterday	*gisteren*	*khis*·tuh·ruhn
today	*vandaag*	van·*daakh*
tomorrow	*morgen*	*mor*·khuhn

Monday	*maandag*	*maan*·dakh
Tuesday	*dinsdag*	*dins*·dakh
Wednesday	*woensdag*	*woons*·dakh
Thursday	*donderdag*	*don*·duhr·dakh
Friday	*vrijdag*	*vrey*·dakh
Saturday	*zaterdag*	*zaa*·tuhr·dakh
Sunday	*zondag*	*zon*·dakh

January	*januari*	*ya*·new·waa·ree
February	*februari*	*fey*·brew·waa·ree
March	*maart*	maart
April	*april*	a·*pril*
May	*mei*	mey
June	*juni*	*yew*·nee
July	*juli*	*yew*·lee
August	*augustus*	aw·*khus*·tus
September	*september*	sep·*tem*·buhr
October	*oktober*	ok·*toh*·buhr
November	*november*	noh·*vem*·buhr
December	*december*	dey·*sem*·buhr

TRANSPORT

Public Transport

Is this the ... to (the left bank)?	*Is dit de ... naar (de linker-oever)?*	is dit duh ... naar (duh *ling*·kuhr·oo·vuhr)
ferry	*veerboot*	*veyr*·boht
metro	*metro*	*mey*·troh
tram	*tram*	trem

platform	*perron*	pe·*ron*
timetable	*dienst-regeling*	*deenst*·rey·khuh·ling

NUMBERS

1	*één*	eyn
2	*twee*	twey
3	*drie*	dree
4	*vier*	veer
5	*vijf*	veyf
6	*zes*	zes
7	*zeven*	*zey*·vuhn
8	*acht*	akht
9	*negen*	*ney*·khuhn
10	*tien*	teen
20	*twintig*	*twin*·tikh
30	*dertig*	*der*·tikh
40	*veertig*	*feyr*·tikh
50	*vijftig*	*feyf*·tikh
60	*zestig*	*ses*·tikh
70	*zeventig*	*sey*·vuhn·tikh
80	*tachtig*	*takh*·tikh
90	*negentig*	*ney*·khuhn·tikh
100	*honderd*	*hon*·duhrt
1000	*duizend*	*döy*·zuhnt

When's the ... (bus)?	*Hoe laat gaat de ... (bus)?*	hoo laat khaat duh ... (bus)
first	*eerste*	*eyr*·stuh
last	*laatste*	*laat*·stuh
next	*volgende*	*vol*·khun·duh

A ticket to ..., please.
Een kaartje naar ... graag. — uhn *kaar*·chuh naar ... khraakh

What time does it leave?
Hoe laat vertrekt het? — hoo laat vuhr·*trekt* huht

Does it stop at ...?
Stopt het in ...? — stopt huht in ...

What's the next stop?
Welk is de volgende halte? — welk is duh *vol*·khuhn·duh *hal*·tuh

I'd like to get off at ...
Ik wil graag in ... uitstappen. — ik wil khraak in ... *öyt*·sta·puhn

Is this taxi available?
Is deze taxi vrij? — is *dey*·zuh *tak*·see vrey

Please take me to ...
Breng me alstublieft naar ... — breng muh al·stew·*bleeft* naar ...

Cycling

I'd like ...	*Ik wil graag ...*	ik wil khraakh ...
my bicycle repaired	*mijn fiets laten herstellen*	meyn feets *laa*·tuhn her·*ste*·luhn
to hire a bicycle	*een fiets huren*	uhn feets *hew*·ruhn

I'd like to hire a ...	*Ik wil graag een ... huren.*	ik wil khraakh uhn ... *hew*·ruhn
basket	*mandje*	*man*·chuh
child seat	*kinderzitje*	*kin*·duhr·zi·chuh
helmet	*helm*	helm

Do you have bicycle parking?
Heeft u parking voor fietsen? — heyft ew *par*·king vohr *feet*·suhn

Can we get there by bike?
Kunnen we er met de fiets heen? — *ku*·nuhn wuh uhr met duh feets heyn

I have a puncture.
Ik heb een lekke band. — ik hep uhn *le*·kuh bant

bicycle path	*fietspad*	*feets*·pat
bicycle pump	*fietspomp*	feets·*pomp*
bicycle repairman	*fietsenmaker*	feet·suhn·*maa*·kuhr
bicycle stand	*fietsenrek*	feet·suhn·*rek*

GLOSSARY

bibliotheek – library

bier – beer

biertje– glass of beer

bitterballen – small, round meat croquettes

broodje – bread roll (with filling)

bruin café – brown *café*; traditional Dutch pub

café – pub, bar; also known as *kroeg*

coffeeshop (also spelt *koffieshop* in Dutch) – cafe authorised to sell cannabis

CS – Centraal Station

drop – salted or sweet liquorice

dwarsstraat – street connecting two (former) canals

eetcafé – *café* serving meals

fiets – bicycle

frites – French fries; also known as *patat*

gezellig – convivial, cosy

gezelligheid – conviviality/ cosiness

gracht – canal

Grachtengordel – Canal Ring

GVB – Gemeentevervoerbedrijf; Amsterdam municipal transport authority

GWK – Grenswisselkantoor; official currency exchanges

hof – courtyard

hofje – almshouse or series of buildings around a small courtyard or garden, such as the Begijnhof

jenever – Dutch gin; also spelled *genever*

kaas – cheese

kade – quay

kerk – church

koffiehuis – coffee house (distinct from a *coffeeshop*)

koninklijk – royal

kroketten – croquettes

markt – town square, market

NS – Nederlandse Spoorwegen; Dutch railway company

OV-chipkaart – fare card for Dutch public transit

pannenkoeken – pancakes

paleis – palace

plein – square

proeflokaal – tasting house

Randstad – literally 'rim city'; the urban agglomeration including Amsterdam, Utrecht, Rotterdam and Den Haag

stamppot – potatoes mashed with another vegetable (eg sauerkraut or kale), served with bacon bits and a smoked sausage

stedelijk – civic, municipal

steeg – alley, lane

straat – street

stroopwafel – thin, syrup-filled waffle

toren – tower

VVV – tourist office

waag – old weigh house

De Wallen – Red Light District

zaal – hall

Behind the Scenes

SEND US YOUR FEEDBACK

We love to hear from travellers – your comments keep us on our toes and help make our books better. Our well-travelled team reads every word on what you loved or loathed about this book. Although we cannot reply individually to your submissions, we always guarantee that your feedback goes straight to the appropriate authors, in time for the next edition. Each person who sends us information is thanked in the next edition – and the most useful submissions are rewarded with a selection of digital PDF chapters.

Visit **lonelyplanet.com/contact** to submit your updates and suggestions or to ask for help. Our award-winning website also features inspirational travel stories, news and discussions.

Note: We may edit, reproduce and incorporate your comments in Lonely Planet products such as guidebooks, websites and digital products, so let us know if you don't want your comments reproduced or your name acknowledged. For a copy of our privacy policy visit lonelyplanet.com/privacy.

OUR READERS

Many thanks to the travellers who used the last edition and wrote to us with helpful hints, useful advice and interesting anecdotes:
Carl Shavitz, Gunnar Gjelstrup, Janine Boeckmann, Jon Kent, Stephen Garone, Yvette van Laar

AUTHOR THANKS

Catherine Le Nevez

Hartelijk bedankt first and foremost to Julian, and to everyone in and around Amsterdam who provided insights, information and good times. *Dank u wel* in particular to Thomas and all in De Pijp. Huge thanks too to my awesome Amsterdam co-author Karla Zimmerman, Netherlands co-author Daniel Schechter, Destination Editor Kate Morgan and all at LP. As ever, *merci encore* to my parents, brother, *belle-sœur* and *neveu*.

Karla Zimmerman

Many thanks to Manon Zondervan, Machteld Ligtvoet and the Amsterdam Press Office, and to Thierry and Julie Lehto, Saskia Maas, Andrew Moskos, Gert-Jan Ruiter and Rachael Teo for sharing their time and excellent info. Deep gratitude to ace co-author Catherine Le Nevez, Kate Morgan and all at LP. Thanks most of all to Eric Markowitz, the world's best partner-for-life, who accompanied me on the journey and drank loads of beers, visited heaps of museums and carried home all of my Dutch chocolates with the patience of a saint.

ACKNOWLEDGMENTS

Cover photograph: 17th century houses and houseboats on Prinsengracht canal, Amsterdam; Frans Lemmens/Getty.

Amsterdam Transport Network Map © GVB Amsterdam. Map designed by Carto Studio, Amsterdam.

THIS BOOK

This 10th edition of Lonely Planet's *Amsterdam* guidebook was researched and written by Karla Zimmerman and Catherine Le Nevez, who also wrote the 9th edition. The 8th edition was written by Karla Zimmerman and Sarah Chandler. This guidebook was commissioned in Lonely Planet's London office, and produced by the following:

Destination Editors Helen Elfer, Kate Morgan

Product Editor Joel Cotterell

Regional Senior Cartographer David Kemp

Book Designer Michael Buick

Assisting Editors Jodie Martire, Monique Perrin, Saralinda Turner

Cover Research Naomi Parker

Thanks to David Carroll, Neill Coen, Dan Corbett, Andi Jones, Anne Mason, Jenna Myers, Karyn Noble, Kirsten Rawlings, Luna Soo, Angela Tinson, Lauren Wellicome

See also separate subindexes for:
EATING P292
DRINKING & NIGHTLIFE P293
ENTERTAINMENT P295
SHOPPING P295
SPORTS & ACTIVITIES P296
SLEEPING P296

Index

Sights 000
Map Pages **000**
Photo Pages **000**

Sights 000
Map Pages **000**
Photo Pages **000**

Sights 000
Map Pages **000**
Photo Pages **000**

EATING

DRINKING & NIGHTLIFE

ENTERTAINMENT

SHOPPING

SPORTS & ACTIVITIES

SLEEPING

Sights 000
Map Pages **000**
Photo Pages **000**

Amsterdam Maps

Sights

- Beach
- Bird Sanctuary
- Buddhist
- Castle/Palace
- Christian
- Confucian
- Hindu
- Islamic
- Jain
- Jewish
- Monument
- Museum/Gallery/Historic Building
- Ruin
- Shinto
- Sikh
- Taoist
- Winery/Vineyard
- Zoo/Wildlife Sanctuary
- Other Sight

Activities, Courses & Tours

- Bodysurfing
- Diving
- Canoeing/Kayaking
- Course/Tour
- Sento Hot Baths/Onsen
- Skiing
- Snorkelling
- Surfing
- Swimming/Pool
- Walking
- Windsurfing
- Other Activity

Sleeping

- Sleeping
- Camping

Eating

- Eating

Drinking & Nightlife

- Drinking & Nightlife
- Cafe

Entertainment

- Entertainment

Shopping

- Shopping

Information

- Bank
- Embassy/Consulate
- Hospital/Medical
- Internet
- Police
- Post Office
- Telephone
- Toilet
- Tourist Information
- Other Information

Geographic

- Beach
- Gate
- Hut/Shelter
- Lighthouse
- Lookout
- Mountain/Volcano
- Oasis
- Park
- Pass
- Picnic Area
- Waterfall

Population

- Capital (National)
- Capital (State/Province)
- City/Large Town
- Town/Village

Transport

- Airport
- Border crossing
- Bus
- Cable car/Funicular
- Cycling
- Ferry
- Metro station
- Monorail
- Parking
- Petrol station
- S-Bahn/Subway station
- Taxi
- T-bane/Tunnelbana station
- Train station/Railway
- Tram
- Tube station
- U-Bahn/Underground station
- Other Transport

Note: Not all symbols displayed above appear on the maps in this book

Routes

- Tollway
- Freeway
- Primary
- Secondary
- Tertiary
- Lane
- Unsealed road
- Road under construction
- Plaza/Mall
- Steps
- Tunnel
- Pedestrian overpass
- Walking Tour
- Walking Tour detour
- Path/Walking Trail

Boundaries

- International
- State/Province
- Disputed
- Regional/Suburb
- Marine Park
- Cliff
- Wall

Hydrography

- River, Creek
- Intermittent River
- Canal
- Water
- Dry/Salt/Intermittent Lake
- Reef

Areas

- Airport/Runway
- Beach/Desert
- Cemetery (Christian)
- Cemetery (Other)
- Glacier
- Mudflat
- Park/Forest
- Sight (Building)
- Sportsground
- Swamp/Mangrove

NIEUWENDAM
SCHELLINGWOUDE
Het IJ
IJ Haven
Rietlandpark
EASTERN ISLANDS
INDISCHE BUURT
Flevopark
WATERGRAAFSMEER
DAPPERBUURT
OOSTERPARKBUURT
TRANSVAALBUURT
Park Frankendael
NOORD
Dijksgracht
Nieuwe Vaart
Entrepotdok
Artis Royal Zoo
Plantage Muidergracht
Singelgracht
Oosterpark
Amstel
CENTRUM
NIEUWMARKT
RED LIGHT DISTRICT
WESTERN CANAL RING
SOUTHERN CANAL RING
Keizersgracht
Prinsengr
Sarphatipark
DE PIJP
Amstelkanaal
WESTERN ISLANDS
JORDAAN
Westerpark
WESTERPARK
OUD WEST
Museumplein
OLD SOUTH
Apollolaan
Beatrixpark
Zuider Amstel Kanaal
NIEUW ZUID
Hugo de Grootgracht
Jacob van Lennepkanaal
Vondelpark
Noorder Amstel Kanaal
DE BAARSJES
Volkstuinenpark Sloterdijkermeer
BOS EN LOMMER
Erasmuspark
Rembrandtpark
2 km
1 mile
0
0
1
2
3
4
5
6
7
8
9
10
11
12
13

AP INDEX

Key on p302

See map p313
See map p310
See map p314
See map p304
Haarlemmer Houttuinen
Haarlemmerstr
Buiten Brouwersstr
Herenmarkt
Binnen Visserstr
Droogbak
Brouwersgracht
Keizersgr
Panaalst
Gouwenaarsst
Nieuwendijk
Smakst
Engelsest
Stromkt
Roommolenstr
Herengr
Herengracht
Langestr
Singel
Koggestr
Spuistr
Korsjespoortst
Teerketelst
Nieuwezijdsarmst
Korte Kolkst
St Jacobsstr
Oude Nieuwstr
Nieuwezijds Voorburgwal
Nieuwezijds Kolk
Kolkst
Oude Brugst
Lijnbaansst
D van Hasseltsst
Mandenmakerssst
Suikerbakkerssst
Nieuwe Nieuwstr
Onze Lieve Vrouwest
St Geertruidenst
Bergstr
Mosterdpotst
St Nicolaasstr
Torensluis
't Hot
Beurspassage
Torenst
Molst
Gravenstr
Zoutst
Damrak
Beursplein
Nieuwe Kerk
Eggertst
Papenbrugst
Damrakst
Valkenst
CENTRUM
Mozes en Äaronstr

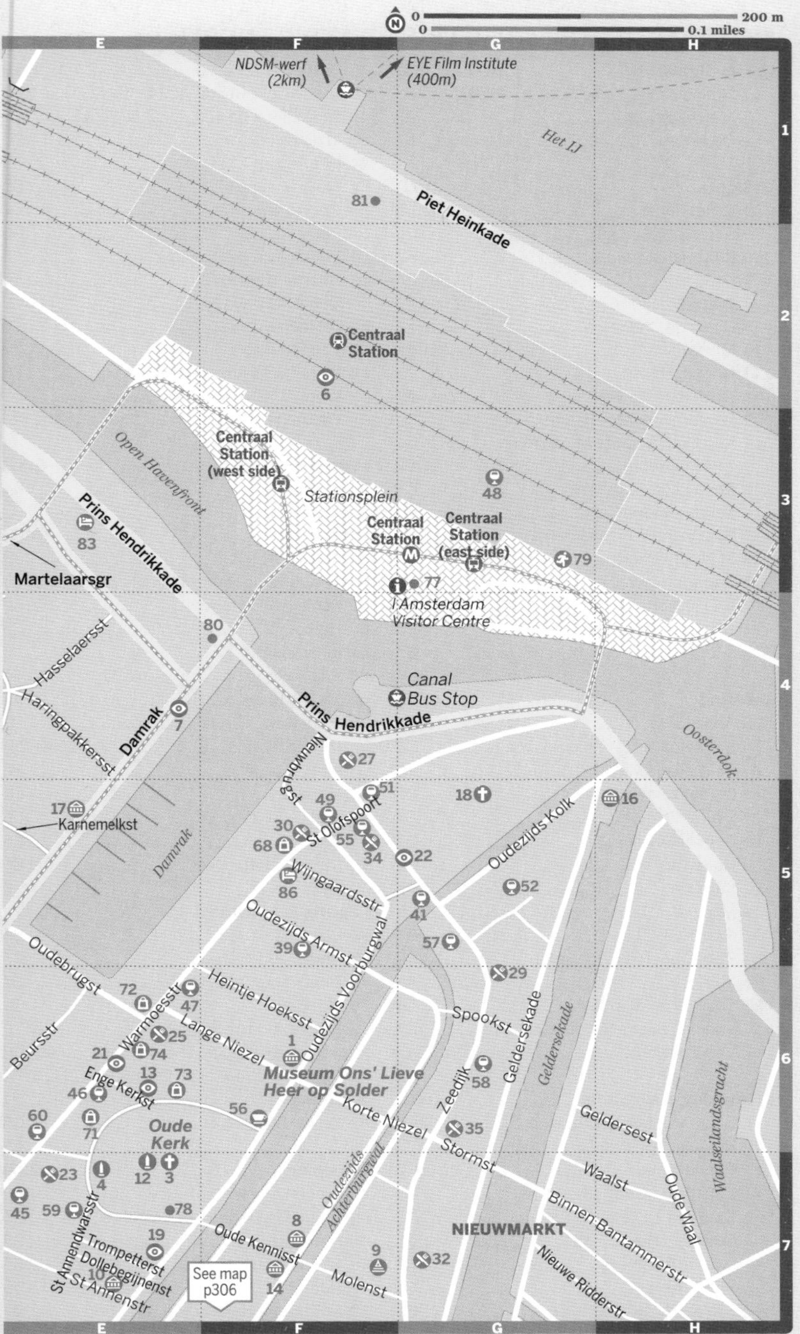

0 200 m
0 0.1 miles
NDSM-werf (2km)
EYE Film Institute (400m)
Het IJ
Piet Heinkade
Centraal Station
Open Havenfront
Centraal Station (west side)
Stationsplein
Centraal Station
Centraal Station (east side)
I Amsterdam Visitor Centre
Prins Hendrikkade
Martelaarsgr
Hasselaersst
Haringpakkersst
Damrak
Canal Bus Stop
Oosterdok
Nieuwbrugst
St Olofspoort
Karnemelkst
Oudezijds Kolk
Wijngaardsstr
Oudezijds Armst
Oudezijds Voorburgwal
Oudebrugst
Warmoesstr
Heintje Hoeksst
Lange Niezel
Spookst
Geldersekade
Beursstr
Enge Kerkst
Museum Ons' Lieve Heer op Solder
Korte Niezel
Zeedijk
Waalseilandsgracht
Oude Kerk
Geldersest
Stormst
Oudezijds Achterburgwal
Waalst
Oude Waal
Binnen Bantammerstr
NIEUWMARKT
St Annendwarsstr
Trompetterst
Dollebegijnenst
St Annenstr
Oude Kennisst
Molenst
Nieuwe Ridderstr
See map p306

MEDIEVAL CENTRE & RED LIGHT DISTRICT NORTH *Map on p300*

MEDIEVAL CENTRE & RED LIGHT DISTRICT SOUTH *Map on p304*

Key on p303

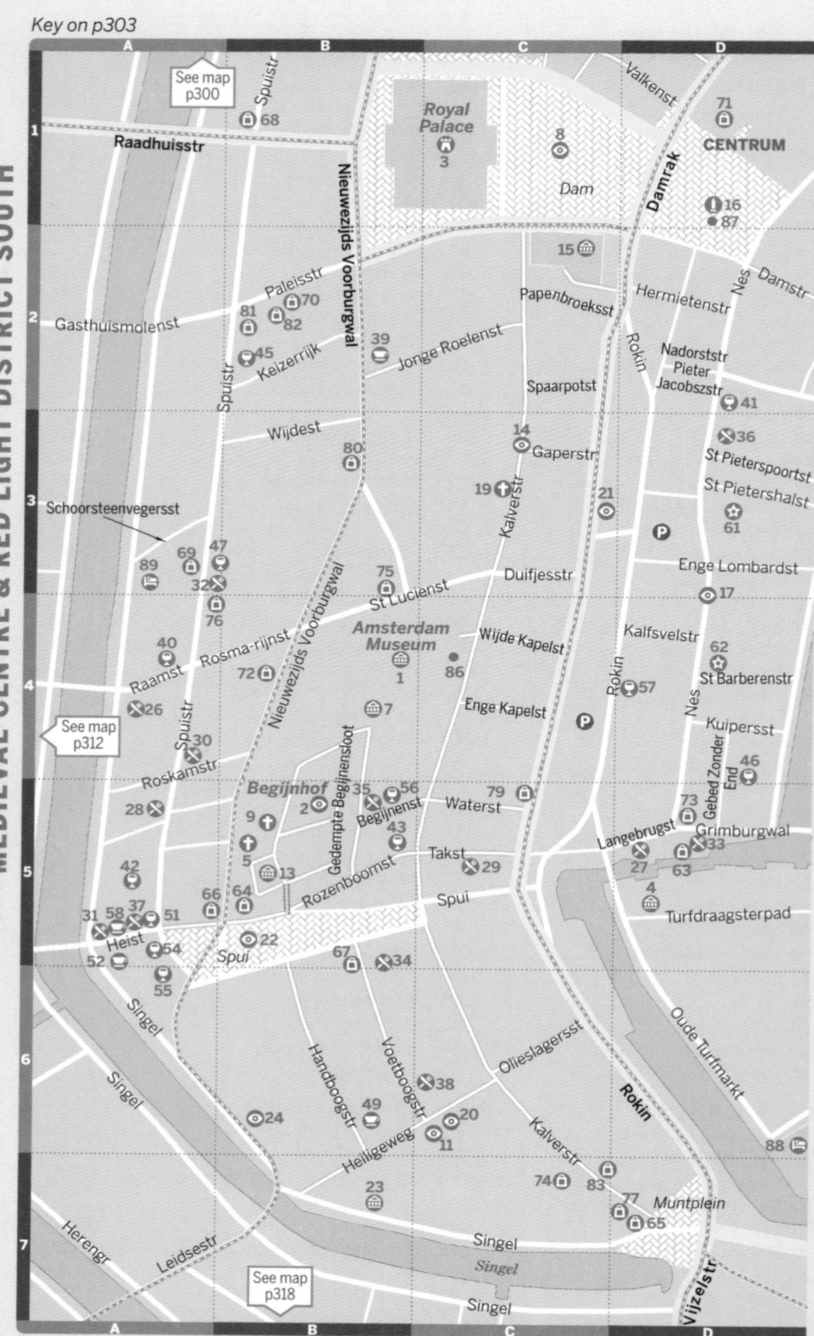

MEDIEVAL CENTRE & RED LIGHT DISTRICT SOUTH
See map p300
See map p312
See map p318
Royal Palace
CENTRUM
Dam
Amsterdam Museum
Begijnhof
Raadhuisstr
Spuistr
Nieuwezijds Voorburgwal
Valkenst
Damrak
Damstr
Nes
Hermietenstr
Papenbroeksst
Rokin
Nadorststr
Pieter Jacobszstr
Gasthuismolenst
Paleisstr
Keizerrijk
Jonge Roelenst
Spaarpotst
Wijdest
Gaperstr
St Pietersspoortst
St Pietershalst
Schoorsteenvegersst
Kalverstr
Duifjesstr
Enge Lombardst
St Lucienst
Rosma-rijnst
Raamst
Wijde Kapelst
Kalfsvelstr
St Barberenstr
Enge Kapelst
Kuipersst
Gebed Zonder End
Roskamstr
Gedempte Begijnensloot
Begijnenst
Waterst
Langebrugst
Grimburgwal
Takst
Rozenboomst
Spui
Heist
Turfdraagsterpad
Singel
Oude Turfmarkt
Olieslagersst
Handboogstr
Voetboogstr
Heiligeweg
Muntplein
Herengr
Leidsestr
Vijzelstr

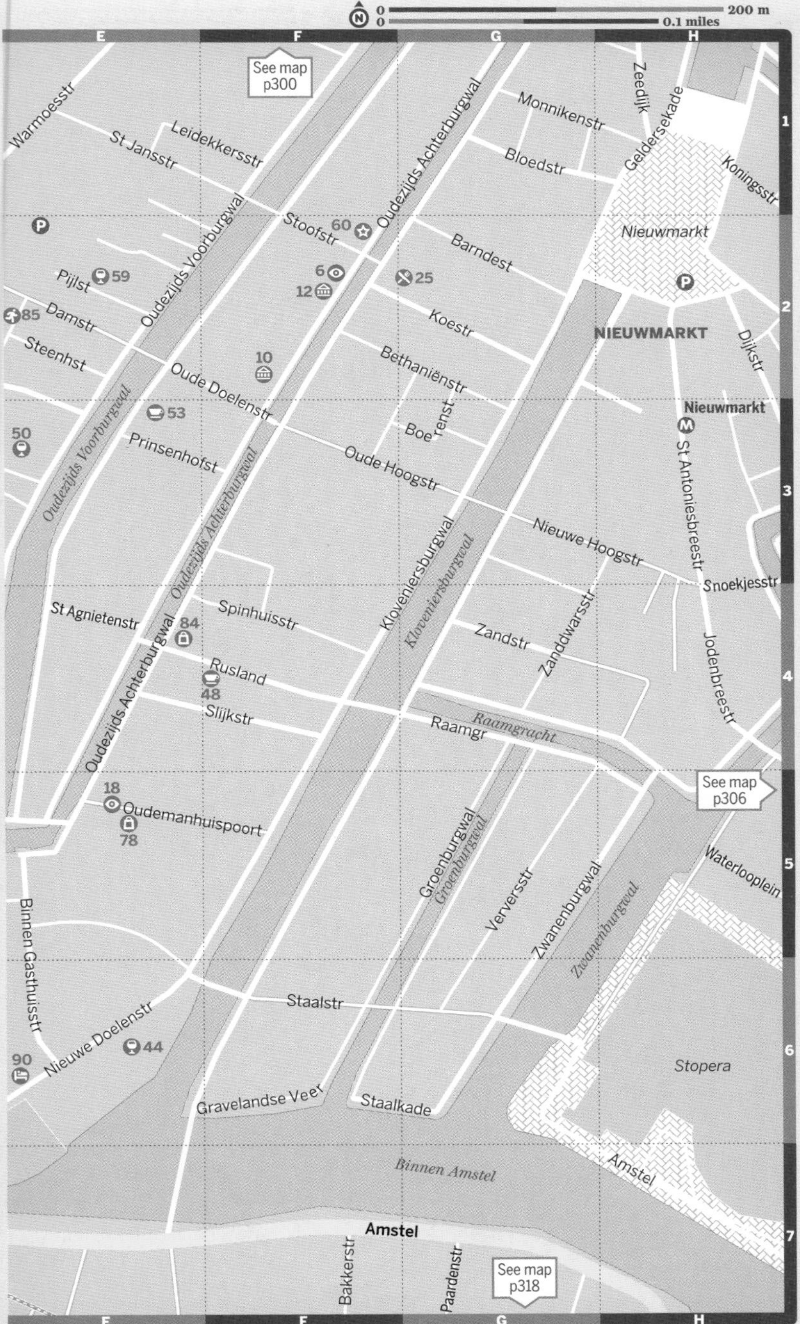
0 200 m
0 0.1 miles
E
F
G
H
1
2
3
4
5
6
7
See map p300
See map p306
See map p318
Warmoesstr
Leidekkersstr
St Jansstr
Oudezijds Achterburgwal
Monnikenstr
Zeedijk
Geldersekade
Koningsstr
Bloedstr
Stoofstr
Barndest
Nieuwmarkt
NIEUWMARKT
Oudezijds Voorburgwal
Pijlst
Damstr
Steenhst
Koestr
Bethaniënstr
Dijkstr
Oude Doelenstr
Boe
renst
Oude Hoogstr
St Antoniesbreestr
Prinsenhofst
Nieuwe Hoogstr
Snoekjesstr
Kloveniersburgwal
St Agnietenstr
Spinhuisstr
Zandstr
Zanddwarsstr
Jodenbreestr
Rusland
Slijkstr
Raamgr
Raamgracht
Oudemanhuispoort
Groenburgwal
Verversstr
Zwanenburgwal
Waterlooplein
Binnen Gasthuisstr
Staalstr
Nieuwe Doelenstr
Stopera
Gravelandse Veer
Staalkade
Binnen Amstel
Amstel
Bakkerstr
Paardenstr
60
6
12
25
59
85
10
53
50
84
48
18
78
44
90

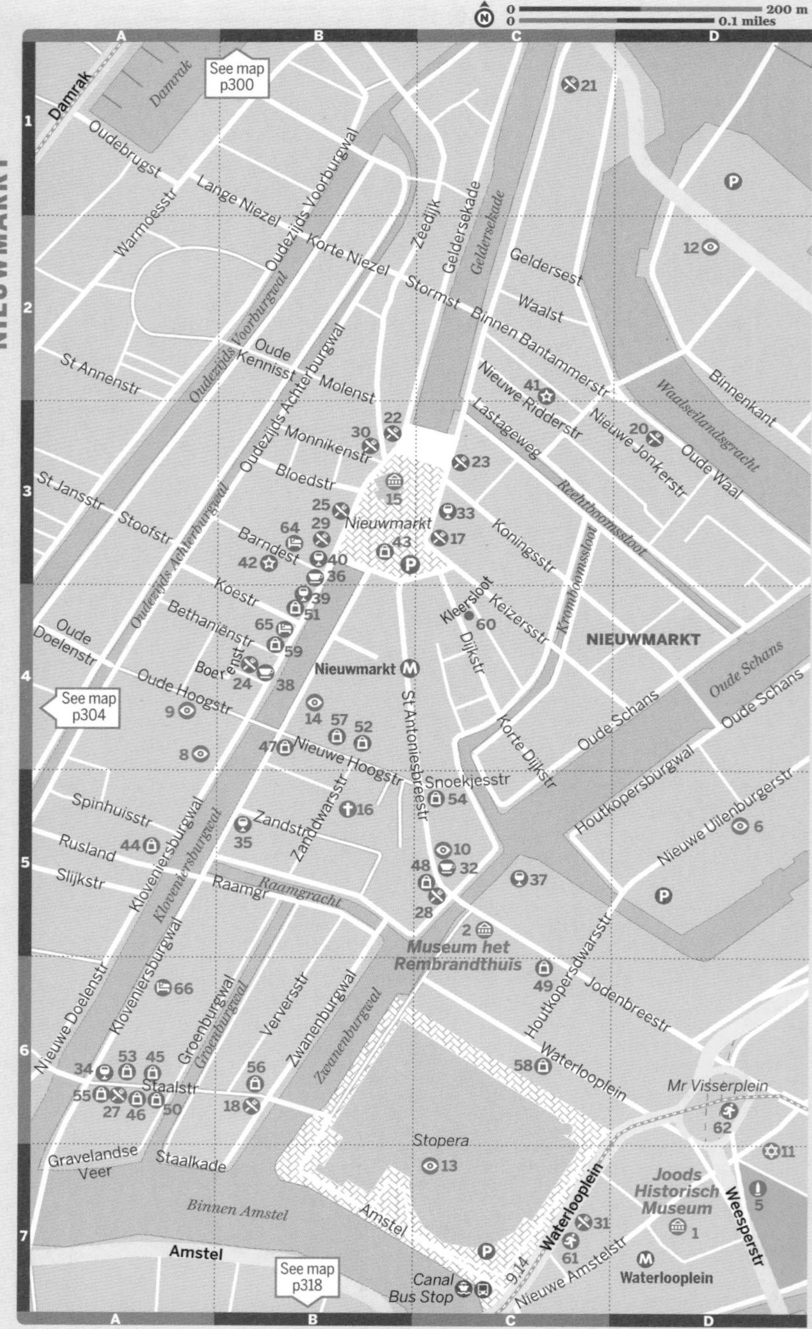
NIEUWMARKT
0 200 m
0 0.1 miles
See map p300
See map p304
See map p318
Damrak
Oudebrugst
Warmoesstr
Lange Niezel
Korte Niezel
Oudezijds Voorburgwal
Oudezijds Achterburgwal
Zeedijk
Geldersekade
Geldersest
Waalst
Stormst
Binnen Bantammerstr
Nieuwe Ridderstr
Nieuwe Jonkerstr
Binnenkant
Waalseilandsgracht
Oude Waal
Lastageweg
Recht Boomssloot
Kromboomssloot
Oude Kennisst
Molenst
Monnikenstr
Bloedstr
St Annenstr
St Jansstr
Stoofstr
Barndest
Koestr
Bethaniënstr
Boerenst
Oude Doelenstr
Oude Hoogstr
Nieuwe Hoogstr
Nieuwmarkt
Koningsstr
Keizersstr
Kleersloot
Dijkstr
Korte Dijkstr
NIEUWMARKT
Oude Schans
St Antoniesbreestr
Snoekjesstr
Zanddwarsstr
Zandstr
Spinhuisstr
Rusland
Slijkstr
Raamgr
Raamgracht
Kloveniersburgwal
Houtkopersburgwal
Nieuwe Uilenburgerstr
Museum het Rembrandthuis
Houtkopersdwarsstr
Jodenbreestr
Waterlooplein
Mr Visserplein
Nieuwe Doelenstr
Groenburgwal
Verversstr
Zwanenburgwal
Staalstr
Gravelandse Veer
Staalkade
Binnen Amstel
Amstel
Stopera
Joods Historisch Museum
Weesperstr
Nieuwe Amstelstr
Canal Bus Stop
9, 14
Waterlooplein

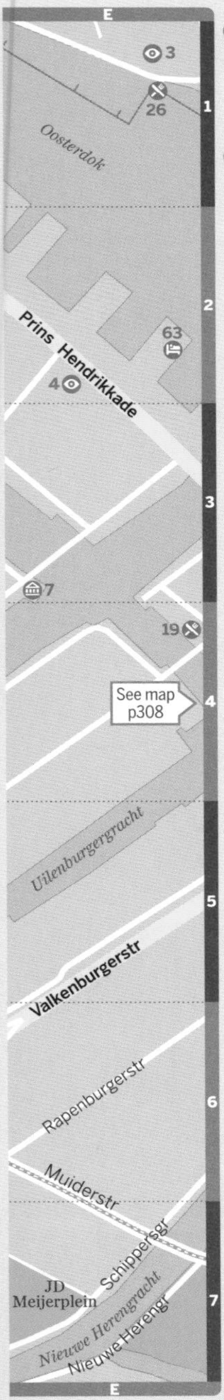
E
3
26
1
Oosterdok
2
63
Prins Hendrikkade
4
3
7
19
See map p308
4
Uilenburgergracht
5
Valkenburgerstr
Rapenburgerstr
6
Muiderstr
Schippersgr
JD Meijerplein
Nieuwe Herengracht
Nieuwe Herengr
7
E

Top Sights (p94)
1 Joods Historisch Museum...D7
2 Museum het Rembrandthuis....C5

Sights (p95)
3 Centrale Bibliotheek Amsterdam.... E1
4 De Appel....E2
5 Dockworker Statue....D7
6 Gassan Diamonds....D5
Kleine Trippenhuis....(see 59)
7 Montelbaanstoren....E3
NAP Visitors Centre ... (see 13)
8 Oostindisch Huis....A4
9 Oude Hoogstraat 22....A4
10 Pintohuis....C5
11 Portuguese-Israelite Synagogue....D7
12 Scheepvaarthuis.... D2
13 Stopera....C7
14 Trippenhuis.... B4
15 Waag....B3
16 Zuiderkerk....B5

Eating (p101)
17 Café Bern.... C3
18 Frenzi.... B6
19 Gebr Hartering....E4
20 Hemelse Modder.... D3
21 Lastage.... C1
22 Latei....B3
Moes....(see 4)
23 Nam Kee.... C3
24 Nyonya.... B4
25 Poco Loco....B3
26 Sea Palace.... E1
27 Sterk Staaltje....A6
28 TisFris....C5
29 Toko Joyce....B3
30 Tokoman....B3
31 Tokoman....C7

Drinking & Nightlife (p105)
Amstelhoeck.... (see 13)
32 Bluebird....C5
33 Cafe Cuba.... C3
34 Café de Doelen....A6
35 Cafe de Engelbewaarder....B5
36 De Bekeerde Suster....B4
37 De Sluyswacht....C5
38 Goa....B4
39 Green Place....B3
40 Lokaal 't Loosje....B3

Entertainment (p108)
41 Amsterdams Marionetten Theater....C2
42 Bethaniënklooster....B3
Muziektheater....(see 13)

Shopping (p109)
Antiques Market....(see 43)
43 Boerenmarkt....B3
44 Book Exchange....A5
45 Droog....A6
46 Filmantiquariaat Cine Qua Non....A6
47 Head Shop....B4
48 Henxs....C5
49 Het Fort van Sjakoo....C6
50 Het Hanze Huis Amsterdam....A6
51 Jacob Hooy & Co....B4
52 Joe's Vliegerwinkel....B4
53 Juggle....A6
54 Knuffels....C5
55 Marbles Vintage....A6
56 Puccini Bomboni....B6
57 't Klompenhuisje....B4
58 Waterlooplein Flea Market....C6
59 Webers....B4

Sports & Activities (p111)
60 Architectuur Tours....C4
61 MacBike....C7
62 TunFun....D6

Sleeping (p230)
63 B&B Le Maroxidien....E2
64 Christian Youth Hostel 'The Shelter City'....B3
65 Misc EatDrinkSleep....B4
66 Stayokay Amsterdam Stadsdoelen....A6

PLANTAGE & THE EASTERN ISLANDS

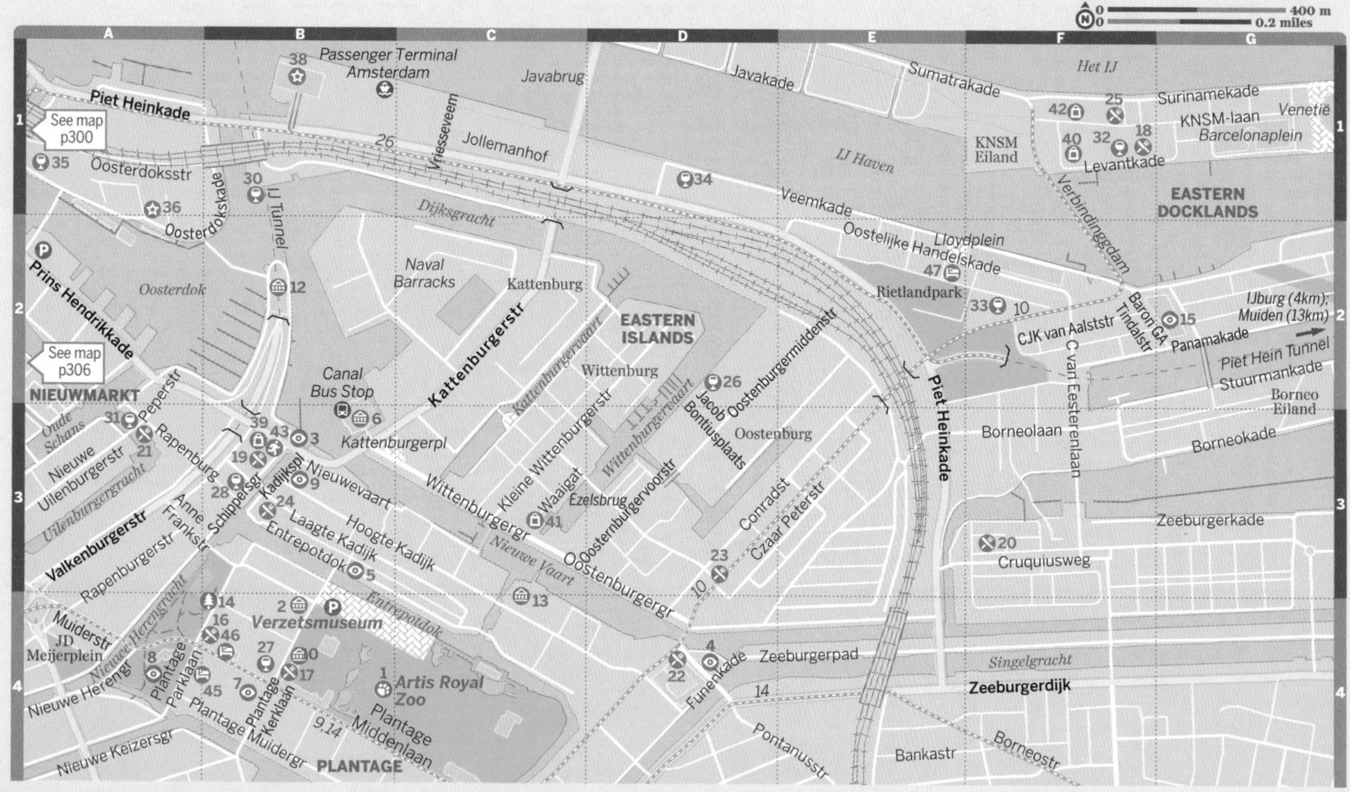

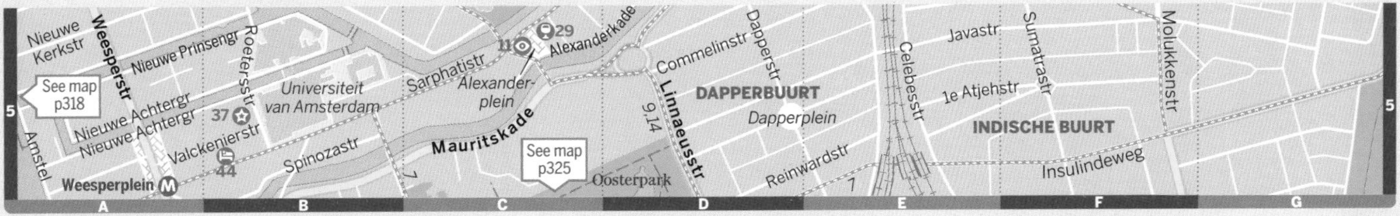

Nieuwe Kerkstr
Weesperstr
Nieuwe Prinsengr
Roeterssstr
Universiteit van Amsterdam
Sarphatistr
Alexanderkade
Alexanderplein
Commelinstr
Dapperstr
DAPPERBUURT
Dapperplein
Celebesstr
Javastr
Sumatrastr
Molukkenstr
1e Atjehstr
INDISCHE BUURT
Nieuwe Achtergr
Valckenierstr
Spinozastr
Mauritskade
Linnaeusstr
Reinwardstr
Insulindeweg
Amstel
Weesperplein
Oosterpark
See map p318
See map p325

Top Sights (p99)
1 Artis Royal Zoo ... B4
2 Verzetsmuseum ... B4

Sights (p97)
3 ARCAM ... B3
4 De Gooyer Windmill ... D4
5 Entrepotdok ... B3
6 Het Scheepvaartmuseum ... B3
7 Hollandsche Schouwburg ... B4
8 Hortus Botanicus ... A4
9 Kadijksplein ... B3
10 Micropia ... B4
11 Muiderpoort ... C5
Muziekgebouw aan 't IJ ... (see 38)
12 NEMO ... B2
13 WerfMuseum 't Kromhout ... C4
14 Wertheimpark ... B4
15 Whale ... G2

Eating (p103)
Café Kadijk ... (see 24)
16 Café Smith en Voogt ... B4
17 De Plantage ... B4
18 De Wereldbol ... F1
19 Éénvistwéévis ... B3
20 Gare de l'Est ... F3
21 Greetje ... A3
22 IJsmolen ... D4
23 Instock ... D3
24 Koffiehuis van den Volksbond ... B3
25 Kompaszaal ... F1
Zouthaven ... (see 38)

Drinking & Nightlife (p106)
26 Amsterdam Roest ... D2
Brouwerij 't IJ ... (see 4)
27 Café Koosje ... B4
Café Orloff ... (see 9)
28 Café Scharrebier ... B3
29 De Groene Olifant ... C5
30 Hannekes Boom ... B1
31 HPS ... A3
32 Kanis & Meiland ... F1
33 KHL ... F2
34 Mezrab ... D1
35 SkyLounge ... A1

Entertainment (p108)
Bimhuis ... (see 38)
36 Conservatorium van Amsterdam ... A1
37 Kriterion ... B5
38 Muziekgebouw aan 't IJ ... B1

Shopping (p110)
39 Datema Amsterdam ... B3
40 De Ode ... F1
41 Frank's Smokehouse ... C3
Imps & Elfs ... (see 42)
42 Loods 6 ... F1
Pols Potten ... (see 42)

Sports & Activities (p111)
43 GlowGolf ... B3

Sleeping (p230)
44 Hotel Allure ... B5
45 Hotel Hortus ... B4
46 Hotel Rembrandt ... B4
47 Lloyd Hotel ... E2

WESTERN CANAL RING NORTH

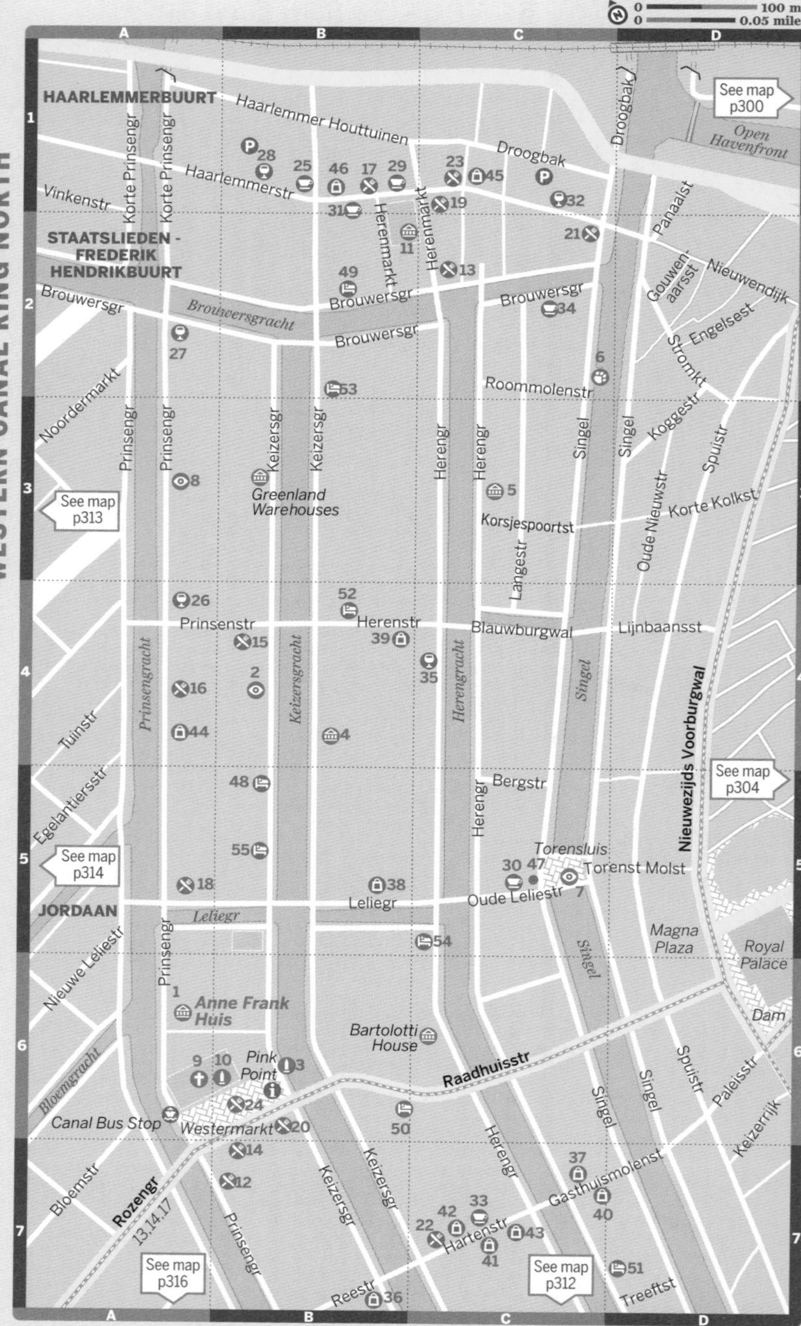

WESTERN CANAL RING NORTH

Top Sights (p114)
1 Anne Frank Huis A6

Sights (p116)
2 De Rode Hoed B4
3 Homomonument B6
4 Huis Met de Hoofden B4
5 Multatuli Museum C3
6 Poezenboot C2
7 Torensluis C5
8 Van Brienenhofje A3
9 Westerkerk A6
10 Westerkerk Bell Tower B6
11 West-Indisch Huis B2

Eating (p118)
12 Bistro Bij Ons B7
13 De Belhamel C2
14 Koh-I-Noor B7
15 Letting B4
16 Pancake Bakery A4
17 Petit Gâteau B1
18 Spanjer en van Twist A5
19 Stout C1
20 Stroopwafel Heaven B6
21 Stubbe's Haring C2
22 Van Harte C7
23 Vinnies Deli C1
24 Wil Graanstra Friteshuis B6

Drinking & Nightlife (p121)
25 Barney's B1
26 Café de Vergulde Gaper A4
27 Café Tabac A2
28 Dulac B1
29 Greenhouse B1
30 Grey Area C5
31 Il Tramezzino B1
32 Jay's Juices C1
33 Screaming Beans C7
34 Siberië C2
35 't Arendsnest C4

Shopping (p123)
36 Amsterdam Watch Company B7
37 Antonia by Yvette C7
38 Architectura & Natura B5
39 BeBoB Design B4
40 Brilmuseum C7
41 Exota C7
42 Gamekeeper C7
43 Hester van Eeghen C7
44 I Love Vintage A4
45 Nukuhiva C1
46 Tenue de Nîmes B1

Sports & Activities (p126)
47 Reypenaer Cheese Tasting C5

Sleeping (p229)
48 Canal House B5
49 Frederic Rentabike B2
50 Hotel Clemens Amsterdam B6
51 Hoxton Amsterdam D7
52 Maes B&B B4
53 Sebastian's B2
54 Sunhead of 1617 C5
55 Toren B5

WESTERN CANAL RING SOUTH

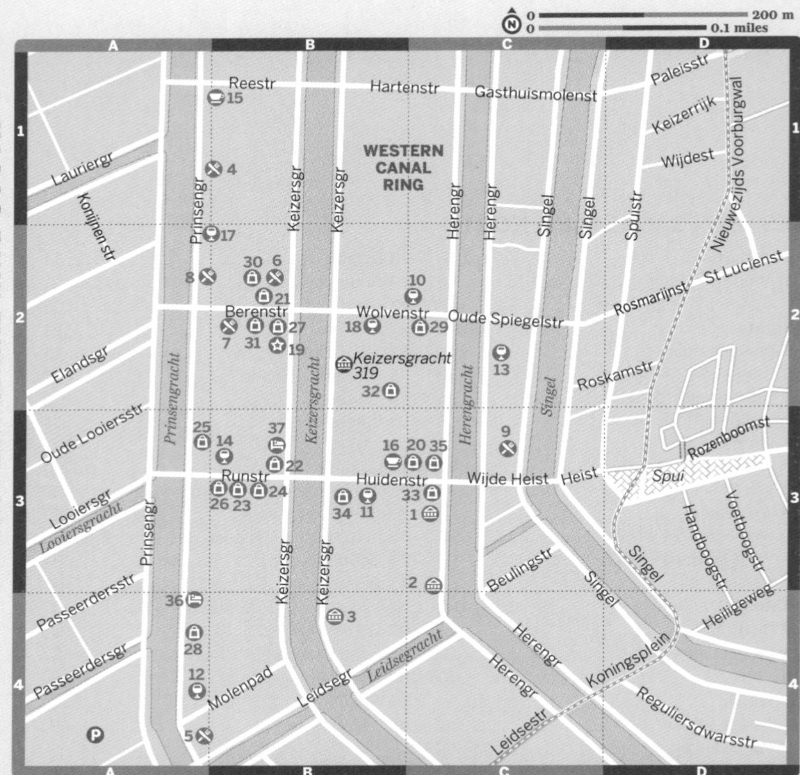

Sights (p116)
1 Bijbels Museum ... C3
2 Het Grachtenhuis ... C3
3 Huis Marseille ... B4

Eating (p118)
4 Café Restaurant van Puffelen ... B1
5 Casa Perú ... A4
6 De Struisvogel ... B2
7 Lunchcafé Nielsen ... B2
8 Pancakes! ... A2
9 Singel 404 ... C3

Drinking & Nightlife (p121)
10 Brix Food 'n' Drinx ... C2
11 Café de Pels ... B3
12 Café Het Molenpad ... A4
13 De Admiraal ... C2
14 De Doffer ... B3
15 Koffiehuis De Hoek ... B1
16 Pâtisserie Pompadour ... B3
17 Vyne ... B2
18 Wolvenstraat 23 ... B2

Entertainment (p123)
19 Felix Meritis ... B2

Shopping (p123)
20 Beadies ... C3
21 Boekie Woekie ... B2
22 Darling ... B3
23 De Kaaskamer ... B3
24 De Witte Tanden Winkel ... B3
25 Denham the Jeanmaker Men's Store ... A3
26 Denham the Jeanmaker Women's Store ... B3
27 Episode ... B2
28 Frozen Fountain ... A4
29 Laura Dols ... C2
30 Marlies Dekkers ... B2
31 Mendo ... B2
32 Negen Straatjes ... B2
33 Scotch & Soda ... C3
34 Van Ravenstein ... B3
35 Zipper ... C3

Sleeping (p229)
36 Andaz Amsterdam ... A4
37 Dylan ... B3

THE WEST

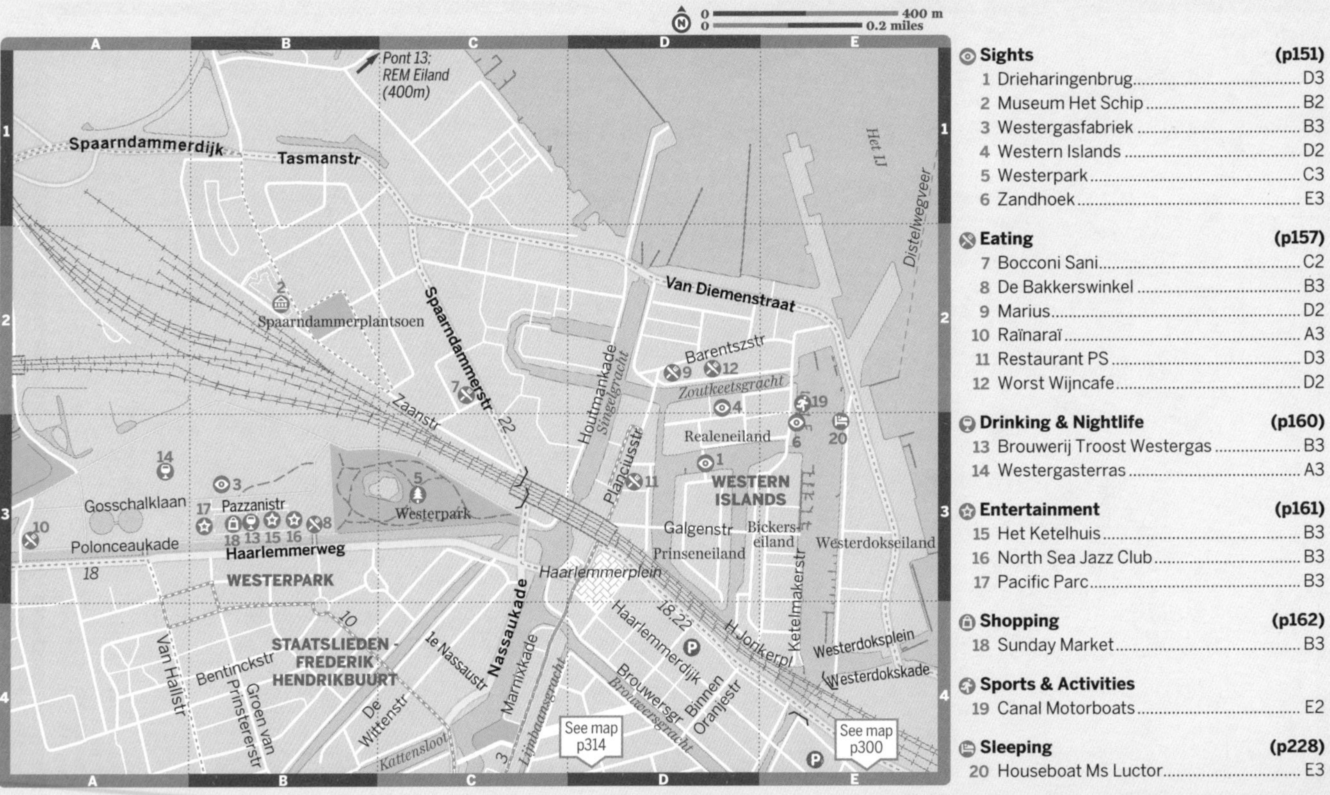

Sights (p151)
1 Drieharingenbrug ... D3
2 Museum Het Schip ... B2
3 Westergasfabriek ... B3
4 Western Islands ... D2
5 Westerpark ... C3
6 Zandhoek ... E3

Eating (p157)
7 Bocconi Sani ... C2
8 De Bakkerswinkel ... B3
9 Marius ... D2
10 Raïnaraï ... A3
11 Restaurant PS ... D3
12 Worst Wijncafe ... D2

Drinking & Nightlife (p160)
13 Brouwerij Troost Westergas ... B3
14 Westergasterras ... A3

Entertainment (p161)
15 Het Ketelhuis ... B3
16 North Sea Jazz Club ... B3
17 Pacific Parc ... B3

Shopping (p162)
18 Sunday Market ... B3

Sports & Activities
19 Canal Motorboats ... E2

Sleeping (p228)
20 Houseboat Ms Luctor ... E3

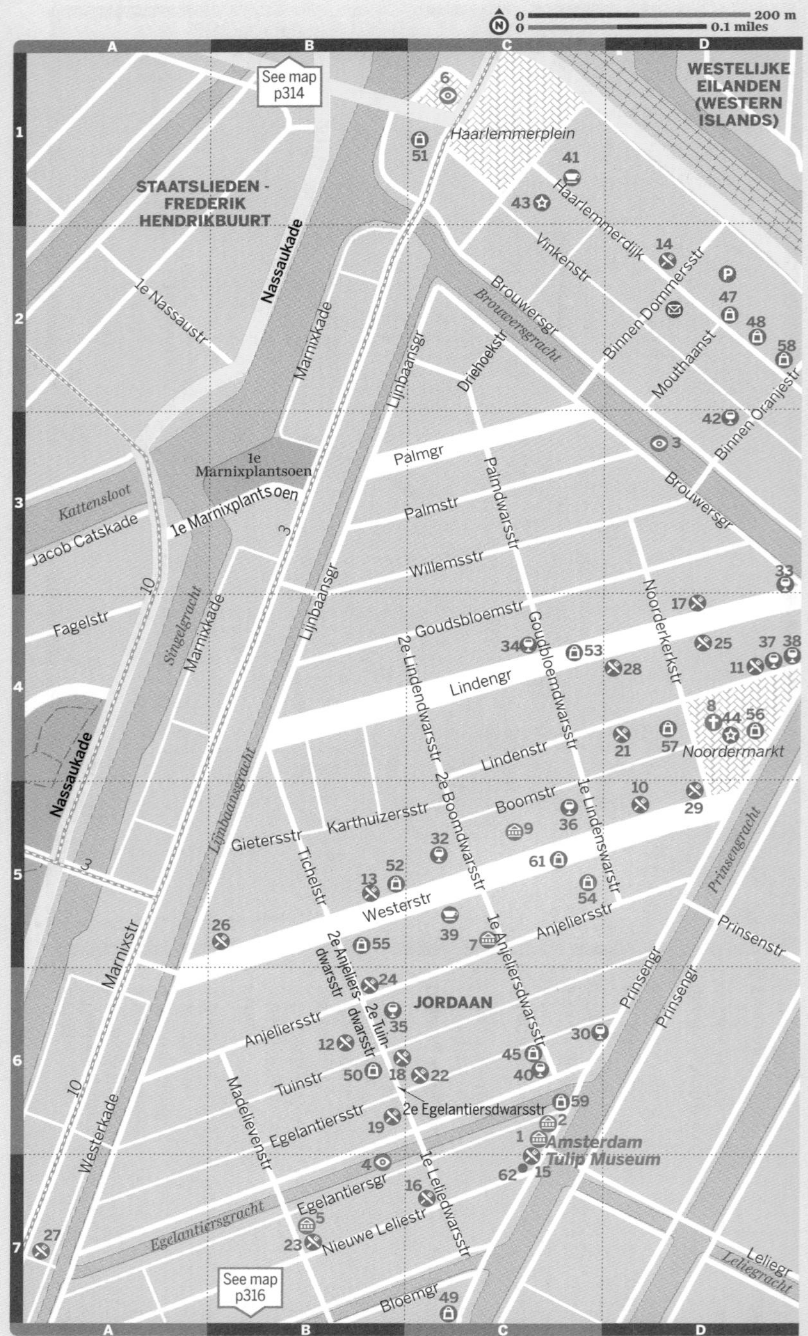
0 200 m
0 0.1 miles
A
B
C
D
1
2
3
4
5
6
7
See map p314
See map p316
WESTELIJKE EILANDEN (WESTERN ISLANDS)
STAATSLIEDEN - FREDERIK HENDRIKBUURT
JORDAAN
Haarlemmerplein
Haarlemmerdijk
Vinkenstr
Brouwersgr
Brouwersgracht
Binnen Dommersstr
Mouthaanst
Binnen Oranjestr
Nassaukade
1e Nassaustr
Marnixkade
Lijnbaansgr
Driehoekstr
Palmgr
Palmstr
Palmdwarsstr
1e Marnixplantsoen
1e Marnixplantsoen
Kattensloot
Jacob Catskade
Willemsstr
Fagelstr
Singelgracht
Goudsbloemstr
Goudbloemdwarsstr
Noorderkerkstr
Lindengr
2e Lindendwarsstr
Lindenstr
Noordermarkt
Boomstr
2e Boomdwarsstr
1e Lindenswarsstr
Karthuizersstr
Gietersstr
Tichelstr
Lijnbaansgracht
Westerstr
Anjeliersstr
1e Anjeliersdwarsstr
2e Anjeliers dwarsstr
2e Tuin dwarsstr
Marnixstr
Prinsengracht
Prinsenstr
Prinsengr
Anjeliersstr
Tuinstr
Madelievenstr
Egelantiersstr
2e Egelantiersdwarsstr
Amsterdam Tulip Museum
Westerkade
Egelantiersgr
Egelantiersgracht
1e Leliedwarsstr
Nieuwe Leliestr
Leliegr
Leliegracht
Bloemgr

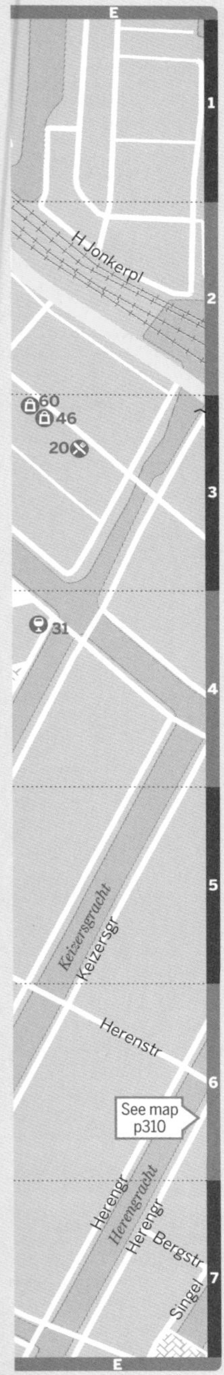

E
1
H Jonkerpl
2
60
46
20
3
31
4
5
Keizersgracht
Keizersgr
Herenstr
6
See map p310
Herengr
Herengracht
Herengr
Bergstr
7
Singel
E

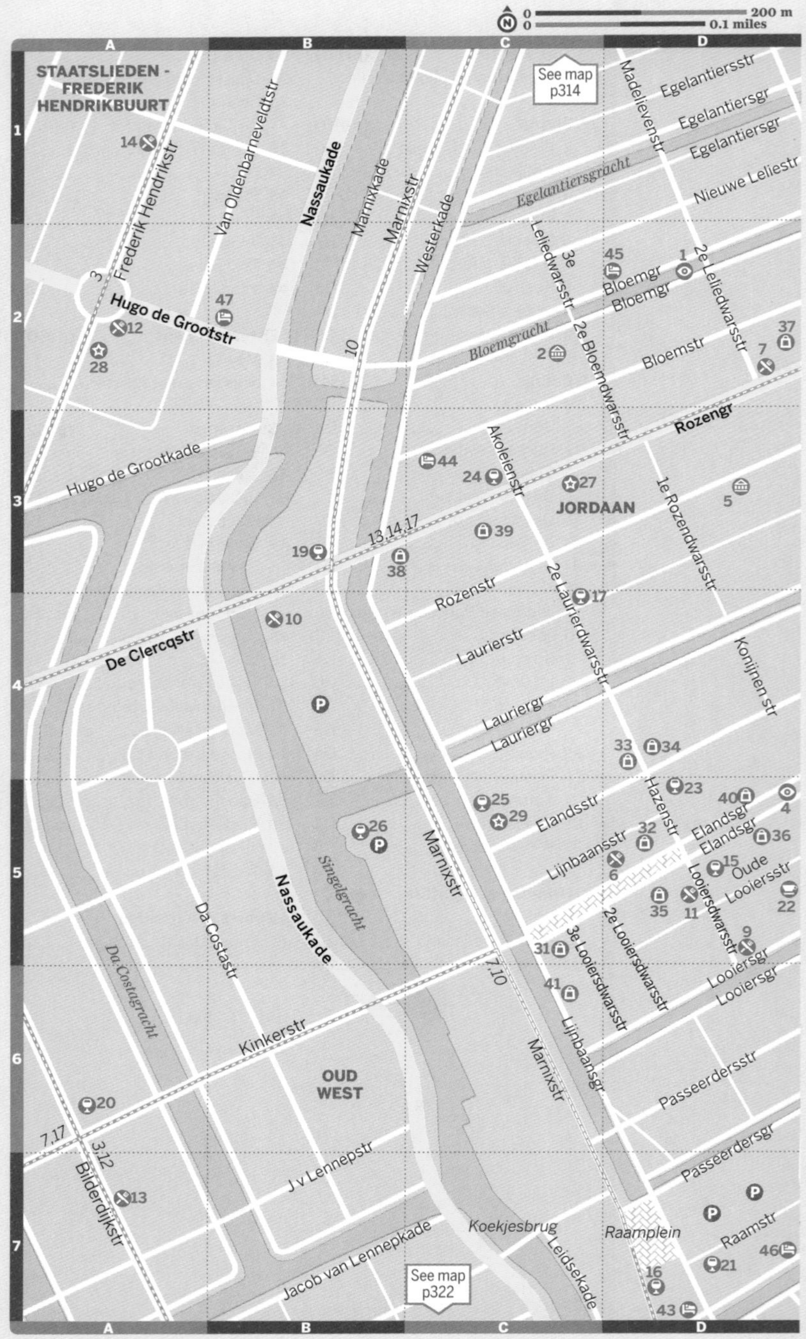
STAATSLIEDEN - FREDERIK HENDRIKBUURT
JORDAAN
OUD WEST
See map p314
See map p322
Frederik Hendrikstr
Van Oldenbarneveldtstr
Nassaukade
Marnixkade
Marnixstr
Westerkade
Madelievenstr
Egelantiersstr
Egelantiersgr
Egelantiersgracht
Nieuwe Leliestr
3e Leliedwarsstr
2e Leliedwarsstr
Bloemgr
Bloemgracht
Bloemstr
2e Bloemdwarsstr
Hugo de Grootstr
Hugo de Grootkade
Akoleienstr
Rozengr
1e Rozendwarsstr
De Clercqstr
Rozenstr
Lauriersr
Lauriergr
2e Laurierdwarsstr
Konijnen str
Hazenstr
Elandsstr
Elandsgr
Lijnbaansstr
Oude Looiersstr
Looiersdwarsstr
2e Looiersdwarsstr
3e Looiersdwarsstr
Looiersgr
Singelgracht
Da Costastr
Da Costagracht
Kinkerstr
Lijnbaansgr
Passeerdersstr
Passeerdersgr
Bilderdijkstr
J v Lennepstr
Jacob van Lennepkade
Koekjesbrug
Leidsekade
Raamplein
Raamstr
0 200 m
0 0.1 miles

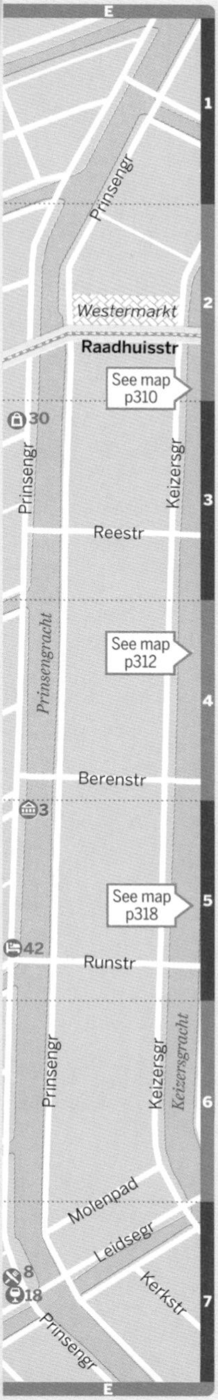

Sights (p149)

1 Bloemgracht D2
2 De Drie Hendricken C2
3 Houseboat Museum............. E5
4 Johnny Jordaanplein............ D5
5 Stedelijk Museum Bureau Amsterdam....................... D3

Eating (p151)

6 Balthazar's Keuken............... D5
Brasserie Blazer.......... (see 31)
7 Broodje Mokum D2
8 Ellis Gourmet Burger............ E7
9 Festina Lente......................... D5
10 Moeders B4
11 Pazzi D5
12 Razmataz.............................. A2
13 Riaz A7
14 Yam Yam A1

Drinking & Nightlife (p157)

15 Café de Jordaan.................... D5
16 Café de Koe D7
17 Café de Laurierboom C4
18 Café Pieper E7
19 Cafe Soundgarden................ B3
20 De Trut A6
21 De Zotte D7
22 La Tertulia D5
23 Saarein D5
24 Struik C3
25 Tripel..................................... C5
26 Waterkant............................. B5

Entertainment (p160)

27 Boom Chicago C3
28 De Nieuwe Anita A2
29 Maloe Melo C5

Shopping (p162)

30 A Space Oddity E3
31 Antiekcentrum Amsterdam C5
32 Arnold Cornelis..................... D5
33 Cats & Things........................ D4
34 Chocolátl................................ D4
35 Jefferson Hotel D5
36 Kaashuis Tromp D5
37 Kitsch Kitchen....................... D2
38 Raw Materials........................ B3
39 SPRMRKT C3
40 Tenue de Nîmes.................... D5
41 Uke Boutique......................... C6

Sleeping (p228)

42 Amsterdam Wiechmann Hotel E5
43 BackStage Hotel................... D7
44 Christian Youth Hostel 'The Shelter Jordaan'........ C3
45 Hotel van Onna D2
46 International Budget Hostel D7
47 Morgan & Mees..................... B2

Key on p320

See map p312
See map p316
See map p322
See map p322
Elandsgr
Oude Looiersstr
Looiersgr
Runstr
Huidenstr
Heist
Singel
Spuistr
Waterst
Takst
Spui
Spui
Prinsengr
Keizersgr
Beulingstr
Singel
Singel
Handboogstr
Voetboogstr
Heiligeweg
Kalverstr
Singel
Singel
Passeerdersstr
Passeerdersgr
Marnixstr
Molenpad
Leidsegracht
Leidsegr
Leidsestr
Koningsplein
Reguliersdwarsstr
Herengr
Herengr
Raamplein
Raamstr
Leidsegr
Lange Leliedwarsstr
Prinsengr
Korte Leliedwarsstr
Leidsestr
Keizersgr
Nieuwe Spiegelstr
Leidsekade
Keizersgracht
Leidseplein
Leidsebosje
Leidsekruisstr
Lange Leliedwarsstr
Korte Leliedwarsstr
Kerkstr
Hirschpassage
Lijnbaansgr
Zieseniskade
Spiegelgracht
Prinsengracht
Max Euweplein
Tesselschadestr
Zandpad
Vondelpark
2e Weteringdwarstr
3e Weteringdwarstr
Weteringstr
Vijzelgr
Lijnbaansgracht
Singelgracht
Stadhouderskade
Vossiusstr
Hobbemastr
Schapenburgerpad
PC Hooftstr
Nieuwe Weteringstr
Weteringschans
Jan Luijkenstr
Van de Veldestr
Paulus Potterstr
OUD ZUID
Weteringcircuit
Honthorststr
Hobbemakade
Boerenwetering
Johannes Vermeerstr
1e Jacob van Campenstr
Museumplein
Museumpl
Quellijnstr
Ferdinand Bolstr

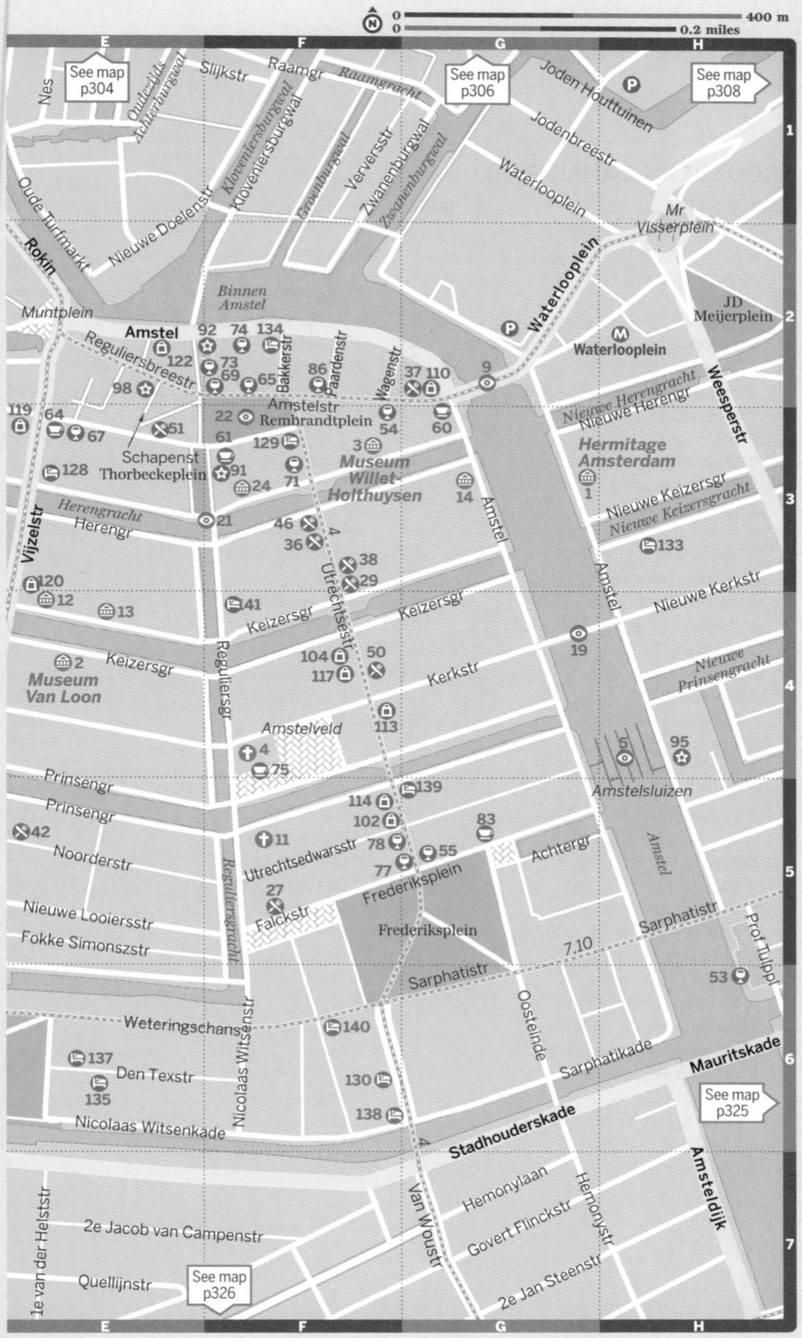

0 400 m
0 0.2 miles
See map p304
See map p306
See map p308
See map p325
See map p326
Slijkstr
Raamgr
Raamgracht
Joden Houttuinen
Jodenbreestr
Waterlooplein
Nes
Oudezijds Achterburgwal
Kloveniersburgwal
Groenburgwal
Verversstr
Zwanenburgwal
Oude Turfmarkt
Rokin
Nieuwe Doelenstr
Mr Visserplein
Binnen Amstel
Muntplein
Amstel
Reguliersbreestr
Bakkerstr
Paardenstr
Wagenstr
Waterlooplein
JD Meijerplein
Nieuwe Herengracht
Nieuwe Herengr
Weesperstr
Amstelstr
Rembrandtplein
Schapenst
Thorbeckeplein
Museum Willet-Holthuysen
Hermitage Amsterdam
Nieuwe Keizersgr
Nieuwe Keizersgracht
Herengracht
Herengr
Vijzelstr
Utrechtsestr
Keizersgr
Keizersgr
Keizersgr
Nieuwe Kerkstr
Museum Van Loon
Reguliersgr
Kerkstr
Nieuwe Prinsengracht
Amstelveld
Amstelsluizen
Prinsengr
Prinsengr
Noorderstr
Utrechtsedwarsstr
Achtergr
Reguliersgracht
Frederiksplein
Nieuwe Looiersstr
Falckstr
Frederiksplein
Sarphatistr
Fokke Simonszstr
Sarphatistr
Prof Tulppl
Weteringschans
Oosteinde
Sarphatikade
Mauritskade
Den Texstr
Nicolaas Witsenstr
Nicolaas Witsenkade
Stadhouderskade
Amsteldijk
Hemonylaan
Hemonystr
Van Woustr
Govert Flinckstr
1e van der Helststr
2e Jacob van Campenstr
Quellijnstr
2e Jan Steenstr
SOUTHERN CANAL RING

SOUTHERN CANAL RING *Map on p318*

Top Sights **(p130)**
1 Hermitage Amsterdam........G3
2 Museum Van Loon........E4
3 Museum Willet-Holthuysen........F3

Sights **(p129)**
4 Amstelkerk........F4
5 Amstelsluizen........H4
6 Amsterdam American Hotel........A4
7 Amsterdam Pipe Museum........B4
8 Blauw Jan........B4
9 Blauwbrug........G2
10 Bloemenmarkt........D2
11 De Duif........F5
12 FOAM........E4
13 Geelvinck Hinlopen Huis........E4
14 Gijsbert Dommer Huis........G3
15 Golden Bend........D3
16 Kattenkabinet........D3
17 Krijtberg........C2
18 Leidseplein........B3
19 Magere Brug........G4
20 Max Euwe Centrum........B4
21 Reguliersgracht........F3
22 Rembrandtplein........F3
23 Stadsarchief........D3
24 Tassenmuseum Hendrikje........F3

Eating **(p133)**
25 Bar Huf........D2
26 Bojo........B4
27 Bouchon du Centre........F5
28 Buffet van Odette........D4
29 Café van Leeuwen........F3
30 De Blauwe Hollander........B4
31 Everything on a Stick........B3
32 Herengracht Restaurant & Bar........C2
33 In de Buurt........B4
34 La Cacerola........D5
35 Lavinia Good Food........D4
36 Lite/Dark........F3
37 Lo Stivale d'Oro........G2
38 Loekie........F3
39 Pantry........B4
40 Pastini........B2
41 Patisserie Holtkamp........D5
Piet de Leeuw........(see 41)
42 Restaurant Fyra........E5
43 Ron Gastrobar Oriental........B3
44 Rose's Cantina........D3
45 Soup en Zo........C4
46 Stacey's Pennywell........F3
47 Stach........C4
48 SupperClub........C2
49 Taste of Culture........B4
50 Tempo Doeloe........F4
51 Van Dobben........E3
52 Van Vlaanderen........D6

Drinking & Nightlife **(p138)**
53 A Bar........H6
54 Air........F3
Back to Black........(see 34)
55 Bar Moustache........G5
56 Bulldog........B4
Café Americain........(see 6)
57 Café Brecht........D6
58 Café de Spuyt........C4
59 Café de Wetering........D5
60 Café Langereis........G3
61 Café Schiller........F3
62 Chicago Social Club........B3
63 Church........B3
64 Coffeeshop Free........E3
65 De Kroon........F2
66 Dolphins Coffeeshop........B3
67 Door 74........E3
68 Eijlders........B3
69 Escape........F2
70 Jimmy Woo........A3
71 Lellebel........F3
72 Lion Noir........D2
73 Montmartre........F2
74 Mulligans........F2

75 NeL F4
76 NJOY B4
77 Oosterling G5
78 Pata Negra F5
Stanislavski (see 99)
79 Suzy Wong A3
80 Sweet Cup C4
81 Taboo Bar D2
82 The Otherside D2
83 Two For Joy G5
84 Up B4
85 Van Dyck Bar B4
86 Vivelavie F2
87 Whiskey Café L&B B4

Entertainment (p142)

88 Bourbon Street Jazz & Blues Club B4
89 Cave B3
90 Cinecenter A3
91 De Heeren van Aemstel F3
92 De Kleine Komedie F2
93 De Uitkijk B3
94 Jazz Café Alto B4
95 Koninklijk Theater Carré H4
96 Melkweg A3
97 Paradiso B5
98 Pathé Tuschinskitheater E2
99 Stadsschouwburg B4
100 Sugar Factory A3
Uitburo & Last Minute Ticket Shop (see 99)

Shopping (p144)

101 Carl Denig C5
102 Centre Neuf F5
103 Cityboek D4
104 Concerto F4
105 Cora Kemperman B3
106 Eduard Kramer C4
107 Eichholtz Delicatessen C3
108 Gone with the Wind D4
109 Hart's Wijnhandel D5
110 Heineken Brand Store G2
International Theatre & Film Books (see 99)
111 Jaski D4
112 Lieve Hemel D3
113 Look Out F4
114 MaisonNL F5
115 Marañon Hangmatten D2
116 Mark Raven Amsterdam Art C3
117 Mobilia F4
118 Reflex Modern Art Gallery C5
119 Shirt Shop E3
120 Skateboards Amsterdam E3
Stadsboekwinkel (see 23)
121 Tinkerbell C4
122 Vlieger E2
123 Walls Gallery C3
124 Young Designers United C2

Sports & Activities

125 MacBike B4
126 Mike's Bike Tours C4

Sleeping (p232)

127 Amistad Hotel B3
128 Banks Mansion E3
129 City Hotel F3
130 Cocomama F6
131 Eden Amsterdam American Hotel A4
132 Hans Brinker Budget Hotel C4
133 Hotel Adolesce H3
134 Hotel Amstelzicht F2
135 Hotel Asterisk E6
136 Hotel Freeland A3
137 Hotel Kap E6
138 Hotel Notting Hill F6
139 Hotel Prinsenhof G5
140 Hotel V F6
141 Seven Bridges F4
142 Seven One Seven B3

Key on p324

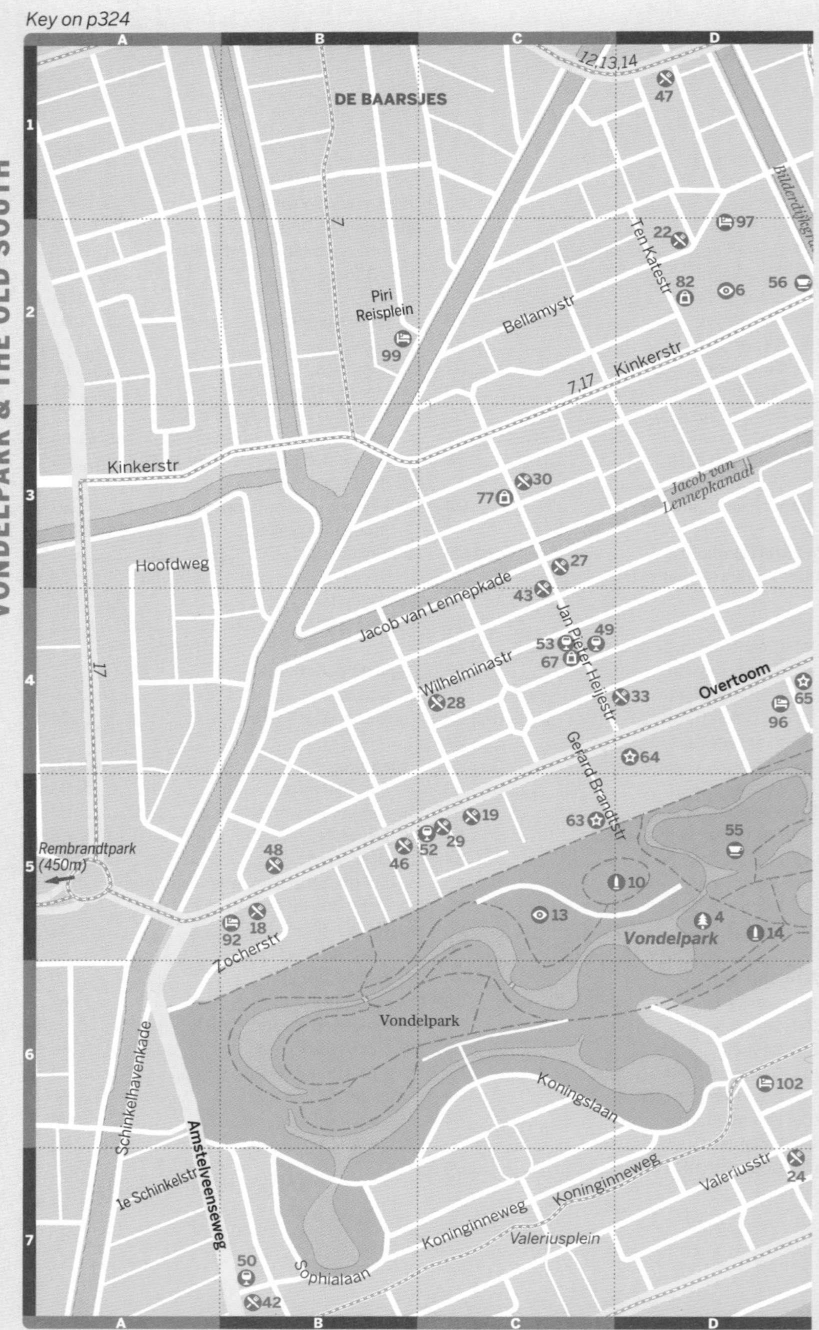

DE BAARSJES
Piri Reisplein
Bellamystr
Kinkerstr
Ten Katestr
Bilderdijkgr
Jacob van Lennepkanaal
Jacob van Lennepkade
Hoofdweg
Wilhelminastr
Jan Pieter Heijestr
Overtoom
Gerard Brandtstr
Rembrandtpark (450m)
Zocherstr
Vondelpark
Koningslaan
Schinkelhavenkade
Amstelveenseweg
1e Schinkelstr
Koninginneweg
Valeriusplein
Valeriusstr
Sophialaan
12,13,14
7,17
17

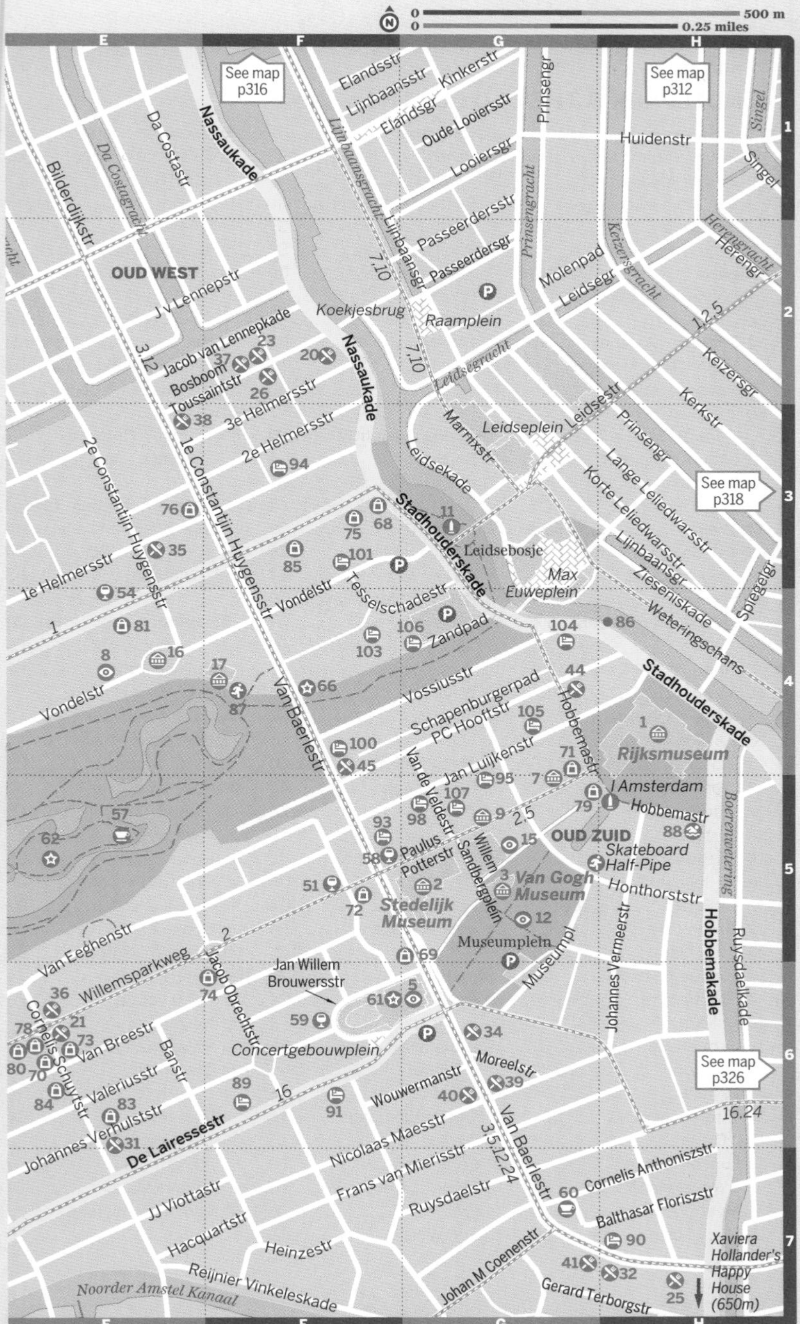
See map p316
See map p312
See map p318
See map p326
OUD WEST
OUD ZUID
Rijksmuseum
Van Gogh Museum
Stedelijk Museum
Leidseplein
Max Euweplein
Leidsebosje
Raamplein
Koekjesbrug
Museumplein
Concertgebouwplein
I Amsterdam
Skateboard Half-Pipe
Jan Willem Brouwersstr
Xaviera Hollander's Happy House (650m)
Nassaukade
Stadhouderskade
Hobbemakade
De Lairessestr
Van Baerlestr
Noorder Amstel Kanaal
0 500 m
0 0.25 miles

VONDELPARK & THE OLD SOUTH *Map on p322*

Top Sights (p167)
1 Rijksmuseum........H4
2 Stedelijk Museum........G5
3 Van Gogh Museum........G5
4 Vondelpark........D5

Sights (p174)
5 Concertgebouw........G6
6 De Hallen........D2
7 Diamond Museum........G5
8 Hollandsche Manege........E4
9 House of Bols........G5
10 Joost van den Vondel Statue........D5
11 Little Woodcutter........G3
12 Museumplein........G5
13 Rose Garden........C5
14 The Fish........D5
15 Van Gogh Museum Library........G5
16 Vondelkerk........E4
17 Vondelparkpaviljoen........F4

Eating (p175)
18 Adam........B5
19 Alchemist Garden........C5
20 Blue Pepper........F2
21 Brasserie De Joffers........E6
22 Breakfast Club........D2
23 Café Toussaint........F2
24 Carter........D7
25 De Bakkerswinkel........H7
26 De Italiaan........F2
De Peper........(see 64)
27 Deegrollers........C3
28 Dikke Graaf........C4
29 Fondue & Fondue........C5
Foodhallen........(see 6)
30 Holy Ravioli........C3
31 IJsboutique........E6
32 La Falote........H7
33 Lalibela........D4
34 l'Entrecôte et les Dames........G6
35 Lunchroom Wilhelmina........E3
Meat West........(see 6)
36 Mech Make & Take........E6
37 Narbonne........F2
38 Pastis........E3
39 Renzo's........G6
40 Restaurant De Knijp........G6
41 Restaurant Elements........G7
42 Ron Gastrobar........B7
43 Saffraan........C4
44 Sama Sebo........G4
45 Seafood Bar........F4
46 Toasty........B5
47 Van 't Spit........D1
48 Zus & Zus........B5

Drinking & Nightlife (p181)
49 BarBrå........C4
50 Café Bédier........B7
51 Cold Pressed Juicery........F5
52 Craft & Draft........C5
53 Golden Brown Bar........C4
54 Gollem's Proeflokaal........E4
55 Het Groot Melkhuis........D5
56 Lot Sixty One........D2
57 't Blauwe Theehuis........E5
58 Tunes Bar........F5
59 Welling........F6
60 Wildschut........G7

Entertainment (p183)
61 Concertgebouw........F6
Filmhallen........(see 6)
62 Openluchttheater........E5
63 Orgelpark........C5
64 OT301........D4
65 Plan B........D4
66 Vondelbunker........F4

Shopping (p184)
67 Beer Tree........C4
68 Bever........F3
69 Broekmans & Van Poppel........G5
70 Buise........E6
71 Coster Diamonds........G4
Darling........(see 6)
72 Edha Interieur........F5
73 Ennu........E6
74 Fretons........F6
75 Friday Next........F3
76 Goochem Speelgoed........E3
77 Johnny at the Spot........C3
Local Goods Store........(see 6)
78 Manwood........E6
79 Museum Shop at the Museumplein........G5
80 Nikkie........E6
81 Pied à Terre........E4
ReCycle........(see 6)
82 Ten Katemarkt........D2
83 Van Avezaath Beune........E6
84 VLVT........E6
85 Women's Outdoor World........F3

Sports & Activities (p186)
86 Blue Boat Company........H4
87 Friday Night Skate........F4
88 Zuiderbad........H5

Sleeping (p233)
89 Collector........F6
90 College Hotel........H7
91 Conscious Hotel Museum Square........F6
92 Conscious Hotel Vondelpark........B5
93 Conservatorium Hotel........F5
94 Flynt B&B........F3
95 Hotel Aalders........G5
96 Hotel de Filosoof........D4
97 Hotel De Hallen........D2
98 Hotel Fita........G5
99 Hotel Not Hotel........B2
100 Hotel Piet Hein........F4
101 Hotel Vondel........F3
102 Neighbour's Magnolia........D6
103 Owl Hotel........F4
104 Park Hotel........G4
105 Poet Hotel........G4
106 Stayokay Amsterdam Vondelpark........G4
107 Van Gogh Hostel & Hotel........G5

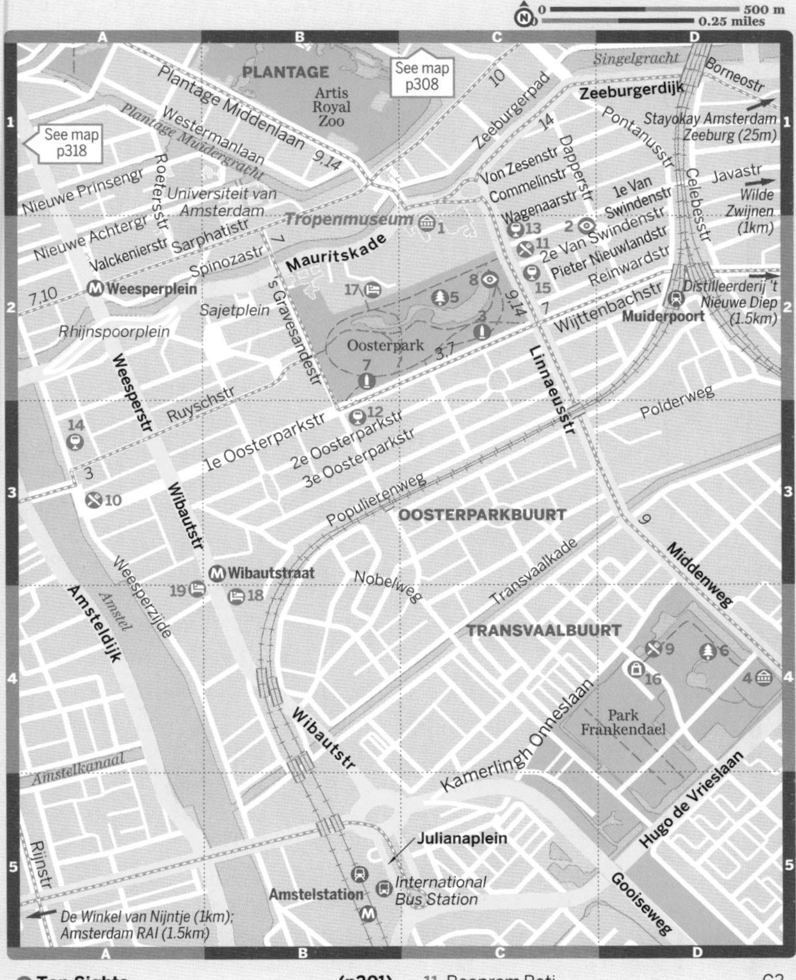

Top Sights (p201)

1 Tropenmuseum C2

Sights (p201)

2 Dappermarkt C2
3 De Schreeuw (T van Gogh memorial)......C2
4 Frankendael House................................D4
5 Oosterpark..C2
6 Park Frankendael..................................D4
7 Slavery memorial...................................B2
8 Spreeksteen C2

Eating (p203)

9 De Kas D4
10 Eetcafe Ibis A3
Merkelbach...(see 4)
11 Roopram Roti...C2

Drinking & Nightlife (p204)

12 Bar Bukowski B3
Canvas ....(see 19)
13 De Biertuin...C2
14 De Ysbreeker..A3
15 Spargo C2

Shopping (p205)

16 De Pure Markt...D4

Sleeping (p230)

17 Generator Amsterdam B2
18 Student Hotel...B4
19 Volkshotel..A4

DE PIJP

N
0 200 m
0 0.1 miles

A B C D E F G
1 2 3 4

Nicolaas Witsenkade
Stadhouderskade
Singelgracht
Amstel
Amsteldijk
Hobbemakade
Boerenwetering
Ruysdaelkade
Heineken Experience
Marie Heinekenplein
1e Jacob van Campenstr
2e Jacob van Campenstr
Quellijnstr
1e Van der Helststr
Frans Halsstr
Daniel Stalpertstr
Saenredamstr
Gerard Doustr
Gerard Douplein
DE PIJP
Albert Cuypstr
Albert Cuypmarkt
Govert Flinckstr
1e Jan Steenstr
1e Jan van der Heijdenstr
Ferdinand Bolstr
Ceintuurbaan
2e Van der Helststr
Van der Helstplein
Van Ostadestr
Rustenburgerstr
Tolstr
Sarphatipark
Nic Berchemstr
1e Sweelinckstr
Hemonylaan
Hemonystr
Van Woustr
2e Jan Steenstr
2e Jan van der Heijdenstr
Sint Willibrordusstr

See map p318
See map p322
See map p325

1 2 4 5 6 7 8 11 12 13 14 16 17 18 19 20 21 22 23 24 25 26 27 28 29 30 31 32 33 34 36 37 38 39 41 42 43 44 45 47 48 49 50 51 53 54 55 56 57 58 59 60 61 62 63 64 65 66 67 68 69 70 71 72 73 74

16, 24
3
4
12